Best Wishes
Jim "Mudcat" Grant

THE
BLACK ACES

THE BLACK ACES

BASEBALL'S ONLY AFRICAN-AMERICAN TWENTY-GAME WINNERS

JIM "MUDCAT" GRANT
with Tom Sabellico
and Pat O'Brien

www.theblackaces.com

Published by The Black Aces, LLC
SAN: 850-5691
One West Street
Farmingdale, NY 11735 USA

www.theblackaces.com

ISBN: 0-9779421-0-4

Printed in the United States of America
By Marathon Press

DEDICATION

Writing this book has caused me to fully realize the importance of so many people in my life. Without some of them I would not be able to read or write. Without others, I would never have had the opportunity to play baseball at the level I did, or at all. Some gave me instruction, some inspiration, some courage, some company. I have discussed in this book the things that some people gave me; some of the things people gave me are only known to them and me; and there are still others who have contributed to my life and even they are not aware of their contribution. I dedicate this book to all of them:

To my mother, Viola Grant, who instilled in me a belief of my self-worth and ability, and a beautiful sense of values;

To Larry Doby, my childhood hero, teammate and roommate; the second African-American to play in the Major Leagues, but first in my heart, and to his wife, Helen, and their children;

To Satchel Paige, who I wish had a chance to perform in the majors during his prime;

To my wife, Trudy Grant;

To my nineteen grandchildren and sixteen great-grandchildren;

To my daughter, Gloria Yvonne Grant, and my son, James Timothy Grant, and my other children;

To my sisters, Johnnie Mae Lopey, Katrina Morgan, Annabell Lewis and Altimease Wrispus;

To my brother, Julius "Swampfire" Grant;

To my nephew, Julius Grant, my niece, Naomi Pressley and her husband, James;

To my aunt, Esther Lee Blackmon, who would catch with me to keep my arm in shape;

To all my family;

To my teachers, Mrs. Vera Lucas Goodwin (Elementary Music and Writing); Mr. Hiram James Goodwin (Math, Algebra, and Baseball Coach); Mrs. Mary Marshall (English); Mrs. Louise Gilbert (Business);

To Mr. Jesse Stanley, Lacoochee Constable;

To Mr. & Mrs. James Irvin, he provided the kids in Lacoochee with baseball gloves and shoes, and she provided us from time to time with steak and sliced tomatoes;

To Mitchell June, a minor league teammate who deserved to be in the majors, and to all my teammates;

To all the Negro League players, and my friends at the Negro League Baseball Museum;

To Maya Angelou, a special friend;

To Dr. Mary McLeod Bethune;

To Patti LaBelle and her mom, "Chubby", who was like a second Mom to me;

To Mavis Staples and family, Pops and Ma Staples, Yvonne, Cleo and Purvis;

To B.B. King, who made my Mom feel real special by providing a seat right near the stage;

To James Moody, O.C. Smith, Duke Ellington, Count Basie, Ella Fitzgerald, and Lionel Hampton;

To Ike Isaac, my childhood best friend;

To Bob Knowling, businessman and mentor;

To Paul Barnett and Brian Barnett, who believed in me and this project; and

To Bruce W. Boyea, President and CEO, Security Mutual, a great friend of The Black Aces.

THE BLACK ACES

BASEBALL'S ONLY AFRICAN-AMERICAN TWENTY-GAME WINNERS

PREFACE

Prepare yourself to take a heart-felt journey with Jim "Mudcat" Grant as he shares his memories and his thoughts on people and subjects very dear to him. Mudcat is a true ambassador for the game of baseball. What he relates in these pages is born of a deep love of both the game and his country, which he has nurtured and cherished throughout his life. He writes from a unique perspective with the emotion and conviction that he has forged over the six decades that baseball has been at the center of his world. You will undoubtedly come away with a deeper knowledge about the great game of baseball and the country in which we live, and an appreciation for the achievements of the players featured in this book.

Mudcat is a natural to tell this story. To begin with, he has the qualifications based on what he accomplished on the field. He is one of The Black Aces, a select group comprised of the only thirteen African-American pitchers to have won twenty or more games in a Major League season. (The other members are Vida Blue, Al Downing, Bob Gibson, Dwight Gooden, Ferguson Jenkins, Sam "Toothpick" Jones, Don Newcombe, Mike Norris, JR Richard, Dave Stewart, Dontrelle Willis, and Earl Wilson.) In addition, Mudcat's experiences off the field, before, during and after his playing career, serve to broaden and enhance his view of life well beyond the myopic view that is sometimes attributed to baseball.

He grew up in a time and place when American society did not allow blacks to enjoy even the most basic expectation of acceptance as an equal member with all of its other citizens, much less that of enjoying the same level of opportunity or attaining a level of accomplishment in any given field of endeavor. He was raised in the deep South in the 1930s and 1940s, when the closed door of Organized Baseball was just one more portal in a very lengthy corridor through which blacks were not permitted to pass.

In April 1947, when Jackie Robinson had just started playing for the Brooklyn Dodgers, Mudcat was eleven years old. Robinson's debut, and that of Larry Doby with the Cleveland Indians just eleven weeks later, expanded the horizon of opportunities for Mudcat and all other black children. For the first time, they were allowed to believe their dreams could come true. As a teenager he experienced the thrill of Robinson, Satchel Paige, and his personal hero, Doby, coming to his area of the world. They came as members of Negro League "All-Star" teams that toured the country playing against other Negro Leaguers or against teams comprised of Major League and minor league white players, a baseball tradition known as "barnstorming." In the summer of 1949, Mudcat was already playing in the Florida State Negro League for his hometown team, the Lacoochee Nine Devils. In that same year, Don Newcombe, who would later become the first black twenty-game winner in the Major Leagues, made his debut with the Brooklyn Dodgers.

Mudcat was signed by the Cleveland Indians in 1954 and already playing in their minor league system before future fellow Aces, Mike Norris and Dave Stewart, were even born. That same year he was a twenty-game winner in the minor leagues. In his first Major League spring training camp, with the Indians, Mudcat roomed with Larry Doby. He became the first black twenty-game winner in the American League before fellow Floridian, Dwight Gooden, had celebrated his first birthday. Bob Gibson, Don Newcombe, Sam Jones, Vida Blue, Al Downing, Earl Wilson, Dave Hoskins and Larry Doby were his teammates at different times during his career. He played in the American League and the National League, and for the Indians and the Dodgers, the teams that signed the first blacks in their respective leagues. He played in the majors, both before and after the Civil Rights Act of 1964, making him one of the relatively few black Major Leaguers with the perspective that playing with, and after, "Jim Crow" can provide.

Now, over thirty years after his retirement as a player, he is very active in baseball alumni affairs. He keeps up with the activities of former players and helps raise funds throughout the country for youth sports programs and many other charitable causes. Tirelessly, he traverses the country spreading the gospel of baseball, and the accomplishments of The Black Aces. He has always appreciated his ability to play the game and understood that his actions, his very existence on a Major League team, may have impacted others, just as the signing of Larry Doby by the Cleveland Indians impacted him.

This book doesn't just tell the stories of The Black Aces. It is a story about America - north, south, east and west. It is the story of the game of baseball and the business of baseball; segregation and integration; discrimination and determination; heroes and cowards; fear, strength, and courage; opportunities denied to some, and seized by others; yesterday, today, and a glimpse into tomorrow, all told against the backdrop of the accomplishments of some of the most successful pitchers of their time. It is the essence of who Jim "Mudcat" Grant is today: preserving true stories of the great game of baseball and the lives of the men who built it, while working with a passionate energy to instill and foster a greater interest in, and appreciation for, the game in today's youth.

Before we go any further, we can provide you with a great insight to this book and Mudcat's vision, by sharing with you his instructions to us on the day we first met to discuss writing this book:

I think we are going to have to be a little more direct in getting humanity and the rest of the players to understand that the integration of baseball came about years ago for the betterment of humanity and we don't know why it was the time. Timing is just about everything, in some circumstances, but let us tell what happened, what went on, the letters, the underground work that happened. I think the current players and the readers will have more respect for what Jackie Robinson and Don Newcombe and those guys did, if they understand some of the background of what happened, what was tried thirty years before then, the connection of the whole thing. That is what we want in place from a historical standpoint instead of just letting it disappear. We need to show the relationship of thirty years before that connected to

now. That's what I would like to do, and have readers appreciate and respect the timing of it all, of the lack of timing of it all, all those years when things could have been different. The public needs to know that there were black ballplayers before Jackie Robinson. Some people don't even know that. So, that's the essence of the strength of the book. It's the historical, not just the passionate, but also the historical part of it, that needs to be told. Now, the passion, the pride, has to come from the book through us. After you start reading it, you're supposed to yell and scream, you're supposed to throw the book up against the wall, you're supposed to cry, you're supposed to do all of those things, and if you do, if we can get people to do that, that means the importance of the book will be even better. It means that this generation will catch up with it; I'm talking about sports fans. There will be some people who will read this who are not sports fans. People are going to want, white people are going to want their children to know this. Whites are not hiding their children now from a lot of things that they hid before. It's okay to discuss this and the book will be a circumstance where at least kids will hear about it. They may not read it, but they will hear about it. They will be more prepared to hear some things that won't frighten them, because now I think, even in Black History Month, when we talk to kids, the white kids, I think some of the things frighten them, keep them from an emotional feeling sometime, keep them from asking questions sometimes, because they are afraid.

We consider ourselves blessed to have come to know 'Mudcat' so closely. We are honored he trusted us to collaborate with him on this project – a project that is so dear to him. We thank him for allowing us into his world, and hope we have justified his decision to work with us on this book.

We spent a great deal of time with Mudcat and delved deeply into the lives and careers of the other Black Aces, who graciously granted us interviews and were generous with their time. We also interviewed and corresponded with many teammates and opponents of The Black Aces, which produced a wealth of memories and information. With the knowledge gained from those players, and from Mudcat's perspective, we will highlight the twenty-win seasons of The Black Aces and celebrate their accomplishments. We will also look back in time to examine the careers of other pitchers who might have attained that same milestone had they been allowed to play in the Major Leagues during the prime of their careers. In researching the lives and careers of the players, we read thousands of articles spanning back over the last hundred years. In many of those publications blacks were referred to as "tan," "colored," "Negro," "Afro-American," and other adjectives. In the context of the time, writing about some of the older players, these adjectives, all widely-used at certain times over the last century, were used in this book within the historic context of their use.

We would like to acknowledge and thank our dear friend, former Major Leaguer Rosendo 'Rusty' Torres, for introducing us to Mudcat and other former players, who have all become close friends, and have helped us to understand the life of a professional ballplayer. They have all been extremely forthcoming in opening up their hearts and minds and sharing their thoughts, remembrances and insights. We also extend our gratitude and appreciation to the many people who wrote to us. We have received mail and e-mail from players and fans from across the country, providing us with numerous remembrances of Mudcat and the other Black Aces. We would be remiss if we did not also acknowledge our appreciation of the work performed by countless beat reporters, columnists, and sportswriters, who preserved for history the contemporaneous thoughts and opinions of players, managers and fans over the past century. Although we have spoken to scores of players over the past two years, a work of this magnitude and detail would not be possible without drawing on their efforts and the myriad newspapers, magazines, and books that published their work.

Even with such a massive body of data, facts and anecdotes at our disposal, however, the one aspect of our research effort that was most revealing, and inspiring, was a visit we made with Mudcat to his hometown of Lacoochee, Florida. Lacoochee is never far from Mudcat's mind or lips, but nothing he had told us about his hometown was as revealing or poignant as the sight of his grandnieces and grandnephews running into his arms, or seeing his eyes light up and grow moist with memories as he narrated our tour of Lacoochee. A heartfelt "thank you" goes out to Mud's twin sister, Johnnie Mae, and his younger brother, Julius (Swampfire), for their warm hospitality during our visit.

One of Mud's objectives in writing this book was to preserve for future generations an inside look at the integration of baseball – past and present - through the stories of select black pitchers, narrated in his voice. Mudcat's close friendship with the players, and his long career in baseball, give this book a special warmth that only he could impart, and provide a unique insight into the subjects it covers.

We must make one very important observation at the outset, which you should keep in mind as you take this journey with him. From the time we originally discussed this project with Mudcat, he made it very clear that despite the segregated conditions he has faced, and the discrimination practiced by some people, he harbors no anger toward anyone. As we interviewed the athletes, and heard story after story of the treatment they endured, or the opportunities they were denied, we not only learned about the events in their lives, but were also enlightened and enriched by the strength of their character under such difficult circumstances. We began to understand Mud's deep feeling that this story is a very positive one. It is not a lament of opportunities lost or unfair realities endured, but a celebration of triumph and accomplishment.

We would like to thank Paul Barnett and Brian Barnett for believing in us and this project and helping to make this book a reality.

We extend our thanks to the librarians at the National Baseball Hall of Fame in Cooperstown, New York, for their help and assistance in sorting through their wealth of files for information on our subjects, specifically Claudette Burke and Fred Berowski. Thanks to Pat Kelly for her help in selecting photos to enhance our words. Thanks also to Christopher Sabellico, Stephen Aspetti, Gina Aspetti, Dave Diamond, Tina Diamond, Dan Kornfeld, and Marcella Nostrand for their help in editing the manuscript, and to Ike Galanoudis for the contribution of his creative genius in designing our cover. But most of all we thank our patient and indulgent families, especially our wives, Paula and Mary, who have endured our many hours of involvement in this project.

Tom Sabellico
Pat O'Brien

INTRODUCTION

There are a number of important reasons why I felt the need to tell the story of my experiences and those of other black baseball players over the last century. One of the most significant ones is my concern that we are losing priceless links to our country's history, and our heritage, as these players age and pass on. Since I initiated work on this book, five pioneers of the game died: Larry Doby, the first black to play in the American League; Earl Battey, one of the first black catchers in the Major Leagues and my catcher during my twenty-win season; fellow Black Ace, Earl Wilson, Negro League star, Ted "Double Duty" Radcliffe, and most recently, my teammate and former All-Star, Vic Power. Their deaths are especially personal losses to me but they are also great losses to future generations, because other than "Double Duty" they never took the full opportunity to express their experiences in their own words. Those experiences are unique pieces of the jigsaw puzzle that makes up our past and, quite honestly, the total picture will always lack a bit of clarity and focus without them. Nothing can be seen in perfect detail with pieces missing, and men like Larry, Earl, "Double Duty," Earl Wilson, and Vic and many others hold important pieces. It seems that not a week or month goes by when I don't learn that another one of my teammates has passed on. Sadly, their part of the puzzle often goes with them.

A people without the knowledge of their history is like a tree without roots.
Marcus Garvey

Another strong motivating factor that fueled my passion for this project is the need to change the commonly held, but totally distorted notion that baseball and America integrated instantly in 1947, resulting in a steady march forward toward a successfully integrated society and a harmonious racial co-existence ever since. Well, there have been a lot of marches over the years, and they have led to some progress, but the notion of ultimate success and harmony has yet to be fulfilled. In fact, it is possible that the playing fields of America, and especially in the area between the foul lines on a baseball field, have been the only places in America where blacks and whites play by the same rules and such a notion holds true. But for sure, off the field and in the mainstream of American society, not much changed for blacks in 1947, other than our expectations. In fact, the 1950s and 1960s were some of the most violent racial times in American history. We all need to look at those times closely, and learn from them so that no other segment of this great society ever faces such violence again.

Lastly, I wanted to commit to writing a celebration of the accomplishments of some great black ballplayers in the hopes that current and future generations will also come to love the game that has given me so much, and that they will understand and respect the sacrifices and work of those who went before them. We need to stir people to action: the people who run Major League Baseball, the people who own teams, the people who run universities, the people who run youth sports leagues, the parents and the children. The great game of baseball, so often used by so many as a metaphor for life and the American dream, will only maintain its exalted status as America's game if it truly reflects America, and all of its many and varied constituent groups.

The late, great black intellectual, W.E.B. DuBois, captured in words a duality that black Americans feel:

It is a peculiar sensation, this double consciousness. One ever feels his twoness - an American, a negro; two warring souls, two thoughts, two unreconciled strivings; two warring ideals in one dark body, whose dogged strength alone keeps it from being torn asunder.
The Souls of Black Folks, by W.E.B. DuBois, Vintage Books, NY 1990

I have always felt and understood this "twoness" but I came to have a greater understanding of its application to my fellow players as I researched this book. Many of the black athletes I spoke with, especially the older ones like Don Newcombe, are very proud of what they accomplished as an African-American. It is important to them that history remembers the fact that they succeeded in an arena where no other blacks had been allowed to even enter. Yet, there is the need for history to also note that the pitchers I have featured in this book were not only successful black pitchers, they were successful pitchers period! They were incredible athletes, fierce competitors and highly accomplished professionals. In a sense, they lived with a separate and similar "twoness" as both a ballplayer and as a black ballplayer. If I were writing this book about all twenty-game winners in the twentieth century, and the pitchers with the greatest impact on the game, these men would play a prominent part in it at any rate, without regard to their color. Their great accomplishments are part of the history of both the game and America itself. It is the context in which that history unfolded and that they attained their success that makes their accomplishments that much greater. Returning to the words of DuBois, I believe it is "possible for a man to be both Negro and American, without being cursed and spit upon by his fellows, without having the doors of opportunity closed roughly in his face."

I have led a remarkable life, with unforgettable experiences, much of it due to my God-given talent, hard work, and my life as a baseball player. It is my hope that you enjoy this book as it was meant to be enjoyed, as a celebration of the accomplishments of the Black Aces, and the story of how they did it, from my view on a Major League pitcher's mound.

James "Mudcat" Grant

CHAPTER 1

BASEBALL DREAMS

BASEBALL, the word and the game still capture me, as they have ever since I first learned to play a simple game of "catch" on the dirt roads of my hometown of Lacoochee, just outside of Dade City, Florida. Lacoochee and I weren't alone in our love of the game. Baseball completely captivated all of America in the first half of the twentieth century, especially in the South where the weather is so accommodating that the game can be played year round. I don't think there was a town in America that didn't have some version of a baseball field back then, even if it was nothing other than a cow pasture. It didn't take much more than a stick and anything that resembled a ball to get a game going. (A real ball was a luxury back then, costing nine cents – almost a full hour's wages! I would often gather up some rags and tie them with string, and use that until it came undone.)

The game of baseball was just perfect for where the mindset of the country and its population were in the first half of the twentieth century. Tens of millions of immigrants had come to America since the 1890s. Many of them, and their children who were born here, embraced the distinctly American game of baseball as a rite of passage, unofficially bestowing American citizenship, but officially incorporating them into the American fabric. This feeling of acceptance in American society through their adoption of America's game was just as important to another sector of new American citizens: American blacks who were enfranchised by the Constitution on paper, but had little to show for it according to how society treated them.

In the 1940s there were probably very few young boys in America who didn't dream of being Joe DiMaggio, or Stan Musial, or Bob Feller. Very few white boys, that is, because it was a time when black kids, referred to then as "colored" or "Negro", couldn't share the same dream of playing baseball in the Major Leagues. It was a time when men, even American-born men, were not allowed to play baseball in the Major Leagues, or in any recognized leagues associated with them (known collectively as "Organized Baseball") because of the color of their skin. It is a part of our history that is often forgotten, maybe because some prefer not to remember it. Even when it is brought to mind, there is a tendency to place it in an era that seems far more distant in our past than its actual place in time, only fifty-eight years ago.

Despite the segregation practiced by Organized Baseball, the game was so popular then – loved by blacks and whites alike - that separate leagues for Negro players were formed and sustained for the first time. The Negro National League, formed in 1920 by Rube Foster (one of the greatest pitchers of all time) was the earliest and most prominent of these ventures. It was his vision and leadership that made this bold attempt a reality and afforded Negro players their first real opportunity to play in the same kind of structured setting that their white counterparts did in Organized Baseball. While the Negro National League, and later the Negro American League, did not have the same stability or financial strength as Organized Baseball, they gave black kids, like me, athletic heroes we could identify with - men like Satchel Paige and Josh Gibson.

About the time I was nine years old, it became clear to me that I had been given a special gift – tremendous athletic ability. I could run, throw and hit as well as, or better than, kids several years older than me. I was blessed with excellent reflexes, strong muscles and superior hand-eye coordination. Things just seemed to come my way. There were other kids who were as good as I was but things didn't happen for them, as I look back and reflect on it. But at that time I didn't realize it, it just seemed to be a way of life for me. I hit home runs. I could catch everything, and when I pitched I could always throw a strike.

I enjoyed playing sports and did so at any and every opportunity. Aware of my athletic skills and as in love with baseball as the rest of the country, I dreamed of being a baseball player, a Negro League baseball player, because that was the best I could achieve at that time. It was the first time I dreamed that I could do something with my life that would extend beyond Lacoochee. In an effort to get there I practiced hard. I always wanted to get better. There was a thrill of getting better and there was one specific thing you knew that would make you better and that was practice. Get your butt out there and practice!

Prior to 1945, I had no reason to ever think I could play in the Major Leagues no matter how hard I practiced. It was one of the expectations society robbed from me, although I didn't realize at the time that something I was entitled to had been taken, and I didn't blame society. As a boy, I didn't have a notion of the frustration that such limitations could cause in a person who had the talent to compete at that level. A man like Josh Gibson was considered by many to be the greatest home run hitter of all time, black or white. Yet, the highest accolade baseball afforded him was his recognition as the "black Babe Ruth." His baseball "twoness" prevented him from being judged on the basis of his own individual baseball talent, and from enjoying the well-deserved opportunity to compete with the Babe on the same field in the Major Leagues. If things were different, Ruth might have become known as the "white Josh Gibson." But society prevented what might have been from happening.

Because of the segregated society in which I was raised, I accepted that the furthest my baseball ability could get me was to the Negro Leagues. I knew, even at that early age, that the world did not view Negro League ball as "real baseball" – the baseball of Joe DiMaggio and Stan Musial. Lacoochee was my whole world and I wasn't really thinking about other black kids in other towns and places throughout America. But I came to learn that I wasn't the only one whose dreams were limited; other black kids felt the same way:

We'd walk eight or nine miles to see these [Negro] teams play, to see them play the Orange [New Jersey] BBC, the local white team. And then they would play the Newark Eagles. You'd go from Orange to East Orange to Newark and on Saturday afternoon for a quarter you

could see great baseball games. So the kids would pick out a star. We'd want to play like Willie Wells or Ray Dandridge or Mule Suttles or Leon Day. Terris McDuffie, Cool Papa Bell, John Henry Lloyd, these were our heroes. ... We'd watch 'em play that shadow ball where they did infield drills without the ball, they put on running contests, throwing contests, pepper where each guy would handle a ball for 15 or 20 seconds, they did all those things that were so skillful – and we wanted to be just like them.
Monte Irvin, The Sporting News, May 1, 1995

People always ask you, did you dream about playing Major League ball? Uh-uh! There were no blacks. You may say when you're out in the backyard that you're Babe Ruth, but you're just saying it because everybody else was saying it. As far as visualizing yourself playing big league ball, it was so far-fetched it wasn't funny.
Chuck Harmon, first African-American to play for the Cincinnati Reds, quoted by Chris Haft, MLB.com, February 12, 2003

I was 16 and already dreaming of a baseball career, but not in organized baseball.
Elston Howard (who grew up in St. Louis)

If I were born ten or fifteen years earlier, I might not have made it to the Major Leagues, not because I wasn't good enough, but because I was black. If I were born ten to fifteen years later, I might not have had to face some of the hurdles I did. However, I am extremely happy I was born when I was. I've heard Don Newcombe say that as the earliest black pitchers in the Major Leagues we were "part of a revolution" and I agree. I am thrilled to have been part of that revolution, not for the fame, but for the pure joy of pursuing that dream, and helping to open the door for others, of all colors, to realize a similar dream.

I always wondered how the door to Organized Baseball was originally shut to blacks. It seemed to me that it had always been that way but I was surprised to learn that wasn't the case. In fact, it really wasn't until an all-black team from Philadelphia had the gumption to knock on that door in 1867 that it was slammed shut for them and many generations to follow. After the Civil War, Organized Baseball, along with the rest of American society, was faced with the task of dealing with the newly freed black population in ways that it had probably never contemplated before slavery was abolished. Would blacks be permitted into mainstream society? Where would blacks fit in? How was society supposed to deal with blacks? How would society deal with blacks? Would they really be treated as equals? Were they equals? Could they fit into white society? All of these issues became known as "the Negro question." Organized Baseball was first called upon to respond to that question when that all-black Philadelphia team, the Pythians, applied for membership to The National Association of Base

3

Ball Players (NABBP), one of baseball's earliest recognized governing bodies. Unfortunately, baseball chose to respond to their request by sidestepping the issue altogether.

The Association, "wanting to avoid any controversy," reasoned that "If colored clubs were admitted there would be in all probability some division of feeling, whereas, by excluding them no injury could result to anyone." So they denied the application as if they were doing blacks a favor. In fact, the very next year, the NABBP compounded that action when it decided unanimously "against the admission of any club which may be composed of one or more colored persons." Although that decision was never memorialized as a formal resolution or written policy of the NABBP, it nonetheless came to be honored by its members and later by the Major Leagues for many years to come. Its convenient, patronizing and racist edict effectively slammed the door to Organized Baseball shut for blacks until 1947. This would not be the only time baseball ducked out of the way of a "high hard one" without "stepping up to the plate" on this important issue.

Because the NABBP's resolution only applied to the admission of new clubs with black players on their rosters, a few individual blacks did play in white Organized Baseball for a time. In 1884, for instance, Moses Fleetwood Walker became the very first black Major Leaguer when he played in the American Association for the Toledo Blue Stockings (the American Association was considered to be a major league at the time). Later that season, his brother, Welday Wilberforce Walker, joined him on the Blue Stockings. In fact, when George Stovey won thirty-five games for Newark in the International League in 1887, there were approximately fifteen blacks competing on white teams in Organized Baseball. That same year, however, the International League barred all future contracts with black players, based on a report that "many of the best players in the League were anxious to leave on account of the colored element." While this ruling was not supposed to affect those blacks already in the League, it had a predictable effect as the Binghamton club immediately released "Bud" Fowler, a very successful black pitcher, who was also batting .350 with 30 stolen bases, and banned him from signing with any other club in the League.

Cap Anson, one of the most gifted and influential players of that time, was one of the "best players in the League" referred to in that report. He was openly racist and it was his agitation and protest, and that of others like him that forced the club owners' hands. Fearing the loss of their white stars, they began to operate under an unwritten and misnamed "gentlemen's agreement," that barred blacks from playing in Organized Baseball. As a result, it wasn't long before there were no blacks in Organized Baseball at all. By the early 1890s, there weren't even any blacks playing on white minor league teams. Later, in 1923, *The Sporting News* acknowledged the existence of the unwritten ban, and how blacks were treated differently than all other races:

In a democratic, catholic, real American game like baseball there has been no distinction raised except tacit understanding that a player of

Ethiopian descent is ineligible ... No player of any other 'race' has been barred. ... The Mick, the Sheeny, the Wop, the Dutch and the Chink, the Cuban, the Indian, the Jap or the so-called Anglo-Saxon – his 'nationality' is never a matter of moment if he can pitch, hit, or field.
"A New Division in Baseball," The Sporting News, December 6, 1923

Blacks would not play in Organized Baseball again until April 1946 (when Jackie Robinson took the field for the Brooklyn Dodgers' AAA team, the Montreal Royals, and Don Newcombe and Roy Campanella did likewise for the Dodgers' Nashua affiliate) and not in the Major Leagues until April 1947 when Robinson made his debut with the parent club. During those fifty-seven years the baseball dreams of thousands of kids just like me were limited by the prejudice of Organized Baseball against blacks. Luckily, I was young enough to outlive the narrow-mindedness that sent thousands of great athletes like Bullet Rogan and Buck Leonard to their graves wondering "What if?" because they weren't permitted to dream, or perform, at the highest levels that their talents clearly warranted.

CHAPTER 2

LACOOCHEE

There are places like Lacoochee. You've never heard of Lacoochee? For one thing, that's the place where Jim (Mudcat) Grant of the Cleveland Indians was born. It's the hypotenuse of a triangle leading from Route 50, west of Orlando, to Federal Highway 301. You can go straight west on 50 and pick up 301, but if you don't take the cutoff, you'll never see Lacoochee. It looks like a mining town which mines no more. The city hall is a weary, ramshackle affair which stubbornly defies the winds. The bridge going into Lacoochee is over a fetid swamp with the stumps of rotted trees looking like wooden tombstones in a village of horror. There isn't much to see in Lacoochee if you should happen to sneeze going through. You wind up, just before you get back on 301, at Shorty's junk yard where the splendid automobiles of yesteryear are eaten by the corrosion of time.
Bob Addie, The Sporting News, March 16, 1963

The picture of Lacoochee that resides in my mind is much more romantic than Bob Addie's description. Baseball, as you may have figured by now, was indeed my first love, and for you to get a clear picture of how that love developed, I need to tell you where the seed of this passion was sown. Lacoochee, Florida was never really a city or a town. It was really just a simple, little place that housed the people who worked for Cummer Sons Cypress Company, a lumber mill company that built Lacoochee around the abundant cypress trees that had been growing in the vast swamps of Pasco County for thousands of years. At a time when the South was suffering economically, before the entire country felt the squeeze of the Depression, Cummer Sons developed a typical company town around the Withlacoochee River and its surrounding swampland. They not only built the lumber mill, and brought in all of the equipment and machinery necessary to process the hewn timber into usable lumber, but also constructed a railroad line to transport the wood. Lacoochee was a by-product of the Cummer Sons enterprise, created to house and accommodate the hundred or so families who eked out their meager living by working for the company. The "company town" consisted of the company store, the company doctor, the company quarters, and the company elementary school, formally known as the Lacoochee Colored School, located in two adjacent row houses that had been converted for use by students.

The workers' quarters were a series of approximately one hundred two-room or three-room houses, and placed in rows, like mass produced cookies on a baking sheet. Considering that Cummer Sons's workers got paid about ten cents an hour for long, hard labor, the quality of their housing was equal to the quality of their income - poor, and there was little else to provide any comfort, except for family. There weren't any utilities: no running water, no electricity, and no telephone. There wasn't any indoor plumbing, just an outhouse behind each of the row houses. There were two water fountains – one near the mill and one in the middle of town, and that's where you got your water. A simple coal stove was all that was provided in each house for cooking and heating, and we used kerosene lanterns for light. Our row house had two bedrooms (we not only shared a bedroom, we shared a bed), a kitchen and a living room with a fireplace.

The quarters were home to all of the black mill workers. The "white part of town" was literally across the railroad tracks. It housed the general store, the post office, and the movie theatre. Workers who were industrious made additional money by harvesting the Spanish moss that hung from the cypress trees. They could earn a penny a pound for the moss, which was used as stuffing for pillows and mattresses. In fact, that practice led to the development of a separate section of town that was called Mosstown, appropriately enough, and the people who lived there owned their own home or trailer.

Many athletes of my generation used their talents to enable themselves and their families to move from the poverty and segregated conditions that existed in their hometowns. Likewise, my ability gave me my first chance to travel beyond Lacoochee. In fact, because I played ball for the Lacoochee Nine Devils, I often traveled outside of the Lacoochee area before I finished high school. No one else my age got farther away from home than the high school grounds. Living in Lacoochee and growing up in Lacoochee it was like night and day whenever I left to go to the outside world. But now, all these years later, I find my heart and mind connecting with Lacoochee constantly. Lacoochee stayed with me throughout all of my travels around this country, and the world, over the last sixty years, and I find that Lacoochee is constantly beckoning me home.

Life was simple in Lacoochee. It just was. Everything was sort of staked out for you as a Negro whose family worked for the mill company. There was a whistle to go to work, there was a whistle to eat meals, and there was a whistle to knock off. Since we had no real source of income, let alone wealth, other than what the family was paid by Cummer Sons, it was understood that our family, extended as it might be, would all live in one of the row houses. It was expected that my siblings and I would attend the row house school, as did all the other "colored" children, and learn enough to grow up to be a lumber mill worker, to grow up learning to follow orders. As I reflect on it, there was never any expectation by the company that blacks would accumulate any wealth. There was no bank in Lacoochee for blacks.

In accordance with the "separate but equal" guideline set down by the United States Supreme Court, the white children of Lacoochee attended a separate, more formal school: the Lacoochee Elementary School. Our educational "system" was certainly *"separate"* from the schooling afforded to whites, but it was far from *"equal."* We used textbooks that were out-of-date "hand-me-downs" from the white school. They lacked covers or backs, pages were torn out of them, and other pages were marked and ripped; in fact, we usually had to combine parts of three or four of these "hand-me-downs" to make a complete book. The same held true for such simple things as chalk and crayons. We were given nubs to work with; finding a crayon or a piece of chalk longer than an inch was like Christmas morning.

I didn't know it or realize it then, but these conditions were just reflections of what most blacks would experience for their entire lives – afforded either inferior resources or no resources at all, making it difficult or impossible to succeed in a world that constantly reminded you that you were "second class" at best. Society gave you no reason or realistic hope to expect to succeed. Expectations were to survive and, for some, the bigotry and racism that created lowered expectations became self-fulfilling prophecies. Society told them they wouldn't and couldn't succeed, and they didn't. But for others, whose elders instilled a desire to excel, dreams endured.

We come from a legacy of people who, when they were told they were nothing and everything around them, every single experience in their life, said, 'You are nobody. You are nothing'. . . . somewhere inside themselves, said, 'I believe I'm better.'
Oprah Winfrey, quoted in "And don't call me a racist", by Ella Mazel, Argonaut Press, 1998

My belief that I could succeed and excel, my voice from within me, came from my mother. I remember my Mom telling me, as a child, that she always thought, always knew, I was blessed the minute I came out of her. She always thought, and maybe there was something that she felt or sensed, that I had come into the world for many missions, and she told me that again and again. Whether she actually felt it or not, it was the source of great confidence for me.

Another one of the most influential people in my life was one of my teachers, Mrs. Vera Lucas Goodwin. She never let the threadbare, impoverished conditions in our small schoolhouse dampen her passion for education, or her passionate and loving drive to see her students learn and flourish. She was a fan of music and culture, and was determined to light a spark in us that would light our way to become more than mill laborers. She was the one who identified and fostered my ability to sing and perform. She gave me my first record, a recording of Johann Strauss, and then she gave me albums by Eddy Arnold, and by John Lee Hooker. She was trying to show me the universal appeal and reach of music in its various forms: from Johann Strauss, a person obviously foreign to kids from Lacoochee, to the lyrics of Eddy Arnold's ballads telling life's stories, to the blues of John Lee Hooker, deep and rich in his culture. She made learning as enjoyable as possible under the circumstances, and above all, she taught us to love to learn. Another important person in my education was Rev. Floyd. He was an activist who was always trying to improve circumstances for the blacks in Lacoochee. He knew the importance of education in Pasco County if black children were ever to have a chance, and his pet project was a new school for the black children in the area.

By the time I was ready for the eighth grade, that new school was finally built. In his honor, the school was called the Floyd Academy Elementary School. (Just as a footnote, we found out some years later, that the Floyd Academy Elementary School, although much more spacious and accommodating than the row house school, was built with inferior lumber that presented such a fire hazard and safety risk the County condemned and demolished it.)

Education wasn't the only area where we weren't given a fair shake. Health care was another one, a very important one. If we were ill, we could see the company doctor, Dr. Walters, but he couldn't do much for us. If we were really ill, there wasn't much hope for us at all. The only hospital in our area was in Tampa and we didn't have money or insurance for anything like that. If you had a serious illness, you just had to suffer through it. You got compensated if you lost a finger or a hand working at the mill. I think the company gave you a hundred dollars if you lost a finger, but there was definitely no insurance. At the company doctor, there was a separate waiting room for "coloreds." Dr. Walters could only see black patients after he had seen the white patients. He became a friend to the Grant family, because my Aunt Esther worked for him. After getting to know him a little better, I could tell that Dr. Walters had some passion, and it bothered him that he had to discriminate against the blacks. He would try to accommodate us by seeing us after hours, or at his home.

The same system of separate and unequal treatment extended to our teeth. We were not allowed to sit in the dentist's chair. If we had to get a tooth pulled, we would have to go to Dade City, where there was a dentist who would see black patients, out on a porch. He would use a rusty piece of equipment (one that had been lying out in the weather) to pull our teeth out, without Novacaine. The dentist was forbidden from using any needles or equipment on blacks for fear of contamination. Our ailments were usually addressed with medicines prepared at home, according to old folk recipes that relied on ingredients taken out of the rain forest around Lacoochee.

When Cummer Sons Cypress Company opened its lumber mill operation in Lacoochee, it insured its success by identifying two natural resources of the South that were cheap and plentiful: Negroes and Cypress trees. Nature had provided thousands of acres of cypress trees, which flourished in the hot, damp climate of the West Coast of Florida; the course of American history provided the Negro population as an available, cheap source of labor. Black men and women had been brought to this country in large numbers as part of the slave industry. After hundreds of years of service to America's white farmers and land owners, and despite the Emancipation Proclamation and the Thirteenth Amendment, Negroes were left by southern reconstruction and deeply embedded custom to be identified as "former slaves" (even if we weren't) and treated as "less than second-class" citizens (which we weren't).

The absence of any kind of fair or equitable educational and employment opportunity in the South forced blacks to be mobile in order to find work where and when an opportunity presented itself. Despite a conservative political base and a strictly segregated society in the South, the great majority of the country's black population continued to make their homes there because of the opportunities for agricultural work. The presence of large cypress forests in Pasco County, and a company with the money to harvest those trees and provide jobs and housing for its labor force, led many blacks to that particular area. One of the many drawn there for those reasons was my father, James Grant, Sr. He and my mother, Viola, moved from South Carolina to Lacoochee because that's where the work was.

The segregation of American society in the South was very structured. We were expected, by society, to know our place – which was likely to be as an uneducated, non-intelligent manual laborer, who had no right to associate with white people. We couldn't even use the same facilities they did. We were to experience the journey of life from the back of the bus – sitting on its uncomfortable benches and leaving the cushy seats up front for the white people. It didn't matter to many of them if we enjoyed the ride or not.

There wasn't much white people would allow us to do in those days. You could be a schoolteacher or an athlete to get away from the manual labor and servant-type jobs, but there wasn't much else they were going to allow you to do. I came from a family of eight. We only had outdoor plumbing. We could see white people live in a way we couldn't dream of, because if we did think we could live like that, we were simply being foolish and we would get depressed at our own lot in life. You have to understand what that could do to a person. A lot of players who came up through Mobile [Alabama] went through the same thing. ... Watching that type of disparity had a direct effect on all of us, and it was just a matter of time before it had to stop. I wanted to make my mark, I wanted people, white people in power especially, to know that I was alive and when it came time for me to confront them, I was going to do that by hitting the baseball. Hard.
Hank Aaron, quoted in Shut Out, A Story of Race and Baseball in Boston, by Howard Bryant, Routledge, NY, 2002, p. 50

Years of trusted service might get a black worker promoted to a slightly better position in the mill, which was respected more highly than the common laborer – like a skidder operator. But, it didn't mean any extra wages, just a little respect. It wasn't really an acknowledgement by management that you had the ability to think, but only that you could be trusted to do a more important job, if still only one designated for "coloreds."

American society's treatment of blacks divided black families for generations. Slavery separated families as owners selected slaves based on the owner's needs, not family ties. When slavery ended, the economic realities of a de facto segregated society continued to break up families as blacks were offered a limited range of jobs, many of which took them far from home for extended periods, such as train porters and domestic help. Others were forced to leave their families behind just to seek decent employment. Despite those deprivations and the lost time and lessons to be learned from those taken or drawn away from their families, we were still blessed to have those lessons that were passed down to us by our elders who survived. They were powerful guidelines for life. I have no memory of my father, who died when I was only two years old, but I know he left me more than my name, James Grant, Jr. My Mom saw to it that I always remembered him. We were taught to be patient, taught to be respectful, taught to build up an endurance, taught how to handle the anger that would naturally well up inside when we were faced with discrimination and hatred. Inside of each of the ancient cypress trees there was a hollow, which was exposed when the trees were harvested. My mother taught me that just like the cypress, there was a place inside me where my endurance dwelled - a place where no man, no society, could reach, unless I let them. She also taught me that there would be a time when I would have to let all of that anger go; to release it in a way that was not hurtful or harmful to myself or others. Otherwise, she cautioned, it would hold me down in a way far more devastating than the prejudice that caused it. So, what you do is you go in the outhouse, or someplace private like that, and you scream, letting out all the emotion, and you come out with a smile on your face. One rule was you never let the person getting to you see the anger. You can't deny that type of emotion – revenge or anger – but the strong side of you, the perseverance and the patience, that's got to win over the other part. My Mom, my uncle and other elders were giving me the lessons to deal with the situations that would come up, because they knew what I would face, since they had been through it all before. They never proclaimed that we didn't have it in us to handle any situation.

The efforts of black elders to preserve community history and family heritage became powerful tools for maintaining dignity and hope in the grim presence of racial segregation. ... Elders invoked their experiences of slavery to strengthen African American resolve in the difficult environment of Jim Crow. They also told stories of the adversities slaves faced in order to encourage and cajole younger blacks to excel. ... Over time, the oral histories of slavery and segregation began to merge into a powerful stream of popular knowledge used to teach young people to be constantly on guard lest they fall prey to capricious actions of white folks.
Remembering Jim Crow, African Americans Tell About Life in the Segregated South, edited by William H. Chafe, Raymond Gavins and Robert Korstad, The New Press, New York, 2001, page 56

My Mom put the world in perspective for me. She led by example and used everyday life as her classroom to teach humility and self-esteem, to teach kindness and respect, for others and for ourselves.

I was the second youngest child in my family. My three sisters, including my twin, Johnnie Mae, and my younger brother, Julius, lived in our two-bedroom company shack along with my Mom, my Mom's brother (Uncle Boy) and me. From time to time my Mom's sister, Aunt Janey, also would take up residence with us.

While almost all the men in Lacoochee worked in some capacity at the lumber mill, most of the women worked at the citrus canning factory, which we all called the "juice plant." That's where Mom worked, in addition to working as a domestic. She even worked at the lumber mill on rare occasions. She was over-working herself to try and keep the family together. When I was thirteen years old, she collapsed over the kitchen stove while cooking breakfast for all of us. Despite the burns she suffered, and her fatigue, she went to work that day. Since I was the oldest son living at home, I knew it was time for me to work to help sustain the household. It was never really a question of where I would work, only when I would start and that time had now come. Although I told them I was 18 (and they probably knew I wasn't) it didn't matter to them. I was one more source of cheap labor, one more person working for the company. In addition to working at the mill, I was picking oranges, and getting paid 15 cents a box. And my sisters and I would sing and dance at the company store on paydays, hoping that the mill workers would throw a few pennies and nickels into the bucket we put out to encourage their donations.

Although money was certainly at a premium for us, and there were times our bellies weren't full, it was the only life we knew. We really didn't know we were hungry or poor, though. Mom cooked chicken and stewed fish, and at times we'd have biscuits and syrup for breakfast. But our meals included possum and coon, which I was never fond of, and all the other staples of a black, Southern "diet", like hog maws and chitlins. (Hog maws are the lining of a pig's stomach and chitlins are a pig's large intestines.) These were foods that were served to slaves as the discards of the pig after the slave masters took all the best parts, like the chops and loins, and the parts they would cure as hams and bacon.

Mom made us understand that we were blessed to have a roof over our heads, however humble, and to have food on our table, however basic. Her philosophy was "Live simple, live prayerful and never ask for more from a person than you would expect from yourself." She also taught us that we can't take a blessing for granted and expect it to continue. She believed that you had to earn the continuousness of the blessing. She helped me to understand that by seeing to it we would help feed others. When we went out to fish, Mom made sure we brought home more fish than we could eat at one meal. She would cook enough for the children to eat. Then, as we ate, she prepared the rest of the food and packaged it with the names of neighboring families on them. She would give each of us four or five packages, and our job was to bring them to our less fortunate neighbors who needed it. Mom gave us explicit directions that when we delivered the food, we couldn't leave it on the porch or give it to any one except the head of the household. That way the person responsible for feeding their family would be the one to pass it out to his or her family. To do otherwise would be disrespectful. We were being taught the blessing of giving, and manners and respect. The lessons impressed upon me by my Mom were priceless and have remained with me throughout my life. The value of those lessons and the memory of Mom are the things that continue to draw me to Lacoochee.

One of our only sources of diversion when I grew up in Lacoochee was to play sports with other kids our age. Baseball and basketball were our two favorite pastimes. We would play basketball out on the old clay court outside the elementary school, and sometimes the elders would rig portable lights up for us to play outside the row house school after dark. But any version of baseball, including stickball, was the first love of all the kids then. We would play out on the dirt roads for our enjoyment and to entertain all the folks sitting out on their porches. We shared whatever primitive equipment we had, and passed it down to the next youngest kid when we got too big.

If we wanted to see a movie, we had to save up the cost of admission: nine cents. Then we would muster up the courage to cross the railroad tracks, because the only movie house within walking distance was in the white part of Lacoochee. Inside the theatre we were reminded of our place in life – separate and apart from the whites. We had to sit in the balcony, the section reserved for "colored only." Although we were segregated, we were safe. It was the walk to the theatre that was dangerous. We knew that as soon as we crossed the tracks the white kids, who knew we would be out on Friday nights, would be lying in wait for us. We would walk along the tracks as far as we could and only cross over at the point closest to the theatre. We would get called all kinds of names. Then, of course, there was the "duking." They would get a hold of our head and ram their knuckles into our skulls for fun. Unfortunately, there really wasn't much we could do about it. You're too far to run back home, so you have to stay there. Your stomach is tied up in knots as to how much you are going to fight, how much you are going to defend yourself, or if you are going to let them beat you up, hoping you can take whatever it was and then go into the movies. We certainly didn't like it but we knew when we ventured out that, if we wanted to see Gene Autry, Andy Devine, the Cisco Kid, or Roy Rogers badly enough, we had to endure the white kids' knuckles and name calling. It came with the territory as a "colored person" in the South in the 1940s. We had two choices: stay home and do nothing, or endure the hazing we would get as part of the cost of going to the movies.

When we got out of the movie house, we encountered the same rituals on the way home until we crossed the track back into "our" section of Lacoochee. We just accepted it as part of our lives. The truth is, in one way or another, we were always having our heads handed to us as blacks growing up in the South, and although it wasn't always physical abuse, it hurt nonetheless. It was the way of life in the South: there was a way that whites thought about blacks, and on the other hand, there was a way that blacks thought about whites. That was passed down from generation to generation. If you were black, you were actually less than a human being to tell the truth. You were treated differently. When you were a kid they called you "boy" and when you became of age they called you "uncle." The practice of segregation, in its full insidious effect, pervaded every aspect of Southern life. But there were some whites that were fine, and very supportive.

It wasn't until the 1940s that American blacks started to migrate from the mills and farms of the South to the larger urban areas of the North. Even though blacks were more densely concentrated in the South, we had no political power or even political representation. In fact, we had little or no civil rights. Most Southerners just didn't consider blacks to be human beings. Those that did, couldn't conceive the notion that blacks had any rights or even feelings. The Civil War had ended, on paper, over seventy years earlier. Slavery had officially ended. But old habits die hard. Deep in the heart of southwestern Florida, in the 1940s, blacks were still controlled by whites, even if they no longer owned us. Perhaps now we got paid for our work, but the meager wages we received barely covered our room and board, which was what our forefathers had received for their work as slaves.

Having been raised in the South, without ever really getting farther than forty miles from my hometown until I was a teenager, I only knew the Southern way .... the way that said blacks had to use separate water fountains, separate bathrooms, and separate waiting rooms. If separate facilities did not exist, we had to do without. We were expected to know that if we used public transportation we were relegated to the back of the bus. If there were no seats remaining in the "back" of the bus, we were expected to stand, even if there were empty seats in the front of the bus. It's just the way it was.

As negative as all of that was, it actually served to build strength and humility in most Southern blacks. It is easy to understand our humility, if you give it some thought. Society treated us as though we were less than human, and therefore we best be humble in society. Yet, while that treatment took away whatever expectations other children could enjoy, it gave black children a sense of appreciation for our elders and for what we did have. It forged our mettle so that we could endure hardship to secure rights. If I wanted to enjoy the right to see Gene Autry ride off into the sunset at the movie theatre, I had to pay nine cents **and** endure the humiliation and beatings regularly visited upon me by the "whites." I made the choice to go see the Gene Autry movies, knowing I would get beat up. Although I could run, I could not hide and I knew that fighting back wasn't really an option either.

Of course, it is just as easy to understand why some of the people treated that way could become angry, enraged and militant. However, blacks who resisted the Southern way in the 1940s and later, too often found themselves at the end of a swinging rope. Even during World War II, while young blacks were fighting and dying along with white soldiers and sailors to defend our freedoms, blacks were being "lynched" in their homelands of Alabama, Mississippi, Georgia, and Louisiana by racist vigilantes for perceived offenses, and sometimes just for being black. I remember one time they arrested a guy for reckless eyeballing. They claimed he was looking at a white woman, and in the newspaper they had a picture of just his eyes.

I tell you this not to seek your sympathy, or to vent any anger. In fact, I don't harbor any anger whatsoever at the things I experienced in my life. I understand, even more so now, that people were acting out a way of life that had been ingrained long before I was born. I believe the Southern whites that taunted me and discriminated against me had no personal hatred for me. They were products of generations of racial feelings that existed in the South. Fortunately for me I had my Mom and Lacoochee.

In 1959, after I had left Lacoochee to play for the Indians, Cummer Sons closed shop, and Lacoochee, which was totally dependent on the mill, teetered on extinction. Knowing what the meager existence was like while I was there, it was hard to imagine how life could get even more difficult, but it did. Since the mill closed, Lacoochee's economy has continuously eroded, almost in synch with the dilapidated, remaining structure of the mill, which stands as a reminder of what happened to the town itself. The silent work whistle and abandoned work areas speak volumes about the lack of work in Lacoochee since 1959. To me, however, Lacoochee is as much a state of mind as it is a place. It existed for me as an anchor throughout all that has happened in my life. It continues its hold on me and calls out to my heart and mind constantly. I go there as often as I can, but sadly, it is not often enough. I still have family in Lacoochee, and just as importantly, my personal and emotional roots run just as deep and strong as they always have.

CHAPTER 3

TWENTY-GAME WINNERS

If you had a pill that would guarantee a pitcher twenty wins, but might take five years off his life, he'd take it.
Jim Bouton, in Ball Four

For a pitcher to win 20 games is like breaking the sound barrier, is like an actor winning the Academy Award, like winning eight Gold Medals, like going around the world in 79 days.
Vida Blue, to Ron Bergman, The Sporting News, Oct. 30, 1973

Making a lot of starts and winning 20 is important because it tells the players around the league that you're consistent. It tells them you have pride in what you do, that you keep yourself healthy and keep your body in shape.
Ferguson Jenkins, to Jerome Holtzman, The Sporting News, April 19, 1969

There are a lot of ways to win 20 games, a lot of pieces. One of the ways is to take the ball every time it's your turn.
Tony LaRussa, Manager

I knew it would ruin my arm, but one year of 25-7 is worth five of 15-15.
Steve Stone

My personal mission, as always, was to win twenty games.
Bob Gibson

People have asked me about the significance of being a twenty-game winner, and, specifically being a black twenty-game winner. In reality, it has no more practical significance than being a nineteen-game winner. Is a pitcher who never wins more than 19 games in a season, like Dock Ellis or Jim Bibby, or 18 like Rudy May, any worse than a pitcher who had a twenty-win season in his career? Probably not, but he is certainly perceived differently. Why? The answer lies somewhere in our love for round numbers and magic plateaus. Ask a hitter who bats .299 how he feels about that .001. You know he wanted it, so he could legitimately claim to be a .300 hitter. I remember that was one of the regrets Mickey Mantle had at the end of his career - that his performance during the last two seasons of his career caused his lifetime batting average to fall to .298, which dropped him from the prestigious

17

list of career .300 hitters. I don't think it really made Mickey any less of a great player, but perception means a lot in baseball.

Being a twenty-game winner or a .300 hitter was, and is, part of common baseball lore. They are the benchmarks; the standards of excellence. At the time I played, 30 home runs was the standard. Now 50 home runs is the standard, thanks to Barry Bonds, Sammy Sosa and Mark McGwire. Funny thing is, back when Willie Mays hit his 50th home run, that achievement didn't raise the standard, because it was Willie. Everybody just expected great things out of him. One hundred runs batted in is another standard for a hitter, just as 20 wins and 200 strikeouts are the standards for pitchers. These statistical achievements came to be commonly accepted measures of success in baseball and everybody worked towards them and continues to work toward them. Every pitcher wants to be a twenty-game winner. **That** is a pitcher! Once you became a member of that club you knew you were in select company, because there weren't a whole lot of guys winning twenty games in one season.

> **Ferguson Arthur Jenkins of the Cubs won 20 games last year, a magic figure that has been the goal of every big league pitcher ever since baseball became an organized sport. To make it all the more remarkable, Fergie achieved it in his first full season as a major league starting pitcher.**
> *Edgar Munzel, The Sporting News, May 4, 1968*

Since 1901, approximately 6,000 men have pitched in the Major Leagues. Blacks have been allowed to play during only 58 of those 104 years. In total, less than 400 pitchers have ever won twenty games in a season. Thus, only approximately 6.6 percent, or roughly one out of sixteen, of all pitchers have ever achieved that milestone.

Only 13 black pitchers have done it, and I am one of them. As one of The Black Aces, I am part of a group that comprises only .0002 of all of the Major League pitchers who have toed the rubber since 1901. There are fewer Black Aces than 300 game winners (22), 500 home run hitters (20) and perfect game pitchers (17). When such a low percentage of people have been able to accomplish such a feat, we have to wonder what makes it so difficult. What does it take to reach that milestone? What are the components that make a twenty-game winner?

The answer is not always the same for every pitcher or even for the same pitcher in different seasons. There are several factors that contribute to attaining and sustaining a record as a winning pitcher. As you study the different kinds of seasons enjoyed by twenty-game winners, you recognize a number of factors contributing to their success:

Making it to the majors as a starter
Getting the starts
Good defensive team

Run support
Health and conditioning;
Manager's game strategy and pitching rotation; and
Luck.

Making it to the majors: This is obviously the most important factor on the list because it is the threshold and is absolutely the most difficult to accomplish. Millions of young men from around the globe dream of standing on a big league mound and pitching. Very, very few are afforded the opportunity. There are only thirty Major League teams, each with a pitching rotation of about five starters, maybe only four of whom will get enough starts in a year to have any realistic chance to win twenty. That means that at most only 120 men can have any shot at this brass ring each year. Needless to say, to become one of those 120 men, you need to possess world class skill, and the determination, discipline and desire to survive the minor leagues and all else that goes with making it to the majors.

Getting the starts: Consider the number of twenty-game winners in the Major Leagues each season over the last eleven years:

2005	4
2004	3
2003	5
2002	5
2001	7
2000	4
1999	3
1998	4
1997	4
1996	3
1995	**NONE**

With all of its incredible talent, the Major Leagues have only produced less than four twenty-game winners a year, on average, during this time. That translates into about three percent of the starting pitchers (roughly one in thirty), just half the average since 1902. When you expand the sample to cover the period from 1950 through 2005, the average number of twenty-game winners per year in the majors rises only slightly to about 6, and that can be traced back to when starting pitchers got more starts because they were part of a four-man rotation, not five. When managers adopted the five-man rotation and clubs fell in love with relief pitcher specialists, taking starters out of the game earlier, the number of twenty-game winners dropped dramatically. The number of twenty-game winners, by decade, shows this:

1950s:	58
1960s:	73
1970s:	96
1980s:	37
1990s:	34

Because of the depletion of Major League rosters caused by the war during the 1940s, and the completely different nature of the game that led to pitchers not only winning twenty games, but thirty, prior to the 1940s, I have not focused on statistics prior to 1950.

On Opening Day in 2000, the rosters of all thirty Major League teams included only twenty-one pitchers who had won twenty games in a season, and only five of those pitchers had done it more than once: Roger Clemens, David Cone, Tom Glavine, Greg Maddux, and Bret Saberhagen. By contrast, there were forty former twenty-game winners in 1975 among only twenty-four teams, and twenty-one of those pitchers had won twenty games more than once.

You get 15 wins a year now, you're considered an elite pitcher.
Tom Glavine, February 2001

So, I think the single most important element of becoming a twenty-game winner in the Major Leagues is getting the starts. Just about every Major League starter has the ability to give himself a chance to win twenty games. If you start forty ballgames you have a chance to win twenty games. For some, that may not ever happen, but, for others like me, that one time, in 1965, it did, and it's heaven when it does. When you look at certain guys out there, like Greg Maddux in his prime, he could win twenty games or more every year, and he has won twenty twice, because he has the talent and he gets the starts. It's a matter of getting the starts. Once you have talent enough to become a starting pitcher in the Major Leagues, and you get the starts, there is a possibility that you can win twenty. Denny McLain is the last pitcher to win thirty games in a season, winning 31 in 1968, when he started 41 games. When asked about what it takes to be a big winner, he emphasized the number of starts:

[You] must get out there every fourth day. Rain or shine, I was out there every fourth day. If there were two rainouts in a row, I'd get out there before someone else. You can't worry about offending anyone. In '68, I pitched the Sunday before the All-Star break and the first day after it. Every time you pitch a fifth day, sooner or later that takes a start away from you. You've got to get out there 40 times.
The Sporting News, July 3, 1971

There's a flip side to this though with a little bit of irony to it. There are good pitchers who have lost twenty games in a season; pitchers who in other seasons might also have won twenty games. Fellow Ace, Sad Sam Jones is one of them, winning twenty in 1959 after losing twenty in 1955. It may seem odd to say it but, in order to lose twenty games you have to be a good enough pitcher that the manager had the confidence to give you the ball often enough to get that many decisions. This reinforces my notion that being good enough to be given the call to start on a regular basis is the number one element in putting together a twenty-win season.

Playing for a team with good defense: Defense is one element of a winning team, and a very important element. As a pitcher, if I had to choose only one strong point for my team, I would select a strong defense. An outfielder's ability to chase down potential extra base hits and convert them to outs is a wonderful thing for a pitcher to behold, as is the arm of an outfielder who can cut down a runner trying to take an extra base. The same can be said for infielders who get to the balls hit in the hole, and turn difficult double plays. They are lifesavers, not just to their team, but to any pitcher's chance of winning twenty, as are the arms of catchers who nail would be base stealers.

In Bob Gibson's fabulous year of 1968, when he had 22 wins, 9 losses, and an unbelievable Earned Run Average (ERA) of 1.12, not one of his teammates was even among the top three league leaders in any major offensive category, including Batting Average, On Base Percentage, Slugging Percentage, Runs Scored, Hits, Total Bases, Home Runs, or Runs Batted In. There were, however, three Gold Glove winners on that team: Dal Maxvill, Curt Flood, and Gibson himself.

Mike Norris, my fellow Ace, feels that the defense played differently depending on the starting pitcher, and that the better you pitched the better they played:

In 1980, we had a horseshit defense on paper in Oakland, but when I got out there and played, they played their asses off. They made plays like a son of a bitch in the outfield. They didn't hit worth a son of a bitch, cause, see this is the difference. They know when a guy is going out pitching good, they know they don't need that many runs to score. When a guy like Kingman goes out to pitch, they go to bed at night; the outfielders go to bed at night. They get their rest, because they know they're going to be running. So, mentally they approach you differently. They know how you are.
Mike Norris interview

Run support: Baseball is a funny game. A starting pitcher can give up only one run and be the losing pitcher in a 1-0 game, and in his next start he can give up 8 runs and be the winning pitcher in a 9-8 game. There's a well-known baseball saying that the double play is a pitcher's best friend, but there is a lot to be said for a grand slam or a six-run inning. In my twenty-win season in 1965 with the Minnesota Twins, unfortunately for me, they did not give me strong defensive support. In fact, they had the lowest fielding average of any team in the Major Leagues that season. But boy did they make up for it at the plate. They led the league in runs scored, with 774, and in team batting, with a .254 average. I was pitching really well on my own, throwing a league leading six shutouts, but it was great sitting in the dugout watching Tony Oliva, Zoilo Versalles and Harmon Killebrew, among others, pound the ball and circle the bases so often. That year, Oliva was the American League batting champ, with a .321 average, and led the league with 185 base hits. Versalles took most of the other honors, winning the Most Valuable Player award, while leading the league in runs scored, total bases, and doubles, and tying for the league lead in triples.

When I was traded to the Pittsburgh Pirates late in my career, in 1971, I was a reliever. The first game I got into I gave up five runs. I remember going into the dugout at the end of the inning and throwing my mitt against the bench. The Pirate skipper, Danny Murtaugh, looked at me and asked, "Can you hold them? Because if you can we'll score some runs." I'll be darned if that bunch of Pirates didn't go out and score eight runs the very next inning, making me a winning pitcher in my first appearance for the team. Now that's what it's like to pitch for a team that can score runs!

You have to rely on your teammates, defense and offense. And, the Cubs we were a little shy of both from time to time. But when I pitched, the guys just mustered up. They put together 2, 3 runs and good defense for me, and I won ball games. And I did it in a small ballpark. So, there were times when if I didn't pitch well, I ended up losing. If I did pitch well, the guys played really hard. So, I mean it was a combination of the two. "Let's do it. Fergie's pitching today, let's give him a couple of good runs against Drysdale or against Seaver or somebody," and I ended up winning some ball games.
Ferguson Jenkins

When Sam Jones finally won twenty games in 1959, his tenth Major League season, he deflected the credit to his teammates, when he noted that the main difference was that "I'm getting more runs."

Health and conditioning: This is a very important component of becoming a twenty-game winner, or of achieving any measure of success in sports. To take advantage of a strong defensive team behind you, or a run-producing team on your side, you need to answer the call every single time it's your turn in the rotation. You need the health to take the mound and the stamina to stay in the game once you get there, long enough to become the pitcher of record.

Pitching a Major League ballgame is a grueling experience. I can't say that a pitcher's body takes the same punishment in the course of a game as a National Football League running back, but certain parts of the pitcher's body, namely the shoulder, elbow and legs certainly do take a pounding. Consider that a pitcher doesn't get a running start like a fullback, or a basketball player attempting a dunk, or a hockey player on a breakaway play. A pitcher starts from a dead stop and uses only a modest windup and his legs, to propel a ball towards home plate at speeds reaching 100 miles an hour. Bob Gibson once commented to a reporter: "Have you ever thrown a ball 100 miles an hour? Everything hurts. Even your ass hurts." Considering that the game is played during the summer months, and that you could be asked to throw in excess of one hundred pitches on a warm, humid day, it is understandable why pitchers need two or three days rest; and why they need to be among the better conditioned athletes on the team.

Guys who had legendary careers, like Nolan Ryan, and like Roger Clemens is having now, knew that they had to be in top shape to stay in the rotation, turn after turn, year after year, throughout their career. It is no secret that these two star pitchers were two of the hardest working players on their respective teams at conditioning themselves. Physical regimen between starts allowed them to make 1,444 starts between them, and Clemens isn't finished yet. That's an awful lot of pitching, and their combined results underscore the importance of staying in such great shape. Together, they amassed: eight twenty-win seasons, two nineteen-win seasons, four eighteen-win seasons, 10,216 strikeouts, and 665 victories and an incredible 1,129 career decisions.

Don Newcombe remembers that when he was with the Newark Eagles, his manager, former Negro League great, Willie Wells (Hall of Fame, 1997), stressed the importance of a pitcher building strong legs, and emphasized running over throwing. Wells, who was also still playing for the Eagles at that time, was a person whose advice was to be heeded. He is considered by many to be the best shortstop never to play a game in the Major Leagues. Wells was an eight-time Negro Leagues All-Star who started as a pitcher before suffering an arm injury. He was a leadoff hitter, who achieved a .328 career batting average. Buck O'Neil, the first officially recognized coach employed by a Major League team, compares him to Alex Rodriguez. Wells is also credited with helping Jackie Robinson learn how to make the pivot play at second base when the Dodgers wanted Robinson to make the transition from shortstop to second base before he left Montreal in 1946.

Newcombe also remembers that early on in his career Jackie Robinson would get after him to run more as a conditioning tool. Robinson felt that Newcombe was tiring late in the game because of lack of conditioning. That started Newcombe on his training regimen, which he reflects on with pride:

I became known for my running. I ran to keep my legs strong – I didn't get tired in the seventh inning, but got stronger. Alston used to compliment me on my strength in the later innings in St. Louis and Cincinnati in the heat. In close games, he'd let me stay in, because I wasn't tired and was a good hitter. We won many games because I knew how to run. I was a hard worker. I didn't have control of my fastball or an outstanding curveball until I worked hard. I'm sure Dodgers like Duke Snider will verify that I was the hardest worker on the team. It was the hard work that again made me one of the toughest pitchers in baseball.
Don Newcombe, We Played The Game, Danny Peary, Editor. New York: Hyperion, 1994.

In April 1970, as Ferguson Jenkins began what would be his fourth straight twenty-win season, he acknowledged the importance of a pitcher's health in the make-up of a twenty-game winner, in his conversation with Edgar Munzel of *The Sporting News*:

The one thing I'm hoping for is good health. That's the most important

factor if you want to be a 20-victory possibility. You can't reach that goal if you're out of action for a few weeks.

In other words, you have to escape hamstring pulls, charley horses, arm trouble, getting hit by a line drive and every other type of injury and ailment.

When your turn comes up to pitch, you have to be ready. And sometimes you may not feel chipper, but you'd better go out there, nevertheless. Every time you fail to pitch, it cuts down on your potential for 20 victories.

A potential 20-game winner has to start at least 35 times. And his chances naturally progress if he starts 40 times.

For the past three years, I've been averaging 40 starts. In 1967, I started 38 games, then 40 in 1968 and last season I had my high of 42 starts.

Manager's game strategy and pitching rotation: Most Major League managers now use a five-man pitching rotation. That means if all five pitchers make every one of their starts the most starts they will get will be 32 or 33. If the manager used a four-man rotation that number would increase to 40 or 41. When I came to the majors, in 1954, it was only a 154 game season, but with a four-man rotation, that still meant 38 or 39 starts if you took the ball every time. It was not uncommon for the great pitchers of the game, Hall of Famers like Bob Feller and Robin Roberts to get 39 or 40 starts. When the Major League schedule grew to 162 games (in the American League in 1961 and the National League in 1962) there were eight more starts for the staff to divide up, but it did not have a significant effect on the number of starts or twenty-game winners.

Workhorses were workhorses, whenever they played, provided their manager gave them the ball. Mickey Lolich of the Detroit Tigers started 169 games in the four seasons from 1971 through 1974, including 45 starts in 1971. He won 79 games during those four years, with 25 wins in 1971. Getting the ball every fourth day increases a pitcher's chance to win twenty games. Consider the following statistics on Ferguson Jenkins' amazing seven twenty-win seasons:

Year	Starts	Wins
1967	38	20
1968	40	20
1969	42	21
1970	39	22
1971	39	24
1972	36	20
1974	41	25

Since the days of Ferguson Jenkins and Mickey Lolich, only one starting pitcher in either league has started more than 39 games (except for a knuckleball pitcher). Jim Clancy started 40 games for the Toronto Blue Jays in 1982 (and had a career high 16 wins). The knuckleball pitchers are a whole different breed, and have to be considered for the anomaly they are. Over the three-year period from 1977 through 1979, Hall of Famer, Phil Niekro started 43, 42 and 44 games, respectively, for the Atlanta Braves, and was the last National Leaguer to start 40 or more games. In the American League, knuckler, Charlie Hough, of the Texas Rangers, was the last one to start 40 or more games, starting exactly 40 in 1987. Prior to that, fellow knuckler, Wilbur Wood, started 182 games over four seasons, beginning with an incredible 49 starts in 1972.

If a manager employs a five-man rotation a pitcher is getting seven to nine less starts than a pitcher on a team with a four-man rotation. That's seven to nine less opportunities to win. Consider that some of a pitcher's starts will be lost to injuries, rainouts, and the need for spot starters due to doubleheaders. As you begin to whittle away a pitcher's number of starts it gets increasingly difficult to reach twenty wins. A winning percentage of .667 is an extraordinary year for a pitcher, but that's what it would take to win twenty games if he only gets thirty starts.

While the number of starts, which is directly affected by the pitching rotation, is critical to a pitcher's chances to win twenty games, the number of games a pitcher gets to finish is also important. Many baseball games are decided in the final inning of a game. The less likely a starting pitcher is to be around in the eighth and ninth inning of a game, the less likely he will get a decision. Once again, the lower the number of decisions a starter gets, the less likely he is to win twenty games. Unfortunately for those starting pitchers who now want to win twenty games, the role of the starting pitcher has continued to evolve on a downward slope. The role of the pitching staff in general has continued to change since 1901. Originally, starting pitchers were given the ball and expected to complete the game they started. In 1901, pitching staffs were completing better than eighty percent of their games. The Philadelphia Athletics pitching staff completed 124 of the 137 games they started. That year, Cy Young started 41 games and completed 38 of them. Most teams only carried seven or eight pitchers, and five or six of them pitched ninety percent of the innings. In 1904, Jack Chesbro of the New York Yankees started 51 games, and completed 48 of them. Finishing the year with a record of 41-12, he was responsible for 53 decisions of the team's 151 games (35%). That year the Boston Red Sox staff completed 148 of their 157 starts, and the St. Louis Cardinals' staff completed 146 games.

When the 1911 New York Giants' pitchers, led by the legendary Christy Mathewson and Rube Marquard, led the National League in complete games with 95, it was the first time that a team in either league, led the league with less than 100 complete games. The teams' reliance on fewer pitchers to do all the work, the endurance of the pitchers, and possibly their familiarity with the hitters (they were playing 154 games against only 7 opponents, seeing each team 22 times in a season), could account for the fact that it was not unusual for six or seven pitchers in each league to win more than twenty games. There were several thirty-game winners in addition to Chesbro, including Smokey Joe Wood (Boston Red Sox), Walter Johnson (Washington Senators), Jack Coombs (Philadelphia Athletics), Jim Bagby (Cleveland Indians), and Grover Cleveland Alexander (Philadelphia Phillies). Walter Johnson had ten consecutive twenty plus win seasons, from 1910 to 1919, and Christy Mathewson ran off twelve straight twenty plus win seasons, from 1903 to 1914.

The number of complete games thrown by Major League pitching staffs continued to decline at a fairly constant pace, as did the number of pitchers who won twenty or more games.

I remember one game when I was pitching for Cleveland against the Red Sox and Birdie Tebbetts was my manager. I was leading by nine runs and Boston scored four runs, then they got three more runs, and Birdie come out there and said, "Hey, if you think somebody else is coming in the game, that's bullshit. You're gonna finish this game, win or lose." Things have changed since then.

When Dizzy Dean won 30 games in 1934 for the St. Louis Cardinals, he was the last pitcher to do so until McLain won 31 for the Detroit Tigers in 1968, and no one has won more than 27 since (Bob Welch, Oakland Athletics, 1990). After 1923, only one team's pitchers would complete more than 100 games in a season – the Chicago White Sox in 1941. Since then, the most games completed by a team's staff is 94, accomplished three times, most recently by the Oakland Athletics in 1980, (fellow Ace Mike Norris, Rick Langford, Steve McCatty, Matt Keough and Brian Kingman) when they were playing "Billyball" with Billy Martin as manager. Mike pitched 24 of those complete games for the Athletics, out of 33 starts, and that is the year Mike won 22 games. Since 1998, no team in the Major Leagues has had more than 17 complete games. (I am not medically qualified to tell if the length of the outings by Oakland pitchers in 1980 was the cause of later problems for those pitchers but in 1983, three years after combining for 93 complete games, Langford, McCatty, Norris, Keough, and Kingman combined for a total of five complete games.)

The following charts visually display the decline in the number of complete games. Chart I represents the number of complete games thrown by the team that led its respective league for the years 1904 to 2005, starting with Boston's 148 and St. Louis' 146 (in 1904), through and including St. Louis' 15 to top the National League in 2005 and the 9 complete games thrown by each of the pitching staffs of the Chicago White Sox, Oakland Athletics, Minnesota Twins and Toronto Blue Jays, to tie for the American League lead.

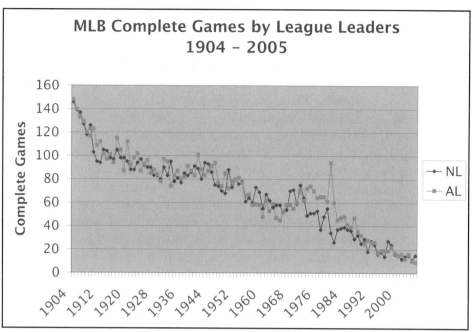

Chart I

Chart II is more dramatic. It represents the sharp decrease in the average number of complete games per Major League team from 1904 (136.63) through 2005 (6.3):

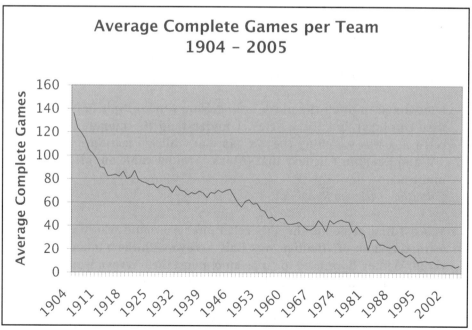

Chart II

I don't believe that lack of ability or conditioning on the part of starting pitchers were the reasons managers stopped letting their starting pitchers complete games they had started. I believe it was just a natural evolution of the game, and to some degree, our society itself. We don't stress endurance as much as we admire dominance. We don't value general practitioners as much as we seek out specialists. During my early playing days it was fully expected that a starting pitcher would complete the game, except on a day when he didn't have his "stuff." On those days, a manager would turn to a relief pitcher who was usually a guy that had been a starter but no longer had the endurance to go more than a few innings. In 1968 the Dodgers used me mainly as a relief pitcher. Although I was a starter for half of the 1969 season with the expansion Montreal Expos, I was a reliever for the remainder of that season with the St. Louis Cardinals, and for the remainder of my career, with the Athletics and the Pittsburgh Pirates. By the late 1950s and early 1960s, baseball was experiencing a new commodity: a pitcher who could completely overpower the opposition for one or two innings: the closer. Starting with Ryne Duren of the New York Yankees (1958) and Dick Radatz of the Boston Red Sox (1962), the use of relief pitchers increased dramatically through the 1960s, 70s and 80s. Duren used a 100 mile per hour fastball to shut down opponents, averaging well better than a strikeout an inning. Radatz never started a game in his seven-year career, but was on the mound to finish the game 297 times. The tradition was continued when the success of Lee Smith, Sparky Lyle, Bruce Sutter, Rollie Fingers and the late Dan Quisenberry made it commonplace for every team to have one pitcher who the manager deemed the most unhittable for one inning, and the ninth inning of just about every game belonged to him.

When I started in the 1950s, (the norm) was the complete game ... when you threw a complete game then, it was 'so what?'"
Roger Craig, former major league pitcher and manager (Arizona Republic)

I screamed to pitch the ninth inning from time to time ... Now it's 'five (innings) and fly. ... Hey, I understand the money, but I'm retro ... I was watching the A's game at Chicago last Saturday on TV, and I couldn't believe that (Mark) Mulder came out after eight innings.
Vida Blue, (Arizona Republic)

When I first came up, the only relief pitcher around who was really attracting a lot of attention was Luis Arroyo with the Yankees. As I recall, Whitey Ford used to go seven innings, then Arroyo would mop up. When I started, you hardly ever saw a relief pitcher. When they gave me the ball at the start of a game, I was expected to keep it. Now, hardly anyone goes the distance any more.
Bob Gibson, quoted by David Moffit, 1982

The newest generation of closers has brought the art form to a whole new level. When Mariano Rivera, of the New York Yankees, and Eric Gagne, of the Los Angeles Dodgers, enter the game in the eighth or ninth inning, it usually means the game is over for their opponent. As a sign of the increased importance of relief pitchers, relievers came to be recognized for their role in the game. Prior to 1977, Jim Konstanty, one of the 1950 Philadelphia Phillies Whiz Kids, was the only relief pitcher to win either a Cy Young Award or the Most Valuable Player Award. He was elected the National League MVP, with a 16-7 record, appearing in 74 games and earning 22 saves. Since 1977, National League relief pitchers have won the Cy Young Award three times: Bruce Sutter in 1979 (37 saves, 2.22 ERA), Steve Bedrosian of the Phillies in 1987 (40 saves), and Gagne in 2003 (55 saves). In the American League, four relief pitchers have won the Cy Young Award: Sparky Lyle of the Yankees in 1977, Rollie Fingers of the Brewers in 1981, Willie Hernandez of the Detroit Tigers in 1984, and Dennis Eckersley of the Athletics in 1992. All of them, except Lyle, also won the American League MVP Award the same season they won the Cy Young Award. Four relievers have been inducted into the Hall of Fame: Eckersley, who was a starter for a good portion of his career; Hoyt Wilhelm, who was a starter for two seasons in the middle of his career, Fingers who was a starter for the first year and a half of his career and never started another game after that, and most recently, Bruce Sutter, who was a true reliever, never having started one game in his career. I think that the Hall needs to continue to acknowledge the evolution of the game and the growing dependence on relief pitchers by inducting some of the other greats who dominated and changed the game, like Lee Smith and Rich "Goose" Gossage, and I believe that will happen soon.

Then there is the issue of the manager himself and his relationship with the starting pitchers, for whatever reason. According to George Crowe, who played for the Cincinnati Reds in 1956, his manager Birdie Tebbetts denied Brooks Lawrence the opportunity to win 20 games, because he did not want a Negro twenty-game winner on his watch. This, despite Lawrence having won thirteen straight games. Tebbetts' view might very well have cost his team the pennant, since they only lost it by two games to the Brooklyn Dodgers. Lawrence only got 30 starts and finished 19-10 with 11 complete games.

I was going for my 20th pitching win the next night, and that's the dividing line for pitchers. That means something. It just seems natural that some guys win 20 games – Juan Marichal, Bob Gibson … but I'll bet they were excited too, the first time.
Phil Niekro, The Sporting News, September 27, 1969

Luck: I think of all the factors that enter into whether a pitcher will or will not win twenty games in a season, luck as a separate factor has to be considered last and least important. I say that because luck, good or bad, will only affect a pitcher's ability to win twenty games in a season if all or most of the other factors are present.

If a pitcher only gets eighteen starts in a season, luck will have nothing to do with him not winning twenty games. In Branch Rickey's famous words, "luck is the residue of design," or "luck is the result when preparation meets opportunity." I believe that most ballplayers understand Mr. Rickey's statement to mean that hard work - in the off season, in spring training, and throughout the season - will result in a better and winning ballplayer and team. Sportswriters and fans will say that a pitcher was "lucky" to win twenty games in a certain year because on the last day of the season he was pitching against the last place team and his team scored ten runs. But it was a combination of many other factors that put that particular pitcher in a position to have "luck" affect him. He was good enough, he had the "stuff," to get to the Major Leagues in the first place. He remained healthy and took enough starts that year to have had nineteen victories by the last game of the season. He played for a team that could score runs. There is also a saying: "people would rather be lucky than good." Now, I certainly wouldn't mind being lucky, but luck will only get you so far on a big league mound. You need to be better than good just to get there. And there is another saying among ballplayers: you make your own luck.

Bob Gibson is the luckiest pitcher in baseball. He is always pitching when the other team doesn't score any runs.
Tim McCarver

All that being said, however, luck does enter into some pitchers making it to twenty wins or not. Bob Gibson was deprived of completing the 1967 season because of a broken leg, but he also lost a chance for another twenty-win season in 1964. He finished the season with 19 victories, and a game he was pitching was called off on account of rain before the game was official, with the Cardinals in the lead.

As you get closer to the goal of twenty wins each play becomes more and more important. Mike Norris remembers feeling added pressure as the victories mounted, and also remembers that luck played a big role in how each of those pivotal plays turned out:

This season went so fast, it was unbelievable. I was already like 17 games, and I was like, whoa. It took me losing one, I got to 17 and I lost a game. Bob Lacey blew one for me. And then I started seeing the magnitude of how difficult this could start being because now at 17 you start getting a little tight. Now you're trying a little harder to do something that you weren't trying so hard, that was coming a little more natural. You're thinking a lot. You're thinking, hell, yeah, you are. Those breaks, man. You gotta get those breaks, man. Luck is so crucial, I mean, you get that pitch on the outside corner or you don't. Line drive down the leftfield line, foul, or fair. Error, you can't control that. Guys playing good behind you, great.
Mike Norris interview

I tried to take a little different approach. I remember my pitching coach Johnny Sain used to say: "Each game you win is a biscuit in the pan." You can't cook another biscuit until the game is over. When that game is over you put that biscuit in the pan. You go game by game. When I won 16, 17, 18, 19, I started hearing things about becoming the first black pitcher to win 20 games in the American League. I thought it was wonderful. I never said, when I was at 15 that I'm going to win 20. I said, I know I'm going to win 16. That's what you go after. You get stopped there, then the next time you go after that one game. You can only count it after you win. So, the pressure is not up front, the pressure is to win the game that you are playing. Those are the kind of pressures that you face. You have to sort of take the other stuff out of it. Everybody knows that sometimes you get on a roll. One time I was 17-2. You get on a roll and it seems like everything comes into fruition and things happen to you. For example, you're losing a ball game 4-0, seventh inning, there's a home run on your side. Nobody does anything in the 8th inning. Two out, there's a walk, an error and somebody hits one out. But, in terms of winning the game, you get down into the seventh inning, you got a two run lead, you're more interested in winning that game that day. You can't let it get away from you. It's not the number that counts in the paper the next day, but winning that game.

Some people think that playing for a winning team is an important factor in a pitcher winning twenty games. Others see this like the question of which came first - the chicken or the egg. I think that pitching is such an integral part of the game, that a quality pitcher who gets the starts can win twenty games even on a losing team. I will grant you that it might not be as easy, because you can be a phenomenal pitcher and not win games because there is no defense behind you, or your team can't score runs, or the team just does not have a winning attitude. Even though it's true that good pitching is one of the key elements of a winning team, even great pitchers can't play all nine positions, or bat in all the runs.

But, there have been twenty-game winners on losing teams, like Mel Stottlemyre who was 20-9 with the 1965 New York Yankees, who were 77-85 (57-76 in games when Stottlemyre was not the pitcher of record). Again, in 1969, Mel was 20-14 and the Yankees were 80-81 (60-67 in games when Stottlemyre was not the pitcher of record). The offense didn't score enough runs when Stottlemyre wasn't pitching to win half the games. The defense and/or relief pitching didn't hold down the opposition sufficiently more than half the time when Stottlemyre wasn't pitching. But Mel still had the "stuff" to have the Yankees come out on top twenty times when he was the pitcher of record. With a better team behind him in general, his job would have been much easier, and his record greater. Mel was a three-time twenty-winner, and won sixteen games several times. With a more potent offense, he would be much more recognized by the fans for the great pitcher he was.

In 1972, Steve Carlton was 27-10 with the Philadelphia Phillies, whose overall record was 59-97 (32-87 in games when Carlton was not the pitcher of record). No other pitcher on the team that year had a winning record, **and no other starting**

pitcher on the team won more than four games, and they were all playing with the same defense behind them and the same lineup.

I think the most famous example of a twenty-game winner on a losing team is Ned Garver, a righthanded pitcher for the 1951 St. Louis Browns. Garver finished the season with a record of 20-12 and the team's overall record was 52-102, which means the Browns were 32-90 in games when he didn't get the decision. He appeared in only 33 games and had 32 decisions. He started 30 games and had 24 complete games. He had the talent; he got the starts. It was amazing! What's even more amazing is that in 1949 he had the most losses in the league – 17, and in 1950 he had the third most losses with 18. In 1951, he was the only pitcher on his team with a winning record, was an All-Star and finished second in the MVP voting. It is the only year in his career when he had a winning record. I guess it was just his year!

It was of course what every kid pitcher dreams about, winning twenty games in the big leagues. When that happened that was the greatest feeling, greatest moment in my professional career – winning the 20th game on the final day of the season. A lot of things have to happen good. That year the team scored some runs for me. Where, the year before, I was second in the league in ERA and only won 13 games. When you're on a team that's not as good as a lot of the rest of them, you have to be a little lucky. I think, the one thing about it, they had some confidence in me. I think, maybe, our players went about it in a little more positive fashion because I was on the mound.
Ned Garver, 20 game winner for St. Louis Browns in 1951

It becomes apparent that different pitchers can, and do, follow different routes to becoming twenty-game winners. Whether they play on teams that are terrific defensively, or are powerhouses offensively, and whether or not they are helped or hindered by luck, I believe that the one constant of a twenty-game winner is that he is talented enough to get the starts at the Major League level, and then has the "stuff" to deliver when he pitches.

CHAPTER 4

DREAMS DEFERRED

What happens to a dream deferred?
Does it dry up
like a raisin in the sun?
Or fester like a sore –
and then run?
from A Dream Deferred, by Langston Hughes (1951)

The real path to a pitcher's mound in a Major League stadium is a lot longer, and more difficult to travel, than the short distance from the dugout to the rubber on the ball field. It is a road that begins countless miles from the ballpark and many years before game day. Just like the route to becoming a twenty-game winner, the path to the Major Leagues doesn't follow any one map or even offer any assurances that you will reach your intended destination. In fact, it is as long and varied, as complex and winding, as humbling and rewarding, as any of the different life-journeys that will be examined in this book. The majority of it is traveled out of the sight of the public. For over a century, it has been traveled by thousands of young men. Some of these eager young men have accomplished a great deal on the mound, rising to various levels of success at different levels of the game, whether as amateurs or Major Leaguers. For all of them it starts with a dream. Many of them have talent but are short on desire. Some are short on talent, but compensate with determination. Some have had their dreams deferred because they were born at the "wrong place at the wrong time." A select few combine their talent with the drive and determination to make their dream a reality even in the face of sometimes overwhelming odds and obstacles. But, each of them, and their individual journeys to the mound, is a vital thread in the fabric of baseball because each has contributed in his own way to making it "America's game." While I salute their efforts, the focus of this book is more limited and will shine a light on two very small, special groups of extraordinarily talented and elite hurlers.

One group is The Black Aces. I was one of the first black pitchers in the American League. In fact, in my rookie year, 1958, I was the only black starting pitcher in the American League. The only other black starters were National Leaguers: fellow future Black Aces, Sad Sam Jones (with the Cardinals) and Don Newcombe (with the Reds), and Brooks Lawrence (also with the Reds). I consider myself fortunate and blessed to have had a successful career in baseball. One thing about baseball is that it is meant for statistics, even more so now than when I played. With the amount of information available due to today's technology, you can isolate and group statistics, and present them in very detailed ways. An announcer in any game can tell you in an instant what a certain batter is hitting against a certain pitcher, when batting in a particular inning, and what the batter's career average is not only for batting, but for batting when he has a certain ball and strike count on him. And the statistics that can be provided in print are in even greater detail. It is great for me because I love the statistics of baseball. Still today I read the box scores of games before I read any stories or articles.

With the great athletes playing in today's game, we constantly hear about new players entering into select groups. In 2004, Ken Griffey, Jr. became the 20th player in the 500 Home Run Club, and Greg Maddux became the 22nd member of the 300 Win Club.

In reflecting on my career, and my statistics, it occurred to me that I too was a member of a very select "club." In the history of the game only thirteen black pitchers have had one or more twenty-win seasons, and I was the first one to accomplish that feat in the American League. The respective journeys of the thirteen Black Aces to the mound are especially important to the game, not just because they made it to the "big show," but also because they did it despite the additional and often overwhelming obstacles that only stood in the path of men of color. I am humbled to be in their company and, while it is a bit awkward for me to speak with such reverence of any group of which I am a member, I am so proud to be one of them. I hope to put any modesty aside so that I can share with you the significance of our collective accomplishments in the broader historical context of the game as it parallels the history of America.

As I looked at the names of the other black pitchers who had twenty-win seasons, and the statistics related to those seasons, it hit me that it took almost twenty years after Jackie Robinson's Major League debut for a black pitcher to become a twenty-game winner in the American League. My mind started racing with questions: What was it like for the players who came before me? What might the great Negro League ballplayers have accomplished if they were allowed to compete? What greatness were we deprived of experiencing because of the "gentlemen's agreement" and Jim Crow laws?

Certainly, I didn't have all the answers to those questions, but I thought it was important for me, as a member of that club, as one of the first black pitchers in the American League, as Larry Doby's former roommate, to examine them and memorialize my recollections and opinions, and to seek out the memories and opinions of the other Black Aces, and the players we played with and against.

In order to fully take measure of these thirteen men, however, I think it is important to first take a look at the careers and experiences of African-American aces who pitched in the Negro Leagues and elsewhere before Jackie Robinson stepped onto a Major League diamond; men who were deprived of their chance to play in the Major Leagues during their prime, or at all, simply because of their race.

Some people think God smiled at Jackie Robinson and chose him to be the black to break baseball's color line. I think it was more like God tapped Jackie on the shoulder and said, "Okay, kid, show me what you got." It was Jackie who smiled, briefly, and then steeled himself to show the world that a black man could compete, and dare succeed, in Major League Baseball. Throughout this book, I will spend more time on Jackie Robinson as he fits into the story chronologically. Suffice it to say, though, that Jackie Robinson's place in the history of the integration of baseball and the integration of America is monumental. Thanks to his discipline, his dedication and his ability, he forged a successful and historic entrance for himself into Organized Baseball. In doing so he blazed a trail that heralded the arrival of black talent in Organized Baseball, and set the stage for the abilities of black players like The Black Aces to be displayed to the world. That being said, we need to turn the spotlight around and remember some of the players who came before Jackie; players who, some believe, were the most gifted to ever pick up a baseball, but who were never given the opportunity to show their talent on the Major League stage. They were never allowed to do what world-class athletes love to do: to compete against the best, to let the game decide their rightful place in its history as the result of open, unrestricted competition.

There are pitchers who would win twenty games a season for any big-league club that would offer them contracts … Only one thing is keeping them out of the big leagues, the pigmentation of their skin. They happen to be colored.
Shirley Povich, Washington Post, 1941

Some of America's greatest ballplayers plied their trade on all-black teams, in Negro Leagues, on the playing fields of Latin America, and along the barnstorming frontier of the cities and towns of the United States, but never within the major and minor league realm of 'organized baseball.
Extra Bases, Reflections on Jackie Robinson, Race & Baseball History, by Jules Tygiel, Bison Books, Nebraska, 2002, p. 51

These men played baseball under the same rules as Major Leaguers. Unfortunately, they were forced to live under a much different set of written and unwritten rules off the field. Negro Leaguers also competed under much more harsh physical conditions, both on and off the field. They often played two or three games in a day and traveled, between games and during the night, in a cramped sedan or bus packed with teammates and equipment, to the next day's contest, because they couldn't get accommodations in the towns they passed through or played in. Consider the recollections of Dan Bankhead, who was the first black pitcher in the history of modern Major League baseball:

Once last year, they [the Memphis Red Sox] pitched me six straight days. I either started or relieved. I was so tired my tongue was hanging out. We rode all night in those dinky buses and then they made you pitch your head off in towns like Grand Rapids, Mich., Peoria, Ill., and other places.

Listen to this. One Sunday I pitched a twelve-inning game in New York. Right after the game we jumped in the bus and started out for Memphis. On the way the darn bus broke down and we had to sit out on the road for about twelve hours. When we finally got it fixed, we started again. We had to make Memphis for a night game. However, when we got to Cincinnati we realized we couldn't make it. We called Dr. [B.B.] Martin [Memphis owner] and explained it to him. He chartered an airplane and we flew to Memphis. We went right from the airport to the ball park. We hadn't seen a bed for four days, mind you. Well, we lost the game. The score was 1-0. I was the pitcher for Memphis. Know what Martin said after the game? He bawled me out. He said I should have won it. He said we didn't do our best.
Dan Bankhead, quoted by Wendell Smith, Wendell Smith's Sports Beat, The Pittsburgh Courier, March 27, 1948

They were forced to eat meals they had packed, like sardines and crackers, because restaurants wouldn't serve them. Don Newcombe remembers that their bus was like a traveling motel to a Negro League team. Besides eating and sleeping on the bus, they would store all their clothes there, and hang their laundry from its windows. Many of the parks they played in would not even allow them to use the dressing rooms so the bus also became a locker room. Without the comfort of air conditioning, blacks would improvise and wrap themselves in sheets soaked in ice water to combat the heat.

Many of them were of equal or better talent than their Major League counterparts but had to accept the limited opportunity that this divide forced upon them. Some found it more difficult to accept than others. Yet, they all excelled at their craft, even if only for the pleasure of a limited audience. Chet Brewer could have been Bob Veale; Leon Day could have been Dock Ellis; Dave Hoskins had he been given a chance could have been a Sad Sam Jones. I mean, Bullet Rogan could throw a ball. He wasn't named Bullet Rogan just for the heck of it. It's the talent they had that led you to believe that given the opportunity they could win twenty games. Their arms were strong. They could start forty games a season; they probably pitched fifty games a season and they pitched year round. They only made a living by playing and pitching. Some historians estimate that official league games only accounted for maybe a third of the actual games the Negro Leaguers played in.

These were the guys that had some success. I am sure that they won a lot of games in the Negro Leagues, and some of the teams they played for weren't like the Kansas City Monarchs, or the Newark Eagles or the Baltimore Elite Giants; they were far lesser teams. Much of what they accomplished on the field would have never been recognized but for the courage of great Americans like Ted Williams. In July 1966, almost twenty years after Jackie Robinson's debut and the demise of the Negro Leagues, on the day Williams himself was inducted into the Hall of Fame, he said:

Baseball gives every American boy a chance to excel. Not just to be as good as anybody else, but to be better. This is the nature of man and the name of the game. I hope some day Satchel Paige and Josh Gibson will be voted into the Hall of Fame as symbols of the great Negro players who are not here only because they weren't given the chance.

Thanks to the momentum created by Williams, the baseball writers saw fit to acknowledge the talent of some of the Negro League players by inducting them into the Hall of Fame. Starting with Satchel Paige who was inducted in 1971, a total of eighteen players, who played all or a majority of their career in the Negro Leagues, have been enshrined in the Hall of Fame, and another dozen early black ballplayers are awaiting formal admission in July 2006.

The experiences of these men laid the groundwork for generations of African-American ballplayers to follow. Their caliber of play under such circumstances helped to eventually turn the heads of the white ownership of Major League teams to the vast pool of Major League quality talent they were missing. It is important to recognize them here not only for their own immense talent but also as a means of expressing the gratitude of those of us who enjoyed the Major League opportunities they never had. In so recognizing them, I also hope to trace the gradual evolution of acceptance of blacks among Major League ownership, acceptance begun and advanced by their successes.

It has been a very difficult process for me to decide who would make the cut for my list of these Early Aces. There are no videotapes to view and precious little game film. Most of their teammates are long gone, and if it weren't for the efforts of the many dedicated historians and researchers who have worked diligently over the last twenty-five years or so to preserve their memories, that important part of baseball history would have been gone as well. My work with the Negro League Baseball Museum in Kansas City, coupled with my work with Buck O'Neil, provided me with some familiarity with the Early Aces. My age also helped since I knew and played with and/or against some of them. Beyond that, I had to delve deeply into the books already written about what is termed "the other half of baseball history." In this regard, I owe a real debt to men such as John B. Holway, Larry Lester, Dick Clark, and James A. Riley. Their efforts have provided me with a wealth of information about this vastly under-recognized part of American history.

After the research was done, more soul-searching was necessary to refine my list of Early Aces. African-Americans have been playing baseball in this country for just as long as any other Americans. There have been scores of African-American pitchers over the years prior to 1947 who likely could have won twenty games in a Major League season, if their skin color and their ancestry did not bar them from competing with their non-black counterparts.

Pitching has always been a key element to any team's success. This was as true in 1886 as it is today for that is when the first prominent African-American pitchers began to make a name for themselves. John "Bud" Fowler may have been the first

African-American professional baseball player in America and Moses Fleetwood "Fleet" Walker may have been the first African-American Major Leaguer, but the first player ever signed to a contract by the first all-black professional team was a pitcher (which suggests that even then it was recognized that "good pitching beats good hitting"). His name was "Shep" Trusty and he was a mainstay of the Cuban Giants, a legendary black team for a number of years in the 1880s. At around the same time, a young lefthander by the name of George Stovey came on the scene. He formed part of the first professional all-black battery with Fleet Walker when they played together for Cleveland of the Western League. Stovey went on to win 35 games for Newark of the International League in 1887, a record that still stands today. They are just a couple of the well-qualified players that I considered.

In later years, there were many others that clearly had the talent. Men such as Dan McClellan, George Wilson, Verdell Mathis, Dave Brown, Ted "Double Duty" Radcliffe, Stuart "Slim" Jones, Webster McDonald, William "Dizzy" Dismukes, Jesse "Nip" Winters, and Andy Cooper, to name just a few. But, I had to make a choice and it would obviously mean leaving a number of early greats off my list. So, to them I say, "Your place in baseball history was secured by what you did on the field and is not diminished by the limitations of my choices here. I'll save a place for you in Volume 2 when I have a few more African-American twenty-game winners in the majors to write about."

One of the problems I faced in coming up with the list of pitchers who are included in The Black Aces, and in my list of earlier pitchers, was to define who was "black" and who was not. That is not as clear-cut an item as it might sound, especially considering the history of that issue within the game of baseball, and American society. During the period of time when blacks were not allowed to play in the Major Leagues, some who would be considered black in other circumstances, or by a mere review of their heritage, were ushered into the game, under the pretense that they were Cuban, or Indian. This was tried unsuccessfully as early as 1901, when John McGraw, manager of the Baltimore Orioles in the newly-formed American League, tried passing off a second baseman with the black Columbia Giants, by the name of Charlie Grant (no relation), as an American Indian by the name of "Chief Tokahoma." League officials, led by Chicago White Sox owner, Charlie Comiskey, didn't buy it, and Grant didn't get to play in the Major Leagues. This issue was not always addressed consistently, nor could it really be, since the Major Leagues were operating under the unwritten "gentlemen's agreement." Where would they turn for a ruling on whether a player was black or not, other than the say-so of the majority of owners? Some players who were one-eighth black were barred from the game, while others, whose ancestry was at least half black, were able to play because of a Latino surname or a light skin color. Famous Negro League pitcher Chet Brewer tells a story that demonstrates how the race issue was sometimes decided:

A young, black boy came to the stadium and stood behind the dugout begging the manager to let him play. The manager turned him away

because he was black. The next day the boy came back, again, telling the manager how good he was and begging the manager to let him play. Again, the manager turned the boy away. This continued for several days. One day, with the boy behind the dugout, the manager found himself with the pitcher due up, no pinch hitter, down by a few runs, with two men on and two outs, and the other team bringing in the best, hard-throwing relief pitcher in the league. He turned to the boy and told him to step to the plate, figuring the boy would strike out, be embarrassed, and leave. To his surprise the young boy hit the first pitch into the left-center field gap and started rounding the bases. As he passed second, the manager was standing on the dugout steps, yelling, "Would you look at that Cuban run!"

And so it went. Black wasn't always black. It all depended on the powers that be, which confirmed that the discrimination against blacks was without basis in fact, but rooted in society.

There were also many great Latino ballplayers playing right alongside African-Americans in the Negro Leagues and elsewhere who suffered the same kind of discrimination. Jose Mendez, Martin Dihigo, Luis Tiant, Sr., and so many others also had the same exceptional talent that would have enabled them to succeed in the Major Leagues, and would have had a shot at a twenty-win season if they ever had the chance. But, they shared a distinction with their African-American teammates that would keep them out of Organized Baseball as well ... their dark skin.

I fully recognize their accomplishments. In fact, they may have achieved their success under even more difficult circumstances than some of the African-American pitchers I have selected. They not only endured the same difficulties and prejudices as their American counterparts because of their similarly dark skin, but also did so in a foreign country where they didn't even speak the language. More significantly, they came here with no prior experience or understanding of the manner in which African-Americans were treated in the United States during those times. It had to be a shock for them to come from their homelands where ballplayers of all colors were treated like "heroes" and "kings," as Willie Wells said, to a country where they were not shown even the most basic respect and dignity that every man deserved. Because of the discrimination against blacks here at the time, many Latino ballplayers objected to any reference to them as "black" or "colored." Specifically, I remember that Vic Power and Minnie Minoso didn't want "Colored" written on their passports under the category "Race." Minnie said, "I'm Cuban. Don't put no colored stuff on my passport!" and Vic would declare, "I'm Puerto Rican, not colored." Meanwhile, at hotels that segregated us by race, Minnie and Vic had to stay with the black ballplayers.

Jose Mendez played in both the Cuban League and the Negro Leagues in a career that lasted from 1908 to 1926. He was a small man who threw a big fastball and was first noticed by American baseball in 1908 when he threw a one-hitter against the Cincinnati Reds, who were then touring Cuba. The following year he is said to have pitched twenty-five straight scoreless innings against other Major League teams touring the island. His play was so outstanding that John McGraw of the New York Giants described him as "better than any pitcher except Mordecai Brown and Christy Mathewson ... and sometimes I think he is better than Matty" and "sort of like Walter Johnson and Grover Alexander rolled into one." McGraw said at the time that he would pay $50,000.00 for Mendez "if he were only white." Mendez is credited with a 44-2 record while barnstorming with the Cuban Stars in the United States in 1909 and also played for a number of all-black teams in the United States, including the Brooklyn Royal Giants, All Nations, and Chicago American Giants. He was signed by J.L. Wilkinson as player-manager of the Kansas City Monarchs in 1920, the first year of play for the Negro National League, and managed them to league pennants in 1924, 1925, and 1926. One of the high points of his time with the Monarchs came during the 1924 champion series against the Hillsdale club, when he pitched in four games resulting in a shutout, two victories and a 1.42 ERA. He retired from baseball in 1926, finishing a career that well deserved the nickname that he earned early on in Cuba, "El Diamante Negro" or The Black Diamond.

Martin Dihigo was beginning his baseball career around the time that Mendez was coming to the end of his. When he first came to the United States as a seventeen-year old with the Cuban Stars in 1923, sportswriter Fay Young of the *Chicago Defender* compared the two, writing that Dihigo was "the best youngster to come off the island (Cuba) since pitcher Jose Mendez." Dihigo went on to not only validate Young's opinion of him but also to become perhaps the greatest all-around baseball player, black or white, (or Cuban), to ever step on a field. He was a big man, around 6'3" and 200 pounds, but he had a real fluid style and agility. He could play every position exceptionally well, and he was great with the bat, hitting over .400 and winning the Negro League home run crown several times.

The greatest player I ever saw was a black man. His name is Martin Dihigo. I played with him in Santo Domingo in winter ball in 1943. I thought I was having a pretty good year myself down there and they were walking him to get to me.
Johnny Mize (NY Giants 1B), on Martin Dihigo

Dihigo is the only man to be inducted into a baseball Hall of Fame in three separate countries, in Mexico where they called him "El Maestro," in his homeland of Cuba where he was known to his countryman as "El Immortal," and in the United States where his grace drew comparisons to DiMaggio, "with a stronger arm." In fact, some have said he had a better arm than Roberto Clemente. It was that same arm that enabled him to compile a career record of 261-138 on the mound, including records of 115-60 in the Cuban League and 119-57 in the Mexican League. He continued to play and dominate the game of baseball through 1945, when he retired.

Luis Tiant, Sr. pitched in the Negro Leagues from 1930 through 1947 and earned a reputation as a "grand master of mound wizardry" during his career. Many of you are probably familiar with his son, Luis Tiant Jr., who enjoyed a long Major League career and still holds the Major League record in holding batters to a .172 average during the 1968 season. Some of you may even remember the poignant moment during the 1975 World Series when father and son were reunited for the first time in fifteen years after Fidel Castro permitted Luis Tiant Sr. to travel from Cuba to Fenway Park to see his son pitch. But, many of you may not know that the son probably learned a great deal of his craft from his father, who was thought to be the better pitcher by many who saw them both play. Tiant Sr. pitched for several Negro League teams, spending most of his time with Alex Pompez' New York Cubans, and was on occasion referred to as the "black Lefty Grove" and the "Cuban Carl Hubbell." He was named to the East-West All-Star game in 1935, and later in 1947 on the basis of a 10-0 regular season record. He was a crafty type of pitcher, using a lot of off-speed pitches that he delivered in a herky-jerky kind of motion. He also had an excellent pick-off move that was considered legal, but which was extremely deceptive, not only to the runner. He may be the only pitcher in baseball history to cause a batter to swing and miss at a pick-off throw made to first base as happened to Goose Curry of the Baltimore Elite Giants. (Curry said he thought he saw the ball coming to the plate, and the umpire said if Curry was stupid enough to swing at it, it was a strike!)

These men are only three of the many Latino aces who I believe could have reached the magic number of twenty wins in the majors if given the chance. Neither they nor any of their dark-skinned Latino brothers have been forgotten, nor would their accomplishments allow them to be. It is very important to me that they receive this brief recognition, and that their families and all of baseball know the high esteem and respect I have for them, even if I can't include them among my African-American aces.

Without further ado, the men that I have selected as the Early Black Aces are Satchel Paige, Rube Foster, "Smokey" Joe Williams, Leon Day, Wilbur "Bullet" Rogan, Hilton Lee Smith, Dave Hoskins, Chet Brewer, Dick "Cannonball" Redding, and Willie Foster. After much consideration, I think they represent the best talent that the Negro Leagues had to offer and were the most likely candidates to have joined our special group. Seven of them, (Satchel Paige, Rube Foster, Leon Day, William Foster, Wilbur Rogan, Joe Williams, and Hilton Lee Smith), are among the eighteen Negro Leaguers in the Hall of Fame.

During my own passage through the world of baseball over the last six decades, I have come to realize that there is not just one course to follow in pursuit of pitching excellence but rather as many as there are men who have given their all in the effort to be part of this wonderful game. While the route to the rubber may have been dramatically different for each of us, including these Early Aces, there are lessons to be learned from those who went before us. I followed my own path to the mound, and now, having looked more deeply into the lives of these other pitchers, I have a greater appreciation for not only their accomplishments, but also the road they followed to secure their place in baseball and society.

CHAPTER 5

ANDREW FOSTER
Rube

Born September 17, 1879 in Calvert, Texas
Died December 9, 1930 in Kankakee, Illinois
Teams: Chicago Union Giants, Cuban X-Giants,
*   Philadelphia Giants, Leland Giants,*
*   Chicago American Giants*
Inducted into National Baseball Hall of Fame 1981
Inducted into Texas Sports Hall of Fame

When the big game shall have become history, there will stalk across the pages of the record a massive figure and its name will be Andrew Foster ... the master of the show ... the smooth-toned counselor of infinite wisdom and somber thought ... Always the center of any crowd, the magnet attracting both the brains and the froth of humanity.
Sportswriter Rollo Wilson's eulogy of Rube Foster

White baseball has never seen anyone quite like Rube Foster. He was Christy Mathewson, John McGraw, Connie Mack, Al Spalding, and Kenesaw Mountain Landis – great pitcher, manager, owner, league organizer, czar – all rolled into one.
John Holway, The Sporting News, August 8, 1981

Rube Foster is a pitcher with the tricks of a Radbourne, with the speed of a Rusie, and with the coolness and deliberation of a Cy Young. What does that make him? Why, the greatest baseball pitcher in the country; that is what the greatest baseball players of white persuasion that have gone against him say. But his color has kept him out of the big leagues, and that is why the Leland Giants and Philadelphia Giants and other teams for the last ten years have had the services of a pitcher who otherwise would be a priceless boon to the struggling White Sox or Highlanders just now.
Chicago Inter-Ocean

Rube Foster is the most finished product that I have ever seen in the pitcher's box.
Frank Chance, Manager, Chicago Cubs

Rube Foster is one of the greatest pitchers of all time. He was the smartest pitcher I have ever seen in all my years of baseball.
Honus Wagner, Hall Of Famer

It is no coincidence that Rube Foster is the first of the many great African-American pitchers that I chose to include among my Early Aces. While his age and tenure would in any event have placed him in that position chronologically, his life and career in the game of baseball, both on and off the field, made that decision easy for me. He so dominated and revolutionized the game, not just blackball but baseball itself, in so many ways during his days as a player, a manager, a team owner, and a league commissioner that my only difficulty was in figuring out how to separate the man from the legend. I realized, however, that there was no way to do that as the two are just too intertwined. Simply put, his accomplishments are the stuff that legends are made of and, in his case, it is a status he well deserves.

Rube Foster was probably the most dominant pitcher in black baseball during the first decade of the twentieth century and ranked in a class with such other greats as Walter Ball, Danny McClellan, and Harry Buckner as the best of that era. He was also a great student of baseball, and particularly of the art of pitching, who later became one of the most successful managers in the game utilizing a "racehorse" style of play that emphasized the running game in ways that nobody had done before. His most enduring legacy though, the one that earned him a reputation as "The Father of Black Baseball," was his vision in establishing the first successful black professional league, the Negro National League, in 1920.

Foster was born in 1879 to Andrew and Sarah (nee Watts) Foster in Calvert, Texas, which was a fairly good sized town just southwest of Waco. His father, a minister and the presiding elder of the African Methodist Episcopal Church in South Texas, was a serious, disciplined man, who introduced his young son to those values early in life. Religion played an important part in young Andrew's childhood as he was required to attend church every Sunday. However, even though he was asthmatic in his youth, he would sneak off to play baseball every Sunday afternoon, which was the beginning of his lifelong love of the game.

Before he finished grade school, his mother died. When his father later remarried and moved into southwest Texas, Rube made the fateful decision as an eighth grader to leave school and run away to pursue a baseball career in Waco and Fort Worth. By his own reckoning, it was a difficult life - riding freight trains from place to place with little expectation that he would be accepted by any black families, as baseball players had the reputation of being "low and ungentlemanly." But he pursued his passion for the game and wound up pitching for the Fort Worth Yellow Jackets as a 17 year old. He was on his way to becoming the bear of a man, with the ready wit and booming voice, who called everyone "Darling," who would leave an indelible mark on the history of baseball.

Rube pitched for the Fort Worth Yellow Jackets from 1897 to 1901. His break came in the latter year when he was 21 and got a chance to pitch batting practice against Connie Mack's Philadelphia A's during their spring training in Hot Springs,

Arkansas. As one blackball veteran named Rogers later related to Wendell Smith of *The Pittsburgh Courier*, "As soon as we saw him pitch one inning, we knew he was great. Our manager, James M. Bright, signed him up and Rube Foster was in the big time."

He pitched a shut out in his first game for the Chicago Union Giants in 1901 but struggled for the rest of that year. It seems that he fell a bit too much in love with his considerable fastball and couldn't win. Rube jumped to a white semi-pro team in Otsego, Michigan for a part of that year with the same results. Perhaps it was that experience that made him realize he had a lot to learn about baseball and turned him into such a student of the game. At any rate, he certainly learned something about pitching that worked very well for him because the following year in 1902, after joining the Cuban X Giants and getting shelled 13-0 in his first game against a white semi-pro team from Hoboken, New Jersey, he is reported to have won his next 44 games in a row and 51 overall for the year. In fact, it is said that he earned his nickname "Rube" that year by outpitching "Rube" Waddell of the Philadelphia Athletics (who had just finished the Major League season with a 25-7 record) in a 5-2 win. He was making $40 a month and, by his own declaration, becoming "the best pitcher in the country."

He backed up that claim in the ensuing years as he dominated all opponents for the rest of the decade. In 1903, he almost single-handedly pitched (and hit) the Cuban X Giants to victory in the first world series in blackball history. The first Major League World Series was being played that year between the Pittsburgh Pirates and the Boston Red Sox, and the Cuban X Giants had challenged the Philadelphia Giants for the championship of blackball. Rube is said to have gone 54-1 during the regular season but did even better in the series as he won 4 games to lead his team to a 5-2 game edge to take the championship. Those victories included a 3-1 win in the first game in which he gave up only three hits and a 12-3 win in the third game in which he knocked out three hits of his own.

Rube jumped to the Philadelphia Giants in 1904 and repeated the prior year's history in a reverse kind of way as he lead them to a series victory over the Cuban X Giants to once again claim the blackball championship for his team. Foster led his team in dramatic fashion in the 1904 series as he overcame illness to pitch two wins in the three-game playoff. In fact, his manager, Sol White, almost begged him to pitch the opening game after the Cuban X Giants taunted that he was afraid of them. All Rube did was take the ball against the great Walter Ball in that game and strike out 18 in an 8-4 victory, and later closed out the series in a third game 4-2 win in which he only gave up two hits. (He also hit .400 in that series.) The Philadelphia Giants also won the blackball world series in 1905 and 1906 with Rube starring on the mound. In fact, he is said to have won 51 of the 55 games that he pitched in 1905.

During these years, Rube established himself as not only an enormously talented pitcher but also as an incredibly smart one. He was a very big man at well over 6 feet tall and 200 pounds, and would grow much larger as he got older. He had a wide repertoire of pitches at his disposal but the nasty screwball that he threw with a submarine delivery was his most effective one. He also had the kind of control that enabled him "to pick buttons off your uniform, one by one," according to one old timer. But, Foster described his approach in a much simpler way: "I don't rely on any kind of ball. I don't use any kind of system. I just size up the batter and give him what I think he can't hit. Sometimes it's a curve and sometime it's a straight ball. And I can tell almost by instinct what's coming off behind me."

However, I believe that simple explanation really contradicts the complicated thought process that was behind everything that Rube did on the mound. In fact, he was really revolutionary in the way he thought about pitching. He often threw a curveball on a 3-2 count, which was against the conventional thinking at that time, reasoning to himself that most hitters wouldn't be expecting it. He also liked to play mind games with hitters, some of which he described in a contribution entitled "The Art Of Pitching" that he wrote for Sol White's Guide To Black Baseball. In it, he described, among other things, his approach when facing a batter with the bases loaded:

Do not worry. Try to be jolly and unconcerned. I have often smiled with the bases full with two strikes and three balls on the batter. This seems to unnerve them.

He also revealed his psychological advice when facing an anxious batter:

...waste a little time on him, and when you think he realizes his position and everybody's yelling at him to hit it out, waste a few balls and try his nerve; the majority of times you will win out by drawing him into hitting at a wide one.

It was also during this period of his career that many of the events that gave rise to his legend were born. (I say events, not stories, because most of them are true.)

While some say that John McGraw, the legendary manager of the New York Giants longed to have Rube pitching for him, it is commonly accepted that he did hire him in 1903 to teach some of his pitchers, including Christy Mathewson, Iron Man McGinnity and others, to throw a screwball. Mathewson learned it so well that it became his famous "fadeaway" pitch and helped him win 34 games in 1903 after winning only 14 in 1902; in fact, he went from a 34-37 record from 1900-1902 to 94-33 over the next three years. McGinnity also won 30 games for the first time in his career in 1903.

Rube was also a master of trickery if he thought it would give him an advantage on the field. One of the more notable incidents that showed his creativity in this regard took place in Philadelphia in 1905 while pitching against an all-white City league team that had a number of Major Leaguers, including A's outfielder Topsy Hartsell. Rube was pitching with a one run lead in the bottom of the ninth, and Hartsel came up with the tying run on third and the winning run on second. The count went to 2-1 when Rube called his catcher, James Booker, to the mound. Booker told Rube to walk the batter in a voice loud enough for Hartsell to hear but it was a set-up and Rube slipped a strike by him instead. Booker played his role and went back out to the mound yelling at Foster for crossing him up. Hartsell was losing his patience with what he thought was a stall and had the umpire caution them to play ball. Foster responded by shouting to the umpire that Hartsell was too close to the plate and had to back off so as not to get hit. Hartsell took the bait and, when he looked down to see where his feet were, Rube threw a strike right down the middle of the plate to strike him out and end the game!

Rube's dominance as a pitcher was recognized in 1911 when he was named by the writers of *The Indianapolis Freeman* as one of only three pitchers to their Negro All-Star Team, the first such election to my knowledge. The other two pitchers were Dan McClellan and Charles Dougherty.

The managerial phase of Rube's career began in 1906 when he left the Philadelphia Giants for the Leland Giants in Chicago, and became their player-manager. He later joined forces with a white saloon owner, John Schorling, (who was also Charles Comiskey's brother-in-law), to take over that team. They renamed it the Chicago American Giants and began a blackball dynasty. Foster raided much of the best talent on the other black teams to assemble one of the greatest teams ever. In 1910, they are said to have won 123 of 129 games, with Rube himself winning 13 games, and from 1910 through 1922, they won all but one championship of black baseball. Their popularity was so great that on one particular Sunday they outdrew both the White Sox (9,000) and the Cubs (6,000) with an attendance of 11,000.

During this period, Rube's genius really had an opportunity to flourish. He was stern and demanding as a manager but he was fair and tolerant as long as he felt his players were giving their all. He emphasized good pitching, sound defense and running, especially the latter. His style of baseball required all of his players to run and be adept at bunting and moving runners. In fact, he had little use for hitters that couldn't hit to left or right as he directed them to. His bold base-running tactics regularly beat out teams that hit for much higher averages and with greater power. He was ruthlessly aggressive and used the bunt, the squeeze play, the hit-and-run, and the bunt-and-run so often and to such advantage that they became the trademarks of his team's offense. In one game against the Indianapolis ABCs, Rube had his American Giants bunt continuously for eight innings to wear the ABCs down and walked away with a 1-0 win. In another game against the same team, they came back from an 18-0 deficit in the seventh inning when Rube had them bunt an incredible 11 times in a row. Frank Forbes, a member of the Indianapolis team, gives some insight as to why Rube's bunting strategy was successful:

He [Foster] built his club with speed. We'd go out there to play those son of a bitches – excuse me – and you know what he does? We don't wake up until the end of the ballgame, but he had drowned the goddamn infield the night before. Those suckers lay down a bunt, it

rolls nine feet and stops. The man's on. My God, by the time you got to the ball the man was on.

Voices from the Great Black Baseball League, by John B. Holway, New York, DaCapo Books, 1992

James "Cool Papa" Bell revealed another reason for Foster's team's success in bunting. He remembers that Foster had built ridges along the lines in the base paths at the Giants' home field, so that bunts would always stay fair.

Foster was also a great strategist and innovator. He pretty much invented the hit-and-run, and certainly perfected it. He also embraced the bunt-and-run, often using it with a man on second and advancing him home. As Dave Malarcher said, "He knew the value of speed and he knew the value of being able to hit into a directed play." He advocated that you won a game in one or two innings, not over a long term, so he emphasized taking advantage of all opportunities when they arose.

Malarcher went on to say that, "If Cobb had a smart manager like Rube Foster to make him fit into the plays, they (the Detroit Tigers) would have won the pennant year after year after year." Now, while I don't doubt that may be true, somehow I just can't envision a Georgia cracker like Cobb allowing himself to be managed by a black man no matter how many pennants it would bring him!

While Foster was a great handler of men, he was also a disciplinarian and was always in total control of a game, often giving signs by blowing smoke rings from his ever-present corn cob pipe. He not only called what pitches were to be thrown but also where they were to be thrown and sometimes even directed with what kind of motion they were to be thrown. Foster was also known to have directed his hitters to take two strikes early in the game to tire out an opposing pitcher.

Foster was as innovative, determined and successful off the field as he was on the mound. In the years leading to 1920, he was the leading voice in the world of black baseball calling for organization. He used the columns of several leading black sportswriters, and wrote himself in the black weeklies, to rally blacks to strengthen the then existing black baseball teams, to honor contracts, and to organize more efficiently, so that the profits of the teams, and more importantly the ownership, would not be lost. On February 13, 1920, Foster convened a meeting at the Colored YMCA in Kansas City. He brought together Negro League leaders, including J. L. Wilkinson (Kansas City Monarchs), John "Tenny" Blount (Detroit Stars), Charlie Mills (St. Louis Giants), Joe Green (Chicago Giants), C.I. Taylor (Indianapolis ABS), and others. At that meeting, Rube presented the group with the corporate charter for the National Negro Baseball League, which would become the first black long-term league in any sport. No longer willing to wait for the others to agree to act, Rube had already incorporated the League in New York, Pennsylvania, Maryland, Illinois, Ohio, and Michigan. Rube's preemptive activity proved to be very fruitful. While he went into the meeting hoping for a league that would start in April 1921, the Negro National Baseball League actually was able to start playing league games on May 1, 1920. Rube developed a motto for the league, which confirmed its importance and identity: "We Are The Ship, All Else The Sea."

Throughout the 1920s, Rube's Chicago American Giants and the Negro National Baseball League did very well. That left Rube to conquer his next target: getting Organized Baseball to lift the color barrier. Unfortunately, Rube was not to be successful in that venture, despite his best efforts. By 1926, Rube began to suffer delusional episodes. He was ultimately deemed to be insane and was institutionalized in Kankakee Sanatorium, where he remained until his death on December 9, 1930. Seven months before his death, the *Chicago Defender* published a photo of Rube with the following statement:

He was the greatest pitcher our Race has ever known. He ranked with Cy Young, Christy Mathewson, Joe McGinnity, and other greats. He was a mastermind of baseball and was ranked by the daily newspapermen as one of the three greatest managers of the country. The other two were John McGraw of the New York Nationals and Connie Mack of the world champion Philadelphia American Leaguers. Foster was also the brains and the founder of the Negro National Baseball League, and it was due to his long hours and hard work plus the worry of running the league that caused him to lose his health.
Chicago Defender, May 3, 1930

Finally, in 1981, more than fifty years after Rube's death, baseball saw fit to enshrine him in the Hall of Fame, recognizing his greatness as a player, a manager, and the founder of the Negro National Baseball League.

CHAPTER 6

JOSEPH WILLIAMS
Smokey Joe
Cyclone

Born April 6, 1886 in Seguin, Texas
Died February 25, 1951 in New York, New York
Teams: San Antonio Black Broncos, Austin Black Senators,
Chicago Giants, New York Lincoln Giants, Mohawk
Colored Giants, Chicago American Giants, Atlantic
City Bacharach Giants, Hilldale Daisies, Brooklyn Royal
Giants, Homestead Grays, Detroit Wolves
Inducted into National Baseball Hall of Fame 1999

If you ever witnessed the speed of a pebble in a storm you have not even seen the equal of the speed possessed by this wonderful Texan Giant. You have but to see him once to exclaim, 'That's a-plenty!'
Frank Leland, Owner, Chicago Giants, 1910

He didn't have a lot of different stuff, but he had a terrific fastball, and perfect control. If he caught you swinging at that ball here at the knees, he raised it up to the belt, then up to the letters, pitch you outside, things like that. He didn't have much of a curve or change of pace, but he had terrific speed.
Bill Holland, Pitcher, Chicago Unions

If I was going to pick a man to throw hard, I'd have to pick Joe Williams. I'd pick him over all of them. They talk about Satchel Paige and them throwing hard, but I think Joe threw harder. It used to take two catchers to hold him. By the time the fifth inning was over, that catcher's hand would be all swollen. He'd have to have another catcher back there the rest of the game.
Sam Streeter, Pitcher, Homestead Grays

Those who saw Joseph "Smokey Joe" Williams pitch have left behind a compelling testament to support the notion that he <u>was</u> the greatest pitcher in blackball history, bar none. As with many of the great Negro stars of the first half of the twentieth century, the historical record of his accomplishments is not as complete as we might like but what there is certainly supports a claim to that lofty throne. Comparisons to other Early Black Aces are inevitable in this regard, particularly to the legendary and most well known of them, Satchel Paige. But, Smokey Joe's claim has some impressive, and even unlikely, backers.

In 1952, for instance, *The Pittsburgh Courier*, a black weekly newspaper, conducted a poll to determine who was considered to be the greatest Negro Leagues pitcher. The poll sought the opinion of a number of veteran Negro League players and sportswriters, who had played with, or watched, all of the greats perform. It didn't just seek the kind of fan vote, or "popularity contest," that was used to select the All-Stars who would play in the annual East-West Game. The result of the players' poll put Smokey Joe at the top of the list as the greatest of them all, even if he only beat Satchel by a margin of 20-19. On at least one occasion, Satchel himself referred to Smokey Joe Williams as "the best pitcher I've ever seen."

While that vote alone might be considered sufficient by some to validate his legacy, Smokey Joe also received a vote of confidence and respect from another highly reputable (in terms of his baseball talent), if infamous (in terms of his racial attitudes) critic, which tells me even more about the kind of talent that he had. The critic was Ty Cobb, "The Georgia Peach," a great baseball player but a man who embodied the worst racial prejudices that the South had practiced for many years. Cobb is said to have considered Smokey Joe to be "a sure thirty-game winner" if he ever pitched in the Major Leagues. It seems to me that such high praise for a black man could not have been an easy thing for a man like Cobb to offer and must have simply been the inescapable truth.

Williams was born to a black father and Indian mother of the Comanche tribe in Sequin, Texas in the late nineteenth century. The date of his birth is a matter of some debate and, while many consider that he came into this world on April 6, 1886, he himself claimed at times to have been born as early as 1876. It is not uncommon for there to be a lack of definite information on the birth date of many of the Early Aces. Back then not every event was officially recorded like it is now. Where I was born, your birth certificate was likely to be written on the bark of the nearest tree. (The actual date of Smokey Joe's birth takes on particular importance in considering the longevity of his playing career and some of the games he pitched when he could have been as old as 40 or 50). His baseball career began down in Texas where he first played for the San Antonio Black Broncos from 1907-1909 and lasted for a quarter of a century through 1932. He is most identified with the New York Lincoln Giants for whom he played from 1911-1923, and later the Homestead Grays.

Smokey Joe was a tall, well-built man standing about 6'5" or 6'6" with very long arms, and weighed over 200 lbs. Similar in build to Walter "Big Train" Johnson, his fastball was also comparable to the pills thrown by Johnson; Dizzy Dean called it "an agitatin' fastball, a real live fastball." In fact, when Williams played for the Homestead Grays from 1925-1932 at the end of his career, Cum Posey, the owner and manager of the legendary team, said that his speed could only be matched by Johnson, or maybe Lefty Grove or Satchel Paige. While it is hard to compare players or eras, some who played with Williams during his early years in Texas have said that he was much faster as a young man than later when he was mowing down batters during the 1920s and 1930s. It was his fastball that earned him his nicknames of "Smokey Joe" and "Cyclone" without question. Baseball historians Rob Neyer and Bill James recently released a comprehensive book entitled *The Neyer/James Guide to Pitchers* (Fireside, 2004) which includes a list of the ten pitchers with the best fastballs of each half-decade, beginning in 1880. I think it is most revealing that Smokey Joe Williams' name appears on the lists from 1905 through 1924, and they list him as number two for the period of 1905 to 1909, only behind Walter Johnson.

Williams also used a few other pitches to keep hitters honest, although he didn't have to use them often. Some have said that he didn't have much of a curve or "drop" ball, but it was good enough to work off that fastball in setting hitters up and keeping them from getting too comfortable in the batter's box. It was a real hard curve that didn't break much but was delivered with the same smooth overhand motion that he used for the fastball, making it tough for a hitter to recognize and distinguish between the two. He also used a change of pace and what is known today as a "slider." But there are also a few other elements that made his overpowering fastball, and these complementary pitches, work so well for him and were important ingredients in the success that he enjoyed: impeccable control, the unmatched ability to move the ball around within the strike zone, and the smarts to make all of these factors work to his advantage.

Smokey Joe was able to dominate both Negro Leaguers and Major Leaguers. He reportedly struck out 27 batters in a single extra-inning game against the Kansas City Monarchs in 1930, while only giving up one hit. That same game featured an 18-year old Josh Gibson as Smokey Joe's catcher, and Chet Brewer as his mound opponent for the Monarchs. Brewer also pitched all 12 innings only giving up four hits, while striking out 19 batters, including ten in a row. The game, considered to be one of the greatest in Negro League history, was one of the first games ever played at night, using the Monarchs' experimental portable lighting system which they moved around the country on twelve trucks, and powered by a whopping 250 horsepower generator! Although I am sure the lighting was dim by today's standards, and may have helped Williams, it is still an extraordinary accomplishment for any pitcher, no less one who was at least 44 years old, depending which birthday you believe. He had a 22 and 7 record, including 12 shutouts, when pitching against Major League teams, and once struck out 20 batters in an exhibition game against the New York Giants. In exhibition competition, Smokey Joe defeated five Hall of Fame pitchers: Grover Alexander, Chief Bender, Waite Hoyt, Walter Johnson and Rube Marquard. (Source: National Baseball Hall of Fame)

His control was said to be perfect. Some of the other aces of the Negro Leagues lavished him with high praise for his control, knowing how important it is to a pitcher's success. Webster McDonald, for instance, described his ability by saying that Williams always threw "right to that spot;" Willie Foster said he could "spot-pitch you to death." In fact, Hall of Famer Judy Johnson said that Williams's ability to hit his spot was so good that "If he walked one man, he'd say his control was bad." He used that control to keep hitters off balance and guessing what pitch was coming next. One of his teammates on the Lincoln Giants, Frank Forbes, described it this way:

> Joe had a lot of control, I mean like he'd cut your throat up here with a fastball inside and then come down on the outside corner on the knees with the next one. He'd move a guy out of the box, see? I'd tell him, "Move 'em around." He knew what I meant. You've got to be a hell of a hitter to dig in on him, especially if you take a full cut at the ball. He'd cut you down. Then you're not in there so firm. Then the next pitch comes outside on you, you can't get to it.
> *Voices from the Great Black Baseball League, by John B. Holway, New York, DaCapo Books, 1992*

In 1951, several weeks after Smokey Joe Williams died, black sportswriter Joe Bostic took the occasion of Williams's death to advocate the admission of Negro League players into the National Baseball Hall of Fame, in Cooperstown, New York. In a column called *Continuing The Plea For Revocation Of James Crow's Membership in Baseball's Hall of Fame*, Bostic wrote:

> The thing which bothers this observer is that so many superlative baseballers will go on to their reward unsung and unhonored despite the fact they were specialists at their respective positions. We find it hard to accept such discrimination as being either in keeping with the moral code of sports or the noble ideal behind the establishment of the shrine at Cooperstown.

> Let's put it another way. If such a violation of the sports code is acceptable to the policy makers at Cooperstown, then the shrine should be blasted to smithereens and torn from its foundations as a blasphemy to the sanctity of the sports ideal.

> The inequity and unfairness of such a setup is graphically underscored by the fact that the immortal Cyclone Joe Williams passed away some three or four weeks ago and fully nine-tenths of the baseball fans of the country knew nothing about it. Ask any informed baseball authority or any pro who had to bat against the man and you'll be told quickly that the Cyclone could throw with any man who ever tossed the little round pellet plateward. Still, despite this great talent, the present Jim Crow setup at Cooperstown can't accommodate Mr. Williams' name even though he were nominated. This is an injustice that cries to be wiped out.

> ... There must be a complete re-examination of ALL ballplayers in the light of the fact that there have been those with extraordinary

talents, even though they performed outside the ranks of organized baseball because the doors were closed to them. Jim Crow was understandable, if not forgivable, in the frankly commercial baseball setup. But Cooperstown takes its genesis in the nobility and dignity of tradition. James Crow can't possibly be an acceptable citizen in such a community. Not unless pollution of the membership body is preferable to purity.

It took twenty years after Williams' death and Bostic's column before the first black was inducted into the Hall of Fame (Satchel Paige in 1971) and another twenty-eight years before baseball finally recognized the talent of "Smokey Joe" Williams by inducting him into the Hall of Fame in 1999. Perhaps fittingly, he went in with another of the great fastball pitchers of all time, fellow Texan, Nolan Ryan.

It has been said that Smokey Joe was to the early part of blackball history what Satchel Paige was to the latter part. Certainly there were similarities in their ability and success on the field, the longevity of their careers, and even in the uncertainty surrounding their ages. But make no mistake, there is no need to draw any comparisons between Smokey Joe Williams and any other ball player in order to recognize his greatness. His talent and accomplishments clearly make him a prime candidate to have joined me and the other twelve Black Aces if the circumstances had been different.

CHAPTER 7

WILBUR ROGAN
Bullet
Bullet Joe

Born July 28, 1889 in Oklahoma City, Oklahoma
Died March 4, 1967 in Kansas City, Missouri
Teams: All Nations, Kansas City Monarchs
Inducted into National Baseball Hall of Fame 1998

Rogans was one of the world's greatest pitchers. ... He was the onliest pitcher I knew, I ever heard of in my life, was pitching and hitting in the clean-up place. ... Oh, yes, he was a number one pitcher, wasn't any maybe so.
Satchel Paige

Rogan was the greatest pitcher that ever threw a ball. He had not only an arm to pitch with, but a head to think with. Rogan was a smart pitcher with a wonderful memory. Once Rogan pitched to a batter, he never forgot that batter's weaknesses and strong points. And don't think Rogan was nicknamed "Bullet" for nothing. That guy had a ball that was almost too fast to catch. He would really burn 'em in there.
George "Tank" Carr, First Baseman, Kansas City Monarchs

Wilbur "Bullet Joe" Rogan may have been the most complete ballplayer that ever lived. In fact, in an age when scouts talk about "five-tool" players, it seems that number is too small to list all of Rogan's tools. What he did during his twenty-year professional playing career with the Kansas City Monarchs, on the mound, at bat, on the base paths, and in the field (even when he wasn't pitching), is astounding. Baseball historian John Holway says, "At the very least, Rogan and Babe Ruth were the two greatest double-threat men, pitching and hitting, of all time. In his heyday, Rogan could win 20 games, bat .400 and slug homers at a pace of 40 per 550 at bats." It is all the more astounding to me when I consider that he was a man of modest physical stature at about 5 foot 6 inches and 160 pounds (or less by some accounts), and that he didn't even start his professional career until he was already thirty years of age. His election to the National Baseball Hall of Fame in 1998 came too late for him to see or enjoy it, but it was no mistake that he was finally recognized with that honor.

Rogan was considered by many of his contemporaries, and others that saw him play, to be the superior pitcher to even his fellow Negro League and Hall of

Fame pitchers, Satchel Paige, "Smokey Joe" Williams, and "Rube" Foster. He had a live, running fastball that was said to be faster than Paige's with a lot more movement and approached those of Bob Feller and Walter Johnson. He also had a sharp curve ball that broke straight down, which he could throw "faster than most pitchers could throw a fastball." In addition, his arsenal included a side-armed curve, a fork-ball, a spitter (when it was still legal!) and a masterful palm ball that he would "just walk … up there" to throw off the timing of those hitters expecting his fastball.

He had a blazing fast ball and a big curve that he could throw harder than most fastballs. Then he was the master of the palm ball – something like a knuckleball if thrown right.
Chet Brewer, quoted in Invisible Men, Life in Baseball's Negro Leagues, by Donn Rogosin, Atheneum, 1985, New York

He didn't use a wind-up, one of the first pitchers not to, and had a nice, easy delivery "straight from the shoulder." He moved the ball around the plate a lot, and while his control was not the greatest, he didn't give up many runs even when he walked a few batters. He was also considered the finest fielding pitcher of his day.

While those talents alone made him an outstanding pitcher, there are two other aspects of his game that really separate him from the crowd in terms of my view of his potential to have won twenty games in the Major Leagues, namely: his bat and, perhaps more importantly, his head. Winning twenty games is no easy task and even the greatest pitchers need every advantage they can get to do it. Those who can help themselves at the plate, have the "smarts" to pitch, rather than throw, and work themselves through difficult situations when their stuff is not at its best, are putting themselves in the best situation they can to have that kind of success.

As a hitter, Rogan stood away from the plate, deep in the batter's box and wielded a heavy bat. While he was not a very big man, his thin legs were powerful and he had tremendous strength in his broad shoulders and wrists. He punished all kinds of pitchers, whether Negro Leaguers, Major Leaguers, or otherwise, throughout his long career. In fact, he was so accomplished as a hitter that he regularly hit in the clean-up spot and played in the outfield when he was not pitching to keep his powerful bat in the game. He hit for both power and average, and was often among the leaders in the Negro Leagues in home runs, batting average and even stolen bases. "Buck" O'Neil, a Negro League legend, paid Rogan the highest compliment when he said, "If you saw Ernie Banks hit in his prime, then you saw Rogan." A pitcher who hits like that can really help himself win games and, during a long season, put himself in a much better position to reach that twenty game plateau, because the manager is not tempted to pinch-hit for him, and he is usually still in the game when it is decided.

Rogan was also a thinking man on the mound. He knew how to adapt to situations, to set up hitters, and not just try to throw the ball by them … he just never wanted to give the batter a good pitch to hit. Newt Allen, who played behind Rogan, at second base, for most of his career with the Monarchs, gave him the edge over Satchel Paige for that reason, saying, "Satchel was just a stuff pitcher; he had the stuff, but Rogan had the brains. I give Rogan the edge because he knew how to pitch." He received a similar endorsement from former Negro League great and Hall of Famer Judy Johnson, who said, "Satchel Paige was fast, but Rogan was smarter."

Rogan may have had the greatest combination of these additional talents of any pitcher that ever lived. These talents, together with his physical ability on the mound, put him at the top of my list as the most likely of these early aces to have joined our elite group of thirteen.

His vast talents didn't just appear one day at the age of thirty however, as he began to play baseball as a boy in Kansas City, Kansas. He was born Charles Wilbur Rogan in Oklahoma City, Oklahoma in 1889 (although it is believed by many that he was really born in 1893 but changed his age to enlist in the Army). As a young child, he moved with his family to Kansas City, after the death of his mother. Black baseball was taking root and flourishing in that area during the first decade of the twentieth century and, as a youngster, Rogan was a devoted fan, particularly of the Kansas City, Kansas Giants who would claim the Negro World Championship in 1909.

He played baseball at the integrated middle school that he attended in Kansas in the early 1900s and first played semi-pro baseball for Fred Palace's Colts in 1908 as a catcher. (By then he was known only as Wilbur Rogan.) The Colts were a highly regarded team of 18 and 19 year olds in the Kansas City area "having a reputation that stand(s) next to the Kansas City, Kansas Giants." It was only three years later that Rogan was playing for those same Giants, his idols and a team that reportedly won 54 straight games while he was with them. His semi-pro experiences in the Kansas City area are significant in his baseball life, not only because of his play, but also because they may have brought him into contact with another young baseball player in the area, a white player named Charles "KC" Stengel, who was playing for another semi-pro team there, the Kansas City Benstons. Stengel is reported to have recommended Rogan to J.L. Wilkinson, the owner of the Kansas City Monarchs, many years later after having seen Rogan play in the Army.

As talented and gifted a ballplayer as he was, Rogan also had a deep love for America and chose to enlist in the Army in 1911 and remained a soldier until 1917. He served in the Philippines and played for the all-black 24th Infantry Regiment team, where another Negro League great, Oscar Charleston, was also stationed. Several years later, in 1915, while with the all-black 25th Infantry in Schofield Barracks, in Hawaii, he joined with such other future Negro League greats as shortstop Dobie Moore, outfielder Oscar "Heavy" Johnson, and first baseman Lemuel Hawkins, to form the legendary 25th Infantry Wreckers, an Army team with a formidable reputation. It was during this time that he began to make a name for himself on the diamond and develop the military bearing and discipline that would later characterize his career and approach to the game. In fact, during one game that the 25th Infantry played against the AAA Portland Beavers of the Pacific Coast League in 1917, Rogan had the kind of outing on the mound that would help to cement his baseball reputation. He pitched a 3-0 shutout, striking out 13 while walking only three batters, against a team that included several former and future major league players. He also stroked a double to help his cause.

He left the Army for a while in 1917, to pitch for the Los Angeles White Sox of the California Winter League, which was the first league to bring together Negro League teams and white professional teams in one league. The white teams were comprised of Major League players who lived in California as well as minor leaguers from the top-rated Pacific Coast League. Rogan's stay in the California Winter League was a short one. He returned to the Army that same year and was assigned to Fort Huachua in Arizona, where he again teamed up with Moore, Johnson and Hawkins, as well as outfielder Hurley McNair and left-hander Andy Cooper, to form an even more dominant team than the one he played with in the Philippines. While there, he had occasion to pitch against an Army team that included Stengel. Stengel, whose "KC" nickname easily had already become "Casey", was so impressed with Rogan that he recommended him to Wilkinson, who signed him in 1917 to play for the All Nations team as a shortstop and leftfielder. He later moved him up to the Kansas City Monarchs as a pitcher, when the Monarchs became one of the first teams in the newly formed Negro National League in 1920.

The rest, as they say, "is history" and, in terms of Rogan's professional baseball career, what a history it is! He went on to play for the Monarchs for the next 19 years, and held the dual role of player-manager from 1926, until he retired from both roles in 1938 at the age of 48. He then worked as an umpire for the Negro American League until 1946, before going to work for the US Post Office.

As a player with the Monarchs he was spectacular. His stats during Negro League play are hard to believe. He hit over .300 in each of the years from 1922 to 1930, averaging .341 in all and reaching highs of .435 in 1923 and .411 in 1924. He also hit a combined .410 during the post-season in 1924, 1925 and 1926. In that same period, he compiled a record of 109-43 on the mound, and went 8-4 in playoff and World Series play. Over the course of his time with the Monarchs, Rogan played all nine positions for the team! In 1929, Chet Brewer was the ace of the Monarchs' pitching staff, but Rogan was still a big contributor to the team's success. He was the starting centerfielder and cleanup batter for the Monarchs as he led the team to its fourth and final Negro National League pennant.

He was a great pitcher. Rogan pitched for Kansas City for more than ten years and averaged at least 30 games a season. I'll tell you how good he was … he was never relieved or knocked out the box once in ten years. That record speaks for itself.
J.L. Wilkinson, Monarchs Owner, quoted by Wendell Smith, Wendell Smith's Sports Beat, Pittsburgh Courier, Sept. 3, 1949

In 1933, when the East-West All-Star game was first held, his all-around play was so well recognized that he was one of the leading vote-getters <u>as both a pitcher and an outfielder</u> in fan voting for the West team.

When it came to playing against white Major League competition in the barnstorming days of the 1920s and 1930s, however, he seemed to reach another level of excellence. He hit .389 over the course of sixteen games against Major League pitching, including the likes of Paul and Dizzy Dean, and Bob Feller. In fact, when he was almost fifty years of age, he went 3-4 against Bob Feller in 1937. In addition, his pitching was so impressive against the major leaguers that Brooklyn Dodger outfielder Babe Herman, who faced him a number of times, later declared that:

> **He was the best colored pitcher I hit against, had one of the best curve balls I ever saw and a good, live fastball. I always said he was much better that Satchel Paige. Satchel was real fast, but he had a lousy curve, and his fastball was pretty straight. Rogan's fastball was just alive! ... his curve ball ... broke straight down. He could field his position good, and he used to hit a few over the fence in that small park they played in in Los Angeles. ... I told Casey Stengel, "The guys they put in the Hall of Fame are a joke. Rogan's the guy [who] ought to go in."**

Herman proved to be prophetic. Rogan was inducted into the Baseball Hall of Fame in 1998, along with my good friend and former roommate, Larry Doby, and black sportswriter, Sam Lacy.

It is impossible to know whether Rogan's best playing days were in his younger years on those impressive Army teams or in later years with the Monarchs. But it's hard not to think about it and, if you assume that the prime years of a man's playing career take place during his twenties, imagine how great a player he actually was in those early days when he was at his physical peak. It's even more difficult to think about Rogan's lost opportunity to show what he might have accomplished if he had been allowed to play against the best competition available in those days, black or white, at the Major League level. Based on his actual performance over such a long career, particularly at the ages when even the most talented of his contemporaries had long since retired, he deserves to be considered as one of the greatest (if not the greatest) player who ever put on a pair of cleats!

CHAPTER 8

DICK REDDING
Cannonball

Born 1891, in Atlanta, Georgia
Died 1948, in Central Islip, NY
Teams: Atlanta Depins (Semipro), Philadelphia Giants,
New York Lincoln Giants, New York Lincoln Stars,
Indianapolis ABCs, Brooklyn Royal Giants,
Chicago American Giants, Atlanta City Bacharachs,
New York Bacharachs

Dick Redding was like Walter Johnson. Nothing but speed. That's the reason they called him Cannonball. He just blew the ball by you. I've seen Redding knock a bat out of a man's hand.
Frank Forbes, Chicago Union Giants, 1914 in <u>Blackball Stars</u>, *by Holway*

If you had a ball club in the big leagues, you wouldn't lose any games at all.
Casey Stengel, to Redding, after playing against him in Bushwick Park, Brooklyn, NY

He was one of the finest men you ever saw. God, he didn't enjoy money, he just enjoyed life. He was just a clean-cut, clean-living man. There'll never be another Dick Redding.
Jake Stephens, in <u>Blackball Stars</u>, *by Holway*

The "Cannonball" … it's a nickname that conjures up the image of a man capable of throwing a fastball through a brick wall, and apparently that is the kind of "cheese" that Dick Redding delivered whenever he pitched. But it seems a bit at odds with the type of man that he was. His ability on the baseball diamond was such that many of his contemporaries felt he was a better pitcher, with a better fastball, than even Satchel Paige. A fastball like that coming at a hitter from a man as big as Redding, who was 6', 4" and well over 200 lbs., suggests that he put the fear of God into his opponents whenever he let one loose … and he generally did when he was on the mound! Yet his personal demeanor and his approach to life make me think of him as a much different kind of person, a "fun-loving, good-natured" man who really embraced both life and the game of baseball. In fact, the other but less famous nickname that the press bestowed on him, "Smiling Dick," seems more appropriate to describe the man, if not the ball player.

He enjoyed a career that lasted from 1911 through 1938 as both a pitcher and a manager during which he was regarded as one of the greatest pitchers in blackball, and perhaps the greatest of all during the period from 1911 through World War I (when he interrupted his baseball career to serve America in combat duty in France). In fact, when Cum Posey, the owner of the Homestead Grays, was called upon in later years to name his all-black team, he gave Redding the nod as the number two man after "Smokey Joe" Williams and just ahead of Paige. The Negro League Committee of the Society of American Baseball Research (SABR) lists Redding as number 21 on its list of the Top 40 Negro League Players, ahead of the likes of Larry Doby, Jose Mendez and Quincy Trouppe. During Redding's twenty-seven year career, there were some amazing highlights ranging from the twelve no-hitters that he threw (although some records give him credit for as many as thirty no-hitters) to the day he is said to have struck out Babe Ruth three times on nine pitches during a 1922 exhibition game! Unfortunately, many of the records and statistics from his earlier (and best) years are sketchy and incomplete, but what's there establishes that Dick "Cannonball" Redding was clearly one of the best pitchers of all time.

On the mound, he didn't have a wide repertoire and relied almost exclusively, at least in his earlier years, on an overpowering fastball and excellent control. He made that fastball even more effective, however, by the way he delivered it. He didn't use a windup but he would turn his back on a hitter, which not only made it more difficult for the hitter to pick up the ball when he released it, but also gave him pause to think about where it might be headed. As pitcher Sam Streeter said, "When a man turns his back, the batter's going to give a little when he comes around." Redding was pretty composed when he pitched and seldom got riled, but he was not above throwing one at your head if you dug in on him. He was a bit of an innovator, employing a "hesitation" pitch long before Paige did and using it to great advantage. He also developed a curveball later in his career, but when that fastball was working for him he didn't need it much.

He was a very hard working man, with great stamina, who often pitched both ends of a doubleheader on consecutive days! As a man and as a manager, though, he was much less imposing and, according to his teammates and those who played for him, was a good-natured fellow who was very well liked. He didn't have any formal education, couldn't read or write, and really wasn't even considered to be a very good manager. But he was effective enough to manage the Brooklyn Royal Giants from 1923-1938.

Dick Redding was just like a big kid. As a manager, I don't think he was that great. But everybody liked him. So they played for him.
Gene Benson, one of Redding's players on the Giants

It even seems Redding's happy disposition occasionally came to light when he was on the mound as one old timer recalled him grinning at a batter as he raised his leg up to deliver that imposing fastball. Even with all of his players' recollections about him, however, it is hard to know a man completely based on such a limited record and Dick Redding's life is no exception. As Ted Page said of him, "He took everything good-natured. He didn't have a care in the world so far as I could see, yet he never had much money or anything like that." But despite all of the good-nature, Redding was subject to the same uncertainties of life that we all face and died alone in a mental hospital in Central Islip, New York at the age of 57. While the details of his illness and death have never really been made clear, it seems he fell ill with a "strange malady" in late 1948 and died before the end of that year. I don't know if he maintained his wonderful disposition up until that time but I want to honor him here as another of my Early Aces in the hope that it will bring out his ever-present smile once again, wherever he is, to know that we remember him so well and fondly for his baseball talent and accomplishments as well as for the man that he was.

Redding's baseball career began in his hometown of Atlanta, Georgia, where he first pitched for his college team at Morris Brown University and then played with a semi-pro team known as the Atlanta Depins. In 1911, when Redding was 20 years of age, he had a chance to pitch batting practice against the National League champion New York Giants during a trip through the South. He took full advantage of that opportunity and made such an impression on their manager John McGraw that McGraw arranged for Redding to join the Philadelphia Giants, who were then managed by Sol White.

If they could have taken colored in the big leagues, John McGraw would have taken Dick Redding.
Jesse Hubbard, Pitcher, Brooklyn Royal Giants

Redding only stayed with the Philadelphia team through July of that year when he left to pitch for the New York Lincoln Giants and immediately began to exhibit the fastball and dominant success that marked his career. During the balance of that 1911 season with the Lincoln Giants, he is said to have won 17 (later revised by some historians to 29) games in a row. That streak was marked by four wins over Rube Foster's Leland Giants of Chicago (including one over the legendary Cuban hurler Jose Mendez) and five no-hitters, and only ended in a 2-0 loss to "Smokey Joe" Williams when Redding gave up two runs in the eighth inning.

"Cannonball" stayed with the Lincoln Giants for the 1912 season, who by then had also acquired the pitching services of "Smokey Joe" for that year. They also boasted such greats as Hall of Famer John Henry Lloyd at shortstop/manager, Spottswood Poles in center and Louis Santop behind the plate. Redding and Williams stayed together on that Lincoln Giants team through 1914, giving them a 1-2 punch in their pitching rotation that was unrivaled at the time and made them one of the greatest black teams that ever took the field.

During his tenure with the Lincoln Giants, Redding really cemented his legacy as one of the greatest pitchers of that era. In 1912, his record was 43-12, with several no-hitters, including one against the Cuban Stars. He is also said to have struck out 25 batters in one game, a game in which he only faced the minimum 27 hitters. The following year, 1913, he showed the same kind of dominance, throwing a perfect game against the Jersey Skeeters (who played in what is now the International League) and striking out 15 of the 18 batters he faced in another game. Among his many amazing performances that year, he struck out 24 batters in a contest against a team in the United States League (then known as a "quasi-major league"), which the New York press described as "undoubtedly ... a record for semi-pro ball" and is said to have bested both the New York Giants and the Boston Braves in separate exhibition contests. (He also pitched for Club Fe in Cuba that winter, and led the league there in winning percentage with a 9-5 record.) His last year with the Lincoln Giants in 1914 was just as successful as he posted a 12-3 record, according to available records.

Redding had a change of scenery for the 1915 season when he jumped across town to the New York Lincoln Stars. The surroundings may have been different but the results were the same. He reeled off 20 straight wins against black and white opponents, including an exhibition win against Connie Mack's Philadelphia A's and three wins over all-star teams made up of some quality former Major League talent. He had a 23-2 record by August of that year when he returned to the Lincoln Giants for a playoff series against Rube Foster's Chicago American Giants. True to form, he pitched them to a series tie, going 3-1 and hitting over .300. His reputation was such that the press began to refer to him as "the Demon pitcher."

He spent 1916 with the Brooklyn Royal Giants and in 1917 he had brief stints with both C.I. Taylor's Indianapolis ABC's and Foster's Chicago American Giants before World War I broke out. His pitching success continued with them as, among other things, he one-hit the All Nations team in one performance and led the American Giants with a record of 13-3 that year (which is said to have included a victory against Dick Rudolph of the Boston Braves who was pitching during the Major League off-season for a barnstorming team of International League players). It was in 1917 that the press bestowed his other nickname, "Smiling Dick," upon him.

His baseball career was interrupted by the outbreak of World War I, and he saw combat duty as a member of the US Army in France during 1918. But, when his tour of duty was over, Redding returned to baseball and joined the Atlantic City Bacharachs as player-manager in 1919. He stayed with the Bacharachs in that capacity through 1922. Whether it was his experience in the war, or the year he spent away from baseball while he served his country, or just his age, Redding was not the same pitcher after World War I as he was before. As one of his contemporaries said, "He faded fast ... but he was just as good as [Smokey Joe] Williams when he was good." In fact, while his record in 1919 was not near his pre-war standard, his losses included a two-hitter against Williams (who threw a no-hitter), a 14 inning 2-1 loss to Carl Mays of the Boston Red Sox, and a 2-1 loss to Jeff Tesreau of the New York Giants (who he later beat 6-4 in a 14 inning re-match).

Although time had taken its toll, Redding still had the ability to rise to the occasion during his post-war years. That was never more evident than in one historic game he pitched for the Bacharachs during the 1920 season. In the first game ever played between two all-black teams in Ebbetts Field, he bested "Smokey Joe" Williams in a 5-0 gem before 16,000 fans. The Bacharachs went on that year to win the "Colored Championship of the East" and play the American Giants for the "undisputed title of black baseball," which actually didn't solve any disputes because the series ended in a four game split. The following year, 1921, the same two teams faced each other in the informal "black World Series," and Redding again showed that he was up to the task as he pitched six no-hit innings against the ace of their staff, Dave Brown, but lost 3-1.

Redding and Williams, the dominant Negro League pitchers of that era, met several times, creating special lasting memories.

One of the most heralded pitching duels of Negro baseball history, [was] between Dick Redding and Smokey Joe Williams in the early twenties ... Redding beat Williams in the first game of a double header 1-0 and then, after a short rest, Williams came back and beat Redding to win the second by an identical score.
Invisible Men, Life in Baseball's Negro Leagues, by Donn Rogosin, Atheneum, 1985, New York

The Eastern Colored League was formed in 1923 and Cannonball signed on as the player-manager of the Brooklyn Royal Giants in that inaugural year. It would be the last and longest stop for him during his long baseball career as he stayed with the Royal Giants for 16 years until 1938 when he retired from baseball. He was again reunited with "Smokey Joe" Williams as a teammate on that 1923 team, but by then Redding was not pitching as much as he had been and Williams was considered their number one man. While his skills, or at least his stamina, may have been fading in those years, his ability to bring it for a few innings was still there. In 1926, Laymon Yokely, who would later establish himself as one of the hardest throwers in the Negro Leagues, was a rookie pitching for Redding's Brooklyn Giants and had an eye-opening first impression of his manager's pitching ability:

Redding was throwing hard then, and he was going out! ... I looked at him and said, 'Going out? Hard as that man throws?' Yeah, he could throw harder than I was, and I was just coming in!

I don't have any doubt that Dick "Cannonball" Redding had what it takes to have been a twenty-game winner in the Major Leagues, particularly in the period of his greatest dominance during the pre-World War I years of his career. His fastball alone seems to qualify him as a bona-fide candidate, and the testament of those who played against him or saw him pitch establish that he was just as good as his reputation suggests. The fact that he was also such a universally liked, and likeable, man, with such a wonderful disposition and approach to life, is really just a bonus for me in counting him among those early Aces who might have reached that wonderful twenty-win plateau in the Major Leagues if given the chance.

CHAPTER 9

WILLIAM HENDRICK FOSTER
Willie
Bill

Born June 12, 1904, in Calvert, Texas
Died September 16, 1978, in Lorman, Mississippi
Teams: Memphis Red Sox, Chicago American Giants,
          Birmingham Black Barons, Homestead Grays,
          Kansas City Monarchs, Cole's American Giants,
          Pittsburgh Crawfords
Inducted into National Baseball Hall of Fame 1996
Inducted into Mississippi Sports Hall of Fame 2003
Inducted into Texas Sports Hall of Fame
Inducted into Alcorn State University Hall of Fame
Inducted into Southwestern Athletic Conference Hall of Fame

Willie Foster's greatness was that he had this terrific speed and a great, fast breaking curveball and a drop ball, and he was really a master of the change of pace. He could throw you a real fast one and then use the same motion and bring it up a little slower, and then a little slower yet. And then he'd use the same motion again, and z-zzz. He was really a great pitcher.
Dave Malarcher, Negro League third baseman and manager

Willie Foster, I think, was the top lefty we have produced. Foster, a giant with a burning fastball, gave our best team fits.
Cumberland "Cum" Posey, Owner, Homestead Grays

He had the same perfect delivery of Herb Pennock, but was faster by far, with a sharp curve, and had what all great pitchers have … control.
Umpire "Jocko" Conlon, Hall of Famer

All the years I played, I never got a hit off him. He threw fire.
Buck Leonard

I always heard him referred to as the black "Lefty" Grove.
Monte Irvin, Hall of Famer

If I could paint you white, I could get $150,000 for you right now.
Hank Greenberg, Hall of Famer

People often speak of "baseball families," who seem to produce far more than their share of athletes blessed with incredible baseball talent, and there are many of them throughout baseball history. Blackball certainly had its share, going back as far as the nineteenth century and continuing right up until the Negro Leagues folded. The earliest one that comes to mind is the Walker family that produced the first two black Major Leaguers in brothers, Fleet and Weldy Walker. Another is the Bankhead family, which had not only five brothers that played in the Negro Leagues (Sam, Dan, Fred, Joe, and Garnett) but can also claim the first black pitcher to ever toe the rubber in the Major Leagues during the modern era, Dan, who did it as a teammate of Jackie Robinson in 1947. But the family that stands out most to me, particularly as a pitcher, has to be the Foster family of Calvert, Texas. They not only brought the great right-hander Andrew "Rube" Foster (see Chapter 5) into this world but dipped into the same baseball gene pool twenty-five years later to give the world my next early Ace, Willie Foster. As you will see in the next few pages, however, Willie was not just Rube's southpaw half-brother but an equally dominant force on the mound, so much so that he too was ultimately inducted into the National Baseball Hall of Fame, in 1996. In fact, when he was inducted, he and Rube formed one of only three sets of brothers to be enshrined in the Hall. (The others are Harry and George Wright, and Paul and Lloyd Waner.)

Willie Foster's accomplishments on the mound were many, and some of his individual performances were legendary. He was the winningest pitcher in Negro League history, notching 137 wins against only 62 losses. He also tossed more career shutouts than any other pitcher in Negro League history, with 34, and was second only to Satchel Paige in career strikeouts. When he had the opportunity to face Major League talent, Willie was certainly up to the task, winning six of the seven games he pitched against Major League All-Star teams during his career. But, the statistic that impresses me the most about him is his record in Negro League post-season play. It was said about him that he was at his best when the stakes were high, and the fact that he had more post-season wins (12) than any other Negro League pitcher tells me that he probably had just the kind of stuff, in his arm, in his head, and in his heart, to win twenty games in a Major League season.

Willie was a pretty big fellow, at about 6' 1" and 195 pounds, and had a variety of pitches at his command. His repertoire included an overpowering fastball, a slider, a fast-breaking drop ball, a slow curve, and a great, deceptive change-up. He enhanced the effectiveness of his pitches by using the same easy motion when he delivered them so that a hitter couldn't pick up a hint of what was coming. His control was so good he once joked that, while Satchel Paige would often warm-up by throwing pitches over a gum wrapper, he could throw his pitches over a matchstick. His teammate and manager, Dave Malarcher, said that Willie was a "carbon copy" of his brother Rube with "identical moves … ball held behind (their) head … just before they take their stride." But, while he surely did learn a lot from his brother early in his career, the pitching mastery that Willie attained was his alone.

This later generation Foster was born on June 12, 1904. Both he and Rube had the same father, Andrew Foster, Sr., but different mothers. Willie's mother was Sarah Lewis, who herself had a family connection to blackball in that her brother, Robert "Bubbles" Lewis, came to own the Memphis Red Sox in later years. At a very early age, Willie moved with his mother and a sister, Geneva, to live with his maternal grandparents in Rodney, Mississippi. Unfortunately, his mother died shortly after their move when he was only four years old and Willie stayed in Mississippi where he was raised by his grandparents. He played baseball in the fields around Rodney as a youngster and grew up big and strong in the process. By his own recollections, he was a strapping six footer and almost at his adult weight when he was only thirteen years old. It was at around that time he took his first step toward the baseball career that he would make his life when, one Saturday morning, he decided to forego his usual baseball game with his friends and instead took a trip to Lorman, Mississippi so he could watch the Alcorn College team play.

As he told it, he hitched up a wagon for the ride and, when he arrived, stood under a tree to watch them. After a while, the Alcorn coach came over to him and asked, "What are you doing here, big fella?" He answered with the same kind of confidence that he later pitched with and told the coach that he could beat any of the players he saw out on the field. When the coach invited him to try, he proceeded to back up his words: "I struck out everybody they had." Willie's performance that day earned him an invitation to join the Alcorn team, and began an association with Alcorn that lasted right up until his death in 1978. It also marked the real beginning of his baseball career because, during the few years he attended Alcorn and played baseball for them, he also played semi-pro ball and began to make a name for himself locally. In fact, his success while later pitching for one of those semi-pro teams in Arkansas led to an invitation to join the Memphis Red Sox, after he had beaten them twice in one series.

By 1923, Willie had hopes of playing for Rube's Chicago American Giants and moved from Mississippi to Chicago seeking a try-out. But, Rube refused him, insisting that he forget about baseball and pursue an education instead. This didn't sit too well with Willie, who became upset with Rube and returned to the South where he signed with the Memphis team owned by his uncle, "Bubbles" Lewis. When Rube heard about his signing, he used his powerful influence and directed Lewis to send Willie to him in Chicago. Lewis didn't have much choice in the matter and, whether it was because Rube wanted Willie under his wing or because he finally recognized his younger brother's talent, Willie wound up back in Chicago. It was a tumultuous year for Willie but he did get some pitching in, finishing with a 5-2 record that included a victory over the Kansas City Monarchs in his only appearance for his brother's Chicago American Giants. The next two seasons proved very similar for Willie as he split his time between the American Giants and the Memphis Red Sox in 1924, going 6-1, and the American Giants and the Birmingham Black Barons in 1925, posting a 7-1 record.

His first full season with the Chicago American Giants came in 1926. Sadly, it was the year that his brother's mental illness caused him to be hospitalized, and Dave Malarcher had taken over as Manager of the team. But, it was the year that clearly marked the arrival of Willie Foster as a premier pitcher. He was still attending college in Tennessee in the early part of the season but joined the team in time to put up twenty-six consecutive victories. His 11-4 ledger in league play during the second half of the Negro National League season led the American Giants to the second half title. That set the stage for one of Willie's most memorable post-season performances against the Kansas City Monarchs who had won the title for the first half of the season. Their playoff series for the league championship came down to a doubleheader, and the American Giants had to win both ends to earn a berth in the blackball World Series against the Bacharach Giants who had won the Eastern Colored League championship. Foster answered the bell to start both games. He beat "Bullet" Rogan in the first game by a score of 1-0, with the only run scoring in the bottom of the ninth. He won the second game, 5-0, again besting Rogan who had decided he would take the start over Chet Brewer when he saw Foster warming up for the second game. Foster was just as impressive in leading his team to victory, five games to four, over the Bacharach Giants in the World Series. He pitched three complete games, including a shutout, earned two victories, and finished with a 1.27 ERA. (Fittingly, John Holway named Willie as the winner of The Rube Foster Award in his work, The Complete Book of Baseball's Negro Leagues, for his performance in 1926.)

Willie followed up the 1926 season with just as much personal success in 1927, and another World Series championship. He posted an overall 32-3 record, including a 21-2 mark in league play, and his post-season performance was just as stellar. Willie went 2-0 with a 2.00 ERA in the Negro National League playoff series against the Birmingham Black Barons, throwing two complete games and a shutout, as the American Giants won all four games played. He also opened and closed the World Series with victories against the Bacharach Giants, sending them to defeat for the second straight year.

While there was not much of an off-season for Negro Leaguers, however long it was Foster did not use it for rest, and maintained the same level of success. He pitched in the California Winter League in 1926-27 and posted a 14-1 mark. He also traveled to Cuba to pitch during the winter of 1927-28 and, while his record was only 6-8, he led the Cuban League in complete games, with 8.

In the ensuing seasons of 1928, 1929, and 1930, Foster put up marks of 14-10, 11-7, and 16-10 for the American Giants, assuming the managerial reins in 1930. One of his more memorable performances during this period came after the 1929 season when he got the chance to face a team of American League All-Stars that included members of the Detroit Tigers, St. Louis Browns, Cleveland Indians and Chicago White Sox. Future Hall of Famer Hank Greenberg and Art Shires, who had just hit .312 for Chicago that year, were among them. Foster pitched both ends of a doubleheader against that team. He lost the first game but won the second, throwing a no-hitter for eight innings. He also struck out nine Major Leaguers on that day, including Shires five times. It was the kind of performance that would secure the place of any pitcher, black or white, as among the best the game had to offer.

Willie's stint with the American Giants was interrupted in 1931, which he split between the Homestead Grays and the Kansas City Monarchs, but he returned to the then Coles American Giants in 1932, after businessman Robert Cole purchased the team. He posted a 15-8 record that year, and pitched the team to the Negro Southern League championship with a 2-0 win over the Nashville Elite Giants in the seventh and deciding game.

Foster's successes continued in 1933 in several different ways. He continued his dominance on the mound, going 9-3 and pitching the American Giants to a pennant in the "new" Negro National League. He also garnered a new honor as the leading vote-getter for the inaugural East-West All-Star Game, with 40,637 fans casting their ballots in The Pittsburgh Courier for him. Willie proved worthy of their confidence in him, as he won the game by a score of 11-7 against a line-up that included future Hall of Famers "Cool Papa" Bell, Oscar Charleston, and Josh Gibson. He also became the only pitcher to pitch a complete game in that classic (as the rules were later changed to limit a pitcher to no more than three innings). His final accomplishment of 1933 came outside of baseball, and probably would have made his brother Rube most proud of him, as he completed his degree in agricultural education at Alcorn State.

At this point in his career, Willie's best days were behind him but his skills were still exceptional. His American Giants won the first half Negro National League championship in 1934 although they lost the league pennant to the second half champs, the Philadelphia Stars, four games to three. The fans recognized his continuing ability that year by again voting him to be the starting pitcher for the West in the East-West All-Star game, with a then record 48,957 votes.

Foster stayed with the American Giants for the 1935 season, going 6-3 in league play and, after spending 1936 with the Pittsburgh Crawfords, he rejoined them in 1937, which was his last full season in the Negro Leagues. He ended his pitching career in 1938, spending some time with the Memphis Red Sox in spring training and later pitching for the Washington Browns, a far less talented blackball team than he was accustomed to, and a white semipro team in Elgin, Illinois.

When his playing days were over, Willie at first moved to North Carolina to sell insurance and later spent some time managing the world-famous Harlem Globetrotters. Ultimately, he found a second career that enabled him to combine two things that were very dear to him during his younger days, baseball and Alcorn State, when he became the baseball coach and later the Dean of Men at Alcorn. He held those positions from 1960 until the time he died in 1978.

While his genes may have given him an advantage, his accomplishments cannot be ascribed solely to any innate gift that God may have given him or anyone else in his family. Many of us have gifts that we don't take the fullest advantage of. What Willie Foster did on the field of play went far beyond what he inherited. He succeeded because he worked and perfected his talent. There is no doubt in my mind that his talent would have put him right there with the rest of us who were fortunate enough to win twenty games in a Major League season.

CHAPTER 10

CHESTER ARTHUR BREWER
Chet
Pop

Born January 14, 1907 in Leavenworth, Kansas
Died March 26, 1990 in Whittier, California
Teams: Tennessee Rats, Gilkerson's Union Giants,
      Kansas City Monarchs, Bismarck Churchills,
      Brooklyn Royal Giants, New York Cubans,
      Philadelphia Stars, Cleveland Buckeyes,
      Chicago American Giants, Carmen Cardinals
Inducted into Mexican Baseball Hall of Fame 1966

Chet was a good pitcher. He had a good fastball, a great curve ball, and, above all, great control. I'd have to rank Chet up there with Bullet Joe Rogan and Hilton Smith.
Sammy Haynes, Catcher, Atlanta Black Crackers & KC Monarchs

Brewer was a finesser. Good curve ball, good control, spotted the ball. … kind of a leader fella.
Buck O'Neil, First Baseman, Kansas City Monarchs

He had three speeds: fast, faster, and out of sight! He threw a pea, an aspirin and one with a tail on it!"
Al McKerlie, catcher for Brewer on the 1952 Carmen Manitoba Cardinals, when Brewer was 45 years old.

In the twenty-four years that Chet Brewer pitched in professional baseball, it seemed that his star was often eclipsed by a more established or more flamboyant teammate. While he played for a dozen or more teams in almost as many countries during his career, he is most closely associated with the Kansas City Monarchs for whom he played in fifteen of those years. During that long career, however, he never got top billing despite his great talents and accomplishments because of the bright lights that shone in front of him. In Brewer's first year with the Monarchs in 1925, "Bullet Joe" Rogan was in his prime as Kansas City's manager, star pitcher, and main gate attraction. Later, Satchel Paige joined the Monarchs and drew the spotlight as the most celebrated man in blackball history. Yet, even in the shadow of these other Aces, there can be no doubt that Chet Brewer was one of the greatest pitchers that ever toed the rubber in the Negro Leagues and, quite likely, in all of baseball.

Brewer was born in Leavenworth, Kansas on January 14, 1907. His father was a Methodist minister and, while Chet once described himself as a "mischievous little so-and-so" as a youth, he also acknowledged that his parents raised him in a good Christian environment and instilled in him a strong sense of the basic values that guided his life through baseball and beyond. When opportunities for work in Kansas fell flat, Chet's parents moved to Des Moines, Iowa.

Des Moines was like a breath of fresh air to us. We got rid of a lot of racial prejudice we found in Kansas. Everything there was either all-white or all-black. We lived in an integrated neighborhood and I went to integrated schools in Des Moines. We blacks could go to movies in Des Moines and not have to sit back with the projector. I have very fond memories of Des Moines.
Chet Brewer (www.desmoineregister.com)

Chet attended West High School in Des Moines, where he played basketball and football, and ran track. He didn't play baseball for the school, since it had no baseball team. But even then his baseball talent must have been evident because, when school was out for the summer, he made the grade as a teen-ager with the Tennessee Rats, a popular black barnstorming baseball team of the 1910s and 1920s (which is thought by many to be the team on which the 1970s book and movie "Bingo Long And His Traveling All-Stars" was based.) Those early days as a barnstorming, teenage ball player were fondly recalled by Chet in an interview he gave to John Holway in 1983, when he said:

We'd come to a town in our Model-T Ford and go up and down the street with a megaphone – didn't have microphones then – and say, "Come out to the ball park," and slept in tents and played and clowned, just like Bingo Long. It was a way to make money. It was the only way we knew how to get the people to come. It was a tough life, but I see these big ball players nowadays complaining. We couldn't eat in the restaurants or sleep in the better hotels, but we still entertained the people. Didn't make much money, but had a lot of fun playing, because we loved the game.

Chet had what today's scouts would call a "perfect pitcher's body," standing long and lean at about 6'4" and 187 pounds. He didn't rely on just one "out" pitch; instead, he "threw everything but the kitchen sink," and did so with great success. He would come at a hitter with a "good, live, running fastball," a "big old rainbow" curve, an overhand "drop" ball, a screwball, a slider, and an emery ball. He had great control, which made each one of these pitches all the more effective because it enabled him to "spot" the ball and work a hitter all around the strike zone: up, down, inside and out. Chet was also known to keep a hitter honest (or "knock our hats off," as Willie Powell said of him) if he was digging in or getting too close to the plate or just getting too comfortable.

Brewer first came on the professional scene in 1924 with the Gilkerson Union Giants. There is no record of what he did that year, but it opened the door to what amounted to a Hall of Fame career. In fact, one of his teammates on that team was the legendary Ted "Double Duty" Radcliffe, who would later assess Brewer's talent as a pitcher to be "in the same league" as both Rogan and Paige.

His play as a youngster with the Rats must have made a terrific impression on some of his opponents because it paved the way for him to join the Kansas City Monarchs in 1925. One of those opponents was The All Nations Team, which he played against when he was about 15. It was a mixture of a traveling entertainment show and barnstorming baseball team that was very popular in the 1910s and 1920s, and brought not just baseball to the towns it traveled to, but also music, dancing and sideshows. Its players included whites, blacks, Asians, Cubans, and even women (one of whom was known as "Carrie Nation"), but despite the distractions many of them were serious baseball players capable of playing at a high level of competition. It was those players who recommended the young Brewer to the team's owner, J.L. Wilkinson, who also happened to own the Monarchs. He sent for Brewer to play for the Monarchs in 1925 based on the "scouting report" that they provided him.

Brewer didn't do much in that first year with the Monarchs, but had a real "breakout" year for them in 1926 when he went 12-1 in league play. Ironically, however, it seems that season may be most notable in blackball history for the game that Chet didn't pitch than for the ones that he did. The Monarchs had won the first half pennant in the Negro National League that year. But they had to face the Chicago American Giants, who had won the second half pennant, in a playoff series to advance to the "black World Series" against the Eastern Colored League champs, the Bacharach Giants. Brewer drew the start in the first game and won; he also won his next start 5-0 to give the Monarchs a 3-1 lead in the series. When the series then shifted to Chicago, the Giants won the first game there and a rainout in the next game forced a doubleheader that would decide the series. "Bullet Joe" Rogan started the first game of that twin bill and, in a classic pitcher's duel with Willie Foster, lost a tough 1-0 decision. With the series now tied at 3-3, Brewer just knew that he would start the second game, and was already warmed up and ready to go; as he said, "I had pitched like a dog all year … and I knew that those guys didn't want to face me." But, when Rogan saw that Willie Foster was warming to go in that second game, he took the ball instead of Brewer and, although he settled down after giving up 3 runs in the first inning, lost the game 5-0 and the 1926 Negro League championship with it.

Chet's best year with the Monarchs was 1929 when he went 17-3 in league play (which included a streak of 31 consecutive innings in which he didn't allow a run) and again helped the Monarchs to the Negro National League championship. He was credited with 30-win seasons in at least three years against all competition, with 30 wins in 1930, 34 in 1933 and 33 in 1934 (during which he is said to have won 16 straight.)

During the early 1930s, Brewer was a pioneer in integrating baseball, by playing integrated ball throughout the Midwest on several different teams. In 1931, he was one of the first black players to play integrated baseball when he played for Crookston, Minnesota, where he won every game he pitched that year. He played integrated ball again, in 1934, with Jamestown, North Dakota, and in 1935, Chet played with an integrated team in Bismarck.

The recognition and respect that he received from players and fans alike as one of the pre-eminent pitchers of his day was evidenced by his selection to both the 1933 and 1934 East-West Game, the Negro League equivalent of the Major League All-Star Game. In fact, he received more votes than every other pitcher except Willie Foster for the 1934 game.

While he continued to pitch in the Negro Leagues through the 1948 season where he ended his Negro League career with the Cleveland Buckeyes (and was again voted to the East-West Game in 1947 and 1948), Brewer also pitched year round for a number of other teams in a number of other leagues, tournaments and countries. He pitched winter ball for 14 years in the California Winter League during the period from 1926 through 1943, pitching against established Major League and prominent minor league talent. Brewer had a career record of 43-13 there, leading the league in wins in 1928 and 1937 and managing the Kansas City Royals from 1943-1946.

Brewer also became the first African-American player to pitch in the Mexican League when he took the field for Tampico in 1938. He compiled a 32-24 career record in 3 seasons there, which included a 17-5 record with a 1.88 ERA in 1938 and a 12-7 record and 2.50 ERA in 1939. During the winter of 1938-39, he established a Mexican League record of 40 consecutive shutout innings, which included two no-hitters.

His pitching journey also brought him to Santo Domingo, Panama, Cuba, Puerto Rico, and even China and Japan, at different points in his career. In 1937, for instance, he bested his Monarchs teammate, Satchel Paige, tossing a one-hitter against the strong Cuidad Trujillo team that had been assembled by the dictator Trujillo himself, with Paige as its ace. Later on, he helped to pitch Caguas to the Puerto Rican Winter championship, including the win in the final, pennant-clinching game.

Throughout his career, he had plenty of opportunity to face Major League talent and he did not disappoint anyone there either as he was the winner in both of his head-to-head starts against touring Major League all-star teams. In the first of those games in 1931, he struck out 13 batters in a complete game 6-2 victory in which he gave up only 6 hits to the likes of the fabled "Big Poison" and "Little Poison," Paul and Lloyd Waner. In October of 1936, he pitched an 11-0 shutout against a team that included future Hall of Famers Jimmy Foxx, Heinie Manush, and Ted Lyons, as well as Doc Cramer and future Red Sox manager, Pinky Higgins, and held the team to only 3 hits in that complete game win; Manush struck out against him three times. But the real opportunity to face Major Leaguers never came to pass for Chet despite the fact that he almost beat Jackie Robinson to the punch as the first African-American to sign a contract to play Organized Baseball in the modern era.

In 1943, the Los Angeles Angels of the Pacific Coast League, offered a tryout to Chet and outfielder, Lou Dials. However, owner Phil Wrigley, son of William Wrigley (owner of the Chicago Cubs), refused to sign either player. (It is believed that Wrigley did not want a confrontation with Commissioner Landis over the signing of a black player.) But, Chet got a second opportunity to enter Organized Baseball in 1945. The Cleveland Indians had a farm team at Bakersfield in the California League at that time and they made a real effort to sign Chet to a contract. Now, that by itself is a pretty significant tribute to the kind of talent that he had since he was already 38 years of age at that time. (By a quirk of fate, this was the same year that Chet managed Jackie Robinson in the California Winter League for the Kansas City Royals.) The Indians went so far as to secure the approval of the Commissioner of minor league baseball, George Trautman, but the matter went no further as their General Manager, Roger Peckinpaugh, would not give his blessing to the idea. If he hadn't stood in the way, baseball history might have been written a bit differently, with Chet Brewer playing a much more recognizable part, as Jackie Robinson only signed his contract with the Montreal Royals later that year.

There is also a bittersweet irony to Chet's last few years in the Negro Leagues with the Cleveland Buckeyes. During those same years, his former teammate, Satchel Paige, was pitching at the Major League level across town for the Cleveland Indians, again in the spotlight and helping the Indians claim the 1948 American League pennant. By then, Hank Greenberg was Cleveland's General Manager and, upon seeing Chet pitch for the Buckeyes, asked, "Who is that guy? He has better control than any pitcher on our club." Little did he know that he could have had Chet on his staff if his predecessor had had the vision and courage of men like Branch Rickey or Bill Veeck, who had brought Paige to the Indians. While Chet did ultimately pitch in Organized Baseball in 1952, as the player-manager of Porterville in the old Southwest International League, his time had passed by then and the opportunity to do so at the Major League level never came his way.

After he stopped pitching, Chet stayed connected to the game he loved. In 1957, he was hired by the Pittsburgh Pirates as a scout of the southern California area for the Hollywood Stars, the Pirates' Pacific Coast League affiliate. Brewer continued to work as a scout for the Pirates organization through 1974. After he retired from the Pirates, he went to Los Angeles, where he and his wife started a baseball program for boys in Watts, to keep them out of trouble. He also ran a semi-pro youth baseball league, known as Chet Brewer's All-Stars, which was a launching pad that helped to develop the talents of such Major Leaguers as Hall of Famer Eddie Murray, 19-game winner Dock Ellis, baseball's first black general manager Bob Watson, Lyman Bostock, Ellis Valentine, Bobby Tolan, George Hendricks, Willie Crawford, Reggie Smith, and Enos Cabell. The program was also very successful in helping dozens of other young men find themselves.

When I consider Chet's baseball talents and accomplishments, it seems to me that whatever shadows may have been cast by some of his contemporaries and teammates, his own star shone just as brightly and earned him a well-deserved place among my Early Black Aces.

CHAPTER 11

LEROY ROBERT PAIGE
Satchel

Born July 7, 1906 in Mobile, Alabama
Died June 8, 1982 in Kansas City, Missouri
Teams: Mobile Tigers, Chattanooga Black Lookouts,
   New Orleans Black Pelicans, Birmingham Black Barons,
   Baltimore Black Sox, Nashville Elite Giants,
   Cleveland Cubs, St. Louis Stars, Pittsburgh Crawfords,
   Trujillo All Stars, Kansas City Monarchs, Memphis
   Red Sox, New York Black Yankees, East Chicago Giants,
   Philadelphia Stars, Chicago American Giants, Cleveland
   Indians, St. Louis Browns, Kansas City Athletics,
   Miami Marlins, Portland Beavers, Springfield
   Redbirds, Atlanta Braves, Indianapolis Clowns
Inducted into National Baseball Hall of Fame 1971

Satchell, elongated and a consummate showman, whose whip-corded right arm rifles a ball plateward with the speed of a bullet, has as fast a ball as any ever uncorked in big league baseball. Shades of "Lefty" Grove ... Walter Johnson ... and other stars of mound fame, come almost unbidden to mind as he marvels at the speed and cunning contained in those long arms of the boy who came to Pittsburgh via Alabama and Tennessee.
Pittsburgh Courier, July 1, 1933

He made his living by throwing the ball to a spot over the plate the size of a matchbook.
Cool "Papa" Bell, Hall of Famer

The first man Satchel pitched to, I thought he was playin' shadowball, cuz I didn't see the ball. I said, now wait a minute, something's wrong here. He wouldn't be playing no shadowball out here during a game, but I can't see it. So I know what I'm gonna do. I'm going down there closer and see, was he throwin' it or not. And I went down there behind the catcher and he was throwin' it but you just couldn't see it, that's how fast it was.
Clifford "Connie" Johnson, Jr., Pitcher, Negro Leagues and Major Leagues

Many a sportswriter have protested against the color discrimination in big league baseball. The owners and managers say that their Southern

training camps would make trouble if Negroes were on the team. But many a shepherd of a limping major league club has made no secret of his yearning to trade more than a couple of butt-sprung outfielders for colored players of the caliber of Satchelfoots Paige.
Time Magazine, June 3, 1940

Barred from organized professional baseball because he is a Negro, Paige has played against many of the major league stars in exhibition games. According to them he has more than proved his ability to play in the big leagues. He won four of six games from Dizzy Dean in a series and Joe DiMaggio says Paige is the greatest pitcher he ever batted against.
Life Magazine, June 3, 1940

They said I was the greatest pitcher they ever saw ... I couldn't understand why they couldn't give me no justice.
Satchel Paige, quoted in his obituary in The Sporting News, 1982

If there was but one household name among the scores of men who played Negro League baseball, it had to be my next Early Ace, Satchel Paige. And I'm not just talking about black households but all of America! He was not just one of the greatest pitchers who ever lived but a true baseball icon and American legend. Satchel Paige was also an accomplished storyteller and down-home philosopher, with a penchant for quotable quotes that may have only ever been rivaled by Yogi Berra; he was a showman and a gate-draw rivaling the best carnival barker that ever sold a ticket to the big top when it came to bringing people out to whatever ballpark he may have been pitching in; and he was a businessman and entrepreneur who was probably the highest paid athlete in the country, black or white, during his time. He was all of those things and more. But, most of all he was one heck of a pitcher.

I have to tell you from the outset that I have a much more personal connection to Satchel than to any of the other Early Aces that I have written about for a lot of reasons, and not just because he was one of the very few of them who actually pitched in the Major Leagues. You see, I not only grew up during the time he was in the prime of his blackball career but also had a chance to talk pitching with him later on when I was a minor leaguer in the Cleveland Indian organization learning the art of pitching. I think that has given me a much different perspective on his career than all of the research that I did about him. Also, like me, Satchel loved to sing and perform. Because of the segregated nature of our road existence as ballplayers, we always found ourselves staying in the same hotels as black entertainers, most of whom were great baseball fans. In Kansas City it was Street's Hotel; in Baltimore, the Smith Hotel; and in Detroit, the Norwood. In my day, I stayed in the same hotels as Duke Ellington, Count Basie, the Staple Singers,

Patti LaBelle, B.B. King, James Moody, O.C. Smith, Ella Fitzgerald and Lionel Hampton, and many other great performers, and got a chance to jam and perform with some of them. Years earlier, Satchel had the opportunity to do the very same thing as he got to sing with the Mills Brothers, at the Crawford Grille, owned by Gus Greenlee, the owner of the Pittsburgh Crawfords.

As a kid growing up in Lacoochee, I can clearly remember hearing about the great Satchel Paige from the grown-ups and, as I got older, reading about his baseball exploits in *The Pittsburgh Courier* and all of the other black newspapers that I used to deliver. In fact, I even got to see him pitch a few times when he came through Florida on barnstorming trips with the Satchel Paige All-Stars. The impressions that his name and reputation left upon me as a youngster elevated him onto a pedestal that is hard to describe. But, the thing that stands out the most in my memory is a conversation that I had with him years later when he took the time to tell me about some of what it took to be a successful pitcher. For me, it was like getting an audience with the Pope when Satchel took me aside one day and shared a few of his secrets to pitching success.

It was in the mid-1950s after Satchel had finished his last Major League stint with the St. Louis Browns. He was probably close to fifty years old at the time and he was still pitching very effectively at the AAA level for the Miami Marlins of the International League. He said, "Let me tell you something, youngster. If you ain't got a titty pitch you can't win in the big leagues." He was telling me that you had to keep a hitter from getting too comfortable up there in the batter's box and let him know he couldn't just wait on a pitch out over the plate. If you bring a fastball up and in over his chest once in a while, a "high hard one," he'd always have that in mind when he faced you again and it would help you, as a pitcher, establish your ownership of the plate, especially the outside part. I'll always remember the way he described it so simply as the "titty pitch" but more so I remember the point he was trying to get across to me as a baseball player, and I heeded that advice as I moved on in my career. Satchel himself seldom hit a batter as he had absolutely pinpoint control but he had such unbelievable speed that he was able to send his message to a hitter whenever he came inside. I tried to do it the same way with the same purpose.

Paige had nicknames for a lot of other variations on his fastball and many of the other great pitches that he included in his arsenal, and the way he described them had as much to do with his colorful reputation as their effectiveness had on his baseball success. He was a tall, slender man at about 6' 4" and only about 180 pounds. But, he threw a baseball with such incredible speed and control that he didn't really even need to develop a breaking ball until many years into his career, after he had arm problems and began to use a bit more guile in his approach to pitching. His success and reputation was based on a fastball that was unmatched and pretty much unhittable from all accounts. He dubbed one variation the "Bee Ball," which just rode straight to the plate, and another the "Jump Ball" because it rose half a foot on its path home. He also threw a "Bat Dodger," the "Hurry-Up Ball," the "Midnight Creeper," a "Four-Day Rider," and even a "Nothin' Ball."

No matter the name though, the results were pretty much the same as Satchel put together a baseball career that literally spanned five decades, during which his pitching earned him a spot in the National Baseball Hall of Fame as one of the first Negro League inductees in 1971.

Satchel was born in Mobile, Alabama, on July 7, 1906, although his exact date of birth seems to be a subject that he enjoyed playing with over the years. Like many other young black kids in that area, he got an early introduction to both the game of baseball and some of life's more difficult lessons. They say he got his nickname of "Satchel" at a very young age when he would pick up a little bit of money carrying passengers' luggage at the Mobile train station. It seems that one day he tried to make off with one of the suitcases but was caught. A friend turned that experience into a nickname that stuck with him throughout his life. A few years later, as a young teenager, he would learn a difficult lesson when he was sent to a reform school after being caught in another theft. While it was a hard time, it was his first opportunity to really play on a school team and he benefited from his stay there, at least in a baseball sense.

When his time at the Mount Meig Reform School was over, Satchel was still a teenager and pitched for a few local semi-pro teams. One was the Mobile Tigers, where his teammates included the fathers of future Major Leaguers Hank Aaron, Billy Williams, and Amos Otis. He threw with the same explosive speed then, but not with the same kind of control that he later developed, and he began to make a name for himself. Ultimately, in 1926, that talent earned him his first professional contract with the Chattanooga Black Lookouts of the Negro Southern League. He was making $50 a month and his legendary career was off to a start.

By the end of the 1926 season, Satchel had followed the lure of a bigger paycheck and moved to the New Orleans Black Pelicans for $85 a month. It was his first raise, a concept that he apparently came to like as he often moved from team to team during his career for bigger and bigger paychecks as he realized the value of his vast baseball talents. At the beginning of the 1927 season, for instance, Satchel was back with the Black Lookouts at an increased salary of $200 a month but finished the season with the Birmingham Black Barons for the yet higher sum of $275 a month. He finished that year with an 8-3 record and stayed with the Black Barons through the 1930 season, refining his talent and building the reputation that would make him one of the biggest gate attractions in black baseball.

In 1931, he moved to the Nashville Elite Giants but ultimately signed on with Gus Greenlee's Pittsburgh Crawfords. He stayed with the Crawfords through the 1936 season and fully reached his stride as a pitcher with them during this period. He won the Crawfords' first game against the Homestead Grays in 1931 and went on to post records of 32-7 and 31-4 for them in 1932 and 1933, respectively. He went 10-1, with a 1.73 ERA, in league play in 1934, and finished his tenure with them in 1936 with a 24-3 record. During this period, Greenlee often "rented" Satchel out to other teams in need of his ability for an important game, but the two often fought over salary, which would ultimately lead to Paige leaving the Crawfords.

Satchel pitched some of his most memorable games during this period though. He pitched in the California Winter League during the 1931 off-season and beat a team of future Major Leaguers, including future Dodger slugger Babe Herman, allowing only one run and striking out eleven batters, including Herman four times. In 1934, while "on loan" from the Crawfords to the Colored House of David team, he pitched them to victory in the Denver Post tournament, known as the "Little World Series," winning three games in five days (two by shutout) and striking out 44 batters in the process. Later that same year, he beat a team led by Dizzy Dean at Los Angeles' Wrigley Field in a classic 13-inning game in which he only gave up two hits and struck out seventeen batters (Dean struck out 15.) In fact, he spent a lot of time barnstorming around the country with his Satchel Paige All-Stars playing against Dean's team.

Paige had become an incredible gate attraction, not only with his pitching ability but also with his showmanship. He was a marketing guy, so the anticipation of seeing him was part of the attraction. We knew that anytime we saw Satchel play that something was going to happen. It's like Willie Mays; you knew that when you saw Willie play you would see something spectacular. Satchel would often advertise his guarantees to strike out the first nine men in an exhibition game, or send the first three batters back to the bench on nine pitches, and invariably he delivered on those guarantees. Another of his stunts was to call in his fielders to sit behind the mound while he mowed down the opposition, and the fans delighted in watching him. I remember hearing that they had a hole in the wall in the Northern League and if you hit the ball in that hole you could get like $100,000. Well, the hole was so small, probably just enough to get a baseball through, but Satchel threw one in there. Yeah. He did all kinds of stuff like that. That was Satchel Paige. He was just an amazing individual. Satchel added to this appeal with his personality and unique ability to turn a phrase, with such lines as trademark, "Don't look back, something might be gainin' on you," one of his famous rules for living.

In 1937, after yet another dispute with Greenlee over salary, Paige accepted an offer from dictator Rafael Trujillo to go to Santo Domingo to play for his team, and Paige recruited many of his Crawford teammates to come play with him. But, Greenlee extracted his revenge for this raid on his players by having Paige banned from Negro League play. As a result, Satchel spent 1938 playing in the Mexican League where he developed a "dead arm" that threatened his baseball career. When he got back to the States, many thought he was washed up and he could not find a team willing to take a chance on him. He wound up signing with the All-Nations team as a gate attraction and touring with his Satchel Paige All-Stars. Most of his time on the field was spent playing first base as he did very little pitching. In the long run, his arm problems turned out to be a blessing in disguise as he was forced to develop a curveball and came up with his famous "hesitation pitch" while struggling to regain his fastball. Paige tried just about everything to bring his arm back to life, including pouring scalding hot water on it. Finally, by 1939, Kansas City Monarch trainer, Frank "Jewbaby" Floyd, came up with an ointment which

Satchel called "snake oil" and which successfully rejuvenated Paige's pitching arm, allowing Satchel to resume the next stage of his incredible career.

I first saw Satchel pitch, probably around 1940, when I was a kid in St. Louis, where he barnstormed against a semi-pro team my older brothers were on. He was fun to watch, kind of a crowd-pleaser. Heck, he sure could pitch. I faced him in my second year in the majors (1948) and he wasn't young then. But he wasn't too bad, either. He came in relief, and was still getting people out.
Yogi Berra, Hall of Famer

The Kansas City Monarchs offered Satchel a contract in late 1939, and he stayed with them until 1948. His accomplishments there were just as impressive as those with the Crawfords as he led the Monarchs to four consecutive Negro American League Championships from 1939 through 1942, and again in 1946. In fact, his arm was so fully back to where it had been that he also played winter ball for Guayama in the Puerto Rican League during the 1939-40 winter season and led that league in wins and strikeouts, going 19-3 with a 1.93 ERA and 208 strikeouts in 205 innings.

By his own estimate, Satchel claimed to have won 2,600 games, including 300 shutouts and 55 no-hitters, during his long and storied career. Based on the record he put up during the twenty-two years that he spent on the mound up until the 1948 season, it would be hard to dispute his claim to be the greatest pitcher that the Negro Leagues had ever seen, even if his numbers were off. But, he seemed to save the best for last because, in July 1948, Bill Veeck of the Cleveland Indians signed Satchel to pitch for the Major League club, and Satchel not only acquitted himself well but played a big part in the Indians' World Series championship that year as the oldest rookie in Major League history.

Paige had watched other black players sign with Major League clubs and, in 1947, he saw Jackie Robinson, Larry Doby, Willard Brown, Hank Thompson, and Dan Bankhead actually take the field at the big league level. He knew that he had Major League ability and felt that he should have been there with them. In fact, it was Paige's name that was most frequently mentioned, in both black and white baseball circles, as the black player with the greatest talent and chance of succeeding at the Major League level. To his disappointment, he was not he first or the second or even the third to get that chance.

But signing Jackie (Robinson) like they did still hurt me deep down. *I'd* been the guy who'd started all that big talk about letting us in the big time. *I'd* been the one who'd opened up the major league parks to the colored teams. *I'd* been the one who the white boys wanted to barnstorm against. *I'd* been the one who everybody'd said should be in the majors. But Jackie'd been the first one signed by the white boys and he'd probably be the first in the majors.
Satchel Paige, Maybe I'll Pitch Forever

But, when Satch's number was called, he embraced it and, at 42 years of age, went 6-1 for the Indians in 1948. His first appearance was on July 21 at Yankee Stadium, and he didn't give up any runs or hits in his one inning of work. He went on to pitch two more shutout innings the next day. After seeing Satchel pitch first-hand, manager Lou Boudreau gained confidence in him, and Satch got his first start on August 3 against the Washington Senators in Cleveland. It was an important outing for the Indians as they were only a game behind the league-leading Athletics. Word got out about Paige's start and 72,562 fans set a Major League attendance record for a night game, as they watched Satchel pitch seven innings in a 4-3 Cleveland win. He followed that up with a 5-0 complete game victory over the White Sox in Chicago on August 13 before another record crowd of 51,013 fans, and beat them again in Cleveland a week later before an even larger crowd of 78,382. Satchel had reached another plateau of baseball success, this time at the highest level possible ... the Major Leagues.

After Bill Veeck sold the Indians and took over the St. Louis Browns he again called on Satchel to pitch in the Major Leagues. Satch pitched for the Browns in 1951, 1952 and 1953, earning an All-Star berth in the two later years. Although Veeck set Satch up with a rocking chair in the bullpen, making fun of his advanced age, Satch showed no signs of old age on the mound. In fact, he was just in the middle of his Major League career. In 1965, in what most people thought of as purely a publicity stunt, Satchel pitched three innings for the Kansas City Athletics. Actually, it was a game they let Satch play in so he could secure a pension. He was 59 years old, at least, yet pitched three scoreless innings, giving up only one hit, to the Red Sox future Hall of Famer, Carl Yastrzemski.

Satch was not the first black to play in the Major Leagues, but in 1971 he did become the first black ballplayer to be inducted into the Baseball Hall of Fame based on his career in the Negro Leagues. I find it very fitting that Satch led the way for the recognition of baseball prowess of many great athletes who were never given the chance to compete in the Major Leagues. And I am ever grateful to Ted Williams for having the courage to speak up and be a leader in having Negro League players recognized in the Hall as full and complete members.

In 1982, while Satch was suffering from emphysema, the Kansas City Parks Department renovated an old ballpark, and held a dedication ceremony, naming the facility The Leroy Satchel Paige Stadium. Satchel attended the ceremony in a wheelchair and stated, "This is the happiest day of my life. Nobody on earth could feel as good as I do now." Satchel died three days later.

Satchel Paige put together a baseball career that established him as a genuine candidate to win twenty games in a season at the Major League level. In fact, it is hard to think that he wouldn't have done it time and time again, particularly if he had been given the chance to pitch during his prime years. His celebrity status and star appeal aside, this man was just unbelievable for his pitching ability, his control, his knowledge of the game, and his approach to the art of pitching. There can be no doubt that he would have been one of us!

CHAPTER 12

HILTON LEE SMITH

Born February 27, 1907 in Giddings, Texas
Died November 18, 1983 in Kansas City, Missouri
Teams: Monroe Monarchs, New Orleans Black Creoles,
*   New Orleans Crescent Stars, Kansas City Monarchs*
Inducted into National Baseball Hall of Fame 2001

The hardest pitcher in baseball for me to hit was Hilton Smith of Kansas City, and there were very few pitchers I respected.
Alex Radcliffe, 3rd Baseman, Chicago American Giants

Hilton Smith was unbeatable there for a spell from 1938 to 1942. Unbeatable! He had more natural stuff, a good rising fastball and an excellent curve ball with good control. My land! He would have been a 20 game winner in the major leagues with the stuff he had. We played against an all-star team the year Stan Musial came up in 1941. … Musial and Johnny Mize said they'd never seen a curve ball like Hilton's curve ball.
Buck O'Neil

You had to be a true fan to know about Hilton Smith. You didn't have to be a baseball fan to know Satchel Paige. But Hilton was great. He had the best curve ball I had ever seen. And he could hit the ball. When he wasn't pitching, he could hit. He wasn't just a pretty good hitter. He was a *good* hitter!
Buck O'Neil

As fine of a pitcher as he was, Hilton also was a great gentleman. He had one of the finest curveballs I ever had the displeasure to try and hit. His curveball fell off the table. Sometimes you knew where it would be coming from, but you still couldn't hit it because it was that sharp. He was just as tough as Satchel was. I'm very, very delighted for his success.
Monte Irvin, Hall Of Famer (After Smith's 2001 HOF Induction)

Hilton Smith represented everything beautiful about sports. The Negro Leagues represented everything beautiful about sports. I'm not talking about the clowning around like you see in movies like "Bingo Long," or the sweet myths like the one about how Cool Papa Bell was so fast, he once hot a line drive up the middle and got hit by the baseball while sliding into second base. No, there was dignity to these men, and that's the part that clutches the heart. They played baseball because they loved it, because they were good at it, and it didn't matter to them that the major leagues would not let them in because they were black, didn't matter that the money was lousy (when the money was actually paid), and hotels wouldn't let them stay, and they often had to drive a hundred miles out of the way to find a restaurant that would let them buy a sandwich. They knew they were good. They played proudly. Hilton Smith knew he was good.

Tom Posnanski, Kansas City Star, March 6, 2001 (After Smith's 2001 HOF Induction)

"A quiet but confident righthander…" Those are the first few words that you will read on the plaque that the National Baseball Hall of Fame put up to honor the next of my Early Aces when the Veteran's Committee elected him in 2001. But, while they may be the right words to describe the man's personal demeanor, I think they are a little misleading about the talent and love for the game that made Hilton Lee Smith one of the best pitchers that ever took the mound in the Negro Leagues. There was nothing "quiet" about either, and his career and accomplishments bear witness to that.

He had a long career in the Negro Leagues beginning in 1932, most of which he spent with the Kansas City Monarchs where he played from 1936-1948. During that time, he was one of the most dominant pitchers in black baseball but was often overshadowed (but seldom outpitched) by his teammate, Satchel Paige. For years, the Monarchs would start Satchel to assure that fans would put their fannies in the seats (and money in the coffers) but, as Satchel often wouldn't go much more than a few innings by then, the team would bring in Hilton early to finish the game and assure a successful outcome. "The old-timers would all say that if you were going to hit anything, you better hit it off Satchel because you weren't going to touch Hilton Smith," according to Bob Kendrick of the Negro League Baseball Museum. Paige himself certainly recognized Hilton's immense ability when, in 1942 amidst press rumors that the Major Leagues were about sign black ballplayers, he responded to a reporter's question by naming Smith first among those Negro Leaguers that he thought would have the most success at the Major League level.

Yet, despite his talent, success, and recognition by fellow ballplayers, Hilton Lee Smith was considered by some to be the "invisible man of black baseball" because of the way that Paige's celebrity and fan appeal kept him from the spotlight. It was a role that Hilton understood and came to accept, even if only grudgingly. As he said in later years:

I just took my baseball serious, I just went out there to do a job. But Satchel was an attraction, he could produce and he'd clown a lot. I

**guess it really hurt me. I tried to get away, but there wasn't anything
I could do about it.**

In fact, Jackie Robinson (who was recommended to the Kansas City Monarchs by Hilton after he saw him play in the California Winter League in 1945) used to tell him that he was going through the same thing with Paige that Jackie had been through with Kenny Washington when he played football for UCLA. Unfortunately for Hilton, he didn't have another sport to turn to and he never eclipsed Satchel's star in the public eye. But the career that I am about to share with you should put you in a better position to understand why Hilton Lee Smith didn't have to stand in any man's baseball shadow as he cast a pretty incredible one himself.

Smith was born in Giddings, Texas, which is in the same area that produced a couple of my other Early Aces, Rube Foster and Smokey Joe Williams, as well as such Negro League stars as Willie Wells and Biz Mackey (a great all-around ballplayer who Smith considered to be the best catcher he ever played with). His father was a schoolteacher but played a lot of baseball, which is how Hilton first came to play and love the game. He also had a couple of uncles who he described as "powerful good ballplayers" that served as baseball role models for him. By the time he was in his early teens, he had shown enough talent that he was playing on their team with and against grown men.

A few years later, he enrolled at Prairie View College and wanted to play baseball there, but he couldn't make the team in his first year. He tells a story about going home between his first and second year there, and pitching for the Giddings town team that makes you wonder how the college coach could have missed his talent. It seems that one of their games that summer was against the Prairie View team, which he shut down in a well-pitched 6-1 victory. He says, "The coach was all over me. … 'How come you didn't come out for the team?' I said, 'I was out there. Didn't you see me?" Well, needless to say, he made the team the next year!

He got his first taste of professional baseball at the semi-pro level in 1931 as a result of his efforts on behalf of the same town team. They traveled to Austin one day where he pitched them to a win over a very good semi-pro team, the Austin Senators. His talent caught the eye of one of the Austin players who had previously played for the Birmingham Black Barons, and it wasn't too long before they asked him to join them. The legendary Chicago American Giants, who were barnstorming through Texas at the time, were coming into Austin and the Senators wanted him to pitch one of the games against them. He accepted their invitation and, in that first appearance for the Senators, went 11 innings for a 5-4 victory. I guess they decided to keep him around after that effort as he then traveled to San Antonio with them where he beat the American Giants once again in only his second game of semi-pro ball. He stayed with the Senators for the rest of that year, traveling with them down to Mexico where the level of play was much higher. His arm was up to the task though, and he continued to enjoy success on the mound.

Hilton made the jump from semi-pro into the full professional ranks as a result of his performance in two games he pitched for the Senators in 1942 against a very good Negro team, the Monroe Monarchs. The Monarchs played in the Negro Southern League, the highest level of Negro League baseball at the time. They had come into Austin and, as Hilton told it:

they heard of this little school boy up there and said, 'Well, we came up here to work him over.' But, we had a great big ball park and I beat them 2-1. They couldn't believe it! They said, 'Well, this big old park, no wonder you won. When you come to Monroe – Monroe had a small park – we'll hit so many home runs off you …' So I went to Monroe the following Sunday and I beat them 4-2."

Those two gems really launched him into the professional game as the Monarchs saw enough to sign him. He stayed with the Monroe team from 1932, when he won 31 games, through 1935, although he occasionally moonlighted for a couple of other teams (the New Orleans Black Creoles and New Orleans Black Crescents) during those years.

When the Negro Southern League was experiencing difficulties in 1935, and money was hard to come by, Hilton traveled with the Monroe Monarchs on a barnstorming trip up into the Midwest. When they got into Bismarck, North Dakota that July, he was approached to join a team the town had put together to compete in the National Baseball Congress tournament in Wichita, Kansas. Bismarck had assembled a formidable team, including Satchel Paige and Chet Brewer, but needed another pitcher if they were going to make a good showing among the great teams, black and white, that came from across the country to compete for that championship. When their offer got to $150 a month, Hilton said, "Yes" and went on to an undefeated season for them that year, including a 5-0 record in the NBC tournament. In 1936, he put together a 4-0 record, all of them shutouts, during tournament play. That success led to his long tenure with the Kansas City Monarchs which began in 1936 and lasted until he retired in 1948.

The career that he enjoyed with the Kansas City Monarchs is what secured his place in baseball history as one of the greatest pitchers that ever played in the Negro League and earned him his place in the National Baseball Hall of Fame. It also made it clear to me that this was a man that would have a great chance to be a twenty-game winner in the Major Leagues, a feat that he accomplished in each of his twelve years with the Kansas City Monarchs. Heck, … twelve years in a row… that kind of streak could even make Fergie Jenkins stand up and take notice!

Hilton's success was particularly impressive during one six-year stretch from 1937-1942. During that time, he put together a 129-28 record that included ledgers of 25-2, 21-3, 25-1 and 22-5 respectively from 1939-1942! In 1937, he threw a no-hitter against the same Chicago American Giants that he had beaten twice as a teenager. In 1941, it is said that he went a perfect 10-0 in league competition. He was voted to the East-West Game in each of these six years, and was the winning pitcher in the 1938 contest. In fact, he is second only to Leon Day in East-West Game strikeouts with 13 (Day holds the record with only one more at 14.)

Long after his playing career had ended, and as Hilton got older, I think he came to lament his lack of recognition a bit. In fact, I think his overall perspective on the game of baseball itself reflected a bit of concern, if not sadness, about the similar lack of recognition that Negro League baseball received following its decline after Jackie signed. He always knew that the public kind of looked at him as "Satchel's relief," and never really put him on the kind of individual pedestal that his talent and performance deserved. But, he also understood that Satchel's showmanship and reputation is what put fans in the seats and paid the bills, including his salary, so he never voiced any real bitterness about it. Instead, I think he relied on a self-assessment of his talent, rather than public acclaim, to provide him with the personal satisfaction of knowing that he was as good as or better than anyone on the mound. As he said,

I pitched against enough Major Leaguers to see if I was on the level. You know, naturally if you never compete with those people, you're always in doubt in your mind whether you're good enough to play against them. But I played against them enough, and they never hit me. So I feel that had I had a chance, I could have pitched in the big leagues.

I think those few words sum up his approach in realizing his own accomplishments and putting them into a perspective that enabled him to recognize just how good he was. It seems to be a very similar approach to the one he took on the field during his playing career. He was "quiet but confident," as his Hall of Fame plaque reads.

In a similar way, I think that Hilton also came to put the fate of Negro League baseball into a similar perspective that enabled him to appreciate its greatness despite his disappointment over its rapid decline after Jackie Robinson signed with the Brooklyn Dodgers. In his words,

You could see it in '46, the first year Jackie went to Montreal, then in '47 Negro baseball began to go back. All the people started to go Brooklyn-ites, everybody who had never known anything about baseball. Whether we were playing here or not, everybody wanted to go over to St. Louis to see Jackie. So it really began to go down, down, down.

In fact, something else he once said about the lack of both recognition and recorded history of Negro League baseball really struck a chord with me and reinforced my resolve to write this book. After his playing career was over, he was asked by a little girl who had heard of him from her father about his days on the field and some of the other questions that inquisitive youngsters have about baseball. She said to him, "Funny, there's no literature or anything. We would like to read about some of the older ballplayers, so we'd know something about them." He responded, "Well, maybe eventually there will be something." As I thought about that simple exchange with that little girl, it sounded more and more to me as if Hilton was expressing the same kind of concern that I have about the need to preserve a precious part of the history of the game, and the terrible loss it would be if we didn't make sure that it is done.

Toward the end of his life, Hilton began to write letters, and send messages and newspaper clippings, to the Hall of Fame touting his career and accomplishments, according to his son, DeMorris Smith. It was out of character for him to do that, but maybe he felt it was his last chance to get the recognition that he deserved. His son couldn't understand it, other than to suggest that maybe he knew he was dying. But, at any rate, he did ultimately receive that recognition when the Veterans' Committee inducted him into the National Baseball Hall of Fame in 2001. Unfortunately, it was eight years too late for him to share in that honor as he died in 1983.

CHAPTER 13

LEON DAY

Born October 30, 1916 in Alexandria, Virginia
Died March 13, 1995 in Baltimore, Maryland
Teams: Baltimore Black Sox, Brooklyn Eagles,
*   Newark Eagles, Baltimore Elite Giants*
Inducted into National Baseball Hall of Fame 1995
Inducted into Puerto Rican Baseball Hall of Fame 1993

People don't know what a great pitcher Leon Day was. He was as good or better than Bob Gibson. He was a better fielder, a better hitter, could run like a deer. And just as good a pitcher. When he pitched against Satchel, Satchel didn't have an edge. You thought Don Newcombe could pitch. You should have seen Day. One of the most complete athletes I've ever seen. If Dwight Gooden can throw as well as Leon for another few years, he'll be in the Hall of Fame.
Monte Irvin, from Holway, Voices From The Negro Leagues

I didn't see anybody in the major leagues that was better than Leon Day. If you want to compare him to Bob Gibson, stuff-wise, Day had just as good stuff. Tremendous curve ball, and a fast ball at least 90-95 miles an hour. You talk about Satchel; I didn't see anybody better than Day.
Larry Doby, from Holway, Voices From The Negro Leagues

Strength and humility have always been the most important principles guiding and sustaining me throughout my life. I learned them early on from the words and deeds of my mother and the many elders who helped to shape the kind of person I would become when I was growing up back in Lacoochee, and I have always recognized that they provided me with the foundation on which I built whatever success I have achieved as both a ballplayer and a man. As I examined the life and baseball career of my next Early Ace, Leon Day, however, it seemed to me that I was looking more and more at a man who personified those important traits in ways that I can only hope that I approached. His achievements on a baseball diamond rival those of almost any player in the history of the game, black or white. But his modesty about them was such that many feel his election into the National Baseball Hall of Fame in 1995 was long and unjustly delayed by his reluctance to even talk about them, much less blow his own horn about them.

    Leon Day has a long and incredible baseball resume. It includes the all-time game strike-out record in both the Negro National League and the Puerto Rican

Winter League. The Negro National League record was accomplished in 1942 against the Baltimore Elite Giants in a night game played at their Bugle Field when they were sent back to the bench 18 times with nothing to show for their efforts, including three such trips by a young catcher named Roy Campanella. At the time, this matched the Major League record of 18, which was held by my friend Bob Feller, and surpassed Dizzy Dean's then National League record of 17. Day set the Puerto Rican Winter League record during the 1939-40 season while pitching for the Aquadilla Sharks when he struck out 19 in an extra inning game. He also struck out 15 batters there in a nine-inning game during the 1941-1942 season, when his season total of 168 strikeouts set a Puerto Rican league record.

He appeared in seven East-West All Star games during his career and holds the career record for strikeouts in that classic with 14. In 1942, *The Pittsburgh Courier* named him to its All-American Team for the Negro Leagues as "Best Pitcher" and, in 1943, named him "The Outstanding Moundsman in Negro League baseball," giving him the nod over Satchel Paige and all of the other great talents of the time. He is the only man, other than Bob Feller, who can claim to have opened a season with a no-hitter as he did against the Philadelphia Stars in 1946 after just having been discharged from the US Army where he served a two-and-one-half year tour of duty during World War II. It was during his Army service that Day pitched what he considered to be one of his greatest games. In 1945 he outpitched Ewell "The Whip" Blackwell, in Nuremburg, Germany, in a game between all-star servicemen, including several Major Leaguers. (Blackwell would go on to be a twenty-game winner and a six-time All-Star with the Cincinnati Reds, leading the National League in wins in 1947.) The crowd for that game was somewhere between fifty and a hundred thousand, depending on whether you spoke to Monte Irvin or Leon.

He had a career record of 76-29 in Negro National League games, and a career winning percentage of .698, better than any of the great pitchers in the National Baseball Hall of Fame (including the HOF's leader, Whitey Ford, who posted a .690 career percentage). He was elected to the Puerto Rican Baseball Hall of Fame in 1993, at a time when they had inducted more American blacks than our own Hall had. And, of course, he was finally given the recognition that he so justly deserved by Organized Baseball when he was elected to join the game's immortals in Cooperstown in 1995.

Yet, with all of those achievements to his credit, Leon Day was such a humble man that he found it difficult to talk about his accomplishments. Some say that getting him to talk about himself was like "pulling teeth." When he did talk of baseball, he would most often talk of the others that he had played with, and of their abilities, rather than shining any part of the spotlight on himself. In fact, the most he was ever heard to utter about his own play was, "I could hold my own." His teammate on the Newark Eagles, Monte Irvin, said of him that, "If he had a fault, it was being too quiet. You almost didn't know he was on the team if you didn't call his name." Monte felt that Day was just as good a pitcher as Satchel Paige but that "he was never the promoter that Satchel was" and should have been in the Hall of Fame much sooner "but he never made any noise." Amazingly, his modesty was such that his wife Geraldine, who he married in the 1960s long after his playing career was over, didn't even know that he had played baseball, much less of his greatness, until one day she overheard him speaking of his career on the telephone!

When I learned all of this about Leon Day, I was moved because I know of the things that he must have faced and overcome to do what he did, as did all black ballplayers of his day. I have a special feeling for his achievement in the face of those obstacles. The combination of strength and humility that he evidenced in the way he played the game, and more importantly in the way he lived his life, render what he did on the field all the more admirable to me. So keep that in mind as I tell you some more about him.

Leon Day was the second of the six children born to Ellis and Hattie Lee Day. He came into this world on October 30, 1916 in Alexandria, Virginia. As was the case with many African-Americans in the early twentieth century, his family moved north from Virginia for better work opportunities and, when he was six months old, they came to Baltimore, Maryland where his father found a job at a glass factory located in a white part of the city called Westport. They lived in a poor, rural all-black area located in the southwestern section of the city known as Mount Winans. Their house had no electricity or running water, and no heat other than a cooking range and pot-bellied stove, and only an outhouse for a toilet. They also had a garden and some pigs outside. "We were poor, but we were never hungry or raggedy. Never," said his sister, Ida May Bolden. When I first read of the way he grew up and the circumstances of his upbringing, it reminded me of how I was reared in Lacoochee, but with an urban twist … poor but proud; not a lot of luxury but always a lot of what was most important.

Leon's introduction to baseball came as a youth when he would often walk the two or three miles from his home to see the Baltimore Black Sox of the Negro National League play at Maryland Baseball Park in Westport. He didn't have the money for a ticket but, like many determined kids, he found a way:

> **I used to go 'over the fence' to see the Black Sox play the Hilldales and all them old teams when I was a kid. An old guy made a little gate in the wall and would let people in for 25 or 50 cents. When he opened the gate to let somebody in, we flew through there behind them. The guy couldn't say nothin', because he was cheatin' himself.**
> *Leon Day, quoted in Holway*

Those trips "over the fence" enabled him to witness the play of many of the greatest talents in the Negro Leagues, particularly one of the Black Sox star outfielders and manager, "Rap" Dixon, and Leon's favorite player, their star pitcher, Laymon Yokely, both of whom who would later help start him down his own path to greatness as a player.

Leon knew at a very early age that he wanted to be a ballplayer and he worked hard to make himself into one. He first played for the Mount Winans Athletic

Club team, the Silver Spoons, when he was only twelve or thirteen years old. By the time he began high school, the game had so consumed him that, against his mother's wishes, he left Frederick Douglass High School at one point because it did not have a baseball team. At around that time in 1934, while playing with the Silver Spoons, a teammate recommended him to "Rap" Dixon, who scouted and signed him to play for the Black Sox for the rest of that 1934 season. As Leon himself later told it:

> **Ever since I can remember, I wanted to play ball. I started playing with the Mt. Winans AC, a team called the Silver Spoons. I was a second baseman, but if the pitcher got in trouble, I'd say, "Give me the ball." One guy there was messin' around playing a little semipro ball. He knew Rap Dixon, who was managing the Black Sox, and he told Rap about me, and Rap came by and picked me up one spring, took me to spring training. That was 1934. That's when I really started playing professional ball – you know, getting paid.**
> *Leon Day, Holway*

In his inaugural season of pro ball, Day got to play under the watchful eye of his idol, Laymon Yokely, who became his mentor. Yokely took a special interest in the young man and took him under his wing. He schooled him in what to do and what not to do, both as a player and as a man, and provided him with valuable lessons about what he could expect on the mound and as a player in the Negro Leagues. Whether it was the student or the teacher, or the combination of the two, the lessons sure stuck - for Leon went on to become one of the greatest pitchers and players in Negro League history.

Day was not a very big man, standing 5', 7" and weighing only about 170 lbs, but he delivered a devastating fastball. His Newark Eagles teammate George Giles said of him, "He looked like he was too small to be a bat boy. Little bitty guy, but oh, could he throw hard." He also had a pretty good curve ball and a change of pace, and very good control. He kind of short-armed that ball in the way that he jerked it from his ear with no wind-up and very little motion, and his delivery was very quick to the plate. Monte Irvin said his curve wasn't too big but was just "a wrinkle, just enough. What would get you off stride was that little hunch just before he threw." Day himself thought that his short-arm technique on the mound was probably a carry-over from his play at second base, where that kind of throwing motion was more natural for an infielder. At any rate, it served him very well throughout his career.

In addition to his prowess on the mound, Day was also an exceptional fielder, even among the "Million Dollar" infield of Mule Suttles, Dick Seay, Willie Wells, and Ray Dandridge that played behind him on the Newark Eagles where he was so good that they considered him a "fifth infielder." He was also a great hitter, and possessed tremendous foot speed. [Day was once clocked at 10 seconds flat in a 100-yard dash while wearing baseball cleats!] He played second base and centerfield when he was not pitching, and he played them as well as any position player of his day. At the plate, he handled the bat so well that he was considered by many as too valuable a hitter to limit to pitching only every couple of days. Sammy T. Hughes, the veteran Baltimore second baseman, said he would have made him into a full-time outfielder so that his team could take advantage of his batting, fielding and base-running skills every day, not just when his turn on the mound came up.

In 1949, Day concluded his Negro League career by pitching for the champion Baltimore Elites, and in 1950 he played in Canada. Finally, in 1951, at the age of 35, Leon Day had a chance to play in Organized Baseball, in the International League with the Toronto Maple Leafs. The Leafs, owned by Jack Kent Cooke, signed Day and infielder Charlie White, to be the first blacks to ever play in a Toronto uniform. Day also played a portion of the 1952 season in the Eastern League with Scranton, before returning to Canada, where he played through 1955.

CHAPTER 14

DAVID TAYLOR HOSKINS
Dave

Born August 3, 1925 in Greenwood, Mississippi
Died April 2, 1970 in Flint, Michigan
Threw Right Handed; Batted Left Handed
Teams: Ethiopian Clowns, Chicago American Giants,
      Homestead Grays, Louisville Buckeyes,
         Cincinnati Clowns, Dallas Eagles, Cleveland Indians
Inducted into Greater Flint Afro-American Hall of Fame - 1983

"With bat, glove, and ball," said Jet magazine, a Negro weekly, "Dave Hoskins has taken his place alongside Texas pioneers of yesteryear who stood tall in the saddle and manipulated six-guns with the speed of a rattlesnake's fangs."
Great Negro Baseball Stars, A.S. Young, 1953

Dave Hoskins is a sentimental favorite of mine to be included in this group of Early Aces. I understand that he did not have the storied pitching career of Satchel Paige or Smokey Joe Williams in the Negro Leagues, and history has not given him credit for having as much impact on the organization of baseball as Rube Foster, but in my opinion Dave Hoskins was one of the most significant individuals in the integration of minor league baseball. Also, since Dave was a contemporary of mine, he is one of the only Early Aces I had the opportunity to see pitch, and from all I know and have seen I believe he had the ability to be a twenty-game winner, if he had a full Major League career as a pitcher.

Dave's family moved from Greenwood, Mississippi to Flint, Michigan, when Dave was eleven years old, at a time when many black families were migrating from the South to industrial areas in the North, in search of employment. Dave quickly made Michigan his new home and made many new friends by excelling on the baseball field. He starred in several sports at Northern High School, and specifically at baseball, in the Flint City League, regularly batting over .400, chasing down fly balls in the outfield, and taking an occasional turn on the pitching mound. By 1942, before Dave had reached his seventeenth birthday, he was signed to a Negro League contract by the Ethiopian Clowns, who wanted Dave for his bat, but used him mainly as a pitcher to complement Roosevelt Davis on the mound.

By 1944, the Homestead Grays had learned about Dave and sought him out to be part of their stellar lineup, which included Buck Leonard, Josh Gibson, Sam Bankhead, "Cool Papa" Bell, Jelly Jackson, Ray Battle, Edward Robinson and

Jerry Benjamin. It didn't take long for the Grays to realize that Dave's bat could make a significant contribution on an everyday basis; although he saw only limited action on the mound (winning both decisions he had), he was a regular in the lineup and batted .355 for the year. Dave was never a teammate of Satchel Paige's in the Negro Leagues, but I remember Dave telling me how much he learned about pitching from watching Satchel, and talking with him.

To give you an idea of just how respected Dave was as a ballplayer, the 1945 edition of *Negro Baseball*, contained an evaluation by sportswriter, Sam Lacy, of which Negro Leaguers were potential Major Leaguers and that list included Jackie Robinson, Larry Doby, and Dave Hoskins. And in April of 1945, when Isadore Muchnick, Boston City Councilman, and Wendell Smith, the Sports Editor of *The Pittsburgh Courier*, were able to pressure the Boston Red Sox into agreeing to try out three Negro League players at Fenway Park, the players selected to attend were Robinson (who was with the Monarchs), Sam Jethroe (Cleveland Buckeyes), and Dave. Unfortunately, the Grays would not grant Dave permission to attend the tryout and Marvin Williams, a 20 year old second baseman with the Philadelphia Stars, went in his place. The "tryout" was pretty much a sham, with the *Courier* having to bear the cost of transporting the players, and the Red Sox not really giving the players much consideration. In fact, the entire affair, which included working out several other white players, took about 45 minutes, and when it was over, it is reported that Hugh Duffy, a Boston scout, commented about Robinson, "What a ballplayer! Too bad he's the wrong color." So, I am quite sure that if Dave had been able to attend the tryout things would not have been much different, only that it might have afforded him some of the attention that Robinson got.

Dave stayed with the Grays for two more seasons (1945 and 1946), and continued to excel as a pitcher and as an offensive weapon, batting over .300. For the next several years Dave moved around quite a bit, from outfield to pitcher, from team to team, and from Organized Baseball to the Negro Leagues and back. He entered Organized Baseball in 1948, with the independent Grand Rapids Jets (Michigan) of the Class A Central League and took his batting eye with him, recording a .393 average. He was the first African-American to play in the Central League, and as well as Dave played for Grand Rapids, I remember him sharing with me that this was the town where he felt the least accepted and where he faced the most discrimination.

The Muskegon club gave me a particularly rough time. There was one pitcher who seemed to take delight in working me over. The first time he pitched to me, he knocked me down. But I got up and knocked a home run off him. The next time I came up, he threw at me until he finally hit me in the back.
Dave Hoskins, The Sporting News, May 14, 1952

In 1949, Dave returned to the Negro Leagues, and was an All-Star with the Louisville Buckeyes.

Dave was back in the Central League in 1950, as a member of the Dayton Indians, an affiliate of the Cleveland Indians, who acquired his "rights" from Grand Rapids. During that year, Dave was hit in the head with a fastball and suffered a concussion that landed him in the hospital, in critical condition, for three days. The baseball that hit Dave in the head also served to make up his mind – to become a full time pitcher:

I was tired of having pitches thrown at me. I made up my mind I would start throwing at other guys.
Dave Hoskins

Dave pitched for the Wilkes-Barre (Pennsylvania) Indians of the Eastern League in 1951.

By the spring of 1952, with the success of Jackie Robinson, Larry Doby, Don Newcombe and Roy Campanella, several other owners and baseball executives were willing to "take a chance" on African-American ballplayers. One such person was Richard W. ("Dick") Burnett, the wealthy owner of the Dallas Eagles of the Texas League, and he made no bones about it. He specifically announced that he was looking to sign a Negro "capable of playing Double-A ball," and held a tryout camp attended by approximately two hundred Negro players, none of which were acceptable to Burnett. At that time, Dallas had a working agreement with the Cleveland Indians, and when Burnett discussed his intentions with his manager, Dutch Meyer, and Cleveland General Manager, Hank Greenberg, the idea of having Dave pitch in Dallas surfaced. Dave had already made an impression on Burnett in person, by retiring all six batters he faced in an exhibition game against Dallas that spring.

Since there had never been a black player in the Texas League, both Burnett and Greenberg had reason to believe that the first black player in the league would face many of the same problems faced by Jackie Robinson in 1946 and 1947, when he integrated the International League and then the majors. So, Burnett and Greenberg conferred with Dave, who accepted the opportunity and the challenge. From his days helping to integrate the Central League, Dave knew what he would be up against, and he felt he could do it. Southern blacks, who were born at the time that Dave and I were born, had an inner resolve that allowed us to take those types of challenges. We had faced tougher times than that growing up. It was sort of a relief from the tough times growing up, even though it was still tough. So, being the only black on the team was something that you had to deal with, a consequence of wanting to live your everyday life, like I knew I was going to get "duked" because I went to the movies.

From the outset, Dave excelled, on the mound, in the batter's box, and as a gate attraction. He won his first five starts for Dallas, beginning with a victory over the Tulsa Oilers on April 13, 1952, and went on to post a league-leading 22 wins, while losing 10, with a stingy 2.12 ERA. He also led the league in complete games (26), and innings pitched (280). In addition, he finished third in the league batting race with a .328 average, and was elected to the league's All-Star team. His performance led the team to the pennant and the way he handled himself led to the Eagles signing Jose Santiago, and to league rival, Oklahoma City, signing Bill Greason, both black pitchers. In fact, in August 1952, Hoskins and Greason faced each other in the first all-black pitching match in Texas League history, before a record crowd of 11,021, more than half of which were blacks. The attendance at that game was extraordinary, but the Eagles had come to expect an increase at the gate when Dave was pitching. His success had brought the game to a new market in Dallas – the black fans:

From his debut victory over Tulsa on April 13 to his two playoff triumphs in September, Hoskins stormed the Lone Star State. By mid-May, the right-handed curveball specialist had posted a 6-2 record, completing all of the games he had started. A left-handed hitter, Hoskins was batting close to .400. The combination established the black pitcher as one of the most popular gate attractions in the history of the Texas League. A tall, thin hurler, whose unusual mannerisms and delivery resembled those of Satchel Paige, Hoskins "continued to help spin the turnstiles" wherever he pitched. In his first appearance at Houston, 11,000 spectators overflowed the stands. In his next start at Beaumont, a record crowd turned out. In both cases, blacks accounted for more than half the throng. Dallas discovered that even on days that Hoskins did not pitch, black attendance remained high. By the season's end, Hoskins had attracted sell-out crowds to every park in the circuit, no mean feat in a year in which overall Texas League attendance continued to decline. Hoskins' spectacular Texas League breakthrough generated immediate repercussions. Throughout the South, minor league teams expressed an interest in signing blacks.
Baseball's Great Experiment, Jackie Robinson and His Legacy, by Jules Tygiel, Oxford University Press, New York, 1997

Hoskins was such a popular attraction at the gate that writers dubbed him "the savior of the Texas League." For example, in twenty-five games (a portion of his starts), 143,935 paid their way to see him pitch. The average was 5,757. In ninety-eight other contests in which Hoskins was not an advertised performer, the Eagles drew an average of 2,157 fans.
Great Negro Baseball Stars, A.S. Young

In 1952 the Dallas Eagles integrated the double-A Texas League when they added pitcher Dave Hoskins to their roster. Hoskins took the circuit by storm, attracting record crowds wherever he performed. By the middle of the season, sportswriters praised him as the "Savior of the Texas League." When the season ended Hoskins had pitched in 32 games, attended by over 180,000 fans, or almost 6,000 per game, more than twice

the average attendance at other league games. Dallas easily led the loop in attendance, and its 1952 figure exceeded that of 1951 by 17 percent.
Earl Mann, Nat Peeples and the failed attempt of integration in the Southern Association, by Kenneth R. Fenster, in Nine, March 22, 2004

Dave attracted so many blacks to the ballpark that he was the reason seating became integrated in Dallas. When Dave pitched the sections of the stands reserved for blacks were always filled to capacity, with a need to have the overflow crowd stand on the field, while many empty seats were available in the white section. That caused Burnett to integrate the stands, accommodating the black fans.

Dave almost didn't get his chance to succeed in Dallas, because in June of 1952, a bill was introduced in the Louisiana legislature to outlaw interracial athletics. The bill's sponsor, Senator B.H. Rogers, had no qualms in stating that the bill was intended to keep Dave from playing for the Eagles when they came into Louisiana. Dick Burnett successfully fought against the bill's passage, stating, "Negroes and whites fight side by side in Korea and I can see no reason why they shouldn't compete together in athletic events," but it was clear that there were people in Louisiana that didn't want blacks playing there against whites. A year later Dave told the Daily Worker about a day in 1952 when he took the mound in Shreveport, Louisiana, and pitched Dallas to victory, despite having received multiple threats against his life:

I got three letters in the same handwriting (last season) telling me to stay out. One said I'd be shot if I as much as sat in the dugout. The second said I'd be shot if I went on the field, even in practice. The third said I would be shot if I went out to pitch the game.
Dave Hoskins, quoted in NY Daily Worker, 1953

It was fairly common for black players to receive death threats when we were on the road. The home crowd, even if they were segregationists, wouldn't go that far, but when you were on the road, as black players in the 1950s and 60s, more so in the 1950s, you always had that feeling that something could happen, and especially in cities like Baltimore and Kansas City. I got threats, we all got them from time to time. It was no different than being razed as a kid, when you felt your life was in danger, that you could be killed anytime. Certainly, one thing for sure, you wouldn't want it to affect or stop you from going out on the field.

I think Jackie Robinson, Don Newcombe and Roy Campanella felt the same way when they went to Cincinnati and all received written notes telling them that if they showed up at the ballpark they would be killed. They talked it over and decided to not only show up but to play. Newcombe pitched a shut out, Campy hit two home runs and Jackie went four for four.

Johnny Sain used to ask me, "How the hell did you guys do it?" It was a continuity of things that allowed you to strengthen yourself. If it was the first time, you thought about it, but the second time, you realized it's going to keep happening, so you developed some strength, and I said, well, if I'm going to die, I'm going to die throwing a fastball 90 miles an hour. That's the way you thought, and you thought about it afterwards a lot of times. You said, "Damn," but then the next time you had the strength and courage to go on back out there again.

Dave survived the death threats and was recognized as an important part of the Eagles team on the field, but he was forced to live a segregated life outside the lines. Whenever the Eagles were on the road, Dave couldn't live or eat with the team. He would stay in "black hotels" or private homes and would room with the team's African-American trainer, John Hobbs, until Santiago joined the team and they became roomies. Dave, Hobbs, and then Santiago, would also be forced to eat their meals in segregated restaurants or on the team bus while the white players dined in restaurants.

Dave's success on the field and at the box office certainly emboldened other owners and league executives to experiment with the integration of their teams and leagues. In 1953, Henry Aaron, at the tender age of nineteen, along with Horace Garner and Felix Mantilla, became the first blacks to play in the South Atlantic (Sally) League, which had teams in Florida, Georgia and South Carolina. They played for the Jacksonville Braves, which was a definite sign of improvement, considering that Jackie wasn't allowed to play in Jacksonville when he was first training with the Dodgers. But not everything changed. Henry's father remembers watching one of his first games:

When Henry came up, I heard fans yell, "Hit that nigger. Hit that nigger." Henry hit the ball up against the clock. The next time he came up, they said "Walk him, walk him."
Herb Aaron

And it wasn't just the fans that sniping racial insults, opposing players and teammates joined in. One of Hank's own teammates said, "A nigger's gonna croak every time" after Henry popped out to end a game. (A Prisoner of Memory, by Mike Capuzzo, Sports Illustrated, November 1992) But in the long run Henry didn't croak. In fact, he won the Sally League MVP award that season, and led the league in batting (.362), doubles (36), runs scored (115), and runs batted in (125).

That same year, the New York Giants signed Bill White, a young infielder from Ohio, and sent him to Danville, Virginia to play for the Danville Leafs in the Carolina League, two years after Percy Miller had a very brief tenure as the league's first black player. White recalls how he was greeted in Virginia:

I had to put up with crap from the fans. I was called names I'd never heard. I rebelled. I yelled back at the name callers. I was only 18 and immature. The more the fans gave it to me, the harder I hit the ball. They eventually decided to leave me alone, which was a victory over bigotry.
Bill White, quoted in Breaking a Barrier, by Michael Hudson, The Roanoke Times, April 1977

African-Americans played baseball well back into the nineteenth century. These young fellows are enjoying a game in a simple pasture down in Apalachicola in my home state of Florida, around 1895. (Photos courtesy of State Archives of Florida, Photographic Collection)

I was baptized in the Withlacoochee River, surrounded by the very same cypress trees that my family and many others processed at Cummer Sons Cypress Company in Lacoochee. (Photos courtesy of West Pasco Historical Society)

Rube Foster, Negro League giant in every way: as imposing physically as he was dominant in the development of early black baseball. He is shown below with Cap Anson (left), of the Chicago White Stockings, whose refusal to take the field with black ballplayers played a major role in Organized Baseball's decision to exclude blacks under the "gentleman's agreement." (National Baseball Hall of Fame Library, Cooperstown, NY)

Smokey Joe Williams shows the long and lean form that enabled him to deliver one of the greatest fastballs in Negro League history. (National Baseball Hall of Fame Library, Cooperstown, NY)

Bullet Joe Rogan, a longtime Kansas City Monarch, shown on the field, (National Baseball Hall of Fame Library, Cooperstown, NY) and, at far right,(below) with fellow Negro League players at the Denver Post Tournament in 1934, the first year integrated teams played in the competition. (left to right, Newt Allen, T.J. Young, Hall of Famer Turkey Stearnes, Eddie Dwight, and Carroll Mothel). (Copyright Source Unknown, National Baseball Hall of Fame Library, Cooperstown, NY)

Cannonball Dick Redding, far right, with early blackball pioneer and historian, Sol White. (National Baseball Hall of Fame Library, Cooperstown, NY)

Chet Brewer had a long career in the Negro Leagues and later, as the founder of The Chet Brewer All-Stars in Los Angeles, influenced the careers of many future major league players, including Hall of Famer Eddie Murray. (Copyright Source Unknown, National Baseball Hall of Fame Library, Cooperstown, NY)

Bill Foster is said by many to be the greatest lefthanded pitcher and the best "money" pitcher the Negro Leagues ever produced. Bill had his greatest success as part of the pitching staff of his brother Rube's Chicago American Giants (Bill is second from left in the group shot below) (National Baseball Hall of Fame Library, Cooperstown, NY)

Satchel Paige, shown here with Indians' President Bill Veeck just days after signing with Cleveland, finally made his Major League debut in July 1948. He would go on to help the Indians win the American League pennant that season, as the oldest rookie in Major League history. (Associated Press)

Satchel's legendary career was recognized when he became the first Negro Leaguer to be inducted into the National Baseball Hall of Fame in 1971. Admission of Negro Leaguers was advanced by Ted Williams' comments in his own induction speech in 1966. (National Baseball Hall of Fame, Cooperstown, NY)

Hilton Lee Smith's "quiet but confident" determination earned him induction into the National Baseball Hall of Fame in 2001. That's him at far left with the 1942 Kansas City Monarch pitching staff, that included Satchel Paige and my old friend, Connie Johnson. (National Baseball Hall of Fame, Cooperstown, NY)

Leon Day is another of the early Aces honored with induction into the National Baseball Hall of Fame (1995). Leon is shown above with Aguadilla of the Puerto Rican League, where he set their all-time single game strikeout record, (National Baseball Hall of Fame Library, Cooperstown, NY) and below with the Newark Eagles, where he set the same record in the Negro Leagues. (Copyright Source Unknown, National Baseball Hall of Fame Library, Cooperstown, NY)

Dave Hoskins integrated the Texas League when he pitched for the Dallas Eagles in 1952. (From the collections of the Texas/Dallas History and Archives Division, Dallas Public Library) He later made it to the majors with the Indians in 1953. (National Baseball Hall of Fame Library, Cooperstown, NY)

"Baseball Has Done It!" That's how Jackie Robinson later described his historic signing with the Montreal Royals on October 23, 1945. Jackie is shown above with Hector Racine, Montreal Royals' Vice-President, and Branch Rickey, Jr., head of the Brooklyn Dodgers' farm system. (Associated Press) Branch Rickey, Sr., Brooklyn Dodgers General Manager (below), was the man who orchestrated this historic signing. (National Baseball Hall of Fame Library, Cooperstown, NY)

My childhood hero and later roommate, Larry Doby, learned of Jackie Robinson's signing while serving with the US Navy in the Pacific. (Copyright Source Unknown, National Baseball Hall of Fame Library, Cooperstown, NY) It wasn't long before he traded his Navy blues for a Cleveland Indians uniform, as the first African-American in the American League. (National Baseball Hall of Fame Library, Cooperstown, NY)

While I believe that Dave's performance in 1952 created more opportunities for blacks in the minor leagues, it earned him a promotion to the majors with the Indians in 1953. It would be difficult for Dave to break into the starting rotation because the Indians had an excellent starting corps, known as the Big Four. That quartet included Hall of Famers Bob Feller, Early Wynn, and Bob Lemon, and All-Star Mike Garcia. Collectively they started 135 of the Indians' 154 games in 1952, with Wynn scoring 23 victories, and Garcia and Lemon 22 each. But it was hoped that Dave would be an effective addition to the remainder of the Indians' pitching staff, referred to as the Little Five, and an occasional spot starter.

Dave managed to appear in 26 games for the Indians in 1953, and posted a 9-3 record. His ERA was pretty much consistent with that of the Big Four, and besides them he had more victories than any other pitcher on the team. Dave also held his own at the plate, batting .259 with two doubles and one homer. It was in the spring of 1954 that I met Dave at Indianville. Both Dave and Sam Jones were there at the time. Sam was trying to work his way back into the majors, Dave was trying to stay up there and break into the rotation, and I was just an 18 year old trying not to be sent home. Dave made the Major League team that year and Sam and I did not, but that would be Dave's last year in the majors. He saw only limited mound time, and after being cut by the Indians in the spring of 1955, Dave was so upset he became physically sick. He only got to pitch a total of 140 innings in the majors. He returned to the minor leagues, playing in Indianapolis, San Diego, and finally back in Dallas, where he was 17-8 in 1958. It was in San Diego that I hooked up again with Dave, in 1957, my last year in the minor leagues. I became very close to Dave. We had an opportunity to spend a lot of time together and he taught me a great deal about pitching. It is mainly based on my personal observations of his talent and knowledge that I feel Dave could have been a twenty-game winner in the majors.

Dave retired at the age of 35 after the 1960 season. Tragically, he died at the very young age of 45, in 1970, leaving behind his wife, Cora, and their daughters, Ruchelle, Lynda and Carolyn.

CHAPTER 15

A NEW DAY DAWNING

Ethnic prejudice has no place in sports, and baseball must recognize that truth if it is to maintain stature as a national game.
...
The greatest untapped reservoir of raw material in the history of our game is the black race.
Branch Rickey

He led America by example. He reminded our people of what was right and he reminded them of what was wrong. I think it can be safely said today that Jackie Robinson made the United States a better nation.
Gene Budig, American League President, 1994-1999

There is a day etched in my memory I will never forget, a day in October 1945. I was awakened by the warm rays of the sun on my face as they penetrated the flimsy window shade and filled the room, on yet another bright, beautiful Florida morning. I had to get up early to deliver and sell newspapers.

The newspapers I delivered were *The Pittsburgh Courier* and *The Baltimore Afro-American*, and occasionally *The Amsterdam News*, a New York paper. They were black weekly papers, commonly referred to as the "colored papers" or the "Negro press." These weeklies, along with *The Chicago Defender* (which I didn't sell), were the top-selling black newspapers in the country. Without telephones or television, we relied primarily on the radio and the black press for state and national news, and "word-of-mouth" for local news. Throughout all the company quarters of Lacoochee there were only two radios, both battery operated. Mrs. Ethel Johnson, respectfully referred to as Mrs. Ethel, owned one of the two radios in town, immediately promoting her to a level of high respect, because she had more immediate contact with the world outside Lacoochee. The weekly black papers provided me with more than news; they were my personal source of income from the time I was eight.

The papers were all printed in the North, and made their way to Lacoochee and other southern destinations through an intricate network of Pullman train porters, who would transfer bundles of papers from train to train on their journeys south. The news was anywhere from one to seven days old when the paper was printed and it took a couple of days for the papers to reach me.

The headlines of all the newspapers in 1945 were primarily filled with stories of World War II and the economic conditions in America. The papers I delivered focused on how those events and conditions affected blacks in our country. But the most important stories to me were those that covered not the battlefield or the boardroom, but the ball field. I loved baseball, all kinds of baseball. I always made sure that I kept one of each paper when I finished my paper route. I couldn't wait to get home and turn to the sports pages to read the box scores.

The World Series had already been played, with the Detroit Tigers beating the Chicago Cubs, but the Negro Leagues didn't follow as strict a schedule as Organized Baseball. The Negro League teams played practically all year round, with barnstorming teams playing in the middle of the season and in the off-season. And they played all over, not just in towns and cities that had teams. So, even in late October I could find out what Satchel Paige and Josh Gibson were doing, and when they might be bringing a barnstorming team to southwest Florida, for it was possible that at any time a game might be scheduled in our area of the world.

I swung my feet around and silently made my way out of the bedroom I shared with my brother, Julius, and Uncle Boy. I tried to be as quiet as a ten-year-old boy could be as I tiptoed past my sleeping Mom, sisters and aunt as I headed toward the front door. The silence I was attempting to maintain broke when I heard my Mom's soft voice, "You be careful out there, James, and come right home when you finished your work." I smiled at the sound of her voice, a comfortable, easy smile that reflected the security I sensed; security created by the love and wisdom that never ceased to come from my Mom.

As I left row house 89 that October morning, and walked to the Greyhound Bus Station in nearby Trilacoochee to pick up my stack of papers, I found myself running. I had to be mindful of what I was doing, because to get to Trilacoochee I had to cross the railroad tracks, to the white part of town. It was early and most people were sleeping, so I would probably be able to avoid the razzing I would normally get from the white kids. Nevertheless, I had been taught to be very careful once I got near those tracks, and to keep my eyes open and my mouth shut. I was aware of where I was but kept thinking about getting to those newspapers. I was full of hope and anticipation, thanks to Mrs. Ethel.

Mrs. Ethel listened to her radio all the time; it was her connection to the outside world. We didn't have any electricity until years later, so Mrs. Ethel relied on a battery (and a bent wire coat hanger in place of an antenna) to pull in any kind of reception. The programming was either gospel music, or rhythm and blues. Every now and then they would report something about Adam Clayton Powell, or some other significant black on the gospel station, but there was no real black news. She was a big baseball fan and listened to whatever games she could get, even before there were Negroes in the Major Leagues. She would listen to the Dodgers and to Harry Caray announce the St. Louis Cardinals' games, because they were on one of the few stations she could get clearly on her radio.

Mrs. Ethel always told us about things she heard on the radio, but we needed to see it in the newspapers to believe it. For as long as I could read, Wendell Smith was writing about the possibility of blacks playing in the Major Leagues. For several months in 1945 his writing was mostly about which Negro League player was most likely to be signed by which professional team. But in October 1945, the news came over the radio first and was then spread by Mrs. Ethel: "The Dodgers signed Jackie Robinson!" As happy as everybody in Lacoochee wanted to be, they had heard encouraging news about integration before, about what was going to happen, but it never came to pass. So, while Mrs. Ethel's news created quite a stir around the town, everybody was suspicious. There was no celebration yet. In fact, people were more skeptical than happy. So, the whole town waited for the paper, because we knew if it is REAL, it would be in the paper. We heard it secondhand from Mrs. Ethel, but we needed to see it and read it. We found it hard to wait until the paper came that warm, sunny October day in 1945.

As I ran down Pine Products Boulevard, I was swept with anticipation. I knew the whole town wanted to believe what we had heard, and was hoping that the papers would confirm the story. When I got the stack of papers, I cut it open and went right to *The Pittsburgh Courier*, and leafed through it until I found Wendell Smith's column. If anybody would have the story it would be Wendell Smith and *The Pittsburgh Courier*. Sure enough, the front page of that October 27, 1945 paper belonged to Jackie Robinson. The headline of that day is burned in my memory: **ROBINSON BREAKS COLOR LINE**. There it was, in print, but I still found it hard to believe. My eyes felt like they were growing and growing. My customers were going to have to wait a few minutes longer for news they had been waiting for for fifty years. This one day I had to read the papers before I delivered them. It was true, Robinson had been signed. The Brooklyn Dodgers, one of the sixteen professional franchises that made up the Major Leagues, had signed an historic agreement, ending a period of segregated play that kept blacks out of Organized Baseball since 1897.

Of course, I can't begin to tell you how happy I am that I am the first member of my race in organized baseball. I realize how much it means to me, my race, and to baseball. I can only say I'll do my very best to come through in every manner.
Jackie Robinson, during press conference after signing contract to play for the Montreal Royals, as quoted in The Pittsburgh Courier, October 27, 1945

After I read the lead article, I gathered up the papers and hurried back into town, yelling out to everyone I saw, "Look what I got. Jackie Robinson! **JACKIE ROBINSON!**" I sold more papers that day than ever before. I was as happy as a ten year old boy could be, but I don't think I could have fully appreciated just what a new day was dawning, for me, for other black children like me, for the black race and for all of America.

A door was opening. The sun was peeking through for the second time that day, in a whole new way. So much raced through my mind. A Negro League player, born in Georgia, raised in California, was signed by a professional team in New York to play in Montreal. This was a story that would truly touch and change not only the entire country but also the world! It was all a little too much for a young boy to process, but what I grasped, for sure, was that the door was now open for me and for every black kid like me, who ever dreamed of being a ballplayer. If the Dodgers could sign Jackie Robinson, the son of a black sharecropper, the limitations on my baseball dreams were now gone. And if that door could open, maybe other doors would open. I fully identified with Jackie Robinson's statement to the press of "I realize how much it means to me." I came to understand the rest of the statement as I experienced how much Jackie's signing meant to "my race, and to baseball", as he said, and to America.

In October 1945, Larry Doby, who would become the first black to play in the American League, was stationed on Mog-Mog, a tiny island, part of the Ulithi Atoll in the Pacific, 900 miles outside of Iwo Jima. He was a sailor, whose duties included unloading incoming ships, and organizing baseball games for other sailors. While sitting in segregated sleeping quarters, separating the white and black sailors, Doby, like Mrs. Ethel, heard about the integration of baseball on the radio:

It came on the radio one night in October while we were sitting there, that Mr. Rickey had signed Jackie [Robinson] to a contract with Montreal. I didn't know much about Montreal at that time, but I knew it was in the International League because the Eagles played in the same park the Newark Bears played in. Then I felt I had a chance to play major league baseball. …. My main thing was to become a teacher and coach somewhere in New Jersey, but when I heard about Jackie, I decided to concentrate on baseball. I forgot about going back to college.
Larry Doby, Pride Against Prejudice, p. 29

Elston Howard, who would become the first black to play for the New York Yankees, and who was a sixteen-year-old stock boy in St. Louis when Jackie signed, recalled his reaction:

A friend of mine came into the store and said, 'Ellie, have you heard the news? Branch Rickey just signed one of your boys. His name is Jackie Robinson.' I felt like dancing all over that floor. The path was opening up. Maybe I could become a major league player.

At thirteen years old, in Washington, DC, Maury Wills, who would become one of the greatest base stealers of all time, had no idea that he could make it to the Major Leagues until the Dodgers signed Jackie:

Not until Jackie Robinson came into baseball could a kid like me have anybody to emulate. Jackie Robinson created the burning desire in me to put all my efforts into becoming a professional baseball player – he and Larry Doby of the Cleveland Indians.
Maury Wills, On The Run, Carroll & Graf, New York, 1991, p. 48

Ed Charles, who I played against in the Florida State Negro League, as a teenager, remembers the influence Jackie Robinson had on him:

My life was impacted with the signing of Jackie Robinson in 1945. I was a thirteen-year old kid then and that kind of thing didn't happen. That was a monumental happening so to speak, because you are talking about the Jim Crow South at that time. I heard it from the elders and it trickled down to the kids. I just couldn't believe it. Montreal trained at Daytona Beach and that meant Jackie would be coming to Daytona Beach, and I would be right there to see him. The park where Jackie trained, Kelly Field, was right across the street from my house. Jackie really had an impact on us. We started saying Jackie opened the door for us, now we can dream about really being Major League ballplayers. We really began to dream in earnest after Jackie was successful with Montreal.
Ed Charles interview

The experiences, and recollections, of just about every black youngster born in the 1920s and 1930s, with hopes of playing the American pastime, were pretty much uniform, as portrayed by the thoughts of one of the greatest players to ever play the game, Willie Mays:

My father said to me, "You're not going into a cotton field, that's number one." That means picking cotton down there, putting it in a sack, carrying it on your shoulder. "You're not going to do that, you're going to play baseball." They always drilled that on me, "You're going to play baseball. You're going to be the best in baseball.
***
I didn't think I would have a chance, because of segregation. I didn't think I would ever get out of Birmingham.
***
[Jackie] Robinson was important to all blacks. To make it into the majors and to take all the name calling, he had to be something special. He had to take all this for years, not just for Jackie Robinson, but for the nation. Because all eyes were on Jackie at that particular time. We were pulling for him. When Jackie came in, I automatically became a Dodger fan, because I wanted to pull for him. I wanted to make sure that he was a very successful guy. [Larry] Doby came in about two weeks after him, and he was in the American League, but we didn't see him that much. Doby didn't get the recognition as being the first black.
Willie Mays interview, achievement.org

Every time I look at my pocketbook, I see Jackie Robinson.
Willie Mays

One of Jackie Robinson's most quoted statements is that you measure the importance of a man's life by his impact on others. Clearly, Jackie's life impacted millions. And it should be made clear that his impact was not just on African-American athletes or African-Americans. He had the ability to emotionally touch all people:

After the game, Jackie Robinson came into our clubhouse and shook my hand. He said, "You're a helluva ballplayer and you've got a great future." I thought that was a classy gesture, one I wasn't then capable of making. I was a bad loser. What meant even more was what Jackie told the press, "Mantle beat us. He was the difference between the two teams. They didn't miss DiMaggio." I have to admit, I became a Jackie Robinson fan on the spot. And when I think of that World Series, his gesture is what comes to mind. Here was a player who had without doubt suffered more abuse and more taunts and more hatred than any player in the history of the game. And he had made a special effort to compliment and encourage a young white kid from Oklahoma.
Mickey Mantle, baseball-almanac.com

Thinking about the things that happened, I don't know any other ball player who could have done what he did. To be able to hit with everybody yelling at him. He had to block all that out, block out everything but this ball that is coming in at a hundred miles an hour. To do what he did has got to be the most tremendous thing I've ever seen in sports.
Pee Wee Reese, baseball almanac.com

By the time I got to the majors Jackie had retired from playing but stayed close to the game doing some broadcasting. Whenever he did a game and I was pitching that day, and even when I wasn't pitching that day, we would sit down and chat. He never got tired of you asking him questions about his life. He was really excited by the fact I played with Larry Doby. I remember in Minnesota, in 1964, when I was traded over there, he did a Twins game and we talked about Larry, and the old Negro Leagues, the Newark Eagles, and the Baltimore Elite Giants, and we talked about the times when black folk went to so many games and the fashions that they wore at the games. If you ran into Jackie, and Jackie was so busy politically and business wise, that was the blessing, that you got a chance to run into him when he was broadcasting games. He didn't broadcast long, but when he did broadcast and when you saw him it was a wonderful thing.

I remember he talked to me about becoming independent. He asked me one time, "How far did you go in college?" and he talked to me about skills of life other than baseball skills. I remember him asking me one afternoon, "What are you going to do after the game?" I really couldn't answer that. He said, "Well, you better start thinking about it." I could have been maybe 30, 31 at that time. We have a tendency to think we're going to play forever and even at the end of your career you say, I'm going to play next year and you never think about what you're going to do after you get through playing the game. He got me to thinking about some of those things, and I started taking marketing classes and entrepreneurship classes.

They call his name in a way no other player's name is called. They plead to shake his hand or ask for his autograph. They touch his clothes as he walks by, unhurrying, pleasant, friendly, cooperative, because Jackie Robinson has never lost sight of what the game has meant to him, and what he has meant, means now, and will always mean to his people.

Milton Gross, baseball-almanac.com

CHAPTER 16

MOVING TOWARDS INTEGRATION

On matters of race, on matters of decency, baseball should lead the way.
Baseball Commissioner A. Bartlett Giamatti

All the nice statements in the world from both sides aren't going to knock out Jim Crow.
Satchel Paige

They say I was born too soon. I say the doors were opened too late.
James "Cool Papa" Bell

Cool Papa Bell is one of the few great Negro League ballplayers whose accomplishments were finally recognized by his induction into the National Baseball Hall of Fame. His phenomenal speed became the substance of baseball legend. Satchel Paige, for instance, enjoyed telling fans that Cool Papa once hit a line drive past Satchel's ear and, by the time he turned around, he saw the ball hit Bell's "ass sliding into second." Almost as unbelievable was Josh Gibson's claim that "Cool Papa Bell was so fast he could get out of bed, turn out the lights across the room and be back in bed under the covers before the lights went out." How I wish sometimes that the integration of baseball moved with that kind of speed.

Obviously, the statements of Satchel Paige and Josh Gibson are exaggerations. (Although, I did have occasion to ask Satchel about Josh's statement, and he suggested it just might be true. With a gleam in his eye, Satch told me that if Josh was talking about gas lamps, rather than electric lights, they glowed for a minute or so after you turn them down.) But, in many people's minds, the integration of baseball was as fast as Cool Papa Bell, accomplished solely by the signing of this one man, Jackie Robinson. In reality though, integration was anything but fast. It was a long, slow, frustrating process, and even after the "switch was thrown" by the Dodgers, the embers of segregation continued to glow brightly for some time and erupt into flames of hostility from time to time.

The fact that Branch Rickey signed Jackie Robinson, in October 1945, to play for the Royals, then a Brooklyn Dodgers' farm team, and then "promoted" Robinson to the Dodgers' Major League club for the 1947 season, is baseball gospel. The day when Robinson took the field for the Dodgers for the first time, on April 15, 1947, is widely recognized as the date when the integration of baseball in America became a reality. The fiftieth anniversary of Robinson's Major League debut was extensively promoted and celebrated by Major League Baseball. As part of the festivities President Bill Clinton appeared at Shea Stadium, on April

15, 1997, for an on-field ceremony honoring Robinson before a game between the New York Mets and the Los Angeles Dodgers (a nice piece of scheduling by Major League Baseball).

With grace and steely determination, he pushed open a door that should never have been closed and held it open for the countless talented young men and women who followed him. *President Bill Clinton, on Jackie Robinson, April 15, 1997*

As Major League Baseball honored Robinson by declaring that his uniform number, 42, would never be worn by future Major Leaguers, Clinton stated that Robinson had "changed the face of baseball and America forever." It was universally proclaimed that Robinson had brought down the barriers of baseball segregation.

He struck a mighty blow for equality, freedom and the American way of life. Jackie Robinson was a good citizen, a great man, and a true American champion.
President Ronald Reagan

History books have recorded that Rickey, Robinson, and the Dodgers integrated baseball. For years, they were devoid of the actual facts of baseball's integration: that it was a long process, and a complicated one. History has a duty to note the significance of not only the first act of integration, but the entire process and the challenges and difficulties endured by blacks as that process has played out.

The actions and character of Jackie Robinson and Branch Rickey, as the principal actor and director, respectively, of the integration of baseball, can not be questioned. The baseball and business sense, and foresight, of Rickey certainly did help to change the face of America, and the courage and strength displayed by Robinson were beyond extraordinary. What has come to be known as Rickey's "Great Experiment" would have failed if Robinson faltered in the field, or in his ability to handle the pressure and emotional stress that came with the burden he assumed. But America must not be fooled into thinking that the integration of baseball was as easy as throwing a switch, or that it was a one act, two-man play, started and completed in 1947, without significant debate and unrest, both prior to and since that date. When blacks were allowed to cross the color line of Organized Baseball, it was a slow, painful journey.

Thousands of excellent athletes were denied the privilege to dream of putting on a Major League uniform, because of their race. Many of those that did dream about it were not allowed to follow those dreams, because the harsh reality of life in America for blacks during the first half of the twentieth century put Major League Baseball on the "other side of the tracks." It was a restricted area that blacks could view, on a limited basis, but could not enter. These statements are not meant to criticize Organized Baseball.

The treatment of blacks in and by Organized Baseball was a product of the times. If anything, baseball was a little ahead of the rest of the nation in 1947 as far as racial integration and its treatment of blacks was concerned. It was not easy physically or emotionally for blacks or whites. Sometimes the pain was caused by the prejudice, and sometimes the pain was a symptom of progress, like a new tooth cutting through. And because baseball is so highly visible in our society, all that happened in baseball became news. That's why I believe that the relations between black and white ballplayers in the early days of integrated baseball helped advance the cause of civil rights in America. Over time, baseball taught America something about the ability of the races to be integrated, and the ability of blacks to play, and to think. Baseball allowed America to see blacks for who we really were: human beings who were different from every other human being in only two ways: our skin pigmentation was darker, and we had been oppressed and stereotyped by society to such an extent that others thought we were inferior intellectually and socially, capable of performing only menial jobs. Baseball provided a stage that allowed America to learn that blacks were not "savages," meant to be confined to second class citizenship. While Hollywood and Madison Avenue perpetuated the stereotype through fictional characters such as Steppin Fetchit, Beulah, and Uncle Ben, baseball was featuring the likes of Jackie Robinson, Henry Aaron, Bob Gibson, and Frank Robinson, who performed so well that there was no question about their place among the greats of the game.

Baseball taught America a great deal about itself. The way that things unfolded, in the time pattern that they did, gave America an opportunity, as painful as it was, to have a long conversation that endured from the 1930s through the 1960s and culminated in the Civil Rights Acts and Voting Rights Act in 1964 and 1965. Branch Rickey didn't just awake one morning and say, "Find me a Negro ballplayer. I think I'll change history." Likewise, Jackie Robinson wasn't simply picked out of a hat to be the first Negro ballplayer in the twentieth century. There were many people who played supporting roles in the integration of baseball and America. Some were actually on stage with Rickey and Robinson, and although they didn't share the spotlight, their tasks were just as difficult and important. Many others also played vital roles in the process of integration. Yet their stories and their names rarely make it to the "Playbill." And if they do, it is only as a footnote.

Baseball has helped to change some of the negative images surrounding Black athletes and Black people, in general. These changes have come about because of the heroic efforts of the Black players themselves, and other people.
Joe Morgan, in Foreword to A Hard Road to Glory, The African-American Athlete in Baseball, Amistad, New York 1988

For at least fifteen years before Jackie Robinson took the field in Brooklyn, the possibility of a player from the Negro Leagues becoming a Major Leaguer was discussed, argued, written about, prayed for, feared, anticipated, dreaded, and planned, by blacks and whites both in and out of baseball. There were obviously many blacks who couldn't wait for the day, and many whites who were dead set against it. Conversely, there were blacks who felt that the Negro Leagues were among the very few successful black business enterprises and while they may have only existed because of segregation, the Negro Leagues would fold if their stars were taken by the Major Leagues. They were also concerned the opportunity for many blacks to play baseball would disappear if the Negro Leagues were no longer there as only a few blacks would likely find employment in Organized Baseball. There were also whites who recognized the inequity of keeping blacks out of baseball, and who realized the talents of players in the Negro Leagues. For sure, the topic was a recurring, and hotly debated one.

As is often the case in social change, the press was leading the charge for the integration of baseball. Beginning in the early 1930s, the Daily Worker, the newspaper of the Communist Party in America, used the existence of segregation to label baseball as a "capitalist controlled sport." (Rickey & Robinson, Chalberg, p. 93). After the 1936 Olympics, the Daily Worker stepped up its attack on Organized Baseball segregation. It hired a twenty-four year old New York University student, Lester Rodney, as its first Sports Editor, and began to run articles directly urging the end of "Jim Crow baseball." He was but one of the many journalists who for years before 1947 led the cry for the integration of baseball as well as the integration of races throughout American society. Sam Lacy, Joe Bostic, and Wendell Smith were leaders in this effort.

In 1938, Sam Lacy interviewed Clark Griffith, owner of the Washington Senators, and asked about the possibility of blacks playing in the Major Leagues. Griffith's response:

Both the commissioner [Landis] and I know that colored baseball is deserving of some recognition in the organized game ... However, I am not so sure the time has arrive yet. ... A lone Negro in the game will face rotten, caustic comments. He will be made the target of cruel, filthy epithets.
Baltimore Afro-American, June 25, 1938

Seemed like a warning from Griffiths rather than a response.

It was Bostic, who wrote for the *People's Voice* and *New York Amsterdam News*, who got Branch Rickey and the Brooklyn Dodgers to tryout Negro Leaguers Dave "Showboat" Thomas and Terris "Speed" McDuffie in 1945, by showing up at Bear Mountain, New York, with the players and Nat Low, a photographer for the *Daily Worker*. At the time, both players were in their late thirties and neither ever made it to the Dodgers, or any other Major League team for that matter. And it was Wendell Smith who accompanied Jackie Robinson to Boston for his famous tryout, and who stopped in to visit Branch Rickey in Brooklyn on the way home from Boston. After that visit it seems that Wendell had the inside track had the inside track on Rickey's intention to bring Robinson into Organized Baseball. Every now and then he would throw a line into his columns that would cause you to think something was happening. When it was widely reported that Rickey was seeking to have Robinson play in a newly formed league on a team called the Brown Dodgers, Smith wrote:

It does not seem logical he [Rickey] should call in a rookie player to discuss the future organization of Negro baseball.
The Pittsburgh Courier, September 8, 1945

The death of Commissioner Landis, late in 1944, and the selection of Albert "Happy" Chandler as Baseball Commissioner, also must be noted as an event that helped integration. When Major League owners voted 15-1 against Rickey's idea to sign Robinson, Chandler approved it anyway. When Chandler was first asked to be the Commissioner, Ric Roberts, a sportswriter for the Pittsburgh Courier asked him if he would allow blacks to play in the Major Leagues. Chandler's response: "If they can fight and die on Okinawa, Guadalcanal, in the South Pacific, they can play baseball in America. And when I give my word you can count on it." (*Invisible Men, Life in Baseball's Negro Leagues, by Donn Rogosin, Atheneum New York 1985, p. 199*)

History must not forget the efforts of players like Dave Hoskins, Rube Foster, and Satchel Paige, which I have written about earlier in this book, and many other individuals who played pivotal roles in the segregation of baseball, like Hank Aaron who integrated the South Atlantic League, Larry Doby, Dan Bankhead, Willard Brown, Hank Thompson, Nat Peeples, Earl Mann, Piper Davis and Fred Valentine. These players were all helping to further the progress of integration in baseball on many different fronts, while Major League Baseball itself still did not yet have its first black player on every team.

Eleven weeks after Jackie Robinson faced his first pitch as a Brooklyn Dodger from the arm of Johnny Sain, the Cleveland Indians signed Larry Doby to become the first African-American to play in the American League. He debuted for the Indians on July 5, 1947. Exactly two weeks later, Bill Veeck, owner of the St. Louis Browns brought up two more African-Americans, Willard Brown and Hank Thompson. They made baseball history collectively and individually. Together they became the first African-American teammates in the history of the Major Leagues when they were both in the lineup in the same game for the Browns on July 20, 1947. Individually, Willard was the first African-American to hit a home run in the American League. Willard started playing for the Monroe, Louisiana, Monarchs and was then a perennial star with the Kansas City Monarchs in the Negro Leagues. Josh Gibson, himself one of the greatest hitters of all times, gave Willard the nickname "Home Run." Both Willard and Thompson were released by the Browns, but Thompson also became the first African-American to play for the New York Giants when he and Monte Irvin joined the team in 1949. And when Thompson faced Don Newcombe, also in 1949, it was the first time in Major

League history an African-American batter faced an African-American pitcher.

Several months after bringing Jackie Robinson up to the Brooklyn Dodgers, Branch Rickey found himself in need of a quality pitcher and Rickey himself scouted the Negro Leagues for talent. He had Don Newcombe under contract in Nashua, but he wanted somebody who could start immediately in the majors. Rickey's search led him to Dan Bankhead, who at the time was pitching for the Memphis Red Sox. Bankhead's baseball career started with the Birmingham Black Barons in 1940 and was interrupted by a three-year stint with the US Marines. He possessed a fastball that led many people to compare him to Bob Feller. Rickey purchased Bankhead's contract from Birmingham and immediately brought him to the Dodgers, where he debuted on August 26, 1947, as the first African-American pitcher in the Major Leagues. His debut was much more successful as a hitter than a pitcher. He homered off of Fritz Ostermueller of the Pirates in his first at bat, but gave up ten hits in 3 1/3 innings of work. After breaking the color barrier for Major League pitchers, Bankhead spent two years in the minor leagues, and then rejoined the Dodgers in 1950.

By April 1949, Jackie Robinson had already played two full seasons in the majors and yet there had still not been an integrated game of professional baseball, or any other sport, played in the city of Atlanta, Georgia, the state where Robinson was born. That changed because of the courage of Earl Mann, the owner of the Atlanta Crackers, who defied the death threats made by Dr. Samuel Green, the Grand Dragon of the Ku Klux Klan, and allowed Jackie Robinson, Roy Campanella and the Brooklyn Dodgers to play a three-game exhibition series against the Crackers at Ponce de Leon ballpark in Atlanta. The series took place April 8th through the 10th and the attendance for the final game has been reported as high as 25,500, the largest crowd ever to attend a baseball game there. The stadium only had seating for approximately 15,000, so Mr. Mann stretched a rope across the outfield and let the fans fill in behind it. Among the many black fans standing beyond that rope was Vernon Jordan, Jr., and his brother and dad. When Dodger catcher Bruce Edwards hit a ball into the crowd for a ground rule double, Vernon's dad survived the pile of spectators pursuing the ball and came up with a souvenir.

I saw a small mountain of what looked like a hundred men who had scrambled to get the ball. Very quickly, the pile grew smaller as each disappointed man got to his feet. From the bottom of the pile came this voice, 'I got it! I got it!' I recognized it instantly. It was my father. That was a heroic moment for all of us.
Vernon E. Jordan, Jr., Vernon Can Read, A Memoir, 2001

Vernon Sr. inscribed the ball with the date and particulars of the game and it has remained in the family as an heirloom and as a relic of that extraordinary day in Atlanta when black and white players played one another for the first time.

In 1950, the Boston Red Sox signed Lorenzo "Piper" Davis, after having purchased his contract from the Birmingham Black Barons for $15,000. The terms of the agreement were $7,500 down and an additional $7,500 to be paid if Davis was still with the Red Sox organization on May 15, 1950. Davis was the first African-American signed by the Red Sox and the circumstances leading up to it and the results of the signing are significant.

For five consecutive seasons starting in 1945, Davis was a Negro League All-Star with the Indianapolis Clowns. The St Louis Browns obtained an option on Davis at the same time they obtained options on Willard Brown and Hank Thompson. However, the unwritten quota system in Organized Baseball at that time only allowed two blacks on a team at a time, so when the Browns brought up Brown and Thompson they left Davis behind. When he refused an offer to play in the minors, his relationship with the Browns was terminated and he returned to the Negro Leagues. Davis became player-manager of the Birmingham Black Barons in 1948, the same year that the Boston Red Sox changed their minor league team in the Class AA Southern Association from New Orleans to the Birmingham Barons, originally the Birmingham Coal Barons, in existence since 1885. The Barons and the Black Barons shared Rickwood Field in Birmingham.

Also that same year, Davis had a rookie on his team named Willie Mays, who grew up in nearby Westfield, Alabama. Mays had all the tools naturally, except the ability to hit a curveball. Davis took him under his wing and helped him with his hitting, resulting in Mays batting .311 in 1949 and .330 in 1950, before being signed by the New York Giants. But before the Giants signed Mays, the Red Sox had a chance at him. They sent super scout Larry Woodall, a Texan, to see Mays and the story has it that it rained the whole time he was there. Instead of staying around to watch Mays, Woodall suggested that the Red Sox sign Davis, which they did. Their two top farm teams were Louisville (Kentucky) and Birmingham and they couldn't send Davis to either to play. Although he could manage a black team in Birmingham he could not play on a team with whites. Codifying what had been the common law in Birmingham, the city council passed an ordinance in 1950 that made it "unlawful for a negro and a white person to play together or in company with each other in any game of cards, dice, dominoes, checkers, baseball, softball, football, basketball, or similar game." So, the Red Sox brought Davis to spring training and then assigned him to Scranton, Pennsylvania.

> **I couldn't stay with the white players. I stayed in the servants' quarters until I found a room in a private home. I ate breakfast in the servants' quarters. In the clubhouse, there was no locker with "Davis" above it. The trainer said I was on the other side . . . the visitors' dressing room. I was the only one in there.**
> *Piper Davis describing his spring training experience with the Red Sox in 1950*

Piper played fifteen games for Scranton and on May 13th, two days before the second installment of $7,500 was due, he was leading the team in batting average (.333), home runs (3), and RBIs (10), but he was released and was told that it was because of economic reasons.

They told me, 'We got to let you go because of economic conditions.' Tom Yawkey had as much money as anyone on the East Coast. I don't talk about it that much. It wouldn't help. Sometimes I just sit there and a tear drops from my eye. I wonder why it all had to happen, why we had to have so much hate.

Piper Davis interview with Jules Tygiel

Just before the 1951 season the Dodgers signed pitcher Joe Black as an amateur free agent and assigned him to the same Montreal farm team where Jackie Robinson started. Midway through the year he was promoted to their team in St. Paul and by 1952 he was on the big league roster as a relief pitcher. Joe had played for Baltimore in the Negro Leagues for seven seasons and at the time he debuted with the Dodgers as a rookie he was already 28 years old. Joe pitched 142 innings, all in relief except for 2 starts, and won the National League Rookie of the Year Award, with a 15-2 record, 15 saves and a 2.15 ERA. The Dodgers won the National League pennant but were strapped for pitching and manager Chuck Dressen turned to the rookie to start Games One, Four and Seven of the World Series against the Yankees. Joe tossed a six hitter in Game One becoming the first African-American pitcher to win a World Series game. Thirteen years later I would become the first African-American pitcher to win a World Series game in the American League. Joe threw a four hitter in Game Four but lost 2-0, and lasted only six innings in Game Seven.

Integration also took a step forward beyond the players in 1951 when Emmett Ashford became the first black umpire in Organized Baseball. Emmett worked in the Southwest International League and would work in the minors for fifteen seasons, before also becoming the first black umpire in the majors, when he was promoted to work in the American League in 1966.

For outfielder Nat Peeples, his date with destiny was April 19, 1954 and the venue was the Class AA Southern Association. He entered the game in the fifth inning as a pinch hitter for the Atlanta Crackers in a game against the Mobile Bears, in Mobile, Alabama, and recaps of the game may have recorded the result of his at bat as a ground out back to the pitcher, but on a far grander scale Peeples' appearance broke the color line in the Southern Association. Peeples started the next game and grounded out three times, reaching base safely only on a base on balls. Before the Crackers returned to Atlanta for their home opener, Peeples was optioned to the Jacksonville Braves of the Class A South Atlantic League. That ended the attempt to integrate the Southern Association. When the Southern Association dissolved in 1961, there had been no other black player to ever play on any team in the association other than Nat Peeples!

Sometimes, it wasn't any premeditated, valiant effort at integration, just people using common sense and acting like ordinary people, without seeing black or white that allowed progress to be made. Consider the story of Fred Valentine, an outfielder in the Orioles organization:

In 1958, I expected to be sent to the Triple A team that spring, but the Orioles signed a bonus baby and he was put on the fast track. That meant I had to go to Wilson, North Carolina. I drove to Wilson, together with two other black players. I was told to go the Cherry Hotel. When I got there and walked in the door, the team's General Manager was waiting for me. As soon as he saw me he said, "You must be Valentine" which wasn't too hard to figure out because I think it had been some time since a black man had been in that hotel that wasn't working there. I told him I was, and that I had two other players in the car, and I offered to go get them. He told me to leave them in the car, because I would not be staying at the Cherry Hotel; blacks were not allowed to stay there at that time. He gave me directions to a boarding house, in a section of town where only black people lived. When we got there three rooms were waiting for us. After a few nights the women who owned the home offered us an apartment for $5 a month, furnished.

I had a very good season in Wilson, probably because I belonged in a higher division of ball. By the middle of the summer I was leading the team in every offensive category, and had developed quite a following. At that time the stands were segregated, and blacks were only allowed to sit in the bleachers, not the grandstands. On one Sunday, so many blacks came out to see me that they added extra seating in front of the bleachers. A few innings into the game there was a tremendous crash which was the sound of the bleachers crumbling under the weight of the capacity crowd. Luckily, no one was hurt, but as they pulled the people out of the mess, the General Manager turned to me, based on my seniority, and asked what I thought they should do. I suggested that the team allow the black fans to sit in the grandstands. I said, "What the heck, this is a small town, and everybody knows each other. I don't think it is a problem." And that is what they did. And as the blacks were making their way into the grandstands, it was clear that whites and blacks knew each other from town, and starting talking to one another. Within a half hour the game was re-started. That was the last day that there were segregated stands in Wilson, North Carolina.

Fred Valentine interview

So, you see that after Rickey and Robinson opened the door to the integration of baseball, there were many other brave people who advanced the cause in many places throughout America. The stories I have included in this chapter are but a sampling of the courageous acts taken that brought about the changes in Organized Baseball that allowed African-Americans to be able to play and compete. Without them and many more like them, none of The Black Aces would ever have found their way to a Major League mound. It is because of all they went through and how they dared to make a difference that I feel so strongly they should not be forgotten, and what they did should not be in vain. Today's children, today's ballplayers, and, in fact, all of us, must remember and celebrate them.

Like Jackie Robinson, Don Newcombe played for the Montreal Royals (1948) before beginning his Major League career in Brooklyn (1949). He went on to have three 20-win seasons, and became the first Black Ace in 1951. Don also earned both the MVP and the first-ever Cy Young Award in 1956, which he proudly displayed (below) to teammate Don Drysdale. (National Baseball Hall of Fame Library, Cooperstown, NY)

Sad Sam Jones was the first African-American to pitch a no-hitter in the Major Leagues (May 12, 1955 for the Cubs against the Pirates). Sam is shown here in spring training with the Giants, in 1959, the year he became a twenty-game winner. (National Baseball Hall of Fame Library, Cooperstown, NY) In San Francisco, Sam befriended Johnny Bushman, a young fan with polio, who became a lifelong friend. (Associated Press)

I notched my first Major League win on April 17, 1958 against Kansas City, and afterwards (above) I was all smiles with teammates Preston Ward (left) and Mickey Vernon. (Associated Press)

I was so proud to put on a uniform every day as a member of the Cleveland Indians (National Baseball Hall of Fame Library, Cooperstown, NY)

Man, what a thrill, to retire the great Mickey Mantle (below) to nail down a victory over the Yankees in a 1961 contest. (Associated Press)

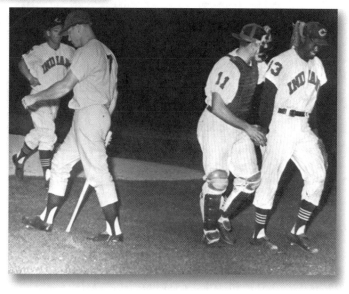

My greatest season was 1965. I got a lot of help that year from pitching coach, Johnny Sain, (above, left) who also coached fellow Black Aces, Al Downing and Earl Wilson. (National Baseball Hall of Fame Library, Cooperstown, NY) Satchel Paige, who taught me the importance of the "titty" pitch earlier in my career, also gave me some reminders during his final Major League stint, with Kansas City in 1965. (Associated Press)

Getting to the World Series with the Twins that year was something I will never forget. Driving a three run home run off Howie Reed to secure my victory in Game Six was almost too good to be true! (Associated Press)

was fortunate to pursue my other love, music, both during and after my baseball
career. Willie Mays joined me during a gig at Basis Street East in New York after
the 1965 season. (National Baseball Hall of Fame Library, Cooperstown, NY) I also
toured for many years with my group, Mudcat and The Kittens, (below, left) (Courtesy
of Mudcat Grant personal collection), and got to meet up with many other athletes
and celebrities including Olympic great, Wilma Rudolph. (Courtesy of Mudcat Grant
personal collection)

I was a successful starter and reliever in the Major Leagues, and was so proud when Hall of Famer Rollie Fingers gave me credit for helping him to become the dominant reliever that he was. (Courtesy of Mudcat Grant personal collection)

My younger brother, Julius "Swampfire" Grant, was also a twenty-game winner, but he accomplished that feat with the Monterrey Sultanes in the Mexican League, where he had a long and successful career. He was recently named as the starting left-handed pitcher on the All-Time Sultanes All-Star Team. Julius also played in the Cleveland organization where we were together for spring training in 1961, but he never made it to the Major Leagues. (Photos courtesy of Pedro Treto Cisneros, former President of the Mexican League)

Many think Bob Gibson's 1968 season was the greatest ever by a pitcher. It started early with a lot of hard work in spring training (above) and, in addition to his remarkable 1.12 ERA, was highlighted by a record setting 17 strikeout performance against the Detroit Tigers in the World Series (below). (Associated Press)

Earl Wilson joined the Boston Red Sox just after they became the last integrated team in the majors in 1959, when Pumpsie Green was called up. (National Baseball Hall of Fame Library, Cooperstown, NY),

In 1962, Earl threw the first no-hitter by an African-American in the American League. (Associated Press)

Earl became a Black Ace when he won his twentieth game for the Tigers, on September 7, 1967. He also belted a two-run homer in that win. (Associated Press)

Ferguson Jenkins' Hall of Fame career began as a teenager in the Philadelphia Phillies organization (Courtesy of Fergie Jenkins Foundation), but his star really shone with the Chicago Cubs where he recorded six straight 20-win seasons. (Courtesy of Fergie Jenkins Foundation)

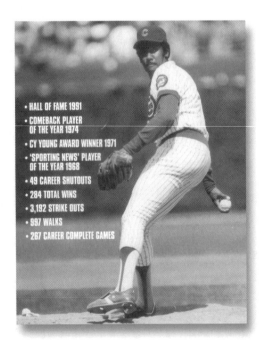

- HALL OF FAME 1991
- COMEBACK PLAYER OF THE YEAR 1974
- CY YOUNG AWARD WINNER 1971
- 'SPORTING NEWS' PLAYER OF THE YEAR 1968
- 49 CAREER SHUTOUTS
- 284 TOTAL WINS
- 3,192 STRIKE OUTS
- 997 WALKS
- 267 CAREER COMPLETE GAMES

Fergie's dad, Ferguson Jenkins, Sr., was an excellent centerfielder with the Chatham All-Stars in Ontario in the 1930s, and Fergie dedicated his own Major League career to his Dad, who never had the opportunity to play in Organized Baseball. (National Baseball Hall of Fame Library, Cooperstown, NY)

Al Downing has always been known as a great student of the game, which was evident at a very young age. Al is shown above (far left) absorbing a few pointers in his home state of New Jersey. (Courtesy of Al Downing personal collection) Al was the very first African-American pitcher ever added to the New York Yankee roster. His joy is obvious (below left) as he packed his bags at AA Binghamton for the trip to New York on July 16, 1961. (Associated Press) It was with the Dodgers (below right) that Al became a member of The Black Aces in 1971. (National Baseball Hall of Fame Library, Cooperstown, NY)

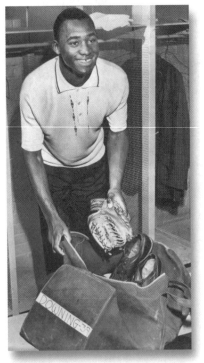

Vida Blue exuded pure left-handed power when he won the Cy Young Award and MVP honors with the A's in 1971. (Copyright Source Unknown, National Baseball Hall of Fame Library, Cooperstown, NY)

Vida nailed down his 20th victory to join The Black Aces elite against the Chicago White Sox on August 7, 1971. (Associated Press).

151

At 6 foot 8 inches tall, with the ability to throw the ball over 100 miles an hour, JR Richard was a very intimidating sight on the mound. He was a consistent winner for the Houston Astros, and it took a stroke to halt his assault on the record books. He was the first righthander in the National League to record 300 strikeouts in a season. (Above: National Baseball Hall of Fame Library, Cooperstown, NY, below: Copyright Source Unknown)

Mike Norris became a member of The Black Aces in 1980, posting a 22-9 record for the Oakland Athletics. He had what many have described as the nastiest screwball in the Major Leagues. (above: National Baseball Hall of Fame Library, Cooperstown, NY; below: Courtesy of Mike Norris personal collection)

Dwight Gooden burst on the scene as a nineteen year old phenom with the New York Mets in 1984, and recorded his 20 win season in 1985 (24-4). His career highlights include the no-hitter he pitched for the New York Yankees in May 1996. (National Baseball Hall of Fame Library, Cooperstown, NY)

Dave Stewart started his career with the Los Angeles Dodgers, but carved a place for himself in baseball history with four consecutive twenty-win seasons while pitching with the Oakland A's. Dave punctuated that success with an outstanding post-season record. (National Baseball Hall of Fame Library, Cooperstown, NY)

Dontrelle Willis brought The Black Aces into the 21st Century when he notched his 20th victory over the Washington Nationals on September 7, 2005 (above). Dontrelle led the majors with 22 wins for the Florida Marlins in 2005, and was selected as a 2005 National League All-Star (below). (Associated Press)

Here I am in the capable and guiding hands of Negro League legend, Buck O'Neil. I greatly admire Buck for having devoted his life to baseball and the memory of all of those guys who played in the Negro Leagues. It is a joy for me to be an Ambassador to the Negro League Baseball Museum in Kansas City, where Buck is the President. (Courtesy of Mudcat Grant personal collection)

*This photo was taken at The Black Aces Golf Tournament in Binghamton, NY, an
annual event sponsored by Security Mutual Life Insurance Company of New York
to raise funds for the Urban League. Pictured, left to right, are Pat O'Brien, me,
Mike Norris, Tom Sabellico, Al Downing, and Vida Blue. (Courtesy of Mudcat
Grant personal collection)*

CHAPTER 17

DON NEWCOMBE
Newk

Born June 14, 1926 in Madison, New Jersey
Teams: Newark Eagles, Brooklyn Dodgers,
Cleveland Indians, Cincinnati Reds
Twenty-Win Seasons: 1951, 1955, 1956
Awards: NL Rookie of the Year - 1949
Cy Young Award - 1956
Most Valuable Player Award – 1956
National League All-Star 1949, 1950, 1951 and 1956

A lot of fans have asked me who's the toughest pitcher I had to face in the majors. I would say Don Newcombe. He had tremendous drive. He loved competition, was a winning-type pitcher. He was the type of man that had great natural ability. He could throw a ball hard. He had great control. He could hit like hell; he was the type of man that everybody would like to be like. Newk was a winner ... He had explosive speed and a big jug-handle curve.
Ernie Banks

He's about as fast as anybody in our league. Even Hal Newhouser, Virgil Trucks, Vic Raschi and Bob Feller aren't any faster.
Ted Williams (1949)

You have to watch him every second. The ball moves on you. He was the most impressive pitcher in this game.
Joe DiMaggio, after facing Newcombe in 1949 All-Star Game

It was a privilege to have played with Don Newcombe, who not only was a great pitcher but a good hitter with power! Don was the kind of pitcher when the game "was on the line" you wanted him to be on the mound for you.
Clyde King

Before he was ten years old, Don Newcombe, his father, Roland, and his three brothers were already attending professional baseball games at Rupert Stadium, in Newark, New Jersey. For 25 cents a ticket, they were permitted to sit in the left-field bleachers (segregated seating reserved for blacks only) and watch the Newark Eagles of the Negro Leagues, or the Newark Bears, the AAA minor league

159

franchise of the New York Yankees. As a boy, Don played sandlot ball and also dreamed of someday being a ballplayer. At nine years old he had already pitched batting practice for a local semi-pro team. His childhood hero was Bob Seeds, an All-Star outfielder with the Newark Bears, who eventually played in the majors with the Indians, White Sox, Red Sox, Yankees and Giants. But, like the rest of us whose dreams were limited by racial reality, his dreams were of being a Negro League player.

My school didn't have a baseball program. But when my older brother started me playing baseball, I knew it was my game. My brother managed a semi-pro team in Elizabeth. I didn't want any part of football after that.

Don Newcombe, as quoted by Vincent X. Flaherty in The Examiner, January 28, 1958

When Don tried out for his junior high school team, near Maplewood, New Jersey, the coach, Hermie Kaufman, told Don he would never make it as a pitcher. He thought Don didn't have the talent and wasn't smart enough, and told him so. Luckily for Don, and for baseball, there were others who encouraged him. Specifically, Newcombe remembers his neighbor, Johnny Grier, who acted like Don's big brother, and kept Don out of trouble. Based on his life experiences, Don has always recognized the need to tell the world about the dangers a ghetto kid can succumb to without a big brother to help keep him on the straight and narrow. Grier taught Don the big windmill windup and high kick that became his trademark.

In 1944, Don was playing checkers in the local barbershop in Elizabeth, New Jersey, with a friend who offered to introduce Don to Abe Manley, an owner of the Newark Eagles. As a result of that checker game and introduction, the Eagles invited Don to a tryout in their spring training camp in Richmond, Virginia. They liked what they saw, and Don realized his dream when he was signed to play with them, at a salary of $175 a month.

After he joined the Eagles, he learned that many of the players in the Negro Leagues were not content to have a league of their own. Having attained the goal of playing ball professionally, they continued to dream, out loud, talking in the clubhouse, on the bus, and in between games, about the possibility that someday blacks would be allowed to reach the ultimate pinnacle of playing in the Major Leagues. Like all true athletes, they yearned to compete against those who were recognized as the very best.

Although Newcombe wasn't aware of it, by 1945 he and his Newark teammate, catcher Roy Campanella, were two of the black athletes Branch Rickey was most interested in bringing to the Major Leagues. Newcombe caught Rickey's attention during the 1945 season, when the native of New Jersey went 14-4 for the Eagles. By that time Newcombe was making $350 a month, double his original salary. Rickey recognized Newcombe as a diamond in the rough – tall, with the ability to throw a 'live' fastball; one with movement, in addition to velocity. He was confident his Dodger coaches could teach Newcombe control and the other fine points necessary to be a winner, because Newcombe already possessed the required raw talent, and he was available for a cheap price.

Prior to the Brooklyn Dodgers signing Jackie Robinson to a professional contract to play for Montreal, Rickey's scout, Clyde Sukeforth, saw Newcombe pitch in an All-Star Game held at Ebbets Field. The game was played between Negro National League players, including Roy Campanella and Monte Irvin, and Major League players, including Eddie Stanky, Buddy Kerr, Ralph Branca, Whitey Kurowski, and Frank McCormick. Newcombe started the game, but only pitched into the third inning when a fastball to Goody Rosen caused severe pain in his elbow. Having to leave the game, his ego was hurting as badly as his elbow. When Sukeforth sought out Newcombe in the Eagles locker room he found him upset and crying, thinking his injury and the resulting short outing had ended his career. It hadn't even really started. Sukeforth told Newk about Rickey's idea to form a Negro League team, the Brooklyn Brown Dodgers, and invited Newk to meet with Rickey the next day in Brooklyn. Newcombe didn't know it, but Sukeforth had also invited Roy Campanella to Rickey's office on Montague Street in Brooklyn. To this day many people think Rickey's promotion of the Brooklyn Brown Dodgers was a smokescreen, to hide his real intentions of bringing black ballplayers to the majors. Smokescreen or not, it was believed by Newcombe and Campanella, so much so that Campanella didn't sign a contract because he was only interested in leaving his current team to go to the majors.

In actuality, Rickey was preparing for the next "wave" in his plan to integrate the Dodgers. Newcombe and Roy Campanella were being groomed to come up to the Dodgers right behind Robinson. Rickey had found an untapped source of baseball talent, and he was about to develop it. After determining that Newcombe had no contract binding him to play for Newark, Rickey signed Newcombe to play for the Brooklyn Brown Dodgers and gave him $1,000. After Rickey signed Jackie to play for Class AAA Montreal, he brought Newcombe and Campanella back to his office. At that time he signed them to Dodger minor league contracts, to play in a lower classification, without designating any specific team.

Because Jackie Robinson made it to the Major Leagues first, not many people know or remember that Don Newcombe and Roy Campanella were also playing in Organized Baseball, in the Brooklyn Dodger organization in 1946. They also got less early press because while Jackie was in spring training in Florida, dealing with Jim Crow face to face, Newcombe and Campanella were not. Rickey was daring enough to run "The Experiment" by having one black ballplayer in the South. He wasn't about to play all his cards at once. Until he could determine a suitable town where Newcombe and Campanella could play, Rickey had them maintain a very low profile. Campanella played winter ball in Venezuela and Newcombe got ready for the 1946 season by working out in a YMCA in New York City.

In addition to physically preparing for their first year in Organized Baseball, Don and Roy mentally and psychologically prepared also. They were in daily contact with Jackie and with either Rickey or Sukeforth. As Jackie dealt with problems he encountered as a rookie black ballplayer in a white man's league, he would talk them out with Newcombe and Campanella, sharing his advice on how to further "The Experiment." That arrangement would continue during the 1946 season. Robinson, with the blessing of Rickey and Sukeforth, would lay down the guidelines for Don and Roy.

Jackie said everything we discussed must remain in the apartment. We discussed all possible incidents that might happen and how we'd handle them. Jackie set the tone. His character, his backbone, his guts – those were the keys. We talked about how things were going, how we needed to change things.
Don Newcombe, as quoted by Hal Bodley in USA Today, April 11, 1997

In Rickey's mind, Don and Roy were not on the same time track to get to the majors as Jackie was. Rickey's original intention was to send Newcombe and Campanella to the Dodgers' Class B affiliate in Danville, Illinois, while Jackie was to be initiated to Organized Baseball at the higher Class AAA level, but in the relative racial calm of Montreal.

Because of what they had already accomplished in the Negro Leagues, Newcombe and Campanella's talent level was above Class C or D. The Dodgers had five Class B teams to which they could assign them, but Rickey knew that he would not be able to send black ballplayers to teams in the southern states, where segregation was still the law of the land. That narrowed his choices to Illinois and New Hampshire. He thought he was safe with Illinois. He was wrong. Despite the fact that Rickey and the Dodgers had built the stadium in Danville, and the Dodgers were among the most active minor league owners in the country, they ran into a fair-weather friend, Tom Fairweather to be exact, who was the President of the Three I League (Illinois, Indiana, Iowa), of which Danville was a member. Fairweather, who was also President of the Class C Western Association and the Class A Western League, told Rickey, "If you send any of those niggers out here, we're going to close down the league." The Three I League was just resuming operations in 1946 after having suspended competition for three years because of World War II. They were back in business and welcoming veterans to play, just not black ones.

The situation Rickey found himself in would occur repeatedly in baseball for the next twenty years. While baseball executives would be free to place white prospects at the classification they felt most suitable for their talent level, and the development of the prospect's career, they would be forced to consider the social ramifications of sending a black prospect to a town where he would not be welcome. Sometimes it kept a black prospect at a lower classification, and other times it meant that a black prospect moved to a higher classification. Some commentators felt that blacks were getting an advantage by "skipping" classifications, moving, for instance, from Class C to Class A ball, because the team's Class B affiliate was in the South. However, there was also a detriment to moving ahead too quickly if the prospect wasn't really ready. The classification system was in place for a reason. If a prospect was being moved from Class C to Class A because of his talent, that was one thing, but if a prospect had to skip a class because of racial considerations, that was something else. The Indians were faced with this exact situation when they signed me in 1954. If I were white, or if there were no segregation problems in the southern states, the Indians would have sent me to their Class D affiliate in Tifton, Georgia. However, they were fearful of the response my presence might cause in Tifton, and decided to send me to their Class C affiliate in Fargo, North Dakota.

Newcombe and Campanella having been refused by Danville, Rickey's next option was to send them to the Dodgers' Class B team in Nashua, New Hampshire, a franchise that had just started in 1946. In Newcombe and Campanella's presence, Rickey's assistant, Bob Finch, phoned Buzzie Bavasi, the General Manager at Nashua, and asked him if he would take two black players. To his credit, Bavasi displayed a great amount of courage, showing disinterest in the racial issue and answering Rickey's question with one of his own, "Can they play baseball?" When Rickey assured him they could, Bavasi responded, "I don't care if they are green with orange spots, or got two heads. If they can catch or hit, send them up." He accepted them as ballplayers, and so they became the first black battery in Organized Baseball in the 20th Century. Not only were they the only black players on the Nashua team, they (and their respective wives) were the only black people in all of Nashua.

As tough as that must have been, to face outright rejection by a league president because of the color of his skin, and then to move to a new town where he was not only a minority but a rarity, Newcombe has always acknowledged that Jackie Robinson had it a lot tougher than he did. Newcombe knows that he was a pioneer, but that Jackie was "the" pioneer. Newcombe is proud to have been among the first blacks to play in the Major Leagues, but has at all times recognized that even though he and Jackie started in the minor leagues the same season, all the focus and attention, both positive and negative, were on Jackie. That didn't mean that Newcombe didn't face racial discrimination, or that Newcombe didn't have hurdles to clear. It only meant that every now and then he was allowed to slip under the radar of the press, while Jackie was in the public's eye from dawn to dusk.

Newk remembers one white batter charged the mound and jumped at him with his spikes aimed at his face, yelling he was going "to grind this nigger's face." Newk, mindful of all that Jackie had to quietly endure, pursuant to Mr. Rickey's instructions, knew that he could not fight back, and he didn't, allowing his teammates, mostly white, including Chuck Connors, to come to his defense.

There is another night that sticks out in Newk's memory. It was a night when Bavasi showed that his courage and integrity were not just words, but were backed up with actions. It was 1946 and Nashua was playing a night game at home, at Holman Stadium, against the Lynn Red Sox. Four individuals stick out in Newcombe's mind from that night: the manager of the Lynn team, Pip Kennedy;

their catcher, Matt Batts; their pitcher, Walter Cress; and Bavasi. Newcombe recalls Kennedy, standing in the third base coach's box, yelling out racial insults at him and Campy all night: "nigger-this" and "nigger-that." One of Branch Rickey's strict rules for his black players during the early days of this Experiment was that they could not retaliate. Some teams, like the Lynn Red Sox, took advantage of that. At the end of the game, Bavasi, who had just finished a three-year stint in World War II as an Infantry Machine Gunner with the Army, had the courage to speak up for his players. When Kennedy and his players appeared at Bavasi's office to collect their road share of the game receipts, Bavasi, with manager Walter Alston at his side, confronted the whole team: "Why don't you say to me right now what you said to them and I'll kick your ass. Go ahead and say it to me. I'll take you on." The Red Sox took their money and left. (Michael Madden, *Boston Globe, March 28, 1997*)

While most writers and baseball historians agree that Rickey had a plan to bring black players to the Major Leagues in stages, with Robinson being the first, there was speculation at the time that Newk, or Campy, could make it to Brooklyn first:

Campanella and Newcombe form the only Negro battery in organized baseball. They are to Nashua and the New England League what Robinson and Wright are to Montreal and the International League. Robinson and Wright, of course, have received more attention in the press because they were the first two Negro players Rickey elected to sign. However, "Camp" and Newcombe are just as important in the drama that is being staged in behalf of Negro players as Robinson and Wright. In fact, it can develop that the two Nashua players will arrive at Ebbets Field in Brooklyn before either Robinson or Wright.

...

Donald Newcombe ... pitched for the Newark Eagles in the Negro National League last year. ... Branch Rickey signed him because he's young, big, and has all the natural ability necessary to get him into the big leagues. He throws a blazing fast ball, a good curve, and has fairly good control.
Wendell Smith, The Sports Beat, Pittsburgh Courier, May 18, 1946

Newk has told me that the people of Nashua, including Bavasi, Alston, and his teammates, were very supportive of him and Campy. Rickey, true to his attention to detail, tried to insure that support by hiring Fred Dobens, the Managing Editor of the local paper, *The Nashua Telegraph*, as the President of the team. Newcombe pitched very well his first season in Nashua, earning a 14-4 record during the regular season and posting two more victories in the playoffs. Most of his success was powered by his fastball. True to the form of the great Negro League pitchers though, Newcombe also demonstrated that he was an exceptional all-around athlete. Newcombe was an excellent hitter, and a better than average fielder. In fact, during the 1946 season, when Alston was ejected from a game and named

Roy Campanella as the interim manager for a game, (making Campy the first black to manage in Organized Baseball, as far as I know), Campy called on Newcombe to pinch hit, and Newk delivered a game-winning pinch-hit home run. That year, both Newcombe and Campanella were referred to in *The Sporting News* as "two of the top prospects in the Brooklyn chain."

Although Newcombe had an excellent season in 1946, it was a difficult year for the Negro Leagues, and the Homestead Grays, in particular. For starters, the signing of Robinson, Newcombe, Campanella and other black stars by Major League teams, took some of the luster out of the Negro Leagues. The Grays, who had dominated the Negro Leagues, winning nine consecutive championships, from 1937 to 1945, faltered in 1946. The Grays' owner, Gus Greenlee, one of the most important figures in Negro League history, died in 1946. Cool Papa Bell and Buck Leonard, Grays' stars, were both past their prime, and their lone remaining superstar was Josh Gibson, who had been diagnosed with a brain tumor causing occasional severe headaches. Despite the illness, and a pair of aging and aching knees, Gibson still led the Negro Leagues in home runs in 1946. Gibson's demise, however, became apparent after the season, when he failed to play winter ball for the first time in his career, and in January 1947, Gibson suffered a fatal stroke.

Based on his 1946 success, Newcombe thought he would be headed to the majors in 1947 to join Jackie. He recalls that several people felt he might be the one to break the color barrier instead of Jackie, because he was such a hard thrower. That built up his hopes and when he learned that the Dodgers wanted him to return to Nashua in 1947, to mature, to work on his curveball (and his tendency to hit white batters), and to keep Rickey's "wave" in place, he contemplated returning to Newark and the Negro League instead.

Eventually, Newcombe did return to Nashua for the 1947 season, and as Jackie blazed the trail in Brooklyn, under the microscope, Newcombe quietly became the best pitcher in the New England League, winning 19 games while only losing 6.

In 1948, Rickey continued implementation of his wave system. He moved Campanella to St. Paul, Minnesota, the Dodgers' other Triple A affiliate, as a warm-up before promoting him to Brooklyn. Newcombe was moved up to Montreal where Robinson had starred in 1946 and Campy in 1947. Newcombe kept the string of stellar performances going by winning twenty games, but not without some controversy. During the International League playoffs, Syracuse catcher Stan West attacked Newcombe after Newk brushed him off the plate. Newcombe, not one to usually back down from a confrontation, gave proof he had been listening to Jackie, when he avoided West's rush at him and refused to fight. That same year, Dan Bankhead, who had become the first African-American to pitch in a Major League game the previous year, won twenty games for Nashua. They were the first black twenty-game winners in the minor leagues. In the playoffs, Newk won three games, and lost one (by a score of 1-0), leading his manager, Clay Hopper, (who also managed Jackie Robinson) to describe him as "the closest thing to Dizzy Dean in fifteen years." In 1948 the Cleveland Indians finally brought Satchel Paige to the Major Leagues. Don has often told me how happy he was for Satchel to finally make it, but how he wished that someone would have given Satch the chance to pitch in the majors when he was in his prime. I think Don also felt that the Dodgers took a little too long in getting him to the majors.

Newk finally made it to the majors on May 20, 1949, and it didn't take long for everyone to realize he was the real thing. On May 22nd, he shut out the Cincinnati Reds, 3-0 in his Major League debut. On July 8, 1949, when Hank Thompson of the New York Giants stepped into the batters box at Ebbets Field to face Newcombe, it was the first time in Major League history a black batter faced a black pitcher. While the significance of that moment was not lost on Newcombe, he was not concerned with being the first black to do this or that, or even the best black pitcher in the Major Leagues. He wanted to be the best pitcher in the Major Leagues. In his rookie season he took great strides toward accomplishing just that. He was selected to the National League All-Star Team, along with Jackie Robinson and Roy Campanella. Newk knew in his heart that he had been ready for the majors, and felt that his selection to the All-Star team justified that feeling. He just found it hard to believe that it was the first time Jackie was selected as an All-Star.

Newk completed 19 of his 31 starts in 1949, posted a 17-8 record, and set a new Dodger pitching record with 31 consecutive scoreless innings of work. He was selected as the National League Rookie of the Year (and he only came up to the majors on May 20th). His brilliant pitching continued in the post-season. He became the first black in the National League to pitch in the World Series, and on October 5, 1949 he matched Yankee hurler Allie Reynolds almost pitch for pitch through eight scoreless innings. Newcombe struck out eleven Yankees, walked no one and gave up only four hits, while Reynolds had nine strikeouts, giving up only two hits and four walks. Reynolds retired the Dodgers in order in the ninth, and in the bottom of the inning, the Yankees' Old Reliable, Tommy Henrich, placed a Newcombe pitch in the right field porch of Yankee Stadium to claim Game One, and the Yanks would go on to win the Series.

When Newk got to the Dodgers he began to get a better, and bitter, taste of what Jackie Robinson was going through. Don had heard racist comments and derogatory remarks before that. We all did. But at the Major League level, the stakes were much higher, and some of the best players in the world saw the infusion of players from the Negro Leagues as a threat to the jobs of existing players. Ballplayers at every level are leery of younger players coming in and taking their jobs. As players get older their reflexes tend to slow down a bit, they lose a step. The beauty of life is that there is always a next generation ready to step up during their prime, who are just a little bit faster, a little bit stronger. That situation was exaggerated when black ballplayers started to become Major Leaguers. In the past the Major Leaguers only had to worry about the next generation stepping up to the plate, but once the color line was crossed replacements could come from a whole new race, and not just rookies, but ballplayers who had been playing professionally already. No ballplayer wanted to lose his job to a new hot-shot kid. For sure, no ballplayer wanted to lose his job to a black man - someone who wasn't even allowed in the league before now. This fear on the part of Major

League players in the late 1940s and early 1950s, that they could be losing their job to a black ballplayer, was definitely an element of the integration of baseball that led to strained and difficult relations between the black and white ballplayers. It happened on the Dodgers, and when it happened it wasn't comfortable. After Jackie Robinson became comfortable at second base, the Dodgers traded Eddie Stanky, and when Roy Campanella joined the team it ended Bruce Edwards chance to be a starter, and caused the Dodgers to convert Gil Hodges to a first baseman. (Truth be told, that one worked out pretty well for Gil, who together with Don, are at the top of my list of players who should have been inducted into the Hall of Fame long ago.)

Black ballplayers were relatively unknown to the American general public. The Negro Leagues didn't get much press or attention, except from the black press and *The Daily Worker*. Were all the black players like Jackie Robinson? Were they all aggressive base runners and hustling ball players? Would they all be playing at his intensity? By virtue of the color of our skin, we were automatically banned together as a "problem" to be dealt with, over and above any racial prejudice that existed, and it did exist. Yet, all Newcombe, or Robinson, or Doby, or the rest who followed, wanted to do was play baseball, and like every athlete who has been blessed with world-class talent and who succeeds, they had a desire to compete against the very best in the world, not hidden on some back road.

Newcombe's first full season in the Major Leagues was 1950, which saw Newk get 35 starts. He improved on his rookie record and just missed becoming a twenty-game winner, getting credit for 19 wins, with four shutouts. In five relief appearances, he earned three saves. On September 6th of that year, Newcombe gave his first Major League display of his awesome arm strength and endurance. The Dodgers needed every win they could get in their pennant race against the Philadelphia Phillies and were a little short on arms. When the Dodgers went head to head with the Phils, Newcombe started both ends of a double-header against them, pitching a total of 16 innings (9 in the opener and 7 in the nightcap), and the Dodgers won both games, but still fell short in the pennant race.

The next year featured a much more memorable pennant race which saw the New York Giants climb back from thirteen and a half games out to end the season tied with the Dodgers. The teams played a best-of-three playoff that went right down to the bottom of the ninth inning of game three and climaxed with Bobby Thomson's famous "Shot Heard Round the World" off Ralph Branca ending the Dodgers' season in a sudden and dramatic fashion. Newcombe got 36 starts in 1951 and went 20-5. He pitched over 270 innings and led the league with 164 strikeouts. But that doesn't tell the whole story of Newcombe's evolution as a pitcher and his importance to the Dodgers.

Just as in 1950, the final series of the 1951 regular season pitted the Dodgers against the Phillies. This time the Phillies weren't in a position to win the National League pennant, but were poised to play the role of "spoiler." The Giants and Dodgers entered the last day of the regular season with identical 95-58 records. The day before, the Giants beat the Boston Braves in the afternoon to move one-half game ahead of the Dodgers. That night, Newcombe, pitching on two days' rest, pitched a complete game shutout against the Phillies, beating future Hall of Famer Robin Roberts. That was Newk's 20th win of the season and kept the Dodgers tied going into the last game of the regular season. On Sunday, September 30, 1951, the Giants were again facing the Braves and the Dodgers were in Philadelphia. By the middle of the sixth inning, the Dodgers were losing 8-5, when they learned that the Giants had beaten Boston. The Dodgers were now a half game back again, and had to win to force a playoff. The Dodgers tied the game in the eighth inning, and brought in Newcombe in relief. Less than twenty-four hours after shutting out the Phillies, Newk was back on the mound in a pressure situation. He was remarkable. He gave up one hit over 5 2/3 innings holding the Phils scoreless, helped by Jackie Robinson's lunging stab of a line drive by Eddie Waitkus ending the 12th inning, leaving the bases full of Phillies. Robinson again rose to the occasion with a home run in the 14th inning to win the game for the Dodgers. Newcombe had pitched 12 2/3 scoreless innings over the two nights.

Three days later, on October 3, 1951, facing the do-or-die situation of the final game of the playoffs, the Dodgers again called on Newk with only two days' rest. He got them to the ninth inning before giving up the ball to Ralph Branca, who gave up the home run to Thomson to end the season. Legions of Dodger fans remember that day with frustration and sadness. Russ Hodges' famous cry, "The Giants win the pennant! The Giants win the pennant!" is burned in their minds, as is the picture of Jackie Robinson, with his hands on his hips, watching Thomson touch all the bases, as the rest of the Dodgers head toward the centerfield clubhouse of the Polo Grounds. But actually, the Dodger organization built steam off that day. They were a force to be reckoned with for years to come.

The 1951 post-season, including the playoff series between the Dodgers and Giants, brought into focus the accomplishments of the limited number of black players that had made it to the Major Leagues. The heroics displayed by Newcombe and Robinson on the last day of the season were typical of their season-long play and their importance to the Dodgers, together with the contributions of catcher Roy Campanella, who was the National League Most Valuable Player that year. For the Giants, Willie Mays was voted the National League Rookie of the Year, and history was made in the World Series that year, when the Giants fielded Mays, Monte Irvin and Henry Thompson, marking the first all-black outfield in World Series play.

Newk remembers that heated pennant race against the New York Giants, and the way pitchers went after batters then. Don hit six batters that year, and he tells you that it had nothing to do with race. If he had to pitch inside to be effective against Willie Mays and he hit him, then so be it. And remember what Satchel Paige told me about the "titty" pitch, and he was throwing in the Negro Leagues, where everybody was black. What has now come to be seen as an act of aggression to be retaliated against was once just part of the game, an important part.

In the prime of his baseball career, Don Newcombe lost two years, 1952 and 1953, to the United States Army. This was Don's second tour of duty for our country, having served briefly in the Navy in 1943. When he returned to baseball in 1954 his rust showed. That year the Dodgers weren't very strong either, and as the Giants won the National League pennant on their way to a World Championship, Newcombe only managed to post a 9-8 record. While '54 was not a good baseball year for Newcombe, it was a crucial year in the history of the civil rights movement. The landmark case of *Brown v. Board of Education* had worked its seven-year trek through the court system to the United States Supreme Court, where lead attorney for the plaintiffs, Thurgood Marshall, Esq., argued that the equal protection guaranteed to all Americans by the Constitution was being violated, when people were made to use separate facilities and institutions based on their color. The decision finally came down, in 1954, when the Supreme Court agreed that "separate was not equal." That decision set off an enormous amount of unrest. As positive as the decision seemed on its face, there was a backlash, especially by Southern states that began to enact new statutes making discrimination legal in their states. Throughout the South people called for Chief Justice Earl Warren to be impeached and Southern states argued that states' rights should prevail over the federal decision. Baseball would be in the thick of this discussion as boys and men on playing fields made efforts to play together, while others made laws to keep them apart.

Back in Brooklyn, with a full spring training under his belt in 1955, Don Newcombe once again became a dominant pitching force in the National League. He won his first ten starts, was 14-1 at the All-Star break, and won his 18th game before he lost his second, a 1-0 heartbreaker he lost to fellow Ace, Sad Sam Jones and the Chicago Cubs. His winning percentage was .800 in 1955, as he became a twenty-game winner for the second time (20-5). Reminiscent of great Negro League pitchers who were excellent all-around athletes, Don also starred at the plate in 1955. He batted .359 with seven home runs and batted in twenty-three runs in only 117 at bats. It would also prove to be the only year that Brooklyn would win the World Championship, but the year was not without controversy for Don. He hadn't been pitching much early in the year, and manager Walter Alston promised him a start. However, the day before the scheduled start, pitching coach Joe Becker asked Don to pitch batting practice. He refused, and took it up with Alston:

> **I went in to argue it out with Alston. "Why don't you just take off your uniform and go home?" he said.**
>
> **I was steaming, "All right, I will!" I yelled, and stormed out of his office.**
>
> **When Campy saw what I was doing, he said, "Boy, don't take that uniform off. Don't ever take it off until a game's over."**
>
> **Jackie Robinson, who probably knows me better than anybody, heard about it when he came in from the field. "You know you're doing wrong," he advised me.**
>
> **But I left anyway. After I got home I received a telegram from Bavasi telling me I was suspended and would be fined.**
>
> *Don Newcombe, Saturday Evening Post, March 9, 1957*

I think this story reveals several important facts: the competitive nature of Newcombe (which may have been one of the reasons Newcombe was not selected to be the pioneer in integrating the Major Leagues), the ability for Robinson and Campanella to see the bigger picture (which may have been one of the reasons Robinson was selected as the pioneer), and the relative lack of leverage on the part of Newcombe, despite having already been a twenty-game winner. Five days after the incident, after serving his suspension, Newcombe pitched a one-hit shutout against the Chicago Cubs.

I was a teammate of Don Newcombe from 1948 to 1958. Of course, Newk's stats speak for themselves, but there's more to the man. I remember how much Roy Campanella meant to Don – Don was one of the early African-Americans in the National League, so he endured many of the indignities of those early years. Campy was able to keep him "controlled" and not let his temper upset him. Newk should be in the Hall of Fame. I know he didn't win 200 games, but he did give two years to the US Army and he was a pioneer in civil rights.
Carl Erskine, Dodger teammate

Newcombe experienced something else of importance in 1955. He witnessed prejudice against another ballplayer - a white ballplayer - who happened to be Jewish. There weren't too many Jewish baseball players at that time, probably just as many as there were blacks, and the Dodgers had a 19-year-old left-handed pitcher named Sandy Koufax who came from Brooklyn. Koufax was wild as many young pitchers were so he didn't see much playing time. But the majors had a rule stating that players who were paid a certain bonus, had to remain on the Major League roster, and couldn't be sent to the minors. So, other players were being shipped to the minors while Koufax sat on the bench not helping the team. Those who were affected, and their friends, focused on Koufax's religion and verbally abused him. It was very similar to the way blacks were getting abused and it made some of the players uneasy, especially Robinson, Newcombe and Campanella, who befriended Sandy, and Don never forgot it.

During the 1955 season, the New York Yankees became the thirteenth of the existing sixteen Major League teams, to field a black player, when Elston Howard joined the Yanks, one of the teams that Jackie Robinson had been very critical of when assessing the progress of integration in baseball. Howard had been playing for the Kansas City Monarchs, where he was a teammate of Ernie Banks. Ellie would become the first rookie to ever hit a home run in his first World Series at bat, the first black MVP in the American League and the first black coach in the American League. The Yanks got themselves a winner and a solid citizen in Howard, one of the finest gentlemen to ever play this game. But although it was a step in the right direction for the Yankees, as far as integration was concerned, there were miles to go. Howard was not able to stay with his teammates at Spring Training until the early 1960s because the Soreno Hotel where the Yanks stayed would not accommodate black players. Finally, the Yankees took a stand and moved from St. Petersburg to Fort Lauderdale to accomplish spring training integration for their team. During his first several seasons Howard also had to stay apart from his teammates in several cities while on the road. His first Yankee manager, Casey Stengel, summed up where race relations really were at in 1955 when he commented about Howard, "When I finally get a nigger, I get the only one that can't run." (Look It Up, Maury Allen, p. 172)

With Howard having made his debut with the Yankees in 1955, the Phillies, the Tigers and the Red Sox remained as the only teams to not have had a black player, nine full seasons after Jackie first played for the Dodgers. In the interim, more than sixty blacks had played in the Major Leagues, including some of the best players of their time and for years to come: Satchel Paige, Roy Campanella, Larry Doby, Minnie Minoso, Newk, Willie Mays, Ernie Banks, Hank Aaron, Orlando Cepeda, Sam Jethroe, Sandy Amoros and dozens more. Despite the success of these players, in the levels of the baseball world below the majors, additional dozens of blacks played on minor league teams, kept out of the majors by unspoken quotas, a disbelief that blacks had the intelligence to play positions like pitcher or catcher, and a general lack of acceptance on behalf of some owners, baseball executives and the populations of some cities.

In the spring of 1956, Curt Flood, who had been signed by the St. Louis Cardinals, traveled from his home in California to Tampa, Florida for spring training. His recollection of his first real encounter with discrimination is disturbing and revealing:

As I floated toward the baggage claim area, [in Tampa] I saw the drinking fountains. One was labeled "White," and the other, "Colored." For a wild instant I wondered whether the signs meant club soda and Coke. The truth stuck, like a door slammed in my face. I had heard of such drinking fountains and here they were. Thank goodness I was just passing through on my way to the Floridian and baseball. ...

[At the Floridian] a black porter emerged from behind the desk and beckoned me. I followed him through the lobby to a side door and found myself on the street. He waved me into a cab and told the black driver, "Ma Felder's."

Until it happens you literally cannot believe it. After it happens, you need time to absorb it. The black cab took me five miles out of town and deposited me at Mrs. Felder's boardinghouse. When I saw who was there – Frank Robinson and four or five other black ball players [Joe Black, Brooks Lawrence, Pat Scantlebury and Charlie Harmon] – my knees began to knock. Rules had been invoked and enforced. I was at Ma Felder's because white law, white custom and white sensibility required me to remain offstage until wanted. I was a good athlete and

might have an opportunity to show it, but this incidental skill did not redeem me socially. Officially and for the duration, I was a nigger.
Curt Flood, The Way It Is, Trident Press, New York, 1971

Back in Brooklyn, Newcombe built on the good feeling of the 1955 season to have a special season of his own in 1956. Newcombe toyed with a thirty-win season, and finished with a 27-7 record; good enough to earn him the National League Most Valuable Player Award and the Cy Young Award. The fact that Don won both of those awards is very meaningful, and symbolic. It was the very first year the Cy Young Award was given out, and at that time there was only one award given for the Major Leagues, not one per league like they do now. Merely eight seasons prior to that date, there were no black pitchers in baseball, and in 1956 when baseball decided to select ONE PITCHER as the best pitcher in the game, it was Don Newcombe, a former Newark Eagle. The Most Valuable Player Award is almost always referred to as the "MVP", but the award, originated in 1931, was formally called the "Kenesaw Mountain Landis Memorial Baseball Award" upon the death of Commissioner Landis in 1944. In fact, the award contains a 10K gold bust of Commissioner Landis. This is ironic, because many people, including Don Newcombe, strongly believe that Commissioner Landis was a racist, who had strong convictions about keeping black players out of baseball. By winning the MVP and Cy Young Awards, Newcombe became the only player in the history of the game to win those awards as well as Rookie of the Year honors. To this day, Don still holds that distinction.

While Newcombe was excelling in Brooklyn, and throughout the National League, Curt Flood had been assigned to the High Point-Thomasville team in the Carolina League, and was feeling the full sting of being a black in the South in the 1950s:

One of my first and most enduring memories is of a large, loud cracker who installed himself and his four little boys in a front-row box and started yelling "black bastard" at me. I noticed that he eyed the boys narrowly, as if to make sure that they were learning the correct intonation. Wherever we played in that league, at home or away, the stadiums resounded with "nigger," "eight ball," "jigaboo" and other pleasantries.

At Fayetteville, NC, I heard spluttering gasps: "There's a goddamned nigger son-of-a-bitch playing ball with them white boys! I'm leaving."...

Most of the players on my team were offended by my presence and would not even talk to me when we were off the field. The few who were more enlightened were afraid to antagonize the others. The manager, whose name mercifully escapes me, made clear that his life already was sufficiently difficult without contributions from me. I was entirely on my own.

We played eight games a week: every night from Monday through Saturday, plus a double-header on Sunday afternoon. Wherever we were, I lived and ate in the local equivalent of Ma Felder's. When we were in transit and the team bus made a dinner stop, I was not permitted in the dining room. I had to go to the back door of the restaurant, like a beggar. I also was barred from the rest rooms. If I needed to relieve myself, the bus would stop along the highway and I would hide from traffic as best I could while wetting a rear wheel.

What had started as a chance to test my baseball ability in a professional setting had become an obligation to measure myself as a man. As such, it was a matter of life and death.

Curt Flood, The Way It Is, Trident Press, New York, 1971

With the completion of the 1956 season, Newcombe had averaged better than twenty wins a season during his first five full seasons with the Dodgers. Newcombe's great year didn't go unnoticed, even by the President of the United States. After the Dodgers lost the World Series to the Yankees, and Newcombe failed to earn a win, thanks in no small part to bad-ball-hitting Yogi Berra, President Eisenhower sent a telegram to Newcombe, care of the Brooklyn Dodgers' front office:

I think I know how much you wanted to win a World Series game. I for one was pulling for you, but I suggest that when you think over this past season you think of the twenty-seven games you won that were so important in bringing Brooklyn into the World Series.

Eisenhower, a heroic World War II general, showed political tact in addressing the telegram to the Dodger front office, leaving it to them to decide if it would offend Newcombe.

When an athlete falls, the depth of his collapse is often gauged by his success just before the fall. If a player ages gracefully and loses his reflexes or skills, the public notices the aging process and accepts it as inevitable. But when a player falls from the heights, like Don Newcombe enjoyed in 1956, to a level of mediocrity, like the 11-12 season he posted in 1957, the drop is too noticeable to place the blame on age. If you talk to Don about it, he won't pull any punches. In the direct manner of speaking he is famous for, Don will tell you that in 1957 his abuse of alcohol caught up to him. Don has a clear recollection of the guys on the Brooklyn Dodgers who steered clear of alcohol – Gil Hodges, Pee Wee Reese and Carl Erskine – but also acknowledges that he had Dodger teammates whose drinking habits, like Don's, shortened their careers and almost shortened their lives.

Don continued to play baseball professionally until 1962. His last year in the Major Leagues was 1960 when he was my teammate and roommate with the Cleveland Indians. When no other Major League team would take a chance on Don he retired from the majors, with a .271 career batting average, and went to Japan where he played for two seasons as a first baseman with the Chunichi Dragons, and was joined by Larry Doby as a teammate. But it wasn't until 1966 that he got on his knees and swore to God that he would not drink alcohol again. Unfortunately, it had already taken its toll, and Don freely admits that in his mind it is his alcoholism that prevented him from his rightful place in Baseball's Hall of Fame.

While there might not be a plaque in Cooperstown for Don, there is no doubt in anyone's mind that he holds an important place in the history of baseball and America. Don Newcombe could have very easily been called upon by Branch Rickey to be the first black player in Organized Baseball in the Twentieth Century. He was young. He was already a professional player. He had a clean background, and he could throw a fastball that caught your attention. Life, and Branch Rickey, had other plans, but for sure, Newcombe was a charter member of the class of players that helped integrate the game and the country.

Willie Mays has been quoted as remarking: "Every time I look at my pocketbook I see Jackie Robinson." This debt is properly assigned. But all black *pitchers* of the Majors owe another, if lesser, debt to Don Newcombe as the man who blazed the way for *them*. Bob Gibson, Ferguson Jenkins, Dave Stewart and so many other men of talent and achievement have been treading in the footsteps of a trail first broken out by big Don Newcombe in 1949.
Guy Waterman, Nine, A Journal of Baseball History and Social Policy Perspective, Vol 1, No. 2, Spring 1993

We, as players, didn't necessarily understand the full impact we had on society while we were playing. Reflecting on it, it becomes more apparent, but while it was happening, it was easier for people outside of the game to appreciate our impact on society. Newcombe holds dear his memories of a very special meeting:

One day I met a man named Martin Luther King, Jr., and we became friends. He told me, "You, Jackie, and Roy will never know how much easier you made my job with what you did on the baseball field." Easier! Here was a man who would be billy-clubbed and thrown in jail, and have police dogs bite him, and have hoses directed at him. Yet we made it easier for him!
Don Newcombe, We Played The Game, 65 Players Remember Baseball's Greatest Era, 1947-1964, Edited by Danny Peary, Hyperion, New York, 1994

After Don retired from baseball he still had a very important battle left to fight – his addiction to alcohol. In his mind, although he had accomplished much during his baseball career, he felt that his career was shortened and his achievements diminished because of his alcoholism. Now that his baseball career was over, Don had to face a decision: would he allow alcohol to now shorten his life and diminish his ability to enjoy whatever he had left, or would he do whatever necessary to defeat this persistent opponent. In 1966 Don came to grips with that issue, and swore off the use of alcohol. Then, like the great competitor and leader he is, Don did something positive with his familiarity with alcohol and its destructiveness. He started speaking to young players about the dangers of addiction. Don was among the first former players to try to educate current players and prospects about alcohol and its addictive nature. For more than thirty years now, Don has been a forceful and effective speaker, educating the public about alcohol use and abuse. He has also remained close to the game and the Dodger organization, working with their community relations department.

Don Newcombe was the first successful black pitcher in Major League Baseball in the twentieth century. If we were to look only at Don's career records, without knowledge of his race, we would remark on his winning percentage, the number of years he won twenty or more games, and the fact that he is the only player in the history of the game to win Rookie of the Year honors, the Cy Young Award (the first ever given) and the Most Valuable Player Award. These are tremendous accomplishments for a Major League pitcher. The mere fact that they were achieved by a black man does not make them more special, except when you consider that no black man had ever accomplished such feats before, or had been allowed to compete. Also, Don was breaking new ground under extremely adverse conditions: having to wait his "turn" to be brought up to the majors, prohibited from rooming or eating with the team, and all of the other restrictions that existed while Jim Crow's name was allowed to remain in the lineup of Major League teams.

Don Newcombe is the one Black Ace I have the most respect for, not to say I have less respect for the others, but I have a robust respect for Don because of where he was, how it was, at that time, and what he accomplished. The respect I have for him encompasses a lot of things. He overcame alcoholism, and he overcame it with a bang, and because he also will say what he thinks. And he's just something a little bit special because he is the first African-American to win 20 games, he was the first Cy Young Award winner. He did play with Jackie Robinson on the Dodgers and Larry Doby on the Newark Eagles and he did pitch during the Satchel Paige era. So, you have to sort of look at those things and realize he is a pioneer and a very special man. That's how I look at Don Newcombe.

CHAPTER 18

SAMUEL EDWARD JONES
Sad Sam
Toothpick

Born December 14, 1925 in Stewartsville, Ohio
Died November 5, 1971 in Morgantown, West Virginia
Inducted into West Virginia Sports Hall of Fame, 1981
Teams: Orlando All-Stars, Cleveland Buckeyes,
*   Cleveland Indians, Chicago Cubs,*
*   St. Louis Cardinals, San Francisco Giants,*
*   Detroit Tigers, Baltimore Orioles*
Twenty-Win Season: 1959
Awards: National League All-Star 1955, 1959

[Sam Jones is] the pitcher I hate most to look at. Man, it's like getting into the batter's box with a snake coiled up on top.
Joe Adcock, Milwaukee Braves, The Sporting News, Sept. 3, 1958

He's got a dozen curves. He has fast curves and slow curves, about six different speeds. And they all break quick.
Dick Groat, Pittsburgh Pirates, The Sporting News, Aug., 3, 1960

"Sad" Sam was one of my teammates in St. Louis, and in my opinion, a pitcher with outstanding stuff. On given days, his curve-ball was superb and he just "froze" some very good National League hitters. Sam was also a friend off the field as well as when in uniform. We shared some good meals, laughs and good conversation.
Wally Moon

For the more casual, or younger, baseball fan, Sam Jones is probably one of the less well-known members of The Black Aces. But for those of us who played with him, and especially those who batted against him, he is an unforgettable character and pitcher. Like Jackie Robinson, Larry Doby and Don Newcombe, Sam Jones began his professional career playing in the Negro Leagues before being given a chance in the majors. However, his path to success was not as direct or short as theirs. In fact, it was more like one of Jones' legendary curveballs. Just when it looked like you knew where it was headed, it changed directions. I was lucky to have Sam's path first cross mine in 1954, when I was a young prospect for the Cleveland Indians. At that time Sam befriended me and from the first time I met him he made me feel comfortable and welcome in his presence.

Sam got the nickname "Sad Sam" much later in life, as a result of having the same name as the Sad Sam Jones who pitched for several teams in the American League, and was a twenty-game winner with the Red Sox in 1921 and the Yankees in 1923. But it didn't take long for sadness to find him as a child. Sam grew up in the Blue Ridge Mountains of West Virginia, in a poverty-stricken, mining community known as The Bottom. When he was just eleven years old, his father, Charles Jones, a coal miner, was killed in an explosion. Sam's mom did her best to provide him with a normal childhood, including sports. He attended Dunbar High School in Fairmont, West Virginia, where he played football and basketball. Oddly enough, he never played baseball until after he quit high school in his junior year and entered the Army.

It was in the Army that Sam developed the habit of chewing on a toothpick, which would later become his trademark and earn him one of his other nicknames. Actually the habit started with wooden match sticks, but Sam found that the sulphur tips were ruining his appetite so he turned to toothpicks. Over the years, Sam got so accustomed to the feel of a toothpick in his mouth that he said he felt "undressed" without one. He kept a pack of toothpicks within reach at all times; he even admitted to sleeping with one. He would limit himself to five toothpicks a day though, chewing on just one for an entire game. He became kind of a toothpick connoisseur:

They've got to be flat. They're the only kind to chew. The round ones are too hard. The flavored ones don't taste good. I've tried peppermint, cinnamon, even strawberry – they can't touch a plain old flat one.

As cheap as toothpicks were, I guess the cost can add up when you go through five a day, every day. But that didn't bother Sam. He was so identified with the toothpick that every spring the Diamond Toothpick Company provided him with a complimentary case of those "plain old flat ones" and that would last him all year.

While in the Army, Jones wasn't allowed to play for the post baseball team – that club was reserved for white players only. Sam's situation was just like that of a lot of other ballplayers in the Army. Their plight, in a way, represented the enforced segregation found in all of the armed services, which was becoming a topic of increasingly heated debate throughout the nation. Blacks were being recruited to fight the enemy and defend our country, being drafted to die on battlefields next to white soldiers, but were not allowed to socialize or live with white soldiers. There are many who believe that discussion of this issue was a significant contributing factor in the ultimate integration of baseball. But not in the Army in 1945, so Sam's play was limited to a company team that just happened to be good enough to beat the post team. It was on that team that Jones first began to pitch from time to time. Like all of us when we started, Sam wasn't really pitching at first as much as he was throwing, but it was a start. He enjoyed the game and in 1946 he began to play with the Orlando All-Stars, a town team in the Florida State Negro League.

In 1947, while playing against the Cleveland Buckeyes, Jones was spotted by Quincy Trouppe, player-manager of the Buckeyes. Trouppe liked what he saw and wanted Jones to play for the Buckeyes. He pursued him, but Jones had just filed re-enlistment papers to stay in the Army for an additional fifteen years. Trouppe was apparently as persuasive with Jones's company commander, Lt. Wilson, as he was with Jones. He convinced the lieutenant to let Sam withdraw his re-enlistment application, clearing the way for him to sign and play with the Buckeyes.

At the time, the Buckeyes featured some really talented ballplayers, including Sam Jethroe, Luke Easter, and Chet Brewer. It was with the Buckeyes that Jones' formal education as a pitcher began. Jones credited Brewer for providing a large part of that education and remembered that Satchel Paige helped him, too. He recalled a game between the Buckeyes and Monarchs, in 1947, when he beat Paige, 1-0. Jones, a 21 year old novice at the time, relied on his fast ball to carry him through that contest, primarily because it was all he really knew how to throw. After the game, Paige told Jones "You'll be a good pitcher, boy, but you got to know how to make a ball move around. You ain't going nowhere with just you and a fastball." (The Ups and Downs of Sam Jones, Dick Schaap, *Sport*, 1960) Sam also credited Paige for teaching him the curveball.

Every time we played against each other, he taught me something. I copied his throwing motion to first base, too. Underhand and easy.
Sam Jones, quoted in The Ups and Downs of Sam Jones, Dick Schaap, Sport, 1960

Jones went 6-3 with the Buckeyes in 1947, helping them win the Negro American League championship. He remained with the Buckeyes in 1948, improving to 15-9, and drew the attention of Bill Veeck's Cleveland Indians, who had already signed Doby and Paige and who were actively scouting a number of additional players from the Negro Leagues. In fact, it was in 1948, when the Indians bought fellow Buckeye, Al Smith, that Jones first began to dream of a break in organized ball for himself. Jones also kept a high profile with the scouts of Organized Baseball by playing winter ball in Panama. In the winter of 1948 – 1949, Jones played with Spur Cola, managed by Sam Bankhead of the Homestead Grays.

After two seasons in the Negro League, Jones was worried about the financial instability of the League and in 1949, he went to pitch for the "semi-pro" Rochester Orioles, of the Southern Minnesota League in Rochester, Minnesota. It was there that he really blossomed as a pitcher. He went an incredible 24-3, with five shutouts and two no-hitters. One of those no-hitters came in the final round of the league playoffs against Austin, when he struck out 15 opposing batters, a big-time performance in a big game. Although he was no longer in Cleveland, his former manager with the Buckeyes, Wilbur Hayes, kept after Indian General

Manager, Hank Greenberg, to take a look at Jones. Greenberg also liked what he saw, and signed Jones in November 1949, for a bonus reported by Jones as "Free breakfast. Bacon and eggs and a cup of coffee. That was it." At the time, Greenberg told *The Sporting News*, "He was very fast, but not only that, he had several different deliveries and each time the ball did something. He was doing things fellows in the majors hadn't learned. The Buckeyes had been trying to get us interested in Sam Jethroe and we let him get away. It could have happened with Jones if Hayes hadn't nagged us into taking a second look." After signing with the Indians, Jones again played winter ball for Spur Cola in the Panama Professional League, turning in another great performance at 10-4 with a league-leading ERA of 2.14.

In 1950, Jones played his first professional organized ball in the United States. The Indians assigned him to the Wilkes-Barre Barons of the Eastern League. Jones was instrumental in helping them win the Eastern League title. He won his first nine decisions and ended the season with a 17-8 record, having pitched 20 complete games. He led the league in strikeouts (with 169 in 219 innings), and had an ERA of 2.71. It looked like Jones was on his way to the majors and he was taking with him his major league ability to strike out opposing batters.

Based upon his performance in Wilkes-Barre in 1950, Jones was invited to the Indians' spring training in Tucson, Arizona, in March 1951. He was one of four Negro players invited to camp that year, the others being Larry Doby, Luke Easter and Harry "Suitcase" Simpson. The four of them, as well as Cuban player Orestes "Minnie" Minoso, could not stay in the same hotel as the white players. They had to live in a private home, owned by Chester Willis, a department head in a laundry operated by Bob Brickman, former Cleveland boxing promoter. As the "elder statesman" of this group of non-white players, Doby was given the responsibility of enforcing the midnight curfew and driving the players to and from the ballpark in a car provided for their use. Other than Doby, they had no supervision off the field. During that spring training camp, Jones worked with Indians' Hall of Fame pitcher, Bob Feller, and credited Feller with showing him how to mask his pitches. Feller saw something in Sam's delivery that was tipping off hitters when the curveball was coming and helped him correct that problem.

When camp broke in the spring of 1951, Jones was assigned to the San Diego Padres of the Pacific Coast League. This was at a time when black ballplayers were still a novelty in many leagues around the country, but were beginning to make inroads in others. In 1951, seven of the eight teams in the Pacific Coast League had at least one black player. Only Seattle, managed by Rogers Hornsby, had yet to integrate. Jones's efforts at San Diego continued to impress the Indians. He started his season by striking out seven of the first nine batters he faced and finished up the year again leading his league in strikeouts, with 246. Sam's record of 16-13 record and ERA of 2.76 were impressive, considering that San Diego finished in sixth place. He also led the Pacific Coast League in complete games (21), shutouts, innings pitched (267) and walks (175).

During that 1951 season, Jones was the subject of much praise:

[Jones] is the best pitcher in the minors this season.
Rogers Hornsby, Manager, Seattle

[Jones] was the best pitcher ever to have worn a Padre uniform.
David Starr, Business Manager, San Diego Padres

[Jones] is a poor man's Bob Feller.
Los Angeles Mirror

In that one game, Jones turned in the best pitching job I have ever seen.
Bryce Tangren, Publicity Director, Hollywood Stars

[Jones] has the best stuff I've ever seen in the Coast League and I go back to 1936.
Bill Jones, Manager, San Diego Padres

He was positively the greatest pitcher I've ever seen in the minor leagues.
Joe Gordon, Manager, Sacramento, Pacific Coast League

At the end of the '51 season, Jones made his Major League debut with the Cleveland Indians. He retired the only two batters he faced in his first appearance, on September 22nd, but lost his first start, against the Tigers. However, he was impressive in defeat, allowing only 4 hits in eight innings. On the basis of Jones's season in San Diego, and his brief work at the Major League level in '51, Indians' skipper, Al Lopez, predicted that Jones would be with the Indians in the majors in 1952.

Sam Lacy, writing in *The Baltimore Afro-American*, on September 25, 1951, introduced Jones to his readers with praise that would be difficult for anyone to live up to:

Take this as wishful thinking if you will, but mark well what is said here today – the Cleveland Indians may be on the verge of uncovering a colored pitcher who will nudge into the shadows the likes of Satchel Paige, the once-promising Dan Bankhead, and even the admittedly great Don Newcombe.
He is a tall, slender young man, who, at 25, is still in the process of graduating from the stage of gangliness and who, since Dec. 14, 1925, has answered to the name of Samuel Edward Jones.

During the winter of 1951-1952, Jones again played winter ball. He was the ace of the staff for San Juan in the Puerto Rican League, and was possibly the best pitcher in the league. By December 30, 1951, San Juan was in first place, with a 28-19 record, and Jones was 10-4, with 119 strikeouts. To put that achievement in perspective, Jose Santiago was second in the league, with only 72. Jones had been complaining of a sore arm, but club officials in Puerto Rico didn't believe him. Their attempted cure for Sam's sore arm was to offer him more money each time he complained. Being the competitor he was, Sam just pitched through the pain for most of the season. But, during the ninth inning of a one-hitter he was throwing on January 20, 1952, he experienced severe pain – enough to finally make him stop. So, with a record of 13-4 and leading the league with 139 strikeouts, Jones left the San Juan team in first place, and returned home to rest up for his spring trial with the Indians.

Great things were expected of Jones in 1952. In February, Hank Greenberg explained to *The Sporting News* that Jones was one reason he was very optimistic about the Indians' chances in the upcoming season:

I've studied Jones' career carefully. During the past year he pitched at San Diego, one game for the Indians and several in Puerto Rico. He undoubtedly pitched more innings than any other professional in the game last season. Yet, he was knocked out of the box only once. He's the chief reason I'm positive our pitching will hold up this year. If there's any slack, Jones is our guarantee to take it up.

When Sam reported to Tucson for spring training, the Indians and the reporters covering the team couldn't wait for games to begin so they could witness Jones' one-two punch of blazing fastballs and breaking curveballs. Unfortunately for Sam, he would have the same problem that faced Dave Hoskins a year later: trying to break into the starting rotation, the Indians' Big Four: Bob Feller, Early Wynn, and Bob Lemon, and All-Star Mike Garcia, whose records in 1951 were 22-8, 20-13, 17-14, and 20-13, respectively.

Greenberg was right on the money when he said that Jones had pitched more innings than any other professional in the game during the 1951 season. Jones pitched approximately 440 innings, **the equivalent of almost fifty complete games!** He threw 267 innings with San Diego, 9 with Cleveland and over 160 in Puerto Rico, without any appreciable rest between leagues. However, while Greenberg was hoping that the number of innings Jones pitched was a sign of his durability, it instead was a cause of his fatigue. Jones couldn't overcome his sore right arm during spring training. His injury prevented him from even being able to pitch batting practice, and the condition wasn't much better during the first half of the season. When his arm allowed him to pitch, it did not afford him any control. A little bit of wildness was always part of Jones's pitching style, keeping batters from digging in against him. But in 1952, he was wild beyond his ability to be effective. Finally, in August, the Indians sent Jones back to the minor league club in Indianapolis. The move seemed to rejuvenate Jones, who went 4-0, pitching four complete games, and in September the Indians recalled him to the Major League club. In all, Jones appeared in only fourteen games for the Indians in 1952, with a 2-3 record. His arm fatigue caused the Cleveland Indians to impose a ban on their pitchers playing winter ball. In October of 1952, Hank Greenberg, in announcing the ban, said, "Jones is a case in point. We have an investment to protect."

Earlier in the year, the Indians made another important policy decision. They integrated the housing at their spring training facility in Tucson, Arizona, and also changed the hotel they stayed at in Chicago during the season so that all of their players could live together throughout the year. They stopped using the Del Prado Hotel in Chicago, which would not accept their black players, and instead booked with the Sherry Hotel. It took four years for the team that signed the first black player in the American League, but progress was being made.

While Jones was with the Indians at the beginning of the 1952 season, his former Buckeye manager, Quincy Trouppe, had a "cup of coffee" with the Indians at the age of 39. His may have been a short stay, but it was long enough for him to be a part of another milestone in the integration of Organized Baseball. On May 3, 1952, in Washington DC, in the seventh inning of a game against the Senators, Jones came on in relief. Trouppe was behind the plate. Their appearance together that day formed the first black battery in the history of the American League.

Jones was on course to be the first effective black pitcher in the American League, considering that he had been preceded only by Satchel Paige who was admittedly well past his prime when he made it to the majors at 44 years old. But Jones' bright future with the Indians was dimmed by his inability to pitch effectively again in 1952. His sore arm, and the success of the Indians' Big Four, combined to put Sam back in the minor leagues with Indianapolis. The Indians, now leery of Jones's ability to bounce back, picked up Art Houtteman from Detroit, as a spot starter. From 1952 through 1954, the Indians' starters combined for a 242-131 record, a .649 winning percentage. Unfortunately for Jones, their success, together with his less than stellar performance in Indianapolis in 1952 (10-12), delayed his return to the majors.

While the Indians were establishing the highest winning percentage in Major League history in 1954 (eventually eclipsed by the 1998 New York Yankees, and then the 2002 Seattle Mariners), Jones was rebounding in the minors. He regained arm strength and became a dominant pitcher again. He finished the season 15-8, with an ERA of 3.78 and 178 strikeouts in 199 innings. He was voted to the American Association All-Star team, and was considered by American Association managers to have one of the best curve balls in the league.

He can beat any club on any given day. He's faster than lightning and his curve ball is really wicked. ... he's got ice water running in his veins and no one will scare him.
Eddie Stumpf, General Manager, Indianapolis

The Indians, content with their starting pitching despite having been swept by the New York Giants in the 1954 World Series, were looking for some offensive power.

So, after the 1954 season, they sent Jones, outfielder Gale Wade and $60,000 to the Chicago Cubs for home run hitter Ralph Kiner. Freed from the Indians' ban on pitching in winter ball, Jones joined the Santurce team in the Puerto Rican League, where his teammates included Willie Mays. Jones, facing Major League hitters, returned to his 1951 form and gave every indication that he was again ready to shine in the majors. He struck out 17 batters in one game, then he pitched two one-hitters within five days. On November 25, he struck out 15 against San Juan and won 2-0. Five days before that he had fanned 15 in a game against Aguadilla. By December 27, 1954, Jones had the most strikeouts in the league with 125, and his closest competitor was Ruben Gomez, with 65. Gomez already had two successful Major League seasons under his belt and was 17-9 with the New York Giants in 1954.

The spring of 1955 was reminiscent of the spring of 1952 for Jones. The Cubs were looking for him to contribute to their Major League pitching depth just as the Indians had. This time Jones produced. Although he had seen Major League action in two previous seasons, it was so limited that, at age 29, Jones was still considered a rookie when he led the Cubs staff in victories in 1955 with 14. But he also had the most losses (20), a victim of the anemic Cub offense that mired them in sixth place in the National League. Despite his losing record, Jones was a dominating pitcher in '55 and was spectacular at times. He held opposing batters to a .206 batting average and led the league in strikeouts (198), coming within seven of the all-time Cub record established by Orville Overall. He beat every other team in the National League at least once.

On May 12, 1955, Jones started a game at Wrigley Field against the Pittsburgh Pirates, and found himself on the mound in the ninth inning without having allowed a hit. Before the game, television announcer Harry Creighton told Jones that if he throws a no-hitter he will buy him a gold toothpick. Both Creighton and Jones laughed at the suggestion. No black pitcher had ever thrown a no-hitter in the Major Leagues. If history was going to be made that day, it appeared that fate would require it to be done in a dramatic way. With the Cubs leading 4-0, and Jones not having surrendered a single hit yet, he walked the first three batters in the ninth, Gene Freese, Preston Ward, and Tom Saffell, to bring the tying run to the plate. With the bases loaded and no one out Sam had to persuade Cub manager, Stan Hack, that he could close it out and should stay in the game. Hack was convinced and left the ball in his hands. Jones then proceeded to strike out Dick Groat, Roberto Clemente, and Frank Thomas, in order! Not only was it the first no-hitter by a black pitcher in the Major Leagues, it was the first no-hitter thrown in Wrigley Field since 1917 (when Jim Vaughn and Fred Tony each pitched no-hit ball for nine innings, in a game eventually determined in extra innings; back then it was called Weegman Park). Coincidentally, it was not the first no-hitter thrown by a Sam Jones. The Sam Jones who played for the Yankees authored a no-hitter in 1923 against the Philadelphia Athletics. And it should be noted that Creighton made good on his promise of the golden toothpick.

In addition to his historic no-hitter, Jones also threw a two-hitter, a three-hitter, a four-hitter and two five-hitters in 1955. In a year-end review of the season, *The*

Sporting News noted that, although Jones could be "wild and erratic," he was "nonetheless brilliant." They gave him credit for possessing "blinding speed and a curve ball that was universally acclaimed the best in the league." (*The Sporting News*, November 9, 1955) Don Newcombe had shown the world that a black man was capable of great success as a starter in the Major Leagues, and many people were now looking for Sam Jones to become the next black twenty-game winner. In fact, at one point in the 1955 season, Newcombe was 18-1, when he faced Jones and the Cubs. Jones tossed a shutout and the Cubs beat Newcombe and the Dodgers 1-0.

The euphoria over Sam's pitching prospects continued on into the spring of 1956. That April, *The Sporting News* selected Jones as the most likely twenty-game winner on the Cubs staff. Cubs' manager, Stan Hack agreed that "if Sam Jones could get better control he would be a cinch to be a twenty-game winner." (*The Sporting News*, May 2, 1956) National League batters were also weighing in with their opinions. The Dodgers' starting shortstop and Newcombe's teammate, Pee Wee Reese, said, "I think there's only one pitcher in the league who has better stuff than [Bob] Friend. He's Sad Sam Jones of the Cubs." (*The Sporting News*, May 9, 1956) The Pirates' Bill Mazeroski conceded that the best pitchers he had seen in his rookie year were Sam Jones and Don Newcombe. (*The Sporting News*, August 29, 1956) Hobie Landrith, who was Jones' catcher in Chicago in 1956, (and would later catch him in St. Louis and San Francisco), said "You've never seen a curveball until you've seen Sam Jones' curveball. If you were a right-handed hitter, that ball started out a good four feet behind you."

In 1956, Jones displayed the fastball and curve ball that everybody was raving about and repeated his 1955 success as National League strikeout king, with 176. His average of 8.38 strikeouts per game was highest by a starting pitcher in modern times, besting Johnny Vander Meer's previous record of 8.05 with the Cincinnati Reds in 1941. Unfortunately, the Cubs didn't have much else going for them in 1956. They were near the bottom of the National League in team batting average, and were weak defensively. Jones won 9 games, and lost 14. Bob Rush was the only starting pitcher with a winning record (13-10). A young Ernie Banks, at 25, and an aging Monte Irvin, at 37, hit .297 and .271 respectively, to provide most of the offense, such as it was. The Cubs only managed to win 60 games and fell to the cellar in the National League.

In the fall of 1956, Jones barnstormed on Willie Mays's All-Negro All-Star team that included Frank Robinson, Hank Aaron, Harry Simpson, Al Smith, Hank Thompson, Gene Baker, Elston Howard, Charlie White, Brooks Lawrence, Joe Black, Connie Johnson, Monte Irvin and Jim Pendleton. They played a 33 game schedule against a team of minor league and Negro League players. They toured throughout the South, including Texas, and they finished up with four games on the west coast. Sam returned from the barnstorming tour to learn that the Cubs had traded him, together with his catcher, Hobie Landrith, to the St. Louis Cardinals. Jones and pitcher Tom Poholsky, who went from St. Louis to Chicago, were the key men involved in the trade.

Sometimes a trade gives a ballplayer new life – a fresh start and a chance to succeed in a new place. I remember Al Oliver telling me that when he was traded from the Pittsburgh Pirates, he requested uniform number "0" to remind him that he was starting over, and he had great seasons, both before and after he was traded. Several of the Aces had their twenty-win season after they were traded, including me. The trade to the Cardinals seemed to have the same kind of beneficial effect on Sam Jones and the Cardinals. Jones gave some of the credit to his use of Satchel Paige's snake oil, the same mysterious concoction that the Kansas City Monarchs trainer, Frank "Jewbaby" Floyd, had used to restore Satchel's arm. Whether it was the trade or the snake oil, sportswriters, opponents and baseball executives were singing Jones's praises over the next two seasons as one of the best pitchers in the Major Leagues:

> **The pride and joy of the staff, however, continued to be Emperor Jones, the fast-firing righthander with the jug-handle-curve. Sam, biting back the discomfort of an arthritic right elbow, suffered the pain of a stabbing defeat, July 23, in the opener of a three-week home stand. But once more he was masterful and overpowering in the three-hit game he dropped to the Dodgers, 1 to 0. Reducing his season's earned run average to an even 3.00, the giant Jones had yielded only seven tallies over a stretch of 49 innings during which he issued just ten walks and fanned 43. The big guy, so often troubled by lack of control in the past, has become magnificent since he zeroed into the strike zone, and for the first 111 inning this season, he'd passed just 36 batters and whiffed 97.**
> *Bob Broeg, The Sporting News, July 31, 1957*

> **In Sam Jones, they've got the best pitcher in the league right now.**
> *Red Schoendienst, Atlanta Braves, quoted by Ted Chapman,*
> *The Sporting News, August 14, 1957*

> **While the Redbirds fell flat in July, big Sam Jones refused to be affected by the distressing slump. The six-foot-four, toothpick-chomping Jones had a perfect 4-0 record in July, beating Los Angeles, Cincinnati, Milwaukee, and the Phils. His record would have been 5-0 except for two unearned runs which prevented him from winning the July 29 game in Philadelphia.**
> **During Jones' all-winning streak, he allowed only eight earned runs in 47 innings and lowered his earned-run rating to a league-leading 2.80 average. With better hitting support, Sam would have had a more impressive won-and-lost record than 8-7.**
> *Jack Herman, The Sporting News, August 6, 1958*

> **The ugly duckling turned into a graceful swan, the cow jumped over the moon – and Sam Jones became a control pitcher.**

Wherever comrades of the toe plate labor in baseball's salt mines, seeking the direction finder that would end their exile, the metamorphosis of Mr. Jones must represent an inspiration. After all, how much wilder could a pitcher be than the man who broke managers' hearts and bases-on-balls records?

If the left-at-the-post Cardinals survive the cut-throat competition to win the National League pennant, it'll be because the Jones who couldn't win at Chicago has combined control and winning so handsomely at St. Louis that he just might be, believe it or not, one of the league's best pitchers and one of its steadiest.

Bob Broeg, The Sporting News, August 20, 1958

The Phillies rate Jones as the toughest pitcher to bat against in the National League because of his wicked curve ball. But last night the veteran had a hopping fast one as his main mound weapon. ... [Richie] Ashburn had open admiration for Jones. "I don't know how this fellow ever loses a game," he said.

Ray Kelly, The Evening Bulletin, August 2, 1958

Many batters call him the toughest to hit in the league and rate his curve as the best since Sal Maglie was in his prime.

Arthur Daley, The New York Times, September 14, 1958

"I've always had trouble hitting against him," said [Stan] The Man [Musial]. "I'm glad he's on our side."

Del Ennis and other Cardinals agree. In fact, Emperor Jones would win – by several landslides – any poll to select "The Pitcher I'd Most Hate to Face."

Bobby Young, an old Brownie now with the Phillies, said, "I'd hate to have to make a living batting against that Jones every day." Other enemy players call Jones "inhuman," then threaten to hide behind water coolers when they're due to bat.

Neal Russo, The Sporting News, September 17, 1958

In fact, the Cardinals' weak hitting (sixth in the eight team league) and weak defense (last in the league in fielding average) did not allow them to survive the competition in 1957 or 1958, and the Milwaukee Braves won the National League pennant in both of those years. But Jones had steadily improved and was among the league leaders in many pitching categories. In 1958, he had the second lowest ERA in the National League (2.88), led the league in fewest hits per nine innings pitched (7.34), and, for the fourth year in a row, the highest average number of strikeouts per nine innings in the National League (8.10). In 1958, Sam also broke Dizzy Dean's Cardinal team record for strikeouts in a season, recording 225 whiffs, which was also good enough to lead the National League. He was the first National League pitcher in 17 years to record more than 200 strikeouts, and his name was mentioned among the elite pitchers in consideration for the 1958 Cy Young Award, together with Warren Spahn, Whitey Ford, Bob Turley, Bob Friend, Billy Pierce and Lew Burdette. (The Award was won by Turley, who was also the winner of the Hickok Athlete of the Year Award in 1958.)

In January of 1959, the Cardinals rewarded Sam with "a substantial increase" in salary. But, before the end of spring training, they then traded him and Don Choate to the San Francisco Giants for Bill White and Ray Jablonski. The Cardinals knew they were parting with a good pitcher, but they felt it was worth the gamble to trade the 33-year-old Jones for the 25-year-old White who had joined the Giants in 1958 after coming out of the service. For a few years, the naysayers were whispering the same things about Jones that they had been saying about Newcombe: he can't win the tough ones. The Giants didn't believe it. From their standpoint, it was viewed as one of the biggest trades they had made in years, acquiring the league's strikeout leader for a prospect. Giants' General Manager, Horace Stoneham, saw Jones as the missing piece that could give the Giants the pennant. Giants' Manager, Bill Rigney, was equally optimistic:

Rigney did everything but turn handsprings when the deal was completed. … "This is the biggest pitching deal we've made in the five years since I've been manager," Rigney said. "I never did have a real fourth starter before. Now I've got one."
Jack McDonald, The Sporting News, April 1, 1959

The Giants didn't win the National League pennant in 1959, although they came awfully close and Jones had a wonderful season. His transformation from a no-control pitcher who led the league in losses in 1955 to a dominant pitcher was complete. In 1959, Sam Jones was voted to the National League All-Star team, and was first or second in the National League in six pitching categories, including wins (21), shutouts (4), and ERA (a career-best 2.82). The latter accomplishment also had some historical significance, baseball-wise, as Jones became the first African-America to win an ERA title in the Major Leagues. It was a long, circuitous route, but on September 12, 1959, while pitching for his fourth Major League team, Sam Jones joined the ranks of The Black Aces, with his twentieth win of the season. It was the first ever twenty-win season by a San Francisco Giant pitcher, and that win also put the Giants in first place, temporarily.

Sam's twentieth win came on his wife Mary's thirty-first birthday. Jones had called her that morning, promising the twentieth victory as a birthday present for her. After the game, Sam said that, except for it being his wife's birthday, the game didn't feel any different from those that resulted in his nineteenth or eighteenth win. He said, "The only time I'll be happy is when we win the pennant. Then I'll be real happy." Sam gave the game ball from his twentieth victory to Johnny Bushman, an 11-year-old boy who was partially crippled by polio and wore leg braces. Sam had met Johnny earlier in the year when he was on the edge of a crowd of kids trying to get Willie Mays' autograph, and his disability put him at a disadvantage in getting close to Willie. Jones stepped up to the boy and introduced himself and they became quick friends. Sam grew fond of the boy because he was so "well-mannered." Over the course of the season, Sam would often give Johnny a ride home, and Sam kept in contact with the young Bushman.

After the 1959 season, Rigney remained just as high about Jones:

"Before we got Sam," says Bill Rigney, the San Francisco manager, "I'd heard rumors that he was tough to handle, that he had trouble winning big games. I was a little worried. But the rumors were all wrong. He was as willing to work as anybody I've ever seen. He was a great competitor. I don't know what we would have done without him."

The Ups and Downs of Sad Sam, by Dick Schaap, Sport Magazine

Jones's season was one to remember. On June 30, he narrowly missed the second no-hitter of his career when official scorer, Charlie Park, ruled that a ball hit by Junior Gilliam and bobbled by Giants' shortstop, Andre Rogers, was a hit rather than an error. It was the only "hit" in the game against Jones, a 2-0 win against Don Drysdale that moved the Giants within half a game of league-leading Milwaukee. Later that season, on September 26, with three games left in the season and the Giants needing to win all three to force a playoff for the pennant, Jones pitched and again did not allow a hit in a seven-inning rain-shortened win against the Cardinals.

When Sam recorded his twentieth victory, his record was 20-12. At that point, Rigney not only relied on Jones to start, but to be his closer on days when he wasn't starting. In September his arm tired a bit, costing him three straight decisions. In all, he appeared in 50 games in 1959, starting 35 of them. He pitched sixteen complete games. Jones finished fifth in the National League MVP voting, ahead of teammate Willie Mays and was the only National League pitcher to receive an MVP vote that year. Milwaukee Brave catcher, Del Crandall, recognized what a great year that Sam had when he commented, "There was a glaring mistake in the vote for Most Valuable Player. They gave it to Ernie Banks, but it belonged to Sam Jones. Sam won it going away." Sam also lost out in the Cy Young Award voting, finishing second to Early Wynn, who was then with the Chicago White Sox. At the time there was only one Cy Young Award given, leading *The Sporting News* to editorialize:

The success of Early Wynn of the Chicago White Sox in winning the Cy Young Award for 1959 brings out forcibly a point *The Sporting News* has made in the past. The Cy Young Award should be duplicated in each league and it should have equal status with the Most Valuable Player Award.

There can be no quarrel with Wynn's election. He was the strong man of a good pitching staff which led the White Sox to their first pennant

in 40 years. Wynn had competition for the Young award from only one man, Sam Jones, who pitched valiantly, in and out of turn, but futilely in an effort to give the Giants a pennant. There was no other pitcher even close in the competition.

As matters stand now, Jones will get little or no recognition for a brilliant effort. Nobody ever remembers for long who finished second in any race. Yet the balloting proves that he was the outstanding pitcher in the National League in 1959.

The Sporting News, November 4, 1959

Sam did win some recognition though: He was selected as the Outstanding Pitcher of the National League on polls conducted by United Press International and *The Sporting News*, and was chosen the Most Valuable Giant for 1959 in two different polls, one by the Giants' Booster Club and one by *The San Francisco Examiner*.

In the winter of 1959, Jones again joined The Willie Mays All-Negro All-Star barnstorming team, along with Don Newcombe, Frank Barnes, Piper Davis, and my good friend, Earl Battey. Bob Gibson remembers

The black squad traveled in a caravan of cars, staying and eating along the way in black neighborhoods. It wasn't always easy to get what we needed and occasionally we resorted to gimmicks, such as sending somebody into a white restaurant wearing a chauffeur's cap. Sam Jones could sometimes pass for white if he wore a hat and didn't say much. So he'd pull a stocking cap over his ears and pretend to be a deaf-mute, ordering hamburgers with sign language.

Stranger to the Game, The Autobiography of Bob Gibson, by Bob Gibson with Lonnie Wheeler, Viking Penguin, NY 1994

It may be a little difficult for young readers today to fathom this situation, but the man who was unquestionably the "outstanding pitcher in the National League in 1959" would have to pose as a white, deaf-mute in order to be served a hamburger in this country.

Sam was rewarded for his twenty-win season with a contract for 1960 that netted him an annual salary of $30,000, the most Sam had ever earned for a season's work. His success on the mound even earned Sam something a little more elusive for a black ballplayer in 1960 season, an endorsement contract with Wilson Sporting Goods Company to help market their A2000 glove.

Sam started the 1960 season just as strong as he finished 1959. On April 12, 1960, Sam started and won the first Major League game ever played at Candlestick Park, beating the Cardinals, 3-1, throwing a three-hitter in front of a capacity crowd that included Vice-President Richard M. Nixon. Later that month, Sam carried another potential no-hitter into the eighth inning against the Cubs, only to give up a home run to pinch hitter, Walt Moryn, with two out. In that same game, Sam ran his career strikeout total to an even 1,000. By the beginning of June, he had thrown a one-hitter, a two-hitter, two three-hitters, a four-hitter and a five-hitter, plus two shutouts. A winless drought during much of July kept Sam from winning twenty again, although many predicted he would. But there were still moments of Sad Sam magic. For instance, in late August, Sam struck out fourteen Phillies in a game, twelve on called third strikes. After that game, Hobie Landrith said, "Jones had the best curve ball I ever saw. It was exploding. At times I felt sorry for those Phillies batters."

Although Sam knew that winning a pennant as a team was more important than his winning twenty games as an individual, reaching the twenty-win mark was still on his mind. This became apparent on September 12, 1960, when Sam got into a heated discussion with Giant manager, Bob Stevens, who removed Sam for a pinch-hitter in the eighth inning of a game he was losing by a run with a runner on first and no one out. Sam said, "How the hell can a guy win twenty games if he gets taken out? Besides I can bunt as well as any guy on the club." Sure enough, Sam did miss the twenty-win mark, but had a successful 18-14 season. After the season, Sam joined 21 of his Giant teammates on a barnstorming tour of Japan. It was Sam's second trip to Japan in three years, having gone there with the Cardinals in 1958.

Sam was strong again in the spring of 1961 to the delight of new Giant manager Alvin Dark, and *The Sporting News* again selected Sam as the Giant pitcher most likely to be a twenty-game winner in the upcoming year. Sam did pitch well in April, but it might have been a sign of things to come when, on April 28, 1961, he lost 1-0 to the Braves when Warren Spahn threw a no-hitter against him. For the second season in a row, after a fast start, Sam had a July slump. He went from June 17 to July 16, 1961 without starting a game, being used only in relief. He only started 17 games the whole year, and finished the season with a disappointing 8-8 record.

Fearing that Sam had passed his prime, the Giants left him unprotected in the expansion draft in October 1961, and he was selected by the Houston Colt 45s. But, during the winter meetings, Sam was traded to the Detroit Tigers and took his toothpick, his curveball and the rest of his repertoire with him back to the American League. The Detroit brass, including former catchers, Rick Ferrell (a club Vice-President) and Bob Scheffing (Manager), were very excited and optimistic about the depth and experience that Jones brought to the Tiger pitching staff. Unfortunately, for Jones and the Tigers, the team's optimism was dealt a harsh dose of reality when Jones was diagnosed with cancer, a "low-grade malignancy" at the lymph glands in his throat and neck, in February and had to undergo X-ray treatments.

His competitive nature drove Jones to continue to train while undergoing treatment, and he took the time away from active duty as an opportunity to learn a new pitch, a slider, from teammate Frank Lary. He made it back to the mound for the Tigers in June and, in his third start as a Tiger, earned his first victory, 2-1, over the White Sox on July 2. In all, Jones only started six games for the Tigers in 1962, and appeared in a total of 30 games, posting a 2-4 record. Sam still had something going for him, though. In 81 innings of work, he struck out 73 batters, an average of better than 8 strikeouts per nine innings.

I can well remember a very embarrassing moment facing Sad Sam in Detroit one Sunday afternoon. By him having this reputation of being a guy that would knock you down, anything you see heading at your body you have a tendency to get down. You don't wait until it plucks you. So this particular day Sad Sam uncorked one of those round house curveballs and it started straight at me, and I just bailed out. I didn't pick up the rotation. I thought it was a fastball coming right at me, not a curve. I'm flat on my back and I hear the umpire holler, "Strike!" I look up and get ready to say, "You got to be out of your cotton picking mind" and the umpire said, "Don't you dare say one word. You didn't even see anything. You were flat on your back."
Ed Charles interview

In addition to his medical problems, which he fought with courage, Sam suffered a hip infection in August 1962 following an automobile accident in West Virginia, which effectively ended his season. Then, a few days before the season ended the Tigers released Sam outright, actually bringing his short tenure with the Tigers to a close. He would not get another start in the Major Leagues.

Sam rebounded to pitch during the winter of 1962-63, while he tried to hook up with a team for the 1963 season. Sam's first choice was to work with Bill Rigney, his old Giant manager, who was now managing the Angels. Sam had his best year under Rigney in 1959 and Rigney had great admiration for Sam. Rigney was able to get Sam invited to spring training with the Angels in '63 on a "look-see" basis. Sam suffered a sprained ankle which landed him on crutches, and eventually even Rigney couldn't convince Los Angeles ownership to take a risk on him. In the first week of April they let him go. Rigney even tried to get Sam placed on a team in Japan, where many players past their prime in the Major Leagues were still playing ball. As the season started, Sam was still without a Major League team, but the Braves were willing to offer him a minor league contract and assign him to their AAA team in Toronto. Sam accepted and made the most of it. By July, the Cardinals, who were in the middle of the pennant race, acquired Sam and assigned him to their AAA team in Atlanta. On July 13, 1963, at the age of 37, Sam pitched seven and two-thirds innings of hitless relief to win both games of a doubleheader for Atlanta. In early August, the Cardinals called Sam back to the Major Leagues. By then he had compiled a 9-4 record in AAA, recording 97 strikeouts in 84 innings, an average of more than 10 strikeouts per 9 innings. A poll of AAA managers named Sam as having the best curveball in that minor league. However, despite recording two victories for the Cardinals during the pennant stretch, without any defeats, Sam only pitched 11 innings in 11 relief appearances, and was released outright at the end of the season by the Cardinals who had fallen short in the pennant race.

Sam remained determined to pitch. During the winter of 1963-64, Sam went to the Dominican League, and pitched for Aguilas Cibaenas. Sam was very effective in the Dominican, playing against future Major League stars, including

Juan Marichal, Bob Veale, Gaylord Perry and Willie Stargell. However, when spring rolled around, none of the Major League teams were willing to place Sam on their roster. Eventually, the Pirates agreed to give Sam a minor league contract and he pitched for Columbus of the International League in AAA. He debuted on April 26, 1964, appearing in both ends of a doubleheader, retiring all ten batters he faced. Sam was named to the International League All-Star team as one of the top relievers in the league. By August 31, he had pitched 82 innings in 52 appearances, all in relief, with a 1.65 ERA. The Baltimore Orioles purchased his contract from Columbus bringing him up for the last month of the season. Sam appeared in seven games for the Orioles, pitching nine innings, with a 3.00 ERA and no decisions. He was released after the season, and would not pitch in the Major Leagues again.

Sam returned to Columbus in the International League where he was a player-coach for an additional three seasons. He had hoped to become a coach at the Major League level, looking for some financial security for his family, but it was not meant to be. The Major Leagues were not really ready yet to open their arms to blacks as coaches. However, Columbus was happy to have Sam back. Larry Shepard, manager of the Columbus Jets, said:

Sad Sam Jones can be as important to this club as Diomedes Olivo was to our 1961 champions. The only reason we have Jones is that most major league managers have a phobia about a pitcher's age.

Shepard proved to be correct. Columbus went on to be International League champions in 1965, and Jones was named the International League's Most Valuable Pitcher. He posted a 12-4 record and 22 saves, and compiled a 3.04 ERA in 77 innings, appearing in 58 games. Sam pitched two more years for Columbus and retired from pro ball after the 1967 season when he was released by Columbus.

In 1971, the cancer that Sam had appeared to have conquered reappeared. He continued to fight but was losing ground, and weight. As the massive tumor took over Sam's body, his weight dropped from 225 pounds to 130. In June, he was admitted to the hospital. By October 1971, word of Sam's terminal illness reached Johnny Bushman, the young man he had befriended in 1959, who at the time was a 23 year old college student still living in San Francisco. Johnny, who had overcome polio but was still using a brace, and whose own father had just died from cancer, boarded a plane and headed to West Virginia to see his hero, Sam. In his luggage, he packed a brand new baseball. He remembered what an impact it had on him when Sam had singled him out from the crowd and gave him the game ball from his twentieth win, and he was about to return the favor. Sure enough, when Johnny got to the hospital to see Sam, he brought the ball with him and gave it to his idol with a hug. Sam's wife, Mary, remembered that Sam was really not an emotional man but, when Johnny showed up and handed him the ball, Sam began to cry. Johnny stayed with the family for a while, and on November 5, 1971, Sam Jones died of cancer at the age of 45.

In 1981, the West Virginia Sports Hall of Fame acknowledged the life and career of Sam Jones, and his contributions to sport, by inducting Sam; a fitting tribute to one of its greatest athletes.

CHAPTER 19

JAMES TIMOTHY GRANT
Mudcat
Coochee

Born August 13, 1935 in Lacoochee, Florida
Teams: Cleveland Indians, Minnesota Twins,
          Los Angeles Dodgers, Montreal Expos,
          St. Louis Cardinals, Oakland Athletics,
          Pittsburgh Pirates
Twenty-Win Season: 1965
Inducted into Reading (Pa.) Baseball Hall of Fame - 2004
Inducted into Cleveland Hall of Fame – 2005
Inducted into Pasco County (FL) Hall of Fame - 2005

**I always felt good playing second base behind Mudcat! From the first
day I met him, I felt comfortable because of the way he accepted me
and as a rookie it was like I'd been there for years. But as I got to
know Mud I realized the depth of the man and all he had overcome,
and what he had accomplished in just getting to the Big Leagues.
What really amazed me were his genuine talents in so many areas
outside the game and his concern for people.**
Frank Quilici, teammate with Minnesota Twins

As you might imagine, this chapter has been the hardest one to write. Sharing
my thoughts with you about some of the greatest pitchers and players to ever play
the game of baseball, many of whom I had the pleasure to watch and to play with
or against, was much easier than trying to condense my life experiences into one
chapter; not just from a writing point of view, but also from an emotional point of
view. My life has been so full and blessed, and I have been so active living it that
taking the time to look back on all that I have seen and experienced has actually
caused me some personal amazement. From my roots in Lacoochee I had no
expectation, no reason to have any expectation, that I would come into contact
with presidents and world leaders, would visit foreign countries, would play in the
World Series, and would experience all the things I did.

Just as baseball was the force behind my first being able to venture outside of
Lacoochee, it was also what enabled me to discuss politics with John Kennedy,
to talk about the civil rights movement with Martin Luther King, Jr., to visit Viet
Nam, to meet thousands and thousands of Americans and share their love for the
game and their country, and to experience so much more. It started on a field in

Lacoochee, where my uncle, Thaddeus Black, one of the best shortstops in the state of Florida, was a starter for the local semi-pro black team, the Lacoochee Nine Devils. There was also a white team called the Lacoochee Nine Devils, but there was no integrated play. Whites didn't play on black teams and whites didn't play against black teams. It was that way in school too. We played in the Florida State Negro League which was like the minor league of the Negro Leagues. Other black teams included the St. Petersburg Pelicans (who Ed Charles played for), Bradenton Nine Devils, Orlando, and the Pepsi-Cola Giants from Tampa.

Because of Uncle Thaddeus, I was the batboy for the Nine Devils from the time I was about eight or nine years old. The other players on the team sort of adopted me as one of their own, and they each showed me how to play their positions. Uncle Thaddeus gave me a three finger glove which I cherished. In fact, I still had it when I tried out for the Indians in 1954.

Before Jackie Robinson was signed, the Nine Devils players would let me take a little batting practice. They let me just slide in there to catch some balls and that kind of stuff, but once he signed then they paid way more attention to me. One time I would go out in the field at shortstop with Uncle Thaddeus, next time I was at third base with Plunk Kelly, then at first base with Fats Richardson. By the time I was 13 or 14, I was playing regularly, mostly third base or shortstop, and I pitched every now and then. Some of the other guys on the team were 18 or 19, but most were in their twenties and some were 35 or 40. They'd give me $10 a game. If I hit a home run they'd pass the hat, and I made another $5 or so.

Mom never wanted me to play ball on Sundays, but I was an integral part of the team. So, Reverend Embry of the Mount Moriah Baptist Church would let me keep my uniform in the parsonage. In the middle of preaching, even if it was one of his most domineering, exciting sermons, it would hit him that the game was about to start. He would gaze down at his watch, look over at me and then turn his head as if to say, "scoot out of here." And I would go to the parsonage, put on my uniform and sprint down to the field which was a couple of hundred feet away. Some of the fans would always be looking out for me over the top of the center field bleachers, waving their hat to let the team know I was coming and I would immediately get put in the game.

From the time I was eight or nine I dreamed of playing baseball. Because of the ban on blacks in the Major Leagues I had no expectation that I could play anywhere but the Negro Leagues. But that didn't stop me from dreaming, although it was almost like you weren't allowed to expect that the dream was going to come true. When I was eight or nine, for a black boy in Lacoochee to dream that he was going to the majors was like dreaming you are going to win the lottery. You would have no right to expect it to come true. But a few years later, after Jackie Robinson and Larry Doby signed, the sun shone a little brighter on my dreams; now I had a chance, an opportunity for my dream to come true, everything kind of changed. For me personally, my dream changed from wanting to play in the Negro Leagues to wanting to play in the majors. We knew the moment that Jackie signed that the opportunity was now there for blacks to play in the Major Leagues. We didn't know when another black would be signed but the opportunity would be there and that's when everything else came into play – the patience that you learned, the blessing, the fortitude, the strength.

The signing of Jackie and Larry made a huge impact at the time it happened, in terms of accomplishments by black men. When they first signed we didn't figure that it meant there would be an influx of black ballplayers all of a sudden leaving the old Negro Leagues to go the majors. We knew the change would not be that sudden. It was more of a feeling of accomplishment that we got one, and when Larry Doby signed we said, oh boy, we got two now, and we looked to see what was going to happen a little bit later. The thought pattern of most of us was that there would still be limitations in terms of the opportunities, but the opportunities were there. We waited for other blacks to be signed for the opportunity to be even bigger. You could only gauge opportunities, especially back in those days, in time. You couldn't gauge them in terms of right now.

Another thing to remember about the signings of Jackie and Larry, is although the impact was huge, and the chance for blacks to play in the majors was shown to be a possibility, it didn't change things in our day to day life. The tracks still separated the white and black sections of Lacoochee, blacks still couldn't go to white schools or drink from white water fountains, and the great Dr. George Washington Carver still couldn't stay in a white hotel. It was a limited great thing that happened, but a great thing nonetheless.

With my dream to play professional baseball still paramount in my mind, my other dream was to become the first one in my family to attend college, hopefully on a sports scholarship. Beside my baseball ability, I was an All-Florida quarterback in 1952 and 1953 and I was also chosen as an All-Florida forward in basketball. My desire to attend college played very well with my Mom who always stressed education. I attended high school at Moore Academy and in my senior year, 1953, we were state baseball champs. During my high school years I continued to play with the Nine Devils and although I didn't know it, I was being watched by Major League scouts from when I was 15. That same year, I got to meet Larry Doby, when he and the Jackie Robinson All-Stars were barnstorming in the area around Tampa, Florida. I was a kid playing on the Florida All-Star Team that played against them. Tampa was one of the places the barnstorming teams came to play; they also played in Miami, in Georgia, and in Alabama. They played about 30 games when they were barnstorming. Whenever they played against the Satchel Paige and Bob Feller All-Stars it was always a sell-out. And that was during the days when blacks had to sit in the bleachers; they couldn't sit in the grandstands, so when the barnstorming team came around, we sort of took over the ballpark. We could sit where we wanted to sit.

Actually, at that time, getting to meet Jackie Robinson or Larry Doby or Don Newcombe was more impressive and important than playing in the game. I saw Jackie and I wanted to talk with him, but he was too busy for me to get close to him. One of the other players said to me, "Well, don't worry about it. You'll get a chance to talk to him a little bit later" and when I looked up it was Larry Doby talking to me. I also got a chance to see some greats like Goose Tatum and Willie Wells and Satchel play in those barnstorming games.

When I was still fourteen years old I got to travel with the Nine Devils to Sylvester, Georgia to play the Sylvester Bulldogs in the Piney Woods League playoffs. After eight innings of play we were ahead by one run and I had struck out about 16 batters already. I was standing next to my manager, Hercules Smith, when this character wearing a raincoat motioned the two of us to come toward him. He had a shotgun under his raincoat and he told us he didn't think we should win since he bet on the other team. When I went out to the mound I continued to pitch the only way I knew and I struck out the first two batters. With that, Smith came to the mound, and called a team meeting. He told the rest of the players what was happening and he instructed me to walk the bases full, giving him time to pack the equipment bags, and relaxing the trigger man. That is exactly what I did and then I threw three fast ones past the next batter to end the game. As prearranged, as soon as I let the last pitch go we all ran for the bus. I didn't wait for the batter to swing or the redneck to shoot. We got in the bus, which was running and we all hit the floor as the driver took off heading for Route 401 South and the safety of Lacoochee. Sure enough, buckshot was tearing at the back window as we drove out of Sylvester.

I am two years older than Mudcat and I remember that in my senior year in high school everybody was talking about this kid from Lacoochee who was striking everybody out and was smoking the ball at the plate. Then I had a chance to go down there to play against him and I realized he was striking everybody out because the lights were so poor nobody could see the ball. But seriously, James was a very talented player as a teenager and had everybody talking about him in that area.
Ed Charles interview

I don't know about the hitters not being able to see my pitches because of the lights but I know there was one catcher who couldn't catch the pitches I was throwing. That was at a state high school tournament for black players down in Daytona, and every ball that the catcher missed hit the umpire flush in the chest. Actually, that turned out to be a very good thing for me because the umpire was former Major Leaguer, Fred "Bonehead" Merkle, who was a birddog scout for the Indians at the time. Merkle knew from the impact of the pitches hitting him that I had the arm strength to be in the majors and without my knowledge Merkle recommended to the Indians that they bring me into camp for a tryout. (Merkle got the nickname "Bonehead" because in a crucial game in 1908 between Merkle's Giants and the Cubs, he failed to touch second base on a potential game-winning hit and while he was celebrating, the Cubs' secondbaseman, Hall of Famer, Johnny Evers, stepped on the base ending the inning. When the game was replayed, Merkle's team lost, costing them the pennant.)

By the time I was 16 the Boston Braves tried to sign me. The Nine Devils played the prisoners in Raiford Prison every Saturday morning, and one of the warden's friends was a Braves scout. During one of our visits to the prison in 1951, the scout came into our dugout and said to me, "We like what we see. How would you like to play professional ball?" The guys started crowding around and I said, "Yeah, I'd like to play." So, he pulled out this long contract, with all these pages. I signed it and he filled out the rest and when he got to where it said "Age" I said "16." I saw his eyes get real big, and he said, "Wait a minute. You're only 16? Excuse me" and he took the contract and ripped it up.

That incident spurred my belief that I could make it to the majors, but unaware that Merkle had recommended me to the Indians, after I graduated high school I headed off to college at Florida A & M University in Tallahassee to pursue a course of study so I could become an English teacher. Because of my baseball ability I had a partial scholarship and I worked as a carpenter's assistant to raise the balance of my tuition. I was in the university library one day and I was looking through a book that contained information on what salary you could expect to make in all of the various professions. It listed the salary for black teachers at about $3000 a year. That sort of settled it for me. The Cleveland Indians had a camp in Daytona Beach, called Indianville, and I was going to find my way into that camp in the spring of 1954. In February of that year I left the college and went to work with my uncle as a carpenter's assistant in New Smyrna Beach, to get a little closer to Daytona, both geographically and economically. What I didn't know is that the Indians were trying to find me.

I was hammering in a roof when I saw my coach, Hiram James Goodwin, drive past the site a few times. I climbed off the roof and hailed him down. He told me the Cleveland Indians had a scout up at Florida A & M trying to find me. Merkle had told them about me and they were interested in taking a look at me that spring. Coach Goodwin said we had to get to Indianville as soon as possible. On the way we drove past Bethune-Cookman College, one of the famous historic black colleges, to pick up Bunky Mathews, a college football coach, who was Mr. Goodwin's ex-teammate, and I got to meet Mary McLeod Bethune, the founder of the college, who had spoken at my high school several times.

When we arrived at Indianville the three of us watched the players taking batting and fielding practice. Every so often Mr. Goodwin or Mr. Mathews would say to me, "Could you do that?" and I would say, "Yeah, I could do that." Afterwards, we approached Mike McNally, the Indians Farm Director who was running the practice. When the coaches introduced me he said, "We got Laddie Placek, our head scout, up at Florida A & M looking for you. You're the guy Fred Merkle has been talking about. He really likes you and we want you to come back in about three weeks when the other lower minor leaguers are coming to camp." At that point, Indian General Manager Hank Greenberg came by and joined the conversation. He told McNally that since I was there already I should stay. He ordered him to put me up in the "barracks" and that was an unbelievable experience. I got to meet Vern Stephens, Hank Foiles, Billy Harrell, Billy Joe Davis, Howard Rodemeier,

Hank Aguirre, Dave Pope, Dave Hoskins, Joe Altobelli, Ed Gasque, Herb Score, and Sam Jones who became a good buddy. They all took me in and I was a "gofer" for three weeks. I went for everything. They played poker and they would send me down to Toby's, a local bar, to pick up the sandwiches and the beer. I would get anything they wanted. If they wanted their shoes shined I would shine their shoes. Everytime I went to do something they would say, "Keep the change." I bet every night I made about twenty bucks. I started sending money to my Mom and she was worried that I was doing something illegal to be getting that kind of money.

When Hank Greenberg had come upon my meeting with Mr. McNally, I really didn't know who he was, or what his background was, or what he had experienced. But I came to learn that Hank himself had suffered the pain of discrimination in Detroit, because when he played he was one of very few Jewish ballplayers. It became my experience that people who suffered discrimination, whether based on race or religion, or disability, like Bill Veeck who had one leg, had a different heart and treated others with much more compassion. I liked Hank, and I came to know and like Bill Veeck also. Bill was always talking to the minority players. He understood our plight. When he talked to you it was a little bit different. Once you've been a victim of discrimination there's nothing you really have to think about because you learn from the history of being treated ugly. So you could look at people, you could look in their eyes, you could hear their tone, of how they thought they were superior and what they thought of you. Bill was one of the first owners of a team to own a motel so that all of his players could stay in the same place during spring training.

When the other "kids" showed up I was transferred down to stay with them, and that started a whole new experience. On the first day we walked out to the field all the other players started calling the new players names as part of a rookie initiation. Because I was black and my spikes and pants were so raggedy they assumed I was from the rural South and they guessed it was Mississippi. Leroy Irby, a firstbaseman, started getting on me saying I was as ugly as a Mississippi Mudcat, the mudcat being the biggest, ugliest of all catfish. In fact, my equipment was so bad that the guys dug a hole and buried it. The next morning we all assembled and the coaches called out all the players' names, telling them what field to report to: "Jim Mobley, Field #4, Mudcat Grant, Field #10, ..." and never having been called anything other than James, right away I think there's another Grant in camp, but they never called "James Grant" so I didn't report to any field. Next morning the same thing happened and I was getting mad that I wasn't being included in the workouts. Then Red Ruffing, Joe Sewell and Spud Chandler called me off to the side.

They said, "They told us you were a hell of a ballplayer, that you worked hard, that you really wanted to be a Cleveland Indian."

I said, "Well, I do."

"Well, hell, we call your name every morning. All you do is go from field to field."

"You haven't called my name."

"Here it is, right here, Mudcat Grant, we call it every morning."

"That ain't my name."

"It is now."

I worked out for about three weeks at third base and shortstop. As a "walk-on" I was placed with the least talented group; definitely the group least respected for the talent we had. We were called The Misfits – guys who hadn't signed contracts yet. They numbered the groups from 1 to 50 and we were number 50. The field we played on was so rocky we called it Iwo Jima. Toward the end of spring training Ruffing and Chandler called me aside again. They told me that the Indians were thinking of telling me to come back next year, but I would have a better chance of staying if I told them I could pitch. Sure enough, McNally came to tell me they were going to release me, but when I told him I could pitch, he gave me a shot to prove it that afternoon. Any chance I had of becoming a starting pitcher in the Major Leagues was a long shot. At that time there were only three African-American starters in the majors, Don Newcombe, Brooks Lawrence, and Bob Trice. Spud and Red felt the deck was stacked against me facing a line-up of upper class players, so they took me in the clubhouse bathroom and gave me tips on pitching. They told me to throw the very first pitch right under the neck of the first batter, who was Cooter Jones. I threw the ball right under his chin and he went down, the bat went out, the ball hit the bat and all of a sudden all of the players looked around and they saw Cooter on the ground and I could see them thinking, "We ain't standing in there." I wound up pitching seven innings and striking out eight batters without giving up any hits or runs. Next thing I know Joe Sewell told me the Indians would be giving me an envelope with a $500 bonus in it, signing me to a contract and sending me to a minor league team. As naïve and happy as I was to be accepted, I signed the contract and when I opened the envelope it was empty. Then I was told I could not be sent to the Indians' Class D team, in Tifton, Georgia, in the Georgia-Florida League, because Tifton didn't allow any mixing of the races. There was absolutely no possibility that I was going to play on the Tifton team. If the Indians had a Class D team in California or the Midwest I would have gone there, but they didn't. They wouldn't send me anywhere south of the Mason-Dixon Line, so they sent me to Fargo, North Dakota. Instead of starting in Class D, I went to Class C.

Before I left for Fargo I went home to Lacoochee to see my Mom and tell her I was going to be in the minor leagues. She said, "When you go to Fargo, there will be many different churches that we don't have in Lacoochee. Here you only know about Baptists and Methodists and the Church of Christ. There will be Jewish people, there will be Catholics, there will be Mormons, there will be Episcopalians, there will be Lutherans, and people of other religions. Since we don't know anything about those churches, I want you to go in to every one of those churches, and I want you to observe, and see what they do and I want you to come back and discuss it with me." I said, "Yes, Mom, I'll do that." So, from the first day I went to Fargo, I started visiting churches. The first church I went into was a Lutheran Church, and then a Mormon church, and so on. I learned what Mass was all about and I read books at every church. I would meet the minister or the priest, and I would say, "My mother asked me to come in here and go to service and find out what you all did." I became a laughingstock of Fargo, because by the time I got to the sixth or seventh church, the pastor said, "Yeah, we've been looking for you. We heard you were coming." By the time I left to go back to Lacoochee I had all of these Bibles and religious medals. I brought them all to Mom and we discussed all of the different religions. She said, "Do you know why I sent you to all these churches?" I said, "No, ma'am, I don't." She said, "Well, you're Baptist and some of your sisters are Methodist, but when you die and go to heaven, if you think that the only people you see in heaven are going to be Baptist and Methodists, God will slap you upside the head." So I learned to respect other religions.

Mom was definitely right about my ignorance of other religions. I remember watching an opposing batter come up to the plate and he slowly and deliberately drew a big cross in the dirt before entering the batter's box. I called time out and asked my catcher to come to the mound. I asked him what the batter had done and he told me he had made the Sign of the Cross, a Catholic religious symbol. I thought for a moment, and I told him to walk back to the plate slowly while I thought of a Baptist sign I could make.

Going from Lacoochee, Florida to Fargo, North Dakota in 1954, I might as well have been going to another planet. First of all, I had never flown before, so that was a new experience for me. And I had been told by two other black players who were also assigned to Fargo, Mitchell June, out of Chicago, and Sonny Logan, out of New York, that there weren't any black people in Fargo. Sure enough, we were the only three blacks in the whole town. Even though we were looked at, it wasn't a look of suspicion; it wasn't a racist thing, it was wonderment. Young children would rub my hair, rub my face, and rub my hand. When the little white kids looked at me it was because they had never been talked to about black people and they had seen very few of us, only on television. The feeling of wonderment wasn't only on the part of the white children. I myself was experiencing something completely new. For the first time in my life, I could drink water at a water fountain, and for the first time I could eat in a white restaurant, and I could stay in the YMCA, where white players also stayed.

Fargo was in the Northern League, and Eau Claire, Wisconsin, (the team Hank Aaron had played for) was also in that League. The year I was with Fargo, Eau Claire had two black ballplayers. The teams got into a bench clearing brawl in the second game of a series after I had shut them out the night before. After the umps got everything under control I was standing near our dugout and this fan yells out at me, "Hey, you nigger!" and I made the mistake of turning around. He continued yelling, "You black nigger! You nigger!" and it seemed like he started foaming at the mouth. I said, that guy's going to have a heart attack, but I just was standing there and I looked at him, and he kept saying, "You nigger! You black nigger! You nigger! You black nigger!" and he was trembling. I was talking to the guys and told them, "That guy is going to have to go to the hospital." He was chanting out like it was a cheer, "You nigger! You black nigger! You nigger! You black nigger!" I said, "That guy got it bad." It didn't affect me one way or the other, but I was concerned he could have had a heart attack and died right there. He was so wrapped up in it, and I was wondering, what happened out there in Wisconsin, or did he come from somewhere else and he was living in Wisconsin now. Usually Wisconsin people didn't act like that, but I'm telling you, he was sweating, he was foaming at the mouth, and he was shaking. I said, "Oh, my God."

When you are pitching and concentrating on the batter and the catcher you can block out the crowd noise, and you can hear the catcher and the catcher can hear you. You can have 50,000 people in the ballpark, but your focus is such, on the game and on that catcher, you can hear what he says. You don't even hear the crowd noise out there. Your focus blocks everything out. I think that you work on it, but don't know it. It's concentration. And if you listened to the crowd you were labeled Rabbit Ears, not to say some guys didn't hear. But when you are not actually playing, or when you walk off the mound and somebody called you a nigger, you're going to hear it.

I had a very successful year in Fargo, and got paid $250 a month. When I wasn't out visiting churches I was busy learning how to become a Major League pitcher. By then, I had talked to Satchel Paige a couple of times and I had met Larry Doby and Jackie Robinson. But it was the other pitchers that really helped me – ones I met when they came through Tampa on barnstorming teams, Brooks Lawrence, and two guys I only knew by their first names: Rabbit, a side-armed pitcher, and Tampa Red. (Red seemed to be the nickname for every light-skinned Negro.) I also learned from two of the pitchers on the Nine Devils: William Grant, no relation, who threw a tremendous curveball, and Cooter Singleton, who could throw a fastball into a teacup. Before I left for Fargo I worked on my pitching with Ruffing, (a Hall of Famer who had four consecutive twenty-win seasons), and Chandler (an All-Star who was a twenty-game winner with the Yankees). Although I had natural ability and had learned a great deal about the game from my time with the Nine Devils, I needed a little more information from these two aces than telling me to throw the first pitch at a batter's chin. My manager in Fargo was Phil Seghi, and there was no pitching coach assigned to the team. That was typical of the minor leagues in the 1950s. The manager served many roles, including pitching coach, batting instructor, team psychologist and chaplain. Once spring training was over, Ruffing was a roving pitching instructor for all the Indians' minor league teams, and I got to talk with him and work with him from time to time during the season. All of that just seemed to work along with the suggestion made by my Mom that someone would be looking after me, that I had a spot in life, and it seemed like I was going to make it despite everything. I never doubted that I would be a Major League ballplayer. I believed in what my mother said, that somebody was paving a highway for me. Not only did I pitch, but I played rightfield, I played second base, I played leftfield. Although I hit well, it was my ability to throw strikes that was making a name for me. In the middle of August I was voted the League's Rookie of the Year. I went on to win 21 ballgames, but I could not participate in the playoffs because of bursitis in my arm.

Jim (Mudcat) Grant, 19 year old Negro pitcher with Fargo-Moorhead, who had won 17 games for the Twins, was named the Northern League's rookie of the year in a pool of managers, umpires and sportswriters, August 16. Grant gained the award by the largest margin in the seven years of the award. He received 67 votes on a 5-3-1 basis to 20 for Bill Robertson, Eau Claire outfielder.

The Sporting News, August 25, 1954

The news got back to Lacoochee and everybody was proud of my accomplishments. Some of the older guys I played against in sandlot baseball, in towns like Brooksville, Florida, wanted to talk with me. They wanted to know all about professional baseball and life outside of Florida. One of my friends came over to Lacoochee to congratulate me, and invited me back to talk to some of the guys at a little session over in Brooksville. On the way there, about fifteen miles outside of Lacoochee, is a little town called Santa Ann, and we stopped there to get a soda at a juke joint that served blacks. The two of us walked in and went toward the back end of the joint and we were drinking our sodas when a Sheriff and a Deputy came in and starting talking to the manager and one of the waitresses. It seemed that some people had caused problems and left just before we came in, so they decided to give us up to the police who started questioning us. I had been away from home for a year and had gotten out of the custom of automatically responding, "Yes, sir" and "Yes, ma'am" when being addressed by a white person. I said "yes" and "no" and that seemed to disturb the Sheriff and the Deputy and he started asking me pointed questions.

"Where are you from?"

"I'm from Lacoochee, Florida."

"Did you cause any trouble?"

"No."

As the word "No" left my mouth I received a sharp, painful blow to my back. I didn't know the cause of the pain but came to learn that the Deputy had walked behind me and kicked me. Instinctively reacting to being hit so hard, I spun around to determine the identity of my attacker, with my fists raised to protect myself. As I turned around he pulled out a .38 caliber revolver, put it in my face, and said, "Damn it, nigger, say 'no, sir' or 'yes, sir.'" In my mind I heard my Mom say, "Don't be no fool." I didn't say anything, but they arrested me and took me to jail for disturbing the peace and being drunk even though to that point in my life I had never drunk alcohol, except for sips of elderberry wine from an uncle's glass at holiday time. My friend drove back to Lacoochee to tell my mother what had happened. She immediately sought the help of Lacoochee's Constable Jesse Stanley, who was white but had a great rapport with the black community. He knew my family real well, since we were born. Mr. Stanley never arrested anybody; if you broke the law he just told you to go to jail. In fact, he never wore a gun. He was also the manager of the white Lacoochee Nine Devils and a great friend of the family.

About an hour after I had been arrested I heard Mr. Stanley in the jail, asking questions about my case. He said, "Why do you have him in here?" And they said, "He was drunk and disorderly." Mr. Stanley said, "He does not disturb anything and he doesn't drink. I've been knowing this family for the longest and I don't like the way he was arrested; I don't like that way that you kicked him. There may be a suit against you, and I want him out of jail, now." I could hear everything that was said, and then there was a silence. I think it was a surprise to the Sheriff and to the Deputy that this white policeman would come and defend me and insist that I get out of jail. After some discussion they finally let me out and that's when I learned that my Mom had made the trip to Brooksville with Mr. Stanley. I was a little embarrassed when I first saw her but she understood that I did nothing that the police said I did. She was angry that he had kicked me and forced me to respond to the point where he really could have shot me. Being kicked and being forced to say, "yes, sir" when the people that were talking to me didn't deserve to hear the words "yes, sir," was the thing that disturbed me the most. When I got home my mother explained to me that it was not me with the problem, it was the Sheriff and the Deputy with the problem, and they needed praying for that evening. And, of course, that's what we did. She forced me, and when I say forced, she told me that I should pray for people like that because they had very serious problems, and I relented, and we prayed together for these two officers.

In 1955, the Indians invited me to spring training camp after the success I had in the minor leagues as a pitcher. When I checked into the hotel, the clerk told me, "Oh, yeah, Mr. Grant, you are rooming with Larry Doby." And I said, "No, I'm not rooming with Larry Doby." He says, "Yes, you are rooming with Larry Doby." and it scared the hell out of me because Larry had always been my hero. So, I repeated in disbelief, "I'm not rooming with Mr. Doby." He said, "Oh, you're rooming with Mr. Doby." The team was at the ballpark by the time I got in. It was about one o'clock in the afternoon. They didn't leave the ballpark back in those days until probably somewhere around about three thirty. So, I go in the room and Larry Doby's stuff is sitting in the room, his shaving kit and his clothes, all fixed in a position of neatness. I didn't know what to do. I wasn't about to change anything, so I just sat there and looked at TV, until I heard a key open the door. I cut the TV off, and when he came in he said, "Oh, you must be Mudcat Grant." I said, "Yes sir, Mr. Doby." He said, "They told me I would be rooming with you." I said, "Yes sir, Mr. Doby." He said, "You want this bed here?" I said, "Yes sir, Mr. Doby." He said, "You want to watch TV?" I said, "Yes sir, Mr. Doby." He said, "Now listen, we got to get rid of this 'Yes sir, Mr. Doby.'" I said, "Yes sir, Mr. Doby." What a roommate he was. He taught me a lot. I went with him on speaking engagements in spring training and I remember him saying, "I'm not the one to pass on accolades, but this kid, I think is going to be a Major League pitcher. He's going to be a good one."

He also taught me about Tucson, Arizona, where we trained. Back in those days you had to read in the paper which restaurant would accept you. We would read the newspaper, and he would say, "We can eat over here." And if we didn't see anything, of course, we ate in a black restaurant, a barbeque place, a little café in the black section of Tucson. But he started teaching me about a whole bunch of things, about life, what I was to face, how I was to not let anything keep me from succeeding, pretty much the same thing I had been taught as a child but Larry reinforced all of what I had forgotten. And it was a constant reminder that you are in a Major League uniform, despite the difficulties you've got to act like a big leaguer and you got to be a big leaguer, and you've got to always play hard, not let worries make your emotions get the best of you, even though Larry was very emotional. A lot of people don't know what emotional torture Larry went through, being one of the first black ballplayers, yet the press not making as much of it as they did about Jackie. Because I roomed with Larry I realized all the things he had to put up with that were similar to what Jackie went through, but it wasn't publicized. It took its toll on Larry; some nights he would just yell and scream. When I got to the big leagues in 1958, I was one of only a very few black pitchers in the league, although there were more black players than in 1948. We still went through strenuous times and realized that there was still a focus on us, but I don't know if I was in Jackie's shoes or Larry's shoes if I would have been able to handle being the first and only black in the league, because at the time they were doing that it was just the two of them and they didn't get help from anybody.

My second year of professional ball, 1955, I was sent to Keokuk, Iowa, to play with the Keokuk Kernels (Class B). From a baseball point of view, my time in Keokuk was very successful. I finished the season there 19-3, leading the league in wins and winning percentage (.864) and tying for the lead in complete games (16). I not only pitched well but batted well enough to play the outfield in several games. On July 4th of that season, I pitched a three hitter against Cedar Rapids and hit three home runs, one in the sixth inning, one in the seventh and one in the eighth. Keokuk was one of the best teams I ever played on. We won the pennant by 22 games over second place Waterloo and then beat Peoria and Burlington in the playoffs to win the championship. In 2001, the 1955 Kernels were voted the 30th Best Minor League Team of All-Time by minorleaguebaseball.com. Including me, the team featured four future Major Leaguers, the others being Russ Nixon, Gordy Coleman, and Bill Dailey.

From a personal point of view, Keokuk was a little bit more prejudiced than Fargo, North Dakota. In Keokuk they didn't want you in some places if you were black. That year there were only two of us on the team, me and Mitchell June. The Kernels' team office was in the Metropole Hotel, but they didn't want us there. They had a place for us to stay with a black lady that had been renting out rooms to ballplayers for a number of years, so we stayed with her instead of staying at the Hotel. And they didn't want us using cabs and public transportation used by the whites, so they gave us a station wagon to use for transportation to go to the ballpark, come downtown, eat, etc. One place where they didn't want us to eat was the Wagon Wheel, a restaurant near the Metropole Hotel. I remember they had some kind of river fly in that area that only lived 24 hours. They came in a certain time of the year, and during the game all you saw were these flies, and they would fly up, they would mate, the female fly would give birth and they both would come back down and die. So, they were all over the field, they were all over the street, they were all over the cars. It was a problem. Mitchell and I went into the Wagon Wheel one day and when I bit into my cheese sandwich something crunched and I didn't like that idea. I opened the sandwich and there were these river flies, dead river flies in there. So, we knew some people in Keokuk would go to some extent to keep us from eating in there. But, since we were paying to eat, we just didn't eat in there any more. They won on that one, but they lost because we were customers like everybody else. That's the way we looked at it.

In 1956, I was in Reading, Pennsylvania, and as I moved from the far Northwest to the middle of the country and then to the East, I thought I would face less prejudice. But Reading wasn't a place that was free of racism. In fact, the most racism that I faced, in terms of being a ballplayer, could have been in Reading. There were places they didn't want you in, and I went in them anyway, because I guess that was just me. If the law says you could go, then why not? My white teammates frequented this place, and one night I went in and sat down. It became obvious that the waitresses weren't going to serve me, but I sat there until closing time. I continued to go back and sometimes I would sit for four or five hours and they would never serve me but I sat anyway. Finally, one of my teammates came over and said, "Mudcat, I don't know why you keep coming in here. They don't want you in here. They are not going to serve you. Why don't you just leave?" So, I said, "But you are my teammate. Why are coming over here to tell me that? Why wouldn't you come over and sit at my table with me? Why don't you go back with your friends, and I'll just sit here?" And that's what I did. Every other night I went in that place and I sat. They never did serve me and I never looked at that teammate for the rest of the season as I had looked at him before. I looked at him as one of "them." But, I think I made a point that humanity is not necessarily the way you think that it is, despite what you may not like about me, the law says that I have the privilege, as long as I have the money, to come in, order anything that I want, as long as I pay for it. That's what the law says.

When you sign a contract you think that baseball is going to be the savior from the humilities that you are going to face. It gives you a sense of false security that now that you are into baseball there are places you are going to be able to eat regardless of your race because, after all, Jackie had made the way. So, we anticipated everybody would look at us and say, "Okay, you're a ballplayer? Come on in!" You think that for a minute, but then after they didn't, you are hurt that you can't go in, that you can't go with your teammates. What are they going to think once they get inside and you're sitting on the bus and they have to bring you a sandwich? It's a hurtful feeling.

You were always aware of the fact that you were black, when I came into the big leagues, because there were stares, there were people that took your money at the counter that didn't want to touch your hand, there were people when you sat next to them on the airplane that sat sideways, away from you. They didn't want to be touching you; like you would give them some kind of disease. There were so many things that we faced back in those days. If you went in a neighborhood where you didn't ordinarily go, in a white area, you were stared at. They were hoping that you left the place. Now it's not as intense as it was back in those days, but you know it's there.

You weren't in denial when it came to pain. You knew how to deal with pain. You knew how to deal with hurt. All the way from the time when you were a little one you knew how to deal with it. It was a hurtful feeling and you tried as much as you possibly could to ignore it to some extent even though it could be prolonged with the white players saying, "Well, we're sorry about that," or some may think we didn't belong in there anyway. So all of that is involved in the pain.

We didn't hold it against the players, but on every team there was always one or two or three or four or five ballplayers that were glad you weren't allowed to go inside a restaurant. So you had different emotions you had to deal with, and again, because of the endurance, because of the space inside that was put there by your experiences as a child, you learned to deal with it. The pain didn't last a long time because you had other things that you had to do. You had accomplishments that you had to make. So, you couldn't afford to let that pain stay there. But it showed up, not only at a restaurant, but it could show up in rides, it could show up at the ballpark where you had to go into certain parts of the ballpark. You couldn't go in the front gate. But, it always showed up. Pain always showed up, everyday, in terms of something that happened. But you didn't express it because you were taught that this is going to happen to you. You can't afford to let this stuff keep you from your accomplishments. So whether you could deal with it or not you learned to deal with it. You know you could have had all kinds of troubles before but once you crossed the line you learned the hard edges of making sure you learned how to deal with it. But I know that there are some circumstances even like that today. It's not as bad as it once was though, because once you had to worry about your life.

In those years the coaches and managers didn't know how to handle it. They didn't know what to say. They just left it up to us to succeed or not succeed. Maybe it was fear to some extent, and you have to remember too that it was a way of life. So, some people in management said, well, they have to deal with it one way or another. There were no black coaches at that time, nobody to turn to, no players' union. There were only a few, rare coaches that said, "Well, I know what you guys are going through, but, you know, you're going to have to go through it." The teams didn't know of any integrated places. They didn't do any research beforehand. It just was what it was. Because they thought we could take it. We've been taking it so long, they just thought we could take it.

The Indians had their eye on my ability to hit and since I loved to play every day I didn't argue with them when they had me alternate between pitching and playing the outfield in Reading in 1956. My pitching stats suffered (12-13), but I managed to bat .325 for the season. That winter I played in the Colombian League for Willard, and I continued to attract the attention of the Cleveland management with both my arm and my bat.

Jim (Mudcat) Grant, young Cleveland-owned pitcher with Willard, is the newest toast of Colombian League fans. Just nine days after tying the all-time loop record with three homers in a game, the Negro righthander gave the customers an even greater thrill by hurling only the second no-hit, no-run game in the ten-year history of the league. ... The Blues' ace faced just 28 batters – one over the minimum – with only two reaching base. He walked the Reds' first batter of the game, Antonio Fang, but a double play erased him. In the eighth inning an error by John Skorupski (Reading) permitted another runner to get on.
Luis A. Bello, The Sporting News, November 11, 1956

Having been successful at Colombia and Class B, my next assignment should have been the Indians' Class AA team in Mobile, Alabama. But because they wouldn't allow blacks to play in the Southern Association, I got kicked up to Class AAA in San Diego, California. It was one of those things. They said, "Well, you can't go down there because you can't play in that league, you can't stay in any hotel there. So, we're going to send you to San Diego." I said, "I'll take it."

Based on what happened in Reading in 1956, and the apparent greater need in the Indians' organization for hitting and position players, Ralph Kiner, the GM at San Diego, told me at the beginning of the season that I would be switched to shortstop. Before the experiment proceeded very far, Indians' starter Herb Score, the best pitcher on the team at the time, was struck in the eye by a line drive off the bat of the Yankees' Gil McDougald. With that injury knocking Score out of the rotation, Kiner came back to me and advised me that the Indians wanted me back on the mound. It was one of those crazy turns or detours that happen in a ballplayer's career, but it was clearly a defining year in my development as a player. During spring training camp that year I had the opportunity to work with and learn from Mel Harder. Harder enjoyed a twenty-year career as a right handed pitcher with Cleveland. He retired after the 1947 season with 223 victories and then coached and managed the Indians. Then when I got to San Diego my pitching coach was Vic Lombardi, who was a teammate of Jackie Robinson's in Brooklyn in 1947 and a teammate of Ralph Kiner in Pittsburgh in 1948. Vic, a lefthanded pitcher, nurtured me, corrected my mistakes, and developed my confidence as a young pitcher. One key, which sounds overly simple, is that they let me pitch. I remember one game going eighteen innings against Sacramento striking out fourteen batters, beating Marshall Bridges 1-0. They didn't baby my arm, instead they helped mature me as a pitcher and a player. Another coach who was very helpful to me was Jimmie Reese, most famous for his years as a coach with the Los Angeles Angels and for being Babe Ruth's teammate. Jimmie wasn't the pitching coach; he was in charge of conditioning and making sure that we all did our share of running which was never a problem for me. Jimmie's real name was Hyam Soloman; he changed it to avoid the discrimination against Jewish players. He started his baseball career in 1919 as a batboy for the Pacific Coast League Los Angeles Angels, played in the majors from 1930 to 1932, and stayed in baseball until his death in 1994 at the age of 92. Playing baseball everyday in beautiful San Diego with that coaching staff was a dream for a kid from Lacoochee. It was in San Diego where I got to spend more time with Dave Hoskins, who was also on the team. Truth be told, they had to drag me off that field when practice was done.

That year I stole a page from Satchel's publicity tricks: I started to name my pitches. I called my fastball my "Comet Ball" and that was the pitch I was basically relying on to be successful in San Diego. I also had a "Kickapoo Pitch" which had me looking in one direction and throwing in another, with a wild leg kick thrown in, very similar to the delivery Dontrelle Willis now uses. I also had a "Hop and Jumper" and a specialty pitch I called a "Cloud Ball" which contained a little moisture.

> **That Grant will develop into one of Cleveland's mound stars seems certain. Padre General Manager Ralph Kiner doesn't see how he can miss. "I've never seen a young pitcher come along so fast as he has." Kiner remarked. "He wants to learn and is willing to take advice. That is a big point in his favor."**
> **There isn't a more popular player on the San Diego team than Mudcat.**
> **...**
> **Pitching and playing in the outfield in the Colombian League last winter, Mudcat hurled a no-hitter, fanned 13 batters in another game and in another he clouted three home runs.**
> *Earl Keller, The Sporting News, August 28, 1957*

> **Rookie Jim (Mudcat) Grant is a virtual cinch to win PCL strikeout honors this season and is also a contender for the honor of leading the league in complete games pitched. When Grant whiffed six while beating San Francisco, 6 to 4, August 31, it gave him 145 strikeouts in 179 innings. He had hurled 14 complete games, only one less than the leader, Vancouver's Erv Palica.**
> *The Sporting News, September 11, 1957*

At the time that second story was written, I was 15-5 with a 2.26 ERA. I finished the season at 18-7, second in the league in wins, and with an ERA of 2.32, third in the league.

By the 1957 season Joe Black's historic Major League career was pretty much over. Joe's contract was owned by Cincinnati, Philadelphia and Washington at different times of the 1957 season and he only appeared in seven games for Washington. However, something Joe did that season had a very large impact on my life. Joe was in San Diego for a game, although I can't remember now who he was playing for at that time. He told me that after the game he had a date and she had a friend, and he invited me to join them. When I left the clubhouse I met up with Joe and headed toward the parking lot where we met his friends: Joe's date, Janella "Johnny" Valentine, who was Miss Bronze of California, and her friend, Trudy. Trudy and I hit it off from the time we met and we started seeing each other pretty regularly. There was only one hitch as far as the Indians were concerned: Trudy was white and they didn't want any black ballplayers dating any white women. I got called in by team management and told that if I wanted to continue my career I had to stop seeing Trudy. I was young and in love, and wasn't quick to accept the team's ultimatum. We snuck around for a while, and I proposed taking Trudy to Mexico to get married. She knew about my lifelong dream to be a ballplayer and didn't want to be in the position where one day I would blame her for my missing my calling in life. So, as difficult as it was, we broke up and went our separate ways, each finding a spouse. Over the years we kept in touch, and as life worked out, years later each of us got divorced, and to this day Trudy and I live together in Los Angeles.

By the time the spring of 1958 rolled around the Cleveland Indians were definitely in need of starting pitching. Herb Score's comeback was questionable at the time. Bob Feller had retired after the 1956 season. Bob Lemon, another of the Indians' Big Four, had a sub-par season in 1957, at 6-11, and no one knew what to expect from him. In addition, Early Wynn had been traded for Minnie Minoso, leaving another gap in the pitching rotation. So the Indians decided to invite nine non-roster pitchers to camp: Gary Bell, Dick Brodowski, Bill Dailey, Julio Guerra, Gene Lary, Donald Schaeffer, Wilbur Striker, Carl Thomas, and me.

Mudcat came to spring training given only an outside chance to stay. It was felt he needed more experience and particularly work on his curve. But Mudcat announced: "Every team I've trained with didn't figure on me when I said hello. But I stayed. I believe I'll fool 'em here, too."
Hal Lebovitz, The Sporting News, April 16, 1958

I made my Major League debut on April 17, 1958, as the starting pitcher for the Cleveland Indians in Cleveland Stadium against the Kansas City Athletics, who were pitching Duke Maas. It was one of the proudest moments of my life. I believe that in 1958, I was the only African-American pitcher in the American League who was starting on a steady basis. In fact, the only other African-American pitchers in the American League who started any other games that year were Charlie Beamon and Connie Johnson, both of whom were with the Orioles and in the last year of their career.

Not only had I made it to a big league pitching mound but I was wearing the uniform of the Cleveland Indians, *the Larry Doby Cleveland Indians*, and Larry was my teammate, having been reacquired by the Indians after spending two years with the Chicago White Sox. I had won about four ballgames by the time we got to Detroit early in the 1958 season. That day I was the starting pitcher and after having been worked on by the trainer I was going out to take batting practice. When I walked out of the dugout towards the batting cage, the people in the bleachers went nuts, yelling and screaming. The noise caught my attention and when I looked out toward the bleachers I saw that from right field all the way around out to left field, from foul line to foul line, the bleachers were full of black people. I said to Larry Doby, "They must have a promotion out here today, or something" because more black fans came to the games in Detroit, Cleveland, Washington, DC, and Chicago, than in other towns, and sometimes the teams hosted promotions aimed to attract even more black fans.

Larry said, "No they ain't got no promotion. Don't you know why they're here?"

So, I said, "No."

"They're here to see you."

"No-o-o-o. They ain't come to see me."

"Yeah-h-h-h, they did. In fact, we don't hit for a few minutes. Let's go out to the bleachers."

So we went out to the bleachers and we walked from foul line to foul line. We started shaking hands with the fans and worked our way toward centerfield. People were sticking their hands through the wire, and the essence of all of that was that by the time we got to the centerfield bleachers, I realized he was right: they were not only there to see Larry, they were there to see me too. It was Detroit, but as a Cleveland Indian both of us had to do well for the black people at that game that day. And you could tell by the look in their eyes where they were coming from, how soulfully they were endeared to us, and that they were pulling for us, not necessarily to defeat the Detroit Tigers, but to do well. And I got this chill about me as we walked all the way around to the left field corner and people reached around the pole, and they were shaking my hand and reaching out to touch me. I shook hands all the way and I remember a little girl, she grabbed my hand and I couldn't pull away so she kept walking, I would stick my hand back through and we walked all the way. I had never experienced that type of feeling and I don't think I have ever felt, from head to toe, the type of tingling inside that I felt when looking at those people, that close to them, looking in their eyes and seeing how they were looking at me - like worshipping me. A black pitcher was in the league, and they were pulling against their home town. People were stomping and clapping, and just going nuts. I don't care what kind of accomplishments that I've had, the rewards that you get from your peers, your teammates and other people respecting you as a player, I never had anything like that. It was unbelievable, and on top of that, my hero, Larry Doby, was walking with me - the great Larry Doby, who had experienced what he had experienced, coming in after Jackie. At that time, reflecting back on it now, I never knew that he wasn't getting the accolades that he should have gotten. It's something that I certainly will never ever forget but I saw it for real. It was a maturing event for me: I knew that I had something other than the game itself to play for, to do well, to make my folks proud of what I was doing, to act well, to act with manners, and that sort of followed me. People always expected me to act that way, and I have been told several times around cities, "Man, you are doing good for us. You're a man for us," that type of thing, because they never heard of me getting in trouble. They heard of me fighting for rights but never getting into any trouble.

Now, sometimes I cry at night because I don't have a picture of that day, that crowd, and Larry and me. I don't have that picture. If I had that picture, it would be great! If I win the lottery of millions of dollars, I would rent Tigers Stadium and I would pay those people to come back. That's a day I never will forget.

That same year I shared an experience of a different kind with Larry in Baltimore, one of the roughest towns back then for visiting black players. The crowds there were pretty tough on us. I was pitching and Larry was playing the outfield. There were always people yelling at us and there were also things thrown at me, but this was one of the best. These guys behind the dugout, and they were the ones yelling the loudest at Larry and I, had a pole which they didn't bring out until the third inning. When Larry was playing the outfield, after the third out was made, by the time I got to the foul line he was just about by my side, and we would walk into the dugout together. We were the only two blacks on the team. In the third inning, these guys finally did what they had come to the ball park to do. They picked up this pole that had a coon tail on it, and shook this coon tail out there. A couple of the other guys on the team saw that thing. And so, me and Larry Doby, we saw it, and we went in the dugout and sat down. I looked at Larry and Larry looked at me, and he motioned for me to go to the bathroom inside the clubhouse. We went in the bathroom and locked the door and Larry said, "Did you see that coontail? That was the biggest coontail I ever seen in my life." I said, "Yeah, I saw it. That was something right there." So we go back out on the bench like we were mad, although we weren't. We thought it was funny. So now, they kept shaking that coontail, and I kept shutting the Orioles out. Around about the eighth inning the coontail disappeared. Larry kind of looked at me and we kind of smiled at one another – that this is the way to do it. The players thought we were mad because we wouldn't smile on the bench, but we went in that bathroom and we laughed like hell.

In the 1950s, and even in the 1960s, there were coaches who felt that blacks were inferior, that we "didn't have it in us" – that we couldn't be quarterbacks or pitchers. Blacks and whites could be absolutely equal but the coach would see them differently. But I had already been taught differently by my family – to believe in myself. I think that is why one of the things that bothered me the most was the lack of respect for my knowledge of pitching a game. Ordinarily, when you were the starting pitcher the manager would give you the other team's lineup and you would go over it with your catcher and your defense. For instance, if you were facing the Yankees you might say, "Bobby Richardson leads off, I want you to play him straight away, because that's what he does, he sprays the ball all over. I'm gonna pitch him inside, but I'm not gonna pitch him a ball he could hit inside. I'm going to make him hit a ball away, but I'm gonna pitch him inside, but I want you to play him straight away. Tony Kubek, he doesn't pull the ball, so let's shade him to the left side. Mickey Mantle comes up, you can play him anywhere you want, because you don't know what the hell he's going to do. But, don't play him to pull, because he'll just hit the ball, the outfield play him straight away, the infield play him over, play him to pull. Yogi Berra, I'm going to throw him strikes. We'll see what he does the first two times at bat and then we'll figure out how we're going to play him, but play him straight away in the beginning. Moose Skowron is always going to hit the ball to right field, so we're going to play him that way, even though you pitch him inside, he's hitting the ball to right field, that's Moose Skowron. Elston Howard, is going to play right field instead of Hector Lopez. Elston Howard loves the ball up and away. Even when he gets jammed sometimes he may hit the ball through the middle or something like that, so you can play him straight away, centerfield shade him a little bit to the right side, that's where I'm going to pitch him." Now, when it was my turn to start, the manager was the one that talked to the team about how he wanted them to play, not the pitcher. That was one of the worst things, and most disrespectful things, that happened to me as a pitcher. Like people thought about black quarterbacks back in those days, people thought about black pitchers the same way, we got lucky a couple of times. Personally, there were worse things that happened to me. There were times when you couldn't drink from the water fountains; there were times when the people from the stands called you names all through the minor leagues; there were times when you had to stay in places that were unclean, filthy, because you couldn't stay in white places on trips along the way in the minor leagues. But from the point of view of not being respected within the game, I found it most hurtful that managers and coaches didn't think I was mentally capable of a pitching game plan and setting my defense. Sometimes it was my own catcher that I had to convince. I remember one specific instance, and I won't name the catcher, since he is still alive. We were ahead by a couple of runs and our opponent had a runner on first. Before every pitch the catcher would look into the manager to see what pitch to call. I was on the mound and I felt that I knew the batter and knew what pitch I felt most confident in. As a pitcher, you throw a pitch to set up the next pitch, and you throw that second pitch to set up another pitch, and that is the game plan you develop in your head. But they were not giving me the credit for being able to do that. The catcher gave me the sign he received from the bench and I shook him off. That happened two or three times. Finally, I nodded in agreement and then threw the pitch I wanted to throw. As expected, it crossed up the catcher, the ball got past him and the runner advanced to second. The catcher came out to the mound and accused me of purposely crossing him up. With my best straight face, I denied it, saying, "I'm your teammate. I wouldn't do that." We went through the same scenario on the next two pitches, with passed balls allowing the runner to score. After the inning, the catcher and I had a scuffle in the dugout, but he came to learn and understand that I was capable of putting together a game plan for pitching to the batters and I was intelligent enough to know what pitchers I wanted to throw.

One teammate who definitely saw me for who was rather than the color of my skin was Gary Bell. I think the first time I met Gary was 1955 in spring training. The Indians had just signed him as an amateur free agent. Thank goodness I didn't have any thought patterns about him being from Texas, because Texas at that time was a racist state. Texas was a state known for indifference to black people, more so than some of the other states. Mississippi was another one, and that's a fact. So the guys from Texas, even though they changed over a period of time, you expect them to have that particular type of discord, I wouldn't call it a hatred, but discord against black folk. But you can't sit back and expect everybody from a certain place to act the same way. Gary never showed me any indifference or negativity. He always was truthful to me. He said, "I ain't been around many black people. I know some of them, but I never been around many." With me, for some reason, we just hit it off, and we were friends from the first day. He hung out with me, I hung out with him. I went to white places, he went to black places with me, but we were always together, and that was a blessing. He didn't have to explain anything to me; I didn't have to explain anything to him. He would tell me things sometimes when we went back, and his white friends would say something, and I would tell him some things, when some black guys would say something about him, but we don't know how and why, we just know that that friendship existed. I didn't have any shortgivings whatsoever in terms of taking him to the black community, and many times they told him, they said, "Gary, you don't have to come down here with Mudcat. You can come down all by yourself" because they saw in him not a black person, but a white person that had humanity inside, and they just had fun with him all the time. That's why baseball was so good to America, because day by day, year by year, people started to see, and this was blacks too, that maybe they're alright.

Gary became one of the best friends I'll ever have. He is a special man. Unpredictable. He's out there, but he has a wonderful heart. I remember rooming with Gary it was probably in 1959 or 1960. They didn't room blacks and whites together in those days. If there were three blacks on the team, you roomed two and one had a single room by himself. So, we decided to break up the crap. We got a room. They didn't hassle us too much but they didn't pay for the room. We had to pay.

I remember being at a segregated water fountain with Gary where there was one spigot marked "White" and one spigot marked "Colored." Gary and I looked underneath the fountain and there was one pipe coming out of the wall feeding both spigots. We called the attendant over and asked him when the White water separated from the Colored water. That was how I could kid with Gary and in poking fun at the silliness of segregation we could help the integration of baseball inch forward.

In 1960, I had another interesting episode in Baltimore. I had thrown close to an Oriole batter, and from the mound I could hear Baltimore manager, Paul Richards say, "Damn nigger!" The next time I got up they threw at me, but I got a hit and went to first base. Jim Gentile played first base for Baltimore and he was upset with Richards' comment, and if you knew Jim Gentile, he was intense, even as a hitter. And he's stomping around first base when I got down there, and he says, "Man, I just want to apologize." I said, "What you need to apologize for?"

He told me that Paul Richards had called me a nigger and that Bob Boyd, who was the only black on the team, had walked down to the other end of the bench. He said, "I don't like it. I don't think that way." And I said, "Well, Jim, don't worry about it." A lot of times, white ballplayers were in a Catch-22 situation – can't say too much about it, and at bat may not have the same concentration, may not have the same intensity because of that incident, and what you try to do, is you try and make sure that they understand that you can take it. You accept the apology for that idiot but you can take it. Later on in the game, Gene Woodling hit a ball that got by the rightfielder who retrieved it and threw it in. The throw got by the third baseman, and I had to back up third base. I called time out and I shot the ball right by Paul Richards' neck. It hit the top of the dugout. He wanted to jump out of there and do something. But then afterwards I felt kind of lousy about it, that I had let him get to me. But, opposing managers and sometimes an opposing ballplayer, sometimes did stuff like that.

On February 1, 1960, four black students from North Carolina Agricultural and Technical College, (Ezell Blair, Jr., Franklin McCain, Joseph McNeil, and David Richmond), tested the Southern Jim Crow restrictions by ordering food at a Woolworth's lunch counter in Greensboro, North Carolina. After the waitress refused to serve them they remained seated at the counter until closing time. They returned the next morning, along with about twenty additional students, and sat at the lunch counter until the store closed. By day three the number of students totaled sixty, including students from Bennett College and Dudley High School. They occupied every seat at the Woolworth's cafeteria counter. By the fourth day, white students joined in the sit-in, and the protest spread to include the lunch counter at S. H. Kress & Co. By day five a battle for the lunch counter seats developed between the students and residents who supported Woolworth's racist policies. The next day Woolworth's received a bomb threat and after evacuating the store, decided to close its lunch counter temporarily. By the end of February Woolworth's re-opened its counter in Greensboro and still refused to serve blacks. In March 1960 the student sit-in at lunch counters refusing to serve blacks had spread to over fifty cities in twelve states. In April Woolworth's and Kress closed their lunch counters but that did not stop the students from sitting at the counters in symbolic protest. Store owners hoped that the end of the college school year would bring an end to the protest, but Dudley High School students took up the cause and spread the sit-ins to the lunch counters of Walgreens and Meyer's. Finally, on July 25, 1960, Woolworth's agreed to serve blacks at its lunch counter and started by serving four of their black employees. Kress followed suit the next day. That same summer, the United States Supreme Court handed down a decision in *Boynton v. Virginia*, ruling that segregation during interstate travel, including at restaurants and rest rooms in bus terminals, was unconstitutional. This led to the revival of the "Freedom Rides" program sponsored by The Congress of Racial Equality (CORE), where blacks would ride buses throughout the South to encourage integration.

In the context of all of these events there were several of my teammates, including Frank Funk, Gary Bell and Barry Latman, who over the course of the

216

summer of 1960 were encouraging me to make some statement about segregation in the South. I resisted at first, and I don't really remember what made me make a statement on this particular day, but in the middle of September we were playing the Kansas City Athletics in Cleveland, and I was in the bullpen for the start of the game. The relievers, the starters who weren't starting that day and the bullpen staff all stood for the National Anthem. As the organist got toward the end of the song I improvised my own ending: "how free can it be when I can't go to Mississippi and sit at a lunch counter." The guys who were goading me to say something were all happy, "Yeah, yeah, that's the way to go." But Ted Wilks, a coach who lived in Texas at the time, was fuming. He got right in my face and said, "If you don't like our country, why in the hell don't you get out?" I responded, "Well, I can get out of the country. All I have to do is go to Texas. That's worse than Russia." Well, you don't tell that to a Texan without a fight. He said, "Well, if we catch your black nigger ass in Texas, we're going to hang you from the nearest tree." With that I threw a punch upside his jaw and down he went. Newcombe was my teammate at the time and he was also in the bullpen. He was one of the players who tried to separate us as we went at it. I was so angry and so upset at Wilks that I just left the bullpen and went down to the clubhouse. I just decided it was best to leave the ballpark. My mistake was not telling the manager, Jimmy Dykes, what had happened. The first Jimmy heard of the incident was when he called the bullpen in the second inning to have me warm up and Wilks told him I left. The next day, Dykes called me in and told me I was suspended for the remainder of the season, which was only about a week. Officially, the team said I was suspended for making derogatory statements about the National Anthem and never mentioned the racial insults spoken by Wilks.

There are times when I think that you should speak up. I've been called an Uncle Tom, because I didn't let things bother me. Not that I didn't figure it was wrong. But, sometimes you have to speak up and sometimes you know when to and sometimes you have to just go with it. If you feel like that's the time, and a lot of times it's spontaneous, when you speak up, and a lot of times you think about it's time for you to speak up. I never really knew the right time to do it. Every time you speak up is the right time to do it, in terms of your own feelings. I never showed any resentment. But, if you want to show some anger, spontaneous anger, in what is happening, you should speak up. This is actually what is happening, and I'm speaking up because it's happening. It's not that it made me bitter, except that that's the way it was. So, if you speak up, then maybe it'll change a little bit, even if it's less than one-half of one percent of an inch. So, I spoke out not in anger but to change things. And the way you speak out on it, people will understand that you can stand on your own, that you could take it, but this is not the right thing that should be happening.

The follow-up to that story also tells you something else about America. After the season Earl Battey got me a gig teaching a seventy-five year old man how to throw a slider, and from that we went on a barnstorming tour in the South. Our first stop was Yazoo, Mississippi, and after my rendition of the National Anthem they were waiting on me in Mississippi. I was sitting in the American League dugout and this man entered the dugout with a young boy behind him. He said, "I want to see Mudcat Grant." I immediately sensed I had trouble on my hands. We didn't carry any guns or nothing like that for protection and there was no stadium security. The only weapon that you could have with you was your spikes. So, you didn't put on your shoes, if you were in my position, until the last minute. As this man approached, I kept one shoe in my hand in case he had a weapon. He said, "You Mudcat Grant?" I said, "Yeah, I'm Mudcat Grant." He said, "You had a little trouble up there didn't you?" I said, "Yeah." He said, "Well, you'll find out that we ain't as hard on niggers down here as you think we are. Can I get your autograph for my boy." I dropped the shoe and said, "Of course" and signed the autograph for his boy.

From Yazoo we headed to Mount Bayou, Mississippi, where we had to pay a toll when crossing the bridge. The tollkeeper looked into the car, which Connie Johnson was driving, and said, "That Mudcat Grant, is he in here?" Straightfaced, Connie said, "No, he ain't in this car" and we headed on to Baton Rouge. We had a one o'clock game in Baton Rouge and then one later that day in New Orleans. The first game went into extra innings which meant we had to speed to get to New Orleans. Connie is driving again, and I am in the car with Earl Battey and Don Newcombe. We're all in uniform, sweaty and cruddy from the game and just anxious to get to New Orleans, when Connie sees a motorcycle cop coming up to stop us. The first thing Connie tells us is to say nothing. Sure enough, the cop stops us and comes up to the car, looks in the window, sees us all in our uniforms, and says, "Goddamn, you niggers are going pretty fast, ain't you? Yeah, all you ballplayers come down here to play?" In his most apologetic voice, Connie says, "Mr. Policeman, us nigger boys, we're hungry, we're trying to get to the next game in New Orleans. We don't know what to do. We're late and we sure could use your help, sir." The officer said, "Well, goddamn it, I'm going to help you guys this time, but don't let me catch you on this highway again" and with that he pulls in front of us and escorts us right into New Orleans. I'll never forget, as soon as his motorcycle got in front of our car and we started to move, Connie yells out to us, "Roll on you son of a bitch!"

My suspension in 1960 wasn't the only time I left the team in a huff over a racist remark. The second time was a game against Kansas City again, only this time we were in Kansas City, in 1961. It was getaway day and we were trying to beat the clock to get to the airport for our flight to California to play the Angels. We were on the verge of losing a doubleheader, down by one run in the ninth inning of the second game when Jimmy Piersall singled and the next batter walked, to put the potential go ahead run on first base. Mel McGaha, the manager, sends me out to pinch run for the runner on first. When I get there, Ray Katt, the first base coach, tells me, "You're the winning run. If this guy hits a tweener, I want you to run like you just stole two watermelons and the man is after you with a shotgun." I thought for a second, my initial reaction being, "How can you say that to me?" because by 1961 I had some sense of freedom in the game, that he wouldn't or

218

shouldn't have said something like that to me, that people didn't think that way anymore. His words really hit me like a jolt of lightning. I guess, now, that Ray being a southerner, and hearing that kind of talk so many times didn't think that what he was saying was offensive, but that's not how it hit me. Finally, I said to Ray, "So, you mean to tell me you want to talk to me about some watermelons?" and then I let him know what was on my mind in no uncertain terms. I called time out and I walked back across the infield real slow. I took slow steps past the pitcher, slow steps past the third base line. Everybody was going nuts, wondering what was happening. When I got to the dugout, McGaha says, "Get your ass back out there." I repeated to him the same profane directive I originally gave to Katt, and then I walked into the clubhouse which was way up a hill in Kansas City. Minutes later Charlie Morris, the Indians' Traveling Secretary, and a wonderful man, runs into the clubhouse, sweating like crazy, and says, ""Gabe [Paul, General Manager], wants to know what's going on. He's got to know what's going on." I tell Charlie the story and he sits down and starts to laugh. Next thing I know he is rolling on the floor and every time he looked up at me he'd start laughing again. It was one of those times when no matter what we did we would laugh. When the game ended, Willie Kirkland, a black teammate, and a funny man, found out what happened. He comes out of the shower, looks at me and says, "Hey, Mud." When I look up he had his both arms cupped like he was holding two watermelons and he breaks out in laughter. Most of the players know this story and to this day some of them will see me and say "Hey, Mud" and they'll cup their arms. But more importantly in terms of race relations, after the game Ray Katt came up to me and he's shaking. He is scared to death that the reporters will find out what happened. So that gave me the opportunity to speak with him about what he did. There are times when you have someone's attention that you can really do some good. Do you want life to change for the worse from that ugly standpoint or do you want to talk to the person that did it? Have a good talk with him, see how he feels, see how the other players feel, the fact that you either said something or did something. Because of Charlie's reaction and the way the players clowned around it was funny, but it wasn't really funny. It wasn't funny at all because I learned something about myself, that I was getting to the point where I wasn't before, that I could be affected by what somebody said, and I let it affect my ability to succeed. I reflected on the lessons that my mother had taught me and realized that even though my getting angry at Ray's comments was a natural reaction, I allowed it to affect my ability to perform and to succeed. I was the fastest pinch runner the team could have used. If the batter did hit a "tweener" I would have scored and we might have won. The guy that took my place couldn't score. So my taking myself out of the game, allowing myself to react in such a way, would have affected the game and my ability to succeed. I needed to use such incidents to motivate me, like Bob Gibson did, not to hold me back.

On the field, we had done pretty well in 1959, challenging the Chicago White Sox for the pennant. Unfortunately, after the season General Manager Frank Lane started to trade off important members of the team. He sent Minnie Minoso to the

White Sox and Cal McLish and Billy Martin to the Reds. Then two days before Opening Day 1960, he made a trade that Indians fans still have not forgiven him for: he let go of the league home run champion, Rocky Colavito, in exchange for the league batting champ, Harvey Kuenn. Lane was telling everybody, "It's like getting steak in exchange for hamburger." We didn't see it that way and neither did the fans. Kuenn lasted one year with the Indians before being traded to the Giants, and eventually the Tribe brought Rocky back. However, with the loss of Minoso, McLish, Martin and Colavito, in 1960 the team performed predictably poorly. Lane's response was to then trade his manager, Joe Gordon, to Detroit, for their manager, Jimmy Dykes.

In the spring of 1961 it looked like there was a chance that my brother, Julius Grant, who had been nicknamed Swampfire, might become my teammate. Julius, who was also known as Little Mudcat, although he wasn't much smaller than me, was a lefthanded pitcher who had a pretty decent fastball. He was 13-8 with Reading in 1960 and the Indians, again needing pitching, invited him to our Major League spring training camp in Tucson. Unfortunately, he didn't make the team and by May, when the Indians' need switched to hitting, they traded Julius to Kansas City for Jim Essegian.

I will never forget another special moment in my life that occurred thanks to baseball. In 1961, we were in Detroit, where the visiting team stayed at the Cadillac Hotel. I was resting in my room when I got a call. The voice on the other end said, "Mudcat, the President would like to see you." I said, "Yeah, sure" and I hung up the phone, positive that one of my teammates was pulling my leg. He called again, and I said, "Man, don't call me no more." A few minutes later there was a knock on my door. I looked through the peephole and there were three guys out in the hall, all with skinny black ties. They definitely looked like FBI/CIA types of guys, so I figured this could be legit and I opened the door. One of them said, "The President would like to see you." They gave me time to dress and took me up to see President John F. Kennedy who was staying in the Presidential Suite of the hotel. He was very friendly and we spoke for a long time. He was a big baseball fan and had read in the papers that we were in town. He knew all about me. We talked about baseball and Martin Luther King, Jr., and conditions in the South, and life in general. He mentioned how he hoped the country would change and that we had a job to do in the country in terms of having a "conversation" on how to get along. But I'd have to admit that most of the conversation we had that day was about baseball. He asked me about sliders and sinkers and stuff like that. As I left, after about an hour, he told me to give him a call when the team played in Washington.

Several months later, after having been to Washington on previous trips and not calling President Kennedy, I am in my hotel in Washington and I get a call from Adam Clayton Powell, who at the time was a Congressman from New York, the only black Congressman in the country. He said, "Man, you were supposed to call the Prez." I said, "Sure enough? I thought he was only being polite." He said, "No, he wants to see you." So, I called the White House and the next day

I was the President's guest in the Oval Office. We talked about Lacoochee and I told him how poor the people were and that there was still no running water in many of the homes, and there was a need for housing and a school. Next thing I know he had several of his assistants in his office with these big books checking to see if Lacoochee was eligible for federal assistance. Within several months the federal government started a project that resulted in a park, a school, housing, and running water. I remember getting a call from my Mom while I was on the road and she said, "James, I want you to hear something." She held the phone next to a toilet and flushed. She was the happiest women in America at that time. The local people were all so overjoyed. They named the park Stanley Park in honor of Jesse Stanley, the constable, and in my honor the street between the park and the new housing was named Mudcat Grant Boulevard.

The 1961 season marked progress for me in my journey to becoming a successful Major League starting pitcher. I posted a record of 15-9 and that gave me confidence to believe that I could win twenty. At the end of that season I was notified that I had to report to Fort Belvoir, Virginia, to serve a one-year stint in the Army. For the first four months of the 1962 season I split my time and my pitching chores between the Army and the Indians. I spent the week with the Army, where I was the manager and starting pitcher for the Fort team, and I would get weekend passes allowing me to join the Indians. By the time I joined the Indians for good, my record was 4-3 with Cleveland and I had made three starts for the Army, including a no-hitter against Lafayette College. My record with the Indians slipped to 7-10 and the main reason for that was that my Army duties deprived me of any spring training, which really hurt me, and then I would only be joining the club on weekends, which didn't allow me to get into any routine.

In 1963, free of the United States Army and any real injuries, and I bounced back to have one of my better seasons. I had the lowest ERA on the team (3.69) and I struck out 157 batters, which would be my career best. I pitched over 229 innings and won 13 games, tied for the team lead with Jack Kralick. It was my sixth season in Cleveland and I was playing for my seventh manager, Birdie Tebbetts. We seemed to have a problem finding a good manager in Cleveland who would stay with the team.

Early in the 1964 season, Early Wynn insisted on tinkering with my delivery. He wanted me to throw overhand although that was not my natural delivery and I was uncomfortable doing it. It was much more natural for me to throw side-armed. I don't know if that was the only reason for my lousy start in 1964, but it was certainly a main contributing factor.

I enjoyed living in Cleveland and with my son getting older I was looking into buying a house in the suburb of Shaker Heights. Since I heard rumors that the Indians were looking to trade me because of my rocky start that season, I asked management what the deal was before I went ahead with the new house. They gave me their vote of confidence (almost always a bad sign) and told me I was part of the Indians' plans. On June 15, 1964, just before the trading deadline I learned that their "plans" were to trade me to the Minnesota Twins, which was the original Washington Senator franchise. It was a difficult thing for me, because it came as such a surprise. I came to the ballpark that day to play against the Twins, and I was sure I was going to get a start, but instead I was traded for pitcher Lee Stange, a player to be named later and an undisclosed amount of money. Twins' owner, Calvin Griffith, had moved the Senators to Minnesota in 1961, when a new franchise moved into Washington. Before I went to Minnesota I already knew about Griffith and his well-publicized racist attitude. He was well known to all the players and to baseball, but I was glad to go to the Minneapolis – St. Paul area because of the attitude of the citizens. They thought less of African-Americans as problems, as the way Griffith may see African-Americans. They didn't have those kind of thought patterns. The population of blacks in Minneapolis – St. Paul wasn't huge, but they lived there with some sense of freedom, and that's what we all liked about Minneapolis when we went up there. There were pockets of freedom, that you felt emotionally, because of the citizens. So, despite Mr. Griffith there was a sense of fresh air in Minneapolis.

In 1978, Calvin Griffith, speaking to a group in Minnesota, gave his reasons for moving the Twins from Washington:

It was when I found out you only had 15,000 black people here. Black people don't go to ball games, but they'll fill up a rassling ring and put up such a chant it'll scare you to death. It's unbelievable. We came here because you've got good, hardworking white people here.

He was just as bad or worse in 1964. You could feel the vibrations of his opinion in terms of black folk. Many owners and general managers might have had opinions, but they sort of kept it to themselves, because they knew if they expressed their opinions all hell would break loose. But sometimes, when they got confident they started blabbing. And then too, sometimes, general managers and owners are not the most intelligent people in the world. We expect them to be, but sometimes they just simply are not. And then there's a breakthrough in terms of thought patterns that they may have. Now, Griffith caught hell for those statements that he made. Minnesota didn't agree with what he was saying. They were appalled at what he said, and they let him know it. I think Rod Carew was on that team at that time. He really got visibly upset at these statements that Calvin Griffith made.

By his own words Griffith treated all blacks differently and he treated me the same way he treated the other black ballplayers. He paid you less. He thought of your value as less, simply because you were black. That was a known factor. I know that he had to be warned, and he had to be convinced that he had to have black ballplayers. When they were the Senators there was Earl Battey, and there was Lenny Green there also. They were the first two blacks with the Washington Senators who then became the Minnesota Twins. In Washington, DC, he had to be made to bring on some black ballplayers, or else he couldn't have played at the new stadium, RFK Stadium. So, we knew how he thought, and despite his success with the Twins his thoughts are not going to change. But we had already lived with the fact that you had to succeed despite who you played for, despite what manager you played for. The only problem we had was our salary, because how he thought wasn't going to change, so that didn't bother us one way or another. Too bad he thought that way, but Mr. Griffith was prejudiced and you knew where he came from. He was that way. That wasn't anything that would stop us from succeeding, but it was motivation to override his thoughts and do something good.

"The Twins have kept me in the league all this time. I'm worried about which team will keep me in the league now." He [Mudcat] was referring to his amazing record against the old Washington Senators (20-5) and the new Twins (6-4). Grant was winning so consistently against the Senators in old Griffith Stadium that they staged "beat Mudcat" days and strung up black cats to decorate the park when Mudcat was to pitch. "I hate to leave Cleveland. I started here and I wanted to finish here. But ball players are like street cars – we come and go. I was always proud to be an Indian. Larry Doby was my idol and I always aspired to play on the team he had been with."
Regis McAuley, The Sporting News, June 27, 1964

Although I knew about the Twins' owner and all that went with playing for him, and I was sad to leave Cleveland after having made my home there for several years and having just purchased a new house, I was glad to go to Minnesota for a couple of reasons. One was that I would be joining one of my best friends in the game, Earl Battey. I met Earl when he was a catcher for the Washington Senators. I beat them on a regular basis, before he got there. Then he got over there in a trade for Roy Sievers – Earl Battey and Don Mincher, who was another wonderful individual, from Alabama. Earl was very learned at that time, he was very bright at that time. Even though I have something in terms of wisdom, I wasn't as bright as Earl in terms of life, in terms of words. I was a little simpler than Earl was, so I learned a lot from him, in terms of politics, in terms of people that he knew that I didn't know. And we became very friendly, like brothers, even though we were opponents. We competed just as hard against one another, but we became closer, like brothers during that time, because of the circumstances. So he knew that I was going to get his ass out, and I knew that he was going to get a base hit if he could. It didn't take long after the game, as soon as you saw one another it was instant.

A second reason I was happy about the trade was I knew that the Twins lineup could score runs for me. Sure enough, in three of my first starts for Minnesota they knocked out 51 hits and scored 32 runs. That was enough support to get me three wins to start off my Twins career.

I said it was nice to be traded to a team that can score like the Twins. They sure made it easier for me to get going again. ... Any pitcher would be happy to be traded to this club. You can just tend to the

pitching and rest assured you won't have to be working on a one-run margin all the time.
Quoted by Max Nichols, The Sporting News, July 25, 1964

Jim (Mudcat) Grant cannot complain about the support he has received from the Twins against the Red Sox since he was obtained in a trade with the Indians in June. Grant started against the Red Sox for the third time as a Twin, September 4, and was a 14-3 winner. In his two earlier starts against Boston, he won by scores of 14-3 and 12-4.
The Sporting News, September 9, 1964

Once I got to Minnesota in 1964 I started to pitch much more effectively. During the first two and a half months of the season with Cleveland I was 3-4 with a bloated ERA of 5.95. After the trade I pitched ten complete games, went 11-9, and brought my ERA down to 2.82, less than half of what it was while with Cleveland.

One definite benefit of pitching for the Twins was the opportunity to be coached by Johnny Sain, probably the most successful pitching coach of all time. Johnny's first project with me was to teach me a new pitch. He discounted the Kickapoo and Hop and Jumper as part of my pitch inventory. He boiled down my repertoire to a fastball, a change of pace and a slow curve, and he wanted me to learn a fast curve, which is similar to the slider. That extra pitch, improved control and the Twins' ability to score runs when I was pitching, were the keys to my becoming a twenty-game winner in 1965. During one stretch in June I went 23.3 innings without issuing a base on balls. In early August of 1965 I was suffering from tendonitis in the knees, a condition they called "housemaid knees." With both knees wrapped I started and won three games in one week, with the Twins scoring 22 runs for me. Even when things seemed bad that year they wound up going well. After I hit a new career high in victories, with 16, by early September, Max Nichols of The Sporting News did a feature piece on me, focusing on the reason for my success:

Why was he having his best year? "Because I'm getting more runs to work with than I've ever had," he said. "These guys have really helped me. I've got to give them credit. It makes a difference working with a lead all the time." Grant also has given Johnny Sain, Twins' pitching coach, credit for helping him improve his curve. ... In his victories, the Twins have scored 111 runs – an average of 6.9 per game. They have scored four runs or more in all but three of his triumphs and never less than three.
The Sporting News, September 4, 1965

On September 25, 1965, I beat my favorite opponent, the Washington Senators, 5-0 on a one-hitter, becoming the first African-American to win twenty games in the American League. I had won eight of my last nine decisions.

I consider myself a very blessed person, so I look at that one stat – 20 game winner - very seriously and I think you have to look at it two ways: spiritually and ordinary. Okay, I was a ballplayer, I got 40 starts. I won 21 games, but that's the only time I won 20 or more. Maybe it was a reward, or a blessing, or something like that. But I got a chance to get in that number one time, and in this small career that I had, I only won 145 games, but look at it this way: I am one of the few pitchers to win 20 and save 20; I'm the first black pitcher to win 20 games in the American League; I led the American League in shutouts in 1965 with 6, I was second in the League with complete games with 14; I was second in the League in appearances in 1970 with 72, for Oakland. Take all of those things piled on in that small career and I consider myself blessed.

When we won the American League pennant in 1965 it was only the third time in seventeen years that the Yankees had not won, and our victory actually ended the Yankee dynasty. They would not win another pennant until 1976. We won the flag by seven games over Chicago, and the Yanks were a full 25 games behind us. We were the only team in the majors to win more than 100 games (102). It was a team effort, with six of our players being selected to the American League All-Star team: Earl Battey, Jimmie Hall, Harmon Killebrew, Tony Oliva, Zoilo Versalles, and me, with Versalles also being selected as the league's Most Valuable Player. As a team we led the league in batting average (.254), runs scored (774), hits (1396), doubles (257), and triples (42). Individually, Oliva led the league in hitting (.321) and hits (185) and Versalles led in runs scored (126) and total bases (308). I pitched fourteen complete games and six shutouts, and started more games that year (39) than in any other year in my career. At the time there was only one Cy Young Award given in the majors, and that was won by Sandy Koufax.

The Dodgers won the National League pennant so we would get to face Koufax, but because Sandy observed Yom Kippur, which fell on the same day as the first game of the Series, we never got to face each other. People have asked me if I wished it could have been me facing Sandy in Game Seven that year. My answer is, "Hell, no!" I knew he would be tougher to beat than Don Drysdale. So, often I say I want to thank Yom Kippur, because it kept Koufax from starting Game One and they started Drysdale, and that kept us from facing each other during the Series. Now, I thought about that when they started writing about the possibility that Sandy might not start because of Yom Kippur. I figured, if I'm going to beat Koufax I may have to beat him 1-0. That's how good he was at that time. But if it's Drysdale, I could beat him 3-2, or something like that. That's the way I thought about it. I recognized talent, and I only won 145 ballgames. Sandy won more, and Gibson and Jenkins won many more. They were all better than me, but at one given time maybe they weren't, and that was the time during the 1965 Series, that I could have a record just as good as Sandy did, and he was on the flip side of it. I know that at least for one week in the opinion of one of my opponents I was comparable to the greats. After I defeated the Dodgers in Game One, Maury Wills told George Vecsey of *Newsday*:

He [Grant] is a lot like [Bob] Gibson. Maybe not quite as fast but pretty much the same.

In the 1965 Series I was probably as good as Koufax. It may have only been during that seven game period, but the record speaks for itself. He won two games, I lost one. I won two games, he lost one. So, at least for that moment, we were equal. I won Games One and Six, and lost Game Four. Sandy lost Game Two and won Games Five and Seven. In Game Six I hit a three run home run off a Howie Reed curveball, only the second home run ever hit by an American League pitcher in a World Series game, and the first since Jim Bagby of Cleveland hit one in 1920. Sandy was basically unhittable in Game Seven, holding us to three hits and shutting us out for the second time in a row.

One place where Sandy and I were not equal was in our ability to capitalize on our on-field success with promotional opportunities. This disparity was captured by veteran sportswriters Phil Pepe and Steve Jacobsen right after the Series:

Jim Grant had come to find the pot of gold. Sandy owns it. It was the day Sport Magazine gave away the Corvette to the outstanding player in the World Series. Sandy Koufax got it because he won two games in the Series. The second one when he pitched with only two days' rest. Jim Grant also won two games in the World Series and he also won his second game pitching with two days' rest, but his was different. His was the sixth game and Sandy's was the seventh and it is part of the story of Jim Grant that he has always been too early. He is too early to get what he really wants, about 50 years too early. Jim Grant is a Negro and the world is not quite ready for Negro heroes and so Jim must struggle because nobody is breaking his neck to sign him for movies and endorsements. He is handsome and he is famous, but he is black ...
Sandy could get $10,000 just for demonstrating the way he soaks his arm in a bucket of ice after he pitches. Jim Grant has the kind of pleasant face that would look good in a television commercial ... if television was ready for his kind of face.
Phil Pepe, October 19, 1985

He won two games and lost one, just as Koufax did. But there were other things even a victory in the seventh game wouldn't have brought Grant. For one thing, he's married. For another, he's Negro. He won 21 games, pitched two complete games in the Series and wears clothes as well as anybody around. But nobody has been around yet to ask him to endorse a product. Being the biggest winner in the American League won't get those fringe benefits for him. Oh, being a big winner got him the exposure on the Johnny Carson television show, singing with the Kittens. It's all right for a colored man to sing on television,

but not to have his picture taken for a sportswear advertisement. Grant is a bright man with a bubbling sense of humor about his sincere musical aspirations and a laugh about a lot of the things that hurt him most.
Steve Jacobsen, Newsday, October 19, 1965

After my twenty-win season in 1965, I thought I was entitled to receive a salary of at least $50,000. Calvin Griffith thought otherwise and that led to my holding out. Finally, I agreed to accept the $35,000 the Twins offered, which was an increase, but not what I was looking for.

During that off-season I began to pursue my second love, music, with much more effort. I had put together a lounge act, called Mudcat and the Kittens, and had scheduled a pretty extensive tour that winter, including a three week engagement on the same bill with Maury Wills, who played banjo, at Basin Street East in New York. Ever since Mrs. Goodwin introduced me to music back in Lacoochee it has been a big part of my life. Back in the late 60s I was seriously considering becoming an entertainer full-time. In addition to my early training I had picked up a lot of information and an additional passion for entertaining through all of my contacts with black entertainers. As we traveled on the road and we were restricted to black hotels, we would find ourselves in the same places as many of the most famous black entertainers who were also not allowed to stay in white hotels. That led to my developing great friendships with many of the top black entertainers.

From 1964 on, violence arising out of racial tension seemed to dominate the headlines for the rest of the decade. Race riots had occurred in the Watts section of Los Angeles during the summer of 1964, and would spill over to the streets of Brooklyn, Chicago, Detroit, Baltimore, Cleveland, Omaha, Atlanta, and Rochester, in 1965 and 1966. In 1967, there were race riots in more than 150 cities throughout the United States, resulting in 83 reported deaths, 66 of which occurred in either Newark or Detroit. The domestic violence seemed to culminate in 1968 with the assassinations of Martin Luther King, Jr. and Bobby Kennedy, both of whom I had an opportunity to meet and grew to admire. I got the chance to meet Rev. King several times. First, he was a minister, and my respect for ministers overbears everything. I admired his courage, because you had to know that a lot of people considered him dangerous to their way of life, and although his life was in danger that didn't seem to bother him. I don't think the world is going to see too many people like Martin Luther King. That's just the way it is. He had no concern for his life and safety. He had concern, of course, for his wife and family, but like he said, "If I have to go, I have to go." His passion for humanity was certainly something that enhanced my passion for humanity; not only his passion for humanity but his passion to improve humanity, for everybody. Even though he was black and he worked so hard for black people, his idea was to encompass everybody into the belief that we should have more respect for humanity and we should work together. That's my take on Martin Luther King, and he probably is the most passionate individual besides my Mom that I really knew of.

The Twins were probably the most integrated team in the American League in the mid 60s, as the St. Louis Cardinals were in the National League. However, whereas the Cardinals under the leadership of Bob Gibson, Bill White and others were a harmonious group, dissension among the Whites, Latinos, and African-Americans, could not be harnessed by new manager, Cal Ermer, and that prevented the Twins from having continued success. Specifically, a discussion between Dave Boswell and Tony Oliva while on the team bus in July 1967 led to heated words from which the team never really recovered. In August of 1967 I was fined $250 for missing curfew, although I was actually in the hotel in a different room. The next day, Ermer pulled me from my assigned start. I immediately asked for a trade. I had had enough of the Minnesota Twins. It took until the end of November for the Twins to find a deal acceptable to them. I was traded to the Dodgers along with 1965 MVP Zoilo Versalles for Ron Perranoski, Johnny Roseboro, and Bob Miller. Since Perranoski was included in the deal, it was widely expected that I would become a relief pitcher with the Dodgers. At the time the trade was announced I didn't care if the Dodgers wanted me to play third base, I was ready to go.

Even if it was Piston, Ga. In the Piedmont League, it would have been better than Minnesota. Spiritually and mentally I'll have peace of mind by getting away from Minnesota, from Griffith and the new manager, Cal Ermer. That team is a mess, mostly because of Griffith and his meddling.
Quoted by Stan Isaacs, Newsday, December 5, 1967

The Dodgers allowed me to compete for a role in the starting rotation in the spring of 1968, and although I did begin the season as a starter, I spent most of my days with the Dodgers as a relief pitcher, a new role for me.

In the off-season between 1968 and 1969, I was contacted by the USO to make three goodwill trips to Viet Nam. The trips were meant as a way to motivate our soldiers and give them some relief and support from America by having them experience some entertainment with ballplayers, Bob Hope, the New Christy Minstrels and other entertainers. I was happy to be able to help and I made all three trips, one with the Commissioner, one with Joe DiMaggio, and one with Willie Stargell and Ron Swoboda, along with some other ballplayers. As far as I'm concerned, they were great trips. We got a chance to understand a little bit more than what we read in terms of Viet Nam, got a chance to mix with the Vietnamese people, got a chance to see more to the point what was happening. You get a chance to see all the problems when it comes to injuries and deaths, when it comes to Agent Orange, which now is a political football in terms of our soldiers being affected by that. But the main experience itself was a good experience. On the trip I made with Stargell and Swoboda, I remember that we were at a Mobile Army Surgical Hospital (MASH), visiting with the soldiers who were patients. They were separated by the severity of their injuries, those that would go back into combat when healed, those who would be sent home when capable, and those who the medical staff considered too injured to transport and who they did not expect to live. One soldier that I spent some time with was in the last category, expected to die there in Viet Nam. He had lost both legs in an explosion caused by a mine he set off. His head was bandaged, his eyes covered, and he was unconscious. Stargell and Swoboda said a few words to him and had moved on to the next patient. I got a chance to spend some time with him and I started by whispering in his ear, "I don't know if you can hear me, but my name is Mudcat Grant, and Ron Swoboda and Willie Stargell and a few other people are over here to spend some time with you guys." Then I read him some letters that had been sent to him and I went on to another hospital.

During that off-season I was chosen by the Montreal Expos in the expansion draft and became the first pitcher to start and win a game for the Expos. Before Opening Day 1969 however, I was reminded yet again that discrimination still existed in sunny Florida. The Expos trained in West Palm Beach and my roommate was former Series rival, Maury Wills. Maury was the subject of a newspaper article and while being interviewed he and the reporter and a photographer went to two different bars to discuss the story and had to leave both establishments because they were told they "didn't serve colored people." *The Herald-Tribune* recorded my comments at the time:

We have been running into situations like this for years and years. I was becoming relieved that these things were finally coming to an end. The fact that Maury and I are allowed to stay at the same hotel as the white players is an encouraging sign of the type of progress made in recent years. But there are still a few public places which prefer to practice discrimination. That's the reason I didn't bring my wife and kids to training camp. We can't live in the type of neighborhood we want because they don't rent to black people.

Things were much better for Maury and I in Montreal as members of the Expos. Actually, I understood what Willie Wells said about playing in Mexico when I was playing in Canada. There was much less racial tension there at the time.

I was sold to the St. Louis Cardinals in June. Sometime in August 1969, I was scheduled to start a home game for the Cardinals, and after batting practice and getting my running in, I went into the clubhouse. I got a message that there were some fans outside who wanted to meet me. I went back outside and there was this soldier with no legs sitting in a wheelchair. I went up and shook his hand and said, "Nice to meet you." He looked at me and said, "I just wanted to tell you, I heard you." He was from somewhere in Missouri, and my trade to St. Louis brought him back into my life. He made a special trip to the ballpark to see me and tell me he heard me. When something like this happens it makes you understand some of the reasons why you would make a trip like I did to Viet Nam and it makes you sleep real good. It also helps you to understand the power and attraction of baseball and all the experiences that had been opened up to me because of my ability to play.

Mud pitched here in Oakland when I was a kid, but he was at the end of his career. What that let me know was that it was possible that a black pitcher could pitch in the big leagues. That's what Mud was to me. He was reality. And then I came to know him later on when I was playing. He was a broadcaster or doing something of that nature then. That was my first impression of him. This was a proud man, and I saw how immaculate he was. He was well dressed and he was well manicured, and I was impressed with that as well.
Mike Norris interview

In December 1969, the Oakland Athletics purchased my contract from the St. Louis Cardinals. The A's also used me in relief, but more as a short man than a long reliever. After I left St. Louis I would never start another Major League game. There is a different philosophy in relief pitching and a different philosophy in starting. There are so many philosophies among starting pitchers, all the way to the point where you have to prepare yourself to pitch a long time, whether it be seven, eight, or nine innings as a starting pitcher. The mentality was, in my day, that you were a nine-inning pitcher. As a relief pitcher, you have to get out of immediate trouble. So, there's two different ways: the long man's philosophy is that you have to hold him until you get some runs. A short relief man's philosophy is that after they get the runs you better hold them, or else you're down at the end of the game. So, what you do in the middle of the game, even though you want to stop the rush, you want to stop the avalanche, until your team can catch up, at the latter part of the game you have to finish them off, otherwise, you are not going to win. You're not so concerned in the middle as to whether you're going to win or lose, but it's to stop the avalanche until your team catches up. Now, they may never catch up, but you're already behind if you're the long man. If you are the starter the philosophy is that you have to pitch deep into the game. You've got to either pitch nine innings, and usually when you pitch nine innings, you're going to win, sometimes you lose; but, the whole way, and I've never been a set-up man, but the short reliever, you're damn right I can explain that. You're in trouble. You don't have time to say, I'm not in trouble. You're either one run ahead, or two runs ahead, or three runs ahead, but you ain't four. If you are the man as the short reliever, you are not so far ahead that they could use somebody else. It is you. It could be one out with the bases loaded, it could be runners on first and third, and the game is on the line. I got to the point where I liked that pretty good. It is sometimes the mentality applied at the right position you are in, because you can't have a long man mentality as a short reliever. When I was with the Athletics I talked with Rollie Fingers a lot about a reliever's mentality, how to prepare yourself, without somebody saying, "Hey, warm up." If you're a short relief man, whatever it takes for you to get ready, that's what you do. And if you're the short man and it seems like you're going to win the game, you could be five runs in front, you can never count on that. You have to get ready, just in case, especially if all of a sudden, now they score two runs. If you're not ready, by that time, then you're not going to be able to pitch in a lot of games, because you can't wait until they call you. That's why now you see short relievers, when the inning is over with, in the 7th or 8th, you see them get up and start to throw. They don't want to have to go, whump, whump, whump. You're not going to be ready. You're arm is not going to be loose. It's going to take more than 8 pitches for it to get loose. No, you've got to do that before, and I think that I was the beginning of doing that, even though no one was paying attention. Around the 7th inning, I'm up and throwing and my arm is going to be loose, and when they call to warm up, you don't have to do that much. That's one of the things that I taught Rollie Fingers. Toward the end of the 1970 season, I was acquired by the Pittsburgh Pirates and made eight appearances for them. Together with the 72 appearances I made for Oakland, my 80 appearances in 1970 placed me among the top fifty pitchers in number of appearances in a single season.

I kept a book on hitters toward the end of my career. But, you didn't forget. You always had a game plan. You knew what the hitters were and what they could do. You knew what pitch they liked, tried to avoid mistakes. But, the game plan was the art of pitching: Make the hitter hit the ball with something on it, so in order to do that now you got to do other things. You got to throw him something else to get him to hit ground balls. But you didn't have to be a rocket scientist on the other hand, especially for some hitters. If I'm in the middle of a ballgame and I got a man on and maybe one run behind, and maybe leading, I got a man on first and third with two outs, Willie Mays, Ted Williams, Frank Robinson, Joe Morgan, Hank Aaron, Roberto Clemente, they ain't gonna hit me. You think I'm gonna throw them something to hit, with a man on first and third, some of the most prolific hitters you've ever seen? I ain't taking no chances, boy. NO! Call me chicken if you want.

In August, 1971, with Pittsburgh heading towards the playoffs, I found myself back with the Oakland Athletics, a move that cost me about $18,000 in World Series money. Oakland again used me in a relief role exclusively. That would be my last work on a Major League mound. In the spring of 1972 I was invited to spring training with the Cleveland Indians but didn't fit in their plans for the year. Instead, I accepted an invitation from Charlie Finley to be a player/coach of the Iowa Oaks.

When the 1972 season was over I began to face the questions which Jackie Robinson had posed to me years earlier: Was I prepared for life after baseball? How would I make my living? Coincidentally, as that phase of my life kicked in, causing me to reflect about Jackie more than usual, Jackie passed away in October of 1972. Thankfully, I had taken Jackie's advice and had studied marketing and entrepreneurship in preparation for life after baseball and I enjoyed working in many different capacities over the past thirty years, including my music. After the 1972 season I began broadcasting Indians games with Harry Jones, becoming the first black sportscaster in Indians history and one of the first on any Major League team. I also served as Community Director for the Indians, Special Marketing Director for Anheuser-Busch in the Cleveland area and Assistant Venue Director for Baseball at the 1984 Olympics in Los Angeles. Then Henry Aaron felt that I still had something left to offer younger players and I put a uniform back on as the pitching coach for the Durham Bulls in the Braves organization.

I have stayed extremely active in baseball alumni activities and I still enjoy putting on a uniform and making appearances. To be honest, it has been a lifelong love affair with baseball and the American people who remain so passionate about the game. I still read the box scores every day, just like I did as a little boy in Lacoochee, and I enjoy getting out to the games as often as I can. I like talking with today's players and I am not bashful about reminding them of how it was back in the 1950s and 1960s. I am ever mindful of what Jackie Robinson and Larry Doby went through which cleared the way for my path to a Major League pitching mound. It is my hope and desire that today's ballplayers do not forget the past.

CHAPTER 20

ROBERT GIBSON
Bob
Hoot

Born November 9, 1935 in Omaha, Nebraska
Team: St. Louis Cardinals
Twenty-Win Seasons: 1965, 1966, 1968, 1969, 1970
Inducted into National Baseball Hall of Fame 1981
National League Cy Young Award 1968, 1970
National League MVP 1968
National League All-Star 1962, 1965, 1966, 1967, 1968, 1969,
*   1970, 1972*
National League Gold Glove 1965, 1966, 1967, 1968,
*   1969, 1970, 1971, 1972, 1973*
Inducted into Creighton University Sports Hall of Fame
Inducted into St. Louis Walk of Fame 1993
Inducted into Missouri Sports Hall of Fame 1997

I used to worship Bob Gibson when I was in high school.
J.R. Richard

The only people I ever felt intimidated by in my whole life were Bob
Gibson and my Daddy.
Dusty Baker

Bob Gibson was one of my baseball idols because he doesn't mess
around out there, he just gets the job done. He's the boss when he's
on the mound.
Vida Blue interview

Bob was the first black pitcher that I saw excel. He was the first one I
saw to have success and was the first one I tried to emulate. His style
of falling off the mound - I tried to do that, I can just remember that
and the fact that he would fight you, hit you and then come down off
the mound and challenge you. I thought that was so gutsy and godly.
In between the lines he was a fierce competitor. I believe I got my
fierceness from him.
Mike Norris interview

233

A friend of mine asked me, "Was Bob Gibson better than you?" and when I responded, "Hell, yeah!" he was sort of stunned. I asked him, "Why are you so amazed?" He said, "Well, you admitted that another pitcher was better than you." Then I really floored him by adding, "He ain't the only one."

Making it to the Major Leagues took talent and drive, and a certain amount of ego, but I would have to be blind or stupid not to acknowledge that differences exist between we mere mortals who were gifted enough to play at the major league level and those who were truly the greats of the game.

Each of the thirteen Black Aces, like each of the earlier Negro League pitchers I profiled, is an integral part of the history of pitching in America. However, I must admit that if I were to select one of the group that was more equal than the others in the history of baseball it would be Bob Gibson. Each of the Black Aces has a uniqueness which makes their collective mosaic fantastic when complete – Newk was the first, a revolutionary; Sam was a throwback before throwbacks were nostalgic; Earl was as much trouble for opposing pitchers as he was for opposing batters; Fergie won the most and won 20 the most times; Vida captured the country's attention and imagination in 1971; Downing and Norris came back to win twenty after people thought they were finished; JR was King in Houston; Stewart owned the ALCS; Gooden's Dr. K persona was like Superman on the mound, and Dontrelle's youthful joy and exuberance brought the Aces into the hip-hop generation, but smack in the middle of the history and geography of baseball is Bob Gibson. Others may have better statistics and accomplished things before he did or things he never did, but all things considered he is looked upon by sportswriters, players, and history itself, as one of the greatest pitchers of all time. In a poll published in *The Sporting News* on October 26, 1996, naming the 100 Best Players in the history of the game Gibby was ranked number 31. Fellow Hall of Famers, Satchel Paige, Sandy Koufax, Steve Carlton and Tom Seaver were ranked 19, 26, 30 and 32, respectively.

In my opinion, Bob Gibson was the greatest pitcher that ever played in the Major Leagues.
Elijah "Pumpsie" Green

Geographically, he was born and raised in the middle of America – Omaha, Nebraska, and he played for a team also located in the middle of America – the St. Louis Cardinals. Chronologically, he came after the most widely recognized trailblazers, like Newcombe and Paige, and helped lead the way into the period of time when black pitchers were dominant in the Major Leagues.

But my opinion of where Gibson sits in the hierarchy of pitchers centers not on time or geography but on the man himself, and his accomplishments. Now, thirty years after Gibson retired as a player, sportswriters and commentators respectfully bring up Gibson's name every time a discussion of great pitching arises and especially if the discussion evolves to include the issue of pitching inside. He is widely regarded as a pitcher who would knock down any batter including his own blood. The reality is that Bob Gibson is one of the greatest money pitchers of all time, of any color, and one of the greatest competitors to ever play the game of baseball. If this book were to be written about the top 13 pitchers of all time, Gibson would be included. If the book were about great pitchers of the 1960's or 70's, Gibson would be on the cover. But I am getting ahead of myself. Before I start to relate how impressed I am with Bob Gibson the baseball pitcher, I need to talk about Bob Gibson the person. Bob's career numbers and statistics, the lore and legend that surround him, and the awe in which players, managers, umpires, fans and sportswriters hold him, are all special, but I know Bob, and I know that how he is viewed and respected as a person is much more important to him than how he is viewed as a baseball player.

Respect, that's the word. Respect. We must respect one another. When Jackie Robinson broke the color line in baseball, he was not respected as a human being, but only because he could play baseball better than most. What we really need in pro sports – and in society – generally, I suppose, is for the white man to respect the Negro for what he is, not merely for his work.
Bob Gibson, quoted by Dwight Chapin, LA Times, July 5, 1968

I hate phonies. I am prejudiced against all those who have contempt for me because my face is black and all those who accept me because of my ability to throw a baseball. I am not proud of that ability. It is not something I earned or acquired or bought. It is a gift. It is something that was given to me – just like the color of my skin.
Bob Gibson, Ghetto To Glory, 1967

All they're saying is I'm a 'special' Negro. That's the only reason some neighbors accept me. It makes me want to vomit. It doesn't excite me when I go into a restaurant and they give me the glad hand because I'm Bob Gibson the ballplayer. They might throw the next Negro out. I'm kind of sensitive about things, and I might sound as if I have a chip on my shoulder. I do. But I didn't put it there. Somebody else did.
Bob Gibson, quoted in Crossing the Line, McFarland & Company

The content of those quotes is straight and direct and they were delivered in such a way as to grab your attention, just the way Bob pitched.

Bob Gibson, the person, showed great courage, discipline and determination, in becoming the great individual he is, and that is really where my story about Bob must begin. Just as my folks had migrated to Florida from Georgia, in search of work, Bob's family had moved to Omaha, Nebraska from Alexandria, Louisiana. Bob and I were both born in the same year (1935) and under some very similar conditions, including poverty. Although I have no memories whatsoever of my father because I was so young when he died, at least he got to hold me and some bonding did occur. Bob never even had that luxury. His dad, Pack Gibson, died of quick consumption, a form of tuberculosis, two months before Bob was born. (Bob was named Pack Robert Gibson, in honor of his dad, and although Bob respected his Dad's memory he was not fond of the name, and changed it to Robert when he became an adult.) That left Bob's mom, Victoria, and his older siblings to raise him. Like me, Bob was the youngest child in his family, and like my mom, Bob's mother persevered through her widowhood to provide as best as she could for her children. She worked at Omaha Lace Laundry and cleaned houses and hospitals in her "spare" time. Although Bob wasn't raised in a company row house, his living conditions were not much better, or bigger. Bob, his mother, and his six brothers and sisters, all lived in a two-room shanty that barely provided any shelter from nature's elements or its creatures. While he was sleeping at home, at the age of four, Bob was bitten on the ear by a rat. Bob's health was in about as sad a condition as his family's living quarters and financial situation. His childhood battles against rickets, pneumonia, asthma, hay fever, and a heart murmur, are well documented.

The father figure in Bob's life was his oldest brother, Leroy, who everyone called Josh, as a reference to the great Negro Leaguer, because of his athletic ability. Bob has often related that when he was being admitted into a hospital as a young boy, he innocently asked his mother and brother if he was going to die. Assuring him that he would be okay, Josh promised Bob a bat and ball when he came out of the hospital. Could Josh have possibly known how prophetic a gift he was to give to Bob? But the real gift was providing Bob with a role model, coach and mentor.

In 1941, Bob's family moved from the shanty into a two-bedroom apartment, in the newly built Logan Fontanelle projects, in the near North End of Omaha, a predominantly black section that technically qualified as a ghetto. The apartments were built with a government grant and occupancy was limited to families with a maximum income of $2,200 for a family of four. The rent was about $18 a month, including electricity, heat and water. Bob has stated that his family, like mine, didn't have a television, but their apartment was located in such a way that he could watch cartoons and cowboy shows, through the window, on his neighbor's set, the only one in the projects.

Bob would spend a good deal of time at the YMCA, playing basketball and baseball on teams they sponsored. Competing in sports came easy to Bob, but his memories of getting to and from the "Y" remind me of my trips to the movie house in Lacoochee:

> **The only difficulty in utilizing the Y was finding a safe way to negotiate the ten blocks between there and the projects. The unwritten rule was never to cross over to the white side of the neighborhood, so we walked straight down Twenty-second Street to Lake, steering two blocks clear of the roughest corner in town.**
> *Stranger to the Game, The Autobiography of Bob Gibson, by Bob Gibson with Lonnie Wheeler, Viking Penguin, NY 1994*

Opportunities weren't many or great for Bob, but Josh continued to see that Bob stuck to the straight and narrow. When Bob experimented with tobacco, at age 12, like many youngsters are tempted to, and Josh found out about it, he gave Bob a shot to the back of the head and a kick in the pants, and that ended that experiment.

Bob quickly acknowledges the impact his brother Josh had on his life, but in retrospect he reflects on which came first, Josh's love of coaching which made Bob a better athlete, or Bob being a great athlete which stirred Josh's interest in coaching. Either way, it became clear that Bob had great talent and Josh had an ability and desire to coach and mentor him. Then in the spring of 1947, when Jackie Robinson became a Brooklyn Dodger, something else became clear – that there was a path to the Major Leagues for a black child, not well-worn or direct, but a path nonetheless.

For both of us, the commitment [to athletics] is probably traceable to a conversation we had when I was eleven. One day late that summer, Josh sat me down in front of our house for a hard lecture on being a professional man. Traditionally, professionalism was and is a matter of education, but at that moment something new was opening up for black people. It was 1947, and Jackie Robinson had just joined the Brooklyn Dodgers. Suddenly, there was the unexpected possibility of a black man being a professional athlete. … Until that time, black kids in most cities had generally played softball rather than baseball. But when Jackie Robinson made the big leagues, we rounded up hardballs, moved the bases back, and began firing overhanded.

Stranger to the Game, The Autobiography of Bob Gibson, by Bob Gibson with Lonnie Wheeler, Viking Penguin, NY 1994

With the breadth of Bob's dreams widened by the signing of Jackie Robinson, fueled by Bob's talent, and encouraged by Josh's coaching and mentoring, Bob started to go places, literally and figuratively. As a result of playing on local teams coached by Josh, Bob got to attend games of the St. Louis Cardinals' minor league team in Omaha. The Cardinals' Bill Bergesch worked with Josh to allow his players to attend games, and also gave him used equipment to use for his sandlot players. As a result of winning local tournaments, Bob got to travel outside of Omaha. He remembers playing in towns throughout Nebraska, Iowa and Missouri.

Most of Bob's opportunity to play baseball came outside of school in local leagues, because, according to what he was told, blacks were not allowed to play baseball at Omaha Technical High School, where Bob attended, despite the fact that blacks made up about half of the student body. However, the real reason for the restriction against blacks on the baseball team was the personal bias and bigotry of the team's head coach, Ken Kennedy. Kennedy would use any excuse to keep a black player from making the roster, making up rules as he went along. In Bob's case, when he tried out for the baseball team as a junior Kennedy told him he was a day late for tryouts, although that clearly was not the case. Bob finally found out the truth about Kennedy from another Tech coach, on the day he was inducted into the Hall of Fame. The baseball team's loss was the gain of coach Dutch White's track team, the best in the state of Nebraska, as Bob ran track and perfected his broad jump skills to the point where he became Omaha City champ, and placed second in the state. By his senior year at Omaha Tech, Bob was offered a contract to play ball with the Kansas City Monarchs, which he turned down to stay in school. That same year, under new head baseball coach, Tom Murphy, Bob and Jerry Parks became the first two blacks to play baseball at Omaha Tech, and they were instrumental in leading the team to the City championship. That summer Bob also led his American Legion Team to the Nebraska State Championship. Bob was mainly used as a catcher and outfielder during his teenage years, though he always found his way to the mound, which was usual for all the better players on amateur teams. No matter where he played in the field, he was a tremendous offensive weapon for every team he played on.

I think I could have batted between .280 and .300 as an everyday player, with twenty to twenty-five home runs a year and thirty to forty stolen bases.
Stranger to the Game, The Autobiography of Bob Gibson, by Bob Gibson with Lonnie Wheeler, Viking Penguin, NY 1994

I remember that there seemed nothing that Gibson couldn't do. In batting practice, he would hit a couple of balls out of the park, then turn around and hit one out left-handed.
Eric Rasmussen, teammate, St. Louis Cardinals

Like me, Bob also loved the game of basketball, and excelled at it, to the point where he dreamed of playing for Indiana University, the team he rooted for and followed. In the fall of 1948, Bill Garrett survived the final cut and became a member of Indiana University's basketball team, becoming the first black athlete to play a varsity sport in the Western Conference. During the 1952-53 season, while Bob was a senior in high school, the "Hurryin' Hoosiers" of Indiana University won the Big Ten Championship. They then went on to become the number one ranked college basketball team in the country, and justified that ranking by winning the NCAA Championship in a thrilling 69-68 win over Kansas. Gibby always loved competition, and always wanted to be the best, so it was a natural for him to want to attend Indiana University and to play basketball there. Bob was a little shocked when the response from the Indiana University coach was "Your request for an athletic scholarship for Robert Gibson has been denied because we already have filled our quota of Negroes." The quota was apparently **one** per class.

So, instead, Bob accepted a basketball scholarship to Josh's alma mater, Creighton University, which was located six blocks from where Bob grew up.

Although there had been other blacks who played basketball for the University, Bob was the first to be given a basketball scholarship, and became the very first person inducted into the Creighton University Sports Hall of Fame. Bob Boozer, two years younger than Gibby, was Bob's teammate on the basketball team at Omaha Tech. He recalls that Gibby "was a terrific basketball player. A lot of people don't realize how good he was." (*The Sporting News*, January 20, 1968) Boozer led Kansas State to the 1958 Final Four, was first team All-American in 1958 and 1959, the first player picked in the 1959 National Basketball Association draft, won a Gold Medal with the 1960 US Olympic team and went on to play 11 years with Cincinnati, New York, Los Angeles, Chicago, Seattle and Milwaukee.

Traveling to away games with his college teammates, by bus, Bob was introduced to parts of the country he had never seen before, and to attitudes that he had never experienced. In his book, *Stranger to the Game*, Bob told of his first real experience with discrimination:

On the train ride to the Tulsa game, which was the fourth of the season, Coach Belford informed me that I wouldn't be able to stay with the rest of the guys. Until then, the color factor really hadn't kicked in because I knew most of my teammates from the Intercity League in high school. One of them, in fact, was my buddy from Tech and the projects, Glenn Sullivan. Given all of that, the idea of not being able to stay where they stayed just didn't compute. I'm sure that if Belford had told me about the situation before we left Omaha, I would have stayed home. But as it was, I couldn't think of anything else to do but cry. When we arrived in Tulsa, we went to a restaurant where they served me in the kitchen. Sullivan walked back there with me, but I wasn't going to eat in the damn kitchen and told Glenn I'd wait until I got to the other side of town, which was where I was supposed to go when the other guys checked into their hotel. Sullivan came with me to my rooming house and offered to spend the night there, but I sent him back over to the rest of the team so I could brood and curse in private.

Bob was just short of the necessary credits to graduate Creighton and although he still had a love for basketball, he became the focus of the scouts of several Major League baseball teams. The Phillies, White Sox and the Athletics all made offers to Bob. Finally, in June 1957, he accepted an offer of $4,000 from St. Louis Cardinals' Bill Bergesch, who was now the General Manager of the Major League team. Although Bob mainly played the outfield when playing for Creighton, he was later fond of saying that he felt he could "get to the majors much faster as a pitcher" because "outfielders are a dime a dozen, unless you're Willie Mays." (*St. Louis Dispatch*, June 15, 1961) Being signed by the Cardinals was a big move, career-wise, for Bob, but he didn't really get to go very far from home. The Cards immediately assigned him to their AAA team in Omaha (American Association). It would be in Omaha, Bob's hometown, where he would meet two men who would figure greatly in his baseball career – Curt Flood, and manager, Johnny Keane. In December 1957, the Cards obtained Flood from Cincinnati and he and Bob quickly developed a friendship that lasted until Card died in January 1997, at the age of 59. Bob's relationship with Keane was special. Johnny recognized Bob's mental and physical ability and showed tremendous confidence in Bob. Their professional relationship was created during three stints in Omaha for Bob and concluded with the seventh game of the 1964 World Series, with Bob and the Cardinals as World Champs.

Bob's first stay at Omaha was rather short. He had early success, winning his first few games, his first professional victory coming on June 23, 1957, a seven-hit victory over Charleston. By the first week in August, the Cardinals moved Bob to their Sally League team in Columbus, Georgia. It was the first time Bob had ever been in the South, and it came at a time when racial tensions were extremely heightened because of the South's reaction to *Brown v. Board of Education*. Southern opposition to the Supreme Court decision, while expected, especially by blacks who had lived in the South, was extreme. From the time the decision was rendered in 1954, it was met with calls for the impeachment of Chief Justice Earl Warren, and it was immediately rejected by Southern elected officials:

Georgians will not tolerate the mixing of the races in the public schools or any of its public, tax supported institutions
Georgia Governor Herman Talmadge

[The ruling is a] flagrant abuse of judicial power
Senator Richard Russell of Georgia

[Brown v. Board of Education is] the most serious blow that has yet been struck against the rights of states.
Senator Harry Byrd of Virginia

These are the statements that elected officials were willing to make in public. You can just imagine what people were actually thinking and saying off the record, and how they were carrying out their feelings. In the years after the *Brown* decision, in a backlash against it, Southern states started to adopt new legislation making segregation, and actually discrimination, the law of the land in the South. The hard fought gains allowing for blacks to play within the structure of Organized Baseball, as accomplished by players like Henry Aaron in the Sally League in 1953, and Nat Peeples for the Atlanta Crackers in the Southern League in 1954, were being threatened, and negated, by legislation making it illegal for blacks and whites to play together in Southern states. In the years after *Brown*, racial tension in the South grew worse instead of better.

1955
It is my request that athletic teams of ... the University System of Georgia not be permitted to engage in contests with other teams where

the races are mixed ... or where segregation is not required among spectators at such events. The South stands at Armageddon. The battle is joined. We cannot make the slightest concession to the enemy in this dark and lamentable struggle. There is no more difference in compromising integrity of race on the playing field than in doing so in the classrooms. One break in the dike and the relentless seas will rush in.
Georgia Governor Marvin Griffith

After the meeting [of Cotton States League directors in Mississippi] league umpires were instructed that Pine Bluff [Arkansas] would forfeit any games in which the Negroes played.
Arkansas Democrat, May 7, 1955

A Negro team which won the South Carolina Little League baseball championship by default because the other 55 white teams in the league withdrew, has been barred from playing in the regional meeting at Rome, Ga. ... Daniel H. (Danny) Jones, the state Little League director, ... issued a statement ... "I am fully convinced that it is for the best interests of the people of our state to continue our way of life and customs on a separate but equal basis, and will do everything I can to preserve that way of life."
Louisiana Weekly, August 6, 1955

1956

The Louisiana Senate and House unanimously pass interposition legislation by a combined vote of 119-0. The legislation is similar to laws previously adopted by Alabama, Georgia, Mississippi, South Carolina and Virginia, and declares that the Supreme Court decision of Brown v. Board of Education is "in violation of the constitution of the United States and the State of Louisiana. It also prohibited "hotels or other lodging places and all public eating establishments from mixing the races," and required "superintendents of public buildings to make sure separate facilities – sanitary, drinking and seating – be provided for whites and Negroes in their buildings."

The Baton Rouge, Louisiana Commissioner of Recreation and Parks declared that African-Americans would not be allowed to play baseball in the city's Goldsby Park. That created a problem for the Class C Evangeline League which had a franchise in Baton Rouge. That problem was "solved" by banishing the league's five black players: Felipe Alou, Ralph Crosby, Sam Drake, Manuel Trabous, and Chuck Weatherspoon.

1957

Two exhibition games between the Kansas City Athletics and the Birmingham Barons, scheduled to be played in Montgomery, Alabama on April 9th and 10th were cancelled because of a ban of interracial sports by the city.

Louisiana's segregation statute leads to the demise of the Shreveport Sports, a minor league team in the Texas League.

Easton, Md. - A Negro father of two children attending a formerly all white elementary school found a homemade bomb of 10 sticks of dynamite on his front lawn. ... Protests to integration of elementary schools in Talbot County have been made by a white citizens' association.
Birmingham News, September 13, 1957

It was into this racially charged atmosphere that Gibby entered when he went to Columbus, Georgia in the summer of 1957, and it didn't take long for it to affect him directly:

There was a particular fan there (Columbus, GA) who used to ride me. He called me 'Alligator Bait.' I laughed for a while. But then I found out. Just for kicks, some of the local folk would tie Negro youngsters to the end of a rope and drag them through the swamps, trying to lure the alligators. Once the alligator got close, the kids would be pulled up out of the water and onto the shore. The alligators would follow and – presumably – get caught. That's where Negroes stood in Columbus.
Bob Gibson, quoted by Dwight Chapin, LA Times, July 5, 1968

At the end of the 1957 season, Bob accepted an invitation from Abe Saperstein to tour with the Harlem Globetrotters. It provided Bob with an opportunity to supplement the small amount of money he had earned in the minor leagues, and a chance to stay in shape playing the game he loved. Over the winter of 1957-58, Bob toured with the Globetrotters for four months, earning $1,000 a month. Several black players, including Piper Davis and Reece "Goose" Tatum before him, and Fergie Jenkins and Satchel Paige after him, also played with the Globetrotters. Bob roomed with the legendary Meadowlark Lemon when the team was trotting the globe.

Bob's first Major League spring training camp with the Cardinals was in 1958, in St. Petersburg, Florida. He was instructed by the team to report to the Bainbridge Hotel, which he did with a good amount of nervous anxiety and eager anticipation of being involved with the team at the Major League level. It didn't take long for Bob to realize that the discriminatory, segregationist policies of the South were stronger than even the Major Leagues:

I rode the train to Florida, sitting solemnly in a seat assigned to black passengers as we rolled through the South. ... I walked across the street from the train station to the Bainbridge Hotel, where the Cardinals stayed. There, I got my first sampling of big league life. When I went up to the desk to register, the clerk advised me that there would be a room waiting for me in a private home on the other side of town. Then he pointed to a door at the end of the hall in the back of the hotel and said that there would be a cab waiting for me on the other side of the door. Curt Flood and a veteran pitcher named Sam Jones and three or four other black players were already at the house when I pulled up in the taxi. ... Sad Sam, who, in the only waking moments in which he wasn't chewing on a toothpick, led the league in both strikeouts and walks.

Stranger to the Game, The Autobiography of Bob Gibson, by Bob Gibson with Lonnie Wheeler, Viking Penguin, NY 1994

The house where we lived was owned by a woman who charged us each $49 a week and provided a couple of meals a day. It was a shame ... and a terrible disappointment. I had traveled more than 2,000 miles and I still had not escaped the ghetto. So this is the major leagues.

From Ghetto to Glory, The Story of Bob Gibson, by Bob Gibson with Phil Pepe, 1970

When spring training ended in 1958, Bob found himself back with Johnny Keane in Omaha. It was Bob's first full season and he used it to show the Cardinal franchise how much promise there was in his right arm and in his heart. In his first start of the season he threw a three-hit shutout against Louisville, without allowing a runner to get to second base. In May of that season he flirted with a no hitter for the first time, retiring the first sixteen batters he faced against the Minneapolis Millers. By June, his success got him sent to Rochester (International League). It took only a month for Cardinal General Manager Bing Devine to recognize Bob's potential: "Gibson has all the equipment to pitch in the majors. He's a strong thrower and a good hitter. He needs only experience to earn a good shot." (*The Sporting News*, July 16, 1958) A month later, Bob came about as close as you can to pitching a no-hitter against Richmond. With one out in the ninth inning Rance Pless singled to end that bid. Having seen Bob pitch for only half a season in the International League, the managers of the League rated Bob's fastball the best in the League.

Bing Devine and the Cardinal organization obviously did not have a problem recognizing raw baseball talent and bringing it on board when they saw it, regardless of race. That was evidenced as early as 1959 by the signing of Sad Sam Jones, Curt Flood, Bill White and Bob. Unfortunately, not everyone in the Cardinal organization was of the same mind and heart. In the spring of 1959, Bob, with some hope of making the Major League team, met the new Cardinal player-manager, Solly Hemus. Hemus, a career .273 hitter, was 39 years old and at the end of his playing career. He was a utility infielder for the Cardinals from 1949 until the middle of the 1956 season when he was traded to Philadelphia, where he played until the end of the 1958 season. Hemus simply did not think that Bob, or any other black player, had the ability to think like a Major League pitcher. Hemus had earned himself the nickname "Little Faubus" after Orval Faubus, the Governor of Arkansas, because of his racist opinions. The following story, which appeared in Red Byrd's column on March 11, 1959, recorded Bob's introduction to Hemus, and tells you something about Hemus and his failure to connect with his non-white players:

Solly Hemus, looking for Ed Oliver one day, approached a ball player and asked, "Are you Olivares?" The player replied, "No, I'm Bob Gibson." And Gibson turned to a teammate and said, "I must have made a helluva impression on the manager. After a week he doesn't even know who I am." The same day Hemus sought out Julio Gotay, young Puerto Rican infielder, who doesn't speak too much English. "Marty Marion will be here." Hemus said. "He help you play shortstop. You watch Grammas, too. He help you. We want you to try to play shortstop." "Hokay, me glad play shortstop," Gotay replied, and then inquired: "You Don Blasingame?"

Gibby quickly sensed that Hemus had no confidence in his ability to think or pitch. Bob started the 1959 season in the minors, but was called up in July, and he won his first start 1-0 over Cincinnati. However, over the remainder of that season and the next, Hemus had Bob going back and forth between the majors and the minors, (Omaha and Rochester), and when he was at the Major League level he shuffled him between the starting rotation and the bullpen. Bob's location and role were never established. He was never made to feel like he belonged at the major league level, and never made to believe that the manager felt comfortable in his ability to pitch. As a result, Bob's pitching suffered.

Solly Hemus' treatment of black players was the result of one of the following, and I won't try to speculate which: Either he disliked us deeply or he genuinely believed that the way to motivate us was with insults. The result was the same regardless. He would goad us, ridicule us, bench us – anything he could think of to make us feel inept. He told me, like he told Flood, that I would never make it in the majors, and went so far as to suggest that I take a shot at basketball instead. He was apparently convinced that I didn't have a thought in my head when I was on the mound, and was not in the least reluctant to insult my intelligence. When the pitchers would meet before a series to review the hitters on the other team, Hemus would say things like, "You don't have to listen to this, Gibson. You just try to get the ball over the plate."
Stranger to the Game, The Autobiography of Bob Gibson, by Bob Gibson with Lonnie Wheeler, Viking Penguin, NY 1994

At one point during the 1960 season Hemus clearly revealed the racist thought patterns he harbored when he spoke with the team the day after an on-field incident between him and Pittsburgh Pirate pitcher, Bennie Daniels, a black. Daniels' first pitch had brushed Hemus back and when Hemus swung at the second pitch, and missed, he let his bat go flying towards the mound. Daniels hit Hemus in the back with the third pitch, and on his way to first base Hemus was screaming at Daniels. "I want you to be the first to know what I said to Daniels yesterday," Hemus told the team. "I called him a black son of a bitch."

End of statement. End of meeting. Not one word of regret … We had been wondering how the manager felt about us, and now we knew. Now we hated him for himself.
Curt Flood, quoted in The Sporting News, March 27, 1971

Over the course of his two seasons under Hemus, pitching as a starter and reliever, on no set schedule, Bob's Major League record stood at 6 and 11.

Two events that changed the course of history for Bob and baseball took place in 1960. Actually one was an event that never happened. The one that did happen occurred during spring training in St. Petersburg, Florida. Despite the fact that after the 1959 season every Major League team had had at least one black player on the roster at some time over the previous twelve years, allowing some people to proclaim that baseball was "fully integrated", our spring training accommodations in Florida were still segregated, except for the Dodgers who had built their own "town" in Vero Beach. And it wasn't just the housing that was segregated. There was a clear sense, very obvious to those of us who had been raised in the South, of how the races were supposed to co-exist. As familiar as it was to us, it was foreign to those black ballplayers who were raised in other parts of the country, where Jim Crow was not a resident. There were black players on the Cardinals who had been raised in different areas of the country, (Bill White was from Florida, Marshall Bridges and Frank Barnes were from Mississippi, George Crowe was from Indiana, and Curt Flood was raised in Oakland, California) and their experiences led to different reactions to Florida segregation. But that is not to say that anybody felt good about it. Most players just weren't comfortable enough to say anything about it. However, when the St. Petersburg Yacht Club sent out an invitation list to certain players for its annual breakfast, and Bill White informed the press that no blacks were invited, the discussion on spring training segregation started in earnest. A motel that would accommodate all of the Cardinal players and their families, regardless of race, was located, and when team leaders, like Stan Musial and Ken Boyer, moved out of their private cottages and moved in with the team to make a point, history was made. Bob remembers that the wives of the Cardinal players got involved, and set up an integrated day care center. Black sportswriters, like Sam Lacy and Wendell Smith, used that incident as the starting point for their crusade to integrate spring training facilities, a crusade that wasn't fully successful until the Minnesota Twins finally became the last team, in 1965, to integrate their spring training camp facilities. It is ironic that it was the St. Louis franchise that got the ball rolling on this issue, because it was in St. Louis, a dozen years earlier, that Jackie Robinson took a stand about not being able to eat in the dining room of the Chase Hotel in St. Louis.

The event that didn't happen that year was the Cardinals trading Bob Gibson. In December 1960, the new Washington Senators drafted Bobby Shantz, the little lefty, from the New York Yankees, in the expansion draft. The Cardinals were trying to acquire Shantz in a trade for Gibson. But the Pirates beat them to the punch and Gibson stayed with the Cardinals.

In 1961, Bob's baseball career was re-born in a sense when the Cardinals changed managers. Not only did the move free Bob from Solly Hemus, it reunited him with Johnny Keane. Keane had always had confidence in Bob, and Bob felt extremely comfortable and self-assured pitching for Johnny. One of Keane's moves was to put Bob in the starting rotation, and Bob was able to pitch without having to worry that every outing would decide whether or not he got another one. Bob got 27 starts and responded by pitching 10 complete games, had his first winning season, at 13-12, and led all National League righthanders with an ERA of 3.24.

Keane handed me the ball and said 'pitch', and that's how it has been ever since. That gave me the chance to prove to myself that I could do it.
Bob Gibson, quoted by Barney Kremenko, May 29, 1965

Bob showed steady improvement in 1962. Johnny gave him the ball for thirty starts and Bob pitched 15 complete games, including a National League leading 5 shutouts. It would be the first of four times that Bob would lead the National League in shutouts. At one point in the season, Bob had a scoreless streak of 22 2/3 innings. His teammate, Hall of Famer, Stan Musial commented to reporters that he "never saw anyone throw as hard as Bob Gibson for nine innings." The League acknowledged Bob's progress by naming him to the All-Star team for both All-Star games played that year. In the first game, played in Washington DC, on July 10th, Bob didn't get a chance to pitch, but in the second game, played in Wrigley Field on July 30, he pitched two innings and gave up one run.

By the beginning of August, with Bob's record at 13-6, *The Sporting News* named Bob as one of the possible twenty-game winners for that season. Sportswriter Neal Russo gave his opinion that Bob had a "good chance of becoming the next great pitcher in the National League." His record improved to 15-13, and he hurled 208 strikeouts. He lowered his ERA to 2.85, fifth best in the league. One method of measuring a pitcher's effectiveness was to see how many low run games he pitched in a season. Under a point system giving pitchers 5 points for a shutout, 4 points for a 1 run game and 3 points for a 2 run game, Bob was tops in the majors in 1962 in low run games, with 55 points. His closest competitor was Jim Kaat with 49. Bob's numbers could have been even better, but he broke the fibula in his right leg in September during batting practice, when his spikes caught in the mud and his leg turned but his foot didn't. In January 1963, former Cardinal, Hal Smith, who at that time was coaching in the team's farm system, said, "I don't see how Bob Gibson ever loses a game. He has the best fastball I ever saw."

As Bob continued to develop and improve so did the Cardinals. With the acquisition of shortstop Dick Groat from Pittsburgh for the 1963, the Cardinals added another piece to the puzzle of what constitutes a contending team. The team was definitely transitioning from the Stan Musial Cardinals to a team that would become the Bob Gibson Cardinals. For the 1963 season the Cardinals carried some players at or near the end of their long careers: Musial was 42 years old, Red Schoendienst (who saw very limited action) was 40, Bobby Shantz and Sam Jones were 37, Diomedes Olivo was 44, and Lew Burdette was 36. But there was a core group of players still in their twenties who would make the team contenders for years to come, including Bob, Tim McCarver, Bill White, Julian Javier, Curt Flood, Dal Maxvill, Mike Shannon and Ray Sadecki. That combination of older and younger players was good enough to bring the Cardinals a second place finish in 1963, six games behind the pennant winning Dodgers who were propelled by Koufax and Drysdale, and then swept the Yanks in the World Series. As for Bob, he continued on his progressive way to becoming a 20 game winner. He finished the season with a record of 18-9, improving on his number of victories from the two previous seasons, 13 and 15, respectively, and drastically improving his winning percentage. For the second straight season he struck out over 200 batters (204) while walking less than 100 (96).

The 1964 baseball season is a memorable one for all baseball fans old enough to have lived through it. Most will remember it as the season when the Philadelphia Phillies suffered one of the worst late season collapses of any team in the history of the game. At the end of play on September 17, 1964, the Phillies just about had the National League pennant wrapped up. The standings were:

Team	Wins	Losses	Games Behind	Games Left
Phillies	89	58	--	15
Cardinals	82	64	6.5	16
Reds	81	65	7.5	16
Giants	81	66	8.0	15

With one day left, at the end of play on October 3, 1964, the standings were:

Team	Wins	Losses	Games Behind	Games Left
Reds	92	69	--	1
Cardinals	92	69	--	1
Phillies	91	70	1.0	1
Giants	90	71	2.0	1

The Phillies had lost 12 of their last 14 games, including 10 in a row, while the Cardinals went 10-5, the Cincinnati Reds went 11-5 and the Giants went 9-5 to get close, but be mathematically eliminated at that point. With one game to go, three teams were still in it, and it was possible that the National League could end in a three-way tie, if the Phillies beat the Reds and the Mets beat the Cardinals. The Phillies mustered whatever they had left to win their last game, tying them with the Reds, but the Cardinals, who had lost the first two games of their three game series to the Mets, (with Gibson losing a 1-0 game to Al Jackson on October 2), beat them 11-5 behind Curt Simmons to clinch the pennant.

Some fans will remember that 1964 marked the last World Series appearance by the New York Yankees until 1976. After winning five straight American League pennants, the Yankees lost their second straight World Series and went into a decade of decline unprecedented in their storied history. Bob Gibson and the Cardinals were the ones who put the final dagger in the pinstripe dynasty of the early 60s.

But before we get to the '64 World Series, I want to talk about how close Bob came to be being a twenty-game winner for the first time in 1964 and how something early in the season came back to bite him. Bob's last start of the season was that 1-0 loss to Al Jackson and the Mets, which followed a 5-1 victory in the first game of a three game sweep of the Phillies. That left Bob with a record of 19-12 for the season, having gone 9-2 after splitting his first twenty decisions. He once again struck out over 200 batters, (setting a new Cardinal record of 245) and decreased his walks allowed to 86. Although he had increased his victory total once again, he fell short of winning twenty. Immediately, sportswriters reminded Bob of the evening of April 25th: in the fourth inning of a game against the Phillies, with Bob and the Cardinals comfortably ahead, 7-1, Bob was ejected from the game for flipping his bat at Phillie pitcher, Jack Balschun, after being hit by a pitch. Earlier in the book, when I wrote about the elements that could keep you from winning twenty games, I listed a poor offense or poor defense, or lack of starts; add getting tossed to the list. In Bob's typical, straightforward manner, his remark on this matter was, "I can't complain about that 1964 season just because I got thrown out of the game. All I had to do was win one of the 12 I lost." (*The Sporting News*, October 3, 1970)

Having won the pennant, Bob was about to enter a stage that he would come to dominate – the World Series. In the first World Series start of his career, Game Two of the '64 Series, Bob was matched up against Mel Stottlemyre, the 19 year old phenom, who, in his first season with the Yankees, won nine straight games, to help the Bombers edge out the Chicago White Sox by one game for the AL pennant. Bob pitched well, recording nine strikeouts, but left the game for a pinch-hitter in the bottom of the eighth inning, with the Yanks leading 4-2. It would be the last time Bob Gibson ever came out of a World Series game. In Game Five, Bob got his introduction to the mound at Yankee Stadium, before 65,633 fans. He carried a 2-0 lead into the ninth inning, but the Yanks rallied to tie the score on a home run by Tom Tresh. In the top of the tenth, Tim McCarver hit a three run homer off of Pete Mikkelsen. Bob stayed in the game and earned the victory by retiring the Yanks in the tenth, on two pop ups and a strikeout – his 13th of the game. Sportswriter Phil Pepe commented that Bob was "pitching like there was a plane outside waiting to take him to Cooperstown right after the game." The Yanks won Game Six, setting the stage for the rubber match between Bob and Stottlemyre and the Yanks and Cards. After eight innings, Bob and the Cards were ahead 7-3, with all three Yankee runs coming on Mickey Mantle's record 18th World Series home run. In the ninth, Bob yielded home runs to Clete Boyer and Phil Linz, closing the gap to 7-5. Johnny Keane visited the mound to give Bob a breather, and at this point most armchair managers were questioning why Johnny wasn't going to his bullpen, but he left Bob in because, in his words, he was "committed to this fellow's heart." Keane's commitment paid off as Bob retired Bobby Richardson on a pop up, making the Cardinals the World Champions!

Bob had set a new World Series record by recording 31 strikeouts in the Series, besting Bill Dineen's record of 28. He was rewarded for his efforts by being named the World Series Most Valuable Player. For that honor, *Sport* magazine gave Bob a new Corvette, which led to an uncomfortable situation:

My initial experience with the Corvette was a bad one, anyway. Just after I got it, I was driving from St. Louis to Omaha when a policeman pulled me over in a small town in Missouri. He said there was a report of a stolen Corvette that matched the description of the one I was driving. I said, "Bullshit." I knew he was just messing with me because he didn't believe that a black man could come by a Corvette honestly. When he asked to see the title papers I said that I didn't have any yet because I'd just won the car for being MVP in the World Series. He then apologized, which policemen and others tend to do when, and only when, they find out they're hassling a public figure. Through baseball, I was able to travel and circulate much more freely than the average black man, but even for me it was not uncommon for bigotry to come barging through. I was with friends and teammates at a suburban St. Louis nightspot around 1964, for instance, when a customer walked over and said to me, "We don't allow niggers in this place." There's no use talking with somebody like that, so I stood up and knocked him over the table.

Stranger to the Game, The Autobiography of Bob Gibson, by Bob Gibson with Lonnie Wheeler, Viking Penguin, NY 1994

Bob started the 1965 season with a new manager, Red Schoendienst, and a new pitching coach, Joe Becker, who had coached Koufax and Drysdale. Whether it was the confidence of being a World Champion, his new coaches, or just Bob's blossoming into the dominant pitcher he was destined to become, he started the season on a tear, winning his first eight decisions, in very convincing fashion. In a game against Milwaukee, the first two batters singled and then Bob retired 26 batters in a row. The next week Bob pitched a one-hitter against the Phillies, yielding only a fourth inning single to Johnny Callison, prompting admiration from some of the Phillies:

Gibson's the toughest pitcher in the league – and that includes Sandy Koufax – when he's right. Gibson has some fast ball. It's always alive.
Clay Dalrymple

Gibson has by far the liveliest arm in the National League. He's as tough as they come. Gibson makes the lefthanders cry and he makes us righthanders cry, too.
Dick Allen

Bob came to my home field, Metropolitan Stadium, for the All-Star Game in 1965, and we each got to pitch two innings for our respective teams. Bob pitched a scoreless 8th and 9th innings, striking out Harmon Killebrew and Joe Pepitone to end the game for the victorious National League, whose pitchers included Juan Marichal, Jim Maloney, Don Drysdale, Sandy Koufax and Turk Farrell in addition to Bob.

With one day to go in the 1965 season, Bob's record was 19-12, identical to his 1964 record, but he had one more chance, getting the start in the final game of the season against the Houston Astros, who were in 9th place, 31 games off the pace of the Los Angeles Dodgers. At the time the Cards were in 7th place, 16.5 games back. When Bob saw the lineup card before the game none of the regulars were playing. Bob tried to get Schoendienst to let Bill White, Curt Flood, Lou Brock and Kenny Boyer play, figuring that they would help his effort to win his 20th, but Red wouldn't go for it. Bob prevailed 5-2 nonetheless, and joined the ranks of twenty-game winners. Bob was a legitimate triple threat that season. As a pitcher, in addition to winning twenty, he had a 3.07 ERA, and broke his own Cardinal record with 270 strikeouts (good for third best in the league behind Koufax (382) and Bob Veale of Pittsburgh (276)). On the field, Bob was a Gold Glove Winner, and at bat he clouted five home runs and knocked in a total of 19. Bob's salary in 1965 was $39,000, **less than half of what Pedro Martinez was paid for one inning of work in 2004** ($17,500,000 divided by 217 innings pitched equals $80,645.16).

Since I was the first African-American to win twenty games in the American League, and I did it in 1965, that was also the first time that there were African-American twenty-game winners in both the American and the National League. It was to signal the start of a period of time when black pitchers had more of a presence than ever before in the Major Leagues.

Having seen Bob first hand for a full season, Joe Becker predicted in the spring of 1966 that Bob "should win 25 – with his stuff." And he wasn't the only one singing Bob's praises.

There's no doubt about it. Gibson has to be the fastest. Oh, on a given day, Jim Maloney might be faster. But, day in and day out, Gibson is faster than any of them. Gibson throws so hard that the umpires miss some of his pitches, calling some for him and some against him.
Grady Hatton, Astros' manager, The Sporting News, June 23, 1966

I much prefer having my left hand beaten up by catching Gibson than have both hands beaten up worse by trying to hit against him.
Tim McCarver, quoted by Neal Russo, The Sporting News, July 9, 1966

Bob may have been fast, but just like in past seasons, halfway through the season his record was just above .500. After twenty decisions he was 11-9. From that point forward, despite losing two weeks to a sore arm, Bob went 10-3 to finish at 21-12, once again reaching a new personal high for victories. When he notched his twentieth win, Bob became only the fourth Cardinal pitcher to win twenty games in back to back seasons and the first since Mort Cooper won twenty or more in three straight seasons: 1942, 1943 and 1944.

Earlier on I wrote about the factors that can help or hurt a pitcher in his effort to win twenty games. Two of the factors were health and luck, which happen to be the factors that combined to prevent Bob from matching Mort Cooper's record of three straight twenty-win seasons. By July of 1967, Bob was cruising along with a 10-6 record, actually ahead of his pace to accomplish another twenty-win season, based on how he historically pitched in the months of July and August. He was on the mound in St. Louis, facing Roberto Clemente, one of the premier players in the game. Bob delivered the pitch with typical Gibson gusto and determination and was falling off the mound to the side in a pose made famous by Bob and immortalized now in a statue outside Busch Stadium. That day a wicked line drive off Clemente's bat made solid contact with Bob's right leg, fracturing his fibula, the same bone he had broken in 1962. When Cardinal trainer, Bob Baumann, got out to Bob on the mound, Bob told him. "Put a piece of tape on it and let me pitch." Not knowing about the break, Bob did keep pitching, to three more batters, until the pain became so intense he collapsed to the ground. The injury cost Bob ten starts. He didn't return to the starting rotation until September 7, 1967, when he pitched five innings in a victory over the New York Mets. Bob pitched three more regular season games, including the pennant clincher, a complete game shutout over Philadelphia. Luckily for the Cardinals, during Bob's stay on the disabled list, Nelson Briles took his spot in the rotation and won nine straight decisions, helping the Cards win their second pennant in four years. What was also fortunate for the Cardinals was that the Commissioner granted Bob special eligibility to play in the post season, even though he was not on the active roster on September 1. In a show of fairness, the Commissioner extended the same dispensation to the Red Sox' Tony Conigliaro, but Tony never played in the Series.

The Series became another showplace for Bob. He continued right where he left off in 1964, with complete game victory after complete game victory. Bob started and successfully completed Games One, Four and Seven of the series, and he seemed to improve with every game. In Game One, in Boston, he held the Red Sox to six hits, and outdueled Jose Santiago, 2-1, with Santiago accounting for the only Boston run with a homer. Four days later, Bob put the Cardinals up three games to one, by throwing a five hit shutout, again beating Santiago. At this point, many people thought the Series was over. Boston's pitching consisted mainly of their Cy Young right-hander, Jim Lonborg, who had won Game Two, and Gary Bell, my old roommate, who had started Game Three, only pitching two innings, and who was used in relief of Santiago in Game Four for an inning and a third. The anticipated matchup between Gibson and Lonborg hadn't materialized, and wouldn't unless Boston forced a Game Seven and pitched Jim on short rest. People were ready to pay to see that matchup. Consider Brent Musburger's comment of October 9, 1967:

> **It's too bad this Series didn't feature a game matching Gibson and Gentleman Jim [Lonborg], the New England assassin. That one would have been worth the $8 it costs to see a series game in person.**
> *Chicago's American*

(Eight bucks! No wonder Bob was only making $39,000 a year.) Well, Lonborg pitched a beauty in Game Five, beating the Cards, 3-1, on a three-hitter, and for Game Six the Red Sox turned to Gary Waslewski, who had a 2-2 record for the year, and hadn't started a game since July 29. Like so many other role players who shine in a World Series, Waslewski rose to the occasion. He gave the Red Sox five and a third innings of four hit pitching and left the game with the Sox winning 4-2. The Cards tied it, but Boston went on to win, setting up the much anticipated Game Seven with Gibson and Lonborg. Bob not only pitched a complete game, three-hitter for the win, he hit a home run off Lonborg in the fifth inning for good measure. For the second time in four years, with Gibson on the mound, the Cardinals were World Champions. Bob's Game Seven victory tied the record of Red Ruffing (Yankees) for five consecutive complete games in World Series competition, and he set a new record of his own, allowing only 14 hits in 27 innings, breaking a record held by the immortal Christy Mathewson since 1905.

> **He never lets up. Never. He challenges you on every pitch. Everybody lets up once in a while, but not him. There are a lot of guys with talent, but his attitude is unique. It's him and you, every pitch. It's like he's telling you, 'Here it is; if you can hit it, go ahead.' It's his best, all the time.**
> *George Scott, sitting on his clubhouse stool, after Game Seven*

> **I think he's the best pitcher I ever faced. I didn't face Koufax often enough to compare them, but I had the feeling that it was just Gibson and me with 55,000 people looking on.**
> *Carl Yastrzemski, 1967 AL MVP, quoted by Brent Musburger, Chicago's American, October 9, 1967*

> **Gibson has to be the best pitcher in the National League. I thought he was the best even when Sandy Koufax was in the league.**
> *Elston Howard, quoted by Ray Kelly, Philadelphia Bulletin, October 13, 1967*

I stayed over an extra day in Boston just to watch Gibson in the seventh game of the Series. It was worth every minute. There's a guy who knows what he's doing.
Earl Wilson, The Sporting News, November 18, 1967

I watched him in the last World Series and he was so great that he even struck me out while I was watching on television.
Joe Torre

He just throws that hard fast ball and hard slider, but doesn't throw too many down the middle. Here's a guy who wants to win 30 games and thinks he can. A great fielder. He knows there is no limit to what he can do.
Clete Boyer, The Sporting News, March 2, 1968

Having won his second World Championship, Bob had every reason to feel good about himself, but that winter he received a piece of mail that reminded him there were still people who didn't see him as a great baseball player, but instead saw him as a black man, a black man they stereotyped as ignorant and illiterate, and unwanted:

a letter from a man in Tampa that year [winter 1967] stands out in my memory. It said: "I guess this will make you and your swollen head several times larger. Why don't you and the other blackbirds on the Cardinals move to Africa where you belong? If you and the other darkies can't read this because of your low mentality, get one of the white players to do it."
Stranger to the Game, The Autobiography of Bob Gibson, by Bob Gibson with Lonnie Wheeler, Viking Penguin, NY 1994

Bob's faith in society was somewhat restored when after sharing that letter with a sportswriter who went public with it, Bob received over 3,000 letters of support.

The start of the 1968 Major League Baseball season was delayed from Monday, April 8 to Wednesday, April 10, to honor the funeral of Martin Luther King, Jr., who had been assassinated in Memphis, Tennessee, on April 4, 1968, by James Earl Ray.

I reeled from the impact of the assassination [of Martin Luther King] – the cold-blooded murder of the one man in my lifetime who had been able to capture the public's attention about racial injustice, break through some of the age-old social barriers, and raise the spirits and hopes of black people across the country.
…

As disturbed as I was about Dr. King, I knew, also that I couldn't let it undermine my pitching. There was a season to play, and I expected a lot out of it.
Stranger to the Game, The Autobiography of Bob Gibson, by Bob Gibson with Lonnie Wheeler, Viking Penguin, NY 1994

If you were to check out the records of the National League pitchers for the first two months of 1968 you would think that something happened to Bob. After ten starts he was sitting with a losing record of 3-5. But if you were a National League hitter, you would know that Bob was at the top of his game. It was the St. Louis bats and defense that were not supporting him. To that point in the season, Bob's ERA was the lowest in the National League, but his teammates had only scored a total of four runs in his five losses. Symptomatic of Bob's season was his May 23rd game against the Dodgers. Bob gave up one hit in eight innings, but lost 2-0 to Don Drysdale.

Then came the streak, one of the greatest pitching exhibitions ever. Starting on June 2 and lasting through August 19, Bob won fifteen consecutive games, and ten of them were shutouts. His ERA during the fifteen game streak was 0.46. Four of his opponents were future Hall of Famers, Fergie Jenkins, Don Drysdale, Juan Marichal, and Phil Niekro:

Date	Team	Loser	IP	H	R	ER	BB	K	Score
6/2	NY	Jackson	9	7	3	3	3	8	6-3
6/6	Houston	Wilson	9	3	0	0	2	5	4-0
6/11	Atlanta	Kelly	9	5	0	0	2	4	6-0
6/15	Cincinnati	Nolan	9	4	0	0	0	13	2-0
6/20	Chicago	Jenkins	9	5	0	0	1	6	1-0
6/26	Pittsburgh	McBean	9	4	0	0	0	7	3-0
7/1	LA	Drysdale	9	9	1	1	2	4	5-1
7/6	San Fran	Marichal	9	6	0	0	4	9	3-0
7/12	Houston	Lemaster	9	3	1	1	0	8	8-1
7/21	NY	McAndrew	9	7	0	0	0	13	2-0
7/25	Phil	Short	9	5	0	0	1	6	5-0
7/30	NY	Selma	9	5	1	1	1	8	7-1
8/9	Atlanta	P. Niekro	9	4	0	0	0	5	1-0
8/14	Chicago	J. Niekro	9	8	1	1	3	7	3-1
8/19	Phil	Fryman	9	2	0	0	2	11	2-0
			135	77	7	7	21	114	

With the streak at six victories, Bob had pitched five consecutive shutouts. He had not let up a run during the whole month of June since beating the Mets, 6-3, on June 2nd. His streak of consecutive scoreless innings stood at 47 2/3 and he was challenging Drysdale's record of 58 2/3 consecutive scoreless innings and six consecutive shutouts. Nobody had pitched five consecutive shutouts since Doc

White (White Sox) in 1904, until Drysdale threw his sixth on June 4, 1968, the same night Senator Bobby Kennedy was shot in Los Angeles.

> **Robert Kennedy's assassination ... was an angry point in American history for black people – Dr. King's killing had jolted me; Kennedy's infuriated me – and without a doubt, I pitched better angry.**
> **...**
> **With forty-seven consecutive scoreless innings, I was actually closing in on the record Drysdale had established just three weeks before. ... When a reporter asked me about the pressure involved in maintaining the streak, I said that I felt more pressure every day just being a Negro in a white society.**
> *Stranger to the Game, The Autobiography of Bob Gibson, by Bob Gibson with Lonnie Wheeler, Viking Penguin, NY 1994*

Thanks to the schedule maker, Bob was facing Don on July 1, with a chance to get within a few innings of the record, and as a member of the Dodgers, I had a front row seat. The stands were packed, as 54,127 fans come to see the showdown at Chavez Ravine. In the very first inning, Bob delivered a pitch that, in my opinion, got by Tim McCarver and allowed Len Gabrielson to score a run to snap the streak. Gabrielson jumped on home plate with both feet to emphasize his understanding of how significant it was to score on Gibson at that time. That would be the only run the Dodgers scored, and although the scoreless inning streak was ended, Bob's consecutive win streak continued.

With the streak at twelve games, Bob was headed to Atlanta to face the Braves. As the coaching staff went over their scouting reports as usual before the series, Atlanta coach, Jim Busby, told Braves manager, Luman Harris, that Tim McCarver had a sore arm and the Braves should be able to steal second base easily. Harris is reported to have responded, "That's just fine, now if you will tell me how in the hell we get a runner to first base [off Gibson]." (*Atlanta Journal*, August 11, 1968).

When the streak ended, Bob's record stood at 18-5, and his ERA was 0.99. In the game Bob lost to break the streak, on August 24th, he struck out 15 batters and lost to the Pirates by a score of 6-4 on three unearned runs. Bob went 4-4 over the final month of the year, finishing with a final record of 22-9, winning at least twenty games for the third time in four years. He started 34 games in 1968 and pitched a complete game in 28 of them. The six times he didn't finish, he was pinch hit for, which means that at no time during the entire season was Bob taken out for a relief pitcher in the middle of an inning. He never had to take that long slow walk off the mound. In fact, that streak was longer than just the 1968 season, it lasted fifty-six starts for Bob. Bob threw 13 shutouts, not only the most in the majors that season, but the most in the Major Leagues since Grover Cleveland Alexander had 16 in 1916. Bob's closest competitor was Drysdale with eight. Bob's final ERA for the season was 1.12, and with that he broke a record of Grover Cleveland Alexander (1.22) that stood since 1915. In addition, for good measure, Bob's total strikeouts, 268, also led the league.

Bob Gibson with a 1.12 ERA. That's almost obscene.
Don Drysdale, quoted by Steve Rushin, in The Season of High Heat, Sports Illustrated, July 19, 1993

I've watched Gibson almost since he first came up and he now has developed complete mastery of three pitches – fast ball, curve and slider. And he is one of the few pitchers who can throw high and get away with it. That's because there's something on every pitch he throws. His control is simply great. His slider is his money pitch. It shakes hands with his fastball.
Al Jackson, pitcher, New York Mets

I hit against Gibson back in 1959 and I hit him then about the way you guys are hitting him now.
Gil Hodges, New York Mets manager, talking to his team

I haven't seen anybody that good during the time I've been in the majors.
Roger Maris, Gibson teammate, The Sporting News, Sept. 7, 1968

Another true measure of Gibson's performance in 1968 is that baseball felt compelled to change the rules of the game after that unbelievable season. What Bob accomplished in 1968 still stands, 37 years later, as a season of pitching excellence that actually changed the game of baseball. While Bob was busy mowing down batters in the National League, over in the American League, Denny McLain was putting together the first thirty-win season for a pitcher since Dizzy Dean in 1934, and there hasn't been one since. Only six batters in the major leagues batted .300 or better in 1968, the American League batting champs, Carl Yastrzemski, and Curt Flood both batted .301 and they didn't have to face Gibson. The others, Pete Rose (.335), Matty Alou (.332), Felipe Alou (.317), and Alex Johnson (.312), batted just over .100, collectively, against Gibson. Bob's 1968 season is still looked upon with awe by today's premier pitchers:

Nobody will have a season like [Gibson] had in 1968. Number 1, nobody will throw 300 innings again because they won't get enough appearances. Nobody will ever throw 28 complete games in a season. I will struggle to get 14. Pedro Martinez won the Cy Young, and everybody marveled at a 1.90. But nobody is ever going to come close to a 1.12. That's one run per game. Somebody might throw

155, 160 innings, but barely qualify for the ERA title. Maybe you could do that. But nobody will ever throw 260 innings and do what he did. To me, it stands with [Joe] DiMaggio's [hitting] streak. You don't understand how unbelievable it is until you start looking at the numbers since then.
Curt Schilling, interviewed by William Ladson, The Sporting News, August 3, 1998

The dominance of these two pitchers in their respective leagues led the lords of baseball to lower the pitching mound by five inches in 1969 and to reduce the size of the strike zone to give hitters a chance. It also hastened talk of a designated hitter, which became the rule in the American League in 1973. Bob was not overly critical of the lowered mounds once the 1969 season started, but he felt that they should still have a slope and not be flat. Both Gibby and McLain won the Cy Young Award and the Most Valuable Player Award for their respective leagues. Bob was the first African-American to win both awards in the same year since Don Newcombe did it in 1956.

It was the last year before the institution of divisional play and playoffs, and it was very fitting that when the two teams met in the World Series, it would also feature a matchup of the winningest pitcher in 34 years against the pitcher with the lowest ERA in baseball history. Baseball fans and sportswriters around the country anticipated a number of pitching duels between Gibson and McLain as the centerpiece of the 1968 World Series. Only Sandy Koufax, who had retired after the 1966 season, and was now doing some broadcasting, saw it differently:

You guys keep writing and talking about the pain with which I pitched. Gibson has constant elbow discomfort. You know something: I can't wait to see what he does to McLain and Detroit today.
Sandy Koufax, quoted by Bob Broeg, St. Louis Post-Dispatch, August 31, 1975

Bob did not disappoint Sandy, or the Cardinals or any of their fans. He was nothing short of awesome in his demolition of the Tigers. Bob shut out the Tigers holding them to five hits and struck out 17 Tigers, a new World Series record. Every starter in the Tiger lineup struck out at least once, and Al Kaline and Norm Cash, the number three and four hitters each struck out three times! McLain on the other hand lasted only five innings, gave up three runs and was the losing pitcher.

I've never seen anyone pitch like that before. Today, he was the best I've ever seen. If he continues to pitch like that, we can't beat him.
Al Kaline

It was the single greatest pitching performance I have ever seen.
Denny McLain, quoted by Steve Rushin, in The Season of High Heat,
Sports Illustrated, July 19, 1993

The two matched up again for Game Four, in Detroit. Bob again held the Tigers to five hits, and one run. McLain didn't make it past the third inning, and was again the losing pitcher. The Tigers made four errors and lost the game 10-1, putting the Cardinals up three games to one. After the Tigers won Game Five, they chose to start McLain for Game Six, and he responded with a complete game victory. That left Mickey Lolich to face Bob for Game Seven. Although Bob again pitched a complete game, his eighth consecutive in Series play, this time he came up on the short end of the score, 4-1. With the game a scoreless tie in the seventh inning, Flood misplayed a ball hit by Jim Northrup, which put the Tigers ahead, and they never looked back. That was to be Bob's last appearance in the World Series. He had nine starts and pitched 81 innings, with 92 strikeouts, and a World Series ERA of 1.89.

Bob continued his domination of the National League in 1969, with his fourth twenty-win season in five years. That year, Bob started 35 games and pitched 28 complete games, winning exactly 20 while losing 13. On July 4th, he was removed from the mound in the middle of the 10th inning in a game against the Cubs. That is significant, because it was the first time Bob had been relieved in the middle of an inning since September 12, 1967. That summer the Baseball Writers Association of America, the same group of sportswriters that decided who gets into the Hall of Fame, voted to select Baseball's Greatest Living Team. Bob was selected as one of three right handed pitchers to make that team, along with Bob Feller and Dizzy Dean. His well-earned reputation was such that even the clergy recognized what they were up against:

After Bob Gibson edged the Padres, 2-1, on August 5, at San Diego, the elevator operator at the ball park said to a priest who had walked aboard, "You weren't working for us, Father." To which the priest replied, "I was, but sometimes it's not enough against Gibson."
The Sporting News, August 23, 1969

After the 1969 season, the Cardinals tried to trade Bob's teammate, roommate and close friend Curt Flood to the Philadelphia Phillies. Flood, a three-time All-Star and seven-time Gold Glove winner objected to the trade and decided to challenge baseball's reserve clause, which, since 1876, gave teams the right to renew a player's contract following each season, barring players from seeking or accepting competing bids from other teams. It allowed teams to buy and sell a player as if he were property. In 1951, Congress had looked into the question of the reserve clause, and ballplayers, including Pee Wee Reese and Lou Boudreau, were called to Washington to testify. At that time the players felt that the reserve clause was important to the game because it prevented the richer teams from luring away players from the poorer teams. But as times changed and players, like all employees, sought more rights and privileges, the luster of the reserve clause for the players began to pale, when they realized how it limited their potential income and restricted their mobility; they realized that what was best for the "game" wasn't necessarily best for the players, individually.

With the Players Association, and its Executive Director, Marvin Miller, behind him, Flood ultimately took the case, Flood v. Kuhn, to the U.S. Supreme Court, but it took until June 1972 to get there and during that all that time Curt did not play. Because Curt was black, there were many people who did not see this case as a ballplayer against the system, but rather as a black ballplayer against the system. It pointed out, in a negative way, what Bob Gibson had been saying about his pitching all along. He wanted America to see him as a successful pitcher, not just always as a successful black pitcher. Curt acknowledged that his experiences as a black ballplayer were different than those of non-blacks, but that it was as a ballplayer that he objected to the reserve clause:

I'd be lying if I told you that as a black man in baseball I hadn't gone through worse times than my teammates. I'll also say, yes, I think the change in black consciousness in recent years has made me more sensitive to injustice in every area of my life. But I want you to know that what I'm doing here I'm doing as a ballplayer, a major league ballplayer.
Curt Flood

The Supreme Court ruled against Curt, ending his case, and effectively ending his Major League career. But the coverage of the lawsuit, and all that surrounded it, heightened players' consciousness of their rights, and is seen as responsible for opening up the game to free agency, the mobility of players, and their greatly increased salaries.

Bob has acknowledged that he used his anger at racial discrimination as a motivator in his pitching performances:

My color influenced me, no doubt, ... but on the mound it was not part of my mental makeup or my game plan. It might, however, have enabled me to understand and utilize intimidation a little better. As a black man, I was a member of a race that had been intimidated by the white man for more than two hundred years, in which time we learned something about the process. When one is intimidated, he resigns himself to the backseat. He defers to his so-called superior, having no other legitimate choice, and allows himself to be dominated. As a major-league pitcher, I had the opportunity, at last, to push off the mound in the other man's shoes.
Stranger to the Game, The Autobiography of Bob Gibson, by Bob Gibson with Lonnie Wheeler, Viking Penguin, NY 1994

I believe it was Bob's anger about the Curt Flood situation that motivated him in 1970. Bob got a second chance to become the third Cardinal pitcher with three straight twenty-win seasons, (besides Dizzy Dean and Mort Cooper), and this time he did it, in style. Bob tied Gaylord Perry for most wins in the league, with 23, his career high, while only losing 7 games. Bob's record is all the more impressive when you take into consideration that the Cardinals as a team were 10 games under .500 and that none of the other four starters had a winning record: Steve Carlton (10 and 19), Mike Torrez (8 and 10), Jerry Reuss (7 and 8), and Nelson Briles (6 and 7). Bob also led the league in strikeouts, with 274, breaking his own Cardinal record, becoming the first National League pitcher to strike out 200 or more batters in eight different seasons. Bob was also very effective at the plate; he batted .303 for the season, and is the last pitcher to hit over .300 and win twenty games in the same season. For his efforts, Bob won his second Cy Young Award, and was named the 1970 Sporting News Pitcher of the Year.

Earlier on in the book, I discussed how the game has changed as to the use of relief pitchers and the fact that starting pitchers aren't on the mound at the end of the game as frequently as in the past, thereby risking more no-decisions and losing possible wins. Consider the number of complete games and the average number of innings per start that Bob compiled in 1968, 1969, and 1970 three of his twenty-win seasons:

Year	Innings Pitched	Starts	Complete Games	Average Innings Per Start
1968	304.7	34	28	8.96
1969	314	35	28	8.97
1970	294	34	23	8.65

Starting in 1971, as Bob's career achievements continued to mount, surpassing those of any other Cardinal pitcher in many categories (and any other pitcher in the Major Leagues in some categories), a series of events prevented him from ever winning as many as twenty games in a season again. In May of 1971, Bob tore a muscle in his right thigh, an injury that placed him on the disabled list to his dismay. This limited his number of starts that season to 31, and reduced the number of innings he pitched by about sixty from previous seasons. The only other season, since 1962, that he saw action that limited was 1967 when he broke his leg. Still, Bob managed a 16-13 record, and after returning from the disabled list he notched career win number 200 in August 1971. Later that month he accomplished something he thought he never would – a no-hitter against the Pittsburgh Pirates, the first no-hitter by a Cardinal since Lon Warneke threw one in 1941.

A player strike shortened the 1972 season by six games and probably cost Bob two starts, and when the season finally began he lost his first five decisions. He came back strong, but missed the 20 win mark, finishing with a 19-11 record. But, again, the season was not without its highlights for Bob. On June 21 he earned his 211th career victory, the most wins ever by a Cardinal pitcher, passing the career total of Jesse "Pop" Haines (1920 – 1937). In July, with an eleven game personal winning streak going, Bob was given the honor of starting the All-Star Game in Atlanta. He pitched two scoreless innings in what would be his last All-Star appearance. In August he hurled his 54th career shutout, placing him ninth on the all-time list of shutout leaders, in the company of legends, Walter Johnson (110 shutouts), Grover Cleveland Alexander (90), Christy Mathewson, (79), Cy Young (76), Eddie Plank (69), Warren Spahn (63), Jim Galvin (57), Ed Walsh (57), and Mordecai "Three Finger" Brown (55), all of whom are Hall of Famers. And Bob didn't waste any time pitching either. In 1972, the average time of his 23 complete games was 1 hour 56 minutes, with the quickest game taking only 1 hour 23 minutes, leading veteran Dodger broadcaster, Vin Scully, to say that Bob pitched like he was double-parked.

In June, 1973, Bob became the All-time Strikeout Leader of the National League, when he recorded his 2862nd strikeout, passing Jim Bunning's record, and leaving him in second place all-time behind only Walter "Big Train" Johnson, who struck out 3509 American League batters during his career with the Washington Senators. Bob would go on to finish with 3117 strikeouts, and at the time he retired he had the most strikeouts by a National League pitcher. He has since been passed by the likes of Nolan Ryan, Roger Clemens, Randy Johnson and Steve Carlton. Currently, Bob ranks 12th among Career Leaders in strikeouts. The end of Bob's career was hastened by the events of August 4, 1973 at Shea Stadium, New York. Bob had reached base safely and when the batter hit a line drive, Bob tried to stop his body and turn back to first to avoid a double play. In the process he tore the cartilage in his knee. Being the competitor that he is, he had centerfielder Bernie Carbo bring him his glove and he attempted to pitch. When he had to place his weight on the leg it crumpled and Bob fell to the ground, forcing him to leave the field.

He was in pain. You could see it on his face, and he still tried to go out and pitch. The man is unbelievable. Most guys would lay right there and let them take him off the field.
Ted Sizemore, Cardinal catcher, quoted by Phil Pepe, Aug. 8, 1973

Bob returned to the mound that season, on September 29, in a victorious start over the Phillies, but the injury lingered into 1974, causing Bob pain and a slow start to his season. By July, 1974, Bob was 3-8 with a 5.18 ERA, and there was talk of Bob going to the bullpen. On July 17, 1974, Bob became only the second pitcher in history to reach the 3,000 strikeout mark, and the only National Leaguer. To this day, only three other National League pitchers have 3,000 or more strikeouts: Steve Carlton, Tom Seaver and Greg Maddux.

In the winter of the off-season between 1974 and 1975, Bob signed his usual one year contract, and announced that 1975 would be his last season, stating:

I'm going to shoot for twenty games. My knee feels better, and I'd like to make that my goal.
Associated Press, St. Louis, January 28, 1975

It didn't turn out that way for Bob. He was only able to complete one of his first ten starts, and in June he finally did make an appearance out of the bullpen, after 303 consecutive starts, a Major League record, since broken by Steve Carlton. On September 18, 1975, Bob retired, with the distinction of having accomplished the following feats:

- He was the All-time Cardinals leader in career wins with 251;
- He was the All-time Cardinals leader in strikeouts for a season with 274;
- He was the All-time National League leader in career strikeouts with 3117, and second overall, behind only Walter Johnson;
- He was the only pitcher to hit two home runs in World Series competition;
- He was the only pitcher to win two Game Sevens in the World Series (1964 and 1967);
- He was the last pitcher to bat over .300 and win twenty games in the same year;
- He had the lowest single season ERA in the history of the game (1.12 in 1968);
- He held the record for most strikeouts in a World Series (31);
- He held the record for fewest hits allowed in three games in a World Series (14);
- He held the record for most strikeouts in a World Series Game (17 in Game One of 1968 Series against Detroit); and
- He held the record for most complete game victories in the World Series.

When it came time for the Baseball Writers Association of America to vote on Bob's credentials for induction into the National Baseball Hall of Fame, in January 1981, he received 84% of the vote, and became only the 11th player in the history of the Hall of Fame to be elected on his first ballot, besides the original five members. I don't really know what the other 16% were thinking about. Also on the ballot with Bob were Juan Marichal and Don Drysdale, neither of which received enough votes to get elected at that time, although both eventually did make it into the Hall. In a moment of candor, at the time of the election, Bob told sportswriter, Bill Madden, why he thought Marichal should have been elected:

Marichal was the best pitcher in baseball when I came up, and there were some pretty good pitchers then, including myself, (Sandy) Koufax, (Jim) Maloney and (Jim) Bunning. I threw harder than he (Marichal) did and I had a better slider, but he was a better pitcher.
Bob Gibson, Daily News, January 17, 1981

When Commissioner Bowie Kuhn introduced Bob on Induction Day at the Hall, he quoted one of Bob's competitors, Ron Fairly of the Dodgers:

There are players that play the game of baseball that attempt to live up to standards. This man [Gibson] sets them.

When it was Bob's turn to talk, he concluded his comments by saying, **I just want to leave you with one thought. One writer asked me a few days ago, what did I want to be remembered as, and I thought about it and I said, "I want to be remembered as a person, a competitor, that gave 100% every time I went out on the field". Sometimes I wasn't too good, but nobody could accuse me of cheating them out of what they paid to see.**

Bob had secured his legacy. Fans and sportswriters who witnessed Bob play could see his competitiveness, his intensity, his desire to win. It was also evident in the things Bob said. On the eve of Game Seven of the 1964 World Series, Bob told sportswriter, Phil Pepe: "I don't want to give them anything ... ever. I want to win this ball game worse than I wanted to win anything in my life." Pepe correctly summed up Bob's competitiveness, his constant desire to win, by writing,

The last time Bob Gibson felt like that was the last time he pitched.
Phil Pepe, World Telegram, October 15, 1964

During Bob's last season, writer Maury Allen, wrote of Bob,

They will talk about him [Gibson] as long as the game is played. They will remember his toughness, his courage, his competitiveness, his style.
...
No one ever threw a baseball with more style, more skill, more drama.
Maury Allen, New York Post, April 24 and June 24, 1975

Those of us who opposed him, or were fortunate enough to be his teammates, know for sure that Bob was the ultimate competitor. So much has been said and written by Bob's contemporaries about this side of Bob, that the best way for me to capture it is to provide you with their words:

If you didn't know him, you might think he was arrogant. But he isn't; it's just his competitive nature.
Tim McCarver, Sunday Daily News, Sept. 29, 1968

There are four guys I've seen who really came to beat you. Maury Wills, Jim Bunning, Frank Robinson ... and Gibson. And Gibson was two miles ahead of the other three.
Lou Brock, quoted by Rich Koster, St. Louis Globe-Democrat, Sept. 2, 1975

He has a vicious competitiveness, he has desire and fantastic ability. That's a nasty combination to oppose. But it's a hell of a thing to have on your side.
Tim McCarver, quoted by Rich Koster, St. L Globe-Democrat, Sept. 2, 1975

Early in my career (1962), Gibby was pitching, I was at shortstop, and he was having a rare inning of giving up a few hits and walks. I went into the mound to try and settle him down a little. Before I could even say one word, Gibby said to me, ""Dal, the only thing you know about pitching is that it is hard to hit! Now get your fanny back out to shortstop and leave me alone!" Needless to say, I never went to the mound again when Gibby was pitching.
Dal Maxvill, teammate

Gibson ... did it with a vengeance that ravaged the batters.
Richie Ashburn, The Sporting News, April 25, 1981

I don't fear anybody. I can honestly say that. I don't fear anybody. There was only one guy I ever felt nervous about and he's not pitching anymore. And that was Bob Gibson.
Gary Matthews, The Sporting News, June 6, 1981

Picking the five toughest pitchers I've ever faced is easy.
Bob Gibson in 1968, Bob Gibson in 1969, Bob Gibson in 1970, Bob Gibson in 1971, and Bob Gibson in 1972. Gibson was the toughest. No one else was even close.
Doug Rader, Dallas Morning News, March 22, 1983

He was tough on people. He'd throw at you *before* you hit a home run. All you had to do was take a full swing, and the next pitch was inside. I remember when Jim Ray Hart went up one of his first times against Gibby. Jim used to look like he was smiling when he stood at the plate. He nicked one off. The next pitch, Gibson broke his collarbone. I don't think anyone ever hit more than five career homers off Gibson, including me. I bailed out a lot against that man. I wasn't getting my shoulder broken up.
Willie Mays, quoted by Art Spander, The Sporting News, March 17, 1986

It is at this point that Bob has concern, when people start to mistake his competitiveness and the anger that motivated and propelled his success for meanness:

I don't appreciate being introduced, as I often am these days, as the world's meanest ballplayer. I don't think that's necessarily a

compliment. It's as if my tombstone is going to read, "Here lies the meanest son of a bitch who ever toed the rubber." I really don't want to be remembered as a bad son of a bitch who pitched a little.
Stranger to the Game, The Autobiography of Bob Gibson, by Bob Gibson with Lonnie Wheeler, Viking Penguin, NY 1994

As a contemporary of Bob's, I could easily understand why the players' memory of Bob was that he was "mean." He flat out wanted to beat you. When the game was on, if you were wearing the other team's uniform you were not a friend, even if off the field you really were Bob's friend. Bob strove to dominate and the way he knew how to do that the best was to claim the outside part of the plate as his. He accomplished that by not making batters too comfortable by not being afraid to pitch inside.

People don't really understand about pitching inside. They think when you throw inside, you are trying to intimidate somebody, you are trying to knock them down, you are trying to hit them. It's none of the above. You pitch inside to make them think inside. If you continually pitch inside, you are not going to get anybody out. But you pitch inside to make the hitter think inside and then you can get them [outside]. I don't care what year you pitched, to consistently get somebody out it has to be out there. But you have to keep him from going out there. When you pitch inside, it's not to hit anybody or scare anybody.
Bob Gibson, interviewed by William Ladson, The Sporting News, August 3, 1998

At this point I should note that it wasn't just Bob who was all business when he took the mound. When I went out there I just cut up and had a ball, like Lew Burdette who used to sing while he pitched. But that wasn't for Bob, or for others. I remember when I was on the Cardinals, Steve Carlton lost a game in Pittsburgh, and I was on the team bus after the game before anybody else got on. Carlton came on and sat across from me. He had a game program in his hands and he kept rolling it up and rolling it up, and then he snarled, "Don't you feel like just killing somebody?" I said, "NO!" Oh, baby, these guys were intense.

Thanks to many sportswriters and baseball announcers, the mythology of baseball now has Bob as the King of Hitting Batters. It is a title that helped intimidate batters while Bob was pitching, but is just not based in fact. Consider the following chart showing the statistics of twelve pitchers, including Bob and me, as concerns the number of batters we faced, the number we hit and how often that happened, through the 2004 season: Bob actually hit 102 batters in his 17 year career – an average of six per year, or one hit batter for every 157.53 batters he faced. By contrast, Pedro Martinez has hit one batter for every 79.90 batters he has faced.

Pitcher	Hit Batsmen	Batters Faced	%age hit	Batters Faced per 1 HBP
Pedro Martinez	**115**	**9,189**	**1.251%**	**79.9043**
Randy Johnson	156	13,864	1.125%	88.8717
Don Drysdale	154	14,097	1.092%	91.5389
Jim Bunning	160	15,618	1.024%	97.6125
Jim Lonborg	105	10,498	1.000%	99.9809
Roger Clemens	147	18,531	0.793%	126.0612
Nolan Ryan	158	22,575	0.699%	142.8797
Greg Maddux	118	16,989	0.694%	143.9745
Bob Gibson	**102**	**16,068**	**0.634%**	**157.5294**
Ferguson Jenkins	84	18,400	0.456%	219.0476
Mudcat Grant	33	10,293	0.320%	311.9090
Sandy Koufax	18	9,497	0.189%	527.6111

As you can see by the chart, I did not hit many batters, although there were times I definitely did plunk somebody to protect one of my own players, or because of something they had done to show us up. I remember that I was pitching a no hitter against the Washington Senators, when infielder Don Blasingame broke up the no-no in the seventh inning with a bunt single. Every time I faced Blasingame after that game I dusted him back or hit him. I even hit him in an Old Timers' Game! And Jim Northrup of the Detroit Tigers says I had a pretty good memory too:

Once I beat Mudcat Grant with a hit in the ninth inning. We played the Twins again the next week and I felt really comfortable against him even though he was a great pitcher. Well, he really decked me. Later, we spoke and he said he wasn't throwing at me. I said to him, "C'mon Mudcat, we both know what you did." We both laughed because that was part of the game.
Jim Northrup, www.angelfire.com

When Bob's playing days were over he was hired by his former teammate and friend Joe Torre, as a pitching and "attitude" coach for the New York Mets, and then followed Joe to become part of his coaching staff in Atlanta. Bob was the perfect man for that job. Off the field, Bob has been active in several business ventures, including banking and restaurants. He has also been very instrumental in helping former players who have fallen on hard times. Bob was one of the first veterans to lend his name and his time and energy to the Baseball Assistance Team, and is still very active in the organization.

In 1999, Major League Baseball sponsored a competition asking fans to select an All-Century Team of the thirty best players to ever play the game. Over two million fans participated and Bob was voted the fifth greatest pitcher of all time, behind only Nolan Ryan, Sandy Koufax, Cy Young, and Roger Clemens.

Bob's competitiveness can be seen in this anecdote about the All-Century Team presentation, which appears on Baseball-Almanac.com:

A common question asked to baseball 'experts' is who would you select to pitch a World Series Game Seven and "Bob Gibson" is often chosen. Gibson was told about this after the ceremony and replied, 'That would be my answer too!"

When Home Run King, Henry Aaron, was asked that question he said, "If I had one game to win, I'd take Gibby."

There were many great World Series pitchers in my day. Whitey Ford was a great World Series pitcher. Mickey Lolich in the times he was in it was great and so were Don Drysdale, Tom Seaver and Jerry Koosman, but I would have to say that Gibson, Marichal and Koufax would be the top three. Gibson, Marichal and Koufax; Koufax, Gibson, Marichal; Marichal, Gibson, Koufax – either way you want to put them, but if I had those three on a team, I would just put their names in a box and pick one out. Understand that is no knock on Gibby, I am placing those three guys in a very special class as the greatest money pitchers of all-time. I wonder if my friend is still flabbergasted at my honest response about me and Gibby.

ROBERT EARL WILSON

Born October 2, 1934 in Ponchatoula, Louisiana
Died April 23, 2005 in Michigan
Teams: Boston Red Sox, Detroit Tigers, San Diego Padres
Twenty-Win Season: 1967
Inducted into Louisiana Sports Hall of Fame

As a player, Earl was one of the better pitchers in Major League ball. I'll never forget the night he threw a no-hitter. As a roomie and friend, we shared some good times and some tough times. Because of the racism in baseball and society in general, we depended on each other as social buddies and confidantes. A good roomie.
Elijah "Pumpsie" Green

He [Earl] was a big, handsome, intelligent, kind man. He was one of baseball's giants, in so many ways.
Jerry Moses, former Red Sox teammate

He [Earl] taught me it's more important what you do outside the field than what you do on it. One of the great teammates that we had, and not only that, a great individual.
Willie Horton, former Tigers teammate, quoted by George Sipple, Free Press, April 26, 2005

He [Earl] was a right-hander who owned a pitcher's disposition – fierce, strong, and fearless. The 1960s were dominated by Bob Gibson and Sandy Koufax, but Pumpsie Green believed that while Wilson may have lacked the overwhelming slider of Gibson or the devastating curve of Koufax, he could be every bit as intimidating. He was totally unafraid to pitch inside or occasionally deck a hitter who leaned out over the plate.
He was a natural athlete. Quick, strong and powerful.
Howard Bryant, Shut Out, A Story of Race and Baseball in Boston, 2002

Earl Wilson's death, which occurred during the writing of this book, increased my passion and desire to finish the project and to start the work of spreading the word about the lives of the Black Aces and the accomplishments of all blacks in baseball.

Of all the Black Aces, Earl Wilson's upbringing is the closest to mine. Earl was born in the southeast corner of Louisiana, about halfway between Baton Rouge and New Orleans, in a little town called Ponchatoula, on the northwest border of Lake Pontchatrain. In conducting my research for the book, I came to learn that the name "Ponchatoula" is from the Choctaw Indian language meaning "hair to hang," derived from the Indian description of the Spanish Moss hanging from the tree limbs in the areas, just as it did off the Cypress trees in Lacoochee. In fact, Ponchatoula was established in 1820, as a logging camp for pine, cypress, and oak trees, in much the same way Lacoochee was used by Cummer and Sons a century later.

Earl was born less than one year before me, and his childhood experiences in Ponchatoula were very similar to mine in Lacoochee. In the late 1930s and 1940s, blacks didn't have standing; we had less than a presence. We were a commodity to help harvest crops, serve as domestic help, and perform the jobs considered too menial for non-blacks. Basically, in the seventy plus years from the time slavery was legally abolished, blacks were still performing the same jobs they did as slaves. Technically, under the law they could no longer be bought and sold like commodities, and could not be forced to work without pay. However, the reality, especially in the deep South, was that the great majority of blacks had very little real chance of breaking free from the virtual chains of slavery which remained part of the Southern culture and social climate.

Ponchatoula is famous for its strawberries. In fact, it proclaims itself to be the Strawberry Capital of the World, so it should not surprise you that Earl's family had been strawberry farmers for several generations. According to Earl's son, Greg Lawrence, Earl "knew from the time he was a little kid that he'd have to figure a way to get out of here [Ponchatoula], because he didn't want to pick up strawberries, too." And although Earl did find a way out of Ponchatoula and strawberry-picking, he, like me, visited his hometown and his Mom quite often.

Earl attended Greenville Park High School, an all-black school located between Ponchatoula and Hammond.

In 1953, Earl had a fantastic season playing for the independent Bisbee-Douglas Copper Kings (in the Class C, Arizona-Texas League). It was while Earl was with Bisbee-Douglas that he suffered a career-altering injury to his catching hand from an opposing player's spikes. While that injury prevented Earl from catching it didn't deter his love for the game or his ability to throw the ball, and throw it hard. Midway through the 1953 season, Earl's manager, Syd Cohen, gave him a chance to start a ballgame. Cohen, who pitched for the Washington Senators in the mid 1930s, and was the last pitcher to strike out Babe Ruth, knew a thing or two about discrimination and not getting a chance. He and his older brother, Andy, an infielder for the Boston Red Sox, were among the first Jewish players to keep their obviously Jewish surname. Seven players before them yielded to anti-Semitic pressure and changed their last name to Kane or Cooney, or some other variation to slip under the radar screen of discrimination.

Earl responded to his first starting chance with a beauty of a game. He pitched eight shutout innings, and gave up only three hits against the Phoenix Senators.

Although he needed relief help to finish, he was credited with the victory. While his position on the field was officially changed from catcher to pitcher, in his mind Earl was still a hitter - that never changed. It would take a little time for Earl to be successful as a pitcher on a consistent basis, and like many of the other Black Aces, he faced several obstacles and detours along the way.

His first step toward the Major Leagues came in 1954, when the Boston Red Sox acquired his contract from Bisbee-Douglas. Although that was a positive step in his trip to the pitching mound of success, the Red Sox' scouting report on Earl was indicative of the team's racial prejudice and the environment Earl would have to endure and overcome to succeed. The report stated that Earl was a "well-mannered colored boy, not too black, pleasant to talk to, well-educated, very good appearance." Just after acquiring Earl, the Red Sox bought the contract of a young infielder, Elijah "Pumpsie" Green, from the Oakland Oaks of the Pacific Coast League.

One day, my manager came in and told me, 'Hey, Pumpsie, you've been sold to the Red Sox. Go to Montgomery, Alabama, and meet their farm team. They have one other black guy there, Earl Wilson. You guys will be roommates.' But that was the one thing I didn't want to do. I wasn't ready to go to Alabama and face the whole color thing, living in different hotels and back alleys, and dealing with what they called 'triple restroom' places: men, women, and colored.
Pumpsie Green, quoted by Ian Browne, MLB.com, Feb. 14, 2003

The Red Sox, by 1954, had a tarnished public image when it came to race relations. Their recent past included the dark stains of the Jackie Robinson tryout, the failure to pursue Willie Mays when he was literally in their hands, and the aborted signing of Piper Davis. Since releasing Davis three days shy of a deadline which would have obligated them to pay the Birmingham Black Barons an additional $7,500, the Red Sox had failed to sign another black player. Al Hirshberg, who wrote for the *Boston Post* and *Boston Herald*, quoted Red Sox manager Pinky Higgins to have said, "There'll be no niggers on this team if I have anything to say about it." What made matters worse for the Red Sox was the progress being made in this area by other teams, even if only superficial it was more than the Red Sox were doing. In 1954, the St. Louis Cardinals (Tom Alston), Baltimore Orioles (Jehosie Heard), Cincinnati Reds (Nino Escalera and Chuck Harmon), Washington Senators (Carlos Paula), and Pittsburgh Pirates (Curt Roberts), all featured the debut of their first black player at the Major League level. That left only the New York Yankees, Philadelphia Phillies, Detroit Tigers and the Red Sox, as Major League teams to have not had a black player on the field. So, while it was not surprising to learn that the Sox' scouting report was patronizing and racist, it was noteworthy that the Red Sox signed Earl to a minor league contract in 1954. The first team he was assigned to was the El Paso Texans in the Class C Arizona-Texas League.

Longtime Red Sox player and coach, Edward "Pop" Popowski, remembers an incident involving Earl that was typical of the obstacles faced on the way to the majors. In 1955, Pop was managing Boston's Class A team, the Montgomery Rebels (Sally League). On the way back from one of those infamous minor league road trips by bus through the South, the team bus pulled into a gas station in Montgomery, Alabama, to give both the bus and the players a chance to rest and fill up. Earl got off the bus and headed toward the water fountain, but was intercepted by the station owner who pointed a pistol at Earl and declared, "If you take a drink, that's the last drink you'll ever take." (*Sarasota Herald Tribune*, Doug Fernandes, August 13, 2000).

Before the 1956 season the Red Sox sent Pumpsie Green to Albany, New York and Earl was first sent to Ocala, Florida, and then joined Pumpsie at Albany, which was in the Eastern League. I was also in the Eastern League that year, playing for Reading. Earl had a 13-2 record that year and a 3.22 ERA. He was the winning pitcher in the Eastern League All-Star game, pitching hitless ball over the last four innings of the game.

That winter our paths crossed again as we were not only in the same league again, but we were teammates. Earl and I both pitched for Willard in the four-team Columbian League. Earl was very successful in Columbia, having started that season pitching 28 consecutive scoreless innings. I was no slouch myself. First I tied the all-time Columbian League record for homers in a game, by hitting three, and then a week later I threw only the second no-hit, no run game in the ten years the league was in existence.

With the Yankees' signing of Elston Howard in 1955, and the Phillies ready to debut John Kennedy as their first black player in 1957, the fact that the Red Sox and Tigers were the only teams without a black player was glaringly obvious, and was not left unnoticed by the press. In January 1957, Hy Hurwitz penned an article for *The Sporting News* under the headline, **Red Sox May Ink Negro in Season or Two:**

The day appears to be coming closer when the Red Sox will have a Negro player on their roster.
***
This winter, the Red Sox have moved two Negro prospects up to their top farm club at San Francisco, [Pumpsie] Green is one of them. The other is Earl Wilson, a tall, husky righthanded pitcher who also was at Albany in 1956.
"We've moved them up," declared Farm Director Johnny Murphy, "because they look like good prospects."
***
"We certainly haven't turned our backs on them," Murphy said. "If a boy is a good prospect our scouts are under orders to sign him, if possible, regardless of his race, color or religion."
***
"Both players have been real gentlemen both on and off the field. They were popular with their teammates and the fans."

In the spring of 1957, the Red Sox, after completing spring training, and just before the start of the season, played against their San Francisco farm team. The three game series drew over 57,000 to the minor league stadium, giving credence to Horace Stoneham and Walter O'Malley's belief that California would support Major League Baseball. After the series, Ed Rumill of the *Christian Science Monitor* commented on San Francisco and Earl Wilson:

Just one word for the crowds. Great. When you come out and see an area like this after being to some other parts of the country which are smaller, I'm sure they've got to have big league baseball. This is a big league town just as the pitcher [Earl Wilson, a Negro righthander] we saw Friday night is a big leaguer.
Quoted by Hy Hurwitz, The Sporting News, April 3, 1957

In another story written that same day by Hurwitz, he gave his own impression of Earl:

The three-game series itself was terrific. The Seals took the opener, 5 to 2, as Earl Wilson, a Negro righthander, made a favorable impression. ***
Wilson was the losing pitcher in the finale. But he's still labeled as a good prospect and is the leading candidate to become the first Negro player in Red Sox history.

Just five days after the Red Sox left San Francisco, it became apparent that Earl was also leaving, but not for a baseball reason. He received notification from the Selective Service System to report for a pre-induction physical. Earl enlisted in the Marines, which delayed his path to the Major Leagues, but allowed him to pitch for the San Diego Leathernecks, the Marine base team. Earl was one of the stars of the team, and was one of the main reasons the Leathernecks won the 1957 All-Marine baseball championship, defeating Parris Island. Earl not only pitched well in the championship series, but in the clinching game he played left field and drove in four runs.

Earl was still with the Marines for the 1958 season and was just as instrumental in the Leathernecks repeating as Marine champions. Over the course of the Marine's regular season, Earl was 16-1, and in the championship series he threw a two-hitter to beat Hawaii, 2-1, on a home run by Floyd Robinson. Floyd, a lefty-hitting, righty-throwing outfielder with power, also went on to enjoy a nine-year Major League career, debuting with the Chicago White Sox in August 1960 where he became an everyday starter through the 1966 season, and he then saw limited action with the Cincinnati Reds in 1967 and the Oakland A's in 1968, before finishing up with the Red Sox in 1968. Earl's won-lost record during his two-year stint with the Marines was 49-2. Earl not only liked pitching in San Diego, he also liked living there. After Earl was discharged from the Marines he settled in San

Diego, and lived there until the early sixties when he became a regular starter with the Red Sox.

While Earl was in San Diego with the Marines, the Red Sox invited Pumpsie Green to their spring training camp, in Scottsdale, Arizona, for the 1958 season. Obviously, the Red Sox didn't learn much from the Dodgers' experience with Jackie Robinson in the spring of 1946. Although they invited a black player to camp, they failed to insure that he would be welcome, let alone comfortable. When Pumpsie arrived at the Safari Hotel, where the players were staying, he was told that they did not accept blacks as guests in the hotel. Pumpsie had to stay at the Frontier Motel, in Phoenix, which was seventeen miles removed from his teammates and the Sox' training camp. Pumpsie came to learn that it was not only the Safari Hotel that was segregated in Scottsdale, but the entire city. The New York Giants, about to become the San Francisco Giants, who had several minority players on their roster, housed all of their players at the Adams Hotel in Phoenix, where all of the players were welcome.

Before the 1958 Major League season started, the Detroit Tigers acquired Ozzie Virgil from the San Francisco Giants in a trade for Jim Finigan. When Virgil, who had played for the Giants in 1956 and 1957, entered a game for the Tigers it left the Red Sox as the only team to have not yet fielded a Negro player. They didn't even have a Negro player on their Major League roster yet, and twelve seasons had been played since Jackie took that first pitch from Johnny Sain.

Although I made it to the Major Leagues (in 1958) ahead of Earl, he was a starting pitcher in Minneapolis, Minnesota before I was. By the time Earl had finished his two years of service to the Marine Corps, the Red Sox had switched their AAA affiliate from the San Francisco Seals of the Pacific Coast League, where Earl never got to throw a pitch, to the famed Minneapolis Millers of the American Association, which played its games in Metropolitan Stadium, the future home of the Twins. The Millers had a proud minor league baseball history, starting from 1902 and ending when Major League Baseball came to Minneapolis in 1960. Fifteen members of baseball's Hall of Fame wore a Millers uniform at some point in their career, including Ted Williams (1938), Ray Dandridge (1949-52), Willie Mays (1951), Monte Irvin (1955), Orlando Cepeda (1957), and Carl Yastrzemski (1959-60). Minnesota was also home to several all-black teams in the early 1900s, including the Minneapolis Keystones and the St. Paul Gophers, the latter having defeated Rube Foster's Leland Giants for the unofficial Negro League championship title in 1909.

Earl spent parts of both the 1959 and 1960 seasons with the Millers and enjoyed success on the mound. He struck out 246 batters in 225 innings over the two years and in 1959 he was 10-2, winning nine straight games, earning him a spot on the American Association All-Star team. As the 1959 season started and the Red Sox were the lone team to have not yet fielded a Negro player, or have a Negro player on their Major League roster, it was clear that the Boston organization was feeling the pressure of their inactivity, and they took action to put a positive spin on their situation. In April 1959, after the Red Sox sent Earl to Minnesota, they optioned Pumpsie Green there also, despite widespread public belief that he was ready to join the Major League squad. That led American Veterans Committee and the NAACP to file charges with the Massachusetts Commission on Discrimination that "the segregation and racial discrimination Green was subjected to by the Red Sox during spring training was unfair, undemocratic and did not afford him the equal opportunity to which Americans are entitled." The Sox had decided to start the season with Don Buddin at shortstop. Buddin was a light-hitting (.237) utility infielder who had already spent part of 1956 and the 1958 season with the Red Sox. Sox Business Manager, Dick O'Connell, responded to the discrimination charges by saying:

> **This is exploitation of a cause which is not just. This is turning into prejudice against whites. It has turned people against Don Buddin, who has undergone a lot of booing for something for which he is not responsible. Green was farmed out for experience. We'd like to have a Negro on our club. We have seven in our farm system, and by next season, Earl Wilson, pitching for Minneapolis now, Green or one of the other Negroes we have should be ready for big league competition.**
> *The Sporting News, April 29, 1959*

Pumpsie is not so sure about the reasons he was sent back to Minneapolis only three days before the 1959 season started, but he is certainly philosophical about it now when he recalls those events:

> **I had a great spring in 1959. I outdid everybody in camp – hitting, fielding, everything. I was in, what they call now in sports, one of those zones. I was hitting everything. Hell, I wasn't that good a hitter. But I was wearing people out. I was in this zone. And I kept it up. Everything was working.**
> **The papers were saying, 'Pumpsie will be in Boston.'**
> **Sometimes it's tough. Number one, they have to find a spot for you. They have guys in positions. For example, if you go to spring training with the Giants and you're a left fielder, I don't care if you hit 1.000, [Barry] Bonds is the left fielder. There's no question.**
> **Hard for me to tell [if it was racial bias]. The manager just said he was going to send me back to Minneapolis, and that was it. … It caused a big stink in Boston because the NAACP got hold of it and they pushed and asked questions. I just wanted to play baseball.**
> **I tried to keep myself positive. I had a great spring and I was looking forward to being back in Minneapolis, because I would get my old roommate back, Earl Wilson. And I would have some company other than at the ballpark. We started the season hot, we broke out on top. Hey, I hadn't cooled off yet. I carried my hot start right on through the spring and up until July, when Boston called me up.**
> *Pumpsie Green, quoted by Bill Kolb, in "Beantown's First Black Sock", Contracostatimes.com*

Earl lost his first start with the Millers in 1959, but by the middle of July he was 9-1, having won nine straight decisions. In addition to being victorious he was dominant. At mid-season he had 108 strikeouts, with 76 of them coming during the 65 innings pitched during his nine straight victories, while he only yielded 16 runs during that time. On top of all of that, Earl led the team in batting, with a .371 average. Over at second base, Pumpsie was doing just as well for the Millers. He was also an All-Star selection that year, batting .320 at mid-season. Both Earl and Pumpsie seemed more than ready to be called up to the majors. Meanwhile, up in Boston, racist Pinky Higgins, who had vowed "there would never be a nigger" on the Red Sox if he had anything to do with it, was still the manager of the team. It seemed like a microcosm of what had happened in all of baseball years earlier, when Commissioner Landis appeared to stand in the way of blacks entering baseball, which only occurred after Landis died and Happy Chandler became Commissioner.

If it wasn't Higgins who was in fact standing in the way of the Red Sox playing a Negro, it was eerily coincidental that less than a week after the Red Sox fired Higgins and replaced him with Billy Jurges they called up Pumpsie Green from the minor leagues. I don't really think it was a coincidence. From what I know of Higgins and baseball, my belief is that the Red Sox were feeling the pressure to integrate the team, and felt forced to bring up Green. Higgins' racist stand could not allow him to be the skipper of the team when it became integrated, to the extent of one player, so he was "re-assigned." Earl had no doubts about Higgins' feelings toward him:

It's not very hard to tell if a guy likes you or dislikes you. It's like if a dog comes in a room, he can tell if a person likes him or dislikes him. It was real, man.
Earl Wilson, quoted by Dan Shaughnessy, Boston Globe, March 28, 1997, "Red Sox Pained by Their Past"

When I broke in, there were some bad guys. [Bucky] Harris [Red Sox General Manager] was a bad guy, and he was friends with Mike Higgins, the manager, and he was a bad guy, too.
Earl Wilson, quoted by Steve Bucklen, The Boston Herald, April 26, 2005

Then on July 21, 1959, in Comiskey Park, Chicago, Pumpsie made Red Sox history by entering a game against the White Sox as a pinch-runner and then playing the field at shortstop. Considering all that had been written and said about Boston not having a black player on the roster, and being the last team to integrate, it was interesting to note that Pumpsie's arrival was not front page news. In fact, the best *The Sporting News* could muster was a small article on Page 19, of the July 29, 1959 edition under the headline, **Bosox Recall Green; First Negro on Club**.

I must note at this point that although Pumpsie did not face all the same obstacles that Jackie and Larry and the very first black pro players faced, he did find himself in uncomfortable surroundings in Boston at first, being the only black player on the team. It is no surprise to me that Ted Williams, nearing the end of his great career, was the first player on the Red Sox to make Pumpsie feel welcome. Before Pumpsie's first game with Boston, as the players paired off to toss a baseball around and loosen up and he anxiously looked around, Ted tossed him a ball and warmed up with him. The reason I say I am not surprised is because I had already seen Ted's acceptance of blacks first-hand. At the end of spring training Cleveland and Boston were scheduled to play an exhibition game in New Orleans. When we got into town, before the bus took the white players to the team hotel, the black ballplayers were dropped off at some other location because we could not room together. However, our bags stayed with all the luggage and were not unloaded until the bus got to the team hotel. Customarily, the black ballplayers would draw straws to determine who was stuck having to go pick up the bags. This time I drew the short stick and summoned a black taxi to bring me to the hotel in a "white" part of town, which he wasn't happy about. When I got to the hotel, the bell captain says to me, "What do you want here, boy?" I said, "I came to pick up my bags," pointing to the grips which I could see sitting in the hotel lobby, just inside the doors. He said, "You have no business here, and you can't enter the hotel." We went around with that conversation one or two more times, when another cab drove up and Ted Williams hopped out of the car. Ted said, "Hey, Mud, what's up?" I said, "Well, Ted, this bell captain said I can't go into the hotel to get our luggage." To my initial surprise but ultimate pleasure, Ted said, "Well, Mud, he's right. You shouldn't go get the bags. He should go inside and carry them out for you." Feeling empowered, I said to the bell captain, "Yeah, boy, go get me those bags." Hearing that the black taxi driver started revving the engine, figuring I was about to cause a riot. The bell captain brought out the bags and the cabbie got me back to where we were staying twice as fast as it took to get to the hotel.

Although by the time Pumpsie got to Boston, blacks had already played for every other Major League franchise, there was still excitement among the blacks in Boston that their home team now had a Negro player. With the same sense of history that I remember my walk around the stadium in Detroit with Larry Doby, Pumpsie talks about first landing in Boston and his first game there on July 24, 1959, when the Red Sox cordoned off a section of centerfield at Fenway so that 1,000 blacks, of the thousands outside trying to get tickets, could see Pumpsie's Boston debut:

We landed in Boston about midnight. We were getting off the plane, and I saw all these lights. I thought those were the lights for us to walk down the ramp, or some airport lights or something normal. Actually, it was for me. Some guys told me, 'Pumps, you really bring 'em out. They got cameras on you.'

The park is already small. They really shrunk it, because they wanted some more of the blacks to come in there. Some of the guys would tease me a little bit, talking about, 'Pumps, you really pack 'em in,'

and all that kinda stuff. Boy, that was the time when my nerves were really going. I wanted to settle down, but I couldn't.

They announce me, and I'm walking up to home plate and I get a standing ovation. On my way up to home plate, I was telling myself, 'Pumpsie, the first pitch you get that you can reach, hit it.' I wanted to hit the ball somewhere. I didn't care about a base hit. I wanted to hit the ball somewhere, because in the back of my mind, I didn't want to strike out after all that standing ovation and have to turn around and walk back to the dugout.

That shouldn't have been a triple. … I had my head down. I was just going. I should have picked up the third base coach. But I ran right through. If he put up the stop sign, I never saw it. And I got another standing ovation.

Pumpsie Green, quoted by Bill Kolb, in "Beantown's First Black Sock", Contracostatimes.com

One week later, the Red Sox called Earl up to the majors, and he made his Major League pitching debut on July 29, 1959. The fact that Earl was 10-1 with the Millers at the time he was called up to the Red Sox, and had already had a successful minor league career, would be reason enough for Earl to have been promoted to the majors. But many people believed, and still believe, that the main reason Earl was brought up at that particular time was because Pumpsie needed a roommate. At the time ballplayers shared a room and no white player was willing to share a room with Pumpsie, causing the team's traveling secretary some headaches and expense. It was nothing new to Pumpsie. He believes that same reason was why he was originally signed by the Red Sox, so that Earl would have a roommate.

On any team, you'd have either two, four, six or eight black players. Never had one, three, five or seven. That's because you had to have a roommate, had to have a pair. So, if you had one black guy who wasn't cutting it, you both went down. That's just the way it was.

Pumpsie Green, quoted by Bill Kolb, in "Beantown's First Black Sock", Contracostatimes.com

Earl secured his first Major League victory on August 19, 1959, by pitching four innings in relief, and helped his own cause with two hits and three runs batted in. That year Earl appeared in a total of nine games for the Red Sox, getting to start four. He was 1-1, with 17 strikeouts in 23.7 innings pitched. The one area where Earl needed work was control. He yielded 31 walks, an average of almost 12 walks per nine innings.

The excitement continued for Earl with his return to the Millers to complete the 1959 season. Having finished in second place, they had made it to the American

Association playoffs, and defeated Omaha and Fort Worth to capture the American Association championship title and advance to the Junior World Series against the International League champs, the Havana Sugar Kings. The first two games were played in Minneapolis; then the Series moved to Havana, Cuba, where Fidel Castro was Premier and baseball was King. There was a tension surrounding the Series, beyond the normal anxiety created by a playoff series, especially one that goes to the seventh and deciding game. It was not unheard of for violence to occur in a Latin American stadium when things didn't go in favor of the home team, as was the case when Satchel was playing for Trujillo. The Millers, under player-manager, Gene Mauch, had a chance to win the series, but couldn't hold the lead in the seventh game.

When the American Association season was finally over, Earl went down to Puerto Rico where he sparkled for the Caguas team managed by my Cleveland teammate, Vic Power. Vic was the hitting star, winning the league batting title for the second time with a .347 average, and Earl was the pitching star, leading the league in victories with 15, while losing only 3, and posting a 2.02 ERA. Together they helped Caguas win the Puerto Rican League championship, and earn a spot in the Caribbean Series, which features the champions of the Puerto Rican, Panamanian, Cuban, and Venezuelan winter leagues. Caguas also featured a young Orlando Cepeda, playing in the shadow of his famous father, Pedro (El Peruche) Cepeda, and a young Juan Pizarro, and was picked by some writers to defeat the favored Cuban team. Earl did his best, twirling a two hitter against Cuba, but they still managed to win that game and the Series. So for the second time in four months Earl left Cuba without a championship.

Based on his combined success in Minneapolis and Caguas (25-5), and the fact that he was up with the parent club in 1959, Earl came to spring training in 1960 expecting to stay in the majors. Unfortunately, when camp broke in early April he was sorely disappointed upon being optioned to Minneapolis again. There, Earl pitched very well again, and was clearly one of the up and coming Red Sox stars, together with teammates Carl Yastrzemski and Chuck Schilling. When August rolled around the Red Sox called Earl back to Boston, and he was determined to stay this time. On August 4, 1960, in Fenway Park, Earl won his first complete game victory, a 9-1 win over the Athletics, in which Earl gave up six hits. Five days later, Earl threw a four hitter against the Indians, winning 6-1. After that game, Ted Williams shared some high praise for Earl with Curt Gowdy, the then-voice of the Red Sox:

He has the stuff, if he can get it over. He may be one of those pitchers who is slow in arriving. But from his first two starts and wins, it would seem that he is about to arrive in a big way.
The Sporting News, August 24, 1960

In all, during the last two months of the 1960 season Earl appeared in thirteen games for the Red Sox, starting nine. He had a winning record of 3-2 and showed better control than he had in the previous season. One note of interest was that fifty-two games into the 1960 season, Pinky Higgins was re-hired as manager of the Red Sox, and despite his earlier pledge, he inherited a team with three black players, Earl, Pumpsie, and Willie Tasby.

As soon as the 1960 season was over, Don Newcombe, Earl and I were teammates on a barnstorming team of American League "All-Stars" that also included Major Leaguers, Pumpsie Green, Willie Tasby, Al Smith (White Sox), Bob Boyd (Orioles), Earl Battey and Lennie Green (Senators), and minor leaguers Harry Simpson, Connie Johnson, Fred Valentine, Ollie Brantley, and Isaac Barnes. We were scheduled to play thirty-three (33) games, throughout North Carolina, South Carolina, Alabama, Florida, Texas, Mississippi and Louisiana, against a National League squad featuring Henry Aaron, Vada Pinson, Curt Flood Bill White and Maury Wills. We also played an exhibition in Syracuse, New York, where Yankee stars, Whitey Ford and Roger Maris joined us.

When the 1961 season rolled around, Earl, with parts of two Major League seasons under his belt, and obviously already accomplished at the AAA level, was fully expectant to stay with the Major League club. Surprisingly, he was optioned to the Red Sox' newest AAA affiliate, the Seattle Raniers of the Pacific Coast League managed by Red Sox legend Johnny Pesky. Earl would spend pretty much the entire season in the minors. He was called back in September, but Higgins never gave him the ball. In the off-season, Earl again played for Caguas in the Puerto Rican League, a circuit that featured such talent as Juan Pizarro, Luis Tiant, Orlando Cepeda, Ossie Virgil, Bob Gibson, Joel Horlen, Julio Navarro, Frank Howard, Lee Maye, Ed Charles, Tony Gonzalez, and JC Martin, in no particular order.

With a total of 22 Major League appearances totaling less than 90 innings under his belt, and a record of 4-3, Earl faced a "do-or-die" situation with the Red Sox in the spring of 1962. He had been in the Red Sox organization for nine years, counting his two years with the Marines, and if he was going to make it to the majors it appeared that it was 1962 or never. The Red Sox must have believed that Earl was ready for the pros in 1962. Even Pinky Higgins seemed to finally be able to recognize Earl's potential and ability rather than his skin color:

Sure, Wilson has been disappointing, but you can't give up on a guy who has an arm as good as his. He's been pitching well in one of the winter leagues, and from the reports we have had, his control has improved a great deal. We could have made a trade for him, if we wanted to, but we feel he'll come through for us.
The Sporting News, February 28, 1962

That was high praise for Earl considering the source. Earl pitched well enough to make the team that spring but not the starting rotation, which was Bill Monbouquette, Gene Conley, Don Schwall, and Galen Cisco. Other pitchers included knuckleballer, Wilbur Wood, Tracy Stallard (who was famous for giving up Roger Maris' 61st home run in 1961), and Dick Radatz (who just recently passed away, and who would go on to become Earl's favorite reliever in both Boston and Detroit). Earl did get a couple of spot starts early in the season and by early June he had cracked the starting rotation.

When Earl took the mound at Fenway Park on June 26, 1962, against the Los Angeles Angels, he had a record of 5-2, having won five of his last six starts. His opponent on the hill that night was Bo Belinsky, who three weeks earlier, on May 5th, had pitched a no hitter against the Baltimore Orioles. By the bottom of the third inning, Earl and Bo were locked in a 0-0 tie, and Earl had allowed only one base runner, on a walk in the second inning. Earl broke the deadlock by lofting a Belinsky pitch over the left field wall. The Red Sox scored a second run in the fourth inning on an error and two singles. Armed with the lead he provided himself, Earl set about retiring the Angel batters. Over the course of the game he walked a total of four batters, and faced only 31. When he got Lee Thomas to fly out to Gary Geiger in center field for the last out of the game, Earl was immediately mobbed by all of his teammates. He had pitched the first no-hitter by a Red Sox pitcher in six years, and the first ever by an African-American in the American League. Earl had arrived on the big league mound to stay, for sure.

That's the greatest thing that ever happened to me. I think God was with me. I had my fast ball working great after the first few innings. Except for a few breaking balls to [Eddie] Yost, I believe I threw nothing but fast balls. I got a big boost from [Frank] Malzone when he caught that foul ball. That was a great catch and it made me feel like I was going all the way. I felt relieved earlier when Runnels made his play on Thomas and that same man gave me a scare as the last out. I thought the ball might hit the bleacher wall. But when I turned and saw Geiger catch it, I think I passed out.
Earl Wilson, quoted in The Sporting News, July 7, 1962

During parts of the 1962 season I was serving in the Army Reserve and played on their baseball team. The day Earl pitched his no-hitter our team had a game at Fort Devens, Massachusetts, which is about a half an hour from Fenway Park. When our game was over I convinced my superior officer to allow me the freedom to take a "side trip" to see Earl. The bus broke down, and we didn't get into Boston until the game was already in the seventh inning. It was well after the game was over by the time I got to a hotel and a beautiful young woman saw me, and figuring that a black man in a hotel in Boston could only be a guest if he was a ballplayer or some other celebrity, she said, "Oh, my God, Earl Wilson! Congratulations on your no-hitter." Without admitting or denying my identity, but basking in the non-truth, I replied with a question, "Did you like that game?" She said, "I loved that game," and I said, "Well, thank you very much."

Earl's no hitter was the brightest spot in his 1962 season, and was one of the only bright spots in the Red Sox' season also, matched by Bill Monboquette's no hitter a little later in the season. The Red Sox finished eighth out of ten teams in the American League that year, with only perennial cellar dwellers, Kansas City and Washington, beneath them. Boston's pitching staff was also ranked eighth out of ten, and they were near the bottom in fielding percentage and in the middle of the pack in hitting. Earl got 28 starts in 1962, his first full season, and finished with a 12-8 record, which was respectable, considering the team was 76-84 overall. Based on Earl's strong showing, the writers who covered the American League for *The Sporting News*, in April 1963, voted Earl as the Most Likely 20-Game Winner on the Red Sox for the coming season.

For the next three years, all with the Red Sox, Earl did not have much luck on the mound, despite pitching fairly well, and the Red Sox didn't have much luck, or hitting, or fielding, or relief pitching either for that matter, besides Radatz. At one point in the 1965 season, Earl had left the game with a lead eleven times and only got one victory. In 1965, sportswriter Larry Claflin memorialized the sad state of Red Sox affairs:

> **With what is probably the worst defensive team in the major leagues and forced to play half their games in a tiny ball park, the Red Sox can hardly be expected to show up well when pitching figures are examined.**
> *******
> **The Boston infield has been notoriously porous all year. The catching is weak. Only the outfield has provided good defense and even that has been bad at times.**
> **In addition, the Red Sox players have made some brutally dumb moves on the field, such as forgetting the count on batters or not knowing how many outs there were, which contributed to pitching woes.**
> *******
> **No pitcher on the club, with the possible exception of rookie Jim Lonborg, has had to survive more bad plays than [Earl] Wilson.**
> *The Sporting News, September 18, 1965*

I didn't help old Earl's problems in 1965. In early September he and I faced each other. We scored a run against him in the first inning on a broken-bat single by Bob Allison, and I made that run stand up, pitching a shutout, and handing Earl his 13th loss of the season, 1-0. I respected Earl's ability and sensed how good he could have been with any kind of support. In fact, I went on record as to Earl's potential, when during the 1965 World Series I told a reporter:

> **He [Earl Wilson] would have won 20 games with our club behind him.**
> *Quoted by Larry Claflin, The Sporting News, December 4, 1965*

From 1963 to 1965, the Red Sox changed managers, from Pinky Higgins to Johnny Pesky to Billy Herman, but the result wasn't much different no matter who the skipper was. In fact, it got worse. In 1963, they finished in seventh place with 76 wins; in 1964 they dropped to eighth place with 72 wins, and in 1965 they finished ninth, winning 62 games and losing 100. Relief pitcher, Bob Duliba, at 4-2, was the only pitcher on the entire Red Sox staff with a winning record, and Earl, at 13-14, was the only pitcher in the starting rotation not to lose eight games more than he won, and was considered the "Ace" of the staff. Earl was looking forward to 1966 being his best season yet, and so was manager, Billy Herman, who had taken over the Red Sox during the 1965 season:

> **I was pleased to see how hard Earl Wilson was working, for example. Not that Earl doesn't always work hard, because he does. But, from the moment he walked on the field, Earl demonstrated that he is determined to have a big year.**
> **You know, Earl could be a big winner this year if he pitches like he did in 1965 and we give him better support. He won 13 games last year, but he could have won at least 18. He pitched well enough to win that many. What pleases me is that he is bearing down just as hard as ever, even though he had some reason to be discouraged last year.**
> *Billy Herman, quoted in The Sporting News, March 12, 1966*

During the off-season, the Red Sox looked into moving their spring training site from Scottsdale, Arizona back to Florida. After being convinced by the town of Winter Haven that they would not face any problems with housing the whole team together or with discrimination against any of their players, the Red Sox entered into an agreement which provided for Winter Haven to build a new spring training stadium (Chain O' Lakes Park) and for the Red Sox to stay there for ten years. During the first month of spring training the agreement was tested.

Pitchers and catchers are traditionally the first players to report to spring training, about a week or so earlier than the other position players. There were no other black pitchers or catchers invited to spring training by the Red Sox in 1966. So for the first ten days or so Earl was the only black player in camp. A few days before the other players were due to arrive, including several blacks, Earl and a few of the other pitchers, Dennis Bennett, Dick Radatz, and Dave Morehead, staying at the Haven Hotel, decided to go shoot pool. After a while they went to a local lounge for a few beers but were told that blacks could not enter. The players then headed for the Cloud Nine Bar, in Lakeland. They gained entrance and sat at the bar. The bartender took Bennett's order and then Morehead, and then turned to Earl and said, "We ain't serving you. We don't serve niggers in here." The players left the bar and returned to the Haven Lounge where their business was accepted.

Within days after the incident, Earl told sportswriter Larry Claflin how he felt leaving the Cloud Nine Bar:

> **That was the longest walk of my life back to my car. Now I wonder where I can go in this town. What places will I be accepted and what places will I not be accepted? I don't want to be accepted just because**

I pitch for the Red Sox. My baseball life has nothing to do with my personal life. I want to be accepted as a human being.
The Sporting News, March 12, 1966

The day after the incident, Boston manager, Billy Herman, issued a statement:

Earl is angry and I don't blame him a bit. All I said to him was to suggest that he be careful what he says and not say anything in anger that he might regret later. As for what happened, let me say that any place that is not suitable for Earl isn't suitable for any player on this team.
The Sporting News, March 12, 1966

Earl's version of what the Red Sox told him was to not talk about the incident, to let it blow over like it never happened:

I'll never forget [former Red Sox executive] Dick O'Connell told me not to do anything or say anything that would hurt me. Of course, me being me, I opened my big mouth and started talking about it.
MLB.com

Having led the team in wins in 1965, Earl was considered the ace of the Red Sox staff. Consider these comments contained in story by Larry Claflin that ran in *The Sporting News* on June 4, 1966:

The Red Sox don't expect Wilson to win 40 games this year, but they do think he is a potential 20-game winner who is just now reaching his pitching peak.
"His physical condition is marvelous," said Herman. "There isn't a player in baseball who takes better care of himself. Earl has a perfect physique. You see him in the middle of winter and he looks in just as good shape as he does in July, when he's pitching every fourth day."
Once the possessor of one of the league's most feared fast balls, Wilson lacks the speed of his youth now. However, he has more savvy on the mound and several other pitches. He uses his change-up effectively, although it still gets him into home-run trouble sometimes. He also worked hard at developing a forkball this spring, a pitch which some people think may be the spitter Frank Robinson hinted at.
Last season, Wilson won 13 games and lost 14, but with a better team or more luck, his record would have been much better. Herman once said that Wilson could have won as many games as Mudcat Grant had Earl been with the Twins instead of the Red Sox.

Despite that high praise, less than one week later the Red Sox traded Earl to the Detroit Tigers for Don Demeter, an outfielder they coveted because of his home run power. (As a side note, Earl went on to hit seventeen (17) home runs for the Tigers and one for the Padres, and Demeter only hit ten (10) home runs for the Red Sox before he was traded to the Indians for my old roommate, Gary Bell, and Demeter then retired after the 1967 season.) Earl was not happy about the trade at the time for two reasons: firstly, he had made his home in the Boston suburb of Roxbury (and was a frequent visitor to *Slade's*, a jazz club owned by Celtic great, Bill Russell) and he now had to uproot himself and leave the only organization he had ever played for; and, secondly, he felt that the trade was not made for baseball reasons, but that he was being shipped out because he had spoken up about the Cloud Nine Bar incident and the racism that continued to exist in Florida in 1966. As hurt as he was, Earl did not verbalize his feelings about the real reason for the trade at that time. One of the things that hurt Earl was the statement of Red Sox' pitching coach Sal Maglie that Earl was "only a .500 pitcher." It is true that Earl's record with the Red Sox was 56-59, but the team record as a whole was a much lower percentage than that. In 1965 the team's winning percentage was .383.

Earl headed to Detroit and made the most of it, literally. Having grown up in the rural South, Earl had never really seen much of any large city except Boston. Even though he had been in the Major Leagues for several years, he only got to see limited sections of the cities he visited on road trips. His move to Detroit was eye-opening for Earl compared to his stay in Boston:

When I finally got to Boston, it wasn't the experience I thought it would be. We were staying at the hotel right across from Fenway, so you're removed from the normal things that happen in the city of Boston. And staying there, you don't venture to a whole lot of places. There were places around that the people I knew hung out at and I would go there. But I didn't go too far. I wasn't looking for no [butt] kicking.

When I first got to Detroit, it was the first time I had seen black folks with their own homes, own businesses, their own new cars. That was impressive to me. I said, 'I would like to live here.' I never did see that in Boston. I don't have the great memories there. But everything was wonderful in Detroit and it became home to me.
Earl Wilson, quoted by Ian Browne, MLB.com, Feb. 14, 2003

It became obvious that something in Detroit agreed with Earl, and that something in Boston had to have been bothering him earlier in the year. Earl was only 5-5 with Boston in 1966 at the time of the trade, and his pitching improved dramatically after he went to Detroit:

	W	L	G	GS	CG	SHO	ERA	BB	SO	IP
Boston	5	5	15	14	5	1	3.84	36	37	100.7
Detroit	13	6	23	23	8	2	2.59	38	133	163.3

His average walks per nine innings pitched dropped from over 3.2 to 2, and his average strikeouts per nine innings pitched increased from under six to over 7.3. During one stretch, Earl won nine games in a row for the Tigers, lifting his season record to 18-9. Then on September 11th, at Kansas City, while fielding a pop bunt in the first inning, Earl suffered a sacroiliac slip and left the game in pain two innings later trailing 2-1. The injury cost him several starts and a chance to be a twenty-game winner that year. Earl not only impressed the folks in Detroit with his pitching, relying mainly on his overpowering, sinking fastball, but he was very productive, and powerful, at the plate. Earl's roommate with the Tigers was slugger Willie Horton, and the running joke was that Earl was helping Willie with his hitting, not the other way around. Earl's first pinch-hit home run won an extra inning game against the Orioles. And if you are into numerology check out this item: Earl hit a grand slam against the Red Sox at Fenway on August 13th, 1966; it was Earl's 13th start for the Tigers; the Tigers won 13-1; and it was Earl's 13th victory of the season. Earl's work in Detroit earned him recognition as the right-handed Pitcher of the Year for the American League in *The Sporting News* poll of the players.

In addition to a good batting eye, Earl always had a good eye for business, and knew how to handle his affairs. He was actually instrumental in how players would eventually negotiate their contracts, with the help of an agent. Earl was involved in a minor automobile accident in Boston in 1964 and sought the help of a local attorney, Bob Woolf, to settle the matter. Earl trusted Bob, and eventually sought his assistance in the preparation of his taxes. When Earl was traded to Detroit and it came time to negotiate a new contract, he asked for Bob's help. But at that time the teams only negotiated with the players, one on one. So as Earl met with Detroit General Manager, Jim Campbell, he had Bob Woolf stay in his apartment next to a phone. At several points in the bargaining session, Earl would leave the room and call Bob. From there, Bob went on to represent hundreds of professional athletes.

As happy as Earl was in Detroit in 1966, things got a lot better in 1967, starting with spring training, when legendary pitching coach, Johnny Sain, was hired by the Tigers. Earl quickly learned what Al Downing learned in New York in 1963 and what I learned in Minnesota in 1965: Sain was a pitching master:

I had five or six different pitching coaches in Boston, so I never really got to know any of them. Sain already told me some things I never thought about. He's got some good theories. He's got me throwing a snapping curve, something I never had before.
Earl Wilson, The Sporting News, March 25, 1967

Beyond the tutelage of Sain, and the comfort level that Earl felt in Detroit, he had the benefit of pitching for a very good team. When Earl first came to the Tigers in 1966, he went from one of the worst fielding teams with the highest ERA in the League, to a team that made 36 fewer errors and had a lower ERA and a higher team batting average. In 1967, the Red Sox not only caught up to the Tigers, but passed them, beating them out for the pennant by one game, fueled mainly by the phenomenal year that Carl Yastrzemski (MVP, Triple Crown, Gold Glove Winner) and Jim Lonborg (Cy Young Award Winner) had. But Detroit was statistically very close to Detroit, with virtually the same team ERA and team fielding percentage. During a seven week stretch of the season, beginning on July 4, Earl went 9-2 keeping the Tigers in the pennant race. He was the pace-setter for pitchers in the majors that season, and was the first twenty-game winner of the year. In fact, Earl won his 20th game earlier in the season than any Tiger since Hall of Famer Hal Newhouser who pitched for Detroit in the mid 1940s. Throughout August and September of that year, Earl's name was constantly mentioned together with Jim Lonborg and Dean Chance whenever the Cy Young Award was discussed.

Earl stood at 6' 3" and had what they referred to as a "menacing" look on the mound. To me and to the rest of the world we knew he had the heart of a fierce competitor. Interestingly, after Earl won his twentieth game, he revealed a different side of himself in an interview with Pete Waldmeir of *The Detroit News*, which was quoted by Joe Falls in *The Sporting News*, September 30, 1967:

It's not that I don't like people. It's just that I'm sort of moody and I like to be by myself. Sometimes I'm not very good to be with anyway. Particularly during the baseball season. I take my baseball pretty seriously. I figure that pitching is 90 percent concentration. So much of it is in your mind ... knowing what you have to do and making every move, every pitch count.

I'm just too nervous – all the time, even when I'm not pitching – to be good company for anybody. I sit in my hotel room and try to watch television, but I can't get my mind off my job. Sooner or later I have to turn it off and go get the newspaper and look to see what the hitters on other teams around the league are doing. The night before I pitch, I wake up often wondering what I'm going to do. You know what? I'm scared.

Earl Wilson

Well, when the season was over, Earl had finished with a 22-11 record, tied with Jim Lonborg (22-9) for most victories in the League, and he led his team's staff in strikeouts (184), complete games (12), innings pitched (264), and games started (38); not too bad for a guy who says he was scared, AND he hit four home runs. Lonborg won the AL Cy Young Award, and both Lonborg and Earl were named by the players to The Sporting News AL All-Star Team. But the prize Earl really wanted, a trip to the World Series against Bob Gibson and the St. Louis Cardinals, was denied to him, as the Tigers fell one game short against the Red Sox.

The riots that had broken out in Birmingham in 1963 and traveled to Watts in 1965 and New York in 1966, reached Detroit in the summer of 1967, at the same time that Earl was pitching his best, in late July. Police raided an illegal bar in the inner city on July 23, 1967. That quickly led to looting, lighting fires and random acts of violence. Within a very short period of time, congregating mobs were conducting a full-scale riot which encompassed fourteen square miles of black neighborhoods in the city. Although the demonstration began as an attack against the arresting police officers it soon spread to mayhem, with black businesses being burned down and/or looted along with white ones. The riots lasted five days before federal troops were able to restore order. By that time 43 people had died, 7,000 were arrested, 1,300 buildings were destroyed and 2,700 businesses looted. The federal Civil Rights Law and Voting Rights Law passed in 1964 and 1965 to outlaw segregation had not cured all the ills in urban black areas. Many people felt that the federal legislation didn't benefit them, and, in fact, hurt black neighborhoods in much the same way that the integration of baseball ultimately killed the Negro Leagues, because the "cream of the crop," those able to climb the social ladder were now leaving black neighborhoods and moving in where they were once not accepted. That left only the socially stagnant lower class left in the inner city, feeling hopeless and angry. The New York Times reports that in 1967 alone, there were almost four dozen riots and countless other disturbances throughout the country that caused injury and damages but didn't rise to the level of a riot. Actually, the success of the Tigers in 1967, and the individual success of Earl as one of the few black pitchers in baseball, was very therapeutic for Detroit. While it did not come clear to curing the tragedy of the human losses or the enormity of the property losses, it did create a certain sense of civic pride in Detroit, where the Tigers stayed in the pennant race until the last day of the season.

In 1968, the Tigers would get another chance and make the most of it, although Earl was hampered by foot and leg injuries over the course of the season. In a game against the Athletics, in Oakland, in late May, Earl slipped making a tag on Bert Campaneris coming down the first base line and injured his heel, causing him to miss four starts. In July he injured his left knee and that injury lingered. In all, Earl missed about six weeks of playing time and posted 13 victories, including his 100th career win. He did win critical games for the Tigers during the pennant drive stretch in September, and contributed with his bat, crushing seven home runs and driving in seventeen runs. Denny McLain and Mickey Lolich both stepped up, becoming pitching stars in the regular season and the World Series. McLain became the first thirty-game winner since Dizzy Dean (1934), winning 31 games while losing 6 and Lolich posted a 17-9 record. Earl got to start Game Three of the Series, but his lack of work in September showed. He walked six batters in less than five innings. He pulled a muscle in his right leg while pitching to Curt Flood in the fifth inning and was removed with the Tigers trailing and took the loss. Gibson pitched a complete game shutout in Game One, and another complete game in Game Four yielding only one run, to put the Cardinals up three games to one. Then Lolich and McLain went to work. Without any help from the bullpen, Lolich won Game Five, McLain (on two days rest) won Game Six, and Lolich (on two days rest) finally defeated Gibson in Game Seven.

In 1969, Earl was again hampered by leg injuries and missed several starts when he suffered a bruised hand deflecting a line drive off the bat of Don Buford, but he managed to post 12 victories and a winning record. It was the eighth straight year he won ten or more games. Although time was beginning to take its toll on Earl's pitching arm, his competitiveness never waned. One example of Earl's desire to win was a rather weird play involving my old teammates, the Twins. Earl struck out to end the inning, but the catcher, Paul Ratliff, a rookie, had not caught the pitch cleanly, trapping it against the ground, and although the umpire did not signal an out the catcher rolled the ball back to the mound and the Twins started off the field. With most of the Twins off the field, Earl took off for first base and then second and then third. When leftfielder, Brant Alyea, a little slow in getting off the field, finally retrieved the ball, Earl had mounted a full head of steam and was charging for home plate. By that time, Leo Cardenas, the Twins shortstop, had run to the plate to take a throw from Alyea, and Earl got caught up in a rundown, and was retired on a play you don't see in many scorecards, 7-6-7, leftfielder to shortstop to leftfielder.

After splitting the 1970 season between the Tigers and the San Diego Padres, Earl retired with a career record of 121-109 and having hit 35 home runs, two shy of Wes Farrell's Major League record for a pitcher. Earl returned to Detroit, where he founded Autotek Sealants Inc., an automotive supplier that produced sound-reduction products. He was the chief executive officer of the company which employed as many as 350 people. The creation and success of that business was a great sense of pride for Earl and rightly so. He was a frequent visitor to Tigers Stadium but did not allow baseball to define him, as he maintained a successful business persona and enjoyed pastimes other than baseball, like jazz music.

As a former player who was able to adjust to life after business and enjoy success off the field, Earl did not forget his roots or his fellow players who were not as successful off the field. He became very active in the Baseball Assistance Team (BAT), and served as its President from 2000 through 2004. During that five-year period the organization dedicated to assisting former players in need raised and distributed approximately $4,000,000.

As we discussed the writing of this book and joint projects among the Black Aces, including the formation of a charitable organization, The Black Aces Foundation, to help preserve the history of blacks in baseball as well as re-generate interest in the game in the inner cities, I spent a lot of time with Earl. He was proud of his accomplishments and happy to be able to use his time in the game in a very positive manner for kids today. I was very saddened when I learned of his sudden death of a heart attack in April 2005. I was honored to be asked to be one of Earl's pallbearers, but had to decline because of my weak hip.

Through hard work and determination this sharp-dressing, jazz-loving, son of a strawberry farmer from Ponchatoulah, Louisiana, became a World Champion, an author of a no-hitter, a twenty-game winner, a highly successful businessman, and the President of the Baseball Assistance Team helping former players. He was a great friend and will be sorely missed.

CHAPTER 22

FERGUSON ARTHUR JENKINS
Fergie

Born December 13, 1942 in Chatham, Ontario
Teams: Philadelphia Phillies, Chicago Cubs, Texas Rangers,
*   Boston Red Sox*
Twenty-Win Seasons: 1967, 1968, 1969, 1970, 1971, 1972, 1974:
Inducted into National Baseball Hall of Fame 1991
Inducted into Canadian Sports Hall of Fame 1987
Inducted into International Afro-American Sports
*   Hall of Fame and Gallery 1992*
National League Cy Young Award 1971
National League All-Star 1967, 1971, 1972

Nothing – and I mean nothing – ever bothers him. …. He knows they can't beat him.
Leo Durocher

Fergie was a pitcher with very little emotion and the guts of a burglar. A great competitor.
Ernie Broglio

Ferguson was a great teammate – laid back and easy going off the field – the ultimate competitor on the field. He could make his slider do anything he wanted it to do! The best fielding pitcher I played with.
Jon Matlack

Ferguson Jenkins is in a class by himself.
Jerome Holtzman

Ferguson Jenkins was born and raised in Canada, and is the only member of The Black Aces born outside the United States. For that reason, some people criticized me when I included him as one of The Black Aces. But when you come to know a bit about Fergie and his family, I'm certain you will see the logic in my thinking.

His mother's ancestors were slaves, brought to the American South from Africa. Although Fergie admits that the family Bible is missing a few details, he knows that members of his Mom's family were among the brave and fortunate who escaped slavery by means of the Underground Railroad. They followed the call of Harriet Tubman and Frederick Douglass and traveled one of the many dangerous routes from the South, through Pennsylvania, Maryland and Delaware, and ultimately into Canada. Most of the routes led to Ontario, Canada, (just east of Detroit, Michigan). It was here that Fergie's parents lived, and where he was born. I can only imagine the courage of those individuals who finally decided to free themselves from the shackles of slavery in an attempt to taste freedom. Every step they took led them further into unchartered territory, with the added fear that anyone they placed their faith and trust in, whether for food, shelter, or directions, might be someone willing to return them to slavery.

Fergie's Dad, Ferguson Holmes Jenkins, was a speedy, left-handed centerfielder, who played baseball for the Chatham Coloured All-Stars and the Ontario Black Panthers in the late 1930s. During that time, he helped them win two Ontario Baseball Association championships. The league he played in was considered semi-pro ball, and the pay was about $35 a week. Several of his teammates were notable Canadian players, including Flat Chase, (a second baseman and pitcher, whose hitting abilities are legendary), A.B. Scott, and Kingsley Terrell.

Fergie Jenkins [Sr.] was a good outfielder. I've seen him catch balls out in the outfield that you'd swear up and down that he would never even get close to. He would dive and catch balls over his head and all kinds of things. And he was good. He could have been in the major leagues.
Kingsley Terrell, an original Chatham All-Star and teammate of Ferguson Holmes Jenkins

Fergie was born too late to see his Dad play, and modestly deflects any suggestion that his Dad had the ability to have played in the Major Leagues. However, Fergie's real feelings about his Dad and his baseball talent come out in Fergie's touching recollection of his thoughts when he took the mound in the majors:

I just told myself, "I'm just playing for my Dad and myself." I always thought in the back of my mind that Dad didn't get an opportunity, but I'm his blood and I'm going out there performing the best I can. "It's you and me Dad, and we're out there."
Ferguson Jenkins

Fergie repeated that sentiment in the speech he delivered at Cooperstown the day he was inducted into the National Baseball Hall of Fame and recognized as one of the greatest players in the history of the game. The reality is that Fergie's Dad, like so many of his black contemporaries, might have had the talent to play baseball in the Major Leagues, but never had the opportunity to find out how far that talent would take him because of the color of his skin. In fact, on some occasions, Fergie's Dad claimed to be an Indian in order to avoid racial discrimination and gain some measure of social acceptance. That proves to me the unfounded nature of prejudice. If certain people even thought you were black, they wanted no part of you, without giving you a chance to be judged on your own. Without changing his appearance or any of his actions, Mr. Jenkins was more accepted when he told people he was Indian rather than black.

Because of his color, Fergie's Dad was denied the dream that his son lived. Instead, he earned a living holding down two jobs, the kind of jobs that blacks were typically relegated to in the Jim Crow era: he worked as a chef and as a chauffeur. It was honest work to be sure, but reflected the limitations that blacks had to live with.

Ferguson is a multi-talented, extremely articulate, individual. The story of his baseball career is a study in consistency, strength, durability and courage. The story of his life off-the-field is not much different. As a child growing up in Canada, one of his childhood idols was Montreal Canadien defenseman, Doug Harvey, one of hockey's premiere players. (Interestingly, Harvey spent parts of four seasons playing baseball in the Class A Border League, including 1949, when he won the batting title and RBI championship.) It was prophetic that Fergie would admire an athlete like Harvey, whose job on the ice was to make it difficult or near impossible for opponents to score, a job that Fergie would come to handle so well in baseball.

During his schoolboy years at Chatham Vocational High School, Fergie played several sports, and won letters in basketball, hockey, soccer, track and golf, but not baseball. He was the Most Valuable Player on the basketball team for three years in a row, and the school's Athlete of the Year for two years (1961-62). He was a complete basketball player, who could handle the ball, defend and score. His basketball idol was Oscar Robertson and, in fact, Fergie tried to emulate his game on the court. That also tells you something about Fergie: his second idol was the perfect teammate - a very gifted, selfless athlete, who would sooner get an assist than score a basket, although able to do either gracefully.

Although he grew up with a love of hockey and basketball that he still harbors, it was the game of baseball that Fergie was ultimately drawn to; he believes it was "in his blood," based on his Dad's experiences. He first played baseball with the Chatham Minor Baseball Association, where he played all positions and hit well, but really excelled as a pitcher.

When I got introduced to pitching, I just thought that it came so easy. I had a good arm. It was kind of a position that I had to do some thinking too, to win on a consistent basis. I knew it took everybody on the team to win, but I seemed to enjoy pitching and really got into it. And I just think that learning the art of pitching came a lot easier than the other two sports. And I had some real success right off the bat. So that was a plus. I think that any athlete when you get into a sport and you don't get defeated right away, (and I started winning right away), it seems like: wow, you're doing this; your team is winning; you're having fun; you're successful at that position ... I just wanted to do it even more. So that's when, I think I really started to take it to heart

that, maybe I can be a pitcher. As a kid I was just a thrower.
Ferguson Jenkins interview

By age fifteen, Fergie was already 6'3", and had drawn the attention of a number of Major League scouts. When Fergie was only sixteen, Gene Dziadura, the area scout for the Philadelphia Phillies, took him under his wing and brought Fergie to a series of open tryouts. Ultimately it was the Phillies who signed him upon his graduation from high school at age 18, in June 1962, for a signing bonus of $6,500, and a monthly salary of less than $400. Consistent with the type of son and person Fergie is, he used the bulk of that to pay off the mortgage on his parents' home. To this day Fergie has no regrets about that! He is quick to tell you that his parents formed an excellent support group for him, and, as a widower with children, he realizes the difficulties children must overcome with only one parent in the household. Fergie regards his Mom and Dad as excellent role models who shaped his character, helped him excel as an athlete, and survive many trying moments as a man.

Fergie drew special strength from his relationship with his Mom, a woman who was legally blind as a result of the difficulties she went through in labor during his birth, yet refused to cave in to her disability. Not only was she an excellent bowler, but Fergie still laughs when he recalls how his blind mother would enter his bed, and correctly say, "Ferguson, you failed to put away your clothes and straighten your room." She is the one who instilled in Fergie the spirit and drive to "Finish whatever you start," and although she didn't have baseball in mind when she said it, Fergie took her message to heart in how he played the game. He started a baseball career that lasted nineteen years at the Major League level. It was a career that took him from Chatham to Cooperstown, during which time he started 594 games, and finished an astounding 267 of them.

As an example of Fergie's dry wit, and the manner in which Mrs. Jenkins and the family chose not to view her blindness as a tragedy or even a disability, Fergie said, "She's my good-luck charm. She's never seen me lose" although Mrs. Jenkins attended several of Fergie's Major League games, including losses. Complementing Fergie's Mom, his Dad was equally supportive from a somewhat slightly different perspective. He supplied Fergie with confidence and the room that a young man with his potential needed to grow and excel. He wasn't overbearing about sports, but provided Fergie with a solid introduction to the game. He gave him an appreciation for the game, and supplied him with all the equipment Fergie would need to master it.

As a Canadian, Fergie was not exposed to the same level of segregation or discrimination as some of us, but that doesn't mean that he was not aware of racial tension, or the history behind it. He needed to look no further than his Dad's baseball career to understand that in the 1940s, even in Canada, blacks did not enjoy one hundred percent freedom of opportunity. While Fergie has no recollection of having suffered any bad experiences as a child because of his race, he was clearly aware he was a minority:

I grew up in the little rural, farm town of Chatham, Ontario. There was like 22,000 people, just blue collar workers. There were factories. We had Libby's and Ontario Steel, and the Decal Company. The people there were hard working. There were a few black farmers; not that many black families, because the year I went to public school there were only three black kids in my class. Then when I went to high school, I was the only black until they bussed black kids in from North Buxton and Shrewsberry. In the 9th and 10th grade I was the only black ballplayer and student for almost a year, a year and a half. Then I left John McGregor and went to CES. There were two other black student-athletes.

Ferguson Jenkins interview

But it didn't take long for Fergie to meet Jim Crow once he started to play professional baseball. His first team assignment was to the Phillies' Class A team in Williamsport, Pennsylvania, where he was initially scheduled to room with Tommy Norwood, a white player. But Norwood was uncomfortable and objected to that arrangement. Fergie quickly found himself sharing an apartment with four other black players, Dick Allen, Richie Haynes, Dick Edwards and Bobby Sanders.

From Williamsport, the Phillies sent Fergie to their Class D team, the Miami Marlins, of the Florida State League, where he got his first taste of the South. Although he was only with the Marlins for a short time, (compiling a 7-2 record in 11 appearances), Fergie experienced first hand the segregated housing, bathrooms, and eating facilities that were still the norm, a full fifteen years after Jackie Robinson and Larry Doby "broke the color barrier," nine years after the Supreme Court declared that separate facilities were not equal (Brown v. Board of Education), and two years after the big push, led by Wendell Smith, to integrate spring training facilities in Florida.

While I was in Miami, Florida, we [blacks] weren't allowed to go to Miami Beach, but we lived at the Sir John Hotel. They had a nightclub called the Sir John Night Beat. Clyde McPhatter, Della Reese, James Brown, and all of the older black musicians played there. It was located in a community known as Overtown, but which was originally called "Colored Town." It was the area west of the railroad tracks, segregated for blacks, because when Miami was being built, in 1896, Jim Crow laws prevented blacks from just living anywhere. They ended up burning it down, I think, in the mid '60s. On the road we stayed in a black neighborhood. We still couldn't stay with the white players.

Ferguson Jenkins interview

The Phillies recognized that Fergie was overqualified for Class D and quickly moved him up to finish the season with their Class AAA team, the Buffalo Bisons, which was much closer to his hometown Ontario. But it wouldn't be long before he was back in the South again.

There was a rule of Major League Baseball in effect at that time, in 1963, called the "first year rule," that required the Phillies to either include Fergie on their major league roster and invite him to major league spring training or risk losing him by exposing him to a draft. At first, the Phillies decided to protect Fergie and that is how he got to spend his spring training in 1963 at Dade City, Florida, not far from my hometown of Lacoochee. He was still prohibited from living with the white players, though, so the club sent him to live with a black family in the area. Fergie told me:

What we used to do was we'd get X amount of dollars for meal money and we'd give some of the money to the family we were living with and we'd eat with them as part of the family, like they had another son. On the road, if we stopped, we stopped at Trailways or Greyhound bus stations, and some of the white players would get off. We would give them money; they'd buy us some hamburgers and get back on the bus with us.
Ferguson Jenkins interview

When camp broke that year, the Phillies, eager to win a pennant, were looking for experienced players in every roster spot, and took a chance on losing Fergie by placing him on irrevocable waivers, choosing to protect some of their veterans. Luckily for them, no one claimed Fergie and he was sent to the Little Rock Travellers, who played in the Coast League. In 1963, Little Rock, Arkansas, was a racially charged environment. It had not cooled down much since September 1957, when it became the focal point of the South's dissatisfaction with the Supreme Court's 1954 decision in *Brown v. Board of Education*. With Little Rock's public schools still segregated, three years after *Brown*, a federal court forced integration upon Arkansas by ordering that nine black students should attend Little Rock's otherwise all-white Central High School. News of this initial attempt at integration caused widespread anxiety and civil unrest not only in Little Rock, but throughout Arkansas, and eventually the entire South. Arkansas Governor Orval Faubus defied the federal court order, and called in the Arkansas National Guard to prevent the black students from entering the school. After ten days, President Dwight Eisenhower called Gov. Faubus to Washington, and got him to agree to use the National Guard to protect the black students, but when Faubus returned to Little Rock he reneged and dismissed the Guard, leaving the students, who continued their attempt to attend the high school, unprotected from the mobs that gathered outside the school. Hatred was evident on the faces of protesters. They threw bricks at the school, breaking windows and doors, and hurled racial insults at the students, who likely suffered more emotional damage than the physical damage done to the school. But those kids endured the event. The mob also took out its anger by beating a number of reporters covering those events. When the National

Guard was demobilized, local police were only able to restore order by evacuating the nine students from the high school. President Eisenhower then realized that Gov. Faubus and the citizens of Little Rock were intent on defying the Court's order to integrate its schools and wouldn't let it happen without federal intervention. He deployed the 101st Airborne Division paratroopers to Little Rock and put the Arkansas National Guard under federal command, surrounding the high school with soldiers armed with rifles and fixed bayonets. With the benefit of that federal protection, the "Little Rock Nine" attended school that day and for the remainder of that school year, but that didn't end the game of "integration tic-tac-toe" being played by Gov. Faubus. Unable to prevent the integration of the Little Rock High School, Faubus closed all of the city's high schools and they remained closed for the entire 1958-59 school year. When the schools re-opened in September 1959, four of the nine students returned, as did the violence, including the bombing of the home of one of the students.

By the time the Phillies sent Ferguson to Little Rock, little had changed in terms of its progress toward racial integration. In fact, it was only in 1963 that blacks were first allowed to play professional baseball in the State of Arkansas at all. Although Ferguson had already played in Miami, it was during his brief stay in Little Rock, his first of three stints with the Travellers, that he began to sense the harsh edges of segregation and racism. He has shared with me the hurt he felt at times when the team went into a restaurant and he was forced to stay behind. He would give money to the white players, who would bring food out to the bus. At times, the black employees of some of those establishments would let him eat in the kitchen, but he wasn't allowed to sit with or ever be seen by the white diners. It was the same type of discrimination Fergie faced in Miami.

Fergie's Little Rock teammate, Dick Allen has vivid memories of the type of discrimination that he and Fergie experienced in Little Rock in 1963, like the scene on opening night at Ray Winder Stadium, when Governor Faubus was in attendance:

When I arrived at the park, there were people marching around outside with signs. One said, "DON'T NEGRO-IZE BASEBALL." Another, "NIGGER GO HOME." They were the same signs that greeted me the day I landed at Little Rock airport. Here, in my mind, I thought Jackie Robinson had 'Negro-ized baseball sixteen years earlier.
Crash, by Dick Allen and Tim Whitaker

As the game started, Allen recited Psalm 23, which his mother had taught him, to gain inner strength. The first pitch was hit to him and he misjudged the ball. Later in the game he hit two doubles and hoped that it made the crowd forget his error. But the worst part of his night was yet to come:

I waited until the clubhouse cleared out before walking to the parking lot. When I got to my car, I found a note on the windshield. It said,

"DON'T COME BACK AGAIN NIGGER." I felt scared and alone, and, what's worse, my car was the last one in the parking lot. There might be something more terrifying than being black and holding a note that says 'NIGGER' in an empty parking lot in Little Rock, Arkansas, in 1963, but if there is, it hasn't crossed my path yet.

Crash, by Dick Allen and Tim Whitaker

By the middle of the 1963 season, Fergie was back with the Miami Marlins, where he achieved a 12-5 record. By the end of that season, the Little Rock fans voted Dick Allen the team's Most Popular Player, and Little Rock sportswriter, Wadie Moore, Jr., remembered

Allen didn't just integrate baseball in Little Rock, he integrated life. Before he got here, black folks who went to the ballpark sat together in a separate section in right field. His being here opened all that up. After him, we could sit anywhere we wanted, and believe me we did just that.

While Moore has fond memories of Dick Allen, Allen's memories of Little Rock in 1963 are a little less rosy:

One night I went to get a cold can of soda from a machine a block away from my rooming house. I was jogging home with the can in my hand. It was a rare off-day and a typically hot Arkansas night. But it had just begun to cool off a bit and I needed to loosen up. Next thing, a squad car comes by and the police put me up against a wall. Then they spread-eagle me against their car. One of the two policemen pulls his gun. They ask me if I stole the can of soda. When I tell them no, they ask me why I was running. I tell them that this is America, and it is my understanding that running is legal in America. The two policemen don't say a word. It was like they had never looked at it that way before. They just let me go. But for weeks afterward I had this vision of catching a bullet in the back just for being thirsty.

Crash, by Dick Allen and Tim Whitaker

Little Rock wasn't the only area in America where racial tensions were exploding, literally. In September 1963, a white man was seen placing a box under the stairway of the Sixteenth Street Baptist Church in Birmingham, Alabama, which was being used by Martin Luther King, Jr., as a meeting hall. That day a bomb exploded at the Church, killing four girls, all age fourteen and under, who were students at Sunday School, and injuring twenty-three others. Robert Chambliss, a member of the Ku Klux Klan, was identified by a witness as the man who placed the bomb at the church. At the conclusion of his trial a year later he was found not guilty of murder, but guilty of possession of dynamite without a permit, resulting in a fine of one hundred dollars and a six month jail sentence.

Under the "first year rule" I mentioned earlier, the Phillies again left Fergie subject to the draft in the fall of 1963, and again he was not claimed. In 1964, Fergie found himself back in the South, this time in a town with ties to the Negro Leagues – Chattanooga, Tennessee, the home of the Class AA Chattanooga Lookouts. That was the name of the old Negro League team Satchel Paige broke in with in 1926 at a salary of $50 per month. Although Ferguson's pay was different from Satchel's, his pitching was not, according to *The Chattanooga News Free Press*, which referred to Fergie as reminiscent of "Satchel Paige in his youth." Fergie showed signs of future greatness while with Chattanooga. He won ten games, while losing six, and struck out 149 batters in 139 innings. His performance earned him election to the Southern League All-Star Team. A review of the All-Star roster reveals several other players who made it to the major leagues, including Roy White and Lee May. Fergie's recollections about how he handled matters in the South, are reminiscent of my enduring getting beat up so I could go to a Gene Autry movie:

When I was playing in the Southern League, they bombed a church in Birmingham where some little kids were at, and all four of the little girls died. We played in Lynchburg, Birmingham, Mason, Chattanooga, and Asheville. There was some pressure at times, but I wanted to be a professional athlete. I wanted to be a major league player. So, if I was confronted, I kind of backed off. But you could tell if somebody was going to get up in your face. At the ballpark, you felt safe - in the outfield somebody would shout something through the fence, I would move in towards the infield. I mean if I turned around and argued, I would probably have gotten rocked or someone would jump the fence, and it would really get ugly. But you kind of stayed away from that situation.
Ferguson Jenkins interview

By August 1964, Fergie was back up with Class AAA Little Rock, where he came close to pitching a no-hitter, yielding only a seventh inning single to Don Landrum.

Fergie began the '65 season in Arkansas again, but finally made it to the majors later that year. He made his debut on September 10, 1965 with the Phillies, holding the Cardinals to two hits in four and one third innings of relief work. Before the season was over he had appeared in seven ballgames.

I used to see Jim Bunning pitch and I'd wonder if the day ever would come - I guess this is the dream of every small boy – when I even would meet him or any other big leaguer. Then one day I not only was Bunning's teammate on the Phils but I replaced Jim as relief pitcher in my first big league game. I won it, too.
Ferguson Jenkins to Edgar Munzel, The Sporting News

During the winter of '65, Fergie pitched for Caguas in the Puerto Rican League. He led the league with a stingy 1.24 ERA, and had a 10-6 record. Despite his excellent showing in Puerto Rico, Phillies' manager, Gene Mauch, who didn't have much faith in Fergie's ability, packaged Fergie in a trade on April 21, 1966, sending him, John Herrnstein and Adolfo Phillips to the Chicago Cubs in exchange for Larry Jackson and Bob Buhl. The trade may have satisfied Mauch at first, but I'm sure the Phillies, and their fans, wish it never happened. Buhl went 6-8 for the Phils, before being released on May 16, 1967, ending his baseball career, and Jackson went 41-45 over three full seasons, choosing to retire after being drafted by the Montreal Expos in the October 1968 expansion draft that also sent me to Montreal.

When Ferguson was young and coming up, some skeptics said he didn't throw hard enough to be a good major league pitcher. I happened to be the minor league pitching instructor when Ferguson was at Chattanooga, and got to see and know him pretty well. I for one, knew the skeptics were dead wrong. I went with him and four other pitchers to Puerto Rico and saw the improvement in his change up and slider and was always praising his fastball and where he threw it. The Phillies made a huge mistake letting him go – but that's baseball. I knew and felt from the start, after seeing him in Double A, that he was and should be a starting pitcher at any level. He had great body control and was a great competitor, who had a terrific career.
Cal McLish

Fergie had tremendous potential because he kept the ball down. He didn't walk many hitters, and he had a great attitude. But Mauch believed that black pitchers buckled under pressure. ... I'll tell you one thing. That kid had great ability, and Mauch traded away one of the best pitchers in the game.
Clay Dalrymple, Phillie catcher and Fergie's teammate, quoted in September Swoon, by William C. Kashatus, The Pennsylvania State University Press, University Park, Pennsylvania, 2004

Fergie was happy to be going to Chicago, where he felt he would have more of a chance to pitch. When he got news of the trade, he and his wife drove all night from Philadelphia to Chicago, and he was an immediate success. In his first appearance he earned a 2-0 victory over the Dodgers, pitching five and a third innings of flawless relief. He even batted in both runs with a home run and a single! Fergie flourished in the Windy City, playing in one of the smallest stadiums in the majors, under manager Leo Durocher. **He went on to be a twenty-game winner for the Cubs in each of his first six full seasons with the team.** Before he was traded, the Phillies had only thought of him as a reliever based on their belief that his ability to throw hard wouldn't allow him to pitch more than a few innings at a clip. They were wrong again! Fergie pitched more than 300 innings in five seasons, and averaged almost 250 innings a year for his career. Fergie was used mainly as a reliever by the Cubs in early 1966, making 48 of his 60 appearances out of the bullpen, although he did get his first Major League start on May 21, 1966. But Leo Durocher could see that Fergie would be dominant as a starter, and wanted to convert Fergie from a reliever. At first, Fergie resisted, because he had become comfortable in his role as a reliever, but by year's end he had become a regular starter in the Cubs rotation. In October, 1966, Durocher told Jerome Holtzman, of *The Sporting News*, "I can't wait until next year. That boy can pitch. And he's going to get better. We haven't seen anything yet."

In 1967, Fergie gave the Cubs a sign of things to come in his very first start of spring training against the Giants. He struck out the first five batters he faced: Tito Fuentes, Hal Lanier, Willie Mays, Willie McCovey and Jim Ray Hart and, after Jesus Alou fouled out, he struck out Ollie Brown to boot. In the first game of the regular season, Fergie faced the Phillies and started to make the trade look bad for them, by hurling a complete game victory. Fergie validated Durocher's belief in his ability to be a quality starting pitcher and rewarded the team by going 20-13, and breaking the Cubs' all-time single season strikeout record of 205 that had been set by Orval Overall in 1909, by striking out 206. He was named to the National League All-Star team, (a first for Fergie), and pitched three innings giving up only one run on a homer by Brooks Robinson, and tying an All-Star record by striking out six batters. Fellow Black Aces, Bob Gibson and Al Downing also appeared in that game. At the end of the season, in a vote conducted by the players, Fergie was named to The Sporting News' 1967 National League All-Star Team.

He became only the third Cub to win twenty games in a season in the preceding twenty years. (Dick Ellsworth went 22-10 in 1963, and Larry Jackson went 24-11 in 1964. Before that no Cub had won twenty games in a season since Hank Wyse went 22-10 in 1945, the last year the Cubs were in the World Series.) Mike McCormick of the San Francisco Giants won the National League Cy Young Award (1967 being the first year that the award was given in each league), and Fergie, and his idol, Jim Bunning, each received one vote of the twenty votes cast. Fergie also received 26 points in the National League MVP vote, with McCormick being the only pitcher to receive more points. The Chicago Baseball Writers named Fergie as the Cubs' 1967 Player of the Year.

Fergie was helped a great deal by pitching coach Joe Becker, who came over from the Cardinals to join the Cubs in 1967. Becker told Fergie what he and the rest of the league had detected in 1966: Fergie was tipping his pitches in the way he held the ball and exposing it before he delivered a pitch in the way his right arm dangled at his side. Becker got Fergie to change his windup so that he started with both of his hands in front of his body, with the ball in his glove. Bolstered by that tip, Fergie recorded another 20 wins, and the Cubs, who had finished eighth in 1966, finished third in 1967.

While Fergie, and other black pitchers like Bob Gibson, Earl Wilson, Al Downing and myself were starting to enjoy success in the Major Leagues, the country was still not making great progress toward integration. As a reminder of how much, or how little, progress the country had made: on August 20, 1967, the United States Senate held its confirmation vote on Thurgood Marshall's nomination for the Supreme Court, and five southern Senators voted against Marshall, calling his nomination a "disgrace to the country" because of his race and his advocacy in Brown v. Board of Education.

At the end of the 1967 season, Ferguson went to Cubs' General Manager, John Holland, to negotiate his salary for 1968. Holland offered Fergie a $10,000 raise. Fergie relates the rest of the story:

I won my 20th game on my last start of the season, and then negotiated my 1968 salary with John Holland. Based on my twenty wins, he gave me a $10,000. raise, and I thought that that was a lot of money. And I said, "If I could do that on a consistent basis, [win twenty], could I double my salary each time?" And he said "I don't think you could do it Ferguson." He said "You've just got to go out there and prove it to the organization. And I said "I know I can do it. If I get enough starts I can win 20 games for this ball club for quite a few years." And he kind of looked at me and sat back at the table and I said "the general manager doesn't believe I could pitch that well." He said, "You know, we have to pay Holtzman, who had 17 wins; we have to pay Billy Williams who hit .340; we have to pay Ernie, we have to pay Santo..." And I said, "You have to pay your 20 game winner here" And then that following year, I had an attorney. He didn't like me, John Holland. Unfortunately, we didn't get along too good. Maybe he did like me, but he didn't like I brought in an attorney to negotiate contracts.

John Holland's statements provided some of the motivation that propelled Fergie to become the winningest black pitcher in the history of the Major Leagues, with 284 victories. The balance of the drive and determination it takes to be so successful already existed within him, nurtured by his parents.

During the 1967-68 off-season Fergie found a way to supplement his income outside of baseball. He became a part-time player and full-time advance publicity man for the Harlem Globetrotters, the professional basketball troop. He accompanied the Globetrotters on a tour around the country, and served as an in-game pitcher as Meadowlark Lemon would slam a home run into the crowd in every arena. When Fergie was asked why he toured with the Globetrotters he revealed a little bit of what made him a consistent twenty-game winner when he responded, "I like to win all the time. It gives me a full head of confidence."

In August 1968, Fergie had only twelve wins, and was several weeks behind his 1967 victory pace. When Jerome Holtzman of *The Sporting News* questioned Fergie about winning twenty, his answer clearly indicated how important that achievement was to him, and how strongly he remembered the Phillies' opinion that he didn't have what it takes:

Every pitcher wants to win 20, but I've got a special reason. If I win 20 again this year, I'd be the only 20-game repeater in our league. Then, nobody could say I just had a fluke year.

Fergie made 40 starts by the end of the 1968 season, tying a Cubs record set by Grover Cleveland Alexander in 1920, and threw 308 innings, the most by a Cub in one year since Charley Root threw 309 in 1927. He also finished with 260 strikeouts, breaking the club record of 236 he himself had set in 1967. While he received virtually no support from the Cubs's offense, Fergie again won twenty, going 20-15, fulfilling his prediction: he was the only pitcher to win twenty games in both the 1967 and 1968 seasons. Fergie became the first Cub to win twenty games in two consecutive years since Lon Warneke ("The Arkansas Hummingbird") did it in 1934-35. Incredibly, five of his fifteen losses ended in 1-0 scores and in ten of Fergie's starts the Cubs failed to score a run. One night in Atlanta, Fergie threw ten shutout innings and left the game while it was a scoreless tie. The Cubs lost 1-0 in 11 innings. Four nights later, Fergie threw a five-hitter against the Cardinals, and Gibson beat them 1-0. (The Cubs were also shutout in the two games between Fergie's starts, failing to score for a National League record-tying 48 consecutive innings.) I discussed with Fergie what it takes to endure a spell like that, where you are pitching your heart out, but the team is just not scoring.

We had four starters at the time, Rich Nye, Kenny Holtzman, Bill Hands and myself, and a lot of times you can't score for everyone. And there were some games that I was opposed by Gibson or Drysdale or Seaver. You know, hey, a ball club is going to get shutout, and shutouts were a very important part of baseball back then, because the other starting pitcher, he'd go out there and he wanted to win. So you wanted to win. My opponent was probably the number one pitcher on the other team, and I seemed to get the ace on every staff. Not always but I did. So, if he was on top of his game, sometimes the Cubs didn't score.
Ferguson Jenkins interview

Fergie again received some consideration in the 1968 National League MVP vote, which was won by Bob Gibson. It was no surprise that Gibson also received all 20 Cy Young Award votes, for his remarkable 1968 season.

In 1969, Jenkins was involved in something new in his career – a pennant race. Paced by the twenty-win seasons of Fergie (21-15) and Bill Hands (20-14), the Cubs and the Mets battled it out during August, but the Amazin' Mets finished much stronger and won the division by eight games. The Cubs won 92 games and finished in second place. It was the third straight year that Fergie won twenty games or more, a feat that hadn't been accomplished by a Cub pitcher since Jim (Hippo) Vaughn did it in 1917, 1918, and 1919. It was also the third straight year Fergie broke the Cubs' strikeout record, besting his 1968 record with 273 strikeouts.

The way the 1970 season started for Fergie, it appeared that his streak of twenty-win seasons was in jeopardy. After his first ten decisions he was 3-7, and getting beat soundly. But thanks to game films, coach Joe Becker, Fergie's Mom, and hard work on Fergie's part, he righted the ship. Mrs. Jenkins stood by Fergie as pessimists started to whisper that the streak was coming to an end, claiming that all that pitching had taken its toll on Fergie's arm. She would call Fergie on days and nights before he pitched and would encourage him, reminding him how good he was. The game films revealed that Fergie was not pushing off the pitching rubber, wasn't driving toward the batter and gaining momentum on his delivery like he had in the past. Once the flaw was detected, Becker and Fergie worked to correct it and, having done so, Fergie reeled off five consecutive victories. However, after he got his pitching mechanics in order, things got a little tense for Fergie. In August, Becker suffered a heart attack and things were touch and go for a while. Then the unthinkable happened in early September: Mrs. Jenkins passed away at the age of 54. Fergie left the team to attend his Mom's wake and funeral. He called Leo Durocher from Canada and asked to take his turn in the rotation on September 16th, the night before the funeral, saying he knew his Mom would have wanted him to pitch, but Leo declined. Then on September 18, 1970, he returned from the funeral and won his 20th game of the season, a complete game victory over Montreal. That made Fergie the only pitcher in the majors to win twenty games in each of the last four seasons, and the first since Juan Marichal accomplished it from 1963 through 1966. That night Fergie said, "Now that I don't have her to talk to anymore, I've got to compile my thoughts by myself. I did that tonight, while I was getting dressed. I told myself, 'Now, go out there and throw hard. Be strong.'"

When the reporters asked Fergie the annual question about what it takes to be a twenty-game winner, he again responded that it was health and making the starts:

You've got to take your turn every fourth day. You can't let little irritants bother you. I've pitched lots of times with a headache or a cold or a sore ankle or hip. And usually late in the year, after pitching a lot of innings, my back aches. Becker told me when he came here, "You can't make any money pitching once a week."
Ferguson Jenkins to Neil Mac Carl, The Sporting News, October 10, 1979

Fergie was 22-16 for the season, pitching 24 complete games of the 39 he started. In his last appearance of the season he struck out the very last batter he faced, for strikeout number 274, (one more than the year before) again setting a new Chicago Cub record for strikeouts in a season. Fergie finished third in the Cy Young Award voting, behind Gibson and Gaylord Perry.

Until the collective bargaining agreement between Major League Baseball and the Players' Association was redrawn in the summer of 1970, players had to negotiate their own contracts with the clubs. The new agreement contained the clause: "A player may be accompanied, if he so desires, by a representative of his choice, to assist him in negotiating his individual salary with his employing club."

304

Fergie was seeking to increase his salary from $65,000 to $100,000, which was the salary then being paid to Gibson and players like Joe Torre, Billy Williams, and Lou Brock. In the spring of 1971, Willie Mays, who was making $135,000 in 1970, signed a two-year deal for $165,000 a year. Fergie, not one to hold out or cause problems, came to terms on a contract that paid him $85,000, with an incentive of $15,000 if he won 20 games again. It appeared that Fergie still believed in his ability to win twenty, and John Holland was still willing to bet against it.

Fergie started the '71 season as if he was going after thirty wins, never mind twenty. In his first sixteen starts, thirteen of them were complete games. Over 136 innings he had 115 strikeouts and only yielded **15 walks**, including intentional passes. John Holland's failure to pay, and respect, Fergie at the same level as Gibson drove him. After a game Fergie would tell reporters, "The front office doesn't think I rank up with Gibson, Juan Marichal and Tom Seaver. But I'm going to prove I do. You'll have to ask Mr. Holland how I rank. He's the one who does the ranking and pays out the money and gives the raises." It may sound odd to say Fergie had a "breakout" year in 1971, after his four straight twenty-win seasons, but he did. His control was impeccable and he was just plain dominant. He had a career high 24 victories, he led the League in innings pitched (325) and complete games (30), was second in the league (to Tom Seaver) in strikeouts (263), and gave up the fewest walks. In 325 innings pitched, he allowed only 37 walks, approximately one walk for every nine innings pitched. Baseball is a game of statistics and in gauging a starting pitcher, it is always a good sign when he has a strikeout-to-walks ratio of 3 to 1, or better. Fergie's strikeout-to-walks ratio in 1971 was 7.11 to 1. To this day, it remains as the best single-season mark for pitchers who struck out at least 200 batters. In fact, he and Cy Young (in 1905) are the only pitchers in the history of the game to ever average over seven strikeouts for every walk they gave up!

Ferguson Jenkins, who I credit along with Bill Hands in showing me how to pitch, had the greatest control of any pitcher before or since. He is, without question, one of the five best right-handed pitchers of the last fifty years.
Ken Holtzman, teammate

Speaking of Cy Young, Fergie had won twenty or more games for four years in a row (1967-1970) and didn't win the Cy Young Award in any of those years. That was one indication of the fact that Fergie played in an era when pitching was dominant in the National League. He was competing against the likes of Bob Gibson, Don Drysdale, Juan Marichal, Tom Seaver, Al Downing and Steve Carlton. For that matter, Marichal, as good as he was, never won one. But 1971 was to be the charm for Jenkins. The Baseball Writers' Association of America finally recognized Fergie by naming him the winner of the National League Cy Young Award for 1971 by a landslide. He received seventeen of a possible twenty-four first place votes, leading second place finisher Tom Seaver to comment,

"How could anyone leave Jenkins off a ballot after the year he had?" It was a clean sweep for the Black Aces, with Vida Blue winning the American League Cy Young.

The Cubs showed their appreciation to Fergie by signing him to a two-year contract, with a salary of $125,000 a year. That made him the highest paid player in Cubs history at that time. (Today there are ballplayer making $16 million a year, which translates to $100,000 a game for an everyday player and approximately $400,000 a start for a starting pitcher, but back in the '71-'72 off-season, paying a ballplayer $125,000 a year still made headlines.)

Fergie followed his phenomenal 1971 season with the typical season that the Cubs had come to expect of him. Despite a labor dispute and strike that shortened the 1972 season by seven games, costing Fergie a couple of starts, he still managed to win twenty games. He started 36 games, his lowest total in six years, and while his control suffered (his walks and ERA were up and his strikeout total down), he was consistent where it counted – in the win column. Fergie went 20-12, and in doing so, he became the first Cub pitcher since Mordecai "Three Finger" Brown, 1906-1911, to win twenty or more games in six consecutive seasons. In fact, Fergie had duplicated a feat accomplished in the modern era only by Warren Spahn, from 1956-1961, while pitching for the Milwaukee Braves. (During two of those years the Braves were good enough to make it to the World Series against the Yankees, winning it all in 1957. During Fergie's streak, the highest the Cubs finished was second place, in 1969, 1970 and 1972.)

Fergie often told reporters that his desire in baseball was to be consistent, like his teammates Billy Williams and Ernie Banks. He recognized their value and contributions not only to the Cubs, but to all of baseball, by playing everyday and by consistently being among the league leaders in many categories. Consistency and durability in sports aren't quite as newsworthy as phenoms who burst on the scene, like Vida Blue and Doc Gooden, but those were the traits Fergie valued and he backed it up year after year with the numbers he put on the board. Arne Harris, who produced the Cubs home games on television, said if he went into the toy business he would make a "Ferguson Jenkins Doll," commenting, "All you've got to do is wind it up and it will win 20 games." Consider Fergie's stats during the six-year twenty-win streak:

Year	Wins	Losses	Starts	Complete Game	Innings Pitched	Strikeouts	Walks	ERA
1967	20	13	38	20	289.3	236	83	2.80
1968	20	15	40	20	308.0	260	65	2.63
1969	21	15	42	23	311.3	273	71	3.21
1970	22	16	39	24	313.0	274	60	3.39
1971	24	13	39	30	325.0	263	37	2.77
1972*	20	12	36	23	289.3	184	62	3.20
*Season shortened to 155 games by labor strike								
Avg.	**21**	**14**	**39**	**24**	**306**	**248**	**63**	**3.00**

Some pitchers disliked pitching in "the friendly confines" of Wrigley Field in Chicago because its dimensions qualify it as a hitter's ballpark, and the wind is usually blowing out to boot. But, Fergie didn't mind the wind blowing against him. Few people realize this, but, actually, as a pitcher, you like the wind blowing out, as long as it is not a gale wind. When the wind is coming from behind you it tends to flatten out your pitches and make them easier to hit. With the wind blowing against you the ball tends to move more. One aspect of Wrigley Field's layout that Fergie found interesting was the proximity of the bullpen to the field:

In Chicago, when you're on the mound, you can hear that bullpen phone ring. I don't care how big a crowd there is, you can hear that bullpen phone ring. You are so close, you're winding up, you hear that ring, or you see somebody getting up, you say, well, I better bear down. So it is just part of what your psyche is all about. Even though pitchers supposedly don't have rabbit ears, we do. We hear a lot of things.
Ferguson Jenkins interview

In typical Fergie fashion he found positives in the small dimensions of Wrigley, saying, "There is always one advantage. If you get lonesome, you can turn around and talk with the center fielder! Nevertheless, the smallness of the park does have its compensations. Most important, it makes you concentrate more." Sparky Anderson, managing the Cincinnati Reds at the time, said that Fergie's winning 20 games for six straight years while pitching in Wrigley should qualify him for immediate entry into the Hall of Fame. After a game against the Cubs featuring six home runs, Sparky said, "Any hitting records made in this park shouldn't count. Everyone says we play good games against each other here, but if anyone pops the ball in the air, it's out of the park."

Fergie had a very disappointing and frustrating season in 1973, ending his streak of twenty-win seasons, and also ending his first tour of duty with the Cubs. Fergie was 14-15 in 1973, causing some to think that the years of pitching over 300 innings had finally taken their toll. Although Fergie started 38 games, he only pitched 7 complete games, which would probably lead the league today but was far short of a typical Ferguson Jenkins year. The Cubs finished in 5th place, with a 77-84 record. It was the Cubs' first losing season since Fergie arrived, and they would not have another winning season until after Fergie retired. Over the seven-year period beginning in 1967, Fergie won 141 games, more than any other pitcher in the Major Leagues. He broke team records that had existed for decades, and was very popular with Cubs fans. But when he failed to win in 1973, and home runs against him started to mount, he began to feel like Wrigley Field was closing in on him, and the fans started asking that proverbial question, "What have you done for us lately?"

As a result, Fergie asked to be traded and, in the off-season between 1973 and 1974, the Cubs accommodated him by sending him to the Texas Rangers for Bill Madlock and Vic Harris. Fergie went from Leo the Lip to Billy the Kid – Billy

Martin. I asked Fergie about the similarities between the two famous managers, and what it was like pitching for them:

Well, Durocher was the kind of guy who'd say, "Here big fellow, here's the ball. Don't give it back until the game is over." And, Billy used to say, "Jenks, it's your game. If you don't feel like you could do it . . . hey"

But, I just think that the confidence pitchers got from old school managers was very important. Don Zimmer was like that and so were Gene Mauch, Leo and Billy. I mean they gave you that opportunity to perform because they had the confidence that you could go out there and do a good job. So I knew they were in my corner. I had a good shot of winning the ball game. You know they're going to leave me in the ball game and stay with me so I had an opportunity to keep my team in the game.

Ferguson Jenkins interview

Fergie obviously felt comfortable with Billy Martin's confidence in him. And Billy wasn't the only one with confidence. Ranger second baseman, Dave Nelson, said, "Just the thought that he's pitching for us gives this team a mental outlook like I've never seen before. When he's on the mound, we just know he can win. Now that's really something different for the Rangers." Fergie pitched complete games in his first seven starts, winning six of them. He made his debut in the American League by throwing a one-hitter against the World Champion Oakland A's. Reggie Jackson, who had not faced Fergie before that season, said, "If we had him on our staff, we could all go home by August 15." He was just as impressive late in the season. After Fergie beat Oakland again in late September, to push his record to 22-11, Reggie wanted to know, "How did that guy ever lose 11 games?" Jenkins closed out the Rangers' season with a 2-1 victory, sealing his seventh twenty-win season with his 25th win of the year, a career high. In his first season in the American League, he was voted the Comeback Player of the Year. He was second in the Cy Young voting, behind Catfish Hunter, (who had an identical 25-12 record) and finished fifth in the American League MVP vote, receiving only one point less than Reggie Jackson.

Major League Baseball enjoyed one of those magical years in 1974. When a pitcher has a career year in victories, has won twenty games or more for the seventh time in eight years, and his name is being mentioned among possible Cy Young and MVP candidates, you would expect that he would get some press, as Fergie did. Similarly, it was in 1974 that Hank Aaron broke Babe Ruth's career home run record, a story that was front page news in papers across the country. Meanwhile, Lou Brock had brought base stealing to a whole new level in 1974, stealing 118 bases, and that was worth writing about. And the Cleveland Indians broke new ground when they announced that Frank Robinson would be player/manager for the 1975 season, making him the first African-American manager in Major League history. But not everybody was okay with the coverage these athletes and events received. In November of 1974, a letter to the Editor of The Sporting News reminded America that bigots still existed:

> **I am getting fed up with *The Sporting News*. Practically all baseball news is about Lou Brock, Henry Aaron, Ferguson Jenkins and other colored players. The same applies to football and basketball. If you continue to praise and glorify all colored players, then my subscription ends. That will be it.**

> **Now, on top of everything, Phil Seghi supplied the straw that broke the camel's back by naming a Negro manager. What will happen if white Cleveland players will not cooperate with Frank Robinson or if fans will not turn out like they did this year? Then, after two or three years of not winning the pennant, how in the world are they going to fire him and replace him with a white manager? It would turn out to be a big discrimination case. In Cleveland, the shoe was on the other foot and Mr. Ken Aspromonte's hands were tied.**
> **When I go through The Sporting News I will not read anything that pertains to colored players in baseball, basketball or football.**

It would turn out that 1974 was Fergie's last twenty-win season. Although he continued to pitch for an additional nine seasons, he averaged only 12 wins a year, going 110-105. After two seasons with the Boston Red Sox, (22-21), he returned to the Texas Rangers, where he enjoyed an 18-8 season in 1978, and in 1982 he returned to the scene of his glory years by rejoining the Chicago Cubs, after eight years in the American League. By that time Fergie had 264 career victories. But before anybody could see Fergie in a Cubs uniform and think he was the Ferguson Jenkins of 1967-1972, he gave them a more realistic expectation:

> **You always want people to remember you for what you did, but I don't want anybody thinking they're going to see the Ferguson Jenkins of the '60s. I was just a tall, skinny guy then – a tall skinny guy who could throw hard.**

> **I'll have to play cat and mouse with the hitters for a while, keep the ball down and brush a few back.**
> *Ferguson Jenkins, The Sporting News, January 2, 1982*

And while he knew how he differed from the past, in that same interview he also had an eye on the future:
> **Winning 300 is a goal of mine. That could mean the Hall of Fame. If it happens, I want it to be in Chicago.**

While Ferguson was not the dominant pitcher or workhorse that he once was, in 1982, he still managed to lead the Cubs in wins (14), games started (34), complete games (4), innings pitched (217.3), strikeouts (134), and ERA (3.15). On May 25, 1982, he became only the seventh pitcher in the history of the game to record 3,000 strikeouts, joining Walter Johnson, Gaylord Perry, Nolan Ryan, Steve Carlton, Bob Gibson and Tom Seaver in that elite club. Yet 1983 was a difficult year for Fergie. He only managed to secure 6 victories against 9 losses, and had over a dozen "no decisions" in a pitching rotation where no starter had an ERA under 4.0 and the bullpen was overworked.

As he went to spring training in 1984 with the Cubs, Fergie had 284 victories to his credit. He wasn't assured of making the roster, but he had a shot at 300 wins, and he wanted to do it as a Cub, if at all. That spring, when it became apparent after a while that he would not make the Cubs roster, Fergie declined offers to be traded. Although he had a desire to reach that 300-win plateau, he wanted to do it with the club that had been such a big part of his success, the Cubs. Since he didn't want to go elsewhere, the Cubs had little choice other than to release him. He understood the move as part of the game:

It was inevitable. The Cubs have young pitchers they're going to look at, and my performance last year wasn't that great.

Interestingly, in 1984 the Cubs won the National League East Division and just missed the World Series, losing to the San Diego Padres in the National League Championship Series.

Fergie wanted to be like Ernie Banks and, in some respects, he was: neither of these great Cub players got to play one game in the post-season. Both of them were consistent and durable players, who gave it their best every time they strapped on the uniform - day in, day out, year in, year out. Neither of them was flashy or controversial, and neither of them got a great deal of media attention during their playing days. That may have been because they never made it to the post-season, or never played in media centers like New York or Los Angeles. When Fergie retired, he had a 284-226 record, but that wasn't all:

- He was the All-time Cubs leader in strikeouts with 2,036 for his career;
- He was the All-time Cubs leader in strikeouts for a season with 274;
- He was the only pitcher in the history of the game to record more than 3,000 strikeouts (3,192) and give up less than 1,000 walks (997);
- He was only the fourth pitcher in history to win more than 100 games in both leagues (the first three were Cy Young, Jim Bunning and Gaylord Perry), since then Nolan Ryan and Dennis Martinez were added to the list; and
- He had defeated 24 different teams at least six times each.

Throughout his career, sportswriters often made comparisons between Ferguson Jenkins and his contemporaries: Bob Gibson, Tom Seaver and Juan Marichal. They were all excellent pitchers whose statistics are actually very similar. Take a look at the following chart which compares their career records, winning percentage, ERA and strikeout totals, and their single season highs in starts, complete games, wins and strikeouts:

	Win	Loss	Pct.	ERA	Yrs	Most Starts	Most CG	Career Ks	Most W/yr	Most Ks/yr
Gibson	251	174	.591	2.91	17	3	28	3117	23	268
Marichal	243	142	.631	2.89	16	30	30	2303	26	248
Seaver	311	205	.603	2.86	20	36	21	3640	25	289
Jenkins	284	226	.557	3.34	19	42	30	3192	25	274

All of these pitchers dominated the National League and have been justifiably inducted into the Hall of Fame. But despite all the similarities there were differences at times in how they were perceived and treated by the press. One difference is that Gibson (three years), Seaver (two years), and Marichal (three years) all played in the post-season and all received a much greater amount of media coverage than Jenkins. Another difference was the number of times these aces were selected as All-Stars. Seaver was a twelve time All-Star, while Gibson and Marichal each participated in the mid-season classic nine times. Fergie was only selected to play in three All-Star games, despite having won twenty games in a season seven times. In 1967, Fergie had already won 13 games and was leading the league in strikeouts by July 1, yet he did not make it to the All-Star team. What looked like a "snub" at first was eventually explained and Fergie was fine with it: he was originally selected by Cardinal Manager, Red Schoendienst, but then dropped in favor of Ernie Banks. In typical Fergie Jenkins style, he took the incident in stride:

I don't think you feel bitter in situations. You're working hard to win; you work hard to get on the All-Star squad and be a representative for your ballclub. But we already had three guys on the team. We had three quarters of the infield. Ernie being put on? No problem. Kenny Holtzman, I think, had 12 wins too that particular year, and none of the Cubs staff got a chance to make an appearance. Managers picked All-Star pitchers, and it wasn't easy. In my era, you had guys – Gibson, Sutton, Seaver, Carlton, Marichal, Koufax, Drysdale – there were so many of those good young pitchers, that a lot of times your name just couldn't make it on the ballot.
Ferguson Jenkins interview

During his career, Fergie would occasionally use Gibson's notoriety to his advantage in his salary negotiations. When sportswriters would ask Fergie if he was comparable to Gibson, Fergie's frequent response would be, "I'm definitely in a class with Gibson. I think my winning twenty every year proves that. The only difference between us is money." (*New York Times*, August 22, 1971) If I had to characterize the difference in the way Gibson and Jenkins were perceived,

I would compare it to the differences between Roger Clemens and Greg Maddux. Gibson, like Clemens, was overpowering, and wore his competitiveness on his face. Jenkins, like Maddux, wore you out. He was cool and he found a way to outlast his opponents.

> **The funniest thing about Fergie – you face him a hundred times and it looks like he isn't doing nothing, as if you could wear him out. The next thing you know, you're 0 for 4. His big thing was that little slider on the outside. It wasn't overpowering or fast or anything like that. But he would give you a little dabble of that, right on the corner. He had such great control.**
> *Ed Charles interview*

Looking back on his career now, and his place among the greats, Fergie is comfortable in the belief that he belongs in a class with Gibson, Marichal, and Seaver, and the stats confirm just that. When Fergie was pitching for the Cubs, Durocher would alter his spot in the rotation so that Fergie would be pitching against the ace of the opposing team as often as he could. It was that feeling of being able to compete against the best in the world in which Fergie delighted (and it was one thing that earlier black pitchers were denied because of the racial ban in baseball).

> **Durocher was that type of manager. I mean, I'd get Carlton or I'd get Drysdale. I never got Koufax, but I'd get Drysdale. And I enjoyed that. Knowing two days before, I'd check the starting box scores and I say "Uh, Koufax, pitched yesterday, I guess I'm going to get Drysdale." Or I get Osteen, you know. So I knew I was going to get a tough pitcher to pitch against me. And I enjoyed that part of it because, my mental toughness and thought process was there. I knew I had to pitch well or I was going to be out of the ballgame quick.**
> **I see a lot of the guys I competed against at golf tournaments and some of the social things we do now. And we talk baseball in some respects. But the competitive part of being a pitcher, pitching against the number one pitcher on the other team, is a part of playing the game I enjoyed. The enjoyable part of it was not proving that you were the best that day, but you had to go out there and try to win.**
> *Ferguson Jenkins interview*

Winning was something Fergie did very well and he was often recognized for his accomplishments during and after his career. In 1967, 1968, 1971 and 1972, Fergie was chosen by the Canadian press as Canada's outstanding male athlete. In 1987 he was inducted into the Canadian Sports Hall of Fame, and in 1992 he was inducted into the International Afro-American Sports Hall of Fame and Gallery. On January 8, 1991, after falling short of the necessary votes in both 1989 and

1990, Fergie finally became the first player from Canada elected to the Na
Baseball Hall of Fame, and was inducted along with Rod Carew and Gaylord I
His reaction to his election was, "This is my world championship right here."
first person he called was his father, Ferguson Holmes Jenkins, who was 84 y
old at the time. Fergie related to me, "I told him I made the Hall of Fame an
started shouting."

Fergie's success on and off the field was the result of traveling a long rc
filled with hard work and sacrifice, during which he endured and rebounded fr
a number of personal tragedies. Four days after Fergie's election to the Hall
Fame, in 1991, his wife died of injuries sustained in an automobile accident. C
year later, tragedy struck again as Fergie's girlfriend took her own life, by carb
monoxide poisoning, and also took the life of Fergie's three-year old daughte
Samantha. Through all of it, Fergie has drawn on the indomitable spirit of h
mother and his religion for his strength. Fergie, who has a tattoo which read
"Trust in God," says, "There are two things in sport, either you win or you lose
Life is like that too. How you get through depends on how strong your faith
is."

After retiring as a player, Fergie coached in Texas, Cincinnati and Chicago.
He thought it was a good way of giving something back to the game, of passing on
to the next generation of players some of the things the older players and coaches
taught him. Fergie enjoyed the chance to enhance some other young player's
career by showing him a certain grip for a pitch, or a follow-through.

Fergie now lives in Arizona with his wife, Lydia. He is active with the Baseball
Players' Alumni Association, and does a great deal of charity work throughout the
country. He is an excellent speaker, bringing with him to the podium the same
calm delivery that he brought to the mound, and the same confidence that he has
something to contribute.

Ultimately, Fergie got his wish. He wanted to be like Ernie Banks, consistent
and durable. He enjoyed a nineteen-year Major League career, and was a consistent
ace as a pitcher, winning twenty games or more seven times during an eight year
stretch. In addition to his Hall of Fame play, Fergie is as well-liked and respected
off-the-field as Ernie is, and that, by itself, is a very high standard of excellence for
any Major League ballplayer to achieve.

Fergie is a gentleman with the strength of a thousand year boulder. What he
went through impressed a lot of people. It was amazing that Fergie went through
what he did and was able to contain the fear, the anger, and still be a gentleman, and
always willing to do something for humanity. He has impressed a lot of people. If
he has the time, he will come to any event you ask him to come to, without asking
anything for it. From a baseball standpoint he had a tremendous, tremendous
record. I am extremely impressed by his stature today, individually, personally and
from a humanitarian standpoint.

CHAPTER 23

ALPHONSO ERWIN DOWNING
Al

Born June 28, 1941 in Trenton, New Jersey
Teams: New York Yankees, Oakland Athletics,
*   Milwaukee Brewers, Los Angeles Dodgers*
Twenty-Win Season: 1971
American League All-Star 1967
Inducted into New Jersey Hall of Fame 1995
Inducted into Trenton Baseball Hall of Fame 1996

Al Downing is a pitcher with a future. ... No young pitcher since Whitey Ford arrived on the scene in 1950 has made such a thumping impression on his teammates and the rest of the American League. ... For the last month, Downing had been the hottest whiff specialist in the league. ... No question about it. Here's a young man you'll be hearing more about.
Til Ferdenzi, The Sporting News, July 27, 1963

He's got fire in his arm.
Elston Howard about his roommate and teammate, Al Downing

Al was such a big part of our Yankee success during his days with the Yankees. A great competitor – a Christian gentleman – outstanding.
Bobby Richardson, teammate, New York Yankees

When I speak to people about any of the individual Black Aces, many of them respond almost instinctively with one or two words that sum up their recollection of him, almost is if I were a psychologist asking them to play a "word recognition" game. As I go down the list of the players, the responses to the players' names vary, and are usually along these lines:

Newcombe	Overpowering, Dodgers, or Boys of Summer
Gibson	Intimidating, 1.13, 1968, or Cardinals
Jenkins	Cool, Canada, Cowboy, or Cubs

But when I mention Al Downing, the response is always either "Aaron" or "Gentleman." Baseball fans who watch and know the game tend to identify Al with the fact that he surrendered Hank Aaron's record breaking 715th home run, moving him past Babe Ruth as the all-time home run king. Al is permanently identified with that historic moment and unfortunately on the losing end of the equation.

But, even that distinction hasn't dulled his great sense of humor or sense of grace, as he noted after the event, and the thousands of questions that were posted to him about it, "I never say 7:15 anymore. I say quarter after seven." (Actually, giving up that home run was nothing to be ashamed of. I am responsible for giving up a few dingers to Henry myself. So, if it weren't for me, Al would have given up home run number 713.) Yet, his memories of Henry Aaron go far beyond that historic home run number 715. Al has shared with me some of his reflections on his early spring trainings played in Florida were under some "hostile conditions," making it difficult for a young, black man to play his best. He warmly remembers that Henry Aaron always treated him with respect and helped him through that time in his life, and left him with a link to Hank that may have been less historic but had far more impact on a personal basis.

For those of us lucky enough to really know Al, we can't help but refer to him as Gentleman Al. He is one of the nicest men you will ever meet. He is a well-spoken, sincere man who can talk knowledgeably and insightfully about baseball with you until the cows come home, even if you just woke him from a deep sleep. Oh, yeah, that is another thing that his teammates will tell you – Al can fall into a deep sleep on about two seconds notice, anywhere, anytime, including the dugout. (I'll give you Al's side of that in a little bit.)

Like Don Newcombe, Al grew up in New Jersey, but fifteen years later. Thus, the experiences of his childhood and adolescence are different from Newk's. To begin with, Al's Mom died in an automobile accident when Al was only seven years old, leaving Al's Dad, Dover, to raise eight children. Al credits his two older sisters and his Aunt Beulah and Aunt Ora with helping to raise and nurture him. Al is also very thankful for the presence of the local Boys Club in his life. After-school programs and day care for children didn't exist in the 1940s and 1950s. The kids in Al's area all gravitated to the Boys Club to participate in various activities, whether it was arts and crafts, or playing basketball, pool, or table tennis. It gave them a chance to compete and a sense of belonging.

As I've explained, in the South, blacks were segregated in every sense of the word, and we knew it. It was just a fact of life. There were separate facilities for "whites" and "coloreds" and very distinct boundary lines for neighborhoods where whites lived and where blacks lived. Slowly, very slowly, over decades of years and books of legislation, blacks and whites started to interact with a little more frequency and tolerance. In the North, it was different. Until blacks started to migrate to the North in the early 1930s and 1940s, northern neighborhoods were populated predominantly by whites, and there were no separate facilities for "coloreds." As the migration from the South increased, blacks started to settle into established neighborhoods in increasing numbers, and a phenomenon which Al has referred to as "northern transitional" took place. Neighborhoods turned from predominantly white to mixed to all black. The same was true for the eastern section of Trenton where Al grew up and started to attend school. Then, when Al was about ten, because a friend of Al's transferred to a new school in the Western section of Trenton, Al transferred with him.

They were learning at a faster pace as I found when I got over there. The make up of the school was predominantly Jewish, and there were also a lot of Irish children, and there was a little black neighborhood around there. So, it was diverse, but I think it was more Caucasian than it was black. As a young kid, it was good for me, because now I was stepping outside of my neighborhood, and you're developing more of yourself, becoming the adult person you will become, and I always felt as a kid it was very important to develop yourself as quickly, as early as you can because it makes you less fearful of moving into new environments. It was one of the first revelations in my life, in terms of your growth period, as you start to expand your horizons.
Al Downing interview

That new environment created at least one situation for Al which definitely would have never happened in Lacoochee in the 1930s or 40s, or even in the 50s or 60s. A progressive thinking teacher conducted a role playing exercise in his class which the children didn't see as a problem, but some of the parents did:

In the fifth grade we had a Thanksgiving Program and my teacher, Mrs. Esther Clark, said, "Well, we're going to have a program about going to grandmother's house, over the hills and through the woods, to grandmother's house we go. We need a father and a mother." And we pretend we have a sleigh, so we sit in chairs, the father and mother sitting in the front. Mrs. Clark said, "Okay, Sherry Kaplan, you will be the mother, and Alphonso, you'll be the father." Of course, at the time you don't think about it. You just say, "Well, okay" and you got this little black kid and this little Jewish girl are going to be mother and father. Kids are sitting in the back. There were parents when they came and saw that program, they went, "Mrs. Clark, what ... ?" To her, that was part of teaching kids. I started to think about it. I said, "Gosh, that's a bold move." I didn't even think about it at the time in terms of it being a bold move. I didn't think about it until years later. Gee, that was a very bold thing to do.
Al Downing interview

As a kid, Al read the columns written by the late Sam Lacy, and other black sportswriters, on the orange colored pages of the *Baltimore Afro-American*, one of the papers I was delivering down in Lacoochee. Like me, Al remembers that when that paper arrived each week he would go through it carefully because it was one of the only sources of information about what was happening in the black communities all over the country and even in Africa. Just as I did, Al went to the sports section and read about the players and the various teams in the Negro Leagues. He has memories of reading about Satchel Paige, of course, and about Dan Bankhead, and Ray Dandridge. He also remembers having a particular interest in reading about Monte Irvin, Larry Doby, Roy Campanella, and Don Newcombe, because they were all playing for teams right around the New Jersey area, the Newark Eagles and the Philadelphia Stars. Al never got to see a Negro League game, but remembers barnstorming teams that came from Philadelphia to play in the area around Trenton.

He also remembers Jackie Robinson coming into the big leagues. Until then, the black community looked upon Joe Louis as their only true sports hero. While Louis continued to be a hero to blacks, Al remembers Jackie adding a whole different dimension, in that he brought hope to many blacks:

People talked about Joe Louis in terms of what Joe could do. Joe was like a stand up citizen, everybody admired Joe Louis. But with Jackie, it was like people started developing phrases about how fast he was – "faster than Jackie Robinson." Jack became a symbol, a symbol of progress, a symbol of a black man being able to rise up, and being able to play this major league game which people said black people could never do, because the whole concept was that they don't have the thought process to play the game of baseball. Yet when you look at the players who were playing baseball up until that point in time, for the most part all of them came from rural areas. There were very few guys like Hank Greenberg and Lou Gehrig. Most guys are coming from these farm areas, strong guys, big, strong guys. Yet no one was questioning their mentality, but with the black players, it was always they weren't smart enough.
Al Downing interview

Those of us who are older than Al, or who lived in more rural areas, all played our youth baseball in "pick-up" games on vacant lots, or played any one of dozens of versions of baseball, like stickball or punchball. The players who were younger than Al and grew up in urban areas had a different experience. Although many of them played a lot of street games, they also had organized youth baseball available to them. Al was sort of caught right in the middle at first. It wasn't until 1947 that Little League had its first franchise outside of Pennsylvania (Hammonton, New Jersey), and by 1951, when Al was ten, there were Little Leagues in New Jersey, but none in the area where he lived. So while other kids were getting their first "official" uniforms, and playing Little League baseball, Al was still playing street ball:

We played with baseballs, but we probably got them because they came over the fence at the park. By that time they were kind of beat up, nobody cared, and then we got old bats that we would paint up; we'd put tacks in them and paint them up. But we'd go to these different neighborhoods and most of them were like public housing developments, and some were kids who lived in surrounding neighborhoods. And we would challenge them to baseball games. We

kids all got along. We probably had skirmishes somewhere maybe, but nothing serious - trivial stuff - nothing in terms of having any racial impact. We didn't have any families fighting families. It was kids playing ball. When you played ball nobody fought. And a lot of it had to do, I think, with the fact everybody knew we had nothing to do for the day in the summer. So go see if these guys want to play a game. Get your team together.

Al Downing interview

It was actually when Al was playing in organized youth baseball that he got his first real eye-opener as far as race is concerned. When he was fourteen years old, he was selected to play on the Babe Ruth All-Star team, which went on to win the New Jersey State Championship, and earn the right to go to Frederick, Maryland to play in the Middle Atlantic States Championship:

We went to Frederick, Maryland to play against teams from New York, Pennsylvania, Delaware, Maryland, and West Virginia. We hadn't been apprised of any social conditions or restrictions in Maryland. We had three black players on our team: William Crossland, Arnold Thomas and myself. When we get to Frederick, we went to the hotel to register and got our little complimentary packages everybody gets. When we started looking for room keys, the three of us didn't have any. We went up to our Coach, George "Puggy" Malone, and said, "Puggy, did they forget our keys?" Then one of the administrators from the League came over to us and said, "This is the situation: the three of you can't stay in the hotel, so we have a family in town that you can stay with, and someone will take you over to their house."

It was disturbing news for young kids to hear. I was 14 and my two friends were 15. They said, "What do you think? What do you want to do?" What could we do? We had no money. We had $10 collectively but that wasn't even the issue. The issue was we were a team and we had played together as a team. So they got the team together and told them the situation. "What do you guys want to do?" Everybody on the team said, "We're going to play." All the guys were very supportive. So everyday we would walk over to the hotel and we would eat and then we'd stay there all day and play and play, and then we'd have practices. Then we would go back to the house where we were living. One night someone brought up the idea, let's go to the movies, not even thinking that this policy existed socially in every aspect of the city. I don't blame the city, because I met people from Frederick years later and it was just how society was in those days. People were living by rules that were established years before. So we get to the movies and we pay for our tickets and the usher looked at me and the other two

black players and said, "You three have to sit in the balcony and you guys can go downstairs." All the white guys on the team just looked at us and said, "They go to the balcony, we'll go the balcony." That was a moment when I knew how special those guys were, and then we all went up to the balcony, and we watched the movie.
Al Downing interview

The exclusion that Al felt that weekend in Maryland stung him because he had not been exposed to it in New Jersey. As a Southerner, this was the way society was structured, and we grew up knowing it. Al expected to be able to stay at the same hotel with his friends and to sit together in the movie house, and was surprised when he couldn't. The expectation of blacks who grew up in the South was to be separated and relegated to facilities that were, in fact, not equal, and if that wasn't the case we were shocked. Al's feelings when faced with this initial circumstance of segregation was not uncommon among the many ballplayers who came from the West, Midwest, or the North, when they first arrived at spring training facilities and found forced segregation. These feelings of uneasy separation were not felt only by black players. Whites who grew up in large urban areas like New York and Chicago, or in other parts of the country where facilities were not segregated, like California, found it difficult to deal with the emotions they felt when their black teammates could not be housed with them, or were not allowed off the bus to eat with them on the road.

On the field, where they were allowed to compete equally, Al's Trenton Babe Ruth Team won the New Jersey State Championship two years in a row (1955 and 1956), and in 1956 his 15-year-old Babe Ruth team won the National Championship in a series played in Portland, Oregon. Al was the starting and winning pitcher in the championship game. Al threw a 1-0 masterpiece to win, but despite his victory, Mickey Lolich, who was on the Portland team, and went on to become a pretty good lefthander in the major leagues himself, was voted the Most Outstanding Player in the Series. Lolich was also courted by the Yankees, but he knew they had signed Al and didn't think they would seriously develop two lefties.

After winning the national championship, Al's team was taken to Yankee Stadium for a presentation at home plate, and while standing on the field his teammates, prophetically, said, "Al, you're going to pitch here one day." Al didn't believe it then, nor was it his ambition at that point to be a major leaguer, but he did allow himself to dream about it:

Yeah, you had dreams about being a professional athlete, but we really thought major league baseball was beyond our comprehension, and our attainment, because we just thought major league baseball players walked on air. Those guys were great. They are the cream of the crop and you don't envision yourself playing it. You don't know, you're 15 years old, so how do you compare yourself to a man 25? You don't.
Al Downing interview

At age 15, Al did not concern himself with thoughts of being a Major League ballplayer, but nevertheless he did all he could to improve his game and especially his pitching ability. He remembers attending every free clinic in his area that he knew of in a constant effort to learn something new about baseball, or a better way to train or play. Al's high school coach, Carl "Kelly" Palumbo, kept his players' minds focused on the present. He taught them fundamental baseball. Al played on as many teams as possible, and worked on his pitching. One of his school advisors, Bill Weaver, who was a birddog scout for the Pittsburgh Pirates, taught Al how to throw a change up. Al continued to improve and, in his junior year, was selected to play on a city-wide high school team.

Al remembers playing for his own high school team in North Jersey tournament. One of their first games was against Montclair High School, which was ranked among the best high school teams in the country, based in large part on the talent of the Haines twins, Richard and Robert, two All-Americans in football and baseball. Al remembers his reaction when he saw them for the first time:

We would go down to Philadelphia and watch the Giants when they came in because we wanted to see Willie Mays. When Willie threw the ball, the ball went "hmmmmmmmmmm." I remember watching Montclair take infield practice, and when we saw Richard Haines throw, we said we'd only seen one guy that could throw like that, it was Willie Mays. We went "oooh."
Al Downing interview

All of the area scouts were at the game to see the Haines twins, but as luck would have it, Montclair knocked Trenton's starting pitcher out in the third inning and Downing was given the ball. He wound up shutting down the Montclair offense, and getting three hits himself, together with the victory. After the game, Bill Yancey, a birddog who was working with Phillies general manager, Roy Hamey, and was following the Haines twins, approached Downing. Yancey himself had been a talented shortstop in the Negro Leagues from 1923 to 1936, playing for several teams, including the New York Lincoln Giants, Hilldale, New York Black Yankees, Brooklyn Eagles and New York Cubans. He also managed in Latin America and helped to develop baseball in Panama in the 1930s. He was an excellent judge of baseball talent, liked what he saw in Al and started to follow him as a player. Yancey even took Al and a teammate down to Philadelphia for a workout. The entry draft hadn't been instituted yet and teams were free to pursue players directly. Yancey took a personal interest in Downing and continued to shadow him. In fact, he got the Phillies to make an offer to Al, but was not happy with the amount they offered and counseled him not to sign.

Meanwhile, Al, who had been President of his high school class for three years, entered Muhlenburg College and continued to play on hometown teams. In 1960, he was the starting pitcher for Trenton in the National Semi-Pro Baseball tournament at Wichita, Kansas. The pitcher for the opposition was Satchel Paige. Al remembers Satchel telling him, "Keep the ball low with men on base and your infielders will help you out of trouble." Paige did induce several Trenton ballplayers to hit into double plays, and defeated Al that day. Al's break came shortly thereafter, when Yancey became the first black scout to work for the New York Yankees. Following their 1960 World Series loss to the Pittsburgh Pirates, the Yankees fired both Casey Stengel, as Manager, and George Weiss, as General Manager. They hired Roy Hamey from the Phillies and Roy asked Yancey to come over to the Yankees with him. On December 9, 1960, the New York Yankees signed Al Downing for a bonus of $16,000, which Al immediately used to move his father and siblings into an eight-room house in the west end of Trenton.

Al was assigned to the Binghamton Triplets Baseball Club, the Yankees' Class A, Eastern League affiliate, at a salary of $250 a month. In February 1961, he headed to Bartow, Florida, for his first professional spring training camp. It would also serve to provide him with his first taste of Florida's racial attitudes for, just like the Babe Ruth tournament in Maryland, Al found that he couldn't stay with the team at their hotel. Instead, he stayed with the McCoys, a local black family.

In 1961, thirteen of the eighteen major league teams trained in eleven Florida cities. All of the clubs – with the exception of the Dodgers – routinely housed their black players in segregated accommodations, usually private homes or boardinghouses in the black districts. By sanction of law and custom, Jim Crow established the standard when dining, lodging, socializing, and traveling.
Baseball's Reluctant Challenge: Desegregating Major League Spring Training Sites, 1961-1964, Jack E. Davis, Journal of Sport History, Vol. 19, No. 2 (Summer, 1992)

Al didn't allow the segregated housing to distract him, however, and impressed his manager, Jimmy Gleeson, so much so that when camp broke, he was invited to stay with the Binghamton club. His professional debut was a two hit shutout and he went on to post a 9-1 record after his first twelve starts.

I was beginning to get very comfortable in my setting, because I realized it was a very competitive league, which was good. There was a lot of talent in that league, but I also knew that I could pitch with anybody in that league. I was never worried about being better than anybody else, I just wanted to be able to pitch with you and compete with you. If I could compete with you, I could beat you as much as you could beat me. That's all I cared about, because whether you win or not depends on how well your team plays over the course of a period of games, but I knew I wasn't going to be embarrassed.
Al Downing interview

Downing definitely wasn't getting embarrassed. In addition to earning nine wins in twelve starts at Binghamton, he had pitched eight complete games, and had an ERA of 1.90. He allowed only 70 hits and 46 walks, while striking out 99 batters, in 98 innings. In his last two starts before the All-Star break that year, he yielded only six hits, while striking out 23 batters. His performance led to his selection as the starting pitcher in the Eastern League All-Star game. However, Downing never made it to that All-Star game. The Yankees, in the middle of yet another pennant drive, and faced with a doubleheader against the Washington Senators, needed a starting pitcher. Ralph Houk decided to bring Al up on the recommendation of Jimmy Gleeson. Houk said, "I had to have a pitcher and it was either the young fellow or a man who had been around seven-eight years without making the majors. If I am going to gamble, I believe in gambling big." (The Sporting News, July 26, 1991)

Houk gambled and Al got the call. On July 19, 1961, Al made his Major League debut, and got his first start, against the Senators. It was an historic day, in that Al became the first African-American to pitch for the New York Yankees, but pitching-wise it was not a day to remember for Al. He didn't make it through the second inning, and although he stayed with the team for the remainder of the year, it was his only start. He appeared in only five games, pitching a total of nine innings, giving up eight runs, walking twelve batters, hitting a batter, and committing a balk. There was good news though, in that he also struck out twelve batters. (Al also got to pitch against Willie Mays and the San Francisco Giants, in a very rare, mid-season exhibition game on July 24, 1961, before 50,000 fans at Yankee Stadium. Al did well against the Giants, and credits that game with helping his confidence level after getting routed against the Senators.)

Al went to spring training with the Yankees in 1962, and was sent down to their Class AAA team in Richmond, Virginia on the day the Yanks broke camp for New York. Except for one inning of "mop-up work," Downing did not see any major league action at all in 1962. However, it would prove to be an interesting year for Al, and for civil rights in America. For starters, Al became the first black to ever pitch for Richmond. Although Al's baseball experiences had provided travel opportunities around the country and he had already experienced spring training in Florida, this would be the first time he actually lived in the South for an extended period of time. Despite the sting of the discrimination he felt when he realized he could not live with his teammates, there were some silver linings for him in living as a boarder with private families. Al told me about his experiences in Richmond, and his connection with an "adopted" elder:

Richmond is like Atlanta, Birmingham, Memphis – with educational institutions there and very strong black communities. When I went to Richmond I was a little intimidated, but feeding on all the experiences I had up to that point I wasn't overwhelmed. I had a friend, Winfield Layton, who coached in the Police Athletic Little League where I played, and he told me, "Son, my niece lives in Richmond. When

you go to Richmond, you look up my niece." I did and she helped me find a place to live, in a black community, in a home owned by a 77 year old fellow who founded the first black bank in Virginia – Walter Banks. I couldn't stay with the white players. The ballpark was also segregated. The black fans had to sit out in rightfield, with no roof over their heads. Everynight I would come home, and I could always tell Mr. Banks was home by the smell of his pipe. And he would say, "Sit down young man." I'd sit on the chair next to him on the porch. He'd say, "How'd you do tonight?" I would tell him about my control problems and my concerns about making it back to the majors. He said, "No, no, just stick with them. You have to be patient, you have to be patient." He always said, "You have to be patient."
Al Downing interview

Al was patient, and he started to notice that his fastball seemed stronger and stronger. While he wasn't very big as a teenager, a growth spurt between the ages of nineteen and twenty-two seemed to significantly increase the speed of his fastball, which in turn led to the need for better control over that pitch so he could put it where he wanted it. He also had to adjust to the level of competition, and learn one of the most important elements of pitching: how to set hitters up and get them out. It took Al the better part of that 1962 season to master those skills.

In his fourth start of the season, on May 12, 1962, Al, at age 20, pitched the Richmond Virginians' first no-hit, no-run game ever in the International League. In typical Al fashion, he downplays the no-hitter, quickly reminding people that the game was a drawn-out affair, with several rain delays. He says, "It wasn't a good no-hitter. I walked about six guys." I didn't know there were any other kind of no-hitters except good, but, if there are, I think most pitchers would take a "bad" no-hitter any day. After that game, Warren "Sheriff" Robinson, the Richmond manager, summed up the status of Al's pitching talent at the time, "He has a world of stuff and his only problem is control. He just misses on a lot of those pitches." Al's teammate, Billy Shantz, was the guy who got him to begin throwing strikes more consistently. Shantz had Al start aiming at one of the catcher's knees, keeping his mind on staying on top of the ball, which really helped to improve his control. On September 8, 1962, Al set a modern-day Richmond strikeout record, when he struck out 15 batters. Though Al was classified mostly as a fastball pitcher, it is interesting to note that in a year-end "managers' scouting report" on the International League in 1962, Al was named, along with Nat Martinez, of Rochester, as having the best curveball in the league.

While Al was paying his dues in the minor leagues in Richmond, Virginia, in five Southern states citizens were required to pay poll taxes in order to vote. Since many blacks could not afford the tax they were being disenfranchised. The poll taxes had originally been enacted in eleven states after Reconstruction, as a means of preventing poor black people from voting, and six states abolished the taxes since 1949 in response to a proposed amendment to the U.S. Constitution to abolish the taxes as a requirement to vote in federal actions. The proposal was finally passed by the United States Senate by a vote of 77-16 in March 1962, taking just as long as the integration of baseball. It then took two years for the Amendment to be ratified, and in 1964 poll taxes were officially illegal under Federal law. Only one state, Mississippi, rejected the Amendment, in December 1962, and never ratified it.

After the 1962 season, like many other American males who were classified 1A by the Selective Service System, Al chose to serve his country by joining the Army Reserve, and he was stationed at Fort Jackson, South Carolina. At that exact time, President Kennedy and Secretary of Defense, Robert McNamara, were dealing with the issue of the integration of the military. The Vietnam War had given rise to a large increase in the number of young Americans drafted, and the issue of desegregating the troops was getting a great deal of attention. The issue had been originally addressed by an executive order issued by President Harry Truman in 1948, but as we have come to see, civil rights and integration issues that began in the 1940s really didn't get dealt with until the 1960s. The Armed Services Committee of the Congress concluded that off-base discrimination reduced military effectiveness, leading Secretary McNamara to pledge that "the military departments will take a leadership role in combating discrimination wherever it affects the military effectiveness" of servicemen. The result was a new directive, published on July 26, 1963, which:

- gave the Assistant Secretary of Defense the "responsibility and authority for promoting equal opportunity for members of the Armed Forces" and
- gave military commanders the "responsibility to oppose discriminatory practices affecting his men and their dependents and to foster equal opportunity for them, not only in areas under his immediate control but also in nearby communities where they may live or gather in off-duty hours.

The directive was seen by many as the administration's most decisive move forward in race relations. But there was no shortage of critics. This is a sampling of the comments directed at McNamara by the press:

It is hard to realize that your office would become so rotten and degraded. In my opinion you are using the tactics of a dictator.... It is a tragic event when the Federal Government is again trying to bring Reconstruction Days into the South. Again the military is being used to bring this about.

* * *

You have, without conscience and with total disregard for the honorable history of the Military of our Great Nation, signed our freedom away.

* * *

We have a bunch of mad dogs in Washington and if you and others

like you are not stopped, our children will curse us. We don't want black grandchildren and we won't have them. If you want to dance with them—you have two legs, start dancing.

Elected officials, especially those from the South, also had plenty to say to McNamara and the Kennedy Administration about the directive:

[The directive] can only be detrimental to military tradition, discipline, and morale. ... It had been apparent for some time that the more extreme opponents of revolutionary civil rights action have wanted to use the military in a posture of leadership to bring about desegregation outside the boundaries of military bases.
Senator John Stennis of Mississippi

[Racial quotas] will take the place of competence for purposes of promotion.
Congressman L. Mendel Rivers of South Carolina

[The drafters of the directive had] one objective in mind—with an almost sataniclike zeal—the forced integration of every facet of the American way of life, using the full power of the Department of Defense to bring about this change.
Congressman F. Edward Hebert of Louisiana

Al came to enjoy his experience in the Army Reserve, and quickly grasped the benefit of the rigorous training he went through, which helped him get in shape for the 1963 season. The one negative about his military training was that his obligations kept him from reporting to spring training in time and cut into his time to prepare for the 1963 season. It was in spring training in 1963 that Yankee coach Johnny Sain, the same person who would work with me in Minnesota, approached Al and told him that he thought Al's curve ball was inconsistent and too "big", giving hitters a chance to measure and hit it. He worked with Al and got him to turn his wrist in such a way that the pitch became tighter and more consistent in reaching its destination. Al learned the delivery and mastered it. He couldn't wait to start working on it with Yankee catcher, Elston Howard. However, the next day Al was shipped back down to Richmond. Al expected to be sent down to AAA though, because he had reported late and really wasn't ready to start throwing in the Major Leagues by Opening Day. Johnny Sain told him, as he packed for Richmond, that it would only be a temporary assignment. His manager in Richmond, Preston Gomez, agreed. By the beginning of June, Gomez told Al that he had called New York and told them that Al was over qualified to be at the AAA level.

Ralph Houk, the Yankee skipper, agreed with Gomez and summoned Al back up to the Yankees. Once again, Houk gave him the ball to start against Washington. This time the result was a lot different as Al won, shutting out the Senators on two hits. From there, he continued to enjoy early success as a starter in 1963. In his second start, he beat the Tigers, giving up seven hits. Later, in consecutive games at the end of June and in early July, Al carried no-hitters into the seventh inning. By the All-Star break, Al was 4-1, and had struck out 58 batters in 51 1/3 innings of work. In fact, he chalked up one of those wins against my Cleveland Indian teammates in early July, striking out fourteen of them in less than eight innings. The early reports on Al were impressive:

The best I've seen since I came over from the National League.
Birdie Tebbetts, Cleveland Indians manager

No question about it. He's got quite an arm.
Al Lopez, Chicago White Sox manager

Al Downing is the best lefthander in the American League right now. He's faster than Steve Barber.
Joe Adcock

He's not going to stop striking 'em out. This guy can throw it by you and he can break your back with the curve ball.
Yogi Berra

I think one of the big things for him is his change-up. He's got the ability to fire that hard one through there on one pitch then come in with one with something just a little softer. He does it with exactly the same motion. It really is a great pitch.
Elston Howard

Al stayed in the Yankee rotation for the remainder of the 1963 season, winning thirteen games and finishing with a 2.56 ERA, fifth best in the league. After Al became a regular starter, the Yankees' rotation, also featuring Whitey Ford, Ralph Terry, and Jim Bouton, became one of the best in the majors, and led the Yankees to yet another American League pennant and a date with the Los Angeles Dodgers in the World Series. The Dodgers' rotation was pretty good too, featuring Sandy Koufax, Don Drysdale, and Johnny Podres, with Ron Perranoski going 16-3 in relief. In fact, it is ironic that Koufax and Downing would match up in the 1963 Series because Al's success during the season was drawing flattering comparisons to Sandy:

His fast curve, also taught to him by Johnny Sain, crackled and dropped sharply as it reached the plate. A black Sandy Koufax was the ballyhoo. He looked over-poweringly good. ...

Al Downing, the rookie, was more devastating than anyone, his potential unlimited. In July he pitched a one-hit shutout, a two-hit

shutout, and a four-hit shutout; in another game he struck out fourteen batters in seven innings. In August he was 5-1, winning a two-hitter, two three-hitters, and a six-hitter, all complete games, his record 11-4 before September in only two and a half months of pitching. Had Downing not sat on the Yankee bench for two months during the 1961 season and hence been ineligible, he would have been the rookie of the year. ...

Downing was a threat to throw a no-hitter every time he took the mound. Al finished with a 13-5 record, ten complete games in twenty-two starts, four shutouts, and an ERA of 2.56. He struck out 171 batters in 175 innings. ...

Downing looked like a black Sandy Koufax, striking out eight or nine batters every game.
Peter Golenbeck, Dynasty

Al may have reminded some people of Koufax, but Koufax WAS Koufax, and in October, the Yankees learned what National League batters had known all season: Koufax was damn near unhittable. Drysdale and Podres were no piece of cake either, and the Yanks lost the Series to the Dodgers. Al got to start Game Two of the '63 Series against Podres. He only pitched five innings, striking out six batters and yielding seven hits. He was victimized by a two run double by Willie Davis in the first inning and a home run by former teammate Moose Skowron in the fourth. It was pretty much academic after the first though, because Podres only yielded one run to the Yankees, and the Dodgers were on their way to a sweep.

Al's performance in 1963 gave baseball people good reason to predict greatness for him. In 1963, Whitey Ford became the holder of the New York Yankee record for most career strikeouts with 1,532. When reporters asked Ford how he felt about the record, he said, "Why get excited about it? In a couple of years, Al Downing will have the record all to himself." In April of 1964, *The Sporting News* selected Al and me as the pitchers most likely to be twenty-game winners for our respective teams. They were a little premature in both cases, but time eventually proved them right.

In 1964, Ralph Houk surrendered the managerial reins of the Yankees to Yogi Berra, while remaining as the team's General Manager. During that season, Houk made these comments about Al:

He's an excellent pupil. He listens and he absorbs..... Just look at Koufax – I hate to mention his name. What was Koufax doing when he was 22? I'd have to say Al is ahead of where Koufax was. ... I've never seen a kid with so much stuff.
George Vecsey, SPORT Magazine

Al was a regular member of the Yankee rotation in 1964, and led the American League in strikeouts, totaling 217. At the age of 23, he was the youngest pitcher to lead the league in strikeouts since Herb Score did it in 1955, at the age of 22. Considering his strikeout total and his level of comfort on the mound, Al felt that he actually pitched better in 1964, starting 35 games and completing 11, than he had in 1963. But his ERA was up to 3.65, and his record, while successful at 13 and 8, didn't meet his expectations. The Yankees, despite the toll that age had taken on a few of their perennial stars, again won the pennant, and Al another chance to pitch in the World Series. He got the start in Game Four and things were looking good early as the Yankees knocked Cardinal starter Ray Sadecki out with three runs in the first inning. Al was cruising until the sixth inning, having only given up two hits. Then, he gave up two more singles but with one out he appeared to get a double play ball that would get him out of the inning. Unfortunately, Bobby Richardson couldn't get the ball out of his mitt and, when he finally did shovel it to Phil Linz, Phil couldn't hang on to it. The result: bases loaded, one out. The next batter, Ken Boyer, cleared the bases with a grand slam, to provide all of the scoring that the Cards needed to defeat the Yankees, 4-3.

As American League hitters started to become familiar with Al, he had to adjust to them, and to think more and throw less. It is a tough task for any pitcher, but Al had two things going for him: his arm, and veteran Yankee catcher, Elston Howard. Ellie grew up in St. Louis, in the shadow of Sportsman's Park, never thinking the major leagues would be open to him, until Jackie Robinson and Larry Doby signed. He was a four-sport athlete at Vashon High School and excelled in all of them. He was the Missouri State Champion in the shot-put, and received many college scholarship offers, but his love of baseball won out, and he stayed in St. Louis to play for the all-black, semipro, St. Louis Braves. It didn't take long for William Dismukes to scout Ellie's talents, and he got Ellie to sign with the Kansas City Monarchs, where Ellie played in 1949 and 1950. From there, Ellie was signed by the Yankees, but first he served in the Army, including some time in Japan. He finally got to play for a Yankee farm team, Muskegon of the Central League in 1952. In 1953, Ellie was back in Kansas City, but this time it was as a member of the Yankees' Class AAA farm team. After a great spring training in 1954, it looked like Ellie was going to become the first black to play for the Yankees that year, but, consistent with the trend that black players had to be better than good, Howard was sent back to the minors for the '54 season. Ellie handled it with class, saying, "I won't lose here. I'll just try my best again to make it." But one sportswriter commented: "For years I defended the Yankees. After watching developments this spring, however, I am convinced they don't want a Negro player; they want a Negro superman." Ellie came close to that in his second year at Kansas City. He batted .331, with 22 homers and 108 RBIs, and was the MVP of the International League. In 1955, Ellie did become the first black to wear pinstripes, and did so with distinction. He had a thirteen-year Major League career, was an All-Star in nine of those years, was the MVP in 1963, and played in ten World Series. In 1969, Ellie became the American League's first black coach with the Yankees, and remained on the coaching staff for eleven years. Throughout that time, Ellie felt that he had been passed over for a managerial spot several times, and thought it was because of his race. Ellie was a fine human being, a superb player and a fine coach. His coaching qualities were evident in the way he handled the young pitching staff the Yankees presented to him in the '60s, with Stottlemyre, Bouton and Downing.

Ellie was particularly influential in Downing's development:

Ellie was the nicest man I've ever met, without a doubt. He didn't say a bad word about anybody and if he did, it was only in the context of what was happening on the field and it was at that moment. He was just one of those guys who never stayed mad long. The first thing we did when we went into every town is we walked to find a fruit stand. Normally, on the way back from the ballpark, we'd go to a fruit stand and Ellie would buy all this fruit. We'd just load up on grapes, peaches, pears and come back to the room, and so that's what you snacked on. You don't need snacks, snacks were your fruit. It was basically a way to keep you from eating junk food, and also to keep some stuff in your system.

The thing that amazed me about Elston is that we'd go into towns and everyone knew him. I mean, we'd go to Chicago, we'd go to Cleveland, we'd go to Detroit, Boston, LA. Ellie loved those men's stores, loved men's clothing. We'd laugh about it – he bought a blue shirt in every town, every store, it was some kind of blue, checks, stripes. Everywhere we went it was like, "Elston, so nice to see you." People loved this guy. He was just a nice man, and well dressed and well liked by everyone.

I was very fortunate. When I first came up Elston and Hector Lopez roomed together. So the Yankees gave us two adjoining rooms. When we went on a road trip, first Hector and I would room and Elston had the single, and then we'd go to the next city, Hector would have the single and Elston and I would room together. I always had a roommate and I always had two guys to talk to me, a hitter and a catcher who was a pretty good hitter. That really facilitated my progress because these guys were talking to me about how you pitch and how you have to handle yourself and the things you have to do when you are out there on the mound and how you have to approach getting the hitter out. So I had Hector talking from a hitter's point of view and Elston talking from a catcher's point of view, and it really was a tremendous help to me. I spent seven seasons as Ellie's roommate.

I would follow him around like a puppy. Every night we would sit in the room and talk about baseball. Talk about pitching, talk about hitters. He would tell me the key to winning in the majors was to think for myself. Basically, with Ellie it was always: "You've got to

think about what you want to do ahead of time; you can't wait until you get in that situation. So, if you know a certain way you want to pitch against a hitter let me know." I said, "Ellie, I trust you." He said, "Why don't you ever shake me off?" I said, "Well, two reasons. I think that I have a feel for the pitches, and I trust what you put down." "But" he said, "one day I'm not going to be back there." I said, "We'll worry about that when it comes."
Al Downing interview

Despite Ellie's work with Al, and suggestions made by pitching coach, Cot Deal, Al had a very inconsistent time of it in 1965 and 1966. Al got 32 starts in 1965, and posted a record of 12 wins and 14 losses, with an ERA of 3.40. At the end of the '65 season there were rumors that the Yankees were ready to give up on Al, and package him in a trade with Roger Maris and Phil Linz for the Cubs' Billy Williams. Instead, the Yankees let go of Deal, and re-hired Jim Turner as the pitching coach. When the spring of 1966 rolled around the Yankee brass was still high on Al's chances:

> **Houk predicted "a great year" for Downing.**
> **"Al's had a control problem," he said, "but with the kind of arm he's got, he should be about ready to mature into a topflight pitcher."**
> **Elston Howard, who will work for the same $65,000 he earned last year, is the president, vice-president and secretary-treasurer of the Al Downing Booster Club.**
> **"Al is really serious about his work," the catcher said. "he's got to improve and he knows the only way to do that is to throw more strikes."**
> **According to Howard, "The best break Downing ever got he'll get in spring training working under Jim Turner. ... He's eager to work with Al."**
> *Til Ferdenzi, The Sporting News, February 5, 1966*

Despite the influence of Jim Turner, Al's inconsistent pitching of 1965 continued in the 1966 season. He had a very difficult spring training, and dropped his first three decisions of the season. But then, everybody on the Yankees was having a tough time in the beginning of 1966. They only won four of their first twenty games, which was enough to get Johnny Keane fired and have Ralph Houk brought back as manager. With Houk at the helm, Al seemed to return to his '63 form, and won his next four starts. But, by season's end, he had his second straight losing season, 10-11.

While people talked about Al's control, he felt the problem was improper conditioning in spring training. Al felt that his arm weakened every season and that it was because he "would go to spring training and start right off throwing hard in batting practice and doing a lot of extra throwing." During the winter of 1966-1967, Al reconsidered his approach to spring training in the hope of keeping his arm strong for the regular season. It appeared that Al was on to something. He didn't begin the 1967 season as a starter but, after two relief appearances, he had pitched 11 innings and given up no runs on six hits, four walks and 12 strikeouts, and caught the attention of management. Yankee catcher, Jake Gibbs, who caught Downing in both of those early season relief jobs, recognized that Al seemed to be much stronger in 1967:

He's got the good fast ball again. The ball moves all the time, while last year there were times when it didn't. It seems that his arm is stronger and the old zip is back.
Jake Gibbs, as quoted by Jim Ogle, The Sporting News, May 13, 1967

Al's success continued through the first half of the 1967 season. By the first of July, he had an unbelievably low ERA, 1.73, and had won four consecutive starts, pitching three complete games, two more than he had in all of 1966. It was a clear sign of his renewed arm strength. Al was selected to the American League All-Star squad, and pitched two scoreless innings, striking out two batters. Fellow Black Aces, Bob Gibson and Ferguson Jenkins also appeared in that game.

Al was making Ralph Houk happy again:

We always knew that Downing had the ability to be a big winner, but we just had to wait until he put it all together. Now it looks as if he has reached maturity as a pitcher and he'll go on from here to be one of the best pitchers in the league.
Ralph Houk, as quoted by Jim Ogle, The Sporting News, July 29, 1967

Others outside of the Yankee organization, were also noticing Al's performance:

Downing has reached his potential and rates as one of the league's best lefthanders.
"He's challenging the hitters now," ex-great Herb Score said while watching Al beat the Indians. "He has confidence in all his pitches and has matured a great deal. I saw him pitch at Richmond and predicted he would be one of the real good ones and he has made it." ...
he has been a model of consistency for the first time in his career. He has eight complete games – as against one last year – and with more batting support would have several more.
Jim Ogle, The Sporting News, August 26, 1967

By July of 1967, Al himself felt that would be the season that he rose to join the ranks of the game's elite pitchers, its twenty game winners. But, from that point forward, what only Al and his teammates knew, was that Al was pitching hurt. His record was 9-5, and he was making every start and completing his games. But everything changed for him. He was pitching in Baltimore when he felt a burning sensation in his arm as he threw a curve ball. Ellie told him, "Okay, we'll stay away from the hard curve, we'll just throw that big curve." But then it started hurting when he threw the fastball too. He knew something was seriously wrong and, by the end of the '67 season, he couldn't throw a baseball fifty feet:

I felt the burning sensation in Baltimore, and I didn't know what it was at the time, and it was never diagnosed as anything. It was just, "You want to take an extra day's rest?" Sure, I took an extra day's rest and didn't throw as much, but it just never got better as the season went along.

I kept taking my turn in the rotation, but I wound up going 5 and 5 the second half of the season. I know, if I had just stayed healthy I would have won 18 or 20 games easily, because I had put things together to the point where I was now ready to go on a roll, but it goes to show you about health. If you don't have the health ...

In those days there was no arthroscopic surgery. More damage was done cutting you open to find out what was wrong with you. There were no MRIs, just x-rays, but a lot of time x-rays were only if there was a skeletal injury. I don't think it showed tendons that were bothering you. So if it wasn't a broken bone or calcium deposit, somebody would say it's tendonitis because they didn't know.
Al Downing interview

Like Sam Jones before him, in 1952, Al had seemed on the verge of a breakout year, only to be derailed by arm trouble. The Yankees sent Al to the Mayo Clinic in Minnesota, where the best orthopedists in the country conducted every test they knew of on Al's arm. But they couldn't come up with any cause or reason for the burning sensation and pain in Al's arm, or for his inability to grip and throw the ball. As it turned out, they seemed to be more interested in Al's ability to sleep almost on command, and prescribed Ritalin, a drug to help him with what they diagnosed as a case of narcolepsy. It wasn't Al's tendency to sleep that concerned him, it was his inability to wake up his "dead arm." Yet the world's best doctors found nothing specifically wrong with it, performed no surgery, and prescribed no medication.

Between his ailing arm and his military obligations, Al didn't get much of a chance to pitch in 1968. For example, he went from May 14th to June 18th without pitching at all, and in order to finally make a two inning appearance on June 18th he had to fly round-trip, coast-to-coast, as his reserve duties sandwiched the weekend leave. But, Al just dealt with it:

So now, all of a sudden, I'm sitting with my arm that won't work, and worrying about sleeping, which I had never worried about before, because I always could control it. Now, it didn't matter. I didn't sleep

when I pitched, only when I didn't have anything to do. If I kept the book, I never slept.

There was nothing else to do. What else am I going to do. I was not pitching. So the issue with my arm was never addressed after that, and it was almost left to, "well, you better get healthy." And how are you going to get healthy if you don't know what you're supposed to do? I spent a lot of time on the DL [disabled list] in 1968, and I also spent a lot of time in Army Reserve meetings. I couldn't pitch, I couldn't throw. Everybody knew that. In total, I pitched only sixty-one innings in '68, starting only 12 games.

Al Downing interview

After the '68 season, it was obvious to almost everybody that something was terribly wrong with Al's arm, but nobody knew what it was. Since nothing specific had been found by the doctors at the Mayo Clinic, the Yankees somehow took the position that Al was therefore not injured. The team's inexplicable position led to an unpleasant negotiation between Al and the Yankees. The team basically told Al that he wasn't pitching like he used to in 1963 and 1964, and that it was not injury-related. Al knew that he couldn't throw because of the pain in his arm. I can tell you that when you can't get a good grip on the seams of the ball you really can't pop the ball, and you have no command of the ball. The parties were far apart on the issue of what was causing Al's ineffectiveness and, as a result, remained far apart on the issue of salary.

I think a lot of it had to do with the fact that ballplayers didn't have any rights. It was like the team said, "We don't have to pay you if we don't want to. If you don't play here, where are you going to play?" I think, that was just how the game was played and I think they felt they still controlled the game. They held all the cards, and they were right.

Al Downing interview

When they finally did come to terms, the Yankees only used Al sporadically during the first half of the '69 season. But, ultimately, in early August, they came to Al and said, "You know, we need you." Despite the way they had treated him, Al responded with six wins between the first week in August and the end of the season, and wound up 7 and 5.

Following the 1969 season, the Yankees traded Al to Oakland, where his pitching coach was Bill Posedel, who had been Sam Jones' coach and who would also coach Vida Blue, Mike Norris and Dave Stewart. Al's stay in Oakland was short though, as he was traded again after about a month with the A's, this time to the Milwaukee Brewers. At that time, the Brewers were really still an expansion team, having moved from Seattle. Because of the way expansion teams were formed, their rosters were often filled with veterans approaching the end of their career, men whose teams did not feel it necessary to protect them from the expansion draft, men like the Brewers' Tommy Harper, Davey May, Max Alvis, Ted Savage, and Phil Roof. Al didn't think he fit into that category, but at least he got a chance to pitch with the Brewers. He pitched well, but didn't receive sufficient offensive support. As a result, he pitched a number of good games, with an ERA of 3.34, and got his pitching confidence back, but posted a 2 and 10 record.

In February of 1971, the Brewers were looking for younger talent and traded Al to the Los Angeles Dodgers for Andy Kosco. Al was happy to be going to Los Angeles, where the climate would be a little warmer, and where he felt the mound was as close to perfect as it gets in the major leagues. Al had pitched at Dodger Stadium when the Yankees played the Angels, who shared that field with the Dodgers before their own stadium was built. I agree with Al. They had good dirt in Dodger Stadium. The mound and infield dirt was crushed brick, and crushed brick didn't break up easily under a player's cleats. And it was almost like hard clay, so your spikes would get good grip. It didn't break up at the mound, it didn't break up on the infield. A lot of guys complained about the infield being too fast. Usually that meant good, pure hops. So, when the ball came it came at you quick, and you had to be ready. The mound was the same way. That dirt did not break up, so there were no holes on that mound. A guy could kick at that mound all he wanted, he couldn't make holes in it. You couldn't make holes in the batter's box either, and a lot of hitters didn't like that, but I loved it. I loved being able to drive off and then you had a good drop so you're coming down at the hitters. The Dodgers had sculpted that mound carefully to give their tall pitchers, like Don Drysdale, Sandy Koufax and Stan Williams, the greatest advantage possible.

When Al reported to Vero Beach, Dodger manager Walter Alston told him, "We want you for long relief." A relief assignment didn't make any difference to Al at that time, as long as he was going to get work and could continue to pitch in the big leagues. Actually, the Dodgers used Al in relief only once during the 1971 season, in late April. The next week, they turned to Al to take a start in place of Bill Singer who was suffering from a migraine headache. The Dodgers were facing the Cardinals and Steve Carlton was on the mound. Steve probably caused a few migraines during his career for both pitchers and hitters. Al rose to the occasion and pitched a gem, leading the Dodgers to a 2-1. After that, Al stayed in the Dodgers' starting rotation.

I thought I pitched very well in 1971. We had a tremendous team and there's no doubt I would not have won 20 games without the team we had. We had a very competitive team. We had Maury Wills, Dick Allen, Willie Davis, Jimmy Lefebvre, and Wes Parker. Tom Haller and Duke Sims were our catchers. We just had a team of veterans, schooled in the fundamentals of baseball; didn't make a lot of mistakes, ground balls they made the plays, whether it's a force out or double play, the plays were made. That's what I always liked, and I won 20, Sutton won 17, and Osteen won 14. We only finished one game out. We didn't score a lot of runs but then, you know, on the Dodger teams

you didn't have to score a lot of runs because you didn't give up a lot of runs.
Al Downing interview

During the 1971 season, Al was asked if he would cherish the Comeback Player of the Year Award, which he was inevitably about to win. In his typical understated fashion, he responded, "It would be more of an honor to win 20 games, and even more of an honor to get into the World Series." (Bob Hunter, Sept. 25, 1971) Unfortunately, for Al and the Dodgers, they fell short of winning the National League Western Division by one game, losing to the San Francisco Giants, in a rivalry that survived coast-to-coast moves by both franchises. But, Al did reach that twenty win milestone, finishing the season with a 20-9 record and a stingy 2.68 ERA. He also led the National League with 5 shutouts and was third in the Cy Young balloting, behind Ferguson Jenkins and Tom Seaver. He even finished tenth in the voting for National League MVP, a strong showing for a pitcher.

I spent most of the 1971 season in the National League, with the Pittsburgh Pirates (who did make it to the World Series that year, but without me) so I got a good opportunity to see Al, and to hear the buzz around the league about the way he was pitching. And since I was in the American League when Al came up with the Yankees in the early '60s, I also had the chance to see the difference in the way he pitched at these different points in his career. One big difference was that Al was not delivering the ball as quickly in 1971. I am not talking about speed to the plate, because Al could still bring it. He had one of the liveliest and best fastballs in the American League when he broke onto the scene, and his pitch still had a lot of giddy-up on it in 1971. But the difference was the speed with which Al was moving his body through his delivery. He had learned to pitch and, in 1971, he was doing a much better job of keeping his head down and his body closed until it was time to deliver the ball. I spoke with Al about it and he told me that when he was younger, Johnny Sain, (who was so helpful to me in Minnesota), told him he was opening up his body much too soon, and worked with him to correct it. Johnny would tell him that when he was delivering the pitch, the back pocket of his uniform pants should be all that the batter saw. That simple lesson helped Al to put his arm in a position to throw the ball, as opposed to "shotputting" it. When Al got to the Dodgers, his pitching coach there, Red Adams, continued to work with Al on this part of his pitching game. He wanted Al to keep his head down, which would allow him to keep his body closed, and then allow his hips to just move naturally toward home plate.

Besides his mastery of a more closed delivery, I asked Al what he thought was the key to winning twenty games in a Major League season:

Health. You've got to stay healthy. You've got to get the starts and the innings, because very few guys win twenty games who pitch less than 200 innings. It just doesn't happen, because if you come out of a game in the sixth inning, you have no chance, hardly, of winning

games. It just doesn't happen very often, because you have too many people that have to come in and hold that lead, and while it will happen periodically, over the course of a season it doesn't happen that often. You lose more than you win. You are more likely to win when you can pitch into the eighth inning. Then you only have to have one guy, maybe, come in and hold the lead for you.

Luck is also a part of winning twenty, but it is a part of the game in general. Luck is being able to pitch on days when the weather is not wet. You don't mind brisk weather; you don't want stifling cold weather, bone-chilling weather like you get in San Francisco. I think in the six and a half years I pitched in the National League, I only saw two days that I pitched in San Francisco that were what you call reasonably good days. Every other game I pitched in San Francisco, it was cold. I mean it was bone-chilling. You can't pitch like that. Juan Marichal, to me, was like a miracle worker, because I went into San Francisco and I'm always thinking, how is it you pitch here?
Al Downing interview

I also asked Al about some of the differences he saw in pitchers now, and the way the game is played, from when he and I were on the hill:

I think it is also a little more difficult to win twenty now, because what the pitchers are asked for is "quality starts." When I played there was no such thing as a "quality start." If you couldn't pitch nine innings on a regular basis, you didn't get to pitch as often. Now, I think, guys pitch to statistics as opposed to pitching to innings. A "quality start" to me is when you walk off the mound with your team leading, and with a good chance to win the game. It's not that you pitched six innings and only gave up three runs. What good is it if your team is losing 3-0? And that is a 4.50 ERA, which was unacceptable when I played.
As a pitcher, you don't go around thinking, "Well, my ERA is this, or that." What you think is, "If a guy is on first, he's not getting to second, or if he's on second, he's not getting to third, and if he's on third, he's not scoring." Your whole idea is don't allow the other team to score, not how much or how little they score.
Al Downing interview

Al went on to pitch very well also in 1972 and 1973. In fact, Al thinks he may have been a better pitcher in the two years after his twenty win season. However, that kind of self-awareness doesn't always show up in a pitcher's won-lost record; he may know it but for one reason or another stats may not show it. Just look at Randy Johnson's 2004 season. He was probably the dominant pitcher in the National League as far as the batters were concerned, but the sportswriters looked

337

to the wins that Roger Clemens and Roy Oswalt were able to put on the board for the Houston Astros.

Of course, no body of work on Al Downing would be complete without spending time on the events of April 8, 1974, when Al gave up home run number 715 to Henry Aaron. Prior to that time, Downing, who had faced Aaron on a regular basis since coming to the National League in 1971, had surrendered two other homers to Aaron. The first was Hanks's No. 676, a solo shot at Dodger Stadium on April 15, 1973, and the second was No. 693, a two-run, sixth-inning shot at Atlanta's Fulton County Stadium. I'll bet there are a good number of pitchers who gave up more than two home runs to Hammerin' Hank over a three year period; probably a few who gave up two in the same game. But, in general, Al was not a pitcher who gave up a lot of home runs. In fact, over his career, Al only yielded 177 home runs, an average of just 16 per year and .7 per game.

But the public will always remember the pitch that yielded number 715 to Henry Aaron. Al's memories were captured by Chris Baud, in *The Trentonian*, and Bob Dolgan, in *The Cleveland Plain Dealer*, 25 years after the historic home run:

"It was a fastball down the middle of the upper part of the plate," Downing said later. "I was trying to get it down to him, but I didn't.

"He's a great hitter. When he picks his pitch, he's pretty certain that's the pitch he's looking for. Chances are he's gonna hit it pretty good. When he did hit it, I didn't think it was out because I was watching Wynn, and Buckner. But the ball just kept carrying and carrying."

But Downing was philosophical about his role in history. ... Naturally, I didn't like giving up the home run," Downing said years later. "But now I take pride in being a part of the historical moment. There's no shame in giving it up."
Chris Baud, The Trentonian

"People say, `I know you threw that pitch deliberately,' said the left-handed Downing. "But that's not true. I was there to shut them down. I was confronted with a great hitter and I challenged him. I wasn't going to let up."
The previous year, Kuhn had warned pitchers he would not tolerate easing up on Aaron after some hurlers hinted they might give him fat pitches.
Downing walked straight to his dugout as pandemonium ensued following the homer. The pitcher had been a teammate of Maris when he broke Ruth's single-season record, but he said far more excitement greeted Aaron's blast.
"The game literally stopped," Downing said. "A ceremony had been scripted. They had a half-hour show with Sammy Davis Jr. on the

field. When Maris hit his homer we had to push him on the field for a curtain call, and that was it."
Bob Dolgan, The Cleveland Plain Dealer

This is how Henry remembered it:

My father threw out the first ball, and then we took the field against the Dodgers. Their pitcher was Al Downing, a veteran lefthander whom I respected. Downing always had an idea of what he was doing when he was on the mound . . . I crowded the plate against him to hit the outside pitch, but at the same time, I knew he would be trying to outthink me, which meant that I had to . . . pick my spot. It didn't come in the second inning, when Downing walked me before I could take the bat off my shoulder.
I came up again in the fourth, with two outs and Darrell Evans on first base. The Dodgers were ahead 3-1, and I knew that Downing was not going to walk me and put the tying run on base. He was going to challenge me with everything he had--which was what it was going to take for me to hit my 715th home run. . . .
Downing's first pitch was a change of pace that went into the dirt. The umpire, Satch Davidson, threw it out, and the first-base umpire, Frank Pulli, tossed Downing another one of the specially marked infrared balls. Downing rubbed it up and then threw his slider low and down the middle, which was not where he wanted it but which was fine with me. I hit it squarely, although not well enough that I knew it was gone.
Henry Aaron, I Had A Hammer, The Henry Aaron Story

With Hank chasing Babe Ruth's home run record through 1973, and ending up only one shy of tying it, people had a long time to express themselves, negatively and positively, towards Hank. Hank remembers that his mail reached the point where he was receiving about 3,000 letters a day, and he acknowledges that while most of it was positive, he received some devastating mail that actually changed him for life and reminded him of how some people still felt:

Dear Nigger,
Everybody loved Babe Ruth. You will be the most hated man in this country if you break his career home run record . . . .

Dear Black Boy,
Listen Black Boy, We don't want no nigger Babe Ruth.

Dirty old nigger man,
Had Ruth played and been at bat as many times as you, old nigger, he

would have hit just short of 1100 home runs. I hope lightning strikes you for trying to blemish Ruth's record. . . .

Dear Hank Aaron,
Retire or die! The Atlanta Braves will be moving around the country and I'll move with them. You'll be in Montreal June 5-7. Will you die there? You'll be in Shea Stadium July 6-8, and in Philly July 9th to 11th. Then again you'll be in Montreal and St. Louis in August. You will die in one of those games. I'll shoot you in one of them. Will I sneak a rifle into the upper deck or a .45 in the bleachers? I don't know yet. But you know you will die unless you retire!

Dear Hank Aaron,
I got orders to do a bad job on you if and when you get 10 from B. Ruth record. A guy in Atlanta and a few in Miami Fla. don't seem to care if they have to take care of your family too.
I Had a Hammer, The Henry Aaron Story

The Dodgers won their division in 1974, and Al got to the post-season again, ten years after the Yanks lost to the Cardinals in seven games. Al earned a victory against the Pittsburgh Pirates in the National League Championship Series, which the Dodgers went on to win to reach the World Series against Vida Blue and the Oakland Athletics. Although Al did not get a full complement of starts during the season, with the Series tied at one game each, he was called upon to start Game Three. He gave up one earned run in three and two-thirds innings of work, and two runs in total, in a game the Dodgers eventually lost 3-2, and Oakland went on to win the Series in five games.

Al stayed with the Dodgers until July of 1977, when he was released and his tremendous career came to an end. During his last few seasons, he never got the opportunity to pitch on a regular basis again, with the Dodgers relying heavily on Andy Messersmith, Don Sutton, and Tommy John. Over the course of his career, Al had proven to be most effective when he got the ball every fourth start.

When his playing days were over, Al stayed close to the game but out of uniform and off the field. He went into the broadcast booth, where he teamed up with Rick Monday as the broadcast team for the Los Angeles Dodgers. With Al behind the microphone fans got an opportunity to witness Al's knowledge of the game from a different perspective.

CHAPTER 24

VIDA ROCHELLE BLUE

Born July 29, 1949 in Mansfield, Louisiana
Teams: Oakland Athletics, San Francisco Giants,
  Kansas City Royals
Twenty-Win Seasons: 1971, 1973, 1975
American League Cy Young Award 1971
American League Most Valuable Player 1971
American League All-Star 1971, 1975, 1977
National League All-Star 1978, 1980, 1981
Inducted into Burlington Baseball Hall of Fame 2001

Vida Blue ranks up there with pitchers like Lefty Grove and Whitey Ford as one of the top 20 lefthanders in history.
Joe Cronin

He popped his fastball too, an overpowering pitch that in the beginning Vida could sink, sail, hop, drop, or dart. Mostly it smoked.
Catfish Hunter, Catfish, My Life in Baseball

When [Vida] pitched against us, one guy would come back from the plate and tell the next batter that the ball was coming in on his fists. The next guy would say the ball was going away from the plate. I think I have the answer. The guys don't see the damn ball. It's just too fast.
Earl Weaver, Baltimore Orioles manager

I'd like to face Blue. I hear he can throw a baseball through a car wash without getting it wet. I'd like to see for myself.
Johnny Bench, as quoted by Pete Waldmeir, July 13, 1971

Swinging at Vida's fast ball is like swinging at sound – that's the sound of the ball hitting the catcher's mitt.
Dave Duncan

"**Vida**" means "life" in Spanish and if ever a child was perfectly suited to his name, it was Vida Blue. His exuberance and love of life became immediately evident to me when I first saw him pitch in 1970, and I still see it in him today.

For many of the Black Aces it took several years (and for some of us, several teams) before we really became pitchers and enjoyed success at the Major League level. That is not unusual in the humbling game of baseball. Young pitchers tend to struggle with Major League hitters. Throughout their years playing in school or in the minors, good pitchers can dominate, but they usually face a degree of shock at the Major League level. There are differences in the level of play as you go up the ladder, but the biggest difference for all players is between AAA and the majors, and it is even more pronounced for pitchers than hitters. Hitters can struggle and even fail at first, but they only need to deal with two or three at bats a game, and there is time between at-bats and games to be coached and make adjustments. For young pitchers, every pitch is a learning experience that can be devastating, especially with an impatient manager or owner, and there's really no one to talk to, or to guide you, between every pitch. The mound can be an extremely lonely place for a young pitcher. Even the greats have struggled early in their career. The Nolan Ryan of the 1969 New York Mets bore little resemblance to the Ryan Express who dominated hitters. Sandy Koufax had a 2-4 record in his second year (1956), and it wasn't until Sandy's ninth season with the Dodgers (1963) that he became a pitching legend, winning a minimum of 25 games a year for the next three years.

But, like Haley's Comet, every so often a brilliant star comes along who shines like a supernova from the moment he comes on the scene. In 1970 and 1971, Vida Blue was just such a phenomenon. In 1970, the Oakland Athletics were another one of the young American League teams trying to jump into the void created by the collapse of the New York Yankees in the late '60s. Their chances of making the post-season were improved by the new divisional structure of the Major Leagues, which placed the Yankees and the powerful and successful Baltimore Orioles in the American League East, and left the West up for grabs. By September of that year, the A's found themselves clinging to an outside chance to win their division, trailing only the California Angels and the first-place Minnesota Twins. When they were able to expand their roster they decided to take another look at their young prospect, Vida Blue. By September 14th, the A's were confident enough in their pitching to release an old-timer like me. I was traded to the Pittsburgh Pirates for the proverbial player to be named later, (who turned out to be Angel Mangual). When I was informed of the trade I was also told I had to leave that day; the Pirates wanted me for a game against the Phillies. As I was in the clubhouse packing I could feel the roar of the crowd in the stadium, and everyone who came through the clubhouse was talking about this young kid, Vida Blue, who was really bringing it. I went down the runway to the dugout and watched Vida pitch for the first time myself. His delivery was explosive and you could see that he drew power from a pair of very strong legs. When the ball hit Dave Duncan's mitt, the "pop" resonated in the stands, and the crowd responded with an audible "ooh-eee!" After three or four pitches, despite all that I had seen in baseball, I found myself part of the crowd, involuntarily yelling "ooh-eee" as Vida delivered another fastball. I remember thinking to myself, "Oh, my goodness. We've got something here."

Within eighteen days of being called up, Vida had a streak of success that was almost hard to believe. He hit his first Major League home run, pitched a one-hitter (against the Kansas City Royals) and then threw a no-hitter (against the Twins) allowing only one walk. Hello major leagues. Vida's presence wasn't enough for the A's to catch the Twins in 1970, but that torrid two and a half weeks was just a little preview of the tornado-like way Vida would tear through the league in 1971, his first full season, and help the A's make it to the post-season. It was his signature season, like 1968 was for Bob Gibson or 1978 for Ron Guidry.

When I came back to the Oakland Athletics from the Pittsburgh Pirates, in August 1971, I couldn't wait to watch Vida pitch again. I not only got to see Vida pitch, but also wound up living with him, as he and Tommy Davis and I shared an apartment. Vida's pitching was all anybody was talking about. He took America by storm, at a time when the country, still stuck in the middle of the Vietnam War, needed a positive diversion. They were even singing songs about him:

If you're looking for a hero that's strong and true,
There's a boy in Oakland by the name of Vida Blue.
He throws a baseball like it was shot from a gun.
Everybody says that he's number one.
That's Vida Blue

In that special season of 1971, at the tender age of 21, Vida Blue became a twenty-game winner. Oh, but that ain't all! He also:

- Was chosen to start the All-Star Game for the American League, and was the wining pitcher;
- Won the American League Cy Young Award;
- Won the American League Most Valuable Player Award;
- Led the league in shutouts, with 8;
- Led the league in ERA with 1.82;
- Led the league in strikeouts per 9 innings, with an average of 8.68;
- Led the league in fewest hits allowed per 9 innings, with 6.03;
- Led the league in fewest combined walks and hits allowed per 9 innings, with 8.57;
- Was second in the league in wins, with 24;
- Was second in the league in complete games, with 24;
- Was second in the league in winning percentage, .750;
- Was second in the league in total strikeouts, 301; and
- Did not commit a single error.

Consider what veteran sportswriters, who had covered many of the greats, were already writing about Vida only two or three months into that 1971 season:

Blue, in other words, is a pitcher who seemingly cannot miss – a left-handed Tom Seaver who could turn the world around for a team that potentially is the best in the American League West.
Paul Corcoran, Copley News Service, May 9, 1971

It's all being done on a single pitch – the most terrifying lefthanded fastball that has been seen since the mutation of Koufax into a television personality.
Newsweek, 1971

What he has done this year has caused him to be called a black Sandy Koufax. Ten consecutive wins – five of them shutouts – and 95 strikeouts in about as many innings is what he has done. ... The style is Marichal without the exaggerated leg kick, a fluid propellant that climaxes in a literal explosion some 60 feet away.
Jack Smith, San Francisco Chronicle, May 27, 1971

Some compare him with Sandy Koufax and others say he is like Sam McDowell; Rico Petrocelli calls him "a lefthanded Bob Gibson. He keeps it coming, just like Gibson."
Phil Pepe, NY Sunday News, May 30, 1971

"Vida has the goods," said [Dick] Williams. "He has such an overpowering fastball that he can win on speed alone. The more he uses his curve and change-up though, the better he will be. Koufax always was fast, but he couldn't control his pitches and never got poise until he got control. This kid has a five-year advantage over Sandy already. He has the control and he has the poise. He's a remarkable young man, and none of it has gone to his head."
Arthur Daley, NY Times, June 1, 1971

They are calling Blue the "Black Sandy Koufax" and it may be a bum rap all the way around. Maybe Sandy Koufax was a Jewish Vida Blue.
Pete Waldmeir, July 13, 1971

By the time the 1971 season was over, the writers had another chance to voice their opinions about Vida's performance when it came time to vote for post-season awards, and they spoke loud and clear. Vida, at 22, became the youngest player to ever win a Cy Young Award and, one week later, became the youngest player in either league to ever win a Most Valuable Player Award. It was only the fifth time in the history of the game that a pitcher had won both awards in the same year, (Newcombe had done it in 1956, as well as Sandy Koufax in 1963, and Gibson and Denny McLain in 1968). It says a lot that three of those five are Black Aces. (Since that time, three more pitchers have accomplished that feat, (Rollie Fingers in 1981, Willie Hernandez in 1984 and Roger Clemens in 1986.)

And baseball wasn't even Vida's best sport! According to Vida, he was better at football. In fact, his eyes still light up when he talks about the beauty of throwing a tight spiral. He speaks from personal experience. As a senior in high school, Vida threw 35 touchdown passes, earning him twenty-five scholarship offers and the nickname "Golden Arm." Blue received scholarship offers from many of the top collegiate football programs, including Grambling, Purdue, Notre Dame, Kansas State, Arizona State, and Southern University. In fact, he actually signed a letter of intent to attend the University of Houston.

Blue also played baseball in high school but didn't start out wanting to be a pitcher. He wanted to play centerfield because of the action, and because of Willie Mays.

As a kid I used to love to play center field and first base. My summer league coach made me pitch. I said, 'Man, that's no fun.' I wanted the action. I wanted to be where the ball was being hit.
Vida Blue, quoted by Mike Berardino, South Florida Sun Sentinel, 2003

But coaches saw Vida's ability and he found his way to the mound. During his senior year, he once struck out 21 batters in a seven inning game! It was lucky for baseball that when the Oakland Athletics drafted Vida with their second pick (27th overall) in the June 1967 amateur draft, he turned down the offers to play football, withdrew from his obligation to the University of Houston and agreed to sign with Charlie Finley's A's. (In that same draft, the Yankees, picking first, didn't even know about Vida and selected Ron Blomberg; the Mets' scout thought Vida was "strong and a good athlete, but he can't throw as well as Jesse Hudson" [Vida's high school teammate] and they selected Gary Gentry; and the Atlanta Braves took Ralph Garr, who went on to become a National League batting champion, and is still a scout for the Braves.) The Athletics knew about Vida because their scout, Connie Ryan, after watching an afternoon game in Ruston, Louisiana (J.R. Richards' hometown), decided to go watch a night game at DeSoto High School in Mansfield, about thirty miles away. Ryan has said that Vida was the best lefthander he saw in nine years of scouting.

Part of the reason Vida opted for baseball over football was the death of his father, Vida Sr., the year he was drafted. His death left Vida as the male head of the Blue household, since he was the oldest of the six Blue children. Vida dropped out of high school in his senior year, to take care of his family. That summer he completed his school work though and earned his diploma. The only football available to Vida was at the college level, and would not have provided him with the instant income he and his family needed. Signing with the Athletics earned Vida a bonus of $25,000 and a job. His mother's concern over the greater risk of injury in football also played a role in his decision.

Vida spent the fall of 1967 in the Arizona Instructional League and was assigned to the Burlington Bees (Iowa) of the Midwest League for the 1968 season. It was the first time Vida lived outside of a totally segregated community. In the 1968 home opener for Burlington, all Vida did was strike out 16 Quad Cities Angels on his way to a 6-1 win. A week later, he struck out 15 Quincy Cubs in only six innings. When he later repeated that feat by striking out 15 Quincy Cubs on August 21 of that year, he set a new club record for the Burlington Bees, with 214 strikeouts, breaking the old record of 201 set by Jim Nash. Vida went further and ultimately led the Midwest League with 231 strikeouts in 152 innings, a record that still stands as the Burlington single-season record. He also hurled a no-hitter during his first full year in professional ball, but he wasn't satisfied with the fact that his record was below .500, at 8 and 11, even though the team itself lost more games than it won.

Vida was promoted to the Birmingham A's (Alabama) of the Southern League in 1969, which was a step up to Class AA. He continued his success on the mound. By mid-season, he was 8 and 2 in 11 starts. He was a unanimous choice for the Southern League All-Star team that played an exhibition game against the Atlanta Braves, but didn't get to pitch in the rain-shortened game won by the All-Stars.

"Sure there was prejudice there [in Birmingham]," [Blue] he said, remembering the obscenities that poured from the stands, "I expected it, Alabama's like that," he shrugged. "I tried not to give them any reason for it. I left everybody alone and stayed to myself, except for my teammates. I just did my job."
Jack Smith, San Francisco Chronicle, May 27, 1971

Those were Vida's thoughts in 1971. Today, he still remembers what it was like to go from Iowa back to the South:

Going to the Southern League was like going three steps back because all the cities in the league were in the South. It was back to that segregated lifestyle that I had growing up in Louisiana. My home base was Birmingham. We played in Montgomery, there was Asheville, there was Charlotte, there was Columbus, Georgia, all mid-sized cities in the deep South.

Being successful, I didn't have many experiences, but I remember one kid I played with, Bobby Brooks, who was from L.A., he played the outfield. I remember him sharing with us he was called everything but a child of God, you know, the curses. The true redneck isn't bold enough to show his face to you, man to man. He is not confrontational. He is confrontational behind a disguise. These groups who have racist beliefs that no one else believes in, I'm sure that they have a problem with people that are different because they don't have any confidence in themselves, I guess. I don't know, but that's what makes the world go round, that we all are different.

One thing I remember, Bobby Brooks, and another black kid, Duane Emerson, and I, we got a house. We found this little old widow, who had just lost her husband and she had a couple of kids, and the tradeoff was three meals a day, we paid rent, she washed our clothes, and we'd cut

her grass, do a little handyman work around the house, and we'd get the kids tickets to the game and stuff like that. It was like having a second mom. She always stayed on our ass and made us walk the straight and narrow, 'cause in '69 I was only going to be turning nineteen that July. So, it was a good experience, because I knew where I was. We lived in a black neighborhood which was where the ballparks were built at that time anyway, so, we could walk to the ballpark. She would come to the games, and we'd go back and have home-cooked meals.
Vida Blue interview

At the end of that 1969 season, Vida was called up to join the A's at the Major League level, but he wasn't really ready yet. He didn't have an effective pitch other than his fastball and that wasn't sufficient to deceive Major League hitters, who smacked 13 home runs off Vida in 42 innings of work.

"Everyone in the ball park knew I couldn't control my breaking ball." **Blue remembered. 'They'd just lean back and wait for my fast ball."** *Ron Bergman, The Sporting News, October 10, 1970*

After the season, Vida entered the Army for a six month stint as part of his Reserve obligation, which kept him out of spring training in 1970. When he did return to the team, they promoted him to the Iowa Oaks in the American Association, the Athletics' AAA affiliate. Vida, young and full of confidence and enthusiasm, thought he was ready for the Major Leagues, and contemplated going back home to Louisiana instead of returning to the minors. It was the advice of elders that kept him on the path:

I thought I should have made the major league team from spring training. I was mad as hell. I do remember calling my mother, telling her I was going to quit and come home, and she had a talk with me and I talked to one of my uncles. My Uncle Ray was a high school athletic director at his school for a long time. He went to Grambling, played a little tight end and he was the head coach of the basketball team, head coach of the baseball team, and he was probably my most inspirational uncle as far as knowing the trials and tribulations of what an athlete goes through. But my mom directly told me, "You can't start and stop. You've got to finish the job." I was mad as hell that I didn't make the team from spring training, and as it turns out, it's probably the best thing that happened to me. In AAA there were guys that had played some major league ball, or guys that had a half a year in major league ball. It really allows you to measure up against these guys and use them as a barometer of how much progress you're making. Of course, I could throw the ball by two-thirds of the people that I faced, but the art of pitching is, number one, getting ahead in the

count, remembering who was a first-ball fastball hitter, remembering the guys that hit the ball to right field, remember what situation guys would give themselves up in, just learning how to pitch, knowing your opponent, knowing when there's a man on second, the way you're taught: man on second with less than one out you got to move him over, so don't pitch that guy outside and allow him a chance to slap that ball to the second baseman. Make him earn that, pitch him inside. If he "inside-outs" the ball and gets under it, he earns it, but just don't be going outside corner. And the Jeff Burroughs of the world, you know that he's a first-ball, fastball hitter, throw him a good curveball if you have it. Use your fastball, but spot it, make it be up and in, or something, just don't throw it down the middle and say, "I don't think you can hit my fastball" because they sure as hell will do that.
Vida Blue interview

In his first start for Iowa, Vida set a new club strikeout record – 14 – and it only took him six and two-thirds innings to do it. Vida's teammates in Iowa included Marcel and Rene Lachemann, Gene Tenace, Tony LaRussa, and Juan Pizarro, who had reported to camp late and was left on the Oaks roster to work himself into pitching shape. Pizarro, a veteran lefty, proved very important to Vida's development because he helped fine tune Vida, specifically working with him on the grip for his curve ball and encouraging him to take a shorter stride when he threw it. His manager, Sherm Lollar, also helped Vida, constantly reminding him to keep his pitches down. Blue responded by winning his first six decisions, averaging 11 strikeouts a game, with a 1.47 ERA. He was 8 and 1 by the All-Star break, when he was named as a starter to the American Association's All-Star team. However, because the Oaks were in first place at the time, they became the team that played the All-Stars from the other teams in the league.

AAA ball turned out to be a great experience for me. You're playing in Oklahoma City, you played against Cesar Cedeno, JR Richards. And Tulsa was the Cardinals; I played against Ted Simmons and Jerry Reuss. Go to Evansville, Indiana; there was Burt Blyleven, talk about a curveball. Indianapolis, talk about Dave Concepcion. Back to the Cardinals, there was a guy named Luis Melendez, who, speaking of a guy that was my nemesis, I bet he hit .555 off me in AA and AAA ball. He had that wide stance, like Roberto Clemente, and just dove into the ball. If you came inside, he'd shorten his stance and yank it down the leftfield line. Denver was still the Texas Rangers. That's where Jeff Burroughs almost hit a ball – there was a Holiday Inn by the old Mile High Stadium – this ball had to go damn near half way to that Holiday Inn. Omaha was the Royals, there was a guy there named Paul Splitorff, and another guy, George Brett, on that ball team.
Vida Blue interview

Late in that 1970 season, Vida was again called up to the majors, but was returned to Iowa after eleven days without ever throwing a single pitch.

Vida completed the 1970 season in Iowa with two consecutive shutouts that included 16 and 11 strikeout performances. He had a 12 and 3 record for the year, and was then returned to the Major Leagues to stay. It was from this point that Vida took off like a rocket, beginning with his one-hit and no-hit performances at the end of the 1970 season. The one-hitter, against Kansas City, was only Vida's second Major League start, yet he didn't yield a hit until allowing a single with two outs in the eighth inning. The no-hitter against Minnesota, eleven days later, delayed the Twins in their effort to clinch the Western Division championship by one day. It was only Vida's fourth Major League start, bringing his 1970 record to a perfect 2-0 and earning him a $2,000 bonus from owner Charlie Finley. In a classy move, Jim Perry and Bill Rigney of the Twins sent Vida one of the bottles of champagne they had on ice for their anticipated celebration. That same day, Vida learned that he was a unanimous choice for the American Association All-Star Team and had been named American Association Pitcher of the Year.

After the 1970 season, Vida spent more time with the US Army, and he valued the physical training he received there:

I went to a place called Fort Bragg, North Carolina, and I was in the best shape of my life. I weighed 185, no body fat. You know, lean, mean fighting machine, all that stuff. Just going on those maneuvers and running with that backpack, and those boots, and that rifle - I made that a fun thing too, because now I got acclimated to life about all these people from different races and backgrounds going to be a part of your life, that's the world. I was like a squad leader, and I used to sing cadence when we would march in formation to my unit. My unit was C82, Charlie Company, Eighth Battalion, Second Brigade. I remember that like it was yesterday. But I had gone to boot camp, and I left boot camp and went to my mother's back in Louisiana for like a week and went straight to spring training. It just so happened, we had a lefthander on our ball team by the name of Tony Pierce, who had had some arm trouble that year and Dick Williams said, as all managers used to say, "I'm going to take the best 25 guys north with me when we break camp." Not only did I get a chance to start, and had a chance to be the opening day pitcher, which was pretty cool, considering we had a guy by the name of Catfish Hunter on the team, a guy named John Blue Moon Odom, who I think had won 16 games that year, and all these guys were established players and I had just come along to just kind of be a part of the fun and the action that was going on, and luckily I was just another piece of the puzzle that made it all work in '71.

Vida Blue interview

A combination of events (including Blue Moon Odom's injury, manager Dick Williams' belief that the Washington Senators had a hard time hitting lefties, and a good showing by Vida in spring training) led to Vida starting the traditional Presidential opener against the Washington Senators in 1971. Unfortunately, a combination of Washington hits earned Vida his first loss as a Major Leaguer that day, by an 8-0 score. He would not lose another game until late in May. In his very next start, he equaled the A's modern-day strikeout record for a nine-inning game by striking out 13 Kansas City Royals and yielding only three hits in a game shortened by rain to six innings. He followed that up with a two-hit, 2-0 victory over the Milwaukee Brewers. In fact, after the Opening Day loss in Washington, Vida reeled off ten straight victories, all complete games in which he gave up six hits or less, including five shutouts. He also conquered the "gopher ball" that had haunted him in 1969; in his first 95 2/3 innings of work in 1971 he only gave up one home run. When he finally did lose to the Boston Red Sox, in Boston on May 28th, this is what some of the winning ballplayers had to say about Vida:

The best fastball I've ever seen. I don't know how I hit it. He gets faster as it gets closer to the plate. I didn't face Koufax, but he can't have anything on that kid. ... [He's like] a lefthanded Bob Gibson. He keeps it coming, just like Gibson."
Rico Petrocelli

He's got good stuff. He's only a baby and he's gonna get better and I hate to see him any better.
George Scott

He's a helluva pitcher. What impressed me was his poise and control. In and out, up and down. He can win without that great fastball.
Carl Yastrzemski

After winning his tenth game, Vida carried two dimes in his uniform pocket on days he pitched. He said it was "to remind me that my goal is to win twenty games. When I went for my tenth, I carried one dime." Asked how he knew he had the right dimes to support his superstition, Vida displayed his sense of humor and his faith when he replied, "They each say, 'In God We Trust.'" (Bob Hertzel, July 14, 1971)

Vida's 1971 salary of $13,000 was just $250 over the then Major League minimum, not out of line for a pitcher who came into the season with a record of 1-1 and only a handful of Major League starts. But, by mid-season, it was apparent to everyone that Charlie Finley was getting the baseball bargain of the century. By June 6th, Vida was 12-2, with 12 complete games, 115 strikeouts in 121 1/3 innings and an ERA of 1.33. Even President Richard Nixon, a huge baseball fan, who was encouraging the country to freeze wages to curb inflation, made the statement that Vida was "the lowest paid superstar in America."

It was clear to Charlie Finley, ever the opportunist and entrepreneur, that Vida was drawing extra thousands of fans to each and every game he pitched. He was baseball's main gate attraction in 1971, and Finley, in his inimitable fashion, wanted to find a high exposure way to reward Vida. So, on June 27, 1971, between games of a doubleheader against the Kansas City Royals, Finley gave Vida a baby blue, convertible Cadillac El Dorado, and had Vida take a spin around the field with his Mom in the back seat. It was the first Major League game Vida's family had ever seen. While Vida was very appreciative of having his family at the game, and the way they were treated, he recalls the incident as somewhat racially insensitive:

When Richard Nixon said I was the "lowest paid superstar in America," is when Mr. Finley turned around and, the guy was not like this, I know he didn't have a racist heart or a racist bone in his body, he was this way with everybody, so it wasn't just blacks and Jews. He was non-discriminating. He went to this local Cadillac dealership, here in Oakland, and he gets me this damn Cadillac, and put vanity plates: "VBLUE." But, at that time all the B movies, Shaft, Superfly, all that stuff was going on. So I said, okay, I'll take the Cadillac you old geezer. I made a good thing out of a bad thing. Atlantic Richfield, ARCO gasoline, used to be the only company sponsoring the jumbo TV screen out in centerfield. So I said, "I can't pay money, I'm still not out of the woods. I can't pay for gas for a Cadillac." This Cadillac had a 22 gallon tank, an El Dorado, powder blue, with a beige top. So he gave me a gas card. I figured I'd fix that geezer's ass. Anytime I'd be in the neighborhood, in the 'hood, the ghetto, buying gas, the next car behind me, I'd tell them, "Pull that car up." I'd fill it up, too. I did that for almost two years. Finley finally said, "Goddamn, are you drinking this gas?" and he took that damn card from me.
Vida Blue interview

Despite the racial implications Vida sensed in receiving the powder blue Cadillac, I think it was pretty well recognized that Finley was not a racist, but just treated everybody in a manner best suited to Finley, without any sensitivity to others. This view of Finley was captured in the following dialogue:

"He [Finley] treats his black players like niggers," said pitcher Vida Blue, growing up far sooner than he should. "It's disgusting."
"Don't feel bad," said ex-A's catcher, Dave Duncan, a white. "He treats his non-black players like niggers too."
Wells Twombly, The Sporting News, October 26, 1974

In another outlandish Finley stunt, he offered Vida $2,000 to change his name to True Blue. Vida also found that offer insensitive, and responded: "I couldn't believe he was serious. Vida was my father's name. I loved my father. He was a good, good man. I enjoy being Vida Blue. When I was a kid my parents called me 'Junior.' Now that my father is dead, I honor him every time the name Vida Blue appears in a headline. Why would I want to be called 'True Blue?' If Mr. Finley thinks it's such a great name, why doesn't he call himself 'True O. Finley?' I won't change. ... [those names] make me feel like a bumper sticker. Just slap it on – True Blue. It may be good for baseball, but I'd rather be just Vida Blue." But as Vida noted, there wasn't a racial motive with Finley, it was just showmanship. He also had "Blue Moon" Odom, "Catfish" Hunter, and "Sugar Bear" Daniels with the A's. In fact, when I got to Oakland, Charlie loved the fact that I had "Mudcat" on the back of my uniform, not "Grant." Remember, this is the same guy who introduced Hot Pants Day at the ballpark, when all ladies in Hot Pants were admitted free. Those taking part in the Hot Pants Parade received certificates for box seats to a future game and prizes for the best Hot Pants included season tickets.

By the time the All-Star break came in 1971, Blue was 17-3 with 17 complete games, and 187 strikeouts. It was the most wins ever by a pitcher at the All-Star break. (The previous record was Bob Feller's 16, in 1941.) It was apparent that Vida would get the ball for the American League and, when Sparky Anderson named Dock Ellis as the National League starter, after Ellis questioned that he would, it was the first time both starting pitchers in the All-Star game were African-Americans. The American League gave Vida enough offensive support (to overcome the runs he surrendered on home runs by Johnny Bench and Hank Aaron) for him to be the winning pitcher.

As we know it now, I was in the Zone. I couldn't do anything wrong. And you get a couple of games under your belt, and you get that confidence that Charlie Finley always talks about – cocky confidence – just cocky enough to know that you're good enough without alienating your opponents. And I started to believe in myself, not that I belonged there but I believed that my ability was at that level, which is always a good thing. I was in that zone, everything worked out. Everything I threw up there they either swung at and missed or hit it to somebody and they made a great play, and I had a great supporting cast, to not sound so conceited about myself, with a Reggie Jackson, and a Sal Bando, and a Gene Tenace, and a Dick Green, and eventually a Don Baylor coming in for first base, and a Catfish Hunter and a Blue Moon Odom, and a Rollie Fingers, don't leave him out. We collectively as a team, man for man, obviously we couldn't challenge the '27 Yankees, but we played together well as a team. We played together as a team, which is so hard to do when you have a multitude of stars on your ball team. And in some kind of way I think the other factor was the one common bond we had was that we were always trying to prove to Charlie Finley that we were better, that we were deserving of more money than he offered us, or than he paid us, and he always dangled the carrot in front of us,

but we were always trying to prove that we were better, that we were worthy of the money that we were making, and then some.
Vida Blue interview

Much of America's attention was on Viet Nam in 1971, as war continued to rage, and the draft had been converted into a lottery system. The race riots that had dominated the headlines during the sixties weren't as prominent, although the country was still reeling from the assassinations of Bobby Kennedy and Martin Luther King in 1968. But racial tension and violence still existed, and stories would be reported that would remind us of those problems. In August of 1971, Vida's pitching success made this 22 year old black from Louisiana the toast of the country, including appearances on the Today Show, on the covers of *Sports Illustrated* and *Time*, and visits with the President. At the same time, Rico Carty, a member of the Atlanta Braves and the 1970 National League batting champion, was beaten by three Atlanta police officers. According to reports, the beating occurred when Carty told police that he and his brother-in-law, who were in one car, had been called "cop-killing niggers" by individuals in a nearby car. As it turned out the "name-callers" were off-duty police officers. Atlanta Police Chief Herbert Jenkins said, "This case involved the worst case of misconduct by a police officer I have ever seen." Atlanta Mayor Sam Maseil suspended the three police officers, saying, "I cannot emphasize too strongly my complete disgust with what is apparently an incident of blatant brutality. Those involved have brought disgrace to our police department, the city and the profession of law enforcement across the country." When I heard of this incident, my mind immediately brought me back to that juke joint in Florida, and I felt the kick in my back and the cold barrel of the gun against my head. I was sad and hurt that seventeen years later some people's minds were still in the same place.

Vida ended the 1971 season with a 24-8 record, a 1.82 ERA and 301 strikeouts. He was the first pitcher since Ewell Russell of the Chicago White Sox, in 1913, to pitch more than 300 innings in his first full Major League season, hurling 312. In the off-season, he won the American League Cy Young Award, by capturing 14 of the 24 first place votes, beating out Mickey Lolich. Blue was the youngest pitcher ever to capture the award. A week later he also became the youngest player ever to win an MVP honor in either league when he was named American League MVP.

During his first full season in 1971, Vida started to feel some of the pressure that the media and the public place on ballplayers. He was young and successful, a new star, and that placed him in the spotlight of the Major Leagues. He made good copy for writers and sportscasters, and the public wanted to know more about him. Who is this young man who can perform like this? Where did he come from? What does he think about the issues facing the country? A 22-year old kid from Louisiana, or from anywhere, can feel a little overwhelmed:

It's a weird scene. You win a few baseball games and all of a sudden you're surrounded by reporters and TV men with cameras asking you

about Vietnam and race relations and stuff like that. I don't even know who I am yet.
Vida Blue, in 1971

At Christmas time, Vida got an opportunity to see what was happening in Vietnam, and other parts of the world firsthand. He was part of the Bob Hope Tour that entertained American serviceman overseas. While the trip was a little different than my trips with the Commissioner, because of the entertainment aspect, it gave Vida the same chance to travel to military bases in Honolulu, Okinawa, Thailand, South Vietnam, Italy, Spain and Guantanamo, Cuba.

At the end of the show, the whole cast would get on stage and sing 'Silent Night.' I would look around while we were supposed to be singing – I really can't sing very well – and I would see the troops with their heads bowed. After the shows, they would mob us and thank us for giving up our Christmas to entertain them.
Vida Blue, quoted by Ron Bergman, The Sporting News, Jan. 22, 1972

Born in 1949, Vida is the first Black Ace born after Jackie Robinson and Larry Doby's debut. Vida was born and raised in the trailer factory and paper mill town of Mansfield, located in the northwest quarter of Louisiana, about thirty-five miles from Shreveport, northwest of Natchitoches and west of Grand Bayou. Vida is one of three Black Aces to hail from the Bayou State. Like Lacoochee, Mansfield's factory and mill employed most of the residents of the town. Vida's Dad was a foundry worker and his Mom was a cleaning woman in a shirt factory. Mansfield's population ranged from 5,000 to 10,000 people, mostly black, and Vida has some definite memories of his hometown:

At the time Mansfield was a pretty segregated area, and my family lived on the poor side of the tracks. I went to an all-black school, an all-black church, and I have friends and relatives all buried in an all-black cemetery. It was a sad commentary to my life, but that's the way stuff was at that time. I don't hold that against anybody. I don't differentiate color. Matter of fact, I probably get on more black people's cases for being racist than I do white people. It's all the same, wrong is wrong. There are two things in life: there's right and there's wrong. When you're wrong, you're wrong. I don't care how much money you have, how many home runs you hit yesterday, how many you hit lifetime, or what kind of car you drive, or how high a hill you live on. Right is right, and wrong is wrong. We all know right from wrong. We all have manners. We just don't use them sometimes.

When I was young, the issues raised by race relations kind of went right over my head like an F16. And looking back at it, it was still

just about basic right and wrong. It was wrong that this lady wasn't able to sit anywhere she wants to sit on the bus. And because of the color of my skin why shouldn't we have the right to vote, and then another one is the water fountains – there's one over here that said "White", and a separate one over here that said "Colored" or would occasionally say "Black." But there's one water line that came out and made a tee. We're drinking the same water, but they were separately marked "Blacks" and "Colored" and "Whites." Now, that just seems so clearly wrong. My parents could not give us an explanation as to why we could not go to the city pool. We're talking about why I still don't know how to swim today because some kid I grew up with drowned in a little sinkhole, which gave me the total fear of wanting to learn how to swim. Yes, my town was segregated, and it was very, very, very racist. This is how I viewed my town. Because you're white doesn't mean you're right, and then we go back to that right and wrong thing again. And again these folks were stupid. The color wasn't black or white, the color was green. That was the color, and they didn't get it.

Our family was not rich, but I never knew, thought, or felt, that we were poor either. All I know is I got a lot of hugs and kisses, and I thought I was one of the Rockefellers. I got a lot of hugs and kisses and that's the stuff that I remember as a kid, and playing ball in the summertime. That was our version of, as we know it now, a gang, if you would, because all the kids in the neighborhood, we played stickball. And that is bizarre to me to hear kids say today, to fast forward to today, that they don't play stickball. I'm like, "You don't play stickball? Get out! You don't take a broom handle and make a taped ball and, you don't do that? What the heck are you doing?" And obviously we're in this high tech age. Everybody is in their room, sending instant messages to their girlfriend or their pal friend across town, and e-mailing and faxing back and forth. But, I'm lucky, I'm glad I grew up when I did grow up. As I said, I didn't know that there was such a thing as rich and poor and middle class and all that stuff.

I didn't play Little League, I played in a t-shirt league. I took a t-shirt, and I would put number 32 on it; the significance of "32" - the guy that was the most prominent black influence on black America was a guy named Jim Brown. It just so happened I said, "Okay, I like him." I didn't know him. I didn't know what he was doing from a political standpoint, a racial standpoint, or making a statement. I just knew that I liked Jim Brown. He wore number 32. He was "bad." So, then anybody that wore number 32 was good. So, it's kind of like kids tell me today, "Hey, when I was playing ball in the neighborhood I was

Vida Blue." These are kids of all ethnic backgrounds. So that applied to me back then. I'm Sandy Koufax, I'm left-handed I wear number 31, and that's how that came about. But, all I did was I played ball in the summertime. I got balls and bats for birthday presents, Christmas presents. I did not own a brand new bicycle until I was 40 years old. I had bicycles but never brand new.

When you're in the neighborhood, even the youngest brother gets to play. You may have to take him on your team, but that's how you learn to play, you play with the older kids all the time. They whoop your ass and beat you up. But you say, "That's okay. I got to get tough." and it makes you a stronger, tougher person. You appreciate that stuff, because you're going to learn to run faster, swing harder, jump higher, do something, because survival is key in that environment.
Vida Blue interview

Baseball, and its many variations, like stickball, punchball, etc., were the predominant games in the neighborhood but, when Vida was introduced to football. He took to it instantly:

I love football. I LOVE FOOTBALL. I like hitting stuff and throwing deep passes and short passes and flair passes and draw plays and all that kind of stuff. I knew I could throw a football. I wanted to be Johnny Unitas, because Johnny U was the most prolific passer at that time. Then the other factor was the guy named Lenny Moore, the running back, and these other guys, and the Colts were the team. Any team that could rival Jim Brown and the boys, you got to sit up and take notice. But, I idolized Johnny U because I enjoyed throwing the football. That is the ultimate for me. I could get a natural high on throwing a football, just when it leaves my hand, the tight spiral that it has. I played cornerback on defense. All the guys on the football team, we were proud to call ourselves "60 minute men" because I kicked off, I punted, I was on the kickoff receiving team, I dropped back deep for punts. I left the field in between quarters to get a play from my coach or at halftime. But that was okay. I wanted to play 60 minutes. Now I'm thinking how much energy and effort it took to do that, which is, I guess, a compliment to the coaches and what they put us through to get us ready and prepared to play the game. But they knew we enjoyed it, and I compliment them for giving us all the time and effort they put into it themselves.
Vida Blue interview

But, even before Vida realized that baseball could provide economic stability for his family, the sport held a special place for him, as it did for most kids in the 1950s. I had the opportunity to talk with Vida about his childhood baseball memories:

> Those were the days. From a geographic standpoint, the Astros were the closest team in proximity to Louisiana. The Cardinals would fade in and out on the radio all the time, but I was a big St. Louis Cardinals fan, with Dick Groat and Ken Boyer, and Mike Shannon and Bill White, and Bob Gibson, of course, and Nelson Briles, and Tim McCarver and all those guys. Those were the days for me. But, the Astros were closer, so you could get them on TV, if it wasn't the Yankees on Game of the Week, from New York. My Daddy used to let me watch the baseball games with him on Sundays, or Saturdays.

> I knew the Negro Leagues existed, and I heard their names; well, the most famous name that I heard was Satchel Paige. He was the legendary, marquee guy, and Cool Papa Bell and those guys. I didn't know that Willie Mays and Hank Aaron played in the Negro Leagues or in the sandlots, or that Jackie Robinson had a stint with those guys, until I got older. I was aware of what that was, but I didn't know the significance of why they did not get a chance to play in the majors. And then you hear about Jackie Robinson, the first player to break the color barrier as it was told to me, but I still didn't know the significance of how and why he was not allowed to play until he was signed by the Dodgers.

> Once I started playing pro ball that obviously became something that I wanted to know about. I couldn't just go read about it, because they didn't have the text they have now, or go to negroleagues.com, like they have now. But you just asked your elders, "Hey man, why didn't he get to play?" "Well, they didn't want blah-blah-blah, and Cool Papa Bell was blah-blah-blah, and this guy was blah-blah-blah." But then you'd hear the stories about when they'd be barnstorming and then you'd get a movie like Richard Pryor made, Bingo Long Traveling All-Stars. You know that is fictional, but it has some merit to it, some of the things they experienced.

> *Vida Blue interview*

During the course of that great 1971 season, Vida often thought of his hometown, and what his on-field success could do for Mansfield:

> If I get extra money from the playoffs and the World Series, I want to help the young blacks in Mansfield get some of the things I didn't have when I was growing up. Don't get me wrong. Generally speaking, I like all people, and I don't consider myself a black leader. But the

young blacks in Mansfield need a playground and a place to hold social events and I'd like to organize a baseball league. I would even like to help some of the poorer families with their financial problems. Kids need food and clothing. I want to give it to them. Being black makes you want to do better. It gave me extra incentive. My mother was born and raised in Louisiana, my father was from Alabama. I'm the only guy from Mansfield ever to make it to the big league.

Vida Blue, as quoted by Samuel J. Skinner, Jr., in No Blues for Vida, Black Sports, September 1971

Being a celebrity here is not helping me unless it can help people there. I hope it can influence the kids, the white kids too, all of them.

Vida Blue, as quoted by Jack Smith, San Francisco Chronicle, May 27, 1971

Vida knew that his success on the field could, and should, translate into economic stability for him and his family, and give him an opportunity to improve conditions in Mansfield. Unfortunately for Vida, he was dealing with the wrong owner, and his contract negotiations for 1972 were taking place at the wrong time. The spring of 1972 was a time of labor unrest in baseball, for the players as a union, behind the leadership of Marvin Miller, Executive Director of the Players' Association, and for Vida, behind the leadership of labor attorney, Bob Gerst. Buoyed by his pitching success, awards, and drawing power, as well as the fact that the A's made it to the post-season for the first time in 40 years, Vida believed that he should be earning $100,000 a year.

You hear these things through the media "Oh, this is a business not a sport" and I took it for face value, and also "You get paid for what you did last season," but when you walk in and deal with Charlie Finley face-to-face and he tells you, "Vida Blue, listen, I don't blame you for wanting more money. Hell, if I was you, I'd want more money too. I know that one out of every ten fans that went through a turnstile in 1971 went to see you pitch. I know you pitched 300 innings. I know you won the MVP and the Cy Young. I know you had eight shutouts. I know you were the starting pitcher in the All-Star Game. I know you won all these awards, but, hell, you might be a flash in the pan. I can't pay you that kind of money. Pigs get fat and hogs go to market, okay?" and that is what he told me.

I thought that I should have been paid what I was asking for. I thought that I was worthy of it. And the fact that Finley could quote my stats, and the fact that as it was noted, one out of every ten fans came to see me, I thought I was definitely worthy of what I was asking. Plus when you get that third party, the agent, speaking for you, now, hell, he'll make you think you could walk on water. And I was 21 going on 22 in '72. I didn't comprehend. Hell, it took Willie Mays seventeen years to do this, but your argument still is that this is the new era, this is the changing of the guard of baseball, and this is a new era of baseball, financially. Guys are going to make $100,000. There were probably more guys making a $100,000 at one time than any other salary, because it was so new and so different. Bob Gibson was making $100,000. I know he had to be. All the marquee players on all the existing teams, within a three-year period, were making between 85 and $100,000. That was the benchmark. That said that you were the guy. On the Orioles, you got to thank Brooks Robinson, Frank Robinson, you got to thank Jim Palmer, you got to thank Dave McNally. So that's four guys there. And on the Giants, you got to thank Mays and McCovey, and Marichal, on the Mets, you got to thank Tom Seaver and Koosman.

It was a bitter and angry time. The frustration was, "Why won't this man give me this money, or pay me what I'm worth?" So, I would go over it in my mind, and that did, to this day change my perception of baseball as I think of it today. Because I all of sudden became this bitter, non-jovial, non-happy-go-lucky guy and I thought of it as a business, and the other thing as far as my attitude was that now public opinion said, "Oh, he's got to prove himself another couple of years." Screw that. I proved myself. You get paid for what you did last year. So, now my attitude changed against the fans, towards the media, because guys would write pro and con articles about the situation and my being a holdout, and I took the position that, hey, that's want I to be paid. Nothing against Charlie Finley. Willie Mays and Willie McCovey, and Hank Aaron made it, and I had a good year I think I should be rewarded accordingly.

It totally changed my life and attitude about baseball. That probably might have been the second time in my life in which I didn't think I wanted to play, or "Okay, I might play this year and then walk away from it." That's stubbornness, when you're at that age, and I'm very stubborn and very proud. I know that, you know I said, "You can't miss what you never had."
Vida Blue interview

In January of 1972, Vida reduced his demand to $92,500, which Gerst had calculated as the average salary of the "top ten" pitchers in baseball. In response, Finley raised his offer to $50,000, with the ultimatum that Vida would have to play for $50,000 or get out of baseball because he would not trade or sell him. When Finley acquired Denny McLain in March of 1972, agreeing in the process to pick up the second year of McLain's contract for $90,000 despite his poor record of 10-

22 in Washington in 1971, it seemed to firm Vida's resolve. Why would Finley pay $90,000 to a pitcher who lost 22 games for someone else, but refuse to pay $90,000 to Vida who won 24 for him, and put a lot of fannies in the seats?

So you won twenty games? Why didn't you win thirty?
Charlie Finley to Vida Blue during 1972 contract negotiations, quoted in
High Inside: Memoirs of a Baseball Wife by Danielle Gagnon Torrez

By the end of March 1972, Marvin Miller completed a vote of the players' union membership, which resulted in 663 of them voting to strike, with only 10 against and 2 abstentions. Meanwhile, Vida's individual negotiations with Finley weren't doing any better. By what would have been the start of the season, Vida publicly stated that he had retired from baseball, and he took a job as Vice-President of Dura Steel Products Corp. Blue had offered Finley ten alternatives to settling their dispute:

- A contract free from the reserve clause;
- A compromise salary between $50,000 and $92,5000;
- Arbitration by the Commissioner's Office;
- Sell or trade him;
- A multi-year contract;
- Deferred compensation;
- An additional bonus for 1971;
- Allow him to play in Japan;
- Appear with him in a television commercial; or
- Pay him a bonus based on attendance.

Finley rejected all of the alternatives with a flat 'no.' The dispute between Finley and Blue became national news. President Nixon even commented on it, and finally Baseball Commissioner Bowie Kuhn stepped in to try and bring the parties together.

Someway, somehow, it came to me that, "Okay, you know what? Let's go back and show them that you could still do this stuff. Just go and re-dedicate yourself." Some kind of way we compromised and settled for 60 something, but, believe it or not, I didn't even get that because Charlie Finley, knowing all the rules and regulations, and by-laws and guidelines that govern Major League Baseball, he claimed that I was physically unable to perform for a period of time, so he docked my pay, so I didn't even get that. And there was a strike for thirteen days. We opened the season in Boston. Then, also what he did, he snookered me: my Mom wanted me to always go to college and get a degree, so the deal was, I got $50,000 salary, he did some renovations to my Mom's house, that she still lives in to this day, and there was going to be some funding for me to go to college. But, the small print, unknown to me, stipulated it had to be used within a certain time frame.

I did not use it, and the guy boldly called me one day, bragging, "Hey, Vida. This is Fin." He always had to identify himself when he got on the phone. "By the way, thanks for saving me that 10 grand that you just saved me." "What the hell you talking about?" "You know you wanted me to put this money in an account that you could go to college? Well, hell, you have not enrolled in school. Thank you very much, the money comes back to me." You know, it wasn't like, "Hey, Vida, listen, I'm sorry to tell you that I don't know why you didn't enroll, I don't know whether you got busy in the off-season, public speaking, appearances, whatever, but I hate to tell you this, but legally these funds come back to me. I'll tell you what. I'll split the difference since you didn't know, or whether you did. I'll give you the benefit of the doubt. I'm all for any person that wants to better himself by going and getting an education." Nah, this guy was, "Thank you very much. Now I gotta go."

He also took it out on Tommy Davis, for introducing me to Bob Gerst. I know for a fact that is why he released Tommy that year. He hated the fact that I used an attorney to help me negotiate. Finley wasn't racist he was just a mean guy. He always had the upper end. But, if he's in heaven, he's still not number one, and if he's in hell, he's definitely prepared for that. So, who knows? But the guy was a very vindictive, evil person and that's sad, because the man, he had some good qualities as far as his ability to recognize talent. Not because he signed me and Reggie, but he was into what he was doing as far as putting his ball team together. He did it in a very shrewd way. He got the most of the players that he signed.
Vida Blue interview

When Blue finally signed on May 2, 1972, for a $63,000 package, he was told of the prediction by his manager, Dick Williams, that he would probably still win twenty games. Prophetically, Vida said, "I'll be lucky if I win ten." The holdout caused him to miss all of spring training and the first six weeks of the season; his first start didn't come until May 28th. A year earlier he was already 10-2, and now he was just taking the mound for his first start. To make matters worse, he had to complete two weeks of military duty in July as part of his obligation to the Reserves, and lost additional pitching time to a twisted, bruised left thigh and necessary dental work. All in all, it was a difficult season for Vida. He only started 23 games, and pitched just 151 innings, less than half his 1971 total. He finished the '72 season with a disappointing 6-10 record. Sportswriters were split on whether Vida's disappointing record in 1972 was the result of his holdout, which most blamed him for, or was a matter of the league catching up to the young pitcher. It was obvious that the negotiating process embittered Vida.

**The fact was, however, that the country kid from Mansfield, La., who
had been signed by Finley himself at the age of 18, was angry, hurt
and confused.**

**"I got it all out of my system," he said of his holdout. "Charlie Finley treated
me like a damn colored boy. He soured my stomach for baseball."**
Tim Horgan, Boston Herald, October 21, 1983

The only real bright spot for Vida in the '72 season was that the A's won the
Division, beat the Tigers in the American League playoffs, and won the World
Series, defeating the Cincinnati Reds in seven games. Even the successful post-
season had some controversy, however, because Vida was not used as a starter in
the playoffs and only as an emergency starter in the World Series. But he did pitch
well, especially in the playoffs when he was on the mound for the pennant clincher
saving the win for "Blue Moon" Odom with four innings of shutout ball. When
reflecting on the ups and down of his pitching success that year, Vida injected a bit
of his Southern ancestral humor. He said, "It's like my granddaddy used to say in
Louisiana: The sun doesn't shine on the same dog's ass every day."

**Vida had the kind of ability to dominate any particular game. Of
all the clutch performances by any of the A's players of that era, I
consider Vida's 4 inning relief appearance in the 5th game of the 72
playoffs to be the single most important reason for the team's run of
World Championships. Coming into a game of that magnitude, under
the extreme pressure, remains my favorite memory of a great pitcher
and an even greater friend.**
Ken Holtzman, teammate

During the 1972 World Series, Jackie Robinson was asked to throw out a
ceremonial first pitch. Vida got to meet Jackie that day, and it was an experience
he still remembers and cherishes:

**I got a chance to meet Jackie Robinson at the 1972 World Series, in
Cincinnati. He came in the locker room and for some strange reason,
to this day, I just said, "Hello Mr. Robinson. Nice to meet you sir." And
he had somebody with him, helping him get around, because he was
losing his eyesight. But I did not ask for his autograph. I didn't want
his autograph; he was bigger than life to me. He was bigger than life.
You know I heard this one story where the Dodgers were barnstorming
and Jackie went out in the field and this guy was heckling him, and I
don't know if this is true, but I'm just sharing with you what sounds
to me so typical of Jackie. So, he comes in, and this guy is calling him
all these terrible things. So, Jackie sticks his head out of the dugout,
says, "Sir, are you the man?" "Yeah, yeah, I am!" So he says, "Shut
up, sit down and act like one then."**

Jackie Robinson was the pioneer. That had to be the ultimate as far as knowing that you could kill him with words but some kind of a way he was able to maintain his character and credibility as a person. He was someone I definitely looked up to as an idol while growing up. My grandfather, like a lot of Afro-Americans of his age and era, were Dodger fans because of Jackie Robinson.
Vida Blue interview

While being interviewed that day, October 15, 1972, Jackie spoke about his disappointment that no black had yet been hired to manage a major league team, and how he'd "like to live to see a black manager." Unfortunately, for everyone, only days later, on October 24, 1972 Jackie Robinson died of a heart attack, never seeing his dream. That same year SPORT magazine named Jackie "The Man of 25 Years of Sports."

When all is said and done, as much as Robinson meant directly to his own people – as an example and inspiration and pioneer – he meant even more to the white society. He did more than any other single human being could do to focus their attention on the inequities of a system in which lily-white baseball was only one small symptom.
Leonard Koppett

Vida's detractors looked at his 1972 performance and claimed that 1971 was a fluke. Vida didn't believe that but he needed to prove to himself that he could come back and be a dominant pitcher again. There was plenty of proof in his performance in 1973.

That kind of cleared that cloud in my head and I just tried to go on with my career and enjoy baseball because I did enjoy it. I enjoyed the traveling, all the big cities and towns. Everybody had established personal relationships in a lot of towns. It was always fun to go to a certain city, to go to a certain restaurant, to go to someone's house or to certain sports bars as we know them now or go to a certain club. That was part of being a pro athlete. I enjoyed that. It was a high profile life and I wasn't going to let Finley ruin that. And I finally came to my senses of wanting to continue to enjoy my life and my career as a player and that's when I tried to put all that stuff aside and tried to focus on being a player.
Vida Blue interview

Vida's renewed focus resulted in his second twenty-win season in 1973. In fact, he won exactly 20 while losing 9. His innings pitched were back over 200; in fact, it began a streak of eight consecutive seasons in which he would pitch 200 or more innings. Despite his return to success on the mound, Vida still had trouble negotiating a contract and an acceptable salary with Finley. I think his experience following that wonderful 1971 season, when he couldn't get paid what he thought he was worth, soured the relationship between Vida and Finley forever. By the spring of 1974, Vida was so tired of negotiating with Finley that he declined arbitration and agreed upon a salary that was less than he wanted. He then announced that he was going to meet with the World Football League about renewing his dream of becoming a pro quarterback.

Even if I have a good year, it would be a hard decision for whether I would play another baseball season. I'm seriously thinking about the World Football League.
Vida Blue, quoted by Ron Bergman, The Sporting News, March 30, 1974

Vida went on and had a pretty good year in 1974 although he was not a twenty-game winner. He started 40 games, a career high, lowered his ERA from the year before to 3.25, and wound up with a 17-15 record. Blue felt that 1974, for him, was a good example of how a manager's decisions can affect a pitcher's chances to be a twenty-game winner. Blue and Hall of Fame teammate, Catfish Hunter, both expressed that A's manager, Alvin Dark, had a tendency to make pitching changes too quickly. When Vida was asked, in October of 1974, how a pitcher as good as he was could win only 17 games, he responded, "With you-know-who as manager, that looks like 34." (Ron Bergman, *The Sporting News*, October 2, 1974). Dark's early hook was even evident in Game 5 of the 1974 World Series, when he pulled Vida in the seventh inning with the score tied at 2-2, with two outs, a runner on first, and a 3-0 count on the batter. To that point, Vida had only yielded four hits to the Dodgers. In the bottom half of that inning Oakland scored and "Blue Moon" Odom was credited with the World Series victory that Vida never got.

When the Major League Baseball season started in 1975, a new milestone was reached in the integration of the game and the country. Jackie Robinson's elusive dream of seeing a black Major League manager was finally realized. In October 1974, Cleveland Indians' executive Ted Bonda named Frank Robinson as the player/manager of the Indians for the 1975 season. At the press conference announcing his hiring, Frank said, "If I had one wish in the world today, it would be that Jackie Robinson could be here to see this happen." In 1975, I had just started my broadcasting career with the Indians, and on Opening Day (April 8) I got the job of announcing the team on the field. There were over 56,000 fans in Municipal Stadium to see the Indians play the Yankees and to greet Frank Robinson as the new manager. I remember feeling the anticipation in the stands mount as I stood on the field; the air was electric in the stadium. After I announced all the players, I yelled out to the crowd, "Are you ready?" and they went wild in welcoming Frank. In a script delivered straight from the heart of a sentimental playwright, Frank, as the designated hitter, hit his 575th home run off Doc Medich in his first at-bat and the Indians defeated the Yankees 5-3. I was happy for Frank, for Jackie, and for baseball.

As it turns out, when the Athletics broke camp in 1975, Vida had not defected to the World Football League, but his star teammate, Catfish Hunter, a free agent, had left for the New York Yankees. When fellow Black Ace, Mike Norris, was lost to arm injury that spring, it was clear that the burden would fall on Vida and "Blue Moon" Odom to carry the pitching load. Blue rose to the occasion and had his quickest start since his whirlwind season in 1971. He was selected to start the All-Star Game again for the American League, and pitched two innings, yielding two runs on back-to-back homers by Steve Garvey and Jimmy Wynn, but he did not figure in the decision. Vida was an impressive 22-11 for the 1975 season with a stingy 3.01 ERA, and was named on a few Cy Young Award ballots.

But not all was positive for Vida in 1975. Shortly before the All-Star break, Reggie Jackson received a piece of mail which contained a threat to kill him if he played in the weekend series against the Kansas City Royals. The same letter threatened to assassinate Vida if he pitched any of the three games against the Royals. (Kansas City and Oakland were really the only two teams fighting for the Western Division championship in 1975, and Oakland eventually won.) The FBI was made aware of the death threats, and although Charlie Finley told the players they could sit out the series, both Jackson and Blue chose to play. Jackson went 6 for 18 over the weekend with two doubles, a home run and four runs batted in. Blue performed equally well under the circumstances. He pitched into the ninth inning in his only start in that series and left the game with a lead, which the bullpen blew. But the A's came back to win the game in the 12th. Unfortunately, these types of threats were not uncommon.

Vida Blue had the most explosive fastball I ever saw in my life. I actually saw him pitch one day and Gene Tenace had to reach out – it was a right handed hitter, if it had been a left handed hitter it would have put a hole in his head. He actually had to leap at the ball. You're a catcher. The ball came in with unbelievable velocity, man. I've never seen anybody like that. Vida was the most powerful lefthanded pitcher I ever saw. It was the most explosive fastball I've ever seen. He had no breaking ball and he could throw two pitches – one pitch, two different ways. That fastball I told you about, a two seam fastball, and a four seam fastball. The four seam went straight up and the two seam went boom. When he really wanted to control it, like when he got behind in the count, 2 and 0, he'd throw that four seam, POW, right down the corner.
Mike Norris interview

For the three year period, 1973 through 1975, Vida was a 59-35, and the Athletics were also enjoying a very successful run. The A's won the American League Western Division for five consecutive years from 1971 through 1975, and won three consecutive World Series from 1972 through 1974. Despite that success, contract negotiations and relations between Finley and his players, already turbulent during the early 1970s, would reach unprecedented levels. In 1976, it became common for players to play well into the season without having a signed contract, and Oakland was one of the teams with the most unsigned players. By the end of May, seven A's were still unsigned, including Vida, Rollie Fingers and Joe Rudi. Two weeks later, on June 15, 1976, Finley tried to trade those three stars by selling them, fearing that he would lose them as free agents at the end of the season since they were unsigned. (At that time, the compensation for free agents had not yet been agreed to.) Finley sold Vida to the New York Yankees for $1.5 million and sold Rudi and Fingers to the Boston Red Sox for $1 million each.

At first the media thought that Vida would be happy to have been free of Finley, but there was a twist to this story. Just hours before the "sale," Finley spoke with Vida about rumors that he was going to be traded. Although Blue was not fond of his relationship with Finley, he liked the Bay area and his teammates and wanted to remain an Athletic. Finley promised Vida he would never be traded and they agreed upon a three-year contract for $500,000. Hours later, Finley delivered Blue to the Yankees, signed for three years. Blue felt betrayed and angry, and once again unhappy with his owner.

When Charlie Finley had his heart operation it took eight hours. Seven just to find his heart.
Oakland A's pitcher Steve McCatty, 1981

Just before Vida was to start his first game for the Yankees in Chicago against the White Sox, Commissioner Bowie Kuhn nullified the sale of the players. He said he was acting under the authority he received under Article I, Section 4 of the Major League Agreement, written in 1921, that allowed him to "pursue appropriate remedies" against parties taking actions not in "the best interests of baseball." Kuhn ordered all three players to return to Oakland, ruling that they were eligible to play for the A's. However, Finley, trying to line up his lawsuit against Kuhn and Major League Baseball, instructed A's manager, Chuck Tanner, not to play any of them. Hell, he didn't even want them in the clubhouse. So three players who were instrumental in Oakland's string of championship seasons were now left with no place to play. While he waited for Finley and Kuhn, or other powers, to decide his fate, Blue said:

Maybe if the Yankees and A's get in the playoffs, I could pitch for both sides. I'd be tired, but that might end all this crap.
All I want to do is play baseball for the next three years. If it's with Oakland, then I'd like for it to be there. If it's with New York, I'd like to enjoy New York.
Ron Bergman, The Sporting News, July 17, 1976

On June 25th, Commissioner Kuhn ordered Finley to play the three players, but Finley refused. It wasn't until the A's players voted on June 27, to strike unless their teammates were allowed to play that Finley relented. When Tanner read the lineup with Rudi's name in it, the players erupted in cheers. They knew that Vida, Fingers and Rudi were vital to any chance they had to win the Western Division.

All in all, Vida didn't pitch for over three weeks as a result of these events, from June 11 to July 2, missing at least four starts. This is that element of luck that I referred to earlier as a component of a pitcher's ability to win twenty games in a season. Vida was pitching exceptionally well in 1976. His ERA was a career low 2.35 (second best in the league behind Mark Fidrych's 2.34). He only gave up 9 home runs all season and, in one stretch, he pitched over 142 innings without giving up a home run. For the second year in a row he finished sixth in the Cy Young Award voting. He ended the season with an 18-13 record. In addition to the three week forced "vacation," other things didn't fall Blue's way in 1976, costing him at least two victories that would have given him another twenty-win season:

With any reasonable luck at all, Blue would have been on his way to a fourth 20-win season. But his luck had been nearly all bad – bloop hits, umpires' calls not going his way, lack of support, relievers not doing their jobs.
Ron Bergman, The Sporting News, October 2, 1976

But Vida echoed Fergie's sentiments that it was all part of the game:
"Sure, I get depressed," Blue admitted. "It lasts for a couple of days. Then I start thinking as long as I know I've given my best, that's all I can do about it. I just wish the results had been better."
Ron Bergman, The Sporting News, October 2, 1976

During the off-season, the Athletics failed to sign any of their six free agents. As a sign of the level of labor unrest in the Major Leagues, especially in Oakland under Charlie Finley, when the 1977 season started, Vida was the only player remaining on their roster from the championship teams earlier in the decade. Vida was fed up with Finley and threatened to sue him for inducing him to sign the three year contract under false pretenses. In April 1977, Vida was traded again, this time to the Texas Rangers for six players and $2.5 million, but again Bowie Kuhn vetoed the trade. By June of that year, Vida made good on his threat and filed a suit against Finley seeking $1.5 million in damages and the nullification of his three-year contract. On the field, Vida may have had a case for a lawsuit against his teammates for lack of support. Vida was 14-19, but in his 19 defeats the A's had scored only 26 runs; less than a run and a half per game. It was so bad that he had five complete-game losses in which the A's scored a total of only four runs.

In December 1977, Finley again tried to trade Vida, this time to the Cincinnati Reds for Dave Revering and $1 million. Again the Commissioner said the transaction raised "substantial questions," and decided to look into it. When he did, this transaction was also voided and Vida remained with Oakland once again. Kuhn issued a fifteen-page decision, stating that he would routinely review any trade which included $400,000 or more in cash. (As a sign of how finances have changed in baseball, $400,000 is now the Major League minimum salary, and trades between teams include millions in cash.) Finally, in March 1978, Finley came up with a trade of Vida that passed muster with Bowie Kuhn. In the first trade ever between the Giants and A's, Vida was sent across the bay to San Francisco for seven players and $395,000.

I was glad to be out of there. "Free at last, free at last," I remember using that quote to somebody. Luckily, I stayed in the immediate bay area with the Giants. It was a big transition coming from the American League to the National League. I was on the up part of my career, probably had leveled off, but I was still feeling good about myself, and knowing that I belonged in the big leagues, and the change of leagues was a challenge for me, "Okay, let's go here."

My '78 team was a great young team. We had Jack Clark, Terry Whitfield, Larry Hearndon in the outfield, three solid outfielders. Jack Clark had bat speed faster than anybody I had ever seen swing the bat. He could hit a baseball, you had to stare and not blink. He could hit a baseball so hard.

And we had a great pitching staff. We had John Montefusco, a young kid named Bob Knepper, a guy named Jim Barr. We had a solid ball team. We had two lefties, two righties, a long left, a long right, short left, short right. We had Randy Moffitt who was the premiere stopper in the major leagues at that time. We had Gary Lavelle, our short lefty. He was our Sparky Lyle in the National League, when we got that lefty-lefty, righty-righty match up late in the ballgame.
Vida Blue interview

Finally free from dealing with Charlie Finley, Vida flourished in San Francisco. He was selected as the National League Pitcher of the Month for June. He was 12 and 4 by the All-Star break in 1978, and credited by many for the Giants' resurgence. The Giants, at the break, were 52-34 and in first place in the National League West. A year earlier, they were 38-48 and trailing the Dodgers by 19 games. The bitterness that had lingered in Vida over his treatment by Finley was gone, and his love for the game resurrected.

The addition of Blue, a 20-game winner across the bay in Oakland, not only added stability, it added confidence. And laughter.
"Vida's a different man now," said a good friend. "He seems so much happier since he's out from Charlie Finley. He always had a devilish sense of humor, but you see it more now."
What you also see, besides the wins next to Vida's name in the stat

sheets, is a guy standing in front of the Giants' home dugout leading the spectators in cheers or his teammates in acceptance.

"He's been terrific," said [John] Montefusco, always a jovial sort himself. "He's openly yelling for everyone. He's got everybody excited. He's always talking about a championship. He's making everyone have a good time."
Art Spander, The Sporting News, June 3, 1978

He's been an inspirational force on this club. Not only has he been our stopper, he's also brought unity to this team. When the trade was made, I knew we were getting a great pitcher, but I had no idea how much he'd contribute when he wasn't throwing.
Joe Altobelli, Giants' Manager, quoted by Nick Peters, The Sporting News, August 26, 1978

Vida finished the season 18-10, again coming so close to winning twenty. In a vote of the players conducted by *The Sporting News*, he was selected as the 1978 National League Pitcher of the Year, over twenty-game winners Gaylord Perry and Ross Grimsley. He finished third in the Cy Young voting, behind Perry and Burt Hooton. In addition to flourishing emotionally and on the field, Vida also flourished financially. In his first non-Finley contract, Vida secured a six-year deal with the Giants that earned him an average annual salary of $700,000. It made him the highest paid pitcher in the Major Leagues.

Vida had a sub-standard 14-14 season with the Giants in 1979, but then rebounded to have All-Star seasons again in 1980 and in the strike-shortened 1981 season. In 1981, Vida had the opportunity to play for Frank Robinson, who was now managing the Giants. Vida was named to the National League All-Star team in 1981. He appeared in relief and pitched a scoreless seventh inning. He received credit for the win when the National League scored in the top of the eighth inning, and became the only pitcher to ever earn a decision for both leagues in the All-Star Game, winning both of them.

In 1982, the Giants completely overhauled their pitching staff. They traded all of their starters, including a deal that sent Vida to the Kansas City Royals together with pitcher, Bob Tufts. Vida had a winning season, 13-12, and the Royals came close to winning the division, falling just three games short of the California Angels. In 1983, Vida was released by the Royals, and was ultimately suspended from baseball for the entire 1984 season, based on a drug conviction.

When I went to Kansas City, that's just something I fell into, there was no rhyme or reason as to why I chose to do what I did. No one made me do it. It was my own bad judgment. And the good part about that, I lived through it. I survived it and I can use that when I go and talk to kids about lifestyle choices. And I talk about me and the reference that I make is, "Hey, man, I won the Cy Young Award and the MVP, and I went to jail for ninety days, a federal penitentiary, for using drugs. What was I thinking? I brought shame and embarrassment to myself, to my family, to my four daughters, to my mother, to my father, whether he's in heaven or hell. I brought shame to my family. And I hope that they will forgive me and I'm sure that they will, and I know that they have. But, the one thing that eats at me every day is, I have never forgiven myself, not fully, not totally, not unconditionally, because no one made me do this." That was the thing to do and not to throw stones, I wasn't the only one doing it. I'm not speaking about just that team. There were a ton of baseball players doing that and other things we shouldn't have been doing, and I just happened to be the one that got caught. But, it's a positive source of reference for me now to think about.

I'm not embarrassed to talk about some of this stuff. It's embarrassing, but I'm not embarrassed to talk about it, because I want the kids to know the positive messages that, yes, I used my worst judgment, it did happen to me but that does not make me a bad person. That does not bring my world to an end. It does not mean I should not continue school, get my GED, or go to college, or become whatever it is that my dream is that I set out to do. It doesn't mean that I have to join a gang, but it means that I can walk away from a gang. It means that I've learned life and love, and I'm just going to try to apply it to my everyday life everyday. You can use it as a powerful message to teach the kids to make good decisions. You went through it, you can survive it. It's not the end of the world if that happens to you.

Actually, having survived and come back from the experience, I learned from it. I learned I am somebody, something more than just a left-handed pitcher. I also learned God loves me.
Vida Blue interview

In 1985, Vida was given a chance by the San Francisco Giants to come back and prove himself. He used that opportunity to prove to Major League Baseball that he was still capable of pitching in the big leagues. At that time, the number of games he might win in a season was not important to him; he was just trying to make the club and survive an entire season, back on a Major League roster. He had some career goals, including 200 wins and 2,000 strikeouts, and he was confident they would come if he could make his comeback stick. And he did. Vida remained on the Giants' Major League roster for all of 1985, finishing the season with an 8-8 record. No other Giant starting pitcher had more victories, and Vida was the only starter that did not have a losing record. The other five starters had a combined record of 32-61. On June 20, 1985, Vida recorded his 2,000th career strikeout against the Astros' Jim Pankovits. Vida also spent the whole '86 season with the Giants, and on April 20, 1986, he threw five shutout innings against San Diego for this 200th victory. After being released by the Giants at the end of the 1986 season, Vida tried to come back with the Athletics in 1987, but retired before the season began.

His final regular season record was 209-161, good enough for 70th all time on the career victory list. He also had 2,175 career strikeouts.

Since 1994, Vida has worked for the San Francisco Giants, serving as the Commissioner of Junior Giants Baseball. More than 250 baseball programs from over 50 cities in northern California participate in the seventeen teams that are included in the program. The Giants' Community Fund provides the equipment and uniforms for the teams, and Vida coordinates all of the life skills programs provided to the children.

As testimony to Vida's enduring appeal and legend, in 2001, keyboardist Page McConnell, who achieved his fame as part of the musical group *Phish,* formed a new trio along with bassist Oteil Burbridge and drummer Russell Batiste and named the group, *VIDA BLUE.* Vida's name was used in the first lines of the band's song, *Electra Glide,* and in June 2004, Vida appeared on stage with the band at San Francisco's legendary Fillmore. It was a combination of music and baseball cultures that did my heart good.

CHAPTER 25

JAMES RODNEY RICHARD
J.R.
King Richard

Born March 7, 1950, in Vienna, Louisiana
Teams: Houston Astros
Twenty-Win Season: 1976
National League All Star 1980

He had the greatest stuff I have ever seen and it still gives me goosebumps to think of what he might have become.
Joe Morgan, Hall of Famer (astrosdaily.com)

J.R. Richard was the most overpowering pitcher. J.R. was the man.
Bruce Froemming, Sport Magazine, June 1993

J.R. is my home boy. He and I are the only two Black Aces with 300 strikeouts in a season. I think he did it twice. But that big old frame itself was intimidating enough for him to be whatever he wanted to be, not only a Black Ace. He's still a big kid at heart.
Vida Blue interview

In one game he threw as hard as anyone I had ever seen. It was scary.
Bill Mazeroski, Hall of Famer

It's a real tragedy, the effect it [the stroke] had on J.R. I'm thoroughly convinced he was destined to be a Hall of Famer. He was still in his prime. It was just tragic.
Tal Smith, Astro General Manager, 1980, quoted in St. Louis Post-Dispatch, July 28, 1996

A few months after Charlie Finley released me, in December of 1971, he called to see if I would sign a minor league contract with the A's. He wanted to keep me in the pack, so to speak, hoping to be able to trade me to a team in need of a relief pitcher, in exchange for some young talent. I was older and a little bit wiser about the workings of the business of baseball by then, so I told him I was making $38,000 with the Indians, although I wasn't, and Charlie offered me $40,000. My gambit worked. I took the $40,000 and headed back to the minor leagues, as much to work with the A's young pitchers and stay visible as trade bait as to actually pitch. Charlie placed me with the Iowa Oaks, in the Eastern Division of the American Association, as a pitcher-coach. I remember feeling quite old when the papers reported that one of my first saves was for Steve Lawson, a 21-year-old rookie who was 16 years younger than me.

Another thing that stands out in my memory from my time with the Oaks is the sight of two exciting prospects playing for Oklahoma City, which was an Astros' farm club at that time. They were catcher, Cliff Johnson, and pitcher, James Rodney Richard. As soon as I saw these guys, I called up the parent team and told them I didn't know how many options were left on Johnson but they should try to get him. I also told them about Richard, but knew that there was no way the Astros would part with a pitcher of his size, strength, and talent.

James Rodney Richard, one of the few men I know big enough to have three first names, was born in Ruston, Louisiana, which is about fifty miles northeast of Vida's hometown of Mansfield, as the crow flies, but you really need to drive through Shreveport (where Dave Hoskins was born), making the distance longer.

The way I was reared in the country, in a family of eight, has given me an appreciation of what it takes to succeed. I played football on Friday night, then got up early Saturday morning and went to work, no matter how sore I was. My father had a little sawmill at home and we children would get our lessons done, then help him make broom handles.

I didn't have it bad growing up. I didn't always have to work; we had some independence. And I was never confronted with the black situation because when you have exceptional ability, you aren't judged by the pigmentation of your skin but by your talent. It's the same if you're rich: people don't look at you as a black guy, but instead they look at your pocketbook, your bank account. As a kid, I was considered an exception, sort of a phenom because I could do things no other kid in the neighborhood did. Nobody said, "J.R. is a black man." They said, "J.R. is a great ballplayer."

But it was hard sometimes developing that ability. For one thing, we didn't have any baseballs. We'd get some pieces of material my mother used to make quilts with, wrap them with tape and play outside the house. Or we'd throw old tennis balls. I used to throw rocks a lot, too. My neighbor, Milton Candle, probably was the first man ever to tell me I could one day become a star. I'd throw rocks at birds in his yard and he'd say, "Son, I've never seen anybody with an arm like yours."
J.R. Richard

The Astros selected Richard right out of Lincoln High School, in Ruston, in the June 1969 draft. His high school baseball statistics were quite unbelievable, especially when you consider that Richard hadn't tried playing baseball until he was 15 years old. Richard proudly recalls that he did not lose a game while pitching for Lincoln High. In fact, he says he did not allow an earned run in high school.

In his senior year alone he struck out 89 batters in 43 innings, and averaged more than 14.5 strikeouts in a seven inning game. Richard played the outfield when not pitching, so they could keep his potent bat in the lineup. During his senior year he batted .378 and belted six home runs. He also tells of the time when he hit four consecutive home runs while pitching a 48-0 shutout.

My thing was to be the very best in the world, to be second to none. That's the way I practiced and the way I played. I gave my best to be that, and it gave back to me.
J.R. Richard (January 31, 2001 interview with Ray Kerby)

As good as Richard was at baseball in high school, he was even more dominant in basketball and football. He was a high school All-American in basketball, and averaged 35 points and 22 rebounds per game as a senior. He claims he had at least 150 college scholarship offers. He also had several big name schools, including Notre Dame, University of Houston, and LSU, chasing him down to accept their scholarship offers. He played all of the line positions as well as quarterback, but was most proficient as a punter. Richard recalls averaging 67.5 yards a kick!

When the 1969 summer draft came around, the Astros knew they had to act quickly and decisively if they wanted Richard. And that is exactly what they did, using their first pick, which was the second pick overall to select him. Richard was then faced with the same problem Vida faced a year earlier … he had to decide whether to pursue a career in football through college or enter the world of professional baseball. We'll never know if the 6' 8", 250 pound Richard would have been like William (The Refrigerator) Perry or not because he chose baseball, immediately signing with the Astros, but he sure had all the tools.

At that particular time I talked to a lot of my coaches and we decided that baseball would be the way to go. Being a middle-class black in those days, we didn't have that much money and the money looked real well at that time, and it was one of the things that helped me make that decision. I have no ill regrets; I'm glad I chose baseball, but I think I could have been one of the first ballplayers to play two sports if I had really went that route because my abilities spoke for themselves. I felt very comfortable with basketball and baseball.
J.R. Richard (Kerby interview)

Richard quickly invested his signing bonus by purchasing 45 acres on the outskirts of Ruston, with hopes of someday developing the land. After signing with the Astros, he spent the remainder of the summer of 1969 with the Covington Astros (Kentucky) in the Appalachian League, where he went 5-4, and struck out 71 batters in 56 innings. Richard's first full season in professional baseball was with the Cocoa Astros, which is the Astros' Class A affiliate in the Florida State League. Even that early in his baseball career, Richard was plagued with injuries, including a deep gash on his pitching hand suffered when he instinctively fielded a line drive bare-handed. While no one could know or have expected that injury would eventually be such a part of Richard's story, they certainly had reason to hope that his first season's performance was a portent of the kind of success he would enjoy as he advanced to higher levels in his baseball career. He struck out 138 batters and only allowed 67 hits in 109 innings of work, and on August 28, 1970, he threw a no-hitter against Daytona Beach, striking out ten batters, and walking only one, winning 2-0. He finished the year with a 2.39 ERA but only a 4-11 record, which I think was more a reflection of the poor team he played on, than of his talent and performance. That season Cocoa finished the season 42 games out of first place that year, going only 43 and 84.

Richard was one of five non-roster players among the twenty-one pitchers invited to the Astros' major league training camp in 1971, as the team tried to improve on its fourth place finish. The team felt Richard's control still needed work and they stayed with a staff that was anchored by Don Wilson, and included Jack Billingham, Wade Blasingame, Larry Dierker, and Ken Forsch. Richard was sent back to the minors, but skipped Class AA, and instead was assigned to Class AAA Oklahoma City of the American Association. He quickly became a pitching force to be reckoned with and captured the attention of the managers, coaches and scouts in the league.

Boy, that's some kind of smoke!
Bob Thurman, Supercout, Kansas City Royals

[Richard's] one of the best prospects in our league, maybe the best.
Jim Williams, Manager, Oklahoma City 89ers

He's the hardest throwing big man I've ever seen.
Del Crandall, Manager, Evansville Triplets

Richard was one of the leading vote-getters in the American Association All-Star Team selection, and was chosen to start the All-Star game. However, his arm stiffened after warming up and he was unable to pitch. That ailment kept Richard sidelined for more than a week. However, it did not stop him from succeeding Vida Blue as the American Association's strikeout leader. On his way to recording 203 strikeouts, he struck out as many as 17 batters in one game. He also led the league in ERA (2.45), and had a 12-7 record.

When the minor league season ended the Astros called Richard up to the majors. On September 5, 1971, he made his Major League debut, starting the second game of a doubleheader against the San Francisco Giants. His introduction to the game started out roughly, when the Giants scored two runs on three hits. With the "butterflies" out of the way, Richard settled down to business and proceeded to strike out fifteen Giants, including striking out the side in the ninth inning, to tie a Major League record for most strikeouts by a pitcher in his first game. Karl Spooner of the Dodgers had accomplished the same feat in 1954, also against the Giants.

In the off-season between 1971 and 1972, the Astros traded away four of their young pitching prospects, Scipio Spinks, Lance Clemons, Bill Greif and Mark Schaeffer. They acquired Dave Roberts from San Diego for Greif, Schaeffer, and Derrel Thomas in December 1971, and just before Opening Day in '72, they acquired Jerry Reuss from St. Louis for Spinks and Clemons. Richard was basically the only young pitching prospect they kept. But, despite his success in his first month as a Major Leaguer, Richard wasn't needed in the starting rotation, with the addition of Reuss and Roberts, and the Astros sent him back to Oklahoma City. Richard continued to strike out batters there at a rate better than one per inning (169 strikeouts in 128 innings), and again had a winning record (10-8). At the end of the season he returned to the Astros and appeared in four games, getting only one start. Richard's manager with the Astros in 1972 was Leo Durocher, who came to the team after leaving the Chicago Cubs and Fergie Jenkins.

Richard split the 1973 season between Houston and its new Class AAA affiliate in the American Association, the Denver Bears. He actually pitched better at the Major League level than in the minors, winning six of eight decisions. However, his season was cut short, and winter ball prohibited, when he separated his shoulder as the result of a motorcycle accident on September 13, 1973.

The rehab necessitated by the shoulder separation had Richard back at Class AA Columbus, of the Southern League, when the 1974 season began, and took longer than expected. It wasn't until July that he was back in Class AAA at Denver. He showed his appreciation for "escaping" Class AA by hurling four consecutive shutouts. He was the only pitcher in the history of the Bears to pitch three consecutive shutouts, then broke his own record by hurling a fourth one, and no one since has matched his streak. In those four games he only allowed a total of 15 hits and struck out 26 batters. In one of those games, against Oklahoma City, his outfielders didn't have a putout. It was reminiscent of the days when Satchel would call in all his outfielders and would put on a show by striking out batters or retiring them on weak grounders to the infielders.

I remember that J.R. pitched in a twilight doubleheader one night, in AA ball in Birmingham, Alabama. One of the kids went to the plate already scared because of J.R.'s reputation and it was difficult to see because of the twilight. He said he never saw the three pitches that J.R. threw, but he heard all three of the pitches. He said he crapped in his pants on the last one because he said he never saw it. All of a sudden – POW – he heard the umpire say, "Strike three." He said to himself, that ball could have killed him because he never saw it. He just thought that was the most incredible thing. Wow, that must have been pretty scary. J.R. had a slider that was a piranha, zoom, zoom.
Mike Norris interview

J.R.'s work at AA ball earned his return to Houston on a permanent basis. When he got there his manager was Preston Gomez who had been helpful to fellow

Ace, Al Downing, when he was in the minors with Richmond. Richard wasn't overpowering when he first came back to Houston, and management didn't quite know what to make of his condition, although they hoped for the best.

> **Even though the shoulder injury was not like a sore arm it was basically the same thing because it hampered J.R.'s throwing. Obviously, he lost something last year. He never showed that real busting stuff he's noted for, except on one or two occasions. I think he's just like Don Wilson, Larry Dierker and all these guys who've had arm trouble from time to time. They don't have quite as much as before they got hurt, but they become better pitchers. This is an old story in baseball. The guy who hurts his arm becomes a better pitcher because he starts to work on other pitches rather than stick to the power stuff. I think this is what has happened to J.R. in a sense.**
> *John Mullen, General Manager, Houston Astros*

It was ironic that John Mullen would mention Don Wilson while speaking about Richard during the winter of 1974, for on January 5, 1975, Wilson, one month shy of his 30th birthday, died of carbon monoxide poisoning in the garage of his home, an apparent suicide. I find it kind of eerie that Wilson and Richard, who in essence replaced Wilson in the Astros' rotation, had many similarities in their lives and their careers:

- Both were born in Louisiana; Wilson being born in Monroe, approximately 30 miles east of Ruston;
- Both were signed right out of high school by the Astros, and neither played for any other Major League team;
- Both were tall and lanky, Richard (6'8") being taller than Wilson (6'3"), and Wilson being slimmer;
- Both were considered "flamethrowers" and strikeout pitchers, Richard striking out 15 in his Major League debut and Wilson tying a Major League record with 18 strikeouts in a game in 1968; and
- Both had remarkably similar career statistics, particularly in terms of their place in Astro history:

Category	Don Wilson	Team Rank	J.R. Richard	Team Rank
ERA	3.15	7th	3.15	7th
Wins	104	6th	107	4th
Hits per 9 innings	7.61	5th	6.88	2nd
Innings Pitched	1748.3	4th	1606	8th
Strikeouts	1283	6th	1493	2nd
Games Started	245	7th	221	8th
Complete Games	78	3rd	76	4th
Shutouts	20	4th	19	5th
Earned Runs	611	7th	562	8th

Richard had an impressive spring in 1975, and did indeed take Wilson's spot in the starting rotation. It was about this time that sportswriters started referring to Richard by his preferred nickname, J.R. It would be the first time he spent the entire season at the Major League level. He started 31 games, going the distance 7 times. He struck out 176 batters, fifth best total in the league. However, his ERA was 4.39, and the team's ERA was 4.09, which could explain why the team's record of 64-97 was the worst in the Astros' fourteen year history. Even though J.R. batted in thirteen runs, a club record for a pitcher, the team's hitting just wasn't strong enough to overcome the runs the pitchers were yielding. The team lost by two runs or less 54 times. More than one third of their games, an unusually high percentage, were decided by only one run, and the Astros lost 42 of those heartbreakers, winning only 16.

The following year J.R.'s control and ERA were much better, but the Astros still were not scoring runs. Typical of what was happening was a game in which J.R. pitched ten innings of shutout ball, but the Astros also failed to score during those ten innings, leaving him with a "no decision." By the middle of the 1976 season, J.R.'s ERA was 2.98, but he had lost eight of his last ten decisions and was 7-9. The coaching staff recognized that early in 1976, hitting, not pitching, was the problem for the Astros.

Throwing the ball is only one part of pitching and J.R. apparently always has been able to throw the ball. But he also has a great attitude and nobody works any harder. He's going to be a real good pitcher. No, take that back. He _is_ a good pitcher.
Mel Wright, Pitching Coach, Houston Astros

During the second half of the 1976 season, J.R. received much more offensive support from his teammates, especially Bob Watson, Cesar Cedeno, Jose Cruz, and Enos Cabell. J.R. proved his durability; he started 39 games, pitched 14 complete games, worked 291 innings, allowed only 221 hits, struck out 214 batters (second highest in the National League), and chalked up a 2.75 earned run average, all career records for him. He was 13-6 in his last 19 decisions, and won the last game of the year for his 20th victory, finishing the season 20-15. But a look at the records of the Astros starters that season will tell you that J.R. had more to do with his wins than the offense did. He was the only starting pitcher on the team that year with a winning record. The only other starter in double digit wins was Larry Dierker and he was 13-14.

J.R. was only the second Astro pitcher to win 20 games in a season, Dierker having won 20 in 1969. To put J.R.'s 1976 success in proper perspective, consider that in the 43 year history of the Astros' franchise only three of their pitchers ever won more than 20 games in a season: Joe Niekro won 21 in 1979, and Jose Lima won 21 and Mike Hampton won 22 in 1999 behind the offensive support supplied by Carl Everett, Jeff Bagwell and Craig Biggio.

Based on the strength of J.R.'s 1976 season, the Astros felt he had arrived as the new ace of their staff and they traded Dierker after the season for catcher, Joe

Ferguson, and outfield prospect, Bob Deverage. That left J.R. as the only probable starter on the staff with more than one year of experience. Joaquin Andujar, Dan Larson, Bo McLaughlin, Joe Sambito, and Mark Lemongello were all rookies in 1976, and Floyd Bannister had no major league experience. It was expected that Joe Niekro would be used in relief. As the 1977 season progressed, J.R. was the only Astro pitcher to take the ball every fifth day, and when it ended, he was the only one with more than 30 starts. After a while, the Astros put Niekro back in the rotation and he was effective at 13-8. But J.R. was clearly the dominant pitcher on the staff, just falling short of a second twenty-win season. He was 18-12, and was the only Astro starter with an ERA below 3.0 (2.97). He again threw 214 strikeouts, which was again good enough for second highest in the league. As more and more sportswriters reported on J.R.'s rise in the ranks of Major League pitchers the superlatives used to describe him were many and varied: "baseball's most dominant hurler," "virtually unhittable," "intimidating," "most feared pitcher in baseball," "overpowering," "feared across the National League," and "one of the best." They clearly indicated that J.R. was recognized as one of the best pitchers in the game.

J.R. was already 6' 8" tall when he signed with the Astros, but at that time he was a relatively skinny 220 pounds. As he matured into a man his body filled in and by 1978, at the age of 28, J.R. was weighing in at over 240 pounds. It was a frightening experience for a batter to face a pitcher of J.R.'s size who threw the ball as hard as he did. With his height and delivery, it felt like he was right on top of you when he released a pitch, and the ball was by you before you knew it. And like many flamethrowers before him, J.R. used a bit of purposeful wildness to discourage any batters who had any thought of digging in when facing him. He was just wild enough to make them think otherwise. Stories of J.R.'s accomplishments are Bunyanesque and confirm his strength (in one game he threw 182 pitches before the Astros could outscore the opposition to earn him a win) and his effective wildness (he once walked 11 men and won).

I've never taken batting practice against him [J.R. Richard], and I never will. I have a family to think of.
Bob Watson, teammate

He is so close to the plate when he finishes his windup that I'm thankful he didn't eat onions before the game.
Richie Hebner, New York Mets, 1978

J.R. wasn't getting it done with his fastball alone though. Many baseball people, including his manager, Bill Virdon, believed that J.R.'s slider, which he threw as fast as his fastball, was his best pitch. In fact, J.R.'s teammate, Nolan Ryan, in his book, *Kings of the Hill: An Irreverent Look at the Men on the Mound*, lists J.R. as Number One on his list of Top Ten Pitchers With the Nastiest Slider. (He listed Fergie as Number Two.)

In 1978, '79, and '80, J.R. cranked it up to another level. In 1978, J.R. surpassed his previous personal high of 214 strikeouts on August 6th and, when he was asked about the possibility of becoming the first right-handed pitcher in the history of the National League to reach 300 strikeouts, his response revealed how important his twenty-win season was to him: "It doesn't matter. I don't care if I only get 150 strikeouts in a season if I can win 20 games. We're looking for winners, not strikeout artists." (The Sporting News, August 26, 1978) But whether he was looking to do it or not, J.R. did indeed become the first right-handed pitcher in the National League to strike out more than 300 batters in a single season. He surpassed Tom Seaver's mark of 289 established in 1971, and led the league in strikeouts with 303. His 1978 record was 18-11 with a 3.11 ERA, 275 1/3 innings pitched and 16 complete games. Opposing batters only managed a paltry .196 batting average against him.

Over the three year period from 1976 through 1978, no righthander in the National League won any more games than J.R.'s 56. Despite his general success, his twenty-win season in 1976, and his record 303 strikeout performance of 1978, J.R. had never received more than a handful of Cy Young Award votes (in 1976 and 1978), and had never made it to the All-Star team. It may have been because J.R. was working under the same conditions as Fergie, on a team that did not receive national attention without being in a pennant race. But 1979 proved to be different as the Astros became a contender, and some overdue attention was finally shed on the phenomenal pitcher J.R. had turned out to be.

In 1979, J.R. broke his own strikeout record, whiffing 313 batters, and becoming the only National League pitcher other than Sandy Koufax to strike out 300 or more batters in two consecutive seasons. But strikeouts were only part of the story. He won 18 games for the third straight year (18-13), had a career high 19 complete games, pitched a career high 292.3 innings, brought his ERA down to 2.71, and only walked 98 batters. In the six-week period after the All-Star break as the pennant race started to heat up, J.R. completed a club-record nine straight games. In those contests he was 8-1, losing 1-0 on a four hitter. He pitched 40 consecutive innings without yielding an earned run, and in total only allowed four earned runs, and never more than one run, earned or unearned in any start. From July 24 to the end of the season, J.R. was scored upon in only 11 innings, and ended the season with a streak of 25 shutout innings!

I wouldn't say for sure it's the best because the year he won 20 games, he was nasty; the year he struck out 300 batters, he was nasty, and this year he is still nasty. Maybe people will realize now that J.R. is probably the best pitcher in baseball.
Enos Cabell, teammate

He's been exceptional. This is the best I've ever seen J.R. pitch over any period of time.
Bill Virdon, Manager

I just kept my goal in mind and kept on doing what I thought would get me to where I wanted to be: to be the best. I think one of the major things that changed was my control. My control became better. I wasn't walking as many guys, I was getting more guys out, and I was throwing more strikes on a consistent basis.
J.R. Richard, to Hollander

Unfortunately, J.R. he did not reach the twenty-win plateau again after 1976, but he did win eighteen games in each of his remaining full seasons (1977, 1978 and 1979). In fact, he might have won twenty again if not for his own wildness. He lost a game 1-0, in which the winning run reached first base on a strikeout and a wild pitch, and lost another 1-0 decision when he walked a batter and then made a wild throw to first on a pickoff attempt. As you have come to see, pitchers have lost the chance to win twenty games in a season many different ways and for many different reasons. What remains constant for every pitcher is that he has a chance to win twenty if he takes the ball every time it is his turn in the rotation, and he maintains a level of consistency. If he can accomplish that, then he also needs to be blessed with a team that can play defense, run the bases well, and has the ability to score at least one more run than he allows. In considering the statements of players about how good a pitcher J.R. was, consider the level of consistency he attained in the years from 1976 through 1979:

	W	L	GS	CG	SHO	IP	H	R	BB	SO	ERA
1976	20	15	39	14	3	291.0	221	89	151	214	2.75
1977	18	12	36	13	3	267.0	212	88	104	214	2.97
1978	18	11	36	16	3	275.3	192	95	141	303	3.11
1979	18	13	38	19	4	292.3	220	88	98	313	2.71

Over the course of that four-year period, the combined batting average of the league against J.R. was below .200. The Astros knew what they had in J.R. and sought to secure his services for years to come. They offered him a four-year contract worth $2.4 million, with incentives which could increase the amount to $3.2 million, and I am sure the Astros would have been thrilled to pay out those incentives if they could get four more years of pitching from J.R. just like the previous four. J.R. probably could have made more money by testing the free agent market, by chose to stay in Houston.

My wife, Carolyn, and I like Houston and wanted to stay there. My teammates had something to do with my decision. So did the fact that we won this season for the first time. [General Manager] Tal Smith

also had something to do with it. He sort of looked out for me and had faith in me back before I got to this position. And I didn't need more money. I was content with what the Astros offered.

J.R. Richard (The Sporting News, October 27, 1979)

A week later the Astros signed free agent Nolan Ryan to a three-year contract worth $4 million. Sportswriters and broadcasters in the Houston area were drooling at the thought of the Astros' rotation for 1980, which would feature the reigning strikeout king from the American League and National League, sandwiched around a knuckleball pitcher (Joe Niekro). When Willie Stargell heard that the Astros had acquired Ryan he called for Commissioner Kuhn to "tie up the deal for the next five years" until Stargell was out of baseball.

J.R. not only had concern and love for the Houston area, which had become his home, but was also aware of global conditions. Beginning in 1979, a period of civil unrest erupted in Cambodia that would last a decade. The situation manifested itself in widespread starvation and disease affecting the Cambodian people and became known as the Cambodian Crisis. In 1980, J.R. became one of the first professional athletes to lend his name and assistance to the cause. He joined with Dave Parker, Paul Molitor, Rod Carew, and Steve Garvey, to make appearances to raise funds for the National Cambodian Crisis Committee.

J.R. started 1980 at a pace even hotter than the way he finished 1979. In his first six games, only four righthanded batters managed a hit off of him. He won four of his first five starts, never yielding as many as five hits. Then in the middle of May he got knocked out of a game in the first inning, the first time that happened to him since 1971. After two more losses, J.R. reeled off five consecutive wins, (including three shutouts), and found himself in the middle of June with a 9-3 record and an ERA of 1.51. From that point things deteriorated for J.R. He failed to complete his next two starts. During a game in Chicago on June 17, J.R. began to feel a tiredness in his throwing arm. He said he felt like he had a "dead arm," and left the game in the fifth inning. Without knowing for sure, J.R. actually diagnosed his condition at the time:

I think it's been a nerve problem and maybe not enough blood was being pumped to my arm. It's sort of like an engine not getting enough gasoline. When that happens, the engine won't run.

The press, the television commentators, the fans, and even J.R.'s teammates began making intimations and accusations about J.R. Most thought J.R. was "jaking it," a baseball term for loafing while faking an injury. Some people were whispering rumors about drug use, and others were accusing J.R. of being jealous of the contract that Nolan Ryan had signed. In actuality, J.R. hadn't missed a start in over three years, and he had bypassed his opportunity to leave Houston for more money in the free agency market only several months earlier. Those things made the rumors and anonymous whisperings all the more hurtful to J.R.

You know what gets me, they talk about me faking! I'd pitched five years in a row without missing a start and they're talking about me faking.
J.R. Richard quoted by Hochman

He didn't pitch again until June 28, in Houston against the Reds. He lasted only 3 1/3 innings, giving up five runs, and left complaining of a "tired arm." The press continued to show no mercy, disregarding J.R.'s record of consistency and performance for the Astros over the previous several seasons.

James Rodney Richard's right arm got better Saturday night. It improved from 'dead' to 'tired.' If his convalescence continues at the current pace, his arm may be 'puny' by the next time he pitches.
Ed Fowler, Houston Chronicle

On July 3, 1980, J.R. worked six innings in Atlanta, giving up two runs on only three hits, before his arm tired. It was good enough to earn him a win, bringing his record to 10-4, and his ERA to 1.96. Although J.R. tired in this game, and had been leaving games earlier than usual throughout the first half of the '80 season, when he was pitching he was the sharpest and most controlled he had been in his whole career. He had 115 strikeouts in 110.3 innings of work, and opposing hitters were batting a measly .160 against J.R. in 1980. Until this game, he had gone 135.3 innings without giving up a home run, then he yielded one to Dale Murphy, and the very next hitter, Chris Chambliss, also homered.

Finally, J.R. was given some recognition for the fabulous job he had done on the mound. He was selected to be the starting pitcher for the National League in the 1980 All-Star Game in Los Angeles, and he still proudly wears a ring from that game. He pitched two strong innings, giving up one hit and striking out three batters.

I was the starting pitcher, and I struck out Reggie Jackson. Everybody said, `Man, he really *is* unbelievable!' That felt good.
J.R. Richard

He had no way of knowing at the time, but that would be J.R.'s last moment of pitching glory on a Major League mound. After the All-Star break, he skipped one turn in the rotation, and then took the mound on July 14 against Phil Niekro and the Atlanta Braves. Again he only managed to pitch 3 1/3 innings, and during that entire time he seemed like he was pitching in a fog. He moved very slowly, and without ease, and his pitches seemed to lumber to the plate. He was nauseous and complained his hands felt cold. He felt numbness in his neck. He was having trouble focusing on the signs from the catcher. Despite his obvious distress, J.R. was actually pitching very well. He had only allowed one hit, and in the second inning he struck out the side in order. Although he was pitching a shutout, Astro manager Bill Virdon had to remove J.R. from the game. The media continued to show no mercy, beginning with a column in the Houston Chronicle the very next day:

Phil Niekro doesn't have a dead arm. Or a tired arm. Or back stiffness. Or shoulder stiffness. Or a stomach ache.
Harry Shattuck, Houston Chronicle, July 15, 1980

In a column written right after that game, but which did not appear in *The Sporting News* until August 2, 1980, Bill Conlin, jumped on the bandwagon:

Now we have the J.R. Richard boondoggle, which peaked July 14 when Astros Manager Bill Virdon was forced to remove his 6-8 All-Star from a game while he happened to be pitching a shutout. Richard, eating a platter heaped with rice, gravy, fried chicken and meatballs, told the press an upset stomach forced him to leave the game. Richard also had been complaining about a "tired arm."
The upshot? J.R. was placed on the 21-day disabled list on July 16.
Hey, stick around, the Season of the Wimp is only half over.

In that same issue of The Sporting News, Ken Picking, took his shots at J.R. in a left-handed way by complimenting his opponent, Phil Niekro:

J.R. Richard may be big and bad, fast and frightening, but Houston's high-powered pitcher cannot come close to matching the courage and sheer determination of Atlanta's ageless and amazing Phil Niekro. Richard, facing the Braves, was firing the ball at 97 miles per hour, but then took an early exit with "nausea" from a pre-game hamburger. Meanwhile, 41-year-old Niekro pitched his heart out with a severely bruised right elbow and defeated the Astros, 2-0, on a two-hitter for his ninth complete game in 21 starts and 225th career victory.

The Astros placed J.R. on the disabled list on July 16, 1980, and had him examined by their team physician, Dr. Harold Brelsford, who proclaimed that the circulation in J.R.'s arm was excellent. He failed to X-ray J.R.'s arteries and simply prescribed rest. J.R. complied and went home to Louisiana for a few days. His old friend, former National League batting champ, Ralph Garr, who grew up four miles from J.R.'s home, had just been released by the California Angels in June. So the two buddies went fishing, which is one of J.R.'s favorite pastimes. Garr remembers that J.R. was very tense and depressed. He didn't want to discuss his pitching arm. He just wanted to fish and relax.

On July 23, 1980, J.R. entered Methodist Hospital in Houston for testing. It was discovered that he had a blockage in the arteries in his right shoulder area. The clot was preventing the flow of blood to his right arm, depriving it of the oxygen-rich blood that made it one of the post powerful pitching arms in the game. The discovery of that blockage made the reason for J.R.'s complaints of a "dead" or "tired" arm very clear. Now a decision had to be made as to how to deal with the blockage. Although it was J.R.'s arm, he was the property of the Houston Astros, and back then players had much less to say about their own medical treatment than they do today. The Astros were in the middle of a pennant race, and J.R. believes that team doctors looked at his condition with a view towards what was best for the team in the short run, not what was best for J.R. in the long run.

Dr. Brelsford, the team physician, and Dr. Charles McCollum agreed that not operating to remove the clot was the right decision, based on their opinion that the clot was not likely to move, and an operation would hamper J.R.'s ability to pitch. They felt that J.R.'s body had started to heal itself by creating a collateral path for his blood to circulate, and that as that collateral system improved, J.R. could continue to pitch, even though it might be for less innings at a time. He wouldn't be able to throw 182 pitches a game in this condition, but the decision was that five innings of J.R. at a time was better for the Astros' pennant chances than shutting him down for the season. That's the way players' lives were handled back then. Baseball first, players' personal concerns second.

The decision not to operate was thus made. J.R. was released from the hospital on July 26, 1980, with instructions to work out under close observation until the team decided it was time for him to come off the disabled list. After leaving the hospital, J.R. was anxious to get back to pitching. The Astros were on the road at that time, so J.R. enlisted the help of former Astro teammate, outfielder Wilbur Howard, who had retired after the '78 season, but was living in the area. They drove to the Astrodome where they worked out under the supervision of former Astro trainer, Jim Ewell. J.R. ran one lap and then threw for about twelve minutes, six softly and six harder, and feeling no pain he sat down to rest. He was sweating heavily, and his right arm was cold and clammy. J.R. figured that if he loosened up his arm with some long tosses, it would help his circulation. So he and Howard went back onto the field and started throwing the ball to each other from a distance of about one hundred feet. After about a half dozen tosses, J.R. wobbled to the ground, and then collapsed on his side. He was feeling dizzy, his head started to hurt, his ears were ringing, his speech was slurred, his fingernails were turning blue. There on the very field where he had struck fear into the hearts of opposing batters, J.R. was felled by a stroke.

By the time an ambulance got J.R. to Methodist Hospital, his heartbeat was irregular and his condition was not stable. He was rushed into intensive care, where doctors realized there was no pulse in his right carotid artery. The clot in J.R.'s artery had grown and was cutting off the blood supply to his arm and brain. His left arm and leg were partially paralyzed. More than his pitching career that was in jeopardy ... J.R. was fighting for his life. Now, without any other option, Dr. McCollum performed an eight-hour surgery on J.R. to remove one of the blood clots, the one that was blocking his carotid artery and his subclavian artery. For days after the surgery, J.R.'s family, Houston players and fans, and the media, held their collective breath. As they started to exhale, their words contained prayers for J.R.'s life, best wishes for his return to baseball, and contrite statements of regret for having doubted his complaints:

Guilt has seized a lot of people in this town who believed in the weeks before his problem was diagnosed ... that Richard was playing his own kind of game. Some wrote or said as much, and if anyone expressed any sympathy, or offered him the benefit of the doubt, no real notice was paid. ... Our concern and shock were mixed with embarrassment and we ought to admit it. ... We judge too fast and we correct ourselves too little and too late. We are too often critics and too seldom reporters.
Mickey Herskowitz, The Houston Post, August 3, 1980

Several members of the Houston media, who earlier had given fans the impression that James Rodney Richard had become a malingerer, apologized publicly after the extent of the pitcher's illness became known.
Bill Conlin, The Sporting News, August 16, 1980

It was not a shining hour for men of good will. The media, myself included, indicted Richard for everything from malingering to drug abuse.
Who shot up J.R.? That was the press box throwaway line. Nor did many of Richard's teammates cover themselves with glory. Few were willing to speak for the record, but there was no lack of "don't quote me, but ..." volunteers.
Bill Conlin, The Sporting News, August 23, 1980

J.R.'s recovery from the physical aspect of the stroke was slow and measured in very small steps, literally. When he was able to put weight on his left leg or begin to move his fingers it made news. While he fought to regain his strength and mobility, J.R. kept an eye on the team's pennant chances. Before a big series with the Pirates in late August, J.R. inspired his teammates by sending a written message, "I'll be pulling for you guys to make the World Series, even if I have to watch." As the days of summer passed, despite some progress in the movement of his arms and legs, it became apparent that J.R. would not pitch again in 1980. Anything beyond that remained to be seen. When J.R. was well enough to leave the hospital for a brief period, the first place he visited was the Astros' clubhouse, where he was warmly received by his teammates. On September 12, 1980, he was released from the hospital, although he still had a long road left on his recovery.

In late September, the Astros were clinging to a two game lead over the Los Angeles Dodgers and a two and a half game lead over the Cincinnati Reds when they opened a three game home series against the Reds. On September 27th, the capacity crowd almost blew the lid off the Astrodome when they saw J.R. walk to home plate with the lineup card. J.R. received a five-minute standing ovation from the fans, the umpires and the players from both teams. He then generated a second wave of applause when he told the crowd, "I'll be back for the World Series here." The Astros won the game, 2-0. The Dodgers managed to tie them at the conclusion of the regular season, and the Astros won the one-game playoff, gaining the right to play the Phillies in the National League Championship Series. J.R. attended the games in Houston and was well enough to throw out the ceremonial first pitch before one of the games. Unfortunately, the Astros didn't make it to the World Series, falling to the Phillies, who went on to become World Champs that year.

Meanwhile, it was determined that J.R. would have to undergo additional surgery. There was a second, larger blot clot still lurking in his right shoulder, and doctors feared that it too might move and cause a second stroke. On October 14, 1980, at San Francisco's California Medical Center, doctors operated on J.R. for 18 hours, and successfully removed the blockage. It took about a month before he was released from the hospital. After that, J.R. was determined to make it back to the pitcher's mound. He immediately began running and exercising his way back into condition, and by January 1981 he began throwing a baseball. While doctors had allowed J.R. to throw they were concerned about his ability to catch or to react to a thrown or batted baseball. The stroke had left him weak in his left side and affected his vision.

You can get a good idea of just how well J.R. was pitching at the time he suffered the stroke, when you look at the year-end statistics for the Astro pitchers for 1981. J.R. pitched less than half the number of games than the other three main starters, yet led the team in shutouts, and had almost as many strikeouts as Joe Niekro who pitched 142 more innings. He had as many complete games (4) as Nolan Ryan, who started 18 more games than he did. And his ERA just speaks for itself.

Player	G	ERA	W	L	GS	CG	SHO	IP	BB	HR	SO
J.R. Richard	17	1.90	10	4	17	4	4	113.7	40	2	119
Joe Niekro	37	3.55	20	12	36	11	2	256.0	79	12	127
Nolan Ryan	35	3.35	11	10	35	4	2	233.7	98	10	200
Ken Forsch	32	3.20	12	13	32	6	3	222.3	41	15	84
Vern Ruhle	28	2.37	12	4	22	6	2	159.3	29	7	55

By the end of February 1981, J.R. was able to once again put on an Astros uniform and join his teammates at spring training in Cocoa, Florida. His arm and legs seemed strong, as did his mind and spirit. He was throwing the ball well, mostly in the high 80s, and letting go of one every now and then that was in the 90 mph range.

I feel strong. ... I hope to pitch this spring, [but] I'm not worried about that. I've set no timetable for myself. I'll take things as they come. But there is no doubt in my mind that I will pitch again. ...
I have no fears. But I never have had any fears. There has never been any doubt in my mind that I would pitch again.
J.R. Richard to reporters at spring training, March 1981

J.R.'s coordination and reflexes were a concern to the team though. Two weeks into the training camp he was unable to hit a ball off a tee. But two weeks later his hard work and determination resulted in visible progress when he was able to actually take batting practice against Bill Virdon, and hit several pitches. By the time the season started, J.R. wasn't "game-ready" and the team made the decision to place him on the 60 day disabled list, but allowed him to travel with the team. He received a warm ovation wherever he went. By the end of May, J.R. was throwing his fastball at a consistent 90 miles an hour. At first it looked like baseball's labor unrest, which interrupted the 1981 season, would afford J.R. the opportunity to pitch in an exhibition game between the Astros and Rangers in preparation for the second half of the season. But Bill Virdon didn't think J.R. was "quite ready," and the shortened season then worked against J.R. actually pitching that year. Despite that assessment, he was making remarkable progress for a man who was near death a year earlier.

He's definitely improved since before the strike. He still gets tired. But he throws more strikes. His velocity is good until he tires. And he's catching the ball a lot better. His hand-eye coordination is improved.
Strech Suba, Astros' bullpen catcher

On September 1, 1981, the Astros added J.R. to the active roster. It was a baseball business move more than anything else because, the Astros ran the risk of losing J.R. as an unprotected player, if he was on the disabled list and not on the roster before November 20. Whatever the reason, it was great to see J.R. back in uniform and on the Houston bench, although he did not pitch at all that year. It's fair to say that J.R. was a little disappointed that the year passed without an opportunity to take the mound in a game, but the rest of the sports world was kind of amazed that he had recovered to the extent he had. Fourteen months after suffering a life-threatening stroke he was in uniform at the Major League level.

J.R. used the 1981 off-season to step up his conditioning program in an effort to get back into the Astros' pitching plans sooner rather than later. He was working out at a rehabilitation clinic in San Diego, California, under the guidance of Dock Ellis, who had retired after the 1979 season. Dock had been my teammate with the Pirates in 1970 and 1971. In '71, he came awfully close to becoming one of the Black Aces himself. He won 19 games and lost 9, posting 28 decisions while he only started 31 games. It was good enough for him to place fourth in the Cy Young Award voting that year for the National League.

When spring training of 1982 rolled around, J.R. was among the first Astro pitchers to report to camp, and unlike the prior year when he worked out individually, he was now working with the rest of the staff, and without the dark glasses he wore in 1981. Unfortunately, that didn't make the prospect of J.R. soon pitching again in the Major Leagues any brighter. A bout of tendonitis during spring training set him back about two weeks. He did take the mound in an intra-squad game, which was a major step considering where he came from, but management didn't feel his reflexes were sharp enough yet to have him pitch in major league competition. J.R. balked at returning to the minors and started the 1982 season in an extended spring training program, which afforded him a game-type environment. By the end of May, J.R. was showing improvement. In one appearance against Gulf Coast (Rookie) League players, he allowed only one earned run and five hits in five innings. It was his most successful pitching outing in two years.

When the extended spring training program ended, J.R. reluctantly agreed to return to the minor leagues and joined the Daytona Beach (Class A) team in the Florida State League. On June 28, 1982, J.R. pitched in a competitive game for the first time in two years. He faced the St. Petersburg Cardinals and lasted four innings and threw 64 pitches. He started off a little rocky, giving up three hits and three runs in the first inning, but then retired nine of the next eleven batters. Four days later J.R. threw 93 pitches and earned a win over Winter Haven. In six innings he allowed only four hits, walked four and struck out three.

By August 2, 1982, J.R. had a 3-1 record in Daytona Beach and was promoted to the Astros' Triple A affiliate in Tucson. On the day he took the mound for his first start there, he received three standing ovations. Again he survived a shaky first inning (38 pitches and three runs), to last into the sixth inning, leaving with a 4-3 lead. In September the Astros called J.R. up to the Major League level, but he did not get an opportunity to pitch there. The progress was slow but it did not shake J.R.'s belief in God or himself. "I'll be back," he said. "Just walking and talking is a miracle. I just believe that time will take care of itself." (The Sporting News, 10/11/82)

In the spring of 1983, J.R. was on the brink of making it all the way back to pitching in the Major Leagues again. He showed up for spring training in terrific shape, having worked all winter to improve his physical and mental condition. Astros manager Bob Lillis was impressed with how hard J.R. had worked to put himself in position to pitch again.

We plan to start him in some intrasquad games, and we plan to pitch him in exhibition games. He's worked hard and he deserves that chance. It may be unlikely he would start the season with us, but not impossible.
The Sporting News, March 7, 1983

J.R. attributed his improvement to "being reborn."

I always thought I was a Christian. But all I was was religious. Now, I've given my life completely to Christ. I can accept whatever he wants me to do and whatever happens in my career. I've only got three goals. One is to bring as many people as possible to Christ; two is to make the club, and three is to just maybe find time to catch me a twenty pounder this spring.
J.R. Richard, The Sporting News, March 7, 1983

Then J.R. suffered a major setback. It started with muscle fatigue in his left leg. Tests revealed that an arterial graft used to replace an artery during his previous surgery was blocked and was not providing enough blood to J.R.'s left leg. He had to undergo additional surgery to replace the graft. It was definitely a roadblock in J.R.'s valiant effort to negotiate a path back to the Major League pitcher's mound, but he would not be deterred. After the surgery, he fought his way back into shape and agreed to once again return to the minor leagues at Class A if that's what it took for him to find his way back to the mound at the Astrodome. During the 1983 season he showed signs of the "old J.R." pitching eight shutout innings in one outing, and also showed signs of an old J.R., giving up seven runs in another abbreviated outing.

When the 1983 season ended so did J.R.'s contract with the Astros. He became a free agent, but no team was willing to take a chance that he would ever make it back to the mound. The Astros signed J.R. to a minor league contract to play with Tucson in the Triple A League. Their general manager Al Rosen, an old Cleveland Indian teammate of mine, explained why:

> **J.R. wants one more chance, and we believe he deserves it. We feel we have a moral commitment to this man because of all the great service he gave to this organization and because what happened to J.R. was not his fault.**
> *The Sporting News, March 5, 1984*

While J.R. was determined to complete his professional comeback, he was at peace with himself as to the effort he had made regardless of the outcome:

> **I can accept whatever happens. I'm putting everything in God's hands. I know He will take care of me. God knows my needs more than I do. He may want me to win baseball games, or He may want me to help save souls by being a preacher or in some other field. He will let me know.**
> *The Sporting News, March 5, 1984*

Actually, it was Al Rosen who let him know. In early April 1984, the Astros made the decision to unconditionally release J.R., ending his major league baseball career. His determined effort to come back had him throwing the ball at 90 mph again, but the Astros were unconvinced that he could pitch at that speed with sustained control and they felt uncomfortable with his reflexes and reactions in the field. By July of that year, J.R. had moved on with his life. He took a job as a car salesman, and devoted himself to his work, his wife and five children, and his faith, which was a foundation for his life.

> **I call what happened to me the Big Trade. I traded baseball for a life of God. I'm going to write a book about this and call it "The Big**

Trade." I'm now very content because of the trade. My family and God have been the main reasons I've kept on going. I accept the fact that the stroke happened because it was an act of God. He wanted it that way.

J.R. Richard quoted by Peter Prisco, The Sporting News, July 30, 1984

If J.R.'s fall from pitching in the Major Leagues was seen as a tragedy, the whole drama was far from being played out. After leaving baseball he went on to work in several different jobs, and his attorneys successfully settled lawsuits filed by him against the doctors who had been treating him prior to his stroke. Then the bottom fell out again for J.R. and this time he lost much more than his place on the pitcher's mound. He lost hundreds of thousands of dollars in an oil-deal scam in California. He went to the Astros for help, looking for an advance payment of salary that had been deferred. The payments were advanced but it cost him a penalty of $300,000. He divorced his first wife, with whom he had five children, and that settlement cost him over $650,000. He had a barbecue business that failed in 1993, costing him his second wife, his car and his home in Houston.

Over the next year and a half J.R. became destitute. He sought the help of friends for an occasional meal and shower, but found himself homeless for weeks at a time, living under the Pierce Elevated Highway, under a bridge that spans Beachnut on State Highway 59 in southwest Houston. One person who helped J.R. at that time was Rev. Floyd Lewis of the Now Testament Church in South Houston. "Even though he was J.R. Richard, when you are down and out, as they say, it applies to everybody. A lot of homeless people don't want to face the responsibility of society. But J.R. refused to be there." (Ben Hochman, The Sporting News, August 5, 1999) Amazingly, J.R. never lost his faith in God:

I realize this: You don't live in homelessness. Homelessness lives in you. You can't sit there in your life and feel sorry about what has happened in your past. Quit dwelling on it. Quit looking for it, because it's gone. Look toward the future. God will help you get out of any situation you're in, but you have to be willing to get out of it yourself. God's not going to fly a turkey to your door. You got to get up and go the supermarket, and then God will help you. If you want to sit there in your feces and your urine, God's going to let you sit there. He said, "You make the first step. I'll help you make the rest of them." How many people out there are stepping toward God? They're stepping toward themselves, not God. And it makes a difference.

J.R. Richard (J.R. Richard: The Human Condition by Dave Hollander, Houston Press (Texas), Sept. 2, 2004)

I trusted the wrong people. I trusted them with my money. I trusted them with my future. I got screwed in business deals. I believed in

people to do what was morally right, and I got screwed. You get to a point in life where you decide to get up and live, or lay down and die. I think life is great. Dying was never an option for me.

J.R. Richard (J.R. Richard Still Throws It Straight, by Ken Hoffman, Houston Chronicle, August 25, 2003)

I always knew God was on my side. I just wasn't on my own side. I am very lucky. Anytime God has enough time to stop by me and put something on my lap and change me to make me a better individual, you have to consider yourself to be very fortunate. God allowed me to get through this to make me a better individual.

J.R. Richard (The Tragedy of J.R. Richard: A story seldom told, by Ben Hochman, The Sporting News, August 5, 1999)

In 1995, J.R. reached the age of 45, which allowed him to access his pension from Major League Baseball, and that was a lifesaver. The monthly income allowed him to rent an apartment and get back up on his feet, financially and literally. That July, the baseball fraternity welcomed J.R. back to the pitching mound, where he pitched two thirds of an inning for the National League in the Legends Game. It wasn't the return to the mound that J.R. had envisioned, but it was a moment I, for one, will never forget. To see that powerful man take the ball in his hand and prepare to pitch on a Major League mound, in uniform, knowing all that he had been through, sent tingles down my spine. That pitcher's mound was only 16 inches high, but it might as well have been ten feet high, for J.R. had actually gotten up from the depths twice, beating physical and financial tragedy.

J.R. does not dwell on his pitching past, nor does he harbor any anger about the stroke he suffered. He accepts it as God's will. But, when he is asked about comparisons to Nolan Ryan or his place in the galaxy of Major League pitchers, J.R. is not bashful or shy about his abilities. He matter-of-factly states he was stopped in the prime of his career and believes that, had he been physically able to complete his career, his statistics and accomplishments would place him as one of the great pitchers in the history of the game:

If I hadn't gotten sick, I could have broken all of Nolan Ryan's records.

J.R. Richard, quoted in Jet, February 13, 1995

I did things to exceed Gibson and I did things to exceed Koufax...I'm not trying to pat myself on the back, but I didn't talk too much, and I let the actions do most of my speaking.

J.R. Richard, quoted in The Sporting News, August 5, 1999

In July, 1993, in a *Sports Illustrated* feature entitled "*What Might Have Been...*", sportswriter Steve Rushin proposed that J.R. would have won the Cy

Young Award in 1980 and would have been elected to the Hall of Fame on the first ballot. In fact, the feature included an illustration of what J.R.'s plaque in Cooperstown would have looked like, complete with the following inscription:

JAMES RODNEY RICHARD
"J.R."
HOUSTON N.L. 1971 TO 1988
REGARDED AS ONE OF THE MOST
INTIMIDATING FIGURES EVER TO TAKE THE
MOUND. 6'8" RIGHTHANDER AVERAGED 261
STRIKEOUTS A SEASON FROM 1976 TO 1986.
PITCHED IN SIX ALL-STAR GAMES. ALL 256
CAREER VICTORIES CAME IN ASTRO UNIFORM

Of all the Black Aces, J.R. was the stingiest when it came to giving up hits. Over his career, he only allowed an average of 6.876 hits per nine innings pitched. That is good enough to place him fifth on the all-time list of pitchers who pitched a minimum of 1000 innings, facing at least 3000 batters and with at least 100 decisions. The only four pitchers above him are Nolan Ryan (6.555), Sandy Koufax (6.792), Pedro Martinez (6.844), and Sid Fernandez (6.851).

By 1999, Nolan Ryan had been retired from baseball for the necessary five-year period that allowed him to be considered for induction into the Hall of Fame. Not surprisingly, he was elected in his first year of eligibility, and was inducted that July. Several thousand miles away, J.R. was actively giving back to his community, working as a minister at the Now Testament Church, to help children at risk. He was helping the Church find people willing to provide financial backing for youth baseball programs with the thought that those kinds of programs would help keep kids from joining gangs.

A movie based on J.R.'s life story, entitled Resurrection, was completed in 2004, and J.R. has plans for a second movie in the works. He has placed his baseball career in proper perspective saying, "That time was that time, and I'm looking forward to my future. My past is my past." (USA Today, July 14, 2004) He starts every day by reading the Bible, and speaks to children at every opportunity, using baseball and his life experiences as a vehicle to teach life skills.

No one will ever be able to know exactly how great J.R. might have been as a pitcher. It certainly appeared that he was on his way to another twenty-win season, and possibly the Cy Young Award, when the stroke he suffered ended his baseball career in 1980. But his faith in God, his belief that God had another mission and purpose for him, and the humility he has shown in redirecting his life, have allowed him to show his greatness as a man. I am truly honored to be able to have J.R. as a fellow Black Ace.

CHAPTER 26

MICHAEL NORRIS
Mike
Black Cat

Born March 19, 1955, in San Francisco, California
Teams: Oakland Athletics
Twenty-Win Season: 1980
American League All-Star 1981
American League Gold Glove 1980, 1981

Michael Norris is without a doubt the finest pitcher in baseball. The spin on his screwball is so tight, its motion so fast, that he's for all intents a left-hander throwing right-handed. The Bretts, the Carews, are up there trying to hit his first and second pitch to save themselves the embarrassment of striking out. We all just sit around waiting for his no-hitter, wondering what 'God,' as we call him, will do tonight.
Matt Keough, quoted by Mark Goodman, Family Weekly, September 27, 1981

He was really a sight to behold in those days [1980]. It was like a celebration every time he pitched. He had that nasty screwball. He was one of those fluid athletes, one of those guys who seemed like he was born to do exactly what he was doing. You know who I thought of when Dwight Gooden had that big year with the Mets a few years ago? I thought of Mike Norris.
Steve McCatty, quoted by Phil Taylor, The National, June 15, 1990

The 1950s are often looked upon as the Golden Age of Major League Baseball. It's a period that I obviously look upon quite fondly because that is when I broke in and I will forever cherish my personal memories of that time. On a larger scale two movements in baseball were happening at the same time then: the continued integration of blacks and the shift of Major League Baseball west of the Mississippi River. Ironically, Mike Norris, the first of The Black Aces born after 1950, was born in San Francisco, California. To be more specific, Mike was born in the Fillmore District, which is also called the Western Addition.

Mike remembers how sports fit in to his growing up in the Fillmore projects, and his first baseball experiences:

I traveled between two sides of the District, which had a Hamilton recreation center and a Hayward recreation center. Being able to play at both of those facilities enhanced my athletic ability extremely. Also I think that helped my character as far as my strength of spirit as a human being, because growing up in a project which had two buildings twelve stories high, there's a lot of kids, and there's a lot of tough kids. So, I had to learn how to take care of myself which gave me some strength that I needed as far as having confidence. I had one little sister. I was the oldest out of the two of us. Being tough was something I had to do because I had to take care of her too when she grew up. So, you had to establish yourself out there sometime.

The large number of kids also gave us an abundance of kids with talent. I started playing sports at seven years old. My Mom let me go downstairs into the play yard finally and in the old days when they choose teams, you used to throw a bat to one another and the last person who held a spot on the bat had the first pick. So, there was two kids still left, and I was one of the last two, and the guy goes, "Ah, I'll take that little guy." So they let me play and I wound up getting three hits out of my first four at bats. So, the next time I went down to play, instead of being the last pick, I was around middle way up into the list. I had moved up in the pecking order, and then I ran into another major leaguer, Jerome White, who is now first base coach of the Minnesota Twins. Jerome was a year older than myself. So, he and I played a lot of ball growing up. There was a lot of competition there.

Then when I finally moved away from that set of projects, to another set of projects, in the Western Addition still, that led to me being on my first organized baseball team, sponsored by Macy's Department Store, when I was nine. The way the coach found out who was going to be a pitcher on the team, was by saying, "Everybody line up on the mound and I'm going to see who throws the hardest and straightest." So, that was me. At nine years old that's how my pitching career began.

Mike Norris interview

At that time, the Fillmore District, also known as the Mo, was close to ninety-nine percent black. As a child, Mike had little or no awareness of cultural diversity, and little or no idea of where his family fit in socially or economically. All of his friends, classmates and neighbors were black, and all lived in the projects. That changed for Mike when he started to go to high school, which required him to take three buses on his trip cross-town.

I wasn't really aware of different races or cultures until the Black Panther Party and the Muslims moved in on the street called Fillmore which was the main street that ran through the Western Addition.

And in order for us to get to school every morning, I would have to go past the Black Panthers and the Muslims, and then I had to go out to the Haight-Ashbury district, so I had to pass through the Muslims, the Hippies, and the Hare Krishnas. So, that's how I started understanding that there were different cultures and different people. But I didn't realize the difference in races until I started playing Joe DiMaggio Ball and I met a friend who is currently my lawyer right now, and he was white. His family invited me out to their home to eat one day. That was the first time I realized that people had garages and two-level homes and dining room tables. I was fourteen at that time. It was mind-blowing to me, man. It was like, WOW. And I came home and tried to explain that to my Mom. She was sitting there looking, and I could look and see she had this look of almost embarrassment, but not quite, but knowing that we didn't have that and couldn't provide that. But, that was my first taste of knowing that we were poor. I would be embarrassed for my friend's father to drop me off at home. Two blocks from where I lived there was a new community of homes, really nice, and I would tell him to drop me off up there and then I would walk back home. So, that was my first experience. That's a friendship that's stayed to this day. Now, the DiMaggio League, was pretty much an integrated league, and that's the first time I had an experience with that.

Mike Norris interview

Mike's first exposure to sports was through his Mom, and the sport she chose was baseball. She would sit Mike down to watch a Giants/Dodgers game on television, making sure he would watch the game in its entirety. From that experience, Mike learned the stances and postures of all the players, and would copy them. When he went out to the play yard of the projects to play Strike Out, (which was a one-on-one baseball game, with the strike zone drawn in chalk on the building wall), he imitated the batting style and pitching delivery of each player on the Giants, or whatever team he wanted to be that day. Mike credits that mimicking ability as key in his attaining consistency as a ballplayer.

As a kid growing up in the early 1960s, Mike was aware of black professional players, and living in San Francisco it is understandable that Mike grew up idolizing Willie Mays. I find it a little sad though that talking with Mike I learned he had no real awareness or understanding as a kid of the importance of the signing of Jackie Robinson or Larry Doby. He remembers hearing about it as part of Negro History Week, but it didn't have any real relevance for him. Later on, when Mike was about 17, he heard Jackie Robinson speak about his experiences in baseball, and he remembers being very impressed with how gracious Jackie was, how Jackie's character and dignity just jumped out at him.

I grew to understand why Jackie was the one chosen, because of his

articulateness and because of the fact he would have been able to take all the bullcrap that was given to him because of his race. I couldn't have done it.
Mike Norris interview

Early on Mike learned the value of playing baseball and the monetary value of being able to play baseball better than the other kids.

I was playing for a team sponsored by the local Chevy dealer, Ellis Brooks, and the coach, bless his soul, he's deceased, his name was Vincent Zuardo. I wasn't a bad kid so I don't want to say he kept me out of trouble, but he kept me focused on baseball, and what he would do for me was for every game I won he would give me $5; if I struck out more than ten batters, he would give me $5; if I got two hits, he would give me $5, and $5 for hitting a home run. So, I could make up to $20 playing a game, and my other friend, who is now my lawyer, his dad, during the summer league would pay me the same thing. So I'd be making $100 during the week sometimes. My mom couldn't afford to give me extra money for anything. She gave me my lunch money and stuff, and bed and clothing. It was pretty good money for 1970, and we weren't hanging out in the streets and we weren't about stealing and robbing like the rest of the kids were doing. That was great. I was actually a professional. I was in high school, thirteen years old.
Mike Norris interview

About that same time, Mike's personal horizons were becoming broader. As he started to play ball at higher levels, he became more aware of racial and social differences among people.

What would happen was because I was so good, I would get picked up by teams that made the playoffs. My team didn't make it, but for the playoffs and the championship, you can add two other players, and I would always be one of the ones picked up, because I could pitch. The teams that made it were generally the white teams. They were the better teams. And that's how I started to realize discipline, how white teams had a little more discipline than the blacks teams had. In other words, when it came down to pressure, the game's getting into the bottom of the sixth, you're losing 3 to 1, I noticed we would do the finger pointing – "It's your fault." "You should have caught this." – and then we had a communication breakdown. I didn't see that on white teams. I saw discipline and togetherness and cohesiveness. And so, once I got to play with them then that rubbed off on me. That enhanced my professional attitude. I had more of a professional attitude than the rest of the kids.
Mike Norris interview

Mike attended San Francisco's Polytechnic High School, a school with a reputation for a rough student body, where on any given day it was very likely that either a fight or a fire would break out. The school was closed before Mike's senior year for earthquake-proofing, and Mike attended Balboa High during his senior year. Like most of the other Black Aces, Mike had multi-dimensional athletic ability, and played baseball, football and basketball in high school. During the Major League Baseball players' strike that spring, Giants' pitching great, Juan Marichal, visited Mike's school, and was the person responsible for teaching Mike how to throw a screwball. Mike was an All-City pitcher in his junior year and upon graduation he was named as the San Francisco Public School Baseball Player of the Year. Several teams were scouting Mike as he played high school ball and local sandlot ball, including the Angels, Dodgers and Indians. One team that was also scouting him, although Mike wasn't aware of it, was the Oakland Athletics, who had assigned scout Cesar Cinabaldi to determine if Mike was worth the cost of a draft pick. The A's, having won the 1972 World Series, had the last pick in the first round of the draft. From the time the draft was started in 1965, until 1986, there were two amateur drafts held per year by Major League Baseball, one in July for graduating high school seniors and first eligible players, then again in January for players graduating mid year and for players previously drafted but unsigned. Since Mike, 17 years old, was graduating midyear, he was first eligible to be drafted in the January 1973 draft. Obviously, Cinabaldi and the A's thought highly of Mike, because they used their first pick to select him.

The A's initially offered Mike a signing bonus of $2,500. At the time he was being guided in his negotiations with the A's by Nate Oliver, a former second baseman with the Dodgers. Oliver felt that the offer was too low and advised Mike to go to college rather than accept the A's offer. Mike enrolled in City College, and within three months the A's got back to him with a new offer of $25,000, but it was more than the money that attracted Mike. This is how he recalls it:

This is how they got me. It's terrible what they did to a kid. They invited me over to the Coliseum, to throw, before they signed me. Now, here I am over in a big league ballpark. They put the big league uniform on me, and I'm throwing in the bullpen, and they get Reggie Jackson to come over and stand there and watch me throw. I'm so pumped up, I'm throwing the crap out of the ball. I could see Reggie winking at them, in admiration of me throwing. He was talking to Wes Stock and Alvin Dark. They're all there. So, after I get through throwing, they're all nodding their heads and I could see them talking. Then they tell me Charlie Finley is on the phone: "I've heard wonderful things about you and I guess I'm going to do this, I'm going to give you what you want. You wanted that $20,000, you got it, and I'm going to throw in an extra $5,000, so you can get clothes. Buy all the clothes you want." I was like, "Wow." So, anyway, that's how they got me.
Mike Norris Interview

It didn't take Mike very long to figure out what to do with his bonus money. He used it to buy a new house for his mother, Mrs. Lula Thomas, moving her out of the Fillmore District ghetto. Mike had basically been raised by his Mom, since his father fell victim to the high amount of violent crime in the Fillmore projects, having been knifed to death when Mike was only seven years old.

Rookies typically sign in June and begin their professional career in one of the short-season Rookie Leagues, but because Mike signed in May, his introduction to professional baseball was with the Burlington Bees (Class A) in the Midwest League, with the intention that he would be shipped to Oakland's Rookie League team in the Northwestern League when their season started. In his first appearance he struck out six of the seven batters he faced and Oakland ditched its original plans to send Mike down to the Rookie League. He remained in Burlington and had an excellent year, throwing a no-hitter and a one-hitter. The one-hitter came against the Quincy Cubs on July 16, 1973, when Mike struck out eighteen batters, including the last seven, and yielded his only hit in the seventh inning.

It just so happens that I was in Burlington when Mike arrived. I was there to perform with the Kittens at The Pizzazz Club. Rene Lachmann, the Burlington manager and an old friend, asked me to pitch batting practice to the team and I did for three days. The pitching coach for Burlington was Bill "Chief" Posedel, who was the pitching coach with Oakland at the major league level when Vida was there, and was also Sam Jones' pitching coach. Posedel saw Mike throw a screwball at about 90 mph, and just about went wild. He knew the pitch was unhittable, but didn't allow Mike to throw it in a game, for fear he would blow out his arm. He limited Mike to throwing a fastball, changeup and curve, but his fastball was so overwhelming at the time that he didn't need to throw the screwball.

Mike's stay in Burlington was the first time he spent any time away from the projects of San Francisco. He had a lot to learn about the country, starting with Midwest weather:

Burlington was a good experience, although I didn't relate too well to that Midwestern weather. The first time I heard thunder and lightning, I ran up under the bed. I never heard nothing like that in my life in San Francisco. I went up under the bed and Claudell Washington, who was my roommate, said "Get the hell up out of there, you little punk."
Mike Norris interview

During that off-season, Mike was recognized by the Northern California scouts as the Northern California Rookie of the Year for his season with the Bees. He was 8-4, with a 2.23 ERA and struck out 130 in 109 innings while only walking 40.

The next year, 1974, Mike advanced to Birmingham (Class AA) of the Southern League, which included franchises in Asheville, Columbus, Jacksonville, Knoxville, Montgomery, Orlando and Savannah. Mike had never been in the South before. His Mom, who was born in Louisiana, and who dated fellow Black Ace

Earl Wilson as a teenager, remembered what it was like and tried to counsel Mike as to what to expect.

> **My mother told me, "Shut your mouth. Go down there and just do your job." But you know, you're 18 years old, you think, that ain't going to happen to me. They don't do that stuff anymore.**
> *Mike Norris interview*

It didn't take too long for Mike to realize that his Mom knew what she was talking about. Race relations had advanced since she was in Louisiana, but in baby steps not strides.

> **The first night we got in, Bob Lacey and I were sitting in a restaurant called Googy's. We were so happy. I don't know, maybe we had a few too many beers or something. An old white woman and an elderly white man were sitting about two tables over from us; they had to be in their 70s or 80s. We were laughing and laughing, having a good time, and the white woman looks up, and says, "Look at that nigger over there, laughing all loud with that nigger lover." The way they can say "nigger," we do it all the time, but the way they say it just sounds mean and that stopped us dead. I couldn't believe that. So, we shut up obviously, and we got up, paid, and left.**

> **During the middle of the season, I went to a place in Georgia, and the hotel is about 15 yards away from this little restaurant. You don't have enough money in the minor leagues to have a good breakfast everyday, but I was pitching that day and I rationed my money so that when I pitched I'd always eat a good breakfast. I'm sitting in the restaurant. One white man comes in, sits down after me. Another couple comes in, sits down after him. Another couple comes in, then another man, and then they order before me. I said, "Damn," because I got to be getting out of there pretty soon to get to the ballpark. So, I said, "Ma'am, could you take my order?" She said, "Nigger, you been bothering me ever since you come in here." I hadn't said one word to her. Then all of a sudden, I don't know what happened in my head, and I swung at her and she ducked and I missed. She was at the counter and she pushed this button up under the counter. Man, before I could get to the door, I'm talking about 15 seconds, not even, here comes two squad cars pulling in, troopers. They come in and talk to her and she's saying, "That nigger this and that nigger that." So they take me outside and I'm thinking, "Where are they going to hang my ass? This could be it." They rode me around the corner and they said, "Alright, now we're going to let you out here. Now go. We know you stay here at the hotel. We know you're a ballplayer, don't go back in that restaurant**

any more, okay, boy?" I said, "Yes, sir." **They let me out and I walked around back to the hotel. No breakfast that morning.**
Mike Norris interview

After a while, like all blacks in the South, Mike adapted to survive. He was rooming with another black player, Claudell Washington, and whenever one of them was going out without the other, they were sure to tell each other where they were headed and with who, and what time they were expected back, so somebody would know when you were missing and where to start looking. Mike came to learn that the one place where he could find a certain amount of serenity was at the ballpark, and even then, he would have fans throwing black cats or watermelons on the field. But all of that was innocuous compared to the final incident Mike experienced in Birmingham:

The last day of the season, I went into a phone booth to call my Mom to tell her what flight I was coming home on the next day. The KKK hit me over the head with a pistol and knocked me out because I was running around with a white woman in the mayor's office. That wasn't good. I was lucky they didn't knock my eyeball out. Anyway, I'm laying in the bottom of the phone booth, white people walking around, "Look at that nigger, bleeding to death." This was three o'clock in the afternoon. They waited until the last day to get me. They said, "Nigger, if you come back here next year you better not mess with that white woman again."

So, I got on the phone with Charlie when I got back home. I said, "You know what, you won't have a pitcher if I have to go back to AA again." He said, "Don't worry about it. I won't send you back there any more. As a matter of fact, I'm going to be sending you to spring training with the big league club next year."
Mike Norris interview

Charlie Finley kept his word and invited Mike to the big league camp in 1975, but didn't place him on the forty-man major league roster. Mike earned that spot himself, and was on the A's big league team on Opening Day 1975, the third youngest player in the majors at age 20. Mike remembers that he helped his own cause in that regard by striking out Hank Aaron on three pitches in a spring training game. After the game, A's manager, Alvin Dark, approached Mike and told him, "Son, you can do things like that, you can pitch for me. You made my ballclub today." Mike was also helped by a series of events that left the A's with a shortage of starting pitchers. Catfish Hunter went to the Yankees, and the team's efforts to sign Juan Marichal and Claude Osteen fell short at the last minute.

Alvin Dark looked upon the arrival of young Mike Norris as a deliverance from heaven. In fact, Dark referred to Mike as "Jeremiah," the child prophet. On April

10, 1975, against the Chicago White Sox, Mike became the 35th pitcher in the history of the Major Leagues to throw a shutout in his pitching debut, but remembers how nervous he felt when climbing that major league mound for the first time:

The first game, I can never forget. I was absolutely shaking on the mound. Before the first pitch I had to get back off the mound. My leg was going like this, knock, knock, knock. "Oh, my God, Lord, stop me from shaking. Everybody in this ballpark has got to see my leg." I stepped off the mound, took a deep breath, and I got back on there, and I'll be damned, my leg had stopped shaking by the time I got on the hill. He answered that prayer.
Mike Norris interview

Mike was feeling much more relieved when the game was over.

This is beautiful. It's like being on a cloud. This is what I was put here to accomplish. I just thank the Lord that I could do it. I'm just glad all this is over. The Lord works in mysterious ways.
Mike Norris quoted by Ron Bergman, The Sporting News, April 26, 1975

In Mike's second start, he only gave up one hit through seven innings, and it began to look like his career was going to start like Vida's. After two outings he owned a shutout and seven innings of one-hit ball. He remembers his anticipation of having another great outing, and how it all changed in the very first inning:

My third start was against the Twins, Tony Oliva, Rod Carew. I'm so pumped up now. I think now I can pitch in the big leagues. I threw a shutout and a one-hitter. Let's go throw something phenomenal. Let's go get another no-hitter or something. I was thinking like this. I was so pumped up that day that everything I threw was rising. If I started it at the waist, it went to the shoulders. If I started it at the letters, it went over the head. I mean, I'm throwing unreal gas. It's rising all over the place, but I can't get it in the strike zone. I walked the first two batters. Now, Carew is up and I got 3 balls and 1 strike on him. And something said, now, okay, get this one down, make sure you get this ball down. I popped to get that thing down, and POW, I just felt it and everything got hot in there. Man, was that some excruciating pain. I looked down and a piece of bone was sticking out, through the skin, through the shirt. Gino [Tenace] had caught me. He came to the mound after I threw the damn thing. He said, "Kid, I called for a fastball. You just threw me a change-up. Did you get the sign?" Then, I'm looking down, blood is coming out of my arm. It was gross. That was my season, man. It was a calcium deposit. It

wasn't even real bone, just calcium that grew on to the bone. Then I started getting dizzy and nauseous. I passed out. The next thing I know I'm in the training room.
Mike Norris interview

Ten days later, surgery was required to remove two calcium deposits from Mike's elbow, and the season that had started with such promise for Mike turned out to be a season of rehabbing his arm. Mike finally made it back to the mound for the A's in September of 1975, tossing two-thirds of an inning in relief. In the off-season, Mike was mentally prepared to return: "I'm ready to go. It's going to be unbelievable. I can throw with anyone in this league right now. It's true. I kid you not." (quoted by Ron Bergman, *The Sporting News*, Dec. 13, 1975), and even showed signs of physical readiness, retiring six batters in a row, with five consecutive strikeouts, as a reliever for a San Francisco winter semipro team. But when the season started, Mike wasn't the same pitcher he was in 1975. He made it to the starting rotation based on a few good outings, and was then sent to the bullpen after a few bad outings.

Starting in June, 1976, and for the next few seasons, Mike did the Finley Shuffle, being sent back and forth from the Major League squad to the minors. It was a move that Charlie used to his advantage, making room on the big league roster from time to time for veteran arms that had a little left to offer, like Stan Bahnsen, Dick Bosman and Dock Ellis. In 1975, Mike had been throwing his fastball at about 95 mph. I can just hear that "POP" of the ball hitting the catcher's mitt as I think about it. But after the injury to his arm the speed was not there. He had lost about 5 mph on his best pitch, and that allowed hitters to get around and make solid contact on balls they used to whiff at. It also seemed like Mike couldn't pitch well when he was healthy and couldn't stay healthy when he was pitching well. On at least two occasions when he was with the Major League club, he suffered injuries (twisted knee, broken wrist) that put him out of commission.

In April 1978, Mike lost his salary arbitration with the A's and his salary was to be $24,000 for the upcoming season. By then, Charlie Finley was giving up on Mike Norris and decided to send him down to AA ball. Mike didn't handle it too well at first, but a conversation with an up and coming rookie spurred him on:

Finley calls me and says, "I'm going to send you to the minors. I'm very disappointed. I don't think you appreciate the big leagues anymore. I think you've had it too good up here. I think you need to go down and smell some bus fumes. I'm going to send you to AA. How does that sound?" "Whatever." So he sends me to Jersey City, New Jersey. The first day I get down there, I checked in to the Holiday Inn, right by the tunnel, and I go to the bar and start drinking. With my mind clouded with alcohol, I think I am putting everything in perspective and I came up with the idea, "I don't want to play anymore." So, I didn't show up

at the ballpark and I stayed in my hotel room for two days, knowing that I'm not making the right decision, and hoping that someone will intervene. If I am good enough maybe they'll come find me and beg me to come back and play or something. So, finally, my girlfriend calls me and convinces me that I need to go to the ballpark.

The first few starts I didn't care about pitching, and I pitched that way. I was 1-5 after six starts. Rickey Henderson was on that team, he hadn't gotten to the majors yet, and he comes up to me and says, "Nor, you're garbage now, man. You used to be a great pitcher. You're garbage now." I looked at him with anger at first, but what he said hit home. You know, nobody wants to be told they're garbage. I thought, "Alright, I'll show his ass." I started doing what I was supposed to be doing. I got to the park early and starting getting myself in shape and did more running and stuff. Being the athlete I was, I was never out of shape anyway, so if I did anything extra I'd be perfect.

So, Rickey's telling me how garbage I am made me want to show everybody I wasn't done yet. So, my third start I come out and although I lost 3-1, I pitched good that night. Then the next start I pitch a complete game and win 2-1. I get a phone call from Mr. Finley the next day, "Well, I see you got your act together. I just wanted to see how long you were going to go down there and pout." He was checking my dexterity and my manhood, to see if I was going to go down there and be pissed because he sent me to AA or was I going to go down there and pitch and come back. So, he brings me back and that was the start of a great friendship with Rickey and I. I began to start getting my major league career back in order. I wanted to stay in the big leagues now.
Mike Norris interview

One thing that Mike started doing to get back in the groove was to throw his screwball more often. As Mike got a little older he realized that while his screwball thrown at 90+ mph was putting a tremendous amount of strain on batters, it was putting an even greater strain on his arm and elbow. He learned how to throw the screwball effectively at a lesser speed, and was successful with it. He earned his way back to the big leagues for the end of the 1978 season and pitched like he belonged there. Unfortunately for Mike's record, the 1978 A's bore little or no resemblance to the A's of the glory days of the early 1970s, and with no support, offensively or defensively, Mike suffered five losses without a victory that season.

In the off-season, Mike played in Venezuela with Mitchell Page and Willie Horton. He continued to work on throwing his screwball effectively and won seven of nine decisions, leading his club to win the Caribbean Series. In the spring of 1979, Mike's pitching continued to be impressive. During the exhibition season, he allowed only one earned run in 26 innings of work. He was back in love with the screwball, and not bashful about it:

> **Get used to this. This is me from now on. When I first came up, I tried to throw it [the screwball] the same way I threw my fast ball, at about 95 miles per hour. It's such a good pitch I don't have to throw it that hard. That's what wrecked my elbow.**
>
> **It's my pitch. The Lord gave me the ability to throw this pitch, and I have to use it. It's my out pitch. I can still blow the fast ball past people, but this is my out pitch.**
>
> *Mike Norris quoted by Tom Weir, The Sporting News, April 14, 1979*

That season was a rebuilding year for Mike, while the A's were still in demolition mode. He pitched more innings that year than he ever had previously, and while experimenting with the screwball he was not yet sharp with his control, as evidenced by 10 wild pitches and 9 hit batsmen. But he was pitching and managed to stay on the big league roster the whole season, except for three weeks in the middle of August, which he spent on the disabled list because he cut up his pitching hand falling down a hill in San Francisco while racing against teammate Rodney Scott. Mike finished the season at 5-8, which looks better when you consider that the A's, managed by Jim Marshall that year, were 54-108 and posted an anemic .239 team batting average. Sportswriters were calling them the "Triple A's" and the "Pathetics."

Mike vividly remembers another conversation with a fellow player that spurred him on, similar to the Rickey incident, but this time it was pitching legend Bob Gibson:

> **I'm pitching in Baltimore. This is the turning point in my career. I got Murray, Singleton and Lowenstein coming up. One ball no strikes to Murray, POW, home run. Ties the game up 3-3. Singleton's up next. Two balls one strike, POW, home run – a walk-off job. That's the first time I ever had a walk-off. That's the weirdest feeling in the world. People are walking past you going off the field, you're going in, like, it doesn't work like that. I'm sitting in the dugout, and it just so happened, Bob Gibson was the color man that year. He comes down and says, "Go in the clubhouse. You're a disgrace." I go, "What, Mr. Gibson?" He went, "You're scared out there." I said, "What do you mean?" He says, "I counted two pitches you threw inside the whole night, and they were by accident." Now I'm a little pissed, "What do you mean Mr. Gibson?" He says, "You know what I used to do? Pick out two of the biggest black guys on the team and pitch them inside, back them off the plate. Those other seven white guys wouldn't think twice about digging in on me after that." I did that the rest of the year**

and I did alright. I think I had two starts left. I went down to winter ball. They got Armas and Conception down there, and I'm knocking these guys, bam, bam. I wind up going 7-1 down there in winter ball, because I claimed the inside of the plate for my own, and it got to the point like, this is so obvious that if you do this the results are terrific, and I never realized how I started expanding the plate once I started getting this part of the plate, the inside. I'm like, Wow.
Mike Norris interview

Propelled by his conversation with Gibson, and encouraged by his off-season accomplishments as the result of claiming the inside of the plate, Mike went into the 1980 season with a mindset of success and confidence. After all he had gone through he was still only 25 years old, and a volatile combination was about to occur: a young, fearless, competitor, eager to prove himself and to become a winner was about to be under the tutelage of one of the fiercest competitive managers in the history of the game, an old timer used to winning – Billy Martin, who was a member of the American League champion New York Yankees the year Mike Norris was born. I knew Billy for many years. We were teammates on the Indians in 1959, and later on he was a coach when I was with the Twins. I know how fiery he was and how much he wanted to win. As I wrote earlier, when talking about Fergie, Billy loved a pitcher who wanted the ball and didn't look for excuses to come out of a game. Fergie, the dependable workhorse veteran pitcher knew how to pitch a tremendous amount of innings in a season. He was a champ at pacing himself. Mike Norris and the rest of the very young A's pitching staff in 1980 were a different story. Rick Langford was the elder statesman at 28; Steve McCatty was 26, Brian Kingman was 25 and Matt Keough was 24. They all thought they were indestructible and invincible, and Billy let them pitch, and pitch and pitch, and pitch some more.

We were just all really wanting to prove that we were major league ballplayers. And I think, just getting the opportunity the way we did, we all were ready for it at that time in our careers.
What happened was, we learned how to pitch to people that third time around the lineup. That's the whole key to why these kids today can't get through the sixth and seventh inning – they don't know how to get through the third time in the lineup. That's when the hitters have timed you. They know basically what you have by then. You've lost about five miles off your fastball, so now you have to be able to learn how to get them out on your own. Now is when you have to get a strikeout or a pop-up in the infield or something like that. Manufacture your own out. And we learned how to do that. And that would enable us to get to the ninth inning. And then it's just a matter of guts from then on. We knew we didn't have a great bullpen, so that was the fire that you lit up under yourself. And then at that point, you

start taking pride in going nine. So it really became virtually almost a joke that we were going nine.

Mike Norris, in Dugout Days, Untold Tales and Leadership Lessons from the Extraordinary Career of Billy Martin, by Michael DeMarco, American Management Association 2001

To go nine was an accomplishment. That's what you set out to do. You didn't rely on bullpens. I learned this from Rollie Fingers: when I pitched, Blue Moon pitched, Glen Adams pitched, Dave Hamilton pitched, when he came in he let the game get tied up and then he would get a win for it. You didn't get paid for saves in those days. That wasn't popular then, wins were popular. That's what Charlie Finley paid you for, wins. He didn't pay for getting saves. When Vida pitched, when Holtzman pitched, when Catfish pitched, Rollie came in and saved their games. He would keep their runners for them on base. When he came in for us, boom, he gave up a hit and let those runs come in. Then he'd stop them and the next inning they'd score a run for him and he'd win. So I learned how to go nine from Rollie. They didn't call him the vulture for no reason. Completing those games made you feel like this, man [Mike pounds his chest].

Mike Norris interview

The A's pitching staff threw 94 complete games that season, with Rick Langford leading the majors with 28. The entire Yankee pitching staff only had 29. St. Louis' staff was tops in the National League with 34, and in the American League the team with the most complete games after the A's was Milwaukee with 48. In Mike's first start, for Billy, in Toronto, he went ten innings in a losing effort, and Billy immediately fell in love.

I can remember the first start I had that year was in Toronto. I pitched ten innings and I lost. I came in that clubhouse and I must have tore that son of a bitch up. I went in that bathroom, I went BAM, cracked the toilet seat, the bathroom door was off the hinges. I lost it. Well, these guys are out here in the clubhouse. They're hearing all this. Billy was having a little meeting with them. He was telling them how well they played in the ballgame, we all stayed in the game pretty good. And then I came out of the bathroom back into the clubhouse, and there's everybody looking at me, like I had lost my mind. "Damn, dude, do you realize we're in here while you were snapping?" That's the look everybody had on their face. And Billy said, "You feel better now?" And I looked around at everybody and I said, "Hell, no! I lost the game." He said, "Don't worry about it partner, because you're the ace of my staff now." I looked around and I'm thinking, you know, "Is

he bullshitting me or what?" My first start. After that, boom. That was it.
Mike Norris interview

According to Mike though, Billy knew what he had in Mike from the times Mike had pitched against Billy's Yankees. Mike specifically remembers one game from 1977, when he was pitching exceptionally well against the Yanks, and was getting everyone out except Thurman Munson, who had timed Mike's fastball perfectly all game:

I'll never forget a game I pitched against the Yankees when Billy was managing them and Thurman Munson was still living. I was throwing hard. I could always remember because Billy at Yankee Stadium stands on that first step and just looks a hole in you. And he's just watching me the whole game, you look over there and he's just watching you. And I can never forget Munson went three for three on me that night. I went into the seventh inning, I'm throwing good, I'm getting everybody else but I can't get Thurman out that night. The first hit Thurman gets off me is a base hit down the third base line. The next one, he hits one in between third and shortstop, a chopper, and then the third one he hit a pea down the third base line again and it hits the stands and shoots back out, not being a fast runner he stayed at first. He stands on first base and he looks over at me. He says, "You gotta be the dumbest son of a bitch I ever seen" because I kept trying to throw fastballs by him and I can't get it by him. So, Billy knew what he had there all along.
Mike Norris interview

One of the things Mike did in 1980 was to not rely as exclusively on his fastball. He began to use the screwball more frequently and with more confidence and control.

That screwball started wearing people out. I would bust them inside, then start going away. I said, this is working great against lefthanders, now what am I going to do about righthanders. I'd bust them in, throw a low screwball in and they'd pull the thing foul. I said, wow, I got a strike like this. This is my strike. That turned my whole career around there. I was able to get a strike whenever I wanted to. I could do the same thing on the other side of the dish. It was just incredible. Waste a pitch? No, not wasting a pitch, you waste a pitch with a purpose. So that's a purpose, okay. That sets up something away, or that sets up something off-speed. Now, they don't just reach out and hit that outside pitch. You make that good pitch outside and you wonder, how the hell did he hit that? They were already out there but once you get them like this [off the plate] then instead of driving that

pitch, all they can do is fleck at it. Now you get a weak fly ball to right instead of a line drive. So this is like a revelation to me.
Mike Norris interview

Mike, Matt Keough and Rick Langford all had fourteen inning complete games while playing for Billy in 1980. It was a throwback to when I was pitching, but no one else in the league except Billy was managing that way.

I'll never forget the fourteen-inning game I pitched. I threw 160 pitches, before Tony Armas hit a grand slam giving us a 6-2 victory. I can remember after the 11th inning, Elrod Hendricks, who was the 3rd base coach looking up at me and shrugged, like "What's going on?" and then the 12th inning and the 13th inning, he gave me the thumbs up sign of approval, right in front of Earl Weaver, he didn't care, because it was phenomenal.
Mike Norris interview

Amazingly, Mike's next start after the fourteen-inning game, he threw 168 pitches in an 11-8 complete game victory. When asked how he did it, Mike responded, "By getting proper rest between starts, and chasing women." On September 16, 1980, in Arlington, Texas, Mike became the A's first twenty-game winner since Vida Blue won 22 games in 1975. Appropriately enough, Mike's twentieth victory was an eleven inning victory over Texas, in a game he was losing 2-0 with one out and one on in the ninth inning, when Mickey Klutts' pinch hit home run sent the game into extra innings. The reaction to Mike's becoming a twenty-game winner was fitting for a guy who had never won more than five in a year and had a losing record the year before.

After winning his 20th, Norris was mobbed on the mound by his teammates. Moments later, in a happy clubhouse, he was sprayed with shaving cream and unceremoniously dropped into the clubhouse showers. It was the happiest day of his career.
Magic 20 for Norris, by Kit Stier, The Sporting News, October 4, 1980

Mike had come all the way back from smelling the bus fumes in Class AA Jersey City to the sweet smell of success on a Major League mound. He became the tenth Black Ace, and looking back at it now he has a deep appreciation for what that means:

Being a guy who won 20 games, it's a dream come true personally. But then I think, socially, politically, it's made me a man that I couldn't have been without baseball. I know that sounds crazy. Let me explain that better. I mean in terms of the way other people perceive me. If it weren't for baseball, I couldn't have some of the advantages that

go along with it. Just like right now, my physical state – I actually get by a little better because of who I am. If I had just been a cripple, with no name, I'd have a tough go of it. But I get help. People are a little more forthcoming. So I earned something as a black man, as my black race looks at me as, instead of just like everybody else. A little more respect, and that means more.

Mike Norris interview

Despite some early season injuries in 1980, Mike made 33 starts, pitched 24 complete games and stayed around long enough to get 31 decisions, going 22-9. Mike pitched 284.3 innings in 1980, in 33 appearances, all starts. That calculates to a phenomenal average outing of 8.62 innings per start. He won his first Gold Glove, gave up the fewest hits per nine innings (6.81), was second in the American League in ERA (2.53), second in strikeouts (180), and second in complete games. Mike praised Billy Martin and his pitching coach, Art Fowler, for his success in 1980:

They have taught me the fundamentals and discipline and give me friendship. If I can't play for Billy Martin, I don't need to be in this game.

Mike Norris quoted by Kit Stier, The Sporting News, October 4, 1980

Unfortunately, for Mike he was also second in the voting for the Cy Young Award. Mike and Steve Stone of Baltimore each received 13 first place votes, with Stone getting a total of 100 points to Mike's 91. Stone had more wins and fewer losses but Mike pitched more innings, had a better ERA and more strikeouts. Mike won his first five starts in 1980, and then lost two 1-0 decisions, one in eleven innings. His ERA after seven starts was an unbelievable 0.52. Mike knew that Stone also had a very good season, but what he had trouble with was that three of the writers who voted for the award completely left Mike off their ballots.

One thing Mike did "win" as the result of this 1980 season was a five-year contract with the Athletics, who signed Mike through the 1985 season.

Mike came to spring training in 1981 aiming to win the Cy Young Award by a landslide. By mid-season, Mike was 9-3, and leading the American League in many pitching categories. In most baseball seasons mid-season is the All-Star break, but in 1981 mid-season was the strike break that I think lasted fifty days, well longer than either side expected. Mike didn't throw during the strike and his pitching performance suffered in the second half. He went 3 and 6 and ended the season with a 12-9 record.

Oakland was in first place in the Western Division when the strike took place. They swept the second half winner, Kansas City, 3-0, in a best-of-five playoff, and then got swept by the Yankees in a best of five American League Championship Series. During the post season of 1981, Mike returned to his 1980 form and was very effective. He pitched Game One of the playoffs in Kansas City and hurled a four-hit, complete game shutout against the Royals, winning 4-0. That performance set the tone for the series, with McCatty pitching a complete game, 2-1 victory in Game Two, and Langford pitching into the eighth inning in the deciding game, winning 4-1, in Oakland. When the A's advanced to the ALCS, and the scene shifted to Yankee Stadium, Norris was again called on to pitch Game One for the visiting A's. Mike remembers the tough greeting he got from the bleacher crowd and how it affected his game:

> **I'm warming up in the Yankee Stadium bullpen, and I'm going, "I got it tonight." On my last warm-up pitch, I hear something like a helicopter, and I got the turtle effect, I put my head into my neck, and all of sudden I heard something on the wall. SPLAT! One of the fans had fired a half-full Southern Comfort bottle down out of the stands at my head. It just missed me and hit the wall just behind me. That would have knocked me to pieces if it hit me. So, I'm like this now <shaking>. First inning, I give up three runs, lose the game 3-1. That's it. If they threw the bottle a half hour earlier, I would have had time to settle down. That's a true story. Not too many people know that story, besides my pitching coach, Art Fowler, and Billy.**
> *Mike Norris interview*

By 1982, Mike's arm started to feel the effects of his extended pitch counts over the two previous seasons. Throwing over 150 pitches per game on too many occasions started to catch up with him, and the other Oakland starters. Mike pitched through pain in 1982, and when he complained of arm trouble the team didn't believe him. He no longer had the ability to go deep into the game and managed only 28 starts and 18 decisions, going 7 and 11. While Mike averaged almost 9 innings per start in 1980, that average dropped to 7.5 innings per start in 1981 and again to 5.9 innings per start in 1982. I think he unintentionally convinced some people of the problem with his arm one day when he was warming up on the mound and threw a ball to the plate that wound up going in the third base dugout. The A's classified Mike's problem as tendonitis in the rotator cuff of his throwing shoulder. They put Mike on the 21-day disabled list, getting him some rest, and had orthopedic surgeon Dr. Frank Jobe examine him. But Mike's emotional nature, and his ability to throw objects (other than a baseball) around a dugout or clubhouse after a loss, led to some whispers questioning Mike's injury. As contrite as the sportswriters were after learning that J.R. Richard was really suffering from an illness and not laziness, they quickly forgot any lesson learned and gave Mike some of the same treatment in the spring of 1983:

> **Sometimes it's hard to figure out if Norris' problem is in his shoulder or his head, but since his great 1980 season, he has been erratic, on and off the field. If he gets serious, the A's get back a topflight pitcher. If his shoulder is worn out or his head is in the clouds, he's just another body.**
> *Peter Gammons, The Sporting News, February 28, 1983*

Mike was known to like his partying, his women, and his gin. But whether those were the items causing him to not pitch well, or his not pitching well and not being believed were the cause of those items, was the question in 1983.

I couldn't get anybody to believe what I was telling them. It was like you writing a story and not having your boss believe it. I became so frustrated by July that I almost felt like quitting after my contract was up. I'm one of the hardest workers here, but if you can't enjoy what you are doing, then why in the hell do it?
Mike Norris quoted by Kit Stier, The Sporting News, April 18, 1983

Things changed when in July 1983, Mike's arm spoke for itself, and people believed:

It was 1983 when I blew my arm out. I kept it going in the 1982 season and there were little rumors and innuendo that I'm using drugs, and I'm on drugs. When next season comes around, it's when I threw it out, against Minnesota. I'll never forget that day. It felt like my shoulder went to the backstop when I threw this one particular pitch. Oh, my God. That was the most excruciating pain I have ever felt in my life. I get out of the inning, and my arm starts twitching. The nerves are going, and I can't stop it. I stick my arm in between my legs, in between innings in the dugout, just so it would stop twitching. Dave Beard was one of my relief pitchers, and he goes, "God damn, Mike, you got to get out of there, man. Look at your arm." I said, "No, Beardie, I'm going to get out there." I was trying to get to the fifth inning so I could get a decision. I went out there to throw the next inning and I couldn't even pick the damn ball up, because the coolness had set in, and that was it. Minnesota was the last game I pitched. That was it. I shut it down for '83. I went under the knife about two months later, in November.
Mike Norris interview

The doctor's report on Mike confirmed that he had tendonitis, and also revealed that he had a shoulder muscle that had "atrophied to the point of being useless" and a possible pinched nerve. *(The Sporting News, August 22, 1983)* Mike didn't know it at the time, nor did the Athletics or anyone else, but that game in Minnesota would be the last time Mike would pitch in the Major Leagues for seven years. Mike underwent surgery to have the nerve damage behind his right shoulder repaired, the first time a ballplayer had this type of procedure. After the surgery in November 1983, Mike disconnected with baseball for awhile and for a few years he had less control over his life than he did over the ball he threw into the dugout:

I think the worst mistake I made was the fact that I didn't have to come to the ballpark at all in '84 and I was under contract until '85.

My drug use probably got to its peak at that point. By not having to go to the ballpark, I stayed home and I drugged all day. Unfortunately at times getting behind the wheel and driving, and I got stopped one night on the freeway, which was probably the start of my court troubles and the start of my having to go to drug clinics. And the drug clinic was the result of the judge sentencing me to programs and such. I was really out of control at that point, because an idle mind is the devil's workshop. I should have been at that ballpark, or at least around the guys. So, that was my biggest mistake there. Before you know it, I'm in and out of drug clinics. I think I went to about five, in all.

Mike Norris interview

In 1985, Mike was rehabbing with Modesto (Class A) in the California League, when he tested positive for codeine. Although Mike claimed he was taking Tylenol with Codeine prescribed by his dentist, because of earlier indiscretions the A's placed him on baseball's alcohol and drug rehabilitation list in July. Barred from the major league team, Mike traveled to the Dominican Republic in October 1985, to pitch for the Licey Tigers. His troubles followed him there and found him before he ever got to report to the team:

I get off the plane and they're searching my bags, no problem. Then all of sudden, they whisk me off into a room. My leather coat is hanging up behind this door in the room. They unzip the coat and I see them pull out a bag of weed. I'm going, "Son of a bitch. That's not mine. I just saw you pull it out and you handed that to him." Well, they kept me in jail for three days. They wound up getting $10,000 out of me, which is what it was all about.

I was sitting in the jail for three days. My mom didn't know where I was. The A's didn't know where I was. The Licey Tigers didn't know where I was. The way I got out was there was a hole in the ground, and after the second day, this big old rat decided to come out of the hole. He's walking around like he owns the cell, and I'm up in the bunk. My biggest fear in the world is a rat. For some people it's snakes, mine is rats. So, I'm losing my mind in there, yelling "get me the hell out of here." I'm getting the creeps. As soon as the rat went back in the hole I jumped off the bed, and kicked the leg on the bed, this was life and death now. I'm thinking about that movie, Midnight Express, and thinking I'm never getting out of here and I'm going to be eaten by this rat. I kick the bed as hard as I can and cut my leg open. They take me to the Infirmary, and I'm hoping I'll run into somebody who speaks English. I get down there, and I tell the doctor what's going on. She doesn't know if I'm lying, but she knows I'm a ballplayer. So she says she will try to get in touch with somebody.

The next day they send me in to court. I don't understand much, but the only thing I understand is this: blah, blah, blah, seis mesa. Six months! I'm going, WHOA! I'm just getting ready to stand up and say something and a big, tall gentleman, about 6'5" with a beautiful light, sky blue, leisure suit comes strolling through the door. He says, "Excuse me, I am with the Licey Tigers, abogado, blah, blah, blah." He's the lawyer. It's like God sent him. He takes the DA in the back room and they stay in there about twenty minutes, and they come out and he goes, "Come with me. You're free." I go, "Cool." So we get outside and he tells me who he is and everything, and blah, blah, blah." It was over just like that.

I pitched well down there that year. I believe it was my childhood, and the experiences I had - those things all came out, so it was survival. That's what that was. After what I went through, with the stitches still in my leg, anybody in their right mind would have got back on the plane and went home. But I knew, if I wanted to play major league baseball again, this is what I had to do.
Mike Norris interview

By Christmas 1985, then Commissioner Peter Ueberroth reached out to Mike and encouraged him to keep working hard and keep his nose clean and he could get back into baseball. At the end of the 1985 winter season, Sandy Alderson, then with the Oakland A's, went down to the Dominican and offered Mike a minor league contract. As a twenty-game winner, who came within a hair's breadth of winning the Cy Young Award, and having just completed a season with a 2.01 ERA, Mike's pride didn't allow him to sign a minor league contract. In hindsight, Mike should have signed the contract and gone to AAA. It probably would have been his fastest route back to a Major League pitching mound.

Out of Major League Baseball for over two years, Mike fell into bad habits with alcohol and cocaine. By New Year's Eve of that year, Mike saw himself hitting bottom and made a determined effort to get his life back in order:

I looked in the mirror one morning and I said, major league baseball player, my ass. You're no better than these dope pushers and junkies. And for the first time in my life I started hanging around people that did that. It was very uncomfortable to realize that I had let myself go to that low state, but, again, that was my bottom, and that's what it took for me to realize and start going up again. And that day, New Year's Day, 1986, I went back to the bar where I had been drinking, and I looked in that bar mirror there, and I looked at myself, major league baseball player my ass. I said, you know what, this is going to be your last drink, your last snort, your last smoke. Well, I wasn't able to stop drinking, but that was my last day that I ever did cocaine, 1986, New

Year's Day. That was the first step, right there. Now, I didn't believe that I was an alcoholic. I knew I was an addict. I accepted that, but I didn't believe I was an alcoholic, because in my eyes an alcoholic was a person that was laying out in the street, and he couldn't stop drinking and alcohol controlled him. I only drank beer. What I didn't realize is that the beer is what got everything started. That beer, and then you want to go see a woman, and then you want to go get some dope, and you lose a lot of judgment as you go, and all the bad decisions follow.
Mike Norris interview

As spring 1986 approached, no Major League team offered Mike a contract – for the majors or the minors. Feeling *persona non grata* and with nowhere to turn, Mike called Harry Stavrenos, the owner of the San Jose Bees, who gave Mike a contract, and put things in perspective for Mike:

Harry told me, "I'm not going to be the guy that releases you out of baseball. If you get released out of here, it's not going to look good. You're already an addict and now you're coming down here and get released. It's not going to look good." That sunk in. So, I got my act together and went out and pitched for him. I pitched well. I went 5 and 0 down there with a 0.9 ERA or something like that.
Mike Norris interview

Eventually the Commissioner of the League would not let Mike play for the Bees. He claimed Mike was making a mockery of the league because no one could hit him. The A's helped Mike find a place on the roster of Hermosillo in the Mexican Pacific League where he pitched with some success. Mike didn't want to go back to Mexico, but could not give up the game. He wound up playing for a semi-pro bar league team on Sundays in San Francisco, which was absolutely no challenge for a player with Mike's ability and knowledge of the game. But the fact that he was back in the Frisco area and well enough to pitch got back to Sandy Alderson, who again approached Mike about signing a minor league contract.

Alderson says, "We're going to give you a AAA contract." "Hell, yes!" That was the winter of '88, comes the spring of '89, they send me to spring training in AA. They said go down there and pitch one game. I shut somebody out, a two-hitter.

What's in my head now is I'm about to get back to the big leagues and I'm going to show all you son of a bitches, blah, blah, blah. Well, instead of pitching seven innings, and getting out of there that night, I pitched the whole nine innings, and I got a tired arm. The next three starts, I'm getting the crap kicked out of me, because I had a dead

arm. So, they throw me in the bullpen. They don't release me because they know I can still throw, because they saw what I can do.

They didn't bring me up that year, at the end of the year, and I was really disappointed, because in AAA, that's what all the guys look forward to.
Mike Norris interview

Though he might have been disappointed at not making it all the way back to the majors in 1989, Mike was ecstatic at getting as far as he did, considering where he came from. That year he told Murray Chass of *The New York Times*, "This is one heck of an ordeal to go through, but it's worth it. I could go out and kiss the grass every morning. That's how much I love this game."

In 1990, seven years after leaving that game against Minnesota, Mike Norris climbed back up on a Major League mound for the Oakland Athletics. It was a terrific personal triumph for Mike and a vindication of the feelings he had all along: that he belonged in the majors. Manager Tony LaRussa had his team on course to win another Western Division title. The aces of the Athletics' pitching staff that year were Dave Stewart, Bob Welch, and Scott Sanderson. Mike was used exclusively in relief and was doing an excellent job. On April 17, 1990, Mike earned his first Major League victory since May 16, 1983. Only Jim Bouton (1970 to 1978) and Fred (Cactus) Johnson (1923 to 1938) had gone a longer period of time between Major League victories. By the All-Star break, Mike had appeared in fourteen games, pitched 27 innings, and was 1 and 0 with an ERA of 3.0. Mike's competitive nature and the desire to pitch and excel took over. During the All-Star break he asked pitching coach Dave Duncan for a start, and Duncan told Mike he was "not good enough to start." Mike defended his position, and the next day the A's released Mike by placing him on waivers. The cold reality of the end of the line started to hit Mike when no other team picked him up. The A's re-signed him and sent him to AAA for the rest of the season, but never called him back up. July 4, 1990 was the last day he toed a major league mound.

In 1991, Mike wasn't willing to throw in the towel and he tried to give it another shot, but there were no takers at the Major League level. He played independent ball up in Reno for about two months and then quit professional baseball forever.

I went into the manager's office one day and I just said, "I'm through." Just going nowhere, I saw the writing on the wall. You got to be able to say, "This is enough." But, it's hard, it's your life. You don't know nothing else. The percentage of ballplayers that get to quit on their own terms may be 2%.
Mike Norris interview

After Mike walked away from the game, at age 36, other than to play in the Senior League for one season, he had no contact with baseball. He maintained his sobriety, and concentrated on raising a family. His daughter was born in 1998.

He missed the game, but there were no offers to coach at any level, so Mike went on without a connection to the game other than his strong love of it. Then while playing golf in Oakland Hills one day in 1999, Mike was walking from his cart to where his ball lay, up a little hill. As he got to the ball he felt weakness in his right leg, and when he swung at the ball his leg gave out on him. He first blamed it on overexertion and he walked back to the cart. But when he got there, he found that his legs were not working. He could not raise his right leg into the cart. This brilliant athlete, who had displayed such balance and agility in the field that he earned the nickname Black Cat, now had no power in his legs and no equilibrium. Mike didn't give in to his body and didn't see a doctor about his condition. He applied the Billy Martin School of Thought and tried to "tough it out." But this time the problem took more than the ample guts Mike displayed.

When he finally got to a doctor, after struggling to walk for almost a month, Mike was told that he was suffering from a condition known as cervical myelopathy – a bruised spinal cord caused by arthritic buildup and a narrowing of the spinal cord. He was told he would require surgery, but that the only surgery available was only successful in improving about 30 percent of the patients who underwent it, with fifty percent evidencing no improvement, and 20 percent actually getting worse. Mike had the surgery in January 2000. They cut several of his vertebrae to widen his spinal canal and relive the pressure on his spinal cord. Several days later complications set in, requiring a second surgery, and Mike was told that he might suffer permanent paralysis. As predicted, after the surgery Mike had real difficulty walking and even standing up. In addition to the myelopathy he was now suffering from paraparesis, partial paralysis of his legs.

Mike needed to be dedicated to his physical therapy routine if there was any chance of getting his legs working again. At first, he had a problem doing that. He shut down, and saw this condition as one more of the recurring roadblocks that kept appearing in his life every so often. Then former teammate and long time friend, Claudell Washington, got wind of the fact that Mike Norris, known as a headstrong fighter, was not fighting this condition, and he got involved in getting Mike back on the right track. Using a cane to steady him, Mike now golfs regularly for exercise. The same drills he uses to develop a better balance in his golf swing help him with his equilibrium. More importantly, his outlook is very positive:

So, right now, what I've done is get my muscles back to life and now I have to get them strong, and I'm in the process of strengthening them. I'm doing okay. I'm going to beat this. I've beat everything that I've taken on in my life, so I don't see why this is going to be any different.
Mike Norris interview

He still has a great love for the game of baseball and a desire to help young kids not only how to play the game but how to prepare for life. I asked Mike what he would say to a young athlete who wants to succeed today and his advice was:

Go to school. Get an education. Be versatile. Always have an option in your life. You're going to need that education to be able to take care of your financial needs or to financially grow. If you don't have the means of knowledge like that then you're going to have to be at someone else's mercy. Education is the best advice I can give someone.
Mike Norris interview

The path that Mike Norris took to the Major League pitching mound seemed easy and direct at first when the versatile, agile teenager was drafted out of high school by the Athletics and hurled a shutout in his first Major League start. But it was ultimately a pretty rough road for Mike, some of it as a result of his own actions. Now he struggles just to walk. Yet he maintains a terrific outlook on life. His distinctive, rolling laugh is as contagious as ever.

Mike may have just missed winning the Cy Young Award by a few votes, and just missed being a .500 career pitcher by one victory, but he has not missed the bigger picture. He has no bitterness about his illness or anger about what might have been.

I've been clean for twenty years ... I feel like God slowed me down so I could see the forest for the trees. This has made me become the responsible person I've always intended to be.
Mike Norris quoted by Ron Salsig, Inside Golf

CHAPTER 27

DWIGHT EUGENE GOODEN
Doc
Dr. K

Born November 16, 1964 in Tampa, Florida
Teams: New York Mets, New York Yankees,
Cleveland Indians, Houston Astros,
Tampa Bay Devil Rays
Twenty-Win Season: 1985
National League Cy Young Award Winner 1985
National League All-Star 1984, 1985, 1986, 1988
National League Rookie of the Year 1984

If you believe those scouting reports, or trust the projections of coaches and managers at the A-ball level, Lynchburg pitcher Dwight Gooden could be the next, well, take your pick: Nolan Ryan or Bob Gibson.
Ron Morris, Baseball America, August 1, 1983

Among pitchers, the one who has most impressed me in the past ten years is Dwight Gooden. Before his injuries slowed him down, Gooden had incredible velocity but, more to the point, he knew how to pitch and compete.
Bob Gibson, Stranger to the Game

Dwight Gooden reminds me of me. He went through a lot of the similar stuff I went through in my life and career. There are a lot of similarities there. He probably could have been the best pitcher out of all of us maybe.
Mike Norris interview

I don't think anybody has ever been as good, as young as he is. His talent is absolutely unlimited. What he does depends on staying healthy, and how long he wants to play. If nothing happens to him, he may set and break all the records realistically within reach.
Sandy Koufax, quoted by Lyle Spencer, New York Post, July 16, 1985

I have mentioned repeatedly that the path to the pitcher's mound in the Major Leagues is not as direct or simple as it appears on the layout of a baseball field, and it has been traveled in many different ways by the thousands of different pitchers who have toed the rubber, some fast, some slow, some direct, and some circuitous. As varied as the route is, there are even more variations in the personalities of those pitchers making the journey. We have come from all corners of this country, and now from all corners of the world; from many different races, different religions, different cultures; from different family compositions, economic classes, and each with our own personal baggage. For those who have been successful, we either learned to place that baggage down when we crossed the foul line on the way to the mound, or we took just enough of it with us to use as motivation to succeed. That is not an easy thing to do, but personal growth, maturity, and success is not easy, and for some people the obstacles to these achievements can be life-threatening.

I have been around ballplayers for over sixty years and it's fair to say that I have seen thousands of pitchers in my life. Yet, when Dwight Gooden took the mound for the New York Mets in 1984, at the age of nineteen, I was impressed. The path he took to the mound seemed like he was shot out of a cannon and landed there, without any problems in the world. But like most of life, as I have come to learn, there is usually more to it than you can see.

Like me, Dwight felt destined to be a Major Leaguer from the time he was a little boy. His dad, Dan Gooden, was a first baseman who played semi-pro ball, and like most dads who loved the game, he nurtured his son's dream that he could get to the Major Leagues.

I guess I was the old man's favorite because I was the youngest of six children. When he was playing ball and coaching, I used to follow him around everywhere. When he coached, the players looked after me. I never had any trouble getting gloves, bats and balls. I guess you could say I grew up around baseball.
Dwight Gooden, quoted by Ron Morris, Baseball America, August 1, 1983

Dwight came from my neck of the woods, the area around Tampa, Florida, and Dan made sure that he saw his share of baseball. Dwight's earliest memory of the majors is witnessing Tiger great, Al Kaline, hit a home run in a spring training game in Lakeland, in 1970. He identifies that as the moment he knew he wanted to be a Major Leaguer. By the time Dwight was ten years old he was good enough to make it to the Belmont Heights Little League team that became National Champions. Although Little League rules at that time required team players to be twelve years old to play in the Little League World Series, Dwight was allowed to travel with the team to Williamsport, Pennsylvania, where they lost the championship to Taiwan.

By the time he was 12, Dwight started pitching, and everybody in the area was buzzing about Dan Gooden's boy, Dwight. He could flat out bring it.

I guess I was 12 when I realized I could throw really hard. I was in the Little League and was overpowering them, striking out 12 or 13 guys

in a six inning game.
Dwight Gooden, quoted by Joseph Durso, New York Times, August 23, 1983

He starred not only in Little League, but Senior League and American Legion ball, before entering Hillsborough High School, where coach Billy Reed had a baseball program that had produced such stars as Lou Piniella, Wade Boggs, Steve Garvey, Fred McGriff, and Tino Martinez. Dwight had a great arm and was a successful pitcher who enjoyed his ability to blow a ball by a hitter, but reminiscent of my teenage years and those of many of the other Black Aces, Dwight enjoyed being a position player, mainly rightfield and third base, where he could still show off his arm, but could get the extra benefits of playing every day and getting to hit. In fact, he believes that if his high school teammate, Floyd Youmans, who also made it to the Major Leagues, hadn't moved to California to live with his father, Dwight would never have gotten the chance to pitch for Hillsborough High as much as he did, sometimes three times a week. In his senior year at Hillsborough, Dwight struck out 135 batters in 74 innings of work and had a 1.52 ERA.

In June 1982, when Dwight was 18 years old, he was drafted by the New York Mets in the first round of the draft, fifth overall, and as proof of the strength of the baseball programs in Tampa, two of the players selected before him, Lance McCullers and Rich Monteleone, were both pitchers from the Tampa area. In all it was a very talented group of players that was drafted that year: including number one pick Shawon Dunston, and a few other players you might have heard of, including: Barry Bonds, Jose Canseco, Bo Jackson, Brett Saberhagen, and Vince Coleman.

The Mets signed Dwight that summer for a bonus of $85,000 and it was obvious that we had come a long way since the empty envelope I received in 1954. Dwight, who was only 17 years old, and had really never spent any time away from home, was then sent to Kingsport, Tennessee, to play for the Kingsport Mets in the Appalachian Rookie League. Although it wasn't as far from home as I was sent when I went to Fargo, it was far enough for Dwight:

I must've called my parents seven times that very first day, and after that, at least ten times a week. I called because I didn't know how to cook, how to wash my own clothes, or fold my laundry. I called because I didn't know how to shop for food, or to open a bank account.
Heat, My Life On and Off the Diamond, by Dwight Gooden with Bob Klapisch, William Morrow and Co., New York, 1999

While still trying to get adjusted to life in Tennessee, Dwight was sent to Little Falls, New York to play for the Mets in the New York-Penn League in upstate New York. It was there that Dwight first felt racial tension and discomfort. The only other black player on the team was Johnny Wilson, younger brother of Mets outfielder, Mookie Wilson. Similar to my experience in North Dakota, the blacks on the team were the only blacks in the whole town.

In 1983, Dwight pitched for the Lynchburg Mets (Lynchburg, Virginia, Class A, Carolina League). He started to develop the intensity and attitude necessary to complement his throwing ability and make himself a Major League pitcher. In August of that season he came within one out of pitching a no-hitter, giving up a two-out, ninth inning single against the Peninsula Pilots.

He pitches like he's been around. He's very confident on the mound. He has shown me a lot of poise and control as much as he has shown me a good fastball and curveball. When you watch him pitch, it is hard to believe he is that young.
Durham Manager Brian Snitker, quoted by Ron Morris, Baseball America, August 1, 1983

He won the Pitcher's Triple Crown in the Carolina League that year, leading the league in wins (he finished with 19 wins and 4 losses), ERA (2.50), and strikeouts, showing a capability that would come to earn him his famous "Dr. K' nickname, fanning 300 batters in only 191 innings. That effort shattered the Lynchburg record of 214 strikeouts by Alan Fitzmorris (1968), and the league record of 275 by Ken Deal in 1947. During the 1983 season, Dwight had his first opportunity to pitch on the mound at Shea Stadium. As part of a promotion highlighting its young talent, the Mets scheduled a game at Shea between Lynchburg and the Salem Red Birds. Dwight got the start and pitched a one-hitter into the ninth inning, before losing the game. When the team returned to Lynchburg, he won his next 14 decisions.

At the end of the 1983 season, Davey Johnson, who was managing the Mets' Tidewater team, brought Dwight up for the International League Governor's Cup playoffs, which he helped them win by throwing a complete game four-hitter against Denver. Davey had first seen Dwight in 1982 when he filled in as the Kingsport manager for a few weeks. He liked what he saw then, he liked it in 1983, and when he was named as the Mets' Major League manager for the 1984 season he began to politic for Dwight's promotion to the majors. Over the reservations of Mets' General Manager, Frank Cashen, Dwight made his much anticipated Major League debut on April 7, 1984, at the age of 19, (the youngest player in the National League), against the Houston Astros.

This is one start I don't want to miss. I've heard all about him, and I'm anxious to see this kid pitch.
Nolan Ryan, quoted by Joseph Durso, The New York Times, April 8, 1984

He won that game, 3-2, and proceeded to have a remarkable rookie year. He broke Herb Score's record for strikeouts by a rookie pitcher, recording 276 K's in 218 innings, establishing his "Dr. K" identity. His strikeouts came at such a phenomenal rate that he established a new Major League record for most strikeouts per 9 innings pitched: 11.394. Since then only four pitchers have achieved a higher average: Randy Johnson, Pedro Martinez, Kerry Wood, and Nolan Ryan. Not bad company when you are talking strikeouts. Dwight also tied a Major League record for strikeouts in two consecutive games, notching 32 in his starts of September 12th and 17th, following his 11 strikeouts in his September 7th start, which gave him a three straight game record 43.

I think the most impressive thing about Gooden is that I saw Koufax and Gibson after they had been in the big leagues for five years. Gibby was wild and even though he threw awfully hard, he had no idea where his fastball was going. It exploded out of the strike zone. Koufax couldn't get his curveball over until 1961. Gooden is the most impressive young pitcher I have ever seen because he is doing it right now and has tremendous poise.
Tim McCarver, quoted by Hal Bodley, USA Today, June 26, 1984

On June 5, 1984, Dwight took a no hitter into the eighth inning against Pittsburgh, and by then he had already pitched five games where he struck out ten or more batters. That year Dwight became the youngest player ever named to the All-Star team, and he combined with Fernando Valenzuela to strike out six consecutive American League All-Star batters, which had never been done before. At the end of the season the buzz created by Gooden was even greater than his anticipated debut in April.

Dwight is a once-in-a-generation pitcher. He's the best thing that has happened to baseball in a long time. Everywhere I go, bartenders, bellmen, waiters, waitresses ... they all ask about Dwight Gooden. They all want to see him pitch.
Keith Hernandez, quoted in The Sporting News, September 10, 1984

They shouldn't try to compare Dwight with Sandy Koufax or Nolan Ryan or anyone else, because there is no comparison. They should be comparing the others with Dwight. There's really no comparison because none of them ever did what Dwight has done. Not at his age. No one.
Davey Johnson, quoted by Jack Lang, The Sporting News, October 1, 1984

He completed his rookie season with a 17-9 record, earning Rookie of the Year honors, and finished second in the National League Cy Young voting behind Rick Sutcliffe. Dwight's performance was key in helping to bring the Mets back to a level of respectability.

All of that set the stage for 1985, a season which *The Sporting News* ranks as the sixth greatest season ever for a pitcher, ranking it one place higher than Gibson's 1968. Although Gibby's year is cited by many as the pinnacle of pitching excellence, mainly because of the 1.18 ERA, Doc's 1985 season is more than worthy of comparison. I'll let you look at the stats for yourself:

Category	Gibson – '68	NL Rank	Gooden – '85	NL Rank
ERA	1.12	1st	1.53	1st
Wins	22	2nd	24	1st
Winning %age	.710	3rd	.857	2nd
Hits per 9 innings	5.85	1st	6.65	1st
Innings Pitched	304.7	3rd	276.7	1st
Strikeouts	268	1st	268	1st
Games Started	34	10th	35	8th
Complete Games	28	1st	16	1st
Shutouts	13	1st	8	2nd

Obviously, an argument can be made for either of those two seasons to be among the best ever by a Major League pitcher. In addition to the statistics I cited there are intangibles on both sides: Gibby won fifteen consecutive decisions and his team won the National League pennant. Doc had only one loss after May 25th, became only the second pitcher since World War II to win the Pitcher's Triple Crown (leading the Major Leagues in Wins, ERA and Strikeouts), and the youngest player ever to win the Cy Young Award.

My fastball rose so much, I swear there were times that I'd throw it at a hitter's belt level, and by the time he'd finished swinging, the ball was around his eyes.
That was a gift, I knew. There's no way a pitching coach can teach you to make a fastball explode like that at the last moment; either you have or you don't. Nolan Ryan did. J.R. Richard did.
Heat, My Life On and Off the Diamond, by Dwight Gooden with Bob Klapisch, William Morrow and Co., New York, 1999

In the middle of that magic season, Hall of Famer, Lefty Gomez, in Cooperstown for Induction Day, commented on Dwight's future:

If he doesn't get hurt he'll be coming here. He's got it. God forbid anything should happen to that kid.
Gomez, quoted by Antone Clark, The Telegram, July 30, 1985

Jim Palmer who himself would be elected to the Hall of Fame, echoed Lefty's thoughts:

He is going to be one of the all-time great pitchers. I know it sounds crazy to say that about someone only in his second season, but frankly, I've never seen anyone like him in the big leagues. Barring injury, he's going to set record books on their ears. His only weakness is holding runners on base, and that won't be too great a problem because in his career there won't be many runners to hold on. He has brains. He

knows the strike zone. He's amazing.
Jim Palmer, quoted by Larry King, The Sporting News, 1985

On August 20, 1985, Dwight shutout the San Francisco Giants on seven hits while striking out 16 batters. That was his 19th victory of the season, and put him in a position to become the youngest pitcher in the history of the game to win twenty games in a Major League season. He did it in his very next start, on Sunday, August 25th at Shea Stadium, beating the San Diego Padres 9-3 for his 14th straight victory. Since 1890, Bob Feller, in 1939, was the only pitcher under the age of 21 to win twenty games in a season.

It's tough enough to win 14 or 15 games. That's a lot of ball games, especially in a five-man rotation and for a young man, only 20. I've never seen a pitcher with a future ahead of him like Gooden has.
Phil Niekro, 3 time 20 game winner and Hall of Famer, quoted by Sam Goldpaper, The New York Times, August 27, 1985

He was by far the greatest pitcher I'd ever seen. I pitched behind him in the rotation, so I always charted his pitches. Those first two years, I swear, it seemed like he was 0 and 2 on 75 percent of the hitters. It was like Little League, where the other team has no chance except to bunt.
Ron Darling, Dwight's teammate, quoted in Sports Illustrated, February 27, 1995

Some days when facing Gooden, you felt like if you hit a foul ball it was a good day.
Tom Herr

After only two seasons in the majors, Dwight "set the standards by which other pitchers are compared" according to *The Sporting News* (April 1986). In Dwight's third season, 1986, he won 17 games, lost 6, struck out 200 batters and had a 2.84 ERA. He was the first modern day pitcher to have 200 strikeouts or more in his first three seasons. He had recorded 58 victories in his first three seasons, an average of more than 19 wins a year. However, he was a victim of his own success. The New York media felt that Dwight was not as overpowering in 1986 as he was in his first two seasons. It was the first time he averaged less than one strikeout per inning and he seemed to be relying on his curve ball more often than his famous fastball. And in 1986 the regular season was the good news for Dwight, who pitched a complete game to clinch the National League pennant for the Mets.

The Mets went on to win the World Series, so Dwight added a World Championship ring to his baseball hardware collection before he reached the age of 22. However, he was 0-3 in the 1986 postseason, with two World Series losses. That off season Dwight's off-the-field problems became bigger news than his on-the-field successes. Rumors began to swirl about Dwight using drugs. In the

November 24, 1986 edition of *The Sporting News*, it was reported Dwight requested "that a drug testing clause be inserted into his contract because he is sensitive to rumors that he is a drug user." Two weeks later Dwight had an "encounter" with the Tampa Police that was reminiscent of when the Deputy kicked me and held the gun to my head in Santa Ann in 1954 because I didn't say "yes sir." But there were differences in the situations. Unfortunately for Dwight, in his situation the police officers were much more physical and that could have been because Dwight had been drinking and resisted his arrest. When tested, his blood alcohol level was .111, slightly above the Florida definition of intoxication. I was sober when I was attacked and although I did not appreciate getting kicked in the back, I heeded my mother's voice in my head telling me that if I gave the Deputy any resistance or grief I would suffer for it physically. Dwight was not as submissive as I was and according to several witnesses he paid for it dearly:

About 10 p.m. Saturday, Daniel Hopkins, 25, ... saw two squad cars, their blue lights flashing, pulling in behind a red Corvette and a silver Mercedes. ... Hopkins watched as a tall black man in light-colored clothes got out of the silver Mercedes. The next morning he found out the man was Gooden.

"Gooden got out of the car first, and he was standing in back, in front of the police car lights, with his hands folded across his chest," Hopkins says. "Two cops came up and they told him to lay across the back of the Mercedes, and then, when he was like that, they searched him."

"Man, why are you searching me? I ain't no druggie!" Hopkins quoted Gooden.

According to police, it was Gooden who first became abusive, accusing them of harassment and refusing to turn over his driver's license.

According to Hopkins, the officers ordered Gooden down on the ground. "I ain't laying down on no goddamn ground!" Gooden shot back. "I ain't no dog."

Gooden was enraged, other witnesses say, and his pals started yelling at the cops.

Even though more squad cars pulled up, Gooden refused to lie on the ground. Officer Larry Scott Wolff, 29, a former high school football star, tried to subdue Gooden with a neck hold that the Tampa police call a "carotid restraint."

They say the technique is intended to "render a person unconscious in a couple of seconds" but is not as dangerous as applying a chokehold. But some police departments say a "carotid restraint" is a chokehold and prohibit officers from using them and all neck restraints because of the danger of fatal injury to a suspect. The one exception is if an officer believes deadly force is necessary.

Wolff, the officer who tried the maneuver, got kicked in the groin by Gooden, police say.

The force used to restrain Gooden stunned some bystanders. "A man turned to me and said, 'I've never seen cops act like that,'" says Dell Barker, 26.

Hopkins says he saw a female officer dash across the street and strike Gooden in the head with an 18 inch flashlight, shattering the glass on the light.

Police regulations in Tampa, as well as elsewhere, prohibit blows to a suspect's head unless deadly force is necessary.

Six to nine policemen wrestled Gooden to the ground, witnesses say. The officers tried to get him to roll over. "He wouldn't," says Jacob Barker, Dell's brother.

Jacob Barker says he heard the cops yell: "Get down, Gooden!"

"The cops started kicking him," Fay says. "He was struggling."

"You could hear the breath going out of him, every time they hit him." Hopkins says.

Once the pitcher was on the ground, witnesses say, they hogtied him with police-issued nylon rope, hands and feet together in an arc behind his back. ...

After police hogtied Gooden, Hopkins says, they sprayed mace in his face. "I saw Gooden with his feet tied up, bleeding from the mouth," says Tim Wertz, 17.

Then, Hopkins says, "they picked him up like a butchered dog," tossing him in the back of a squad car. All of these witnesses were white.

Clem Richardson and Sydney P. Freedberg, Knight-Ridder Newspapers, December 24, 1985

In January 1987, Dwight pled no contest to the charges against him and was given three years probation and 180 hours of community service to the Police Athletic League. Things started to slide further downhill from there for Dwight. In April of 1987, he tested positive for cocaine. That resulted in Dwight entering the Smithers Alcoholism and Treatment Center, his first attempt to rid himself of addiction, which would not be successful, mainly because although they would sober Dwight up, they didn't reach his mind.

I spent those twenty-eight days in the rehab program, the whole time thinking that I didn't belong there. That was an awful mistake on my part.
Heat, My Life On and Off the Diamond, by Dwight Gooden with Bob Klapisch, William Morrow and Co., New York 1999

Dwight's alcohol consumption was setting him up for the use and abuse of cocaine leading to his destruction, much the same way his curveball used to set up hitters to be demolished by his legendary fastball. But the hitter always lived to come back to the plate again. Dwight's game with alcohol and cocaine was much more serious, deadly, in fact. But he seemed to act as if he thought he had nine lives. After his stay at Smithers, Major League Baseball tested Dwight for drugs two or three times a week. He managed to avoid problems with Major League Baseball for a while by sticking to alcohol as his drug of choice. Addictive and destructive though it may be, it was not a prohibited substance, so Dwight used it.

If I won, I went out drinking to celebrate. And if I lost, I went out drinking to forget about it.
Dwight Gooden, quoted in Sports Illustrated, February 27, 1985

The resiliency of youth, especially for a gifted athlete, allowed Dwight to continue to perform remarkably well. In 1989, when Dwight was only 24, an age when most pitchers are still in the minor leagues, or whose careers are already over, he earned his 100th victory. That made him the third youngest pitcher to accomplish that goal.

Dwight is a freak of nature to us normal guys. You can't emulate what he has accomplished.
David Cone, teammate, The Sporting News, July 3, 1989

Dwight missed two months of the 1989 season, from the middle of July to September because of a torn muscle in his shoulder. Despite that injury, in 1990 a panel of the best hitters in the National League, (Tony Gwynn, Lonnie Smith, Mark Grace and Pedro Guerrero), voted Dwight as the best pitcher in the National League. Through the 1991 season, Dwight's lifetime record was 132-53, a .713 winning percentage, and that was the lowest his winning percentage had been at the end of any year in his eight-year career to that point. In 1990, Dwight came very close to having another twenty-win season, posting a record of 19-7. In 1991, Dwight's season ended early, on August 22, when he suffered a torn labrum and partial tear of his rotator cuff, requiring surgery.

By Dwight's own admission, eventually even he hit his limit:

I didn't think it happened before, but in '92 and '93 all the drinking started to affect my performance. It was cumulative. After a while, abusing your body catches up to you. I'd be the first to admit it.
Dwight Gooden, Sports Illustrated, February 27, 1985

Dwight's affected performance reflected in his pitching records. In 1992, Dwight had his first losing season in his career, going 10-13, and he followed that with an equally subpar 1993, at 12-15. It was enough to cause Dwight to make public his thoughts about the end of his career.

I'm not going to keep going just for a paycheck. For a long time, every year was fun for me. I guess I got spoiled. Then 1991 got bad, '92 got

**worse and last year was pure hell. I've said that if it's not fun, it's time
to get out. That time may be getting close.**
Dwight Gooden, The Sporting News, December 6, 1993

But buoyed by a strong spring training, Dwight's outlook seemed to be quite different:

**It's the thing that keeps me going. Within myself I visualize that I can
picture myself pitching 10, 15 games in a row, winning 10, 15 games in
a row, picture the crowd rooting me on to 20 wins. I picture it and I
know that I can do that. And that keeps me going. It's not like I say,
'Oh, man, all those days are over with.' The day I feel that way, it's
time to get out of the game.**
Dwight Gooden, The New York Times, April 28, 1994

Unfortunately for Dwight the strength of his spring training was lost on an injury to his toe suffered in the 1994 opener. That led to missed starts and a poor record, at 3-4, when it was revealed in June that his drug tests were positive. It was the first time in seven years that Dwight tested positive in the drug tests administered by Major League Baseball. This time, in addition to rehab, Baseball Commissioner Bud Selig ordered that Dwight be suspended for the remainder of 1994, and subsequently suspended him for all of 1995. It was a very low point in Dwight's life. His only connection to baseball during that time was coaching his son's team in the North Seminole Little League.

In 1996, Dwight returned to baseball and to the Big Apple, wearing the uniform of the New York Yankees. George Steinbrenner was an owner who had decided to give Dwight another chance, just as he had given a chance to Dwight's former Met teammate, Darryl Strawberry. Dwight was given a spot in the rotation but before the end of April he was moved to the bullpen, with a record of 0-3 and an unacceptable ERA of 11.48. It appeared that his 22 months away from the game were too much to overcome. But when David Cone, another former Met teammate who was now wearing pinstripes, was diagnosed with an aneurysm in an artery in his shoulder, Gooden somehow stepped up. Then a storyline developed that seemed scripted by Hollywood. On the afternoon of May 14, 1996, Dwight received a call from his sister informing him that their Dad, who was already undergoing daily dialysis for failed kidneys, needed double-bypass surgery. Dwight was to fly to Tampa the next morning. They Yankees gave Dwight the option of skipping his turn in the rotation that night against the Seattle Mariners. Dwight decided to take the ball and dedicate his efforts to his Dad. Several hours later Paul Sorrento popped up to shortstop and when the ball came down into Derek Jeter's mitt, Dwight Gooden had pitched the first no-hitter of his career. The next day Dwight's Dad had the surgery and Dwight was there to greet him in the recovery room. Dwight brought with him all the New York papers with the coverage of the game and he presented his Dad with the game ball.

In the spring of 1997, Dwight suffered a hernia which was originally misdiagnosed, causing him to miss most of the first half of the season. The Yankees decided not to pick up his option for 1998, but Dwight was able to land a spot with the Cleveland Indians. Dwight spent two seasons with Cleveland as a spot starter, with a record of 11-10 over the two years. In 2000 he started the season with the Houston Astros, and was then sold to the Tampa Bay Devil Rays before a return engagement with the Yankees, where he spent most of his time in the bullpen.

When Dwight announced his retirement from baseball after failing to make the Yankees' 2001 team, George Vecsey wrote an article in *The New York Times* that mentioned Dwight's potential to be like two other Black Aces, Bob Gibson and Don Newcombe:

He could throw so easily, and hitters raved about his curveball. He could have been Bob Feller or Bob Gibson, two legends who draw huge crowds when they appear at old-timers' functions. Gooden can still make his mark. ...
He doesn't have to be a Feller or a Gibson. Out in Los Angeles there is a man named Don Newcombe who came up to the Brooklyn Dodgers belatedly when the color lines were relaxed, and for a time looked like the greatest pitcher in Dodger history, until he drank himself out of the major leagues. Years later, Newk sobered up – on his own, which not everybody should try. For nearly a quarter of a century, Newcombe has been working with the Dodgers in community relations as well as being a role model for Dodger employees who might have a substance problem.
George Vecsey, The New York Times, March 31, 2001

Unfortunately, Dwight's troubles with addiction were not over. As I complete this book, Dwight is completing a rehab program in Florida. From what I can see this is the most serious attempt made by Dwight to come to terms with his addiction. Dwight Gooden was a good kid. I loved to watch him pitch, especially when he first came up. I got excited at the prospect of him becoming a pro since he came from the same area I did. I remember how impressed everybody was with his talent and ability. I was reminded of that as I researched this book. Every Major Leaguer who saw him, including some of the greatest pitchers in the game, whose quotes I have included in this chapter, thought he was the best they ever saw. They all believed that he was destined for Cooperstown and the Hall of Fame. But somewhere on that path to the mound, Dwight got lost, which was tragic for such a gifted kid. However, life being what it is, I am sincerely hopeful that this time Dwight will be able to recover from his addiction, and go on to do the great things that Don Newcombe did. I believe that Dwight still has an awful lot to contribute and it would be a remarkable and celebrated comeback, on par with JR's return from his physical and financial problems, and Mike Norris's return to the mound after seven years.

432

CHAPTER 28

DAVID KEITH STEWART
Dave
Smoke

Born February 19, 1957 in Oakland, California
Teams: Los Angeles Dodgers, Texas Rangers,
     Philadelphia Phillies, Oakland Athletics,
     Toronto Blue Jays
Twenty-Win Seasons: 1987, 1988, 1989, 1990
World Series Most Valuable Player – 1989
American League Championship Series MVP – 1990, 1993
American League All-Star – 1989

Respect is the first word anyone uses about Stew.
Dennis Eckersley, A's teammate and Hall of Famer

There is more to [Dave] Stewart than a fastball, a forkball and a menacing stare. There is fortitude, resiliency and compassion. There is the one trait we seek in each other; there is humanity.
Art Spander, The Sporting News, October 16, 1989

There may be pitchers in the A.L. with better velocity or better pitches, but no one will battle you any harder than Stew. It's like going to war against him. You can't let yourself get intimidated by that scowl of his, but sometimes you have the feeling he'd like to strangle you if you get a hit off of him.
Kirby Puckett, quoted by Dave Nightingale, The Sporting News, July 9, 1990

He [Stewart] is exactly what all of us want major leaguers to be. He's the teammate who is going to pick up the guy that's having a tough time. ... He's the teammate that's going to reach into his pocket to fund a team party because he wants a lot of unity.
Tony LaRussa, Oakland Athletics Manager, St. Louis Post-Dispatch, July 26, 1995

You know how much I love my hometown of Lacoochee. Now imagine how dearly Dave Stewart must hold his hometown of Oakland in his heart. In addition to being his place of birth, Oakland is where Dave's baseball career blossomed, at a time when most people thought it was already over. Dave is the only Black Ace who excelled at the Major League level in the same town where he was born. He grew up in a "tough" section of town, on Havenscourt Boulevard, about a mile from the Oakland Coliseum pitcher's mound, but his route to the mound of pitching success was anything but short, direct or easy. It was long, with curves that took him off-road, and at several junctures it looked like his efforts would fall short; but he bounced back from a very rough beginning to become a dominant Major League pitcher in the late '80s and early '90s, and a spectacular post-season success.

As a kid growing up in Oakland in the late '60s and early '70s, Dave was a big fan of the Athletics. He was a member of Reggie's Regiment, the Reggie Jackson fan club. He would walk over to the stadium, jump the fence and watch as many games as he could. When he wasn't watching Reggie, Vida or Blue Moon Odom pitch he was playing baseball himself, on Fruitvale Field, thanks to the coaches and volunteers who ran the Boys Club in Oakland.

I was a menace as a kid, a fighter, a rebel without a cause. They couldn't contain me. My mom kept switching me to different, stricter schools, but I didn't get any better. For some reason, and I'm still not sure why, I just didn't like people in general. I loved my family – there were seven of us, five girls [Ed. Note: Dave actually has six sisters] **and two boys – but I couldn't get along with anyone else. I suppose a part of it was that I would look at other kids and see they had more than I had. I'd had to work after school regularly since I was 12. Even in high school, where I played football, basketball and baseball, I pumped gas after practice.**
Dave Stewart, quoted by Ron Fimrite, Sports Illustrated, October 5, 1987

Dave has shared with me that some of his childhood acquaintances now reside in San Quentin Federal Penitentiary and he readily admits that if it were not for youth baseball, neighborhood coaches and organizations like the Boys Club, he could just as easily have been a career convict himself instead of a Major Leaguer.

My circle of friends stayed with our own dreams because we had strong family backgrounds and because we were always playing sports, especially at the Boys' Club. My parents had strong values of right and wrong.
I was tempted by the street life. I admit I experimented a little. But every time I got to the brink of getting in trouble, I pulled back. Sure, there was a lot of stuff happening on the street; the projects across 14th Street housed one of the biggest drug operations in the country. But it wasn't hard staying away from drugs or trouble. I had the Boys' Club and sports. There was a heck of a lot more good available to me

434

than there was bad.
Dave Stewart, quoted by Peter Gammons, Sports Illustrated, November 6, 1989

Dave is not the only professional athlete to call Oakland home. Rickey Henderson, who was Dave's teammate with the A's and the Blue Jays, first played baseball with Dave in the Oakland American Legion League. Other Major Leaguers to come from Oakland include Joe Morgan, Frank Robinson, Curt Flood, Vada Pinson, Willie Stargell, Lloyd Moseby, and Gary Pettis. Dave is quick to acknowledge that it was people like Howard Bess, his Little League coach, and Bob Howard, his Physical Education teacher and coach at St. Elizabeth's High School, that made a difference in his life.

Bob Howard, my coach at St. Elizabeth's High, made me change my personality. What everybody else did, I didn't want to do. One day, he sat me down and told me, 'I care a lot about you as a young man. But it's up to you to go to school and get out, or be satisfied with being a failure. You can do something with yourself.' He was the first person outside of my family who became a positive influence in my life.
Dave Stewart

Dave's Mom, Nathalie Stewart, worked at a local cannery, and his Dad, David, who died in 1972, was a longshoreman. Dave remembers his Dad as a hardworking man, who didn't want Dave to be a ballplayer because he didn't think he would be able to provide for his family. So, Dave's older brother, Gregory, is the one who taught him baseball. Dave attended St. Elizabeth's High School in Oakland, and like several of the Black Aces before him, he was accomplished in several sports. He was an excellent linebacker and a star basketball forward. He had twenty-six (26) football scholarship offers, but baseball was Dave's first love, and he excelled as a catcher in high school.

Following the route of most post-1965 ballplayers, Dave entered baseball via the draft system. But unlike Vida, J.R. and Mike Norris, Dave was neither a high draft choice nor a bonus baby. In fact, he was drafted by the Los Angeles Dodgers in the 16th round of the June 1975 draft, after graduating from high school. Dave immediately learned that professional baseball was as much a business as a game, when the Dodgers sent him to Bellingham, Washington, and immediately began transforming him from a catcher to a relief pitcher.

After spending the balance of 1975 and all of 1976 in Bellingham, Dave was promoted in 1977 to Class AAA and a starting pitching role with the Albuquerque Dukes of the Pacific Coast League. Yet in 1978, he took a step backward, to Class AA, pitching for San Antonio, (where he notched 14 victories), and then as a September call-up he made his Major League debut for the Los Angeles Dodgers on September 22, 1978, closing out a game by pitching two shutout innings. But that was to be his last Major League action for a long time. The good news was his season in San Antonio earned him a return trip to Albuquerque and AAA, but the bad news is that is where he stayed for the 1979 and 1980 seasons. Although he was called up to the majors at the end of each season, he did not get to play at all. In 1980, he led the Pacific Coast League in games started, with 29, and pitched 202 innings. He was 15 and 10 with a 3.70 ERA.

In the spring of 1981, Dave's career with the Dodgers almost came to an end before it really started. A player who is on a team's 40-man roster, but not on the 25-man Major League roster is deemed to be on "optional assignment." That means that during his first three years he can be sent up and down between the majors and minors as many times as the club sees fit, but after that he is out of options. He must be placed on waivers and clear them before a team can send him down to the minors again. Being placed on waivers means that other teams in the Major Leagues, in the reverse order of their standings, have three business days to claim the player. If no team claims him the player is said to have cleared waivers and can be sent down. By 1981, the Dodgers had no options left to send Dave down to the minors without placing him on waivers. As spring training ended and the Dodgers made their final cuts Dave was told he was last man cut and he was being placed on the waiver list. In fact, he was packing his bags to go when he learned that the team had decided to release Don Stanhouse instead, and they put Dave in the bullpen.

Dave enjoyed some success with the Dodgers in 1981. He started out very strong by winning his first Major League game in his first appearance, and did not allow a single run in his first eight appearances, over a total of 12.6 innings. Over the course of the strike-shortened season he made 32 appearances all in relief, earning six saves and posting a 2.49 ERA, with a 4-3 record. He also collected his first World Championship ring in 1981, a rare feat for a rookie, as the Dodgers won four straight games from the Yankees after dropping the first two. Dave appeared in the first two games, pitching 1.6 scoreless innings. He didn't pitch in the League Championship Series against the Montreal Expos, but did get some work against the Houston Astros in the Divisional Series made necessary by the strike. The Dodgers won that series after losing the first two games in Houston, both losses being attributed to Dave, who pitched a total of two-thirds of an inning in relief and gave up the winning runs to the Astros in the bottom of the ninth in Game One and the bottom of the eleventh in Game Two.

In 1982, Dave had a chance to spend time with Dodger legend, Sandy Koufax, my World Series buddy from 1965. It was Koufax who taught Dave how to throw the split-fingered fastball:

I had a hard fastball and a hard breaking ball, but Sandy felt that if I had a pitch that broke on a downward plane, it would be better. I started working with it and started getting ground-ball outs with it. *Dave Stewart, Knight Ridder Tribune, Oct. 16, 1993*

But more importantly, Sandy taught Dave about the emotions of pitching:

He told me, 'Pitching is making a batter fear you. Put one inch of fear in a man, and you've won the battle. I don't know if batters necessarily fear me, but they think about me.'
Dave Stewart, quoted by Art Spander, The Sporting News, May 23, 1988

Dave learned the mechanics of the split-fingered fastball, but didn't have the confidence to use it in game situations yet in the 1982 season. Relying on just his fastball, Dave split his time between the bullpen and the starting rotation, starting 14 games and appeared in a total of 45 games, pitching 146.3 innings. He was above .500 again, with a 9-8 record. His best winning percentage with the Dodgers was in 1983, when he went 5 and 2, basically all in relief again. From the time the 1982 season ended there were rumors that Dave would be traded to the Texas Rangers as part of a trade that would bring catcher Jim Sundberg to the Dodgers. Despite all the rumors, the teams couldn't pull off the trade, and by July 4th, Dave was in the running for the National League Rolaids Relief Man Award. He was 5 and 2 with eight saves, and was contending with Steve Bedrosian of the Atlanta Braves, Jeff Reardon of Montreal, and Gary Lavelle of the San Francisco Giants for billing as the top reliever in the League. But on August 19, 1983, Dave was traded to the Rangers. Sundberg was not part of the trade, and I'm positive that in retrospect Dave wishes he was never part of the trade either.

During the remainder of the 1983 season Dave performed very well for the Rangers. Manager Doug Rader immediately made Dave a starter and during the six weeks he was with the Rangers that season he started eight games and pitched the first two complete games of his Major League career. He had a stingy ERA of 2.14 and matched the 5 and 2 record of the earlier part of the season with the Dodgers, making him 10-4 for the season.

Dave and the rest of the Rangers' pitching staff (Charlie Hough, Frank Tanana and Danny Darwin) got off to a rough start in 1984 and never recovered. Dave lost his first six decisions and then lost a few turns in the rotation to injuries. He was throwing a forkball, which is similar to the split-fingered fastball, but which drops instead of rises. After opposing batters took a few forkballs deep for home runs, Doug Rader's criticism stopped Dave from throwing either the split-fingered fastball or the forkball. By season's end, Hough was the only starter with a winning record (16-14) and no one had an ERA lower than the 3.25 posted by Tanana. By late August Dave was taken out of the starting rotation and was asked to be a middle reliever. He completed the season with a 7 and 14 record and a generous ERA of 4.73.

Things turned from bad to worse for Dave in Texas as the calendar moved from 1984 to 1985. Dave started the season in the bullpen and by the beginning of May, Doug Rader lost confidence in him. Dave was definitely not pitching well, but when he complained of discomfort in his right elbow, it was dismissed as an excuse for his ineffectiveness. Rader basically removed Dave from pitching in situations where the game was on the line. The dispute between player and manager went public, with Rader stating to the press that Dave's pitching was ineffective. That led to Dave asking to be traded rather than buried in the bullpen. By the time the Rangers accommodated him he was 0-6 and it was the middle of September. They traded him to the Phillies, who had been trying to obtain him for more than a year.

When Dave got to Philadelphia he continued to complain about his right elbow. The Phillies' team doctor looked into Dave's complaints and determined that he indeed had bone chips in his elbow requiring surgery. He only pitched a total of 4.3 innings for the Phils in four appearances with no record and went under the knife on October 2nd, 1985. When the 1986 season rolled around the Phils signed Dave to a one year contract for $400,000 and were hopeful that he would make a full recovery from the surgery. Dave was only used very sparingly, in middle relief, for a total of 12 innings in 8 appearances in the first month of the season. On the 9th of May the Phils gave Dave his unconditional release, and it looked like his route to the pitcher's mound had been aborted.

I sat in a room, lights off, for three days without eating. All I wanted to do is play ball.
Dave Stewart, quoted by Peter Gammons, Sports Illustrated, May 16, 1988

Then two weeks later Oakland came back into Dave's life and life came back into Dave's arm and pitching career. Oakland was playing on the road, in Baltimore, and Dave went to Memorial Stadium with the hope that he could convince either team to give him a tryout. The Orioles said, "No" but the Athletics gave Dave a workout and then signed him to a Triple-A contract on May 23, 1986. After one three-inning appearance with their minor league team in Tacoma (Pacific Coast League), Dave was called up to the majors as a relief pitcher. For the first several weeks with the team Dave was used sparingly and not in any situations where the game was on the line. Having gone that route in Texas and Philadelphia, he was not looking forward to doing it again and seriously thought about quitting. He attributes teammate Dusty Baker with encouraging him to stay the course. Stew and Dusty were teammates in Los Angeles and were reunited in Oakland in 1986. Baker saw Dave's frustration in 1986 when he first came to the A's, and told him to hang in there.

Luckily for Dave, his return to his hometown was soon followed by the team hiring Tony LaRussa as their new manager, their third of the year. LaRussa's first act was to name Dave as the starting pitcher against Boston, in Fenway Park, against Roger Clemens. Dave rewarded Tony's confidence by earning his first victory in two years. He then won his next two decisions and nine of his first ten, including the first shutout of his career. Stewart and LaRussa would be a winning combination for the Athletics for the rest of the decade and beyond. Part of that success is attributable to Dave Duncan, who noticed Stewart throwing his Sandy Koufax forkball on the sidelines, and gave Stew the confidence to use it in a game. Dave finished the 1986 season with a 9 and 5 record. That was quite an accomplishment considering that his combined record for all of 1984, 1985 and the first month of 1986 was 7 and 20. Oakland welcomed Dave home, and he demonstrated his comfort at being there by pitching at a whole different level.

His success as a starter for Oakland blossomed even further in 1987. It was then, in his first full season with the Athletics, that Dave earned his status as a member of The Black Aces. But that didn't come easy either. With 19 victories under his belt, Stew failed on four straight occasions to win his 20th, throwing two complete games in the process. But he continued to persevere, didn't miss a start the whole year and finished with a 20-13 record. He was the only twenty-game winner in the majors that season besides Clemens, who won the Cy Young Award with a 20-9 record. Dave notched his twentieth win on September 30 with a 4-3 victory over Cleveland. After the game, Dave gushed, "I feel like crying. I'm happy. I've got a lot of different thoughts right now." I am sure some of those thoughts were that his success absolved him from all the talk that he was "washed up" and that he finally showed the real Dave Stewart to the world. Dave finished third in the American League Cy Young voting behind Clemens (Boston) and Jimmy Key (Toronto).

Stew started the 1988 season with a flourish, winning his first eight decisions. By the middle of May sportswriters were comparing his success rate to Denny McLain's thirty-one win pace of 1968. He was a workhorse in 1988, pitching a league high 275.7 innings. He pitched 14 complete games, notched 192 strikeouts, and posted a 21-12 record in 37 starts. Those stats earned him a place on the 1988 Sporting News All-Star Team as the right-handed pitcher of the year. Dave again received consideration in the Cy Young Award voting, but finished fourth behind Frank Viola (Minnesota), teammate and now Hall of Famer, Dennis Eckersley, and Mark Gubicza (Kansas City).

Although Mark McGwire and Jose Canseco, popularly known as The Bash Brothers, got most of the press for their outstanding hitting performances in 1988, the Oakland pitching staff was equally impressive, leading the league in team ERA (3.44). That combination of pitching and offense was good enough to capture the American League Western Division Title. Stew started two games in the ALCS which the A's swept over the Red Sox to gain a berth in the World Series. This was the beginning of a phenomenal run for Dave in the ALCS. He earned one win, posting a 1.35 ERA, with 11 strikeouts in 13.3 innings over the two games, helping place the A's in the Series. Stew also started two games in the World Series, and although he pitched well, allowing only 5 runs in over 14 innings of work, Dave didn't win a game and the A's didn't win the Series, losing to the Dodgers, led by a gimpy home-run hitting Kirk Gibson and an unbelievable Orel Hershiser.

In 1989, Stew again excelled early in the season, starting off by winning seven of his first eight decisions, and ten of his first twelve. For the three-year period, starting with his first victory for Oakland on July 7, 1986, Dave won more games than any other pitcher in the Major Leagues. He was 60-32 over 103 starts.

Stew was recognized as one of the game's premier pitchers in 1989 when he got the nod as the starting pitcher for the American League in the 1989 All Star Game played at Anaheim. Although Stew had a rough first inning, giving up two runs, he was bailed out by Bo Jackson who made a great running catch with two runners on and two outs, and then in the bottom of the first Jackson hit a line drive home run followed by a Wade Boggs homer to even the score. Nolan Ryan came on in relief and the American League went on to win the game.

On September 13, 1989, Dave already had 19 wins and left a game against Milwaukee in the ninth inning with a 6-4 lead, turning it over to Dennis Eckersley. In uncharacteristic fashion, Eck surrendered a two-run homer to Greg Vaughn, denying Stew of his 20th victory. Five days later Stew again tried to become the first pitcher in the American League to be a 20-game winner three years in a row since Jim Palmer had four straight for Baltimore 1975 through 1978. Again, Stew left the game in the bottom of the ninth, this time against Cleveland, winning 2-1, and he handed the ball to Eckersley. Again, Eckersley yielded a game-tying home run, costing Stew his 20th win. Finally, on September 22, 1989, Stew defeated the Twins, 5-2, earning his 20th win of the season and the 100th victory of his career.

Asked about how he approached winning twenty games in a season, Dave revealed that he didn't start out the season thinking about winning twenty, but rather broke the season down into months in his mind, and set a goal of winning four games a month out of a possible six starts:

If I happen to win five, great. If I win six, that's even better. But I have to go with what's reasonable and I think 4-2 is reasonable.
It's tough to say you're going to win 20 games when the season starts, because then you've put yourself in a position of having to win 20 before you win one. In small quantities, you're able to reach goals.
Dave Stewart, quoted by Kit Stier, The Sporting News, August 21, 1989

With his third twenty-win season under his belt, Dave returned to his favorite venue – the American League Championship Series, this time against Toronto. Dave again got two starts and this time earned two victories, upping his ALCS career record to 3-0. He yielded only 13 hits and five runs over 16 innings, helping the A's win consecutive American League flags and a return trip to the World Series.

The 1989 World Series is one that will always be easily remembered. For starters, it pitted the A's against their cross-town rivals, the National League Champion San Francisco Giants. It was the first time the Giants were in the World Series since 1962, when their championship hopes came to rest in Bobby Richardson's glove as he snared Willie McCovey's Game Seven, ninth inning line drive to end the game, 1-0, and the Series. The A's, having lost in 1988, were seeking their first title in 15 years. They hadn't won since 1974 when they beat the Dodgers in five games, the last of their three consecutive World Championships, during the heyday of Vida Blue. The Series started in Oakland and Tony LaRussa gave the Game One assignment to Dave who threw a complete game gem, shutting out the Giants 5-0, allowing only five hits and walking only one batter. After Mike Moore, Rick Honeycutt and Eckersley, combined on a four-hitter against the Giants in Game Two the Series shifted to San Francisco.

That is when the suspense and drama off-the-field was much greater than the game. During the pre-game warm-ups, as over 60,000 fans packed into Candlestick Park, on October 17, 1989, an earthquake measuring 7.1 on the Richter scale shook the Bay Area to its core. LaRussa told me that when he first felt the vibrations he thought it was the fans, but as he saw the light stanchions begin to sway he knew it was something much more significant and dangerous. Power was lost in the ballpark and immediately the most important of games, a World Series confrontation, became meaningless behind the concerns of the possible devastation, death and destruction that could result from the earthquake. The players and fans were remarkably calm, and Baseball Commissioner Fay Vincent quickly cancelled the game, insuring that all fans could vacate the park during the remaining hours of daylight. Outside the park, the earthquake had not been as forgiving. Buildings were burning, roads and bridges had collapsed, and injuries and fatalities were being reported.

Dave left Candlestick in his uniform and drove to find his two sisters. After driving for three hours and determining that his family and home were safe, Dave turned his attention to all the victims of the earthquake. He spent many hours visiting emergency workers and handing out A's jerseys and merchandise to people affected by the quake.

It was something that anyone would do. Oakland is my home. I had the resources and I had the time.
Dave Stewart, quoted by Jack Chevalier, The Philadelphia Tribune

The Series was postponed for ten days, with Game Three being played at Candlestick park on October 27th. Pre-game ceremonies were extremely emotional. As the Gatlin Brothers performed the National Anthem, 62,000 fans stood and cheered area emergency workers, the real heroes of the disaster recovery effort, who were honored on the field and asked to throw out the ceremonial first pitch.

Without people like that, we could have had more deaths. They stuck their necks out and went in there and didn't care what happened to themselves. They just went out there and did the best they could to bring people out. They should be honored, not just in ball parks, but all around the U.S.
Dave Stewart

LaRussa gave the ball to Dave again and he responded by holding the Giants to three runs in seven innings. He received tremendous offensive support from Dave Henderson (two home runs), Jose Canseco, Carney Lansford and Tony Phillips, as the A's won, 13-7. Dave became the first pitcher in the history of the game to win two Championship Series games and two World Series games in one year. After the A's swept the Giants by winning Game Four, Dave was named the World Series MVP.

After winning the World Series for Oakland, Dave's pride for his hometown was clearly evident:

In a way I feel the way athletes feel at the Olympics when they say they've won for their country. I won those games for my teammates and for myself, but I also won them for my community. I won them for that guy over there, and those kids on the corner, and that elderly woman next to them. I won them for the parks and recreation people, the teachers, the police, my Little League coach and all the people who helped shape my character and baseball skills. There are more than 300,000 people in this town who tonight can say, 'We're Number One,' and mean it.
Dave Stewart, quoted by Peter Gammons, Sports Illustrated, November 6, 1989

While it was right that Dave be recognized for his excellent pitching during the World Series, it was off-the-field that Dave Stewart proved he was a champion in 1989. He showed a warm, humanitarian side of him that was never revealed during game conditions, hidden by his game face death stare. He rose above the gigantic stage of the World Series and put the game in perspective by his approach to the San Francisco earthquake and the people who perished or were hurt, whose homes were lost, and those who served so valiantly to protect and restore. Troubled by the disaster, and the resulting damage to his hometown, Dave could not sleep at night. Every night he would go over to the area where a 1.25 mile portion of the top deck of the Cypress Structure freeway had collapsed, in West Oakland, trapping homebound, rush hour commuters. He would talk to area residents and offer whatever assistance he could, even if at times it was only a shoulder to lean on, or an ear to listen.

One of the most severe and touching stories I remember from the earthquake, was that on the roadway where the two-tiered freeway had collapsed, there was a woman who had died in her vehicle and her body was covering her son who had been injured. The only way they could reach the boy to save him, was to actually saw the woman's body, which they did. I remember visiting the boy in Children's Hospital. His arm was badly injured, and ultimately had to be amputated. A few years ago, as a man in his young 20s, he came up to me and introduced himself, and reminded me who he was, and told me that he never forgot my visit to him in the hospital.
Dave Stewart

It should also be noted that Dave's devotion to the Oakland community was not created by the earthquake and that he never drew attention to his community activities. Long before the 1989 quake, Dave was very active in Oakland area charities, especially those creating opportunities for children. He sponsored youth softball and baseball teams, a girls' track team and a dance troupe. He is on the Board of Directors of the Oakland Boys Club. In addition, Dave generously contributed to St. Elizabeth High, United Way, Cystic Fibrosis Foundation and Multiple Sclerosis Society. Every February, Dave would sponsor a "Picnic in the Park" at the Oakland Coliseum to benefit the Oakland Boys and Girls Clubs.

A lot of people are ashamed of what's happened to my city. They call it 'Cokeland.' They talk about drugs and violence. I want the children in Oakland to grow up feeling they have the same kind of chance that I had. I feel for the people who've suffered in Oakland and for the people who lost loved ones in the earthquake. We can't replace that. We're only a baseball team.

But the A's are a lot like the people of Oakland. The cream rises to the top. The A's battled back, just like the people of Oakland. And I hope we can make them feel a little bit better about their situation. I love this city, and I love this team, and the only team that's going to beat the A's is the A's.

Dave Stewart, quoted by Bob Verdi, The Sporting News, Nov. 13, 1989

In 1990, Dave was recognized for his efforts by Major League Baseball, who presented him with the Roberto Clemente Award, an annual award given to the player who best exemplifies baseball on and off the field.

I couldn't possibly write about Stew without mentioning his famous "Death Stare" and this is probably as good a place to mention it as any, because those who don't know Stew would find it hard to believe that a player who looks so fierce and competitive on the mound could be so warm, kind and compassionate off the mound. Dave's patented look, the "Death Stare", consisted of Dave pulling his cap down low, forming a hood over his eyes which he fixed on home plate with a stare that seemed to be able to paralyze batters. Fellow Black Ace, Mike Norris, told me that he was the one who taught Dave to wear his hat that way to create "tunnel vision to the plate", but Stew remembers that it was Sandy Koufax who actually suggested that he bring his hat down low on his forehead, limiting his vision, so that he could concentrate on a smaller area.

Many sportswriters and announcers realizing that Stew was actually quite pleasant and easy-going off the field, attributed intimidation as the motivating factor behind the Death Stare – Stew's equivalent of Ryne Duren throwing a warm-up pitch into the screen or Al "Mad Hungarian" Hrabosky turning his back to the batter and whipping himself into a frenzy. But Stew claims that the Death Stare wasn't so much about psyching the batter out as it was about psyching himself up:

I don't think it's so much intimidation as just being prepared to do

what you have to do to win. I wish it was as easy as putting on a face. Intimidation comes from building success, not from putting a face on. When you start having success and run off five, six wins in a row, all well-pitched games, you feel better. You know you're pitching well. All of a sudden, you build yourself a wall that people can't break.
Dave Stewart, quoted by Gorden Edes, Boston Globe, March 31, 2000

For the third straight year, Dave finished as a bridesmaid in the Cy Young Award voting. He was the only American League pitcher besides winner Bret Saberhagen (Kansas City Royals) to receive a vote from each of the 28 writers. He received one First Place vote, twenty-four Second Place votes and three Third Place votes. Saberhagen, who was 23-6 with a 2.16 ERA, received 27 First Place votes.

In 1990, Dave followed his established pattern for becoming a repeat twenty-game winner: getting a quick start out of the "gate." He won his first five starts in April, making him 19-0 with one no-decision in twenty April starts since April 15, 1987, his last April loss. In his first seven starts of the season, he yielded no more than two earned runs in any game. He was recognized for his early success by being named the American League Pitcher of the Month for April 1990.

On June 29, 1990, Stew entered the record books together with former teammate, Dodger starter Fernando Valenzuela, as they became the first two pitchers to throw no-hitters on the same day, one in the American League and one in the National League. (On April 22, 1898, Ted Breitenstein of the Cincinnati Reds no-hit the Pittsburgh Pirates and Jim Hughes of the Baltimore Orioles no-hit the Boston Beaneaters. At that time all four of those teams were in the National League). Stew struck out 12 Toronto Blue Jays at SkyDome in Toronto, winning 5-0, while Valenzuela beat the St. Louis Cardinals, 6-0, in Los Angeles. "This was the highlight of my career" Stewart said at the time. "Winning 20 games, that's something because they don't have to vote on 20 wins. But I thought after winning a World Series and the MVP award that you couldn't top that. This does." (*The Sporting News*, July 9, 1990)

In a July 1990 survey of the American League's top four hitters – Kirby Puckett, Carney Lansford, Wade Boggs and Julio Franco – Dave Stewart was ranked as the second best pitcher in the League, again finishing behind Saberhagen, but this time tying him for first place votes with one each, with Bert Blyleven and Charlie Hough also getting a first place vote each. It was a definite sign of the respect that these hitters had for Stew.

On September 14, 1990, Stew threw a five-hitter against the Twins, beating them 9-1. That was his 20th victory of the season, making him the first American League pitcher since Jim Palmer to win at least 20 games in a season for four consecutive years. It was one of Stew's most productive seasons. He achieved a career high in victories (22), and led the American League in innings pitched (267), games started (36), complete games (11), and shutouts (4). Stew finished third in the Cy Young Award voting, as three Athletics placed in the first five spots, with teammate Bob Welch (27-6) winning the Award, and closer Dennis Eckersley placing fifth.

The 1990 American League Championship Series pitted the Athletics against the Boston Red Sox, which meant that Stew and Roger Clemens would get to face off in Game One. Ever since Clemens bested Stew for the Cy Young Award in 1987, Stew seemed to be on a personal mission to prove to the world, and especially the baseball writers, that he was every bit as good as Roger Clemens.

I don't think Stewart has gotten the respect he deserves. Clemens is dominant in one way. But Stewart is dominant in another. I've never seen anyone who was so consistent. He takes the same stuff to the mound every start, and every time he starts, the A's think they're going to win.
Dave Duncan, A's pitching coach, quoted by Peter Gammons, Sports Illustrated, May 16, 1988

Dave Stewart is a special man. He won twenty games or more for us in four consecutive seasons. He was our pitching and spiritual leader.
Tony LaRussa, Manager, Oakland Athletics

In their five face-to-face match-ups leading into the ALCS, Stew was 5-0 against Clemens. The first game of the ALCS proved to be the pitching duel it was promoted as, as a Wade Boggs homer off Stew in the fourth inning provided the only run of the game until the seventh inning. By then, Clemens had left the game, with a 1-0 lead. A Rickey Henderson sacrifice fly in the seventh and a Carney Lansford RBI single in the eighth gave the A's the lead, and then they pounded the Red Sox bullpen for seven runs in the ninth. Stew would get a second start in the ALCS, winning Game Four and clinching the Series, allowing only one run in eight innings of work. For his two victories, during which he surrendered only 8 hits in 16 innings, with a 1.12 ERA, Stew was named the Most Valuable Player for the 1990 ALCS.

The 1991 season started typically for Dave Stewart. He won his first start, making him 20-0 in twenty consecutive April starts. Then things started to turn for Stew. His streak of 166 straight starts without missing a turn in the rotation was ended by a pulled muscle in his lower left rib cage that led to him being placed on the disabled list for the first time in his career. He only had one complete game all year, leading to 13 no-decisions, as many as he compiled in the three previous years combined. Dave lost his last start of the year, leaving him 11-11 for the year. It was pretty much a complete team breakdown, as the A's went from AL champs to a disappointing fourth place finish in the Western Division. When asked what happened to his perennial twenty-game winner, Tony LaRussa commented, "Every once in a while, even Frank Sinatra had to clear his throat." The final event of the disappointing year came after the season was over and Dave had to undergo arthroscopic surgery in an effort to repair torn cartilage in his left knee.

Dave's problems in 1992 started even before the first pitch of the regular season. Taking his turn at bat in an exhibition game against the National League Cubs, Dave re-injured his left rib cage, sidelining him for several days. Unfortunately, it was a sign of things to come over the course of the season. He was already rehabbing the surgically repaired knee, the rib cage was tender, and he would develop a tender right elbow that placed him on the disabled list again midway through the season. Dave thought his elbow problems came from a new no-windup delivery the A's wanted him to use because they felt he was tipping his pitches in 1991. Dave felt that the new windup put extra pressure on his elbow and any gain wasn't worth the pain. He began to realize what most good pitchers realize when they get to be about 35 years old – he couldn't just rely on blowing a fastball by the hitters anymore. He had to set hitters up with his pitch selection and location. Dave managed to have a winning season, posting a 12-10 record, and the A's were able to capture the AL Western Division again, with the identical 96-66 record that Toronto captured the Eastern Division title with. When the two teams met in the ALCS, Stewart again pitched well, starting two games, and winning his only decision, to go 6-0 in ALCS competition. But it wasn't enough for the A's to overcome Toronto, who went on to beat the Atlanta Braves in the World Series.

Toronto not only took the 1992 ALCS from Oakland, they also took Dave Stewart. In the off-season the Blue Jays signed Dave as a free-agent, ending a six and a half year relationship between Stew and the A's that was mutually beneficial to both sides. Dave was 116-71 while with the A's, and they won four AL Western Division titles in six years. Unfortunately for Dave, the change in scenery did not alter the way his April luck had soured since the end of his 20-0 April run during his twenty win seasons. For the third straight year he suffered an early season injury and was placed on the disabled list. In 1992, it was a tear in the flexor muscle of his right elbow, suffered at the end of spring training, that delayed Stew's Blue Jay debut for a month. Injuries nagged at him throughout the season, with a groin pull late in the season being the most serious. Through it all, Stew managed to accomplish a 12-8 record while appearing in only 26 games, his lowest appearance total in his professional career, except for his cameo appearance with the Dodgers in 1978 when he appeared in only one game.

Without a twenty-game winner, behind the pitching of Pat Hentgen, Juan Guzman, a young Al Leiter, and a number of different starters, and fueled by an offense with a .279 season batting average, the Blue Jays won the AL Eastern Division, and that placed Stewart right where he wanted to be – back in the ALCS. As if a switch were thrown, when the ALCS started, Stew returned to his post-season form, winning both of his starts against the Chicago White Sox, including the pennant clincher in Game Six. That ran Stew's ALCS record to a perfect 8-0. For the second time in four years, Dave was named the Most Valuable Player of the ALCS.

I'm about six years older, and I throw with less velocity, no doubt about it. I used to throw between 90 and 94 miles an hour. Now, on

a good day, I'm maybe 91. But I'm smarter. It doesn't show in the stats, but I have a better idea how to set up hitters and get them out. I know how to finish them off with my second or third pitch instead of just my fastball. I can trick hitters, too.
Dave Stewart, quoted by Michael Martinez, Knight Ridder Tribune, Oct. 16, 1993

However, he could not carry his performance into the World Series, where he was 0-1 in two starts, but the Blue Jays defeated the Phillies in a Game Seven thriller which featured Joe Carter's walk-off home run, the first of its kind since Mazeroski sent the Yankees home in 1960.

That would be Dave's last winning season as a player. He appeared in 22 games for the Blue Jays in 1994, finishing with a 7-8 record and a 5.87 ERA. He became a free agent at the end of that season, and returned to Tony LaRussa and the Oakland Athletics at the beginning of the 1995 season. In fact, Stew got there just in time to be given the ball for Opening Day. He had been 5-0 in Opening Day assignments for LaRussa during his first tour of duty with the Athletics. This time the Blue Jays spoiled his debut. As the season went on it became clear to everyone, including Dave, that his time on the mound was growing short. On July 17, 1995 he made his last appearance, and without much fanfare he abruptly retired. Over the season, he appeared in a total of 16 games, going 3-7.

Dave had a career record of 168-129, going 138-94 with four consecutive twenty-win seasons, three World Series championships, two ALCS MVP trophies, and a World Series MVP trophy, all earned after the Phillies had given up on him and issued his unconditional release.

Although Dave's time on the mound had come to an end, he was far from finished with baseball. His love for the game and his desire to remain involved, led him to work in the Commissioner's Office, then as a special assistant to Oakland General Manager Sandy Alderson, and then to be hired by the San Diego Padres as an assistant to General Manager Kevin Towers. It was ground-breaking territory, because despite Jackie and Larry having "broken" baseball's color barrier fifty years earlier, in 1997 Dave was one of only a very few blacks in baseball's front office. While baseball celebrated the golden anniversary of Jackie's debut, it gave rise to a discussion of racism in baseball, and the relative lack of blacks in the game. In fact, it was noted that 1997 was the first time since 1947 that the Dodgers themselves did not have any African-Americans in their everyday starting lineup or pitching staff, and there was a lower percentage of blacks in the game in 1997 than there was in 1959, the year the Red Sox became the last integrated team with the signing of Pumpsie Green. When they asked Dave about it in 1997, he stated:

It's an issue that blacks don't need to know – because we live it every day – but others do. It's just like talking about AIDS and drugs, you're just making people aware, that's all. It's not being militant.
We're not on a dang mission, but there should be equality in baseball.

The bottom line is that it's not the same for the black as it is for the white, from the field to the front office. But you've got to have players talking about it.
Dave Stewart, The Sporting News, April 21, 1997

By the end of the 1997 season, Dave was the top candidate to become the Padres' pitching coach. While he was very confident he could do the job, his real desire was to become the club's General Manager, and he was afraid that coaching would delay that from happening.

I have to set new ground, I have to earn the respect of other general managers and these so-called baseball people. So for me, that's more of a challenge. This (being a pitching coach) is challenging, but as a black man it's not easy to accomplish that goal (being a General Manger). And just how many GM jobs turn over? Bottom line is, there aren't that many. So to achieve it as a black man is an accomplishment in itself. And just to do it is not good enough. I want to do a good job.
Dave Stewart, quoted by Bernie Wilson, AP Online, March 19, 1998

The Padres and Stewart worked out an arrangement that allowed Dave to remain as a special assistant to the General Manager while assuming duties as the team's Major League pitching coach. From the outset, in his first spring training, he instilled a little bit of the Bob Gibson/Dave Stewart competitiveness in his young pitchers: he fined two of his pitchers for fraternizing with players from the opposing team before a game. He wanted his pitchers to be a "mystery" to opposing batters. Dave stressed mental discipline to all of his pitchers. He preached six cardinal rules of pitching:
- Throw first-pitch strikes
- Don't waste 0-2 pitches
- Work out of jams
- Work deep into a game
- Work quickly
- Bear down in the first, fifth and ninth innings

Stew's efforts bore obvious results for the Padres and their pitchers. The pitching staff's ERA dropped from 4.98 in 1997 to 3.63, and the Padres won the National League Western Division Title, beat the Astros in the Division Series and the Braves in the NLCS before losing the World Series to the New York Yankees. After the Series was over, Stew returned to the Toronto Blue Jays organization in the capacity of Assistant General Manager.

Over a three year period, through November 2001, Stew served the Blue Jays in several different capacities including pitching coach, advisor to the general manager, assistant general manager and director of player personnel. But when the Blue Jays by-passed Stew for the vacant General Manager's position in 2001 and hired J.P. Ricciardi, Stew resigned as assistant general manager and made no bones about why he quit:

> **They think the only people capable of doing these jobs are white people, not minorities.**
>
> **I'm not just speaking for me, I'm speaking for a lot of minority candidates who have not been given the opportunity. The system doesn't work. The playing field is never going to be equal. The man I work for here, Paul Godfrey, told me he would like me to take on his manager's job before he hired Buck Martinez.**
>
> **Why was it OK to hire me to manage his club, but not OK for me to be his general manager? It's just little messages. I made it perfectly clear this is the direction I wanted to be in. It's just little signs that it's perfectly acceptable for me to be on the field, but there's discomfort with me being in front-office management.**
>
> *Dave Stewart, quoted by Ronald Blum, AP Online, November 15, 2001*

At the time, of the thirty Major League Baseball teams, only one team, the Chicago White Sox had an African-American general manager, Ken Williams, and there were no general managers of Latin American descent, even though a quarter of the players in the game came from Latin American countries. After Stew left the Blue Jays, he joined Davey Lopes' staff as the pitching coach for the Milwaukee Brewers, the team owned by Acting Commissioner Bud Selig, who was working to insure that minorities were included in the hiring process for front office positions.

In 2003, Dave added another line to his impressive resume when he was named as the pitching coach for the 2003 USA Baseball Olympic Qualifying Team.

Dave's newest career is as a player agent. After negotiating contracts for several minor league players in the summer of 2003, Dave was approved by the major league players' union as a player agent. His first Major League contract negotiation, ironically enough, was with the Oakland A's, when he represented All-Star third baseman Eric Chavez, and successfully negotiated a six-year, $66 million contract extension, the richest contract in franchise history.

CHAPTER 29

DONTRELLE WAYNE WILLIS
D Train
Trelle

Born January 12, 1982 in Oakland, California
Teams: Florida Marlins
Twenty-Win Season: 2005
National League Rookie of the Year 2003
National League All-Star – 2003, 2005

He reminds me of Dwight Gooden. Dave Parker used to talk about himself, saying there's only one of him every ten years that comes down the pike. Well, here he (Willis) is.
Bill Robinson, Baseball Digest, December 2003

I think he's a little more advanced than me as far as pitching talent goes. I was more of a chucker than a pitcher. The sky's the limit for him.
Vida Blue

If you don't like Dontrelle, you don't like people.
Brad Penny, teammate

Dontrelle's the best pitcher I've ever seen.
Cliff Floyd, former teammate

He's going to be special, because he has that hunger in him where he wants to be better every year.
Mike Redmond, teammate

There's a charm about him, that joy of being there. He has all the makings of a star.
Tim McCarver

It's refreshing to see a guy so in awe of the big leagues, with such charisma.
Derrek Lee, former teammate

By September 1, 2005, after years of interviews and research that went into the writing of this book, I was just about finished when I received a call from a sportswriter telling me Dontrelle Willis had just beaten the Mets for his 19th victory of the year, and inviting me to go to be on hand for his next start in Washington, DC, as he went for his 20th win. Boy, how I wanted to be there that night, but I was still recovering from a bout with pneumonia and my doctor absolutely forbid me to fly. So, I parked myself in front of my television, with my phone near at hand so I could discuss the game and the situation with my fellow Black Aces and the many sportswriters who were calling to get my reactions about Dontrelle's imminent membership in our proud group.

By the fifth inning, Dontrelle had knocked out more hits with his bat (two) than he had allowed on the mound (one). He was pitching a shutout, with a five-run lead. I considered myself pretty safe in feeling that history was about to be made, but just like I had to read the *Pittsburgh Courier* to confirm Mrs. Johnson's rumor off the radio that the Dodgers signed Jackie, I needed to see for myself that when the game ended Dontrelle would earn his 20th win. By the time Dontrelle came out of the game, the Marlins were comfortably in the lead, 8-1. Over the course of the night announcer Buck Martinez mentioned two or three times that Dontrelle was attempting to become the first twenty-game winner in Marlins' history and only the 13th African-American to do so, and my heart swelled with pride. When the final out was recorded with the Marlins winning 12-1, I watched Dontrelle step out of the dugout to greet and thank every single one of his teammates. He had a grin that was as wide as America for all to see, and although nobody was watching me at the time, I was wearing the exact same grin. Within minutes my phone was buzzing. I spent the next two hours talking with fellow Black Aces, with sports reporters and with Dontrelle's Mom, Joyce Harris, who is an extraordinary woman. Her love for Dontrelle, her dedication to him, and her contribution to his baseball success are a huge part of his story.

The next day I was able to fully realize the significant impact that ballplayers can have on our society, no matter how old you are or what your life experiences are, when I received a call from Dontrelle himself. He called to tell me how excited he was to become a Black Ace, that he understood the historic significance of his accomplishment and he wanted to be a part of our group and our efforts. After the phone call I forgot I had pneumonia. In my heart and my head I was that little ten-year old boy running down Pine Products Boulevard the morning I first saw Jackie's picture in the *Pittsburgh Courier*. History was happening again, and this time I was able to touch it first-hand. Here I was, a seventy-year old man, a fifteen year major league veteran, who had met presidents. Yet speaking to Dontrelle, who is young enough that he could easily be my grandbaby, made me feel so special.

I'm dumbfounded right now, very ecstatic just because of how my teammates felt for me today. They were pulling for me. I'm kind of breath taken. It's historic. It's a beautiful thing, not only for baseball, but for my team. Hopefully we'll just keep going.
Dontrelle Willis, quoted by Brad Kurtzberg, elitestv.com, after winning his 20th game

452

Two weeks later, when my health allowed, I flew to New York together with fellow Black Ace, Al Downing, to meet Dontrelle at Shea Stadium and to greet him into the Black Aces. He was just as full of the exuberance and love of life and baseball he demonstrates when you watch him on television. As I described our Black Aces project to him he responded joyfully, "I want to be part of it. I want to be part of all of it."

Dontrelle hails from the Bay Area in California, an area rich in Black Aces history and tradition, with Vida, Mike, and Stew all having won 20 at least once with Oakland, and Sad Sam Jones having won his twenty there while pitching for the Giants. Dontrelle also comes from a baseball family. His Mom played softball at an elite, tournament level, and was a power-hitting catcher, and if you know your softball, the catcher is usually the "quarterback" of the team. When she was pregnant with Dontrelle she continued to play well into her seventh month of pregnancy, and soon after Dontrelle was born went right back out on the field, while little Dontrelle watched from his playpen. He literally grew up on a softball field, watching his Mom play, and the same passion for the game she inherited from her father, Frank Guy, who played in the Negro Leagues in Texas, was passed on to Dontrelle.

Joyce's love for softball was surpassed by her love for Dontrelle and the Oakland Athletics. They were her team, especially when Vida Blue was on the mound. In fact, Joyce remembers being at the game when Charlie Finley presented Vida with the blue Cadillac (and she gets a special kick out of the fact that her son's manager, Jack McKeon, once managed Vida and the Athletics, in 1977.) It was especially exciting for Joyce to hear that when Dontrelle won his 20th game, he was the youngest lefthander to do so since Vida did it in 1971. I have enjoyed talking with her about the Athletics, particularly when she told me she had even have rooted for me during my time there in the Bay Area. Although it definitely made me feel my age, I was honored to hear her tell me that I was her Dad's favorite player.

Dontrelle has told me that his mother is the one person who was most instrumental in teaching him the mechanics of the game, and instilling in him his love for the Oakland Athletics and the Negro Leagues. She once gave him a Negro League jersey as a gift, explaining that each time he wore it he showed respect for the Negro players who came before him, and were the pioneers who withstood so much, enabling him and other blacks to play the game at the Major League level today.

I feel very fortunate at this stage of my life to have had an opportunity to meet and speak with Dontrelle and his Mom. So much of their relationship brings me back to Lacoochee and the bond between my Mom and I. Like my Mom, Dontrelle's mother was a single parent who filled many roles in his life. She was the breadwinner in the family, first working as a supervisor for United Parcel Services before becoming an iron worker. Dontrelle still calls her frequently to share the excitement of his career and to stay grounded in the importance of family. They have told me that when Dontrelle was a boy, he and his Mom regularly attended the True Vine Missionary Baptist Church in West Oakland, where to this day, Pastor Zach Carey still offers up a prayer for Dontrelle every Sunday. He kneels in silent prayer before each game and each bullpen session, and as a special dedication to his Mom, Dontrelle writes her name on the underside of the bill of all his baseball caps.

By the time Dontrelle was nine years old he was a pitching star in local youth leagues. I like to imagine that if youth baseball was less structured in the 1990s, and was more of the sandlot game it was when I was a kid, Dontrelle would have been allowed to play with much older players, just like I did. But, although the structure of the league limited his competition to kids his own age, he was performing at a whole different level. Dontrelle's high school coach, Jim Saunders, remembers that when Dontrelle was still at Longfellow Elementary School he would hang out around the high school baseball field and watch the team practice. By the time he worked his way through Wood Middle School and the Alameda Little League, Dontrelle had already figured out how to throw a sharp breaking ball, and then started working on a motion that would be deceptive to the batters. Day after day, he and his friends played their own version of baseball, using a broomstick as a bat and swinging at a tennis ball. Their strike zone is a now famous red square painted on the parking lot wall of the apartment house where Dontrelle lived, and Joyce still lives. He tinkered with different ways to contort his body and hide the ball from the batter as long as possible. He incorporated a high leg kick, turning his back to the batter and a three quarter arm delivery into his motion, and still uses most of those elements in his delivery, a delivery very reminiscent of my "Kickapoo Pitch."

Growing up in Alameda, near the Oakland Coliseum, and with Joyce's influence, it was natural that Dontrelle would became a fan of the Athletics, and that a pitcher would be his favorite player. By the time Dontrelle was old enough to have a baseball idol, Vida had retired and Dave Stewart was "The Man" in Oakland. Dontrelle marveled at Stewart's game demeanor, from the "Death Stare" to the fact that he just didn't give in to batters. Dontrelle still admires Stew's career, but his mother's love for Vida is more present in Dontrelle's delivery and the fact that he wears Vida's number 35 on his uniform. Baseball men have compared Dontrelle to some of the great pitchers in the game, including Vida:

> **He reminds me a little of Fernando Valenzuela and a little bit of Juan Marichal with the head movement and the leg kick. ... I think any team in the major leagues would love to have him. He's left handed, he's competitive. He throws strikes and he's an attraction.**
> *Jim Kaat, National Public Radio, July 31, 2003*

> **He's a lot like Juan Marichal and Vida Blue. He's a new colorful personality coming into the game.**
> *Jack McKeon, Baseball Digest, December 2003*

Vida himself sees some of the similarities, and goes beyond that in his praise of Dontrelle:

I was more over the top, completely. If you were to compare the releasing of the ball, he would be more a la Randy Johnson. The leg kick, if you did a visual, side by side, you might see shades of Vida Blue. Or you might see shades of Dontrelle in mine. Just watching him throw the ball, he really hides it. It's explosive. At the last second, the ball is on you. His knack for throwing with a high kick and maintaining his balance is an art in itself.
Vida Blue, quoted by Mike Berardino, South Florida Sun-Sentinel, 2003

Dontrelle dismisses the comparisons with the kind of humility that shows what a great young man he is, saying "I can't be compared. I haven't earned the right, but I'm trying." (TIME Magazine, 2003)

In 1996, Dontrelle began attending Encinal High School, alma mater of Willie Stargell. In fact, the baseball field there is named after Willie. By the time Dontrelle was a junior he was already the star of the varsity baseball team. In his senior year, 2000, he posted a 12-1 record, and recorded 138 strikeouts in 94 innings, with an ERA of 0.82, and he could get his fastball up there at 90 miles an hour or better. In addition, he batted .621, with 64 hits, 12 home runs and 49 RBI. That was good enough to get Dontrelle named 2000 California High School player of the year, and got the scouts howling, especially Steve Hinton of the Cubs, who selected Dontrelle in the eighth round of the 2000 draft. Dontrelle's first professional team was the Cubs' Arizona League team in Mesa (Rookie Class), managed by former Cub, Carmelo Martinez. During the short rookie league season, Dontrelle, used as a middle reliever, was 3-1.

His first full season in professional ball was 2001, with the Boise Hawks of the Northwest League (Class A – Short Season). During that season, Dontrelle was used exclusively as a starter. He recorded eight victories, second best in the league, and helped Boise finish in first place, holding opposing batters to a .217 average. Dontrelle was named to the Northwest League All Star team, and was cited by several opposing managers as Boise's most valuable player in a poll that appeared in *Baseball America.*

Dontrelle spent the majority of the 2002 spring training season with the Cubs, hoping to move up the minor league chain until he reached the parent club in Wrigley Field. All of that changed suddenly in the last week of spring training. The Cubs, who felt they were close enough to compete in their division that year, needed a starter with Major League experience and a proven closer. So they traded Dontrelle and Julian Tavarez to the Marlins for Matt Clement and Antonio Alfonseca. It appeared at the time that Chicago got the better of the deal, because Dontrelle was shipped to the minor leagues (the Kane County Cougars, Midwest League, Class A) and Tavarez had a rough time with the Marlins, but sometimes it takes years to analyze the ultimate benefits of a trade like that.

Meanwhile, Dontrelle enjoyed immediate success with the Cougars. He won his first four decisions, including a no-hitter on May 1, 2002 against Beloit. Then, after losing back to back starts, he rolled off six more victories, not allowing even one earned run during 21 innings of pitching during the first three of those victories. That type of pitching earned Dontrelle the honor of being named the Marlins' Organizational Pitcher of the Month for both May (3-2, 1.45 ERA) and June (4-0, 0.75 ERA). In late July Dontrelle was promoted to the Jupiter Hammerheads (Florida, High Class A), where he finished the season with a 2-0 record in five starts before going on the disabled list because of a strained left shoulder on August 21. His ERA with the Cougars was 1.83, good enough for the Midwest League ERA title and also earned him a slew of pitching honors, including:

- Marlins' Minor League Pitcher of the Year;
- *Sports Weekly* Minor League Pitcher of the Year;
- Midwest League All-Star; and
- Midwest League *Baseball America* Class A All-Star.
- *Baseball Digest* Pitcher of the Year

While the spring of 2002 only saw Dontrelle change Major League organizations, the spring of 2003 almost ended his career and his life. One night, after driving his girlfriend home, Dontrelle accelerated his Mustang onto Highway 101 in Palo Alto. As he entered into traffic from the entrance ramp, at about 65 mph, Dontrelle lost control of the car when one of his rear tires blew out. The car smashed into the highway guard rail and bounced back into traffic, flipping over several times before coming to a stop. All traffic stopped as other motorists ran from their cars to see the wreck and determine how badly Dontrelle was injured. Miraculously, secured by his seat belt, he was not thrown from the vehicle and he suffered no injuries. He then crawled out of the car through the smashed back window, his only way out. The incident tells me that Dontrelle is blessed and he is a survivor. The fact that on his way out of the car the only possession he saved from it was his Bible may explain why.

Less than two weeks later Dontrelle brought his irrepressible smile and love of the game to the Marlins' spring training camp in Jupiter, Florida. Based on his success at high Class A in 2002, the Marlins were hoping that Dontrelle would start the 2003 season in the Class AA Southern League with the Carolina Mudcats (it must have been destined that we would hook up) and work his way to AAA, with a possible late season call up when the Major League rosters are expanded after September 1. But, Dontrelle never saw AAA and he never even saw June in AA. After making six starts for the Mudcats, resulting in 4 wins, no losses and a 1.49 ERA, Dontrelle was called up to the Major Leagues on May 6 when injuries to Mark Redman and A.J. Burnett left the Marlins way short in the pitching department.

Dontrelle remembers walking into the Marlins' clubhouse and seeing his first Major League uniform, bearing number "35", that of his mother's hero, Vida Blue.

That scene was like a dream for Dontrelle, but the status of the team at the time was more like a nightmare. After one month of play they were six games under .500 (15-21) and headed in the wrong direction. They had lost their last six games in a row and only the Mets (14-20) kept them out of the National League East cellar, but not for long. Two days after Dontrelle's debut, a six inning no decision against Colorado which the Marlins eventually won, the team fired manager Jeff Torborg and hired Jack McKeon. The team promptly lost seven of the first ten games McKeon managed and found itself in last place in the East with a 19-29 record. It was the low water mark for the Marlins that year. One of those games was Dontrelle's first Major League loss, and his first loss in over a year after winning thirteen straight decisions!

The Marlins went on to have the best record in baseball for the period from May 23rd to the end of the season, and edged the Philadelphia Phillies for the NL Wild Card spot. Some people pointed to the change in managers, others to the addition of young slugger, Miguel Cabrera, and others to the promotion of Dontrelle. Truth be told it was probably a combination of those items, together with any number of other tangibles and intangibles that go into creating a winning baseball team, but Dontrelle's contribution must certainly be given credit for some of it. The Marlins had a record of 19-8 in the 27 games Dontrelle started that year, and he pitched deep enough into a sufficient number of games to record 20 decisions, going 14-6 in his rookie season. Using a mesmerizing motion which still contained elements of the delivery he concocted in the Alameda playgrounds, Dontrelle had batters off their timing and unprepared to swing at his sinking fastball. At one point in the season he won eight consecutive decisions, with an ERA of 1.05 during that stretch. He was one of only four pitchers since 1920 to win eight of his first ten starts before reaching the age of 22, the others being Paul "Daffy" Dean (St. Louis, 1934), Mark "Bird" Fidrych (Detroit, 1976), and Fernando Valenzuela (L.A. Dodgers, 1981).

By the All-Star break, Dontrelle was 9-1 with a 2.08 ERA, and when Kevin Brown of the Dodgers had to be scrapped from the National League All-Star squad, Dontrelle was named in his place. That made him the youngest pitcher selected to a Major League All-Star team since Dwight Gooden in 1985.

I remember watching Dontrelle pitch in 2003 and maybe even more importantly I remember watching him play and interact with his teammates. His enthusiasm for the game, his smile and the way he would cheer on and congratulate teammates was great to see. It was a throwback to my playing days and something that seems missing from baseball and sports in general for the most part now. I wasn't the only one who noticed. The fans were going wild for Dontrelle. He developed a following at the ballpark and through the media. Every time Dontrelle recorded a strikeout at home the Marlins would blast the sound of a train whistle over the stadium speaker system. Everybody wanted to know when the "D-Train" was coming into their town. When Dontrelle was pitching at home, attendance was easily double the team's normal average draw, and the story was the same on the road. Fans would show up wearing conductor hats and bib overalls like those worn by train engineers. In one game against the Milwaukee Brewers, in excess of 10,000 walk-up tickets were sold, an extraordinary number for that town and that team.

> **Every ballpark he goes to, there are probably seven writers who want to talk to him. And every radio station and every TV station. It reaches the point where you say, 'Wait a second. Time out. Can I breathe?'**
> *Mark Fidrych, 1976 AL Rookie of the Year*

In a similar fashion to other Black Aces, it should be noted that Dontrelle was succeeding at the plate as well as on the mound. He batted .241 for the season and was always a threat to get a base hit, not the automatic out that most pitchers are as batters. In June he became the first Marlins' rookie to throw a one-hitter shutting down the Mets, and over the course of the season he had the seventh highest batting average by a National League pitcher. His performance earned him the National League Rookie of the Year award, following in the footsteps of the first Black Ace, Don Newcombe (1949), and Dwight Gooden (1984). Of particular interest to me, because of my love for Larry, Dontrelle was also the winner of the 2002 Larry Doby Award, as the Negro Leagues Baseball Museum National League Rookie of the Year. For good measure, *Baseball America* named him as the Top 21 Year Old in Organized Baseball.

> **Dontrelle Willis was undeniably the rookie sensation of 2003, capturing the fancy of fans and media across the nation. The refreshingly talkative and charismatic youngster who just turned 21 sparked the previously unheralded Florida Marlins to an unexpected appearance in postseason competition.**
> **Few rookie pitchers since the sadly brief glory days of eccentric Mark Fidrych of the Detroit Tigers a quarter of a century ago have made opening splashes matching that of left-hander Willis in winning 14 of his 20 decisions for the Marlins. Willis's startling emergence paralleled those of two other relatively recent pitching phenoms, Dwight Gooden in 1984 and Fernando Valenzuela in 1981.**
> *George Vass, Baseball Digest, December 2003*

Dontrelle had never pitched a full professional season prior to 2002, and had never been involved in a Major League pennant race. It was a lot for a twenty-one year old rookie to experience. By the end of the season he had thrown 197 innings, new ground for him, and his arm was feeling it. He got one start in the Divisional Series, against San Francisco, and one start in the NL Championship Series, against the ill-fated Cubs, and came away with one decision – a loss. After McKeon watched Dontrelle surrender 6 earned runs in 2.3 innings against the Cubs, he decided the rookie's stamina had about reached its limit and decided he would only use him in relief. After the Marlins took the National League Championship Series from the Cubs, Dontrelle made three relief appearances against the Yankees in the 2003

World Series and pitched brilliantly. He shut down the vaunted Yankee offense, yielding no runs in 3.7 innings, and helped the Marlins become World Champs.

Unfortunately for Marlins fans and players, in the winter of 2003-2004, their front office repeated the "fire sale" they held after their first World Championship in 1997. They purged the team of many of the great players that helped them win (including Moises Alou, Jeff Conine, Devon White, Al Leiter, and Kevin Brown). This time the players taking the one-way trip out of Miami included Ivan "Pudge" Rodriguez, Juan Encarnacion, Braden Looper, Derrek Lee and Ugueth Urbina. In addition to the off-season departures, starter Brad Penny was traded in a multi-player deal that brought Paul LoDuca to the Marlins, but the loss of another starter focused the spotlight more intently on Dontrelle, who was pitching in his first complete season in the big leagues. He led the team in starts (32) showing he had the endurance it would take to someday be a twenty-game winner, but the results were not there for him in 2004. He started the season with a flourish, winning his first three decisions and not allowing an earned run in 19.3 innings. He threw some spectacular games and even flirted with perfection (for 6.7 innings against Cincinnati), but without the run support he enjoyed in 2003, and with his ERA a little elevated, his record slipped to 10-11.

Having felt the effects of a full season in the majors, Dontrelle decided to whip his body into shape to increase his endurance. He followed a rigorous off-season training schedule under the guidance of veteran teammates Al Leiter and Jeff Conine. He also threw all winter long, using neighbor and teammate, centerfielder Juan Pierre as his catcher.

I feel great, ... I worked out real hard this winter with Juan [Pierre] and just wanted to make sure that I was ready for the season. It was killing me, though. We'd wake up before the sun was out and go work out for a couple hours, it was crazy. I didn't like it at all. Now I feel great, but it was really tough. I just wanted to discipline myself in some way this winter. I feel like I'm in really good shape right now. This spring I felt real good and now I feel great too.
Dontrelle Willis, thinkexist.com

Dontrelle's hard work showed immediate results when the 2005 season started. He began the season with six consecutive victories, and was named the National League Pitcher of the Month for April. It wasn't until his 25th inning of work that he was even scored upon. In the middle of the season Major League Baseball publicized that a World Baseball Classic would be held in March 2006 with players representing their native countries, and it was announced that Dontrelle would be playing for the United States team.

Dontrelle wound up setting a Marlins' club record with 22 victories, which led the Major Leagues. He tied St. Louis' Chris Carpenter for the National League lead in complete games with seven and led the Major Leagues with five shutouts. Dontrelle finished second in the National League Cy Young Award voting to

Carpenter, with Carpenter having 132 points and Dontrelle 112. Dontrelle did win Major League Baseball's 2005 Warren Spahn Award as the best left-handed pitcher in the game, edging out Andy Pettitte for the award, based on number of wins, strikeout total and ERA. And just as this book went to press, Dontrelle was named by *Baseball Digest* as the 2005 Pitcher of the Year.

As a hitter, Dontrelle led all Major League pitchers with 24 hits and 14 runs scored. On more than one occasion, Dontrelle's manager, Jack McKeon, placed Dontrelle higher in the lineup than the customary ninth spot reserved for pitchers. In fact, on September 22, 2005, McKeon batted Dontrelle seventh in the lineup. It was the first time a pitcher batted seventh or higher in a Major League lineup since Steve Renko of the Montreal Expos batted seventh against the San Diego Padres on August 26, 1973.

McKeon, age 74, and his bench coach, Harry Dunlop, age 71, are two career minor-league catchers, who have each spent more than fifty years in the game of baseball. Although neither of them ever got to play in the majors, they have seen their share of pitchers, and great ones at that. McKeon, before being called upon to manage the Marlins, had managed the Royals, the Padres, the Reds, and the Athletics, and while with Oakland he managed Black Aces, Vida Blue and Mike Norris. Dunlop has the distinction of having been the catcher in the only game in professional baseball history where the pitcher struck out twenty-seven batters while throwing a no-hitter. (It was May 13, 1952, and the pitcher was Ron Necciai, 19 years old, pitching for the Appalachian League Bristol (Virginia) Twins.) Despite their many years in the game, or maybe because of that, both Jack and Harry are very impressed with Dontrelle:

> **Dontrelle is just a great kid, who works like hell at this game. He takes pride in all areas of the game. Just watching him play the game makes you feel so good. I tell you what, this kid could play any position, and hit.**
> *Jack McKeon interview*

> **Dontrelle never makes an excuse. He plays the game the way it was meant to be played, with the enthusiasm of the kids on the sandlot. I've seen guys with better "stuff" but they don't command it as well as he does. And he is sincere in wanting to be better with every outing. He has a maturity and confidence beyond his years.**
> *Harry Dunlop interview*

Dontrelle's pitching coach with the Marlins is another veteran of the game, Mark Wiley, who is in his 36th year in pro ball. Mark made it to the majors with the Minnesota Twins, San Diego Padres and Toronto Blue Jays, but the majority of his tenure in the pros has been as a pitching coach, with the Orioles, Indians, and Royals before joining the Marlins. He sees many positives in Dontrelle, and great strides just in the last year:

Dontrelle has fun working and that is a key to his development. He is the first one to show up out on the field to start working. Juan Pierre got a left handed catcher's mitt, and you always see Dontrelle throwing to Juan. They do that even in the off-season. He is in tremendous shape and had a great workout routine. Over the course of this season [2005] his slider has gotten much better and so has his ability to hold on runners. He has a sense of changing speeds, making his pitches much more effective. He sees exactly what the batter is doing and adjusts. He throws a change up at three different speeds. Maybe most importantly he makes everyone on the team play at a higher energy level, and he has tremendous fun doing it. He has a great deal of confidence, and he is always giving credit to his teammates. He loves to compete and he loves this game.

Mark Wiley interview

What veterans like McKeon, Dunlop, and Wiley see in Dontrelle can be quickly absorbed by watching Dontrelle play the game, and interact with his teammates and the press. He appreciates the blessing of talent he has been given and takes himself seriously enough to know that through hard work he can remain as one of the top pitchers in the game. But he is down to earth enough to remember that it is a game that can be fun to play.

Baseball is not as complex as people make it, at least not for me. I try to break things down as simple as I can, as far as going about my work every day. I go out there, I throw the ball, I have a good time and I leave everything on the field. That's all that you can ask from a ball player, bottom line.

Dontrelle Willis, quoted by Jill Lieber, Baseball Digest, August 2005

I guess it was fate that the completion of this book took long enough to include Dontrelle's twenty-win season. I am very pleased that it did!

CHAPTER 30

EPILOGUE

Thanks to the success of Dontrelle Willis, leading the Major Leagues with twenty-two wins in 2005, and the successful season of C.C. Sabathia with the Indians, this final chapter is much different than I envisioned it would be when I started writing. We had gone so long, since 1990, without an African-American twenty-game winner and the number of blacks playing the game, specifically pitchers, has dwindled to a level below what it was when I was playing fifty years ago. There were so few black starting pitchers my fear was that a successful black starter was a thing of the past, a baseball dinosaur, gone the way of Sunday doubleheaders and Ladies' Days.

I was concerned that all that was endured by Jackie Robinson and Larry Doby and the other pioneers of baseball's integration would be reduced to a footnote in the history of baseball, and what was accomplished by a select few pitchers would be lost in the game's sea of statistics.

I am very encouraged not only by what Willis and Sabathia have done on the field, but in how they have embraced the history of The Black Aces. People, and especially today's players, must recognize and appreciate the progress of integration that has changed what today's black pitchers can expect from the game, as opposed to what we faced over the long course of years since Jackie and Larry first stepped on the field, and how that occurred.

I marvel at the thought that today, in every city players travel to, not only does the whole team stay in one hotel, blacks, whites, Latinos, Asians alike, but the accommodations are first class. No longer does any player, of whatever race, have to stay on the bus while his teammates go into a restaurant. No longer does any player have to pretend to be of a different race, or pretend to be a deaf mute, or suffer any other indignity just to be served. Gone are the days when a player would sit at a table in a lounge by himself for hours without being served, because of his race, while his teammates partied across the room.

I take some measure of pride in knowing that much of that progress is directly traceable to the courage and drive of men like Bob Gibson, Bill White, Dave Hoskins, Sam Jones, Don Newcombe, and all of the other Black Aces, and many, many others who played this game. This book would be considerably longer if I detailed the stories of all the players who faced hatred and discrimination and stared it down, each in their own way, so that they could succeed and so that others coming behind them could also succeed, hopefully without having to face the same hurdle. In addition to The Black Aces, dozens and dozens of other players faced discriminatory practices and yet strove to succeed: black players like Al Jackson, Dock Ellis, Blue Moon Odom; Latino players like Luis Tiant,

Felipe Alou, Vic Power, and many others. Things they did on the field have been measured and recorded in baseball's statistical records. But, many of the things they did both on and off the field, acts which took tremendous courage, so that they could compete and so that the rules of society could be changed, may never be known.

I often wonder if I would have been able to take that mound in Cleveland in 1958 if Jackie Robinson had failed The Great Experiment in 1947, or if Larry Doby hadn't been successful. Would black pitchers have ever been accepted if Don Newcombe didn't have the determination and guts to succeed as he did, or if Sam Jones hadn't stayed the course? Would teams have ever been able to live in integrated quarters if Bob Gibson and Bill White didn't have the strength and fortitude to challenge the St. Louis Cardinals to be better?

Today I can eat at any restaurant in Dade City, something I couldn't do as a boy. Today, I can sit anywhere on the bus, something I could not do as a young man. Today, I can stay in any hotel, something I could not do as a Major League ballplayer. Yes, changes have occurred in our society, changes created through the brave efforts of many people. It is my hope and desire that this country continues to go forward, and that the game I love continues to capture the imagination of today's youth as it captured me. It creates a joy in me to think that on some city street, a kid is throwing a ball against a wall, to an imaginary batter, thinking in his mind that he is Dontrelle Willis, and hearing an announcer declare, "Dontrelle wins again!" with the sound of an umpire yelling, "Strike three, yer out!" in the background. It is my hope that performances such as Dontrelle's will create a renewed interest in the game.

As far as we have come, I am saddened by the fact that there are cities and towns that do not have baseball programs for kids today. I know that there are many other games and diversions available to children today, but baseball has always been such a central part of American life that I still believe that each and every kid should have the opportunity to learn and to play the game. I believe that the lack of black ballplayers in the Major Leagues can be directly traced back to the lack of programs for kids in inner cities and other areas. This past year I spoke with the Athletic Director at Bethune-Cookman College, one of the historic black universities. I was surprised, but not shocked, to hear that there was not even one black ballplayer on the college baseball team.

I am determined to re-energize the interest of today's black youth in baseball. The first step was to write this book. Today's youth needs to know more about what happened in America, and to remember the lesson that baseball taught America: that blacks and whites had more similarities than differences, that most of what drove segregation was unfounded fears.

Baseball has done more to move America in the right direction than all the professional patriots with their billions of cheap words.
Monte Irvin, Hall of Famer, quoted in Baseball Has Done It, Jackie Robinson, New York, Lippincott, 1964

As white and black ballplayers began to play together, and eat together, and travel together, we all learned that there was really nothing to be afraid of or hateful about.

Rich Ashburn told me his attitude on race was forever changed during a game when he spiked [Jackie] Robinson with a hard slide into second while breaking up a double play.
"It was unintentional, but I really got him good," Ashburn told me. "My spikes tore through his stocking and laid him open. He was bleeding pretty good. I thought to myself running to the dugout, 'That guy plays as hard as anybody I've ever seen. I just laid him open and he didn't even bat an eye.' He just walked back to his position. His blood was red, the same color as mine, and I realized at that moment that white or black, we were all human beings who bleed the same color and we just better get along."
Bill Conlin, Philadelphia Daily News, September 24, 2002

The second step is already underway. I have spoken with the other Black Aces and we are prepared to visit every corner of this country, from tiny hamlets like my beloved Lacoochee to giant metropolises like New York City, from east coast to west, from north to south. We will include areas of the country where The Black Aces were born, like Louisiana and Nebraska, New Jersey and California, and where they played. We will bring with us our love for the game, our desire to share the rich heritage of blacks in baseball, and our hope that young black kids will embrace the game and grow from it, just as we did. I am extremely confident that the combined efforts of The Black Aces will have a very positive effect. We will still be following the advice of Jackie Robinson, defining the importance of our lives by the impact we have on the lives of others. Those we touch may or may not ever make that trip to a Major League pitching mound but, thanks to Jackie and Larry and those who came before us, the trip has been made possible. We will secure and protect their legacy to today's youth, making the mound within their reach, and help to show them the way.

BIBLIOGRAPHY

Aaron, Hank, with Furman Bisher. <u>Aaron, The autobiography of the greatest home-run hitter of the modern era.</u> New York: Crowell Company, 1974.

Aaron, Hank, with Lonnie Wheeler. <u>I Had A Hammer: The Hank Aaron Story</u>. New York: Harper Collins, 1991.

Adelson, Bruce. <u>Brushing Back Jim Crow, The Integration of Minor-League Baseball In the American South.</u> Charlottesville: University Press of Virginia, 1999.

Allen, Dick and Whitaker, Tim. <u>Crash, The Life and Times of Dick Allen.</u> New York: Ticknor & Fields, 1989.

Ashe, Arthur, Jr. <u>A Hard Road To Glory: Baseball, The African-American Athlete In Baseball, Putting The Record Straight: Forgotten Facts</u>. New York: Amistad Press, 1988.

Bak, Richard. <u>Turkey Stearnes And The Detroit Stars: The Negro Leagues In Detroit, 1919-1933</u>. Detroit: Great Lakes Books, 1994.

Baldassaro, Lawrence and Johnson, Richard A., Editors. <u>The American Game, Baseball and Ethnicity.</u> Illinois: Southern Illinois University Press, 2002.

Bankes, Jim. <u>The Pittsburgh Crawfords</u>. Jefferson, North Carolina: McFarland & Company, 2001.

Barber, Red. <u>1947: The Year All Hell Broke Loose</u>. New York: Da Capo Press, 1982.

Berkow, Ira. <u>The Minority Quarterback, and Other Lives in Sports.</u> Chicago: Ivan R. Dee, 2002

Briley, Ron. <u>Class at Bat, Gender on Deck and Race in the Hole.</u> North Carolina: McFarland & Company, 2003.

Bronson, Eric, Editor. <u>Baseball and Philosophy, Thinking Outside the Batter's Box.</u> Chicago: Open Court, 2004.

Bruce, Janet. <u>The Kansas Monarchs: Champions Of Black Baseball</u>. Lawrence, Kansas: University Press Of Kansas, 1985.

Bryant, Howard. <u>Shut Out, A Story of Race and Baseball in Boston.</u> New York: Routledge, 2002.

Burns, Ken and Geoffrey C. Ward. <u>Baseball: An Illustrated History</u>. New York: Alfred A. Knopf, Inc., 1994.

Burns, Ken, Geoffrey C. Ward, and O'Connor, Jim. <u>Shadowball: The History Of The Negro Leagues</u>. New York: Alfred A. Knopf, Inc., 1994.

Campanella, Roy. <u>It's Good To Be Alive.</u> New York: Dell Publishing Co., 1959

Capuzzo, Mike. "A Prisoner of Memory." <u>Sports Illustrated</u>, November 1992

Chadwick, Bruce. When The Game Was Black And White: The Illustrated History Of Baseball's Negro Leagues. New York: Abbeville Press, 1992.

Chafe, William H., Gavins, Raymond, and Korstad, Robert, Editors. Remembering Jim Crow, African Americans Tell About Life in the Segregated South. New York: The New Press, 2001.

Chalberg, John C. Rickey & Robinson. Wheeling, Illinois: Harlan Davidson, Inc., 2000.

Clark, Dick and Lester, Larry. The Negro Leagues Book. Cleveland, Ohio: SABR, 1994.

Cottrell, Robert Charles. The Best Pitcher In Baseball: The Life Of Rube Foster, Negro League Giant. New York: New York University Press, 2001.

Davis, Jack E. "Baseball's Reluctant Challenge: Desegregating Major League Spring Training Sites, 1961-1964." Journal of Sport History, Vol. 19, No. 2, Summer 1992.

DeBono, Paul. The Indianapolis ABCs. Jefferson, North Carolina: McFarland & Company, 1997.

DeFord, Frank. "Coochie Coos Another Tune." Sports Illustrated, April 8, 1968, Vol. 28, No. 14, p. 56

DeMarco, Michael. Dugout Days, Untold Tales and Leadership Lessons From the Extraordinary Career of Billy Martin. American Management Association, 2001.

Devaney, John. "How Mudcat Changed His Acts." Sport, September 1965.

Dixon, Phil and Hannigan, Patrick J. The Negro Baseball League: A Photographic History. Mattituck, New York: Amereon House, 1992.

Dixon, Phil S. The Monarchs 1920-1938 Featuring Wilber "Bullet" Rogan. Sioux Falls, South Dakota: Mariah Press, 2002.

DuBois, W.E.B. Souls of Black Folk. New York: Vintage Books, 1990.

Echevarria, Roberto Gonzalez. The Pride Of Havana: A History Of Cuban Baseball. New York: Oxford University Press, 1999.

Fenster, Kenneth R. "Earl Mann, Nat Peeples and the failed attempt of integration in the Southern Association." Nine, March 22, 2004.

Flood, Curt, with Richard Carter. The Way It Is. New York: Trident Press, 1971.

Fox, William Price. Satchel Paige's America. Tuscaloosa, Alabama: University Of Alabama Press, 2005.

Freese, Mel. Charmed Circle: Twenty-Game Winning Pitchers In Baseball's 20th Century. Jefferson, North Carolina: McFarland & Company, 1997.

Frommer, Harvey. New York City Baseball: The Last Golden Age. New York: First Harvest/HBJ, 1992.

---. Rickey & Robinson: The Men Who Broke Baseball's Color Barrier. New York: Macmillan Publishing, 1992.

Gates, Henry Louis, Jr. and Kwame Anthony Appiah, Editors. <u>Africana: Civil Rights – An A-Z Reference Of The Movement That Changed America</u>. Philadelphia: Running Press, 2003.

Gibson, Bob, with Phil Pepe. <u>From Ghetto to Glory, The Story of Bob Gibson.</u> Englewood Cliffs, NJ: Prentice-Hall, Inc., 1968.

Gibson, Bob, with Lonnie Wheeler. <u>Stranger To The Game: The Autobiography Of Bob Gibson.</u> New York: Viking Penguin, 1994.

Golenbock, Peter. <u>Dynasty, The New York Yankees, 1949-1964.</u> Englewood Cliffs, NJ: Prentice-Hall, Inc., 1975.

Gooden, Dwight with Bob Klapisch. <u>Heat, My Life On and Off the Diamond.</u> New York: William Morrow and Co., 1999.

Haegele, Katie. <u>Monte Irvin.</u> New York: Rosen Publishing, 2002.

Hall, Alvin and Peter M. Rutkoff, Editors. <u>The Cooperstown Symposium On Baseball And American Culture 1997 (Jackie Robinson).</u> Jefferson, North Carolina: McFarland & Company, 2000.

Heaphy, Leslie A. <u>The Negro Leagues: 1869-1960.</u> Jefferson, North Carolina: McFarland & Company, 2003.

Hinton, Chuck. <u>My Time At Bat: A Story Of Perseverance.</u> Largo, Maryland: Christian Living Books, 2002.

Holway, John B. <u>Blackball Stars: Negro League Pioneers.</u> New York: Carroll & Graf, 1989.

---. <u>Black Diamonds: Life In The Negro Leagues From The Men Who Lived It.</u> Westport, Connecticut: Meckler Books, 1989.

---. <u>Josh And Satch: The Life And Times Of Josh Gibson And Satchel Paige.</u> New York: Carroll & Graf, 1991.

---. <u>Smokey Joe And The Cannonball.</u> Washington: Capital Press, 1983.

---. <u>The Complete Book Of Baseball's Negro Leagues: The Other Half Of Baseball History.</u> Fern park, Florida: Hastings House Publishers, 2001.

---. <u>Voices From The Great Black Baseball League.</u> New York: Da Capo Books, 1992.

---. <u>Voices From The Negro Leagues: Conversations With 52 Baseball Standouts.</u> Jefferson, North Carolina: McFarland & Company, 1998.

---. <u>The Power And The Darkness: The Life Of Josh Gibson In The Shadows Of The Game.</u> Bridgewater, New Jersey: Replica Books, 1996.

Howard, Arlene, with Ralph Wimbish. <u>Elston and Me, The Story of the First Black Yankee.</u> Columbia, Missouri: University of Missouri Press, 2001.

Howard, Darrell J. <u>"Sunday Coming" Blackball Baseball In Virginia.</u> Jefferson, North Carolina: McFarland & Company, 2002.

Hudson, Michael. "Breaking A Barrier." The Roanoke Times, April 1977.

Hughes, Langston, "A Dream Deferred", 1951.

Hunter, James "Catfish" and Keteyian, Armen. Catfish, My Life in Baseball. McGraw-Hill, 1988

Jordan, Vernon E., Jr. with Annette Gordon-Reed. Vernon Can Read, A Memoir. Basic Civitas Books, 2001.

Kahn, Roger. The Boys Of Summer. New York: Harper & Row, 1972.

Kashatus, William C. September Swoon, Richie Allen, the '64 Phillis, and Racial Integration. University Park, Pennsylvania, The Pennsylvania State University Press, 2004.

Kelley, Brent. Voices From The Negro Leagues: Conversations With 52 Baseball Standouts. Jefferson, North Carolina: McFarland & Company, 2000.

---. The Negro Leagues Revisited: Conversations With 66 More Baseball Heroes. Jefferson, North Carolina: McFarland & Company, 2005.

---. "I Will Never Forget", Interviews with 39 Former Negro League Players. Jefferson, North Carolina: McFarland & Company, 2003.

Kolb, Bill. Beantown's First Black Sock. Contracostatimes.com

Lamb, Chris. Blackout: The Untold Story Of Jackie Robinson's First Spring Training. Lincoln, Nebraska: University Of Nebraska Press, 2004.

Lanctot, Neil. Negro League Baseball: The Rise And Ruin Of A Black Institution. Philadelphia: University Of Pennsylvania Press, 2004.

Leonard, Buck, With Riley, James A. Buck Leonard: The Black Lou Gehrig. New York: Carroll & Graf, 1995.

Lester, Larry. Blackball's National Showcase: The East-West Game 1933-1953. Lincoln, Nebraska: University Of Nebraska Press, 2001.

Light, Jonathan Fraser. The Cultural Encyclopedia Of Baseball. Jefferson, North Carolina: McFarland & Company, 1997.

Lomax, Michael E. Blackball Entrepreneurs: 1860-1901. Syracuse, New York: Syracuse University Press, 2003.

Loverro, Thom. The Encyclopedia Of Negro League Baseball. New York: Checkmark Books, 2003.

Malloy, Jerry, Editor. Sol White's History Of Colored Base Ball, With Other Documents On The Early Black Game, 1886-1936. Lincoln, Nebraska: University Of Nebraska Press, 1995.

Mazel, Ella, Editor. "And don't call me a racist." Argonaut Press, 1998

McNary, Kyle. Black Baseball: A History Of African-Americans And The National Game. London: PRC Publishing Ltd, 2003.

McNeil, William F. Baseball's Other All-Stars. Jefferson, North Carolina: McFarland & Company, 2000.

---. Cool Papas And Double Duties: The All-Time Greats Of The Negro Leagues. Jefferson, North Carolina: McFarland & Company, 2001.

---. The California Winter Leagues: America's First Integrated Professional Baseball League. Jefferson, North Carolina: McFarland & Company, 2002.

Metcalfe, Henry. A Game For All Races: An Illustrated History of the Negro Leagues. New York: Metro Books, 2000.

Moffi, Larry, and Jonathan Kronstadt. Crossing The Line: Black Major Leaguers, 1947-1959. Jefferson, North Carolina: McFarland & Company, 1994.

Monteleone, John J., Editor. Branch Rickey's Little Blue Book, Wit and Strategy from Baseball's Last Wise Man. New York: MacMillan, 1995

More, Joseph Thomas. Pride and Prejudice, The Biography of Larry Doby. New York: Praeger Publishers, 1988.

Myers, Walter Dean. The Journal of Biddy Owens, The Negro Leagues, Birmingham, Alabama 1948. New York: Scholastic Inc., 2001.

Nack, William. The Breakthrough. Sports Illustrated, May 5, 1997.

Neyer, Rob and James, Bill. The Neyer/James Guide to Pitchers. Fireside, 2004

O'Neil, Buck, Steve Wulf, and David Conrads. I Was Right On Time: My Journey From The Negro Leagues To The Majors. New York: Fireside Books, 1996.

O'Toole, Andrew. The Best Man Plays, Major League Baseball and the Black Athlete, 1901-2002. Jefferson, North Carolina: McFarland & Company, 2003.

Overmyer, James. Queen Of The Negro Leagues: Effa Manley And The Newark Eagles. Lanham. Maryland: Scarecrow Press, 1998.

Paige, Leroy Satchel, with David Lipman. Maybe I'll Pitch Forever, A Great Baseball Player Tells the Hilarious Story Behind the Legend. Lincoln, Nebraska: University Of Nebraska Press, 1993.

Parrott, Harold. Lords Of Baseball. Atlanta: Longstreet Press, 2001.

Peary, Danny, Editor. We Played The Game, 65 Players Remember Baseball's Greatest Era, 1947-1964. New York: Hyperion, 1994.

Peterson, Robert. Only The Ball Was White. New York: Gramercy Books, 1970.

Rampersad, Arnold. Jackie Robinson: A Biography. New York: Alfred A. Knopf, Inc., 1997.

Reilly, Edward J., Editor. Baseball and American Culture, Across the Diamond. New York: The Hawthorne Press, 2003

Reisler, Jim, Editor. Black Writers/Black Baseball: An Anthology Of Articles From Black Sportswriters Who Covered The Negro Leagues. Jefferson, North Carolina: McFarland & Company, 1994.

Ribowsky, Mark. A Complete History Of The Negro Leagues: 1884-1955. New York: Citadel Press, 1995.

---. Don't Look Back: Satchel Paige In The Shadows Of Baseball. New York: Da Capo Press, 1994.

Riley, James A. The Biographical Encyclopedia Of The Negro Baseball Leagues. New York: Carroll & Graf, 1994.

---. History of Black Baseball and the Negro Baseball Leagues. Negro Leagues Baseball Museum, 1996.

Robinson, Jackie, with Alfred Duckett. I Never Had It Made. New York: Putnam, 1972.

Robinson, Jackie, with Charles Dexter, Editor. Baseball Has Done It. New York: J. B. Lippincott & Company, 1964.

Robinson, Frank with Dave Anderson. Frank, The First Year. New York: Holt, Rinehart, Winston, 1976.

Rogosin, Donn. Invisible Men: Life In Baseball's Negro Leagues. New York: Kodansha America, 1995.

Rossi, John P. A Whole New Game, Off the Field Changes in Baseball, 1946-1960. McFarland & Company, Inc., North Carolina 1999.

Rushin, Steve. "The Season of High Heat." Sports Illustrated, July 19, 1993.

Rust, Art, Jr. "Get That Nigger Off The Field", A sparkling informal history of the Black Man in Baseball. New York, Delacorte Press, 1974.

Sanford, Jay. The Denver Post Tournament. Cleveland, Ohio: SABR (Rocky Mountain Chapter) and The Denver Post, 2003.

Schaap, Dick. "The Ups and Downs of Sad Sam." Sport Magazine.

Scott, Simon. Jackie Robinson And The Integration Of Baseball. Hoboken, New Jersey: John Wiley & Sons, 2002.

Shropshire, Kenneth L. In Black And White: Race And Sports in America. New York: New York University Press, 1996.

Silber, Irwin. Press Box Red, The Story of Lester Rodney, The Communist Who Helped Break The Color Line in American Sports. Philadelphia, PA: Temple University Press, 2003.

Simon, Scott. Jackie Robinson and the Integration of Baseball. New York: John Wiley & Sons, 2002.

Simons, William. "Jackie Robinson and the American Mind: Journalistic Perceptions of the Reintegration of Baseball." Journal of Sport History, Vol. 12, No. 1 (Spring 1985)

Skinner, Samuel J., Jr. <u>No Blues for Vida.</u> Black Sports, September 1971.

Snyder, Brad. <u>Beyond The Shadow Of The Senators, The Untold Story of the Homestead Grays and the Integration of Baseball</u>. New York: Contemporary Books, 2003.

Stargell, Willie and Bird, Tom. <u>Willie Stargell, An Autobiography.</u> New York: Harper & Row, 1984.

Steinhorn, Leonard and Diggs-Brown, Barbara. <u>By The Color of Our Skin, The Illusion of Integration and the Reality of Race.</u> New York, Plume Books, 1999.

Torrez, Danielle Gagnon. <u>High Inside: Memoirs of a Baseball Wife.</u> Putnam Publishing Group, 1983.

Turcotte, Dorothy. <u>The Game Is Easy, Life Is Hard: The Story Of Ferguson Jenkins. Jr.</u> Grimsby, Ontario: The Fergie Jenkins Foundation, 2002.

Tygiel, Jules, Editor. <u>The Jackie Robinson Reader: Perspectives On An American Hero.</u> New York: Dutton Books, 1997.

Tygiel, Jules. <u>Baseball's Great Experiment: Jackie Robinson And His Legacy.</u> New York: Oxford University Press, 1997.

---. <u>Extra Bases: Reflections On Jackie Robinson, Race, & Baseball History</u>. Lincoln, Nebraska: University Of Nebraska Press, 2002.

---. <u>Past Time: Baseball As American History</u>. New York: Oxford University Press, 2000.

Van Hyning, Thomas E. <u>Puerto Rico's Winter League</u>. Jefferson, North Carolina: McFarland & Company, 1995.

Veeck, Bill With Ed Linn. <u>Veeck As In Wreck: The Autobiography Of Bill Veeck</u>. Chicago: University Of Chicago Press, 1962.

Verducci, Tom. "Blackout, The African-American Baseball Player is Vanishing. Does he have a future?" <u>Sports Illustrated</u>, July 7, 2003, p. 56.

White, G. Edward. <u>Creating the National Pastime, Baseball Transforms Itself, 1903-1953.</u> Princeton, NJ: Princeton University Press, 1996

White, Sol. <u>Official Baseball Guide.</u> Amereon Ltd., 1907

Wills, Maury and Celizic, Mike. <u>On The Run, The Never Dull and Often Shocking Life of Maury Wills.</u> New York: Carroll & Graf, 1991.

Wilson, Nick. <u>Voices From The Pastime</u>. Jefferson, North Carolina: McFarland & Company, 2000.

Young, A.S. "Doc". <u>Great Negro League Baseball Stars, and how they made the major leagues.</u> New York: A.S. Barnes and Company, 1953.

Newspapers, Periodicals, Miscellaneous:
Associated Press
Baseball America
Baseball Digest

Black Sports
Birmingham News
Chicago's American
Chicago Inter-Ocean
Christian Science Monitor
Copley News Service
Family Weekly
Free Press
Inside Golf
Jet
Knight-Ridder Newspapers
Knight-Ridder Tribune
Life Magazine
National Public Radio
Newsday
Newsweek
Nine: A Journal of Baseball History and Social Perspective
Refocus Films, Westport, CT – There Was Always Sun Shining Someplace
Society for American Baseball Research Negro League Committee
Saturday Evening Post
Sport
Sports Illustrated
The Amsterdam News
The Arizona Republic
The Arkansas Democrat
The Baltimore Afro-American
The Boston Globe
The Boston Herald
The Chicago Defender
The Cleveland Plain-Dealer
The Dallas Morning News
The Des Moines Register
The Detroit News
The Examiner
The Herald Tribune
The Houston Chronicle
The Houston Post
The Houston Press
The Kansas City Star
The Los Angeles Times
The Louisiana Weekly
The National
The New York Amsterdam
The New York Daily News
The New York Daily Worker
The New York Post
The New York Times
The Philadelphia Bulletin
The Philadelphia Daily News
The Philadelphia Tribune
The Pittsburgh Courier
The Roanoke Times
The St. Louis Globe-Democrat
The St. Louis Post-Dispatch
The San Francisco Chronicle

The South Florida Sun Sentinel
The Sporting News
The Telegram
The Trentonian
The Washington Post
Time Magazine
USA Today

Websites:

AP.org
Achievement.org
Angelfire.com
Astrosdaily.com
Baseball-almanac.com
Baseballhalloffame.org
Baseballlibrary.com
Baseballreference.com
Contracostatimes.com
Desmoinesregister.com
Elitestv.com
Mlb.com
Outoftheshadows.net
Thinkexist.com

Interviews with:

Vida Blue
Ed Charles
Al Downing
Harry Dunlop
Ryne Duren
Joyce Harris
Ferguson Jenkins
Jack McKeon
Don Newcombe
Mike Norris
JR Richard
Jim Robinson
Dave Stewart
Frank Tepedino
Rosendo Torres
Jules Tygiel
Fred Valentine
Mark Wiley
Earl Wilson
JR Richard Interview by Ray Kerby, January 31, 2001

Correspondence with:

Gene Alley
Yogi Berra
Ted Bowsfield
Rocky Bridges
Ernie Broglio
Jim Coates
Carl Erskine
Chuck Essegian

Elijah Pumpsie Green
Tom Herr
Ken Holtzman
Dalton Jones
Jim Kaat
Clyde King
Jerry Koosman
Jim Landis
Tony LaRussa
Jon Matlack
Dal Maxvill
Bill Mazeroski
Wally Moon
Bobby Morgan
Ross Moschitto
Ivan Murrell
Frank Quilici
Eric Rasmussen
Bobby Richardson
Ray Sadecki

Hall of Fame Dossier of Clippings on:

Vida Blue
Chet Brewer
Leon Day
Al Downing
Andrew Foster
William Foster
Bob Gibson
Dwight Gooden
Mudcat Grant
Dave Hoskins
Ferguson Jenkins
Sam Jones
Don Newcombe
Mike Norris
Satchel Paige
Dick Redding
JR Richard
Wilbur Rogan
Hilton Lee Smith
Dave Stewart
Joe Williams
Earl Wilson